The
MACARTHUR
BIBLE
HANDBOOK

John MacArthur

Thomas Nelson Publishers
Nashville

Published by Thomas Nelson Publishers, a Division of Thomas Nelson, Inc., P. O. Box 141000, Nashville, Tennessee, 37214.

Published in association with the literary agency of Wolgemuth & Associates, Inc.

All Scripture used is taken from the *New King James Version*. Copyright © 1979, 1980, 1982 by Thomas Nelson, Inc. Used by permission. All rights reserved.

Material for all introductory text, notes, commentary, maps, and charts are taken from the following sources: *How to Get the Most Out of God's Word* by John MacArthur, Jr., © 1997 by Word Publishing, *The MacArthur Quick Reference Guide to the Bible* by John MacArthur, © 2001 by John MacArthur (published by W Publishing Group), *The MacArthur Student Bible* (John MacArthur, general editor) © 2000 by Word Publishing, *The MacArthur Study Bible* (John MacArthur, general editor) © 1997 by Word Publishing. W Publishing Group (Word Publishing) is a division of Thomas Nelson, Inc. All material used by permission.

Produced with the assistance of The Livingstone Corporation (www.LivingstoneCorporation.com). Project staff includes Christopher Hudson, Pete Gregory, Mary Horner Collins, Kirk Luttrell, Ashley Taylor, Rosalie Krusemark, and Greg Longbons.

ISBN 0-7852-4968-0

Printed in the United States of America

03 04 05 06 07 — 9 8 7 6 5 4 3 2 1

CONTENTS

Index of Tables, Charts
    and Maps....................................v

How to Use the MacArthur
    Bible Handbook...........................ix

Introduction to the Bible xi

How We Got the Bible xvii

How to Study the Bible xxv

Guides to the Biblical Books:

Introduction to the Pentateuch 1

Genesis.......................................7

Exodus 19

Leviticus....................................29

Numbers 41

Deuteronomy...............................49

Joshua.......................................55

Judges 63

Ruth...71

1 and 2 Samuel 85

1 and 2 Kings 99

1 and 2 Chronicles 111

Ezra...121

Nehemiah 129

Esther 137

Job 143

Psalms 153

Proverbs 161

Ecclesiastes 169

Song of Solomon.........................175

Isaiah 183

Jeremiah...................................193

Lamentations 201

Ezekiel 207

Daniel......................................217

Hosea 223

Joel 227

Amos 233

Obadiah 237

Jonah 241

Micah 247

Nahum 251

Habakkuk 255

Zephaniah 259

Haggai 263

Zechariah 267

Malachi 273

Introduction to the
    Intertestamental Period 281

Introduction to the Gospels..............289

Matthew....................................303

Mark 315

Luke..327

John 339

Acts 351

Romans 363

1 Corinthians 373

2 Corinthians 383

Galatians 391

Ephesians..................................399

Philippians 407

Colossians 415

1 Thessalonians...........................423

2 Thessalonians...........................431

1 Timothy 437

2 Timothy 445

Titus 451

Philemon 457

Hebrews 461

James 471

1 Peter 479

2 Peter 487

1 John...495

2 John...505

3 John 509

Jude 513

Revelation 517

Appendices:

Overview of Theology 527

The Character of Genuine
    Saving Faith 539

Read Through the Bible in a Year 541

Monies, Weights, and Measures..........545

Topical Index 547

Index of
TABLES, CHARTS AND MAPS

Hebrew Old Testament xx

Chronology of Israel in the Pentateuch 2

Chronology of Old Testament Patriarchs and Judges 4-5

Garden of Eden 7

Adam to Israel's Twelve Tribes 8

How Old Were the Patriarchs? 9

Nations of Genesis 10 15

Egyptian Pharaohs 20

The Life of Moses 21

The Plan of the Tabernacle 23

The Furniture of the Tabernacle 24

The Exodus from Egypt 26

The Levitical Offerings 31-35

Jewish Feasts and Christ Fulfills Israel's Feasts 37

Placement of Tribes in the Israelite Encampment 41

The Conquest of Canaan 56

Joshua's Preparation for Ministry 57

Israel's Judges 64

The Judges of Israel 66

The Period of the Judges 67

The Story of Ruth 72

The Family Tree of Ruth 73

Kinsman-Redeemer 74

Harmony of the Books of Samuel, Kings, and Chronicles 77

Chronology of Old Testament Kings and Prophets 82-83

The Kingdom of David 86

The Life of David 87

The Life and Ministry of Samuel 88

The Philistine Threat 89

Plot Development of 2 Samuel 96

The Spread of Solomon's Fame 100

The Divided Kingdom 101

The Babylonian Empire 102

The Kings of Israel and Judah 103

Solomon's Temple 104

The Chronicles' Sources 111

The Temples of the Bible 112-13

Post-Exilic Returns to Jerusalem 122

Time Line of Nehemiah 130

Jerusalem in Nehemiah's Day... 131

Seven Attempts to Stop Nehemiah's Work 133

Jewish Feasts 138

The Historical Chronology of Esther 138

Biographical Sketch of Job 143

A Comparison of Satan's Theology with That of Job's Friends........... 145

God's Challenge to Job... 146

Historical Background to Psalms by David.. 154

Types of Psalms 155

Messianic Prophecies in the Psalms 157

Notable Teachers in Scripture.. 161

The "Vanities" of Ecclesiastes 1:2; 12:8... 171

Locations in the Song of Solomon 176

Local Color in the Song of Solomon 177-78

Couples in Love.. 179

God's Judgment on the Nations.. 185

Isaiah's Description of Israel's Future Kingdom................................ 186

Fulfilled Prophecies from Isaiah 189

Major Trials of Jeremiah 193

Babylon Dominates 194

Illustrations of God's Judgment.. 196

Second Kings, Jeremiah, and Lamentations Compared 202

Ezekiel's Temple 207

Ezekiel's Sign Experiences 210

The Holy District.. 214

The Ultimate Restoration of Israel.. 234

God's Judgment on Edom 239

Ten Miracles in Jonah 243

The Temples of the Bible 264

Outline and Chronology of Haggai 266

Zechariah's Visions 269

The Coming of Christ 276

Chronology of the Old Testament 279

Introduction to the Intertestamental Period 281

Expansion Under the Maccabees 282

Roman Control of Palestine 283

Chronology of Intertestamental Period 284-85

Chronology of the New Testament 287

Introduction to the Gospels 289

The Roman Empire in the New Testament Era 290

Harmony of the Gospels 291-98

A Brief Overview of Christ's Life 299

A Brief Overview of Christ's Ministry 300

The Ministry of Jesus Christ 301

Christ's Passion Week 302

The Parables of Jesus 307

Christ's Trails, Crucifixion, and Resurrection 311

The Baptism of Jesus 316

The Life of Jesus 318

The Miracles of Jesus 320

The Plan of Herod's Temple 325

New Testament Women 330

Palestine 340

The Seven Signs 341

The "I AM" Statements 343

Titles of Jesus 345

The Career of the Apostle Paul 357

Paul's First and Second Journeys 358

Paul's Third and Fourth Journeys 359

Major Sermons in Acts 360

Ministry of the Apostles 361

Ministries of the Holy Spirit 361

The Nations of Pentecost 362

The City of Rome 364

Kingdom-Style Mentoring 365

Appearances of the Risen Christ 377

The Agora of Corinth 389

The Cities of Galatia 392

Law and Grace 394

The City of Ephesus 399

The Glories of Christ 417

The Preeminence of Christ 418

Titles of Christ 419

Communities with Christian Churches 424

A Comparison of Emphases in 1 and 2 Thessalonians 432

A Comparison of Paul's Two Roman Imprisonments 446

Timothy's Ministry 447

How Love Works in Philemon 458

Christ's Superiority 464

James and the Sermon on the Mount 472

Faith Alive 473

Suffering in Divine Perspective 482

Living Among Pagans 483

The Life of Peter 488

The Life of John 496

Profile of an Apostate 515

The Seven Churches 518

The Seven Churches of Revelation 519

How to Use the

MACARTHUR
BIBLE
HANDBOOK

The Bible is an extraordinarily intricate and complex book. Study and appreciation of Scripture can be a daunting task. The *MacArthur Bible Handbook* has been designed to facilitate informed study and advanced understanding of Scripture through an accessible format. It does not replace your Bible; it simply offers you a source of answers for the kinds of questions that might discourage your personal study. By checking the *Handbook*, you should be able to get back quickly to the Bible.

If you already own a study Bible, you will note many similarities between the *MacArthur Bible Handbook* and your Bible notes. There are, however, some features you will probably not find in your study Bible. In any case, having these materials at your side as you study the Scriptures will help you to stay focused on God's Word itself.

QUICK TUTORIAL

1. Take a look at the Contents. As you read the entries, note which ones seem unfamiliar to you. Turn to those features and make sure you keep a mental record of what you find. Entries like harmonies and chronologies will be of great value to you when you are studying certain parts of Scripture.

2. Open to one of the Bible book entries. Note the features that you will find in each of those introductions:

- **Title and Its Meaning**
- **Author and Date of the Book**
- **Background and Setting**—historical notes about the book
- **Key People in the Book**
- **Historical and Theological Themes**—broad biblical themes throughout the book
- **Key Doctrines in the Book**—central teachings in the book
- **God's Character in the Book**—key aspects of God's character illustrated
- **Christ in the Book**—how Christ can be found in that book
- **Key Words in the Book**—significant words used
- **Interpretive Challenges**—difficult themes or concepts in the book
- **Outline**—formal structure of the book
- **Meanwhile, in other parts of the world…**—global historical context of the book
- **Answers to Tough Questions about the book**
- **Further Study**—basic questions for reflection as you read

Using the *MacArthur Bible Handbook* may seem a little awkward at first, but with practice, you will find it to be a rich resource of information as you study God's Word.

 ««« ix »»»

The Bible is a collection of 66 documents inspired by God. These documents are gathered into two testaments, the Old (39) and the New (27). Prophets, priests, kings, and leaders from the nation of Israel wrote the OT books in Hebrew (with two passages in Aramaic). The apostles and their associates wrote the NT books in Greek.

The OT record starts with the creation of the universe and closes about 400 years before the first coming of Jesus Christ.

The flow of history through the OT moves along the following lines:

- Creation of the universe
- Fall of man
- Judgment flood over the earth
- Abraham, Isaac, Jacob (Israel)—fathers of the chosen nation
- The history of Israel
- Exile in Egypt—430 years
- Exodus and wilderness wanderings—40 years
- Conquest of Canaan—7 years
- Era of Judges—350 years
- United Kingdom—Saul, David, Solomon—110 years
- Divided Kingdom—Judah/Israel—350 years
- Exile in Babylon—70 years
- Return and rebuilding the land—140 years

The details of this history are explained in the 39 books divided into 5 categories:

- The Law—5 (Genesis—Deuteronomy)
- History—12 (Joshua—Esther)
- Wisdom—5 (Job—Song Of Solomon)
- Major Prophets—5 (Isaiah—Daniel)
- Minor Prophets—12 (Hosea—Malachi)

After the completion of the OT, there were 400 years of silence, during which God did not speak or inspire any Scripture. That silence was broken by the arrival of John the Baptist announcing that the promised Lord Savior had come. The NT records the rest of the story from the birth of Christ to the culmination of all history and the final eternal state; so the two testaments go from creation to consummation, eternity past to eternity future.

While the 39 OT books major on the history of Israel and the promise of the coming Savior, the 27 NT books major on the person of Christ and the establishment of the church. The four gospels give the record of His birth, life, death, resurrection, and ascension. Each of the four writers views the greatest and most important event of history, the coming of the God-man, Jesus Christ, from a different perspective. Matthew looks at Him through the perspective of His kingdom; Mark through the perspective of His servanthood; Luke through the perspective of His humanness; and John through the perspective of His deity.

The Book of Acts tells the story of the impact of the life, death, and resurrection of Jesus Christ, the Lord Savior—from His ascension, the consequent coming of the Holy Spirit, and the birth of the church, through the early years of gospel preaching by the apostles and their associates. Acts records the establishment of the church in Judea, Samaria, and into the Roman Empire.

The 21 epistles were written to churches and individuals to explain the significance of the person and work of Jesus Christ, with its implications for life and witness until He returns.

The NT closes with Revelation, which starts by picturing the current church age, and culminates with Christ's return to establish His earthly kingdom, bringing judgment on the ungodly and glory and blessing for believers. Following the millennial reign of the Lord Savior will be the last judgment, leading to the eternal state. All believers of all history enter the ultimate eternal glory prepared for them, and all the ungodly are consigned to hell to be punished forever.

To understand the Bible, it is essential to grasp the sweep of that history from creation to consummation. It is also crucial to keep in focus the unifying theme of Scripture. The one constant theme unfolding throughout the whole Bible is this: God for His own glory has chosen to create and gather to Himself a group of people to be the subjects of His eternal kingdom, to praise, honor, and serve Him forever and through whom He will display His wisdom, power, mercy, grace, and glory. To gather His chosen ones, God must redeem them from sin. The Bible reveals God's plan for this redemption from its inception in eternity past to its completion in eternity future. Covenants, promises, and epochs are all secondary to the one continuous plan of redemption.

There is one God. The Bible has one Creator. It is one book. It has one plan of grace, recorded from initiation, through execution, to consummation. From predestination to glorification, the Bible is the story of God redeeming His chosen people for the praise of His glory.

As God's redemptive purposes and plan unfold in Scripture, five recurring motifs are constantly emphasized:

- the character of God
- the judgment for sin and disobedience
- the blessing for faith and obedience
- the Lord Savior and sacrifice for sin
- the coming kingdom and glory

Everything revealed on the pages of both the OT and NT is associated with those five categories. Scripture is always teaching or illustrating: (1) the character and attributes of God; (2) the tragedy of sin and disobedience to God's holy standard; (3) the blessedness of faith and obedience to God's standard; (4) the need for a Savior by whose righteousness and substitution sinners can be forgiven, declared just, and transformed to obey God's standard; and (5) the coming glorious end of redemptive history in the Lord Savior's earthly kingdom and the subsequent eternal reign and glory of God and Christ. It is essential as one studies Scripture to grasp these recurring categories like great hooks on which to hang the passages. While reading through the Bible, one should be able to relate each portion of Scripture to these dominant topics, recognizing that what is introduced in the OT is also made more clear in the NT.

Looking at these five categories separately gives an overview of the Bible.

1. THE REVELATION OF THE CHARACTER OF GOD

Above all else, Scripture is God's self-revelation. He reveals Himself as the sovereign God of the universe who has chosen to make man and to make Himself known to man. In that self-revelation is established His standard of absolute holiness. From Adam and Eve through Cain and Abel and to everyone before and after the law of Moses, the standard of righteousness was established and is sustained to the last page of the NT. Violation of it produces judgment, temporal and eternal.

In the OT, it is recorded that God revealed Himself by the following means:
- creation—primarily through man—who was made in His image
- angels
- signs, wonders, and miracles
- visions
- spoken words by prophets and others
- written Scripture (OT)

In the NT, it is recorded that God revealed Himself again by the same means, but more clearly and fully:
- creation—the God-man, Jesus Christ, who was the very image of God
- angels
- signs, wonders, and miracles
- visions
- spoken words by apostles and prophets
- written Scripture (NT)

2. THE REVELATION OF DIVINE JUDGMENT FOR SIN AND DISOBEDIENCE

Scripture repeatedly deals with the matter of man's sin, which leads to divine judgment. Account after account in Scripture demonstrates the deadly effects in time and eternity of violating God's standard. There are 1,189 chapters in the Bible. Only four of them don't involve a fallen world: the first two and the last two—before the Fall and after the creation of the new heaven and new earth. The rest is the chronicle of the tragedy of sin.

In the OT, God showed the disaster of sin—starting with Adam and Eve, to Cain and Abel, the patriarchs, Moses and Israel, the kings, priests, some prophets, and Gentile nations. Throughout the OT is the relentless record of continual devastation produced by sin and disobedience to God's law.

In the NT, the tragedy of sin becomes clearer. The preaching and teaching of Jesus and the apostles begin and end with a call to repentance. King Herod, the Jewish leaders, and the nation of Israel—along with Pilate, Rome, and the rest of the world—all reject the Lord Savior, spurn the truth of God, and thus condemn themselves. The chronicle of sin continues unabated to the end of the age and the return of Christ in judgment. In the NT, disobedience is even more flagrant than OT disobedience because it involves the rejection of the Lord Savior Jesus Christ in the brighter light of NT truth.

3. THE REVELATION OF DIVINE BLESSING FOR FAITH AND OBEDIENCE

Scripture repeatedly promises wonderful rewards in time and eternity that come to people who trust God and seek to obey Him. In the OT, God showed the blessedness of repentance from sin, faith in Himself, and obedience to His Word—from Abel, through the patriarchs, to the remnant in Israel—and even Gentiles who believed (such as the people of Nineveh).

God's standard for man, His will, and His moral law were always made known. To those who faced their inability to keep God's standard, recognized their sin, confessed their impotence to please God by their own effort and works, and asked Him for forgiveness and grace—there came merciful redemption and blessing for time and eternity.

In the NT, God again showed the full blessedness of redemption from sin for repentant people. There were those who responded to the preaching of repentance by John the Baptist. Others repented at the preaching of Jesus. Still others from Israel obeyed the gospel through the apostles' preaching. And finally, there were Gentiles all over the Roman Empire who believed the gospel. To all those and to all who will believe through all of history, there is blessing promised in this world and the world to come.

4. THE REVELATION OF THE LORD SAVIOR AND SACRIFICE FOR SIN

This is the heart of both the OT, which Jesus said spoke of Him in type and prophecy, and the NT, which gives the biblical record of His coming. The promise of blessing is dependent on grace and mercy given to the sinner. Grace means that sin is not held against the sinner. Such forgiveness is dependent on a payment of sin's penalty to satisfy holy justice. That requires a substitute—one to die in the sinner's place. God's chosen substitute—the only one who qualified—was Jesus. Salvation is always by the same gracious means, whether during OT or NT times. When any sinner comes to God, repentant and convinced he has no power to save himself from the deserved judgment of divine wrath, and pleads for mercy, God's promise of forgiveness is granted. God then declares him righteous because the sacrifice and obedience of Christ is put to his account. In the OT, God justified sinners that same way, in anticipation of Christ's atoning work. There is, therefore, a continuity of grace and salvation through all of redemptive history. Various covenants, promises, and epochs do not alter that fundamental continuity, nor does the discontinuity between the OT witness nation, Israel, and the NT witness people, the church. A fundamental continuity is centered in the cross, which was no interruption in the plan of God, but the very thing to which all else points.

Throughout the OT, the Savior and sacrifice are promised. In Genesis, He is the seed of the woman who will destroy Satan. In Zechariah, He is the pierced one to whom Israel turns and by whom God opens the fountain of forgiveness to all who mourn over their sin. He is the very One symbolized in the sacrificial system of the Mosaic law. He is the suffering substitute spoken of by the prophets. Throughout the OT, He is the Messiah who would die for the transgressions of His people; from beginning to end in the OT, the theme of the Lord Savior as a sacrifice for sin is presented. It is solely because of His perfect sacrifice for sin that God graciously forgives repentant believers.

In the NT, the Lord Savior came and actually provided the promised sacrifice for sin on the cross. Having fulfilled all righteousness by His perfect life, He fulfilled justice by His death. Thus God Himself atoned for sin, at a cost too great for the human mind to fathom. Now He graciously supplies on their behalf all the merit necessary for His people to be the objects of His favor. That is what Scripture means when it speaks of salvation by grace.

5. THE REVELATION OF THE KINGDOM AND GLORY OF THE LORD SAVIOR

This crucial component of Scripture brings the whole story to its God-ordained consummation. Redemptive history is controlled by God, so as to culminate in His eternal glory. Redemptive history will end with the same precision and exactness with which it began. The truths of eschatology are neither vague nor unclear—nor are they unimportant. As in any book, how the story ends is the most crucial and compelling part—so with the Bible. Scripture notes several very specific features of the end planned by God.

In the OT, there is repeated mention of an earthly kingdom ruled by the Messiah, Lord Savior, who will come to reign. Associated with that kingdom will be the salvation of Israel, the salvation of Gentiles, the renewal of the earth from the effects of the curse, and the bodily resurrection of God's people who have died. Finally, the OT predicts that there will be the "uncreation" or dissolution of the universe, and the creation of a new heaven and new earth—which will be the eternal state of the godly—and a final hell for the ungodly.

In the NT, these features are clarified and expanded. The King was rejected and executed, but He promised to come back in glory, bringing judgment, resurrection, and His kingdom for all who believe. Innumerable Gentiles from every nation will be included among the redeemed. Israel will be saved and grafted back into the root of blessing from which she has been temporarily excised.

Israel's promised kingdom will be enjoyed, with the Lord Savior reigning on the throne, in the renewed earth, exercising power over the whole world, having taken back His rightful authority, and receiving due honor and worship. Following that kingdom will come the dissolution of the renewed, but still sin-stained creation and the subsequent creation of a new heaven and new earth—which will be the eternal state, separate forever from the ungodly in hell.

Those are the five topics that fill up the Bible. To understand them at the start is to know the answer to the question that continually arises—Why does the Bible tell us this? Everything fits into this glorious pattern. As you read, hang the truth on these five hooks and the Bible will unfold, not as 66 separate documents, or even two separate testaments—but one book, by one divine Author, who wrote it all with one overarching theme.

My prayer is that the magnificent and overwhelming theme of the redemption of sinners for the glory of God will carry every reader with captivating interest from beginning to end of the story. Christian—this is your story. It is from God for you—about you. It tells what He planned for you, why He made you, what you were, what you have become in Christ, and what He has prepared for you in eternal glory.

John MacArthur

Ever since Eve encountered Satan's barrage of doubt and denial (Gen. 3:1–7), mankind has continued to question God's Word. Unfortunately, Eve had little or no help in sorting through her intellectual obstacles to full faith in God's self-disclosure (Gen. 2:16,17).

Now the Scripture certainly has more than enough content to be interrogated, considering that it's comprised of 66 books, 1,189 chapters, 31,173 verses, and 774,746 words. When you open your English translation to read or study, you might have asked in the past or are currently asking, "How can I be sure this is the pure and true Word of God?"

A question of this kind is not altogether bad, especially when one seeks to learn with a teachable mind (Acts 17:11). The Scripture invites the kinds of queries that a sincere student asks. A whole host of questions can flood the mind, such as:

- Where did the Bible come from?
- Whose thinking does it reflect?
- Did any books of the Bible get lost in time past?
- What does the Scripture claim for itself?
- Does it live up to its claims?
- Who wrote the Bible—God or man?
- Has Scripture been protected from human tampering over the centuries?
- How close to the original manuscripts are today's translations?
- How did the Bible get to our time and in our language?
- Is there more Scripture to come, beyond the current 66 books?
- Who determined, and on what basis, that the Bible would be composed of the traditional list of 66 books?
- If the Scriptures were written over a period of 1,500 years (ca. 1405 B.C. to A.D. 95), passed down since then for almost 2,000 years, and translated into several thousand languages, what prevented the Bible from being changed by the carelessness or ill motives of men?
- Does today's Bible really deserve the title "The Word of God"?

Undoubtedly, these questions have bombarded the minds of many. A study of the Scriptures alone settles all questions to the extent that there is no need to be bothered by them again. Scripture gives this assurance.

SCRIPTURES' SELF CLAIMS

Take the Bible and let it speak for itself. Does it claim to be God's Word? Yes! Over 2,000 times in the OT alone, the Bible asserts that God spoke what is written within its pages. From the beginning (Gen. 1:3) to the end (Mal. 4:3) and continually throughout, this is what Scripture claims.

The phrase "the Word of God" occurs over 40 times in the NT. It is equated with the OT (Mark 7:13). It is what Jesus preached (Luke 5:1). It was the message the apostles taught (Acts 4:31; 6:2). It was the Word the Samaritans received (Acts 8:14) as given by the apostles (Acts 8:25). It was the message the Gentiles received as preached by Peter

(Acts 11:1). It was the word Paul preached on his first missionary journey (Acts 13:5,7,44,48,49; 15:35,36). It was the message preached on Paul's second missionary journey (Acts 16:32; 17:13; 18:11). It was the message Paul preached on his third missionary journey (Acts 19:10). It was the focus of Luke in the book of Acts in that it spread rapidly and widely (Acts 6:7; 12:24; 19:20). Paul was careful to tell the Corinthians that he spoke the Word as it was given from God, that it had not been adulterated, and that it was a manifestation of truth (2 Cor. 2:17; 4:2). Paul acknowledged that it was the source of his preaching (Col. 1:25; 1 Thess. 2:13).

Psalms 19 and 119, plus Proverbs 30:5–6, make powerful statements about God's Word that set it apart from any other religious instruction ever known in the history of mankind. These passages make the case for the Bible being called "sacred" (2 Tim. 3:15) and "holy" (Rom. 1:2).

The Bible claims ultimate spiritual authority in doctrine, reproof, correction, and instruction in righteousness because it represents the inspired Word of Almighty God (2 Tim. 3:16,17). Scripture asserts its spiritual sufficiency, so much so that it claims exclusivity for its teaching (cf. Is. 55:11; 2 Pet. 1:3,4).

God's Word declares that it is *inerrant* (Pss. 12:6; 119:140; Prov. 30:5a; John 10:35) and *infallible* (2 Tim. 3:16, 17). In other words, it is true and therefore trustworthy. All of these qualities are dependent on the fact that the Scriptures are God-given (2 Tim. 3:16; 2 Pet. 1:20,21), which guarantees its quality at the Source and at its original writing.

In Scripture, the person of God and the Word of God are everywhere interrelated, so much so that whatever is true about the character of God is true about the nature of God's Word. God is true, impeccable, and reliable; therefore, so is His Word. What a person thinks about God's Word, in reality, reflects what a person thinks about God.

Thus, the Scripture can make these demands on its readers.

> So He humbled you, allowed you to hunger, and fed you with manna which you did not know nor did your fathers know, that He might make you know that man shall not live by bread alone; but man lives by every word that proceeds from the mouth of the LORD.
>
> *Deut. 8:3*

> I have not departed from the commandment of His lips; I have treasured the words of His mouth more than my necessary food.
>
> *Job 23:12*

THE PUBLISHING PROCESS

The Bible does not expect its reader to speculate on how these divine qualities were transferred from God to His Word, but rather anticipates the questions with convincing answers. Every generation of skeptics has assailed the self-claims of the Bible, but its own explanations and answers have been more than equal to the challenge. The Bible has gone through God's publishing process in being given to and distributed among the human race. Its several features are discussed below.

REVELATION

God took the initiative to disclose or reveal Himself to mankind (Heb. 1:1). The vehicles varied; sometimes it was through the created order, at other times through visions/dreams or speaking prophets. However, the most complete and understandable self-disclosures were through the propositions of Scripture (1 Cor. 2:6–16). The revealed and written Word of God is unique in that it is the only revelation of God that is complete and that so clearly declares man's sinfulness and God's provision of the Savior.

INSPIRATION

The revelation of God was captured in the writings of Scripture by means of "inspiration." This has more to do with the process by which God revealed Himself than the fact of His self-revelation. "All Scripture is given by inspiration of God. . ." (2 Tim. 3:16) makes the claim. Peter explains the process, ". . . knowing this first, that no prophecy of Scripture is of any private interpretation, for prophecy never came by the will of man, but holy men of God spoke as they were moved by the Holy Spirit" (2 Pet. 1:20,21). By this means, the Word of God was protected from human error in its original record by the ministry of the Holy Spirit (cf. Deut. 18:18; Matt. 1:22). A section of Zech. 7:12 describes it most clearly, ". . . the law and the words which the LORD of hosts had sent by His Spirit through the former prophets." This ministry of the Spirit extended to both the part (the words) and to the whole in the original writings.

CANONICITY

We must understand that the Bible is actually one book with one Divine Author, though it was written over a period of 1,500 years through the pens of almost forty human writers. The Bible began with the creation account of Genesis 1,2, written by Moses about 1405 B.C., and extends to the eternity future account of Revelation 21,22, written by the apostle John about A.D. 95. During this time, God progressively revealed Himself and His purposes in the inspired Scriptures. But this raises a significant question: "How do we know what supposed sacred writings were to be included in the canon of Scripture and which ones were to be excluded?"

Over the centuries, three widely recognized principles were used to validate those writings which came as a result of divine revelation and inspiration. First, the writing had to have a recognized prophet or apostle as its author (or one associated with them, as in the case of Mark, Luke, Hebrews, James, and Jude). Second, the writing could not disagree with or contradict previous Scripture. Third, the writing had to have general consensus by the church as an inspired book. Thus, when various councils met in church history to consider the canon, they did not vote for the canonicity of a book but rather recognized, after the fact, what God had already written.

With regard to the Old Testament, by the time of Christ all of the OT had been written and accepted in the Jewish community. The last book, Malachi, had been completed about 430 B.C. Not only does the OT canon of Christ's day conform to the OT that has since been used throughout the centuries, but is does not contain the uninspired and spurious Apocrypha, that group of fourteen rogue writings written after Malachi and attached to the OT about 200–150 B.C. in the Greek translation of the Hebrew OT called the

Septuagint (LXX), appearing to this very day in some versions of the Bible. However, not one passage from the Apocrypha is cited by any NT writer, nor did Jesus affirm any of it as He recognized the OT canon of His era (cf. Luke 24:27,44).

By Christ's time, the OT canon had been divided up into two lists of 22 or 24 books respectively, each of which contained all the same material as the 39 books of our modern versions. In the 22-book canon, Jeremiah and Lamentations were considered as one, as were Judges and Ruth. Here is how the 24-book format was divided.

The Hebrew Old Testament

Law	Prophets	Writings
1. Genesis	A. *Former Prophets*	A. *Poetical Books*
2. Exodus	6. Joshua	14. Psalms
3. Leviticus	7. Judges	15. Proverbs
4. Numbers	8. Samuel (1 & 2)	16. Job
5. Deuteronomy	9. Kings (1 & 2)	
	B. *Latter Prophets*	B. *Five Rolls (Megilloth)*
	10. Isaiah	17. Song of Solomon
	11. Jeremiah	18. Ruth
	12. Ezekiel	19. Lamentations
	13. The Twelve (minor prophets)	20. Ecclesiastes
		21. Esther
		C. *Historical Books*
		22. Daniel
		23. Ezra-Nehemiah
		24. Chronicles (1 & 2)

The same three key tests of canonicity that applied to the OT also applied to the NT. In the case of Mark and Luke/Acts, the authors were considered to be, in effect, the penmen for Peter and Paul respectively. James and Jude were written by Christ's half-brothers. While Hebrews is the only NT book whose authorship is unknown for certain, its content is so in line with both the OT and NT, that the early church concluded it must have been written by an apostolic associate. The 27 books of the NT have been universally accepted since ca. A.D. 350–400 as inspired by God.

PRESERVATION

How can one be sure that the revealed and inspired, written Word of God, which was recognized as canonical by the early church, has been handed down to this day without any loss of material? Furthermore, since one of the Devil's prime concerns is to undermine the Bible, have the Scriptures survived this destructive onslaught? In the beginning, he denied God's Word to Eve (Gen. 3:4). Satan later attempted to distort the Scripture in his wilderness encounter with Christ (Matt. 4:6,7). Through King Jehoiakim, he even attempted to literally destroy the Word (Jer. 36:23). The battle for the Bible rages, but Scripture has and will continue to outlast its enemies.

God anticipated man's and Satan's malice towards the Scripture with divine promises to preserve His Word. The very continued existence of Scripture is guaranteed in Isaiah

40:8, "The grass withers, the flower fades, but the word of our God stands forever" (cf. 1 Pet. 1:25). This even means that no inspired Scripture has been lost in the past and still awaits rediscovery.

The actual content of Scripture will be perpetuated, both in heaven (Ps. 119:89) and on earth (Is. 59:21). Thus the purposes of God, as published in the sacred writings, will never be thwarted, even in the least detail (cf. Matt. 5:18; 24:25; Mark 13:3; Luke 16:17).

> So shall My word be that goes forth from My mouth; it shall not return to Me void, but it shall accomplish what I please, and it shall prosper in the thing for which I sent it.
>
> Is. 55:11

TRANSMISSION

Since the Bible has frequently been translated into multiple languages and distributed throughout the world, how can we be sure that error has not crept in, even if it was unintentional? As Christianity spread, it is certainly true that people desired to have the Bible in their own language, which required translations from the original Hebrew and Aramaic languages of the OT and the Greek of the NT. Not only did the work of translators provide an opportunity for error, but publication, which was done by hand copying until the printing press arrived ca. A.D. 1450, also afforded continual possibilities of error.

Through the centuries, the practitioners of textual criticism, a precise science, have discovered, preserved, catalogued, evaluated, and published an amazing array of biblical manuscripts from both the Old and New Testaments. In fact, the number of existing biblical manuscripts dramatically outdistances the existing fragments of any other ancient literature. By comparing text with text, the textual critic can confidently determine what the original prophetic/apostolic, inspired writing contained.

Although existing copies of the main, ancient Hebrew text (Masoretic) date back only to the tenth century A.D., two other important lines of textual evidence bolster the confidence of textual critics that they have reclaimed the originals. First, the tenth century A.D. Hebrew OT can be compared to the Greek translation called the Septuagint or LXX (written ca. 200–150 B.C.; the oldest existing manuscripts dates to ca. A.D. 325). There is amazing consistency between the two, which speaks of the accuracy in copying the Hebrew text for centuries. Second, the discovery of the Dead Sea Scrolls in 1947–1956 (manuscripts that are dated ca. 200–100 B.C.) proved to be monumentally important. After comparing the earlier Hebrew texts with the later ones, only a few slight variants were discovered, none of which changed the meaning of any passage. Although the OT had been translated and copied for centuries, the latest version was essentially the same as the earlier ones.

The NT findings are even more decisive because a much larger amount of material is available for study; there are over 5,000 Greek NT manuscripts that range from the whole testament to scraps of papyri which contain as little as part of one verse. A few existing fragments date back to within 25–50 years of the original writing. NT textual scholars have generally concluded that (1) 99.99 percent of the original writings have been reclaimed, and (2) of the remaining one hundredth of one percent, there are no variants substantially affecting any Christian doctrine.

With this wealth of biblical manuscripts in the original languages and with the disciplined activity of textual critics to establish with almost perfect accuracy the content of the autographs, any errors which have been introduced and/or perpetuated by the thousands of translations over the centuries can be identified and corrected by comparing the translation or copy with the reassembled original. By this providential means, God has made good His promise to preserve the Scriptures. We can rest assured that there are translations available today which indeed are worthy of the title, The Word of God.

The history of a full, English translation Bible essentially began with John Wycliffe (ca. A.D. 1330–1384), who made the first English translation of the whole Bible. Later, William Tyndale was associated with the first complete, printed NT in English, ca. A.D. 1526. Myles Coverdale followed in A.D. 1535, by delivering the first complete Bible printed in English. By A.D. 1611, the King James Version (KJV) had been completed. Since then, hundreds of translations have been made—some better, some worse. Today, the better English translations of the Hebrew and Greek Scriptures include: (1) New King James Version (NKJV); (2) English Standard Version (ESV); (3) New International Version (NIV); and (4) New American Standard Bible (NASB).

SUMMING IT UP

God intended His Word to abide forever (preservation). Therefore His written, propositional, self-disclosure (revelation) was protected from error in its original writing (inspiration) and collected in 66 books of the Old and New Testaments (canonicity).

Through the centuries, tens of thousands of copies and thousands of translations have been made (transmission) which did introduce some error. Because there is an abundance of existing ancient OT and NT manuscripts, however, the exacting science of textual criticism has been able to reclaim the content of the original writings (revelation and inspiration) to the extreme degree of 99.99 percent, with the remaining one hundredth of one percent having no effect on its content (preservation).

The sacred book which we read, study, obey, and preach deserves to unreservedly be called The Bible or "The Book without peer," since its author is God and it bears the qualities of total truth and complete trustworthiness as also characterizes its divine source.

IS THERE MORE TO COME?

How do we know that God will not amend our current Bible with a 67th inspired book? Or, in other words, "Is the canon forever closed?"

Scripture texts warn that no one should delete from or add to Scripture (Deut. 4:2; 12:32; Prov. 30:6). Realizing that additional canonical books actually came after these words of warning, we can only conclude that while no deletions whatsoever were permitted, in fact, authorized, inspired writings were permitted to be added in order to complete the canon protected by those passages.

The most compelling text on the closed canon is the Scripture to which nothing has been added for 1,900 years.

> For I testify to everyone who hears the words of the prophecy of this book: If
> anyone adds to these things, God will add to him the plagues that are written

in this book; and if anyone takes away from the words of the book of this prophecy, God shall take away his part from the Book of Life, from the holy city, and from the things which are written in this book.

Rev. 22:18,19

Several significant observations, when taken together, have convinced the church over the centuries that the canon of Scripture is actually closed, never to be reopened.

1. The book of Revelation is unique to the Scripture in that it describes with unparalleled detail the end-time events that precede eternity future. As Genesis began Scripture by bridging the gap from eternity past into our time/space existence with the only detailed creation account (Gen. 1, 2), so there was a parallel silence after John delivered Revelation. This also leads to the conclusion that the NT canon was then closed.

2. Just as there was prophetic silence after Malachi completed the OT canon, so there was a parallel silence after John delivered Revelation. This leads to the conclusion that the NT canon was then closed also.

3. Since there have not been, nor now are, any authorized prophets or apostles in either the OT and NT sense, there are not any potential authors of future inspired, canonical writings. God's Word, "once for all delivered to the saints," is never to be added to, but to be earnestly contended for (Jude 3).

4. Of the four exhortations not to tamper with Scripture, only the one in Revelation 22:18,19 contains warnings of severe Divine judgement for disobedience. Further, Revelation is the only book of the NT to end with this kind of admonition and was written over twenty years after any other NT book. Therefore, these facts strongly suggest that Revelation was the last book of the canon and that the Bible is complete; to either add or delete would bring God's severe displeasure.

5. Finally, the early church, those closest in time to the apostles, believed that Revelation concluded God's inspired writings, the Scriptures.

So we can conclude, based on solid Biblical reasoning, that the canon is and will remain closed. There will be no future 67th book of the Bible.

WHERE DO WE STAND?

In April, 1521, Martin Luther appeared before his ecclesiastical accusers at the Diet of Worms. They had given him the ultimatum to repudiate his unwavering faith in the sufficiency and perspicuity of the Scriptures. Luther is said to have responded, "Unless I am convicted by Scripture and plain reason—I do not accept the authority of popes and councils, for they have contradicted each other—my conscience is captive to the Word of God.... God help me! Here I stand."

Like Martin Luther, may we rise above the doubts within and confront the threats without when God's Word is assailed. God help us to be loyal contenders of the faith. Let us stand with God and the Scripture alone.

THE BIBLE

This book contains: the mind of God, the state of man, the way of salvation, the doom of sinners, and the happiness of believers.

Its doctrine is holy, its precepts are binding, its histories are true, and its decisions are immutable. Read it to be wise, believe it to be saved, and practice it to be holy.

It contains light to direct you, food to support you, and comfort to cheer you. It is the traveler's map, the pilgrim's staff, the pilot's compass, the soldier's sword, and the Christian's charter. Here heaven is open, and the gates of hell are disclosed.

Christ is the grand subject, our good its design, and the glory of God its end. It should fill the memory, rule the heart, and guide the feet.

Read it slowly, frequently, and prayerfully. It is a mine of wealth, health to the soul, and a river of pleasure. It is given to you here in this life, will be opened at the judgment, and is established forever.

It involves the highest responsibility, will reward the greatest labor, and condemn all who trifle with its contents.

> *For this reason we also thank God without ceasing, because when you received the word of God which you heard from us, you welcomed it not as the word of men, but as it is in truth, the word of God, which also effectively works in you who believe.*
>
> *1 Thess. 2:13*

How   to   Study

THE BIBLE

Here are tips on how to get the most out of the study of this "divine handbook." These pointers will help answer the most crucial question of all, "How can a young man cleanse his way?" The psalmist responds, "By taking heed according to Your Word" (Ps. 119:9).

WHY IS IT IMPORTANT TO STUDY THE BIBLE?

Why is God's Word so important? Because is contains God's mind and will for your life (2 Tim. 3:16, 17). It is the only source of absolute divine authority for you as a servant of Jesus Christ.

It is infallible in its totality: "The law of the LORD is perfect, converting the soul; the testimony of the LORD is sure, making wise the simple" (Ps. 19:7).

It is inerrant in its parts: "Every word of God is pure; He is a shield to those who put their trust in Him. Do not add to His words, lest He rebuke you, and you be found a liar" (Prov. 30:5,6).

It is complete: "For I testify to everyone who hears the words of the prophecy of this book: If anyone adds to these things, God will add to him the plagues that are written in this book; and if anyone takes away from the words of the book of this prophecy, God shall take away his part from the Book of Life, from the holy city, and from the things which are written in this book" (Rev. 22:18,19).

It is authoritative and final: "Forever, O Lord, Your word is settled in heaven" (Ps. 119:89).

It is totally sufficient for your needs: ". . . that the man of God may be complete, thoroughly equipped for every good work" (2 Tim. 3:16,17).

It will accomplish what it promises: "So shall My word be that goes forth from My mouth; it shall not return to Me void, but it shall accomplish what I please, and it shall prosper in the thing for which I sent it" (Is. 55:11).

It provides the assurance of your salvation: "He who is of God hears God's words ..." (John 8:47; 20:31).

HOW WILL I BENEFIT FROM STUDYING THE BIBLE?

Millions of pages of material are printed every week. Thousands of new books are published each month. This would not be surprising to Solomon who said, "Be admonished. . . . Of making many books there is no end" (Eccl. 12:12).

Even with today's wealth of books and computer helps, the Bible remains the only source of divine revelation and power that can sustain Christians in their "daily walk with God." Note these significant promises in the Scripture.

The Bible is the source of truth: "Sanctify them by Your truth; Your word is truth" (John 17:17).

The Bible is the source of God's blessing when obeyed: "But He said, 'More than that, blessed are those who hear the word of God and keep it'" (Luke 11:28).

The Bible is the source of victory: ". . . the sword of the Spirit, which is the word of God" (Eph. 6:17).

The Bible is the source of growth: "As newborn babes, desire the pure milk of the word, that you may grow thereby" (1 Pet. 2:2).

The Bible is the source of power: "For I am not ashamed of the gospel of Christ, for it is the power of God to salvation for everyone who believes, for the Jew first and also for the Greek" (Rom. 1:16).

The Bible is the source of guidance: "Your word is a lamp to my feet and a light to my path" (Ps. 119:105).

WHAT SHOULD BE MY RESPONSE TO THE BIBLE?

Because the Bible is so important and because it provides unparalleled eternal benefits, then these should be your responses:

Believe it (John 6:68,69)
Honor it (Job 23:12)
Love it (Ps. 119:97)
Obey it (1 John 2:5)
Guard it (1 Tim. 6:20)
Fight for it (Jude 3)
Preach it (2 Tim. 4:2)
Study it (Ezra 7:10)

WHO CAN STUDY THE BIBLE?

Not everyone can be a Bible student. Check yourself on these necessary qualifications for studying the Word with blessing:

- Are you saved by faith in Jesus Christ (1 Cor. 2:14–16)?
- Are you hungering for God's Word (1 Pet. 2:2)?
- Are you searching God's Word with diligence (Acts 17:11)?
- Are you seeking holiness (1 Pet. 1:14–16)?
- Are you Spirit-filled (Col. 3:16)?

The most important question is the first. If you have never invited Jesus Christ to be your personal Savior and the Lord of your life, then your mind is blinded by Satan to God's truth (2 Cor. 4:4).

If Christ is your need, stop reading right now and, in your own words with prayer, turn away from sin and turn toward God: "For by grace you have been saved through faith, and that not of yourselves; it is the gift of God, not of works, lest anyone should boast" (Eph. 2:8,9).

WHAT ARE THE BASICS OF BIBLE STUDY?

Personal Bible study, in precept, is simple. I want to share with you five steps to Bible study which will give you a pattern to follow.

STEP 1—**Reading.** Read a passage of Scripture repeatedly until you understand its theme, meaning the main truth of the passage. Isaiah said, "Whom will he teach knowledge? And whom will he make to understand the message? Those *just* weaned from milk? Those *just* drawn from the breasts? For precept *must be* upon precept, precept upon precept, line upon line, here a little, there a little" (Is. 28:9,10).

Develop a plan on how you will approach reading through the Bible. Unlike most books, you will probably not read it straight through from cover to cover. There are many good Bible reading plans available, but here is one that I have found helpful.

Read through the OT at least once a year. As you read, note in the margins any truths you particularly want to remember, and write down separately anything you do not immediately understand. Often as you read you will find that many questions are answered by the text itself. The questions to which you cannot find answers become the starting points for more in-depth study using commentaries or other reference tools.

Follow a different plan for reading the NT. Read one book at a time repetitiously for a month or more. This will help you to retain what is in the NT and not always have to depend on a concordance to find things.

If you want to try this, begin with a short book, such as 1 John, and read it through in one sitting every day for 30 days. At the end of that time, you will know what is in the book. Write on index cards the major theme of each chapter. By referring to the cards as you do your daily reading, you will begin to remember the content of each chapter. In fact, you will develop a visual perception of the book in your mind.

Divide longer books into short sections and read each section daily for 30 days. For example, the gospel of John contains 21 chapters. Divide it into three sections of 7 chapters. At the end of 90 days, you will finish John. For variety, alternate short and long books, and in less than three years you will have finished the entire NT—and you will really know it!

STEP 2—Interpreting. In Acts 8:30, Philip asked the Ethiopian eunuch, "Do you understand what you are reading?" Or put another way, "What does the Bible mean by what it says?" It is not enough to read the text and jump directly to the application; we must first determine what it means, otherwise the application may be incorrect.

As you read Scripture, always keep in mind one simple question: "What does this mean?" To answer that question requires the use of the most basic principle of interpretation, called the analogy of faith, which tells the reader to "interpret the Bible with the Bible." Letting the Holy Spirit be your teacher (1 John 2:27), search the Scripture He has authored, using cross references, comparative passages, concordances, indexes, and other helps. For those passages that yet remain unclear, consult your pastor or godly men who have written in that particular area.

STEP 3—Evaluating. You have been reading and asking the question, "What does the Bible say?" Then you have interpreted, asking the question, "What does the Bible mean?" Now it is time to consult others to insure that you have the proper interpretation. Remember, the Bible will never contradict itself.

Read Bible introductions, commentaries, and background books which will enrich your thinking through that illumination which God has given to other men and to you through their books. In your evaluation, be a true seeker. Be one who accepts the truth of God's Word even though it may cause you to change what you always have believed, or cause you to alter your life pattern.

STEP 4—Applying. The next question is: "How does God's truth penetrate and change my own life?" Studying Scripture without allowing it to penetrate to the depths of your soul would be like preparing a banquet without eating it. The bottom-line question to ask is, "How do the divine truths and principles contained in any passage apply to me in terms of my attitude and actions?"

Jesus made this promise to those who would carry their personal Bible study through to this point: "If you know these things, blessed are you if you do them" (John 13:17).

Having read and interpreted the Bible, you should have a basic understanding of what the Bible says, and what it means by what it says. But studying the Bible does not stop there. The ultimate goal should be to let it speak to you and enable you to grow spiritually. That requires personal application.

Bible study is not complete until we ask ourselves, "What does this mean for my life and how can I practically apply it?" We must take the knowledge we have gained from our reading and interpretation and draw out the practical principles that apply to our personal lives.

If there is a command to be obeyed, we obey it. If there is a promise to be embraced, we claim it. If there is a warning to be followed, we heed it. This is the ultimate step: we submit to Scripture and let it transform our lives. If you skip this step, you will never enjoy your Bible study and the Bible will never change your life.

STEP 5—Correlating. This last stage connects the doctrine you have learned in a particular passage or book with divine truths and principles taught elsewhere in the Bible to form the big picture. Always keep in mind that the Bible is one book in 66 parts, and it contains a number of truths and principles, taught over and over again in a variety of ways and circumstances. By correlating and cross-referencing, you will begin to build a sound doctrinal foundation by which to live.

ERRORS TO AVOID

As you interpret Scripture, several common errors should be avoided.

1. Do not draw any conclusions at the price of proper interpretation. That is, do not make the Bible say what you want it to say, but rather let it say what God intended when He wrote it.

2. Avoid superficial interpretation. You have heard people say, "To me, this passage means," or "I feel it is saying. . . ." The first step in interpreting the Bible is to recognize the four gaps we have to bridge: language, culture, geography, and history (see below).

3. Do not spiritualize the passage. Interpret and understand the passage in its normal, literal, historical, grammatical sense, just like you would understand any other piece of literature you were reading today.

GAPS TO BRIDGE

The books of the Bible were written many centuries ago. For us to understand today what God was communicating then, there are several gaps that need to be bridged: the language gap, the cultural gap, the geographical gap, and the historical gap. Proper interpretation, therefore, takes time and disciplined effort.

1. *Language.* The Bible was originally written in Greek, Hebrew, and Aramaic. Often, understanding the meaning of a word or phrase in the original language can be the key to correctly interpreting a passage of Scripture.

2. *Culture.* The culture gap can be tricky. Some people try to use cultural differences to explain away the more difficult biblical commands. Realize that Scripture must first be viewed in the context of the culture in which it was written. Without an understanding of first-century Jewish culture, it is difficult to understand the gospel. Acts and the epistles must be read in light of the Greek and Roman cultures.

3. *Geography.* A third gap that needs to be closed is the geography gap. Biblical geography makes the Bible come alive. A good Bible atlas is an invaluable reference tool that can help you comprehend the geography of the Holy Land.

4. *History.* We must also bridge the history gap. Unlike the scriptures of most other world religions, the Bible contains the records of actual historical persons and events. An understanding of Bible history will help us place the people and events in it in their proper historical perspective. A good Bible dictionary or Bible encyclopedia is useful here, as are basic historical studies.

PRINCIPLES TO UNDERSTAND

Four principles should guide us as we interpret the Bible: literal, historical, grammatical, and synthesis.

1. *The Literal Principle.* Scripture should be understood in its literal, normal, and natural sense. While the Bible does contain figures of speech and symbols, they were intended to convey literal truth. In general, however, the Bible speaks in literal terms, and we must allow it to speak for itself.

2. *The Historical Principle.* This means that we interpret in its historical context. We must ask what the text meant to the people to whom it was first written. In this way we can develop a proper contextual understanding of the original intent of Scripture.

3. *The Grammatical Principle.* This requires that we understand the basic grammatical structure of each sentence in the original language. To whom do the pronouns refer? What is the tense of the main verb? You will find that when you ask some simple questions like those, the meaning of the text immediately becomes clearer.

4. *The Synthesis Principle.* This is what the Reformers called the *analogia scriptura.* It means that the Bible does not contradict itself. If we arrive at an interpretation of a passage that contradicts a truth taught elsewhere in the Scriptures, our interpretation cannot be correct. Scripture must be compared with Scripture to discover its full meaning.

WHAT NOW?

The psalmist said, "Blessed is the man who walks not in the counsel of the ungodly, nor stands in the path of sinners, nor sits in the seat of the scornful; But his delight is in the law of the Lord, and in His law he meditates day and night" (Ps. 1:1,2).

It is not enough just to study the Bible. We must meditate upon it. In a very real sense we are giving our brain a bath; we are washing it in the purifying solution of God's Word.

This Book of the Law shall not depart from your mouth, but you shall medi-
tate in it day and night, that you may observe to do according to all that is writ-
ten in it. For then you will make your way prosperous, and then you will have
good success.

Josh. 1:8

Here is the spring where waters flow,
    To quench our heart of sin:
Here is the tree where truth doth grow,
    To lead our lives therein:
Here is the judge that stints the strife,
    When men's devices fail:
Here is the bread that feeds the life
    That death cannot assail.
The tidings of salvation dear,
    Comes to our ears from hence:
The fortress of our faith is here,
    And shield of our defense.
Then be not like the swine that hath
    A pearl at his desire,
And takes more pleasure from the trough
    And wallowing in the mire.
Read not this book in any case,
    But with a single eye:
Read not but first desire God's grace,
    To understand thereby.
Pray still in faith with this respect,
    To bear good fruit therein,
That knowledge may bring this effect,
    To mortify thy sin.
Then happy you shall be in all your life,
    What so to you befalls:
Yes, double happy you shall be,
    When God by death you calls.

(From the first Bible printed in Scotland—1576)

(From John F. MacArthur, Jr., *The MacArthur Study Bible*, [Dallas: Word Publishing], 1997.)

Introduction to the
PENTATEUCH

The first five books of the Bible (Genesis, Exodus, Leviticus, Numbers, Deuteronomy) form a complete literary unit called the Pentateuch, meaning "five scrolls." The five independent books of the Pentateuch were written as an unbroken unity in content and historical sequence, with each succeeding book beginning where the former left off.

The first words of Genesis, "In the beginning God created ... " (Gen. 1:1) imply the reality of God's eternal or "before time" existence and announce the spectacular transition to time and space. While the exact date of creation cannot be determined, it certainly would be estimated to be thousands of years ago, not millions. Starting with Abraham (ca. 2165–1990 B.C.) in Genesis 11, this book of beginnings spans over 300 years to the death of Joseph in Egypt (ca. 1804 B.C.). There is then another gap of almost 300 years until the birth of Moses in Egypt (ca. 1525 B.C.; Ex. 2).

Exodus begins with the words "Now these are the names" (Ex. 1:1), listing those of the family of Jacob who went down to Egypt to be with Joseph toward the end of Gen. (Gen. 46ff.). The second book of the Pentateuch, which records the escape of the Israelites from Egypt, concludes when the cloud of the LORD, which led the people through the wilderness, descends upon the newly constructed tabernacle.

The first Hebrew words of Leviticus may be translated, "Now the LORD called to Moses" (Lev. 1:1). From the cloud of God's Presence in the tabernacle of meeting (Lev. 1:1), God summons Moses in order to prescribe to him the ceremonial law, which told Israel how they must approach their Holy God. Leviticus concludes with, "These are the commandments which the LORD commanded Moses for the children of Israel on Mount Sinai" (Lev. 27:34).

Numbers, much like Leviticus, commences with God commissioning Moses at the tabernacle of meeting, this time to take a census in preparation for war against Israel's enemies. The book's title in the Hebrew Bible accurately represents the content— "Wilderness." Due to lack of trust in God, Israel did not want to engage its enemies militarily in order to claim the Promised Land. After forty additional years in the wilderness for their rebellion, Israel arrived on the plains of Moab.

Despite the fact that it was "eleven days' journey from Horeb by way of Mount Seir to Kadesh Barnea" (Deut. 1:2), the journey took Israel forty years due to their rebellion against God. Moses preached the Book of Deuteronomy as a sermon on the Plains of Moab in preparation for God's people to enter the land of covenant promise (Gen. 12:1–3). The title Deuteronomy is from the Greek phrase *deuteros nomos*, meaning "second law." The book focuses on the restatement and, to some extent, the reapplication of the law to Israel's new circumstances.

Chronology of Israel in the Pentateuch

Date	Event	Reference
Fifteenth day, first month, first year	Exodus	Exodus 12
Fifteenth day, second month, first year	Arrival in Wilderness of Sin	Exodus 16:1
Third month, first year	Arrival in Wilderness of Sinai	Exodus 19:1
First day, first month, second year	Erection of Tabernacle	Exodus 40:1,17
	Dedication of Altar	Numbers 7:1
	Consecration of Levites	Numbers 8:1–26
Fourteenth day, first month, second year	Passover	Numbers 9:5
First day, second month, second year	Census	Numbers 1:1,18
Fourteenth day, second month, second year	Supplemental Passover	Numbers 9:11
Twentieth day, second month, second year	Departure from Sinai	Numbers 10:11
First month, fortieth year	In Wilderness of Zin	Numbers 20:1, 22–29; 33:38
First day, fifth month, fortieth year	Death of Aaron	Numbers 20:22–29; 33:38
First day, eleventh month, fortieth year	Moses' Address	Deuteronomy 1:3

Moses was the human author of the Pentateuch (Ex. 17:14; 24:4; Num. 33:1,2; Deut. 31:9; Josh. 1:8; 2 Kin. 21:8); thus, another title for the collection is "The Books of Moses." Through Moses, God revealed Himself, His former works, Israel's family history, and its role in His plan of redemption for mankind. The Pentateuch is foundational to all the rest of Scripture.

Quoted or alluded to thousands of times in the OT and in the NT, the Pentateuch was Israel's first inspired body of Scripture. For many years, this alone was Israel's Bible. Another common title for this section of Scripture is *Torah*, or Law, a term that looks at the didactic nature of these books. The Israelites were to meditate upon it (Josh. 1:8), teach it to their children (Deut. 6:4–8), and read it publicly (Neh. 8:1ff.). Just before his death and Israel's move into the Promised Land, Moses set forth the process by which public reading would make its way into human hearts and change their relationship with God, and ultimately their conduct:

> *Gather the people together, men and women and little ones, and the stranger who is within your gates, that they may hear and that they may learn to fear the LORD your God and carefully observe all the words of this law.*

Deut. 31:12

The relationships between the commands is important. The people must: (1) gather to hear the law in order to learn what is required of them and what it has to say about God; (2) learn about the Lord in order to fear Him based on a correct understanding of who He is; and (3) fear God in order to be correctly motivated to obedience and good works. Good works performed for any other reason will be improperly motivated. The priests taught the law to the families (Mal. 2:4–7) and the parents instructed the children within the home (Deut. 6:4ff.). Instruction in the law, in short, would provide the right foundation for the OT believer's relationship with God.

Because the Israelites' knowledge of the world in which they lived came through the Egyptians, as well as their ancestors the Mesopotamians, there was much confusion about the creation of the world, how it got to its present state, and how Israel had come into existence. Genesis 1–11 helped Israel understand the origin and nature of creation, human labor, sin, marriage, murder, death, bigamy, judgment, the multiplicity of languages, cultures, etc. These chapters established the worldview that explained the remainder of Israel's first Bible, the Pentateuch.

The later portion of Genesis explained to Israel who they were, including the purpose God had for them as a people. In Genesis 12:1–3, God had appeared to Abraham and made a three-fold promise to give them a land, descendants, and blessing. Years later, in a ceremony typical to Abraham's culture, God recast the three-fold promise into a covenant (Gen. 15:7ff.). The remainder of Genesis treats the fulfillment of all three promises, but focuses especially on the seed or descendants. The barrenness of each of the patriarchs' chosen wives taught Israel the importance of trust and patience in waiting for children from God.

The rest of the Pentateuch looks at the way in which the promises of Genesis 12:1–3 expand in the Abrahamic Covenant and achieve their initial stages of fulfillment. Exodus and Leviticus focus more on the blessing or relationship with God. In Exodus, Israel meets the God of their fathers and is led forth by Him from Egypt to the Promised Land. Leviticus underscores the meticulous care with which the people and priests were to approach God in worship and every dimension of their lives. Holiness and cleanness come together in simple and practical ways. Numbers and Deuteronomy focus on the journey to and preparation for the Promised Land. The Pentateuch treats many issues related to Israel's relationship with their God. But the underlying theme of the Pentateuch is the initial, unfolding fulfillments of God's promises made to Abraham.

Chronology of Old Testament Patriarchs and Judges

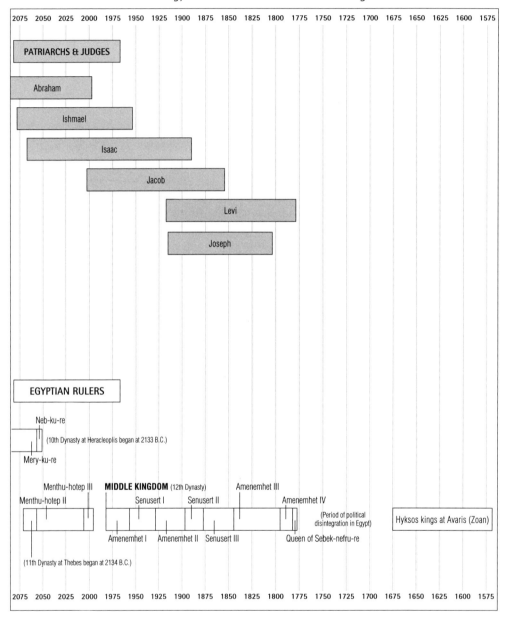

Chronology of Old Testament Patriarchs and Judges

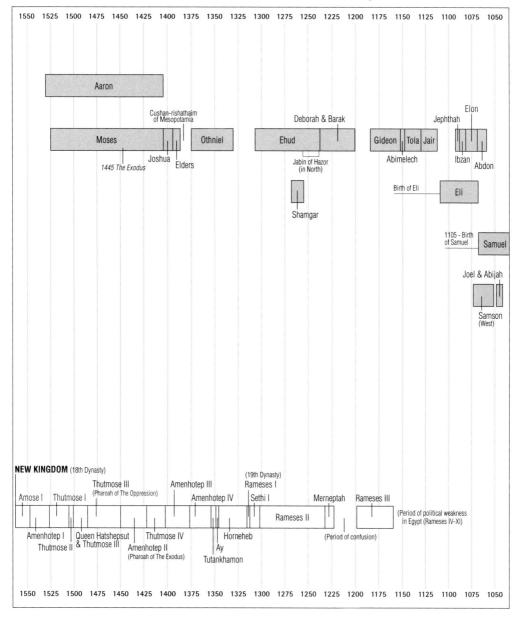

GENESIS
The Book of Beginnings

TITLE

God started everything. The Bible doesn't begin with an argument for God's existence; it begins by accepting that our existence depends on God. The ancient Greek translation of the Old Testament (called the Septuagint, or LXX) titled this first book *Genesis*, meaning "origins." Eventually, English translators borrowed the word directly. The title used in Hebrew texts simply highlights the very first word, which means "in the beginning."

The Garden of Eden

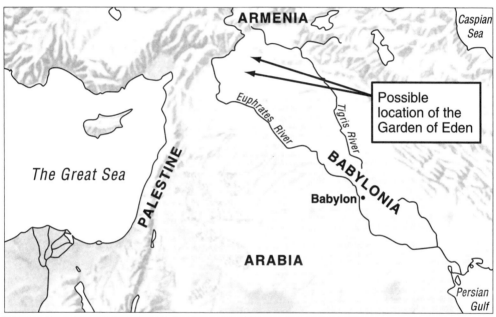

The Garden of Eden may have been located near the Tigris River, which the Bible calls Hiddekel (2:14).

AUTHOR AND DATE

Although Genesis does not name its author, and the events described in the text end almost three centuries before his birth, both the OT (Ex. 17:14; Num. 33:2; Josh. 8:31; 1 Kin. 2:3; 2 Kin. 14:6; Ezra 6:18; Neh. 13:1; Dan. 9:11,13; Mal. 4:4) and the NT (Matt. 8:4; Mark 12:26; Luke 16:29; 24:27,44; John 5:46; 7:22; Acts 15:1; Rom. 10:19; 1 Cor. 9:9; 2 Cor. 3:15) designate Moses as the author. In addition, Moses' educational background makes him the likely candidate (Acts 7:22).

No compelling reasons have been offered to challenge Mosaic authorship. It's estimated that Moses wrote Genesis in approximately 1445 to 1405 B.C. For a brief biographical sketch of Moses, read Exodus 1–6.

BACKGROUND AND SETTING

The initial setting for Genesis is eternity past—before there was time. God, by willful act and divine word, spoke all creation into existence, furnished it, and finally breathed life into a lump of dirt that He fashioned in His image to become Adam. God made human beings the crowning point of His creation; that is, companions who would enjoy fellowship with Him and bring glory to His name.

The historical background for the early events in Genesis is clearly Mesopotamia. While it is difficult to pinpoint precisely the historical time frame in which this book was written, Israel first heard Genesis sometime prior to crossing the Jordan River and entering the Promised Land (ca. 1405 B.C.).

Genesis has three distinct and sequential geographical settings: (1) Mesopotamia (chapters 1–11); (2) the Promised Land (chapters 12–36); (3) Egypt (chapters 37–50). The time

Adam to Israel's Twelve Tribes

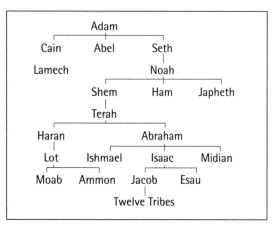

frames of these three segments are (1) creation to 2090 B.C.; (2) 2090 to 1897 B.C.; (3) 1897 to 1804 B.C. It's notable that Genesis covers a longer span of history than any other book of the Bible.

KEY PEOPLE IN GENESIS

Adam and Eve—the original human beings (1:26–5:5)
Noah—the faithful builder of the ark (6:5–9:29)
Abraham and Sarah—the parents of a nation called God's chosen people (12:1–25:8)
Isaac and Rebekah—the original members of a new nation (21:1–35:29)
Jacob—the father of the twelve tribes of Israel (25:21–50:14)
Joseph—the preserver of his people and the nation of Egypt (30:22–50:26)

HISTORICAL AND THEOLOGICAL THEMES

In this book of beginnings, God revealed Himself and a new way of viewing the world to the children of Israel, which contrasted, at times sharply, with that of Israel's neighbors. The author made no attempt to defend the existence of God or to present a thorough explanation of His person and works. Rather, Israel's God distinguished Himself clearly from the alleged gods of her neighbors. Theological foundations are revealed which include God the Father, God the Son, God the Holy Spirit, man, sin, redemption, covenant, promise, Satan and angels, kingdom, revelation, Israel, judgment, and blessing.

Genesis 1–11 reveals the origins of the universe, i.e., the beginnings of time and space and many of the firsts in human experience, such as marriage, family, the Fall, sin, redemption, judgment, and nations. Genesis 12–50 explained to Israel how they came into existence as a family whose ancestry could be traced to Eber (hence the "Hebrews"; Gen.

How Old Were the Patriarchs?

ADAM 930 years (Gen. 5:5)

SETH 912 years (Gen. 5:8)

ENOSH 905 years (Gen. 5:11)

ENOCH 365 years (Gen. 5:23)

METHUSELAH 969 years (Gen. 5:27)

LAMECH 777 years (Gen. 5:31)

NOAH 950 years (Gen. 9:29)

~~~The Flood~~~

SHEM 600 years (Gen. 11:10,11)

EBER 464 years (Gen. 11:16,17)

TERAH 205 years (Gen. 11:32)

ABRAHAM 175 years (Gen. 25:7)

ISAAC 180 years (Gen. 35:28)

JACOB 147 years (Gen. 47:28)

JOSEPH 110 years (Gen. 50:26)

The patriarchs who lived before the Flood had an average lifespan of about 900 years (Gen. 5). The ages of post-Flood patriarchs dropped rapidly and gradually leveled off (Gen. 11). Some suggest that this is due to major environmental changes brought about by the Flood.

10:24–25) and even more remotely to Shem, the son of Noah (hence the "Semites"; Gen. 10:21). God's people came to understand not only their ancestry and family history, but also the origins of their institutions, customs, languages, and different cultures, especially basic human experiences such as sin and death.

Because they were preparing to enter Canaan and dispossess the Canaanite inhabitants of their homes and properties, God revealed their enemies' backgrounds. In addition, they needed to understand the actual basis of the war they were about to declare, in light of the immorality of killing consistent with the other four books that Moses was writing (Exodus, Leviticus, Numbers, and Deuteronomy). Ultimately, the Jewish nation would understand a selected portion of preceding world history and its own national background as a basis by which they would live in their new beginnings under Joshua's leadership in the land, which had been promised to their original patriarchal forefather, Abraham.

Genesis 12:1–3 established a primary focus on God's promises to Abraham. This narrowed their view from the entire world of peoples in Genesis 1–11 to one small nation,

Israel, through whom God would progressively accomplish His redemptive plan. This underscored Israel's mission to be "a light to the Gentiles" (Is. 42:6). God promised land, descendants (seed), and blessing. This three-fold promise became, in turn, the basis of the covenant with Abraham (Gen. 15:1–20). The rest of Scripture bears out the fulfillment of these promises.

On a larger scale, Genesis 1–11 set forth a singular message about the character and works of God. In the sequence of accounts which make up these chapters of Scripture, a pattern emerges that reveals God's abundant grace as He responded to the willful disobedience of mankind. Without exception, in each account God increased the manifestation of His grace. But also without exception, man responded in greater sinful rebellion. In biblical words, the more sin abounded the more did God's grace abound (cf. Rom. 5:20).

One final theme of both theological and historical significance sets Genesis apart from other books of Scripture, in that the first book of Scripture corresponds closely with the final book. In the Book of Revelation, the paradise that was lost in Genesis will be regained. The apostle John clearly presented the events recorded in his book as future resolutions to the problems that began as a result of the curse in Genesis 3. His focus is upon the effects of the Fall in the undoing of creation and the manner in which God rids His creation of the curse effect. In John's own words, "And there shall be no more curse" (Rev. 22:3). Not surprisingly, in the final chapter of God's Word, believers will find themselves back in the Garden of Eden, the eternal paradise of God, eating from the tree of life (Rev. 22:1–14). At that time they will partake, wearing robes washed in the blood of the Lamb (Rev. 22:14).

CHRIST IN . . . GENESIS

JESUS' ENTRANCE INTO HUMANITY was planned from before the beginning of time. God softened the punishment of the curse that resulted from the sin of Adam and Eve by offering a promise that someday a Seed would rise up to crush the serpent (3:15). Even though death came through Adam, Christ's coming brought life to humankind (Rom. 5:12–21).

Genesis goes on to trace the first lines in God's divine blueprint for Jesus' birth. From the peoples of the earth, God singled out Abraham to be the father of a chosen nation. This nation continued through Abraham's son Isaac, and then through Isaac's son Jacob, concluding with the account of Jacob's son Joseph. Genesis reveals God's continual protection over the earliest people in Christ's lineage.

KEY DOCTRINES IN GENESIS

Most of the central teachings of Christianity have their roots in the Book of Genesis.

God the Father—the authority of God in creation (1:1–31; Ps. 103:19; 145:8,9; 1 Cor. 8:6; Eph. 3:9; 4:6)

God the Son—the agent of God in creation (1:1; 3:15; 18:1; John 1:1–3; 10:30; 14:9; Phil. 2:5–8; Col. 1:15–17; Heb. 1:2)

God the Holy Spirit—the presence of God in creation (1:2; 6:3; Matt. 1:18; John 3:5–7)

God as one yet three—the Trinity (1:1,26; 3:22; 11:7; Deut. 6:4; Is. 45:5–7; Matt. 28:19; 1 Cor. 8:4; 2 Cor. 13:14)

Genesis

God: Hebrew plural ᵓelohim—1:1,12; 19:29; 24:42; 28:3; 35:11; 45:9; 50:24—the most used Hebrew term for God. The basic meaning is "the Almighty." The Hebrew usage of this term in Genesis is called "the plural of majesty." Unlike a normal plural, the Hebrew uses this plural to mean "the Fullness of Deity" or "God-Very God!" The plural form of this word has traditionally been recognized as indicating the plural nature of God. God is one, but God is also three distinct persons: the Father, the Son, and the Holy Spirit.

Heavens: Hebrew *shamayim*—1:1,8,9; 2:1; 8:2; 11:4; 14:22; 24:3; 28:12. The Hebrew word for heavens may refer to the physical heavens, the sky and the atmosphere of earth (2:1,4,19), or to the dwelling place of God (Psalm 14:2), the spiritual heaven. The expression is related to the term for "to be high, lofty." The physical heavens of creation testify to God's glorious position and also to His creative genius (Psalm 19:1,6).

Land: Hebrew ᵓerets—1:1,10; 4:16; 12:1; 13:10; 41:36; 31:3; 35:12. The common OT word for land possesses several shades of meaning. In essence, all land belongs to God as its Creator (Psalm 24:1). When God promised the Israelites the land of Canaan, it was His to give. The land of Canaan was so representative of God's covenant with the Israelites (12:1) that it became one of their identifying characteristics—the "people of the land" (13:15; 15:7).

Seed: Hebrew zeraᶜ—1:11,29; 13:15,16; 15:18; 17:19; 28:14; 48:19; 32:12. The Hebrew word for seed can literally mean a plant's seed (1:11,12), or can figuratively mean one's descendants (13:15). In Genesis, it refers specifically to the coming Messiah, in God's promise that the woman's Seed would crush the serpent (3:15; Num. 24:7; Is. 6:13; Gal. 3:16). As such, the term takes on great importance in the Bible: Through Abraham's seed, both collectively in Israel and singularly in Christ, God would reach out to save His people (15:3).

Human beings—created in Christ's image yet fallen into sin and needing a Savior (1:26; 2:4–25; 9:6; Is. 43:7; Rom. 8:29; Col. 1:16; 3:10; James 3:9; Rev. 4:11)

Sin (the Fall)—the infection of all creation with sin by rebellion toward God (2:16,17; 3:1–19; John 3:36; Rom. 3:23; 6:23; 1 Cor. 2:14; Eph. 2:1–3; 1 Tim. 2:13,14; 1 John 1:8)

Redemption—the rescue from sin and restoration accomplished by Christ on the cross (3:15; 48:16; John 8:44; 10:15; Rom. 3:24,25; 16:20; 1 Pet. 2:24)

Covenant—God establishes relationships and makes promises (15:1–20; 17:10,11; Num. 25:10–13; Deut. 4:25–31; 30:1–9; 2 Sam. 23:5; 1 Chr. 16:15–18; Jer. 30:11; 32:40; 46:27,28; Amos 9:8; Luke 1:67–75; Heb. 6:13–18)

Promise—God commits Himself into the future (12:1–3; 26:3,4; 28:14; Acts 2:39; Gal. 3:16; Heb. 8:6)

Satan—the original rebel among God's creatures (3:1–15; Is. 14:13,14; Matt. 4:3–10; 2 Cor. 11:3,14; 2 Pet. 2:4; Rev. 12:9; 20:2)

Angels—special beings created to serve God (3:24; 18:1–8; 28:12; Luke 2:9–14; Heb. 1:6,7, 14; 2:6,7; Rev. 5:11–14)

Revelation—*Natural revelation* occurs as God indirectly communicates through what He has made (1:1–2:25; Rom. 1:19,20). *Special revelation* occurs when God directly communicates Himself as well as otherwise unknowable truth (2:15–17; 3:8–19; 12:1–3; 18:1–8; 32:24–32; Deut. 18:18; 2 Tim. 3:16; Heb. 1:1–4; 1 Pet. 1:10–12)

Israel—Jacob's God-given name that became the name of the nation he fathered; inheritors of God's covenant with Abraham (32:28; 35:10; Deut. 28:15–68; Is. 65:17–25; Jer. 31:31–34; Ezek. 37:21–28; Zech. 8:1–17; Matt. 21:43; Rom. 11:1–29)

Judgment—God's righteous response to sin (3; 6; 7; 11:1–9; 15:14; 18:16–19:29; Deut. 32:39; Is.1:9; Matt. 12:36,37; Rom. 1:18–2:16; 2 Pet. 2:5,6)

Blessing—a special benefit or a hope-filled statement to someone about their life (1:28; 9:1; 12:1–3; 14:18–20; 27:1–40; 48:1–20; Num. 6:24–27; Deut. 11:26, 27; Ps. 3:8; Mal. 3:10; Matt. 5:3–11; 1 Pet. 3:9)

GOD'S CHARACTER IN GENESIS

Many of God's character traits are first revealed in Genesis.

God is the Creator—1:1–31

God is faithful (keeps promises)—12:3,7; 26:3,4; 28:14; 32:9,12

God is just—18:25

God is long-suffering—6:3

God is loving—24:12

God is merciful—19:16,19

God is omnipotent—17:1

God is powerful—18:14

God is provident—8:22; 24:12–14,48,56; 28:20,21; 45:5–7; 48:15; 50:20

God is truthful—3:4,5; 24:27; 32:10

God is wrathful—7:21–23; 11:8; 19:24,25

INTERPRETIVE CHALLENGES

Grasping the individual messages of Genesis that make up the larger plan and purpose of the book presents no small challenge since both the individual accounts and the book's overall message offer important lessons to faith and works. Genesis presents creation by divine fiat, *ex nihilo*, i.e., "out of nothing." Three traumatic events of epic proportions, namely the Fall, the universal Flood, and the Dispersion of nations are presented as historical backdrop in order to understand world history. From Abraham on, the pattern is to focus on God's redemption and blessing.

The customs of Genesis often differ considerably from those of our modern day. They must be explained against their ancient Near Eastern background. Each custom must be treated according to the immediate context of the passage before any attempt is made to explain it based on customs recorded in extrabiblical sources or even elsewhere in Scripture.

OUTLINE

Genesis by content is comprised of two basic sections: (1) Primitive history (Gen. 1–11) and (2) Patriarchal history (Gen. 12–50). Primitive history records 4 major events: (1) Creation (Gen. 1–2); (2) the Fall (Gen. 3–5); (3) the Flood (Gen. 6–9); and (4) the Dispersion (Gen. 10–11). Patriarchal history spotlights four great men: (1) Abraham (Gen. 12:1–25:8); (2) Isaac (Gen. 21:1–35:29); (3) Jacob (Gen. 25:21–50:14); and (4) Joseph (Gen. 30:22–50:26).

The literary structure of Genesis is built on the frequently recurring phrase "the history/genealogy of" and is the basis for the following outline.

I. **The Creation of Heaven and Earth (1:1–2:3)**

II. **The Generations of the Heavens and the Earth (2:4–4:26)**
   A. Adam and Eve in Eden (2:4–25)
   B. The Fall and Its Outcomes (chap. 3)
   C. Murder of a Brother (4:1–24)
   D. Hope in the Descendants of Seth (4:25–26)

III. **The Generations of Adam (5:1–6:8)**
   A. Genealogy—Seth to Noah (chap. 5)
   B. Rampant Sin Prior to the Flood (6:1–8)

IV. **The Generations of Noah (6:9–9:29)**
   A. Preparation for the Flood (6:9–7:9)
   B. The Flood and Deliverance (7:10–8:19)
   C. God's Noahic Covenant (8:20–9:17)
   D. The History of Noah's Descendants (9:18–29)

V. **The Generations of Shem, Ham, and Japheth (10:1–11:9)**
   A. The Nations (chap. 10)
   B. Dispersion of the Nations (11:1–9)

VI. **The Generations of Shem: Genealogy of Shem to Terah (11:10–26)**

VII. **The Generations of Terah (11:27–25:11)**
   A. Genealogy (11:27–32)
   B. The Abrahamic Covenant: His Land and People (12:1–22:19)
       1. Journey to the Promised Land (12:1–9)
       2. Redemption from Egypt (12:10–20)
       3. Division of the land (chap. 13)
       4. Victory over the kings (chap. 14)
       5. The covenant ratified (chap. 15)
       6. Rejection of Hagar and Ishmael (chap. 16)
       7. The covenant confirmed (chap. 17)
       8. Birth of Isaac foretold (18:1–15)
       9. Sodom and Gomorrah (18:16–19:38)
       10. Philistine encounter (chap. 20)
       11. Isaac's birth (chap. 21)
       12. Abraham's act of faith with Isaac (22:1–19)

C. Abraham's Promised Seed (22:20–25:11)
    1. Rebekah's background (22:20–24)
    2. Death of Sarah (chap. 23)
    3. Isaac's marriage to Rebekah (chap. 24)
    4. Isaac the only heir (25:1–6)
    5. Death of Abraham (25:7–11)

VIII. **The Generations of Ishmael (25:12–18)**
IX. **The Generations of Isaac (25:19–35:29)**
    A. Competition Between Esau and Jacob (25:19–34)
    B. Covenant Blessings to Isaac (chap. 26)
    C. Jacob's Deception for the Blessing (27:1–40)
    D. Blessing on Jacob in a Foreign Land (27:41–32:32)
        1. Jacob sent to Laban (27:41–28:9)
        2. Angel at Bethel (28:10–22)
        3. Disagreements with Laban (29:1–30)
        4. Promised seed (29:31–30:24)
        5. Departure from Aram (30:25–31:55)
        6. Angels at Mahanaim and Penuel (chap. 32)
    E. Esau's Reunion and Reconciliation with Jacob (33:1–17)
    F. Events and Deaths from Shechem to Mamre (33:18–35:29)

X. **The Generations of Esau (36:1–37:1)**
XI. **The Generations of Jacob (37:2–50:26)**
    A. Joseph's Dreams (37:2–11)
    B. Family Tragedy (37:12–38:30)
    C. Vice Regency over Egypt (chaps. 39–41)
    D. Reunion with Family (chaps. 42–45)
    E. Transition to Exodus (chaps. 46–50)
        1. Journey to Egypt (46:1–27)
        2. Occupation in Goshen (46:28–47:31)
        3. Blessings on the twelve tribes (48:1–49:28)
        4. Death and burial of Jacob in Canaan (49:29–50:14)
        5. Death of Joseph in Egypt (50:15–26)

ANSWERS TO TOUGH QUESTIONS

1. How does the Bible challenge or agree with current scientific theories?

Scientific theories, by their very definition, are subject to change and adjustment. Scripture remains as God's revealed, unchanging declaration of truth. The Bible was not written as a challenge to any particular scientific theory, but scientific theories have often been designed to challenge or undermine biblical statements. They either agree with Scripture or are mistaken.

The description in Genesis 1:1 that "God created the heavens and the earth" yields three basic conclusions: (1) creation was a recent event measured in thousands not millions of years ago; (2) creation was *ex nihilo*, meaning that God created out of

The Nations of Genesis 10

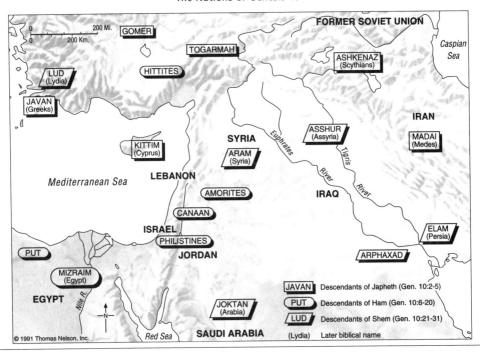

Genesis 10 is called the "Table of Nations" and is structured in terms of the descendants of the three sons of Noah: Japheth (vv. 2–5), Ham (vv. 6–20), and Shem (vv. 21–31). Many names mentioned in chapter 10 are identifiable with nations of ancient times, some of which have continued down to the present.

MEANWHILE, IN OTHER PARTS OF THE WORLD...

Until after the Flood (chapters 6–9), world events center in the Middle East. Populations expand widely after Babel (chapter 11). By the time of the Patriarchs (about 2150 B.C.), Egypt is the world power. Egyptians are already using papyrus and ink for writing.

nothing; (3) creation was special, with light and time being the first of God's creative acts, since the day-count (1:5) began before the creation of sun and moon (1:16).

2. What do Christians mean when they talk about the Fall?

The Fall refers to that moment in time when human beings first disobeyed God. Chapter 3 tells the painful episode. What Eve set into motion, Adam confirmed and completed by joining her. They sinned together. The willful decision of Adam and Eve created a state of rebellion between the creation and her Creator. In the Fall, our first ancestors declared us on Satan's side.

The Bible makes it clear that the Fall brought sin into every subsequent person's life (Rom. 5:12). Our capacity for sin is inborn. We are sinners before we have the opportunity to sin. Not only are we sinners because we sin; we first sin because we are sinners. Why? Because we have all inherited the effects of Adam's fall.

3. How significant is the Flood in the overall biblical history?

The Bible treats the Flood as a worldwide event directly brought by God as a judgment on the sin of humanity. The Flood hangs like a warning cloud over all of subsequent history. Fortunately, that cloud also holds a rainbow of God's promised grace.

The Flood illustrates several important aspects of God's character and God's relationship with His creation: (1) God retains ultimate control of world events; (2) God can and will judge sin; (3) God can and does exercise grace even in judgment; (4) an even more universal and final judgment will be carried out on the world based on God's timetable.

4. Why did God cause the multiplication of languages and the dispersion of peoples in Genesis?

After the Flood, human civilization again began to spread across the earth. Later, the people decided to establish a city in tribute to themselves and as a way to keep from spreading across the earth (11:4). This was a double, prideful rebellion against God. First, their city, with its proposed tower, was to be a monument to their self-reliance. Second, the permanence of their settlement represented an effort to disobey God's direct command to inhabit the whole earth.

Because God purposed to fill the earth with custodians, He responded to the people's prideful rebellion. They had chosen to settle; He forced them to scatter. Their cooperation and self-reliance had been based on their shared language. Instead of using all their resources to obey God, they misused them for disobedience. God chose to complicate communication by multiplying the languages. The location where this confusion took place became known as Babel (related to a Hebrew word meaning "to confuse"). Later it became Babylon, the constant enemy of God's people, and throughout Scripture the capital of human rebellion against God (Rev. 16:19; 17:5).

5. How are we to interpret the Bible (narratives in Genesis) when the customs of ancient peoples seem so different than our own?

Three tools help us in the task of interpreting events that happened so long ago and so far away: (1) The best interpretive tool in understanding a Bible passage is its immediate context. Surrounding verses will often yield clues to the observant about foreign or unusual details in a particular account. (2) One part of the Bible often explains, expands, and comments on another part. An ever-growing familiarity with all of Scripture will equip a student with significant insight into the culture of those who lived the history. (3) Some insight can be gained from ancient sources outside of Scripture, but these only supplement our primary sources in the Bible itself.

Once we are at home in the exotic and unfamiliar contexts of Scripture, we meet people in the Bible pages who are very much like us. These are not aliens, but our ancestors across the ages. Their struggles are ours. Their failures are all too familiar to us. The God who spoke to them still speaks to us.

FURTHER STUDY ON GENESIS

1. How important is it to acknowledge God's creative role in the origin of the universe as described in Genesis?
2. What role do Adam and Eve play in the history of the human race?
3. How much would we know about God if we only had the Book of Genesis?
4. What biblical significance is given to such events as the eviction from the Garden of Eden, the Flood, the Tower of Babel?
5. How does God's promise to Abraham (12:1–3) affect the whole world?
6. Who are the heroes of this book? Why?

EXODUS
The Great Escape

TITLE

The descriptive title "Exodus" was given to the second book of Moses by the ancient translators of the Greek OT. The title is simply the Greek expression meaning "a going out," which delightfully understates God's great acts on behalf of His chosen people. The departure of Israel from Egypt is the dominant historical fact in Exodus.

In the Hebrew Bible, the opening words, "And (or Now) these are the names," served as the title of the book, and suggests that this book was to be accepted as the obvious sequel to Genesis, the first book of Moses. Hebrews 11:22 commends the faith of Joseph who, while on his deathbed (ca. 1804 B.C.), spoke of the "departure" or the "exiting" of the sons of Israel, looking ahead over 350 years to the Exodus (ca. 1445 B.C.).

AUTHOR AND DATE

The Book of Exodus was written approximately 1445 to 1405 B.C., and there is little doubt that Moses was the author. Moses followed God's instructions and "wrote all the words of the LORD" (24:4), which included at the least the record of the battle with Amalek (17:14), the Ten Commandments (34:4, 27–29), and the Book of the Covenant (20:22–23:33). Similar assertions of Mosaic writing occur elsewhere in the Pentateuch (the first five books of the OT): Moses is identified as the one who recorded the "starting points of their journeys" (Num. 33:2) and who "wrote this law" (Deut. 31:9).

The OT confirms Mosaic authorship of the portions mentioned above (see Josh. 1:7, 8; 8:31,32; 1 Kin. 2:3; 2 Kin. 14:6; Neh. 13:1; Dan. 9:11–13; and Mal. 4:4). The NT also concurs by citing Exodus 3:6 as part of "the Book of Moses" (Mark 12:26), by assigning Exodus 13:2 to "the law of Moses," which is also referred to as "the law of the Lord" (Luke 2:22,23), by ascribing Exodus 20:12 and 21:17 to Moses (Mark 7:10), by attributing the law to Moses (John 7:19; Rom. 10:5), and by Jesus' specifically declaring that Moses had written of Him (John 5:46,47).

At some time during his forty-year role as Israel's leader, beginning at 80 years of age and ending at 120 (7:7; Deut. 34:7), Moses wrote down this second of his five books. More specifically, it would have been after the Exodus and obviously before his death on Mt. Nebo in the plains of Moab. The date of the Exodus (ca. 1445 B.C.) dictates the date of the writing in the 15th century B.C.

Scripture dates Solomon's fourth year of reign, when he began to build the temple (ca. 966/65 B.C.), as being 480 years after the Exodus (1 Kin. 6:1), establishing the early date of 1445 B.C. Jephthah noted that, by his day, Israel had possessed Heshbon for 300 years (Judg. 11:26). Calculating backward and forward from Jephthah, and taking into account different periods of foreign oppression, judgeships and kingships, the wilderness wanderings, and the initial entry and conquest of Canaan under Joshua, this early date is confirmed and amounts to 480 years.

Scripture also dates the entry of Jacob and his extended family into Egypt (ca. 1875 B.C.) as being 430 years before the Exodus (12:40), thus placing Joseph in what archeologists have designated as the 12th Dynasty, the Middle Kingdom period of Egyptian history, and placing Moses and Israel's final years of residence and slavery in what archeologists have designated as the 18th Dynasty, or New Kingdom period. Further, Joseph's stint as vizier over all of Egypt (Gen. 45:8) prevents his having served under the Hyksos (ca. 1730–1570 B.C.), the foreign invaders

CHRIST IN . . . EXODUS

As God DELIVERED THE NATION OF ISRAEL out from Egyptian slavery, a new foundation was laid by the presentation of the law. The focus of Exodus remains twofold: (1) a description of the redemption of God's people; (2) the formation of the chosen nation through whom Christ would enter the world. The law prepared Israel to receive Christ, its promised Messiah and King.

who ruled during a period of confusion in Egypt and who never controlled all of the country. They were a mixed Semitic race who introduced the horse and chariot as well as the composite bow. These implements of war made possible their expulsion from Egypt.

BACKGROUND AND SETTING

Eighteenth Dynasty Egypt, the setting for Israel's dramatic departure, was a politically and economically important period of Egyptian history. Thutmose III, for example, the Pharaoh of the Oppression, has been called the "Napoleon of Ancient Egypt," the ruler who expanded the boundaries of Egyptian influence far beyond natural borders. This was the dynasty that over a century before, under the leadership of Amose I, had expelled the Hyksos kings from the country and redirected the country's economic, military, and diplomatic growth. At the time of the Exodus, Egypt was strong.

Egyptian Pharaohs

Ahmosis I	1570–46 B.C.	Amenhotep IV	1379–62 B.C.
Amenhotep I	1546–26 B.C.	Smenkhkare	1364–61 B.C.
Thutmose I	1526–12 B.C.	Tutankhamon	1361–52 B.C.
Thutmose II	1512–04 B.C.	Ay	1352–48 B.C.
Thutmose III	1504–1450 B.C.	Horemheb	1348–20 B.C.
Hatshepsut	1504–1483 B.C.	Rameses I	1320–18 B.C.
Amenhotep II	1450–25 B.C.	Seti I	1318–04 B.C.
Thutmose IV	1425–17 B.C.	Rameses II	1304–1236 B.C.
Amenhotep III	1417–1379 B.C.	Merneptah	1236–1223 B.C.

Moses, born in 1525 B.C. (80 years old in 1445 B.C.), became "learned in all the wisdom of the Egyptians" (Acts 7:22) while growing up in the courts of Pharaohs Thutmose I and II and Queen Hatshepsut for his first forty years (Acts 7:23). He was in self-imposed Midianite exile during the reign of Thutmose III for another forty years (Acts 7:30), and returned at God's direction to be Israel's leader early in the reign of Amenhotep II, the pharaoh of the Exodus. God used both the educational system of Egypt and his exile in Midian to prepare Moses to represent his people before a powerful pharaoh and to guide his people through the wilderness of the Sinai peninsula during his final 40 years (Acts 7:36). Moses died on Mt. Nebo when he was 120 years old (Deut. 34:1–6), as God's judg-

The Life of Moses

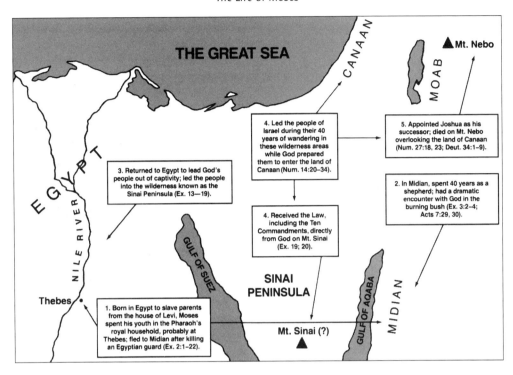

THE GREAT SEA

▲ Mt. Nebo

CANAAN

MOAB

EGYPT

NILE RIVER

GULF OF SUEZ

SINAI PENINSULA

GULF OF AQABA

MIDIAN

Thebes

Mt. Sinai (?)
▲

1. Born in Egypt to slave parents from the house of Levi, Moses spent his youth in the Pharaoh's royal household, probably at Thebes; fled to Midian after killing an Egyptian guard (Ex. 2:1–22).

2. In Midian, spent 40 years as a shepherd; had a dramatic encounter with God in the burning bush (Ex. 3:2–4; Acts 7:29, 30).

3. Returned to Egypt to lead God's people out of captivity; led the people into the wilderness known as the Sinai Peninsula (Ex. 13—19).

4. Led the people of Israel during their 40 years of wandering in these wilderness areas while God prepared them to enter the land of Canaan (Num. 14:20–34).

4. Received the Law, including the Ten Commandments, directly from God on Mt. Sinai (Ex. 19; 20).

5. Appointed Joshua as his successor; died on Mt. Nebo overlooking the land of Canaan (Num. 27:18, 23; Deut. 34:1–9).

ment was on him for his anger and disrespect (Num. 20:1–3). While he looked on from afar, Moses never entered the Promised Land. Centuries later he appeared to the disciples on the Mt. of Transfiguration (Matt. 17:3).

KEY PEOPLE IN EXODUS
Moses—author of the Pentateuch and deliverer of Israel from Egyptian slavery (2–40)
Miriam—prophetess and older sister of Moses (2:7; 15:20,21)
Pharaoh's daughter—the princess who rescued baby Moses from the water and adopted him (2:5–10)
Jethro—Midian shepherd who became Moses' father-in-law (3:1; 4:18; 18:1–12)
Aaron—brother of Moses and first high priest of Israel (4:14–40:31)
Pharaoh—unnamed Egyptian leader at the time of the Exodus (5:1–14:31)
Joshua—assistant to Moses and military leader who led Israel into the Promised Land (17:9–14; 24:13; 32:17; 33:11)

HISTORICAL AND THEOLOGICAL THEMES
In God's timing, the Exodus marked the end of a period of oppression for Abraham's descendants (Gen. 15:13), and the beginning of the fulfillment of the covenant promise to Abraham that his descendants would not only reside in the Promised Land, but would also multiply and become a great nation (Gen. 12:1–3,7). The purpose of the book may be

expressed like this: To trace the rapid growth of Jacob's descendants from Egypt to the establishment of the theocratic nation in their Promised Land.

At appropriate times, on Mt. Sinai and in the plains of Moab, God also gave the Israelites that body of legislation, the law, which they needed for living properly in Israel as the theocratic people of God. By this, they were distinct from all other nations (Deut. 4:7,8; Rom. 9:4,5).

By God's self-revelation, the Israelites were instructed in the sovereignty and majesty, the goodness and holiness, and the grace and mercy of their Lord, the one and only God of heaven and earth (see especially Ex. 3,6,33, 34). The account of the Exodus and the events that followed are also the subject of other major biblical revelation (cf. Pss. 105:25–45; 106:6–27; Acts 7:17–44; 1 Cor. 10:1–13; Heb. 9:1–6; 11:23–29).

KEY DOCTRINES IN EXODUS

Covenant promises—God's promise to Abraham to preserve his heritage forever (12:1–3,7,31–42; Gen. 17:19; Lev. 26:45; Judg. 2:20; Ps. 105:38; Acts 3:25)

The nature of God—human beings cannot understand God completely but can come to know Him personally (3:7; 8:19; 34:6,7; 2 Sam. 22:31; Job 36:26; Matt. 5:48; Luke 1:49,50)

The Ten Commandments—the basic truths of God (20:1–17; 23:12; Lev. 19:4,12; Deut. 6:14; 7:8,9; Neh. 13:16–19; Is. 44:15; Matt. 5:27; 19:18; Mark 10:19; Luke 13:14; Rom. 13:9; Eph. 5:3,5)

KEY WORDS IN Exodus

Delivered: Hebrew *natsal*—3:8; 5:18; 21:13; 22:7,10,26; 23:31—this verb may mean either "to strip, to plunder" or "to snatch away, to deliver." The word is often used to describe God's work in delivering (3:8) or rescuing (6:6), the Israelites from slavery. Sometimes it signifies deliverance of God's people from sin and guilt (Ps. 51:14). In 18:8–10, however, the word is a statement of God's supremacy over the Egyptian pantheon of deities.

Consecrate: Hebrew *qadash*—28:3,41; 29:9, 33,35; 30:30; 32:29—this verb means "to make holy," "to declare distinct," or "to set apart." The word describes dedicating an object or person to God. By delivering the Israelites from slavery in Egypt, God made the nation of Israel distinct. Through His mighty acts of deliverance, God demonstrated that the Israelites were His people, and He was their God (6:7). By having the people wash themselves at Mt. Sinai, the Lord made it clear that He was claiming a special relationship with them (19:10).

Washing: Hebrew *rachats*—2:5; 19:10; 29:4, 17; 30:18,21; 40:12,30—washing or bathing. The term was used in both religious and cultural settings. The ancient custom of washing a guest's feet was a part of hospitality still practiced in the NT period (Gen. 18:4; John 13:5). Ritual washing was an important step in the purification of the priests for service in the tabernacle (40:12). Washing with water symbolized spiritual cleansing, the preparation necessary for entering God's presence (Ps. 26:6; 73:13). The OT prophets used this imagery of repentance (Is. 1:16; Ezek. 16:4). In the NT, Paul describes redemption in Christ as "the washing of regeneration" (Titus 3:5).

GOD'S CHARACTER IN EXODUS
God is accessible—24:2; 34:4–7
God is glorious—15:1,6,11; 33:18–23; 34:5–7
God is good—34:6
God is gracious—34:6
God is holy—15:11
God is long-suffering—34:6
God is merciful—34:6,7
God is all-powerful—6:3; 8:19; 9:3, 16; 15:6,11,12
God is provident—15:9–19
God is true—34:6
God is unequaled—9:14
God is wise—3:7
God is wrathful—7:20; 8:6,16,24; 9:3,9,23; 10:13,22; 12:29; 14:24,27; 32:11,35

INTERPRETIVE CHALLENGES
The absence of any Egyptian record of the devastation of Egypt by the ten plagues and the major defeat of Pharaoh's elite army at the Red Sea should not be reason to question whether the account is historically authentic. Egyptian historiography did not permit records of their pharaohs' embarrassments and ignominious defeats to be published. In

The Plan of the Tabernacle

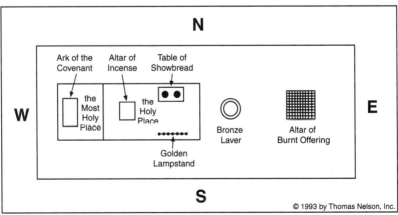

The tabernacle was to provide a place where God might dwell among His people. The term *tabernacle* sometimes refers to the tent, including the Holy Place and the Most Holy Place, which was covered with embroidered curtains. But in other places it refers to the entire complex, including the curtained court in which the tent stood.

N

Ark of the Covenant | Altar of Incense | Table of Showbread

the Most Holy Place | the Holy Place

W — E

Bronze Laver | Altar of Burnt Offering

Golden Lampstand

S

© 1993 by Thomas Nelson, Inc.

This illustration shows relative positions of the tabernacle furniture used in Israelite worship. The tabernacle is enlarged for clarity.

The Furniture of the Tabernacle

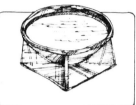

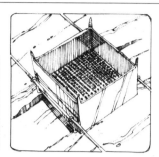

Ark of the Covenant
(Ex. 25:10–22)
The ark was most sacred of all the furniture in the tabernacle. Here the Hebrews kept a copy of the Ten Commandments, which summarized the whole covenant.

Bronze Laver
(Ex. 30:17–21)
It was to the laver of bronze that the priests would come for cleansing. They must be pure to enter the presence of God.

Altar of Burnt Offering
(Ex. 27:1–8)
Animal sacrifices were offered on this altar, located in the court in front of the tabernacle. The blood of the sacrifice was sprinkled on the four horns of the altar.

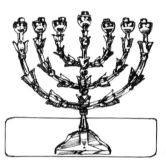

Golden Lampstand
(Ex. 25:31–40)
The gold lampstand stood in the holy place, opposite the table of showbread. It held seven lamps, flat bowls in which a wick lay with one end in the oil of the bowl and the lighted end hanging out.

Table of Showbread
(Ex. 25:23–30)
The table of showbread was a stand on which the offerings were placed. Always in God's presence on the table were the 12 loaves of bread representing the 12 tribes.

Altar of Incense
(Ex. 30:1–10)
The altar of incense inside the tabernacle was much smaller than the altar of burnt offering outside. The incense burned on the altar was a perfume of a sweet-smelling aroma.

recording the Conquest under Joshua, Scripture specifically notes the three cities that Israel destroyed and burned (Josh. 6:24; 8:28; 11:11–13). The Conquest, after all, was one of takeover and inhabitation of property virtually intact, not a war designed to destroy. The date of Israel's march into Canaan will not be confirmed, therefore, by examining extensive burn levels at city-sites of a later period.

Despite the absence of any extrabiblical, ancient Near Eastern records of the Hebrew bondage, the plagues, the Exodus, and the Conquest, archeological evidence confirms the early date. All the pharaohs, for example, of the 15th century left evidence of interest in building enterprises in Lower Egypt. These projects were obviously accessible to Moses in the Delta region near Goshen.

The symbolic significance of the tabernacle has generated much reflection. Attempts to link every item of furniture and every piece of building material to Christ may be appealing to some, but if NT statements and allusions do not support such connections then it is probably unwise to assume such connections. The tabernacle's structure and design for efficiency and beauty are one thing, but finding hidden meaning and symbolism is difficult to prove. How the sacrificial and worship system of the tabernacle and its parts meaningfully symbolize the redeeming work of the coming Messiah must be left to those NT passages that clearly address the subject.

OUTLINE
I. Israel in Egypt (1:1–12:36)
    A. The Population Explosion (1:1–7)
    B. The Oppression under the Pharaohs (1:8–22)
    C. The Maturation of a Deliverer (2:1–4:31)
    D. The Confrontation with Pharaoh (5:1–11:10)
    E. The Preparation for Departure (12:1–36)
II. Israel on the Road to Sinai (12:37–18:27)
    A. Exiting Egypt and Panicking (12:37–14:14)
    B. Crossing the Red Sea and Rejoicing (14:15–15:21)
    C. Traveling to Sinai and Grumbling (15:22–17:16)
    D. Meeting with Jethro and Learning (18:1–27)
III. Israel Encamped at Sinai (19:1–40:38)
    A. The Law of God Prescribed (19:1–24:18)
    B. The Tabernacle of God Described (25:1–31:18)
    C. The Worship of God Defiled (32:1–35)
    D. The Presence of God Confirmed (33:1–34:35)
    E. The Tabernacle of God Constructed (35:1–40:38)

MEANWHILE, IN OTHER PARTS OF THE WORLD...
The Iron Age in Syria and Palestine begins. Also, people in Mediterranean and Scandinavian countries perfect the art of shipbuilding.

The Exodus from Egypt

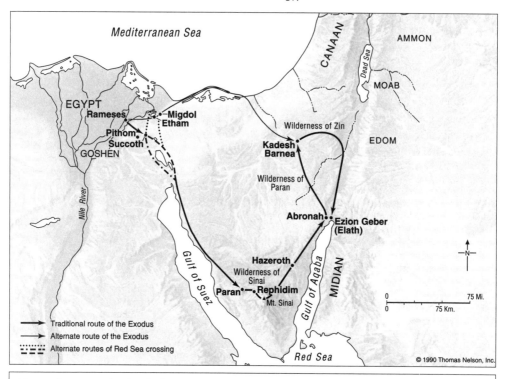

The precise route taken by the Israelites to Mt. Sinai after their departure from Egypt is uncertain. As the map indicates, scholars have proposed both northern and southern routes, with the southern path the most likely. It took approximately two months to reach Sinai, where the Israelites encamped for roughly ten months during the period of divine revelation.

ANSWERS TO TOUGH QUESTIONS

1. Why don't the Egyptian historical records acknowledge the devastation of the plagues, the defeat of the army, and Israel's escape that occurred during the Exodus?

The absence of references to Israel in the available Egyptian historical records should come as no surprise. Most of these records exist in the form of official inscriptions in the tombs and monuments of ancient leaders. Such public and lasting memorials were rarely used to record humiliating defeats and disasters. Interestingly, one of the subtle proofs of the truth of Scripture is the way in which it records both the triumphs and the tragedies of God's people. The Bible offers as many examples of failure as it does of faith.

2. How are we in the twenty-first century supposed to think about the astonishing miracles that Exodus so matter-of-factly reports, such as the burning bush, the plagues, God's presence in the pillar of fire and cloud, the parting of the Red Sea, and manna, to name a few?

The scientific materialism of many twenty-first-century people makes it difficult for them to consider any so-called miracles. If the laws of nature and science are considered supreme, the existence of a personal Supreme Being who is above the laws of nature and able to override them becomes impossible to imagine. Examples of miracles do little to convince someone who is already convinced that miracles are impossible.

Miracles can demonstrate God's existence; they don't prove it. Human beings display an amazing ability to come up with alternate explanations for God's activity in history. The situation is not that twenty-first-century people can't believe in miracles; rather, it is that twenty-first-century people often won't believe in miracles.

For Christians, the matter is settled by faith. In becoming Christians, we had to believe in the central miracle: God came in the flesh, Jesus Christ, who lived, died, and rose from the dead to reign eternally as Lord and Savior. In the light of that miracle, the miracles of Exodus become less a matter for speculation and more a matter of wonder and worship. They are examples of the lengths to which God went to communicate to people. Even twenty-first-century Christians are humbled and awestruck by God's amazing power!

3. Are the Ten Commandments outmoded expectations or divine demands?

People make a serious error when they speak about "not breaking the Ten Commandments." History amply displays the fact that people persist in breaking themselves on the Ten Commandments. The commandments represent God's absolute and unchanging standard despite any arguments over their interpretation and application.

The title "Ten Commandments" comes from Moses (34:28). The emphasis on God Himself speaking and writing these words makes unacceptable any theories of Israel's borrowing legal patterns or concepts from surrounding nations.

The Ten Commandments may be grouped into two broad categories: the vertical—humanity's relationship to God (20:2–11); and the horizontal—humanity's relationship to the community (20:12–17). By these Ten Commandments, true theology and true worship, the name of God and the Sabbath, family honor, life, marriage, property, truth, and virtue are well protected.

4. Why all the specific details about the Tabernacle and what do they mean for us today?

Ever since God dictated the blueprints of the Tabernacle to Moses, people have wondered about the significance of the exact details. Several terms are used to indicate times in the Bible when events, persons, or things represent larger ideas: typology and foreshadowing. For example, the sacrifice of the lambs in the OT had not only a limited immediate significance in understanding the cost of forgiveness, but this practice also foreshadowed the eventual sacrifice of the Lamb of God, Jesus, on the cross.

Because at least some parts of the tabernacle hold special significance—the Ark representing God's covenant with His people—students of Scripture have looked for other possible deeper meanings. It's tempting to establish connections between every item of furniture and every piece of building material to Christ. But if NT statements do not support such connections and typology, students ought to proceed with caution. The beauty and efficiency of the Tabernacle's design present a tribute to God's creative character, but those who look for hidden meaning in every tent peg and covering stitch run the risk of missing the big picture in the details. The NT points repeatedly to the awesome fact of God's presence with people as represented in the Tabernacle. Other NT lessons (particularly the Book of Hebrews) help identify the intended symbols and deeper meanings.

FURTHER STUDY ON EXODUS
1. What are the highlights of Moses' early life?
2. In what different ways did God make Himself known throughout Exodus?
3. What were the ten plagues that afflicted the Egyptians?
4. How did the plagues relate to the gods worshiped by the Egyptians?
5. How does the law summarized in the Ten Commandments show us we need God's help?
6. Which of the Ten Commandments direct our relationship with God and which direct our relationships with other people?

LEVITICUS
The Blueprint for Redemption

TITLE

The original Hebrew title of this third book of the Law is taken from the first word, translated "And He called." Several OT books derive their Hebrew names in the same manner (e.g., Genesis, "In the beginning"; Exodus, "Now these are the names"). The title "Leviticus" comes from the ancient scholars who produced the Latin Vulgate version of the Greek OT (LXX). The orginal title *Leuitikon* means literally "matters of the Levites" (25:32,33). While the book addresses issues of the Levites' responsibilities, much more significantly, all the priests are instructed in how they are to assist the people in worship, and the people are informed about how to live a holy life. NT writers quote the Book of Leviticus over fifteen times.

AUTHOR AND DATE

Authorship and date issues are resolved by the concluding verse of the book, "These are the commandments which the LORD commanded Moses for the children of Israel on Mount Sinai" (27:34; cf. 7:38; 25:1; 26:46). The fact that God gave these laws to Moses (cf. 1:1) appears fifty-six times in the 27 chapters of Leviticus. In addition to recording detailed prescriptions, the book chronicles several historical accounts relating to the laws (see 8–10; 24:10–23). The Exodus occurred in 1445 B.C. (see Exodus: Author and Date) and the tabernacle was finished one year later (Ex. 40:17). Leviticus picks up the record at that point, probably revealed in the first month (Abib/Nisan) of the second year after the Exodus. The Book of Numbers begins after that in the second month (Ziv; cf. Num. 1:1).

BACKGROUND AND SETTING

Before the year that Israel camped at Mt. Sinai: (1) the presence of God's glory had never formally resided among the Israelites; (2) a central place of worship, like the tabernacle, had never existed; (3) a structured and regulated set of sacrifices and feasts had not been given; and (4) a High-Priest, a formal priesthood, and a cadre of tabernacle workers had not been appointed. As Exodus concluded, features one and two had been accomplished, thereby requiring that elements three and four be established, which is where Leviticus fits in. Exodus 19:6 called Israel to be "a kingdom of priests and a holy nation." Leviticus in turn was God's instruction for His newly redeemed people, teaching them how to worship and obey Him.

Israel had, up to that point, only the historical records of the patriarchs from which to gain their knowledge of how to worship and live before their God. Having been slaves for centuries in Egypt, the land of a seemingly infinite number of gods, their concept of worship and the godly life was severely distorted. Their tendency to hold on to polytheism (belief in many gods) and pagan ritual is demonstrated in the wilderness wanderings, e.g., when they worshiped the golden calf (cf. Ex. 32). God would not permit them to worship in the ways of their Egyptian neighbors, nor would He tolerate Egyptian ideas about morality and sin. With the instructions in Leviticus, the priests could lead Israel in worship appropriate to the Lord.

Even though the book contains a great deal of law, it is presented in a historical format. Immediately after Moses supervised the construction of the tabernacle, God came in glory to dwell there; this marked the close of the Book of Exodus (40:34–38). Leviticus begins with God calling Moses from the tabernacle and ends with God's commands to Moses in the form of binding legislation. Israel's King (God) had occupied his palace (the tabernacle), instituted His law, and declared Himself a covenant partner with His subjects.

CHRIST IN ... LEVITICUS

GOD'S EXPLICIT INSTRUCTIONS about offerings within Leviticus point towards the final substitutionary sacrifice of Christ. Because the sacrifices of the people represented only temporary removal of Israel's sins, they needed to be repeated continually. Jesus lived a perfect life on earth and presented Himself as the final sacrifice for all humankind. In contrast to the OT Passover feast celebrated annually, believers constantly celebrate the "feast" of the new Passover—Jesus Christ, the Passover Lamb (1 Cor. 5:7).

No geographical movement occurs in this book. The people of Israel stay at the foot of Sinai, the mountain where God came down to give His law (25:1; 26:46; 27:34). They were still there one month later when the record of Numbers began (cf. Num. 1:1).

KEY PEOPLE IN LEVITICUS

Moses—prophet and leader who acted as God's mouthpiece to explain His law to Israel (1:1; 4:1; 5:14; 6:1–27:34)

Aaron—Moses' brother and first high priest of Israel (1:7; 2:3, 10; 3:5,8,13; 6:9–24:9)

Nadab—son of Aaron, in training to become a priest, died because of disobedience to the Lord's commands (8:36; 10:1,2)

Abihu—son of Aaron, in training to become a priest, died because of disobedience to the Lord's commands (8:36; 10:1,2)

Eleazar—son of Aaron who succeeded him as high priest of Israel (10:6–20)

Ithamar—son of Aaron who also became a priest (10:6–20)

HISTORICAL AND THEOLOGICAL THEMES

The core ideas around which Leviticus develops are the holy character of God and the will of God for Israel's holiness. God's holiness, mankind's sinfulness, sacrifice, and God's presence in the sanctuary are the book's most common themes. With a clear, authoritative tone, the book sets forth instruction toward personal holiness at the urging of God (11:44, 45; 19:2; 20:7,26; cf. 1 Pet. 1:14–16). Matters related to Israel's life of faith tend to focus on purity in ritual settings, but not to the exclusion of concerns regarding Israel's personal purity. In fact, there is a continuing emphasis on personal holiness in response to the holiness of God (cf. this emphasis in chaps. 17–27). On over 125 occasions, Leviticus indicts mankind for uncleanness and/or instructs on how to be purified. The motive for such holiness is stated in two repeated phrases: "I am the LORD" and "I am holy." These are used over fifty times.

The theme of the conditional Mosaic Covenant resurfaces throughout the book, but particularly in chap. 26. This contract for the new nation not only details the consequences for obedience or disobedience to the covenant stipulations, but it does so in a manner scripted for determining Israel's history. One cannot help but recognize prophetic implications in the punishments for disobedience; they sound like the events of the much later Babylonian deportment, captivity, and subsequent return to the land almost 900 years after Moses wrote Leviticus (ca. 538 B.C.). The future implications for Israel's disobedience will not conclude until Messiah comes to introduce His kingdom and end the curses of Leviticus 26 and Deuteronomy 28 (cf. Zech. 14:11).

The five sacrifices and offerings were symbolic. Their design was to allow the truly penitent and thankful worshiper to express faith in and love for God by the observance of these rituals. When the heart was not penitent and thankful, God was not pleased with the ritual (cf. Amos 5:21–27). The offerings were burnt, symbolizing the worshiper's desire to be purged of sin and sending up the fragrant smoke of true worship to God. The countless small details required within the rituals was to teach exactness and precision that would extend to the way the people obeyed the moral and spiritual laws of God and the way they revered every facet of His Word.

The Levitical Offerings

Name
(1) Burnt Offering (olah, Heb.): a. Sweet aroma; b. Voluntary.

Scripture References
Lev. 1:3-17; 6:8–13.

Purpose
(1) To propitiate for sin in general (1:4).
(2) To signify complete dedication and consecration to God; hence it is called the "whole burnt offering."

Consisted of
According to wealth:
(1) Bull without blemish (1:3-9);
(2) Male sheep or goat without blemish (1:10–13);
(3) Turtledoves or young pigeons (1:14-17).

God's Portion
Entirety burned on the altar of burnt offering (1:9), except the skin (7:8).

Priests' Portion
Skin only (7:8).

Offerer's Portion
None.

Prophetic Significance
Signifies complete dedication of life to God:
(1) On the part of Christ (Matt. 26:39-44; Mark 14:36; Luke 22:42; Phil. 2:5-11).
(2) On the part of the believer (Rom. 12:1,2; Heb. 13:15).

The Levitical Offerings

Name
(2) **Grain Offering** (minhah, Heb.): a. Sweet aroma; b. Voluntary.

Scripture References
Lev. 2:1-16; 6:14–18; 7:12,13.

Purpose
The grain offering accompanied all the burnt offerings; it signified one's homage and thanksgiving to God.

Consisted of
Three types:
(1) Fine flour mixed with oil and frankincense (2:1-3);
(2) Cakes made of fine flour mixed with oil and baked in an oven (2:4), in a pan (2:5), or in a covered pan (2:7);
(3) Green heads of roasted grain mixed with oil and frankincense (2:14,15).

God's Portion
Memorial portion burned on the altar of burnt offering (2:2,9,16).

Priests' Portion
Remainder to be eaten in the court of the tabernacle (2:3,10; 6:16-18; 7:14,15).

Offerer's Portion
None.

Prophetic Significance
Signifies the perfect humanity of Christ:
(1) The absence of the leaven typifies the sinlessness of Christ (Heb. 4:15; 1 John 3:5).
(2) The presence of oil is emblematic of the Holy Spirit (Luke 4:18; 1 John 2:20,27).

The Levitical Offerings

Name

(3) **Peace Offering** (shelem, Heb.): a. Sweet aroma; b. Voluntary.

Scripture References

Lev. 3:1-17; 7:11–21, 28-34.

Purpose

The peace offering generally expressed peace and fellowship between the offerer and God; hence it culminated in a communal meal.

There were three types:

(1) Thank Offering: to express gratitude for an unexpected blessing or deliverance.

(2) Votive Offering: to express gratitude for a blessing or deliverance granted when a vow had accompanied the petition.

(3) Freewill Offering: to express gratitude to God without regard to any specific blessing or deliverance.

Consisted of

According to wealth:

(1) From the herd, a male or female without blemish (3:1–5);

(2) From the flock, a male or female without blemish (3:6-11);

(3) From the goats (3:12–17).

> Note: Minor imperfections were permitted when the peace offering
> was a freewill offering of a bull or a lamb (22:23).

God's Portion

Fatty portions burned on the altar of burnt offering (3:3-5).

Priests' Portion

Breast (wave offering) and right thigh (heave offering; 7:30–34).

Offerer's Portion

Remainder to be eaten in the court by the offerer and his family:

a. Thank offering—to be eaten the same day (7:15).

b. Votive and freewill offerings—to be eaten the first and second day (7:16-18).

> Note: This is the only offering in which the offerer shared.

Prophetic Significance

Foreshadows the peace which the believer has with God through Jesus Christ (Rom. 5:1; Col. 1:20)

The Levitical Offerings

Name

(4) **Sin Offering** (hattat, Heb.): a. Non-sweet aroma; b. Compulsory.

Scripture References

Lev. 4:1–5:13; 6:24–30.

Purpose

To atone for sins committed unknowingly, especially where no restitution was possible.

> Note: Num. 15:30, 31: The sin offering was of no avail in cases of defiant rebellion against God.

Consisted of

(1) For the high priest, a bull without blemish (4:3-12).

(2) For the congregation, a bull without blemish (4:13–21)

(3) For a ruler, a male goat without blemish (4:22-26).

(4) For a commoner, a female goat or female lamb without blemish (4:27–35).

(5) In cases of poverty, two turtledoves or two young pigeons (one for a sin offering, the other for a burnt offering) could be substituted (5:7-10).

(6) In cases of extreme poverty, fine flour could be substituted (5:11–13; cf. Heb. 9:22).

God's Portion

(1) Fatty portions to be burned on the altar of burnt offering (4:8-10,19,26,31,35).

(2) When the sin offering was for the high priest or congregation, the remainder of the bull was to be burned outside the camp (4:11,12,20,21).

Priests' Portion

When the sin offering was for a ruler or commoner, the remainder of the goat or lamb was to be eaten in the tabernacle court (6:26)

Offerer's Portion

None.

Prophetic Significance

Prefigures the fact that in His death:

(1) Christ was made sin for us (2 Cor. 5:21);

(2) Christ suffered outside the gates of Jerusalem (Heb. 13:11-13).

The Levitical Offerings

Name
(5) **Trespass Offering** ('asham, Heb.): a. Non-sweet aroma; b. Compulsory.

Scripture References
Lev. 5:14–6:7; 7:1–7.

Purpose
To atone for sins committed unknowingly, especially where restitution was possible.

Consisted of
(1) If the offense were against the Lord (tithes, offerings, etc.), a ram without blemish was to be brought; restitution was reckoned according to the priest's estimate of the value of the trespass, plus one-fifth (5:15,16).
(2) If the offense were against man, a ram without blemish was to be brought; restitution was reckoned according to the value plus one-fifth (6:4-6).

God's Portion
Fatty portions to be burned on the altar of burnt offering (7:3-5).

Priests' Portion
Remainder to be eaten in a holy place (7:6,7).

Offerer's Portion
None.

Prophetic Significance
Foreshadows the fact that Christ is also our trespass offering (Col. 2:13).

KEY DOCTRINES IN LEVITICUS

Sacrifice—God required sacrifices from the people to atone for sin (1:3, 9–13; 16:3; 17:8; 19:5; Ex. 29:34; Deut. 16:5,6; Judg. 11:31; Ps. 66:13–15; Matt. 5:23,24; Rom. 8:3; 12:1; Heb. 2:17; 1 John 2:2)

Holiness—the attribute that summarizes God's perfect character; Israel was called to be holy as God is holy (11:44,45; 19:2; 20:7,26; 21:6–8; Ex. 6:7; 19:6; Ps. 22:3; 99:5; Is. 41:14–16; 1 Thess. 4:7; 1 Peter 1:14–16)

Offerings—forms of worship to God, to give expression of the penitent and thankful heart (1:1–17; 2:1–16; 3:1–17; 4:1–5:13; 5:14–6:7; Gen. 4:4,5; Deut. 16:10; 1 Kin. 18:33–40; Job 42:8; 2 Cor. 5:21; 2 Tim. 4:6)

Israel as God's holy nation—the people through whom Christ would enter the world (26:42–46; Gen. 15:12–21; Ex. 19:5,6; 2 Sam. 7:13; 23:5; Heb. 8:6–13)

KEY WORDS IN

Leviticus

Offering: Hebrew *qorban*—2:3; 4:35; 6:18; 7:14,33; 9:4; 10:14—this Hebrew word is derived from the verb "to bring near" and literally means "that which one brings near to God." The fact that the Israelites could approach to present their gifts to God reveals His mercy. Even though the people were sinful and rebellious, God instituted a sacrificial system in which they could reconcile themselves to Him. The sacrifices foreshadowed Jesus' death on the cross, the ultimate offering, the offering that ended the need for any others. Through Christ's sacrificial death, we have once for all been reconciled to God (Heb. 10:10–18). An appropriate response to Jesus' death for us is to offer our lives as living sacrifices to God (Rom. 12:1).

Memorial Portion: Hebrew ʾazkarah—2:2,9,16; 5:12; 6:15; 23:24; 24:7—a memorial portion of a grain offering was a representative portion burnt on the altar in place of the whole amount. The rest was a gift to the priest, to support him in his ministry. The word for *memorial portion* is related to the Hebrew verb *zakar*, which means "to remember." It signifies the worshiper's remembering of God's gracious character and generosity, especially God's remembering and blessing of the worshiper.

Blood: Hebrew *dam*—1:5; 3:17; 4:7; 8:15; 9:9; 16:18; 17:10; 20:11—related to the Hebrew word ʾadom, which means "red" (Gen. 25:30) and refers to blood. This may be the blood of animals (Exodus 23:18) or human beings (Gen. 4:10). The word *blood* may also represent a person's guilt, as in the phrase "his blood shall be upon him"; that is, he is responsible for his own guilt (20:9). The OT equates *life* with *blood* (Gen. 9:4; Deut. 12:23), which vividly illustrates the sanctity of human life (Gen. 9:6). According to the NT, "without shedding of blood there is no remission" of sin (Heb. 9:22). Thus the emphasis on blood in the OT sacrifices pointed to the blood that Christ would shed, i.e., the life that He would give on our behalf (Rom. 5:9; 1 Cor. 11:25,26).

Jubilee: Hebrew *yobel*—25:9,12,30,40,54; 27:18,24—literally means "ram" or "ram's horn" (Ex. 19:13; Josh. 6:5). The term is associated with the Year of Jubilee in Leviticus 25:10 and Numbers 36:4. The fiftieth year was a "jubilee" year for the Hebrews, marked by the blowing of a trumpet (25:9). During that year, the Israelites were instructed to practice freedom and liberty: debts were canceled; slaves were freed; the land rested; family property was redeemed (25:10–17). The fact that Jesus quoted Isaiah 48:8,9 seems to indicate that Jesus equated His earthly ministry with the principles of the Year of Jubilee (Luke 4:18,19).

GOD'S CHARACTER IN LEVITICUS
God is accessible—16:12–15
God is glorious—9:6,23
God is holy—11:44–45
God is wrathful—10:2

Jewish Feasts and Christ Fulfills Israel's Feasts

Feast of	Month on Jewish Calendar	Day	Corresponding Month	References
Passover	Nisan	14	Mar.Apr.	Ex. 12:1-14; Matt. 26:17-20
*Unleavened Bread	Nisan	15-21	Mar.-Apr.	Ex. 12:15-20
Firstfruits	Nisan or Sivan	16 6	Mar.-Apr. May-June	Lev. 23:9-14 Num. 28:26
*Pentecost (Harvest or Weeks)	Sivan	6 (50 days after barley harvest	May-June	Deut. 16:9-12; Acts 2:1
Trumpets, Rosh Hashanah	Tishri	1, 2	Sept.-Oct.	Num. 29:1-6
Day of Atonement, Yom Kippur	Tishri	10	Sept.-Oct.	Lev. 23:26-32; Heb. 9:7
*Tabernacles (Booths or Ingathering)	Tishri	15-22	Sept.-Oct.	Neh. 8:13-18; John 7:2
Dedication (Lights), Hanuhhah	Chislev	25 (8 days)	Nov.-Dec.	John 10:22
Purim (Lots)	Adar	14, 15	Feb.-Mar.	Esth. 9:18-32

*The three major feasts for which all males of Israel were required to travel to the temple in Jerusalem (Ex. 23:14-19).

The Feasts (Leviticus 23)	Christ's Fulfillment
Passover (March/April)	Death of Christ (1 Corinthians 5:7)
Unleavened Bread (March/April)	Sinlessness of Christ (1 Corinthians 5:8)
Firstfruits (March/April)	Resurrection of Christ (1 Corinthians 15:23)
Pentecost (May/June)	Outpouring of Spirit of Christ (Acts 1:5; 2:4)
Trumpets (Sept./Oct.)	Israel's Regathering by Christ (Matthew 24:31)
Atonement (Sept./Oct.)	Substitutionary Sacrifice by Christ (Romans 11:26)
Tabernacles (Sept./Oct.)	Rest and Reunion with Christ (Zechariah 14:16–19)

INTERPRETIVE CHALLENGES
Leviticus is both a manual for the worship of God in Israel and a theology of Old Covenant ritual. Complete understanding of the ceremonies, laws, and ritual details prescribed in the book is difficult today because Moses assumed a certain context of historical understanding. Once one understands the detailed requirements of OT worship, the question arises as to how believers in the church should respond to them, since the NT clearly replaces OT ceremonial law (cf. Acts 10:1–16; Col. 2:16, 17), the levitical priesthood (cf. 1 Pet. 2:9; Rev. 1:6; 5:10; 20:6), and the sanctuary (cf. Matt. 27:51), by way of instituting the

New Covenant (cf. Matt. 26:28; 2 Cor. 3:6–18; Heb. 7–10). Rather than try to practice the old ceremonies or look for some deeper spiritual significance in them, the focus should be on the holy and divine character behind them. This may be part of the reason that Moses' explanations of the prescriptions for cleanness offer greater insight into the mind of God than do the ceremonies themselves. The spiritual principles behind the rituals are timeless because they are embedded in the nature of God. The NT makes it clear that from Pentecost forward (cf. Acts 2), the church is under the authority of the New Covenant, not the Old (cf. Heb. 7–10).

OUTLINE

I. Laws Pertaining to Sacrifice (1:1–7:38)
    A. Legislation for the Laity (1:1–6:7)
        1. Burnt Offerings (chap. 1)
        2. Grain Offerings (chap. 2)
        3. Peace Offerings (chap. 3)
        4. Sin Offerings (4:1–5:13)
        5. Trespass Offerings (5:14–6:7)
    B. Legislation for the Priesthood (6:8–7:38)
        1. Burnt Offerings (6:8–13)
        2. Grain Offerings (6:14–23)
        3. Sin Offerings (6:24–30)
        4. Trespass Offerings (7:1–10)
        5. Peace Offerings (7:11–36)
        6. Concluding Remarks (7:37–38)

II. Beginnings of the Priesthood (8:1–10:20)
    A. Ordination of Aaron and His Sons (chap. 8)
    B. First Sacrifices (chap. 9)
    C. Execution of Nadab and Abihu (chap. 10)

III. Prescriptions for Uncleanness (11:1–16:34)
    A. Unclean Animals (chap. 11)
    B. Uncleanness of Childbirth (chap. 12)
    C. Unclean Diseases (chap. 13)
    D. Cleansing of Diseases (chap. 14)
    E. Unclean Discharges (chap. 15)
    F. Purification of the Tabernacle from Uncleanness (chap. 16)

IV. Guidelines for Practical Holiness (17:1–27:34)
    A. Sacrifice and Food (chap. 17)
    B. Proper Sexual Behavior (chap. 18)
    C. Neighborliness (chap. 19)
    D. Capital/Grave Crimes (chap. 20)
    E. Instructions for Priests (chaps. 21–22)
    F. Religious Festivals (chap. 23)
    G. The Tabernacle (24:1–9)
    H. An Account of Blasphemy (24:10–23)

I. Sabbatical and Jubilee Years (chap. 25)

J. Exhortation to Obey the Law: Blessings and Curses (chap. 26)

K. Redemption of Votive Gifts (chap. 27)

MEANWHILE, IN OTHER PARTS OF THE WORLD...
The Olmec culture in Mexico develops, and construction begins on the Mexican Sun Pyramid.

ANSWERS TO TOUGH QUESTIONS

1. Why did God have so many specific rules for the Israelites?

God's purpose was to create a separate, holy people (11:44–45). Their lives were to reflect His character and contrast with the behavior of their neighbor nations. They were to obey God's rules even when they didn't necessarily understand the reasons.

Looking back over history, we can often see that God had several reasons behind His rules. One of the interesting discoveries about the Levitical rules for cleanliness is that they measure up to recent standards of hygienic living. They require very similar precautions to those taken by medical personnel today in order to prevent infections and the spread of diseases. God did not ask His people to behave in ways that were at all harmful to them.

2. What does the phrase *type of Christ* mean when used to describe someone or an event in the OT?

Certain persons and practices recorded in the OT serve as hints, clues, and illustrations of what Jesus Christ would accomplish by His life, death, and resurrection. In most cases, the similarities or parallels are highlighted in the NT. The following events and practices, some introduced in Leviticus, prefigure Christ:

the ark—Genesis 7:16; 1 Peter 3:20,21

atonement sacrifices—16:15,16; Hebrews 9:12,24

the brazen serpent—Numbers 21:9; John 3:14,15

the mercy seat—Exodus 25:17–22; Romans 3:25; Hebrews 4:16

the Passover lamb—Exodus 12:3–6, 46; John 19:36; 1 Corinthians 5:7

the red heifer—Ephesians 2:14,16

rock of Horeb—Exodus 17:6; 1 Corinthians 10:4

scapegoat—16:20–22

Tabernacle—Exodus 40:2,34; Hebrews 9:11; Colossians 2:9

veil of the Tabernacle—Exodus 40:21; Hebrews 10:20

3. To what degree should believers today submit to the rules and regulations God gave the people of Israel?

A believer's understanding of the OT must be shaped by Jesus and the NT. Jesus talked about this when He said, "Do not think I came to destroy the Law or the Prophets. I did not come to destroy but to fulfill" (Matthew 5:17).

In relation to the OT ceremonial law, the Levitical priesthood, and the sanctuary, the NT records a number of instances of how this fulfillment by Jesus worked itself out in individual understanding and practice (Matt. 27:51; Acts 10:1–16, Col. 2:16,17; 1 Pet. 2:9; Rev. 1:6; 5:10; 20:6). The very institution of the New Covenant in and by Jesus (Matt. 26:28; 2 Cor. 3:6–18; Heb. 7–10) places the OT in a new light.

The most profitable study in Leviticus focuses on the truths contained in the understanding of sin, guilt, substitutionary death, and atonement by noting features that are not explained or illustrated any place else in the OT. Later writers of Scripture, especially the NT, build on the basic understanding of these matters provided by Leviticus. The sacrificial features of Leviticus point to their ultimate, one-time fulfillment in the substitutionary death of Jesus Christ (Hebrews 9:11–22).

FURTHER STUDY ON LEVITICUS

1. How many different kinds of sacrifices and offerings can you identify in Leviticus?
2. What does the term *holy* mean, and in what ways is it used in Leviticus?
3. In what ways do the laws in Leviticus contribute to healthy living?
4. What kinds of sacrifices and offerings are a part of your relationship with God?

NUMBERS
Travelogue of a Wilderness Journey

TITLE
The English title "Numbers" comes from the Greek (LXX) and Latin Vulgate versions, the ancient translations compiled by Bible scholars. The ancient Greek title given was *arithmoi*, from which we get the English word *arithmetic*. Latin translators later gave the book the title *numeri*, which English has borrowed as its general word *numbers*. This designation is based on the numberings that are a major focus of chaps. 1–4 and 26. The most common Hebrew title comes from the fifth word in the Hebrew text of 1:1, "in the wilderness [of]." This name is much more descriptive of the total contents of the book, which recount the history of Israel during almost thirty-nine years of wandering in the wilderness. Another Hebrew title, favored by some early church Fathers, is based on the first word of the Hebrew text of 1:1, "and He spoke." This designation emphasizes that the book records the Word of God to Israel.

Placement of Tribes in the Israelite Encampment

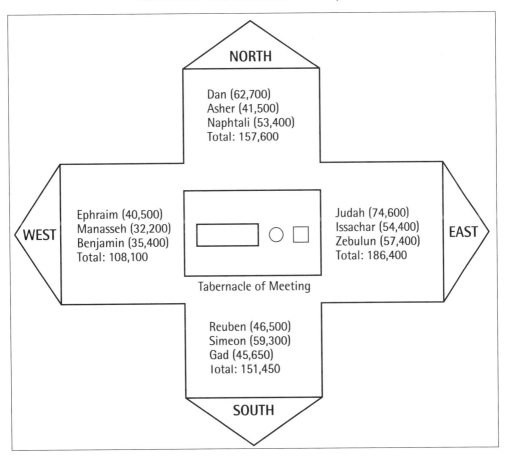

NORTH

Dan (62,700)
Asher (41,500)
Naphtali (53,400)
Total: 157,600

WEST

Ephraim (40,500)
Manasseh (32,200)
Benjamin (35,400)
Total: 108,100

Tabernacle of Meeting

Judah (74,600)
Issachar (54,400)
Zebulun (57,400)
Total: 186,400

EAST

Reuben (46,500)
Simeon (59,300)
Gad (45,650)
Total: 151,450

SOUTH

AUTHOR AND DATE

Numbers is the fourth of the first five books of the Bible which are collectively called the Law or the Pentateuch. This collection of writings is ascribed to Moses throughout Scripture (Josh. 8:31; 2 Kin. 14:6; Neh. 8:1; Mark 12:26; John 7:19). The Book of Numbers itself refers to the writing of Moses in 33:2 and 36:13.

Numbers was written in the final year of Moses' life. The events from 20:1 to the end occur in the fortieth year after the Exodus. The account ends with Israel poised on the eastern side of the Jordan River across from Jericho (36:13), which is where the conquest of the land of Canaan began (Josh. 3–6). The Book of Numbers must be dated ca. 1405 B.C., since it is foundational to the Book of Deuteronomy, and Deuteronomy is dated in the eleventh month of the fortieth year after the Exodus (Deut. 1:3).

BACKGROUND AND SETTING

Most of the events of the book are set "in the wilderness." The word "wilderness" is used forty-eight times in Numbers. This term refers to land that contains little vegetation or trees, and because of a scarcity of rainfall, it cannot be cultivated. This land is best used for tending flocks of animals. In 1:1–10:10, Israel encamped in "the wilderness in Sinai." It was at Sinai that the Lord had entered into the Mosaic Covenant with them (Ex. 19–24). From 10:11–12:16, Israel traveled from Sinai to Kadesh. In 13:1–20:13, the events took place in and around Kadesh, which was located in "the wilderness of Paran" (12:16; 13:3,26), "the wilderness of Zin" (13:21; 20:1). From 20:14–22:1, Israel traveled from Kadesh to the "plains of Moab." All the events of 22:2–36:13 occurred while Israel was encamped in the plain to the north of Moab. That plain was a flat and fertile piece of land in the middle of the wasteland (21:20; 23:28; 24:1).

CHRIST IN . . . NUMBERS

THE NT REMAINS A SOURCE OF INSIGHT into the presence of Christ in the Book of Numbers. In chapt. 21, verses 4 through 9, the Israelite people who looked upon the serpent lifted up by Moses were healed. John describes this as a picture of the Crucifixion: "And as Moses lifted up the serpent in the wilderness, even so must the Son of Man be lifted up" (John 3:14). The manna that sustained the people also illustrated Christ as the Bread of Life (John 6:31–33). Furthermore, the rock that brought water to the people was also a type of Christ. Paul's letter to the Corinthians refers to this rock as "that spiritual Rock that followed them, and that Rock was Christ" (1 Cor. 10:4).

The greatest portion of the book describes the events leading up to the first failed conquest of the Promised Land in the second year after the Exodus as well as the final preparations for the second conquest almost four decades later. In between, the tragedy of thirty-seven wasted years is emphasized by being largely ignored. All incidents recorded in 1:1–14:45 occur in 1444 B.C., the year after the Exodus. Everything referred to after 20:1 is dated ca. 1406/1405 B.C., the fortieth year after the Exodus. The laws and events found in 15:1–19:22 are undated, but probably all should be dated ca. 1443 to 1407 B.C. The lack of material devoted to this thirty-seven-year period, in comparison with the other years of the journey from Egypt to Canaan, communicates how wasted these years were because of Israel's rebellion against the Lord and His consequent judgment.

KEY WORDS IN

Numbers

Sacrifice: Hebrew *zebach*—6:17; 7:17,29,47,59,77; 15:3,5,8—from a verb meaning "to slaughter for an offering." According to the law of Moses, a priest would offer sacrifices on behalf of a worshiper by burning them on the altar (Ex. 20:24). Sacrifices could either be grain offerings (the first fruits of the harvest) or animal sacrifices. Animal sacrifices under the law served one primary function—to cover or atone for sin (Lev. 22:21; Heb. 9:22). The sin of an individual was symbolically transferred to the sacrificed animal, thereby providing a temporary substitutionary atonement that had to be repeated annually because it only partially dealt with sin (Heb. 10:4). Ultimately, all sacrifices in the OT point forward to and are types of the final, all-sufficient sacrifice made by Christ (Is.53; 1 Cor. 5:7; Heb. 9:10).

Anointed: Hebrew *mashach*—3:3; 6:15; 7:1,10,84,88; 35:25—a verb meaning "to wet or dab a person with olive oil." Kin., priests, and prophets were anointed at the beginning of their service (8:12; 16:32; 2 Samuel 2:4; 5:3; 1 Kin. 19:15,16). This ritual identified a person or object as set apart for God's special purposes. During the Exodus, many holy objects were anointed, including the tabernacle itself. Anointing oil was an exquisite and expensive blend of oil and spices (7:1). This special oil symbolized the consecration of the tabernacle and its furnishings to God.

Vow: Hebrew *neder*—6:2,21; 15:3; 21:2; 30:2-3,9,13—a vow. A vow to God is a voluntary commitment to do something that pleases Him or to abstain from certain practices to demonstrate devotion to Him. A vivid example of a vow in the OT is the Nazirite vow (6:1–21). Scripture admonishes the believer against making rash vows, since they are made before God, the righteous and holy Judge (Eccles. 5:4). The reason for the warning is that a vow made to Him is binding and must be fulfilled.

Elders: Hebrew *zaqen*—11:16,24,25,30; 16:25; 22:4,7—a word that means "aged" or "old." In the OT, the word *elder* refers to either an aged, feeble person (Gen. 44:20; Job 42:17) or to a mature person who had authority within the Israelite community (Ex. 3:16; Josh. 8:33). Elders could serve as judges (Ex. 18:12), advisers (Ezek. 7:26), and ruling officials (Deut. 19:12; Ruth 4:2). Their position was one of great honor (Prov. 31:23; Is. 9:15). In addition to age (Hebrew tradition states that an elder had to be a man at least fifty years of age), an elder had to demonstrate his maturity by fearing God, being truthful, and not coveting (Ex. 18:21).

KEY PEOPLE IN NUMBERS

Moses—great prophet and leader who acted as God's mouthpiece to explain His Law to Israel (1:1,19,48; 5:1,4,5,11—and over two hundred other references)

Aaron—Moses' brother and first high priest of Israel (1:3,17,44; 2:1; 3:1–10; 12:1–5; 20:23–29)

Miriam—sister to Moses and Aaron, also songwriter and prophetess; stricken with leprosy because of jealousy toward Moses (12; 20:1; 26:59)

Joshua—Moses' successor as leader of Israel; one of the only two people to see both the Exodus from Egypt and the Promised Land (11:28; 13; 14; 26:65; 27:15–23; 32:11,12,28; 34:17)

Caleb—one of the men sent to scout Canaan; faithful to God in his desire to conquer the land; one of the only two people to see both the Exodus from Egypt and the Promised Land (13–14; 26:65; 32:12; 34:19)

Eleazar—son of Aaron who succeeded him as high priest of Israel (3:1–4; 4:16; 16:36–40; 20:25–29; 26:1–4,63; 27:2,15–23; 32:2; 34:17)

Korah—Levite who assisted in the Tabernacle; killed because of his rebellion against the Lord (16:1–40; 26:9)

Balaam—prophet and sorcerer who halfheartedly obeyed God; attempted to lead Israel into idol worship (22:1–24:25; 31:7,8,16)

HISTORICAL AND THEOLOGICAL THEMES

Numbers chronicles the experiences of two generations of the nation of Israel. The first generation participated in the Exodus from Egypt. Their story begins in Exodus 2:23 and continues through Leviticus and into the first fourteen chapters of Numbers. This generation was numbered for the war of conquest in Canaan (1:1–46). However, when the people arrived at the southern edge of Canaan, they refused to enter the Land (14:1–10). Because of their rebellion against the Lord, all the adults 20 and over (except Caleb and Joshua) were sentenced to die in the wilderness (14:26–38). In chaps. 15–25, the first and second generations overlap; the first died out as the second grew to adulthood. A second numbering of the people commenced the history of this second generation (26:1–56). These Israelites did go to war (26:2) and inherited the land (26:52–56). The story of this second generation, beginning in Numbers 26:1, continues through the books of Deuteronomy and Joshua.

Three theological themes occur througout Numbers. First, the Lord Himself communicated to Israel through Moses (1:1; 7:89; 12:6–8), so the words of Moses had divine authority. Israel's response to Moses mirrored her obedience or disobedience to the Lord. Numbers contains three distinct divisions based on Israel's response to the word of the Lord: obedience (chaps. 1–10), disobedience (chaps. 11–25), and renewed obedience (chaps. 26–36). The second theme is that the Lord is the God of judgment. Throughout Numbers, the "anger" of the Lord was aroused in response to Israel's sin (11:1,10,33; 12:9; 14:18; 25:3,4; 32:10,13,14). Third, the faithfulness of the Lord to keep His promise to give the seed of Abraham the land of Canaan is emphasized (15:2; 26:52–56; 27:12; 33:50–56; 34:1–29).

KEY DOCTRINES IN NUMBERS

Rebellion against God—resulted from Israel's coupling with heathen nations (14:26–38; Ex. 34:6,7; Josh. 24:19; Ps. 32:1–7; Hos. 10:9,10; 2 Thess. 2:3; Jude 1:14,15)

Inheritance of the land—God secured the Promised Land for His people (16:14; 26:52–56; Lev. 14:34; 1 Chr. 28:8; Ezra 9:10–12; Ps. 16:5,6; Joel 3:2; Col. 1:11,12; 1 Pet. 1:4)

Divine authority given to Moses—Moses spoke the words of God and led Israel (1:1; 7:89; 12:6–8). God also gave authority to others of His prophets (Jer. 5:12,13; 1 Cor. 1:10) and to Jesus (Matt. 29; 9:6; Mark 6:12; Luke 10:22)

Israel's sin and judgment from the Lord—God does not have favorites; Israel's sin demanded punishment (11:1,10,33; 12:9; 14:18; 25:3,4; 32:10,13,14; Lev. 10:2; Deut. 9:22; 2 Kin. 1:12; Ps. 78:21; 106:15; Jon. 4:2; John 3:18,19; Rom. 5:9; 1 John 4:17,18; Rev. 20:11–15)

Faithfulness of God to His covenant—when God's people are unfaithful, God remains faithful (15:2; 26:52–56; 27:12; 33:50–56; 34:1–29; Josh. 11:23; 14:1)

GOD'S CHARACTER IN NUMBERS
God is long-suffering—14:18
God is merciful—14:18
God is provident—26:65
God is true—23:19
God is wrathful—11:1,33; 12:9–10; 14:37,40–45; 16:31,35; 21:6; 25:9; 32:14

INTERPRETIVE CHALLENGES
Four major interpretive challenges face the reader of Numbers. First, is the Book of Numbers a separate book, or is it a part of a larger literary whole, the Pentateuch? The biblical books of Genesis, Exodus, Leviticus, Numbers, and Deuteronomy form the Torah. The remainder of the Scripture always views these five books as a unit. The ultimate meaning of Numbers cannot be separated from its context in the Pentateuch. The first verse of the book speaks of the Lord, Moses, the tabernacle and the Exodus from Egypt. This assumes that the reader is familiar with the three books that precede Numbers. Still, every Hebrew manuscript available divides the Pentateuch in exactly the same way as the present text. In them the Book of Numbers is a well-defined unit, with a structural integrity of its own. The book has its own beginning, middle, and ending, even as it functions within a larger whole. Thus, the Book of Numbers is also to be viewed as a singular work.

The second interpretive question asks, "Is there a sense of coherence in the Book of Numbers?" It is clear that Numbers contains a wide variety of literary sources and forms including census lists, genealogies, laws, historical narratives, poetry, prophecy, and travel lists. Nevertheless, they are all blended to tell the story of Israel's journey from Mt. Sinai to the plains of Moab. The consistency of all these elements within Numbers is reflected in the outline below.

A third issue deals with the large numbers given for the tribes of Israel in 1:46 and 26:51. These two lists of Israel's men of war, taken thirty-nine years apart, both put the number over 600,000. These numbers demand a total population for Israel in the wilderness of around 2.5 million at any one time. From a natural perspective, this total seems too high for the wilderness conditions to sustain. However, it must be recognized that the Lord supernaturally took care of Israel for forty years (Deut. 8:1–5). Therefore, the large numbers must be accepted at face value.

The fourth interpretive challenge concerns the heathen prophet Balaam, whose story is recorded in 22:2–24:25. Even though Balaam claimed to know the Lord (22:18), Scripture consistently refers to him as a false prophet (2 Pet. 2:15,16; Jude 11). The Lord used Balaam as His mouthpiece to speak the true words He put in his mouth.

OUTLINE

I. **The Experience of the First Generation of Israel in the Wilderness (1:1–25:18)**
   A. The Obedience of Israel toward the Lord (1:1–10:36)
      1. The organization of Israel around the tabernacle of the Lord (1:1–6:27)
      2. The orientation of Israel toward the tabernacle of the Lord (7:1–10:36)
   B. The Disobedience of Israel toward the Lord (11:1–25:18)
      1. The complaining of Israel on the journey (11:1–12:16)
      2. The rebellion of Israel and its leaders at Kadesh (13:1–20:29)
         a. The rebellion of Israel and the consequences (13:1–19:22)
         b. The rebellion of Moses and Aaron and the consequences (20:1–29)
      3. The renewed complaining of Israel on the journey (21:1–22:1)
      4. The blessing of Israel by Balaam (22:2–24:25)
      5. The final rebellion of Israel with Baal of Peor (25:1–18)

II. **The Experience of the Second Generation of Israel in the Plains of Moab: The Renewed Obedience of Israel toward the Lord (26:1–36:13)**
   A. The Preparations for the Conquest of the Land (26:1–32:42)
   B. The Review of the Journey in the Wilderness (33:1–49)
   C. The Anticipation of the Conquest of the Land (33:50–36:13)

MEANWHILE, IN OTHER PARTS OF THE WORLD...
The Chinese begin to create elaborate sculptures with bronze.

ANSWERS TO TOUGH QUESTIONS

1. The size of Israel's population provokes questions about the accuracy of the numbers in Numbers. Did that many people wander in the wilderness? How did they survive? How did they manage themselves?

Twice during the wilderness wanderings a census of the people of Israel was taken (1:46; 26:51). Each time the resulting total count of fighting men exceeded 600,000. These numbers indicate a population for Israel in the wilderness of around 2.5 million people at any time. Viewed naturally, this total appears too high to sustain in wilderness conditions.

Before concluding that Moses inflated the numbers, several factors must be considered. First, the Lord supernaturally took care of Israel for forty years (Deuteronomy 8:1–5). Second, God also spelled out sanitary practices that prevented the kind of health crises that might have occurred under those conditions. Third, while Israel wandered in the wilderness for forty years, they moved camp only about forty times. Spending about a year in each campsite preserved some grazing for the herds while keeping the people's pollution to a manageable amount. Each census was meant to be an accurate accounting of God's people. They ought to be taken at face value.

2. Chapter 21, verses 4 through 9, records an infestation of fiery serpents that attacked the people. Moses was instructed by God to create a bronze serpent and hang it on a pole. When bitten people looked at the serpent on the pole, they were healed. Wasn't this some kind of idol worship?

The circumstances leading up to the casting of the bronze serpent were all too familiar. The people were tired and discouraged. Angry with God, they complained to Moses. They were convinced that things couldn't get any worse, but God showed them otherwise. He sent fiery serpents among the people, and some of the Israelites died. Others suffered painful bites.

Realizing their mistake, the people came in repentance to Moses and begged for help. They were not worshiping the bronze serpent but were acting in faith, in obedience to God's and Moses' directions.

3. Why does a pagan and greedy prophet like Balaam receive so much attention in the biblical story?

Balaam, whose story is recorded in 22:2–24:25, does seem to receive special treatment. Even though Balaam claimed to know the Lord (22:18), Scripture consistently refers to him as a false prophet (2 Pet. 2:15,16; Jude 11). Apparently, God placed such a priority on the message that the character of the messenger became a secondary consideration. The Lord used Balaam as His mouthpiece to speak the true words He put in his mouth. God had a purpose for Balaam despite the pagan prophet's own plans.

4. What are modern readers to do with Balaam's talking donkey (22:22–35)?

Several observations come to mind when a question like this is asked. First, the question assumes that ancient readers had fewer problems with talking donkeys than modern people do. This incident was not recorded as a commonplace occurrence but as something unusual and noteworthy. Second, one can just as easily wonder why God didn't (or doesn't) use talking animals more often—we would all probably be better off. Third, why not recognize God's sense of humor in this account? Fourth, God's display of patience and persistence in these events ought to provoke in us a sense of humble worship. Fifth, the incident, unusual as it may be, should be accepted at face value as true.

FURTHER STUDY ON NUMBERS

1. What considerations were behind the numbering of the people as they crossed the wilderness?
2. What events led up to God's decision to turn His people back into the wilderness for forty years?
3. In what different ways did the Israelites rebel against God?
4. What benefits could have been accomplished during the forty years in the desert?
5. What principles are illustrated by the plague of fiery serpents in the wilderness (21:4–9)?
6. In what ways does the episode with Balaam illustrate the character of God (22:2–24:25)?

DEUTERONOMY
The Great Review

TITLE
The English title "Deuteronomy" comes from the incorrect translation in the Greek Septuagint (LXX) of "copy of this law" in 17:18 as "second law," which was later translated again as *Deuteronomium* in the Latin version (Vulgate). The original Hebrew title of the book is translated "These are the words," from the first two Hebrew words of the book. This Hebrew title is a better description of the book since it is not a "second law," but rather the record of Moses' words of explanation concerning the law. Deuteronomy completes the five-part literary unit called the Pentateuch, the first five books of the Bible.

AUTHOR AND DATE
Moses has been traditionally recognized as the author of Deuteronomy, since the book itself testifies that Moses wrote it (1:1,5; 31:9,22,24). Both the OT (1 Kin. 2:3; 8:53; 2 Kin. 14:6; 18:12) and the NT (Acts 3:22,23; Rom. 10:19) support the claim of Mosaic authorship. While Deuteronomy 32:48–34:12 was added after Moses' death (probably by Joshua), the rest of the book came from Moses' hand just before his death in 1405 B.C.

The majority of the book is comprised of farewell speeches that the 120-year-old Moses gave to Israel, beginning on the first day of the eleventh month of the fortieth year after the Exodus from Egypt (1:3). These speeches can be dated Jan.–Feb., 1405 B.C. In the last few weeks of Moses' life, he committed these speeches to writing and gave them to the priests and elders for the coming generations of Israel (31:9,24–26).

BACKGROUND AND SETTING
Like Leviticus, Deuteronomy does not advance historically, but takes place entirely in one location over about one month of time (cf. Deut. 1:3 and 34:8 with Josh. 5:6–12). Israel was encamped in the central rift valley to the east of the Jordan River (Deut. 1:1). This location was referred to in Numbers 36:13 as "the plains of Moab," an area north of the Arnon River, across the Jordan River from Jericho. It had been almost forty years since the Israelites had exited Egypt.

The Book of Deuteronomy concentrates on events that took place in the final weeks of Moses' life. The major event was the verbal communication of divine revelation from Moses to the people of Israel (1:1–30:20; 31:30–32:47; 33:1–29). The only other events recorded were: (1) Moses' recording the law in a book and his commissioning of Joshua as the new leader (31:1–29); (2) Moses' viewing of the land of Canaan from Mt. Nebo (32:48–52; 34:1–4); and (3) his death (34:5–12).

The original recipients of Deuteronomy, both in its verbal and written presentations, were the second generation of the nation of Israel. All of that generation from 40 to 60 years of age (except Joshua and Caleb, who were older) had been born in Egypt and had participated as children or teens in the Exodus. Those under 40 had been born and reared in the wilderness. Together, they comprised the generation that was on the verge of conquering the land of Canaan under Joshua, forty years after they had left Egypt (1:34–39).

KEY PEOPLE IN DEUTERONOMY
Moses—leader of Israel; instructed the people on the law of God but was not allowed to enter the Promised Land (chapters 1–5; 27; 29; 31–34)
Joshua—Moses' successor; guided Israel into the Promised Land (1:37,38; 3:21–28; 31:3–23; 32:44; 34:9)

HISTORICAL AND THEOLOGICAL THEMES
Like Leviticus, Deuteronomy contains much legal detail, but with an emphasis on the people rather than the priests. As Moses called the second generation of Israel to trust the Lord and be obedient to His covenant made at Horeb (Sinai), he illustrated his points with references to Israel's past history. He reminded Israel of her rebellion against the Lord at Horeb (9:7–10:11) and at Kadesh (1:26–46), which brought devastating consequences. He also reminded her of the Lord's faithfulness in giving victory over her enemies (2:24–3:11; 29:2,7,8). Most important, Moses called the people to take the land that God had promised by oath to their forefathers Abraham, Isaac, and Jacob (1:8; 6:10; 9:5; 29:13; 30:20; 34:4; cf. Gen. 15:18–21; 26:3–5; 35:12). Moses not only looked back but he also looked ahead and saw that Is-

CHRIST IN . . . DEUTERONOMY
DEUTERONOMY SPEAKS DIRECTLY of the coming of a new Prophet similar to Moses: "The Lord your God will raise up for you a Prophet like me from your midst, from your brethren. Him you shall hear" (18:15). This Prophet is interpreted as the Messiah, or Christ, in both the OT and NTs (34:10; Acts 3:22,23; 7:37).

Moses illustrates a type of Christ in several ways: (1) Both were spared death as babies (Ex. 2; Matt. 2:13–23); (2) Both acted as priest, prophet, and leader over Israel (Ex. 32:31–35; Heb. 2:17; 34:10–12; Acts 7:52; 33:4,5; Matt. 27:11).

rael's future failure to obey God would lead to her being scattered among the nations before the fulfillment of His oath to the patriarchs would be completed (4:25–31; 29:22–30:10; 31:26–29).

The Book of Deuteronomy, along with Psalms and Isaiah, reveals much about the attributes of God. Thus, it is directly quoted over forty times in the NT (exceeded only by Psalms and Isaiah), with many more allusions to its content. Deuteronomy reveals that the Lord is the only God (4:39; 6:4), and that He is jealous (4:24), faithful (7:9), loving (7:13), merciful (4:31), yet angered by sin (6:15). This is the God who called Israel to Himself. Over 250 times, Moses repeated the phrase, "the LORD your God" to Israel. Israel was called to obey (28:2), fear (10:12), love (10:12), and serve (10:12) her God by walking in His ways and keeping His commandments (10:12,13). By obeying Him, the people of Israel would receive His blessings (28:1–14). Obedience and the pursuit of personal holiness is always based upon the character of God. Because of who He is, His people are to be holy (cf., 7:6–11; 8:6,11,18; 10:12,16,17; 11:13; 13:3,4; 14:1,2).

KEY DOCTRINES IN DEUTERONOMY
The Promised Land of Israel (1:8; 6:10; 9:5; 29:13; 30:20; 34:4; Gen. 12:7; 15:5; 22:17; Ex. 33:1; Lev. 18:24; Num. 14:23; 34:1–15; Josh. 24:13; Ps. 105:44; Titus 3:5)

The Lord's faithfulness to give Israel victory over its enemies (2:24–3:11; 29:2,7,8; Num. 21:3,33,34; Josh. 1:7; 10:8–12; Judg. 1:1–4; 1 Kin. 2:3; Ps. 18:43; Rom. 8:37; 1 Cor. 15:54–57; 1 John 5:4)

Israel's rebellion against the LORD (1:26–46; 9:7–10:11; Ex. 14:11; Num. 14:1–4; Ezra 4:19; Ps. 106:24; Jer. 5:6; Ezek. 18:31; Dan. 9:24; 2 Thess. 2:2; Jude 1:11,15)

The scattering of Israel as judgment from God (4:25–31; 29:22–30:10; 31:26–29; Lev. 26:33; 1 Kin. 14:15; Neh. 1:8; Ps. 106:25–27; Eccles. 3:5; Jer. 9:15,16; Amos 9:8)

Holiness of God and His people—God declares Israel His chosen people (7:6–11; 8:6,11,18; 10:12,16,17; 11:13; 13:3,4; 14:1,2; Ex.19:5–6; Prov. 10:22; Amos 3:2; Mic. 6:8; Matt. 22:37; Rom. 12:1; 1 Tim.1:5; 1 Pet. 2:9)

GOD'S CHARACTER IN DEUTERONOMY

God is accessible—4:7
God is eternal—33:27
God is faithful—7:9
God is glorious—5:24; 28:58
God is jealous—4:24
God is just—10:17; 32:4
God is loving—7:7,8,13; 10:15,18; 23:5
God is merciful—4:31; 32:43
God is powerful—3:24; 32:39
God is a promise keeper—1:11
God is provident—8:2,15,18
God is righteous—4:8
God is true—32:4
God is unequaled—4:35; 33:26
God is unified—4:32–35,39,40; 6:4,5; 32:39
God is wise—2:7
God is wrathful—29:20,27,28; 32:19–22

INTERPRETIVE CHALLENGES

Three interpretive challenges face the reader of Deuteronomy. First, is the book a singular record, or is it only a part of the larger literary whole, the Pentateuch? The remainder of the Scripture always views the Pentateuch as a unit, and the ultimate meaning of Deuteronomy cannot be divorced from its context in the Pentateuch. The book also assumes the reader is already familiar with the four books that precede it; in fact, Deuteronomy brings into focus all that had been revealed in Genesis to Numbers, as well as its implications for the people as they entered the land. However, every available Hebrew manuscript divides the Pentateuch in exactly the same way as the present text, indicating that the book is a well-defined unit recounting the final speeches of Moses to Israel, so it may also be viewed as a singular record.

Second, is the structure of Deuteronomy based on the secular treaties of Moses' day? During the last thirty-five years, many evangelical scholars have supported the Mosaic authorship of Deuteronomy by appealing to the similarities between the structure of the book and the ancient Near Eastern treaty form of the mid-second millennium B.C. (the approximate time of Moses). These secular suzerainty treaties (i.e., a ruler dictating his will to his vassals) followed a set pattern not used in the mid-first millennium B.C. These treaties usually contained the following elements: (1) preamble—identifying the parties to the covenant; (2) historical prologue—a history of the king's dealing with his vassals; (3) general and specific stipulations; (4) witnesses; (5) blessings and curses; and (6) oaths and covenant ratification. Deuteronomy, it is believed, approximates this basic structure. While there is agreement that 1:1–5 is a preamble, 1:5–4:43 a historical prologue, and chaps. 27,28 feature blessings and cursings, there is no consensus as to how the rest of Deuteronomy fits this structure. While there might have been a covenant renewal on the plains of Moab, this is neither clearly explicit nor implicit in Deuteronomy. It is best to take the book for what it claims to be: the explanation of the law given by Moses for the new generation. The structure follows the speeches given by Moses. See Outline.

Third, what was the covenant made in the land of Moab (29:1)? The majority opinion posits this

KEY WORDS IN

Deuteronomy

Statutes: Hebrew *choq*—4:1,14; 5:1; 6:1; 7:11; 10:13; 16:12; 28:15; 30:16—conveys a variety of meanings in the OT, including a verb that means "to decree" or "to inscribe" (Prov. 8:15; Is. 10:1; 49:16). It often refers to commands, civil enactments, legal prescriptions, and ritual laws decreed by someone in authority—whether by humans (Mic. 6:16) or by God Himself (6:1). The Law of Moses includes commandments (*miswah*), judgments (*mispat*), and statutes (*choq*) (4:1–2). Israel was charged to obey God's statutes, and they had pledged to do so (26:16–17).

Swore: Hebrew *shaba‘*—6:13; 7:8; 10:20; 13:17; 19:8; 29:13; 31:7—the verb translated *swore* is related to the word used for the number seven. In effect, the verb means "to bind oneself fully"; that is, "seven times." In ancient times, oaths were considered sacred. People were promising to be faithful to their word no matter what the personal cost. The OT describes God as taking an oath (Gen. 24:7; Ex. 13:5). He was not forced to do this; He did not have to swear in order to ensure His own compliance with His word. Instead, He made an oath so that His people would be assured that His promises were completely trustworthy.

Worship: Hebrew *shachah*—4:19; 8:19; 11:16; 26:10; 30:17—this most common Hebrew word for *worship* literally means "to cause oneself to lie prostrate." In ancient times, a person would fall down before someone who possessed a higher status. People would bow before a king to express complete submission to his rule. Following the example of the ancient people of faith, true Christian worship must express more than love for God; it must also express submission to His will.

Cursed: Hebrew *’arar*—7:26; 13:17; 27:15,20,23; 28:16,19—literally means "to bind with a curse." A curse is the opposite of a blessing. It wishes or prays illness or injury on a person or an object. God cursed the serpent and the ground after the sin of Adam and Eve (Genesis 3:14,17). Jeremiah, in despair, cursed the man who brought news of his birth (Jeremiah 20:14–15). The seriousness of God's covenant with His people is illustrated by the threat of a curse on any who violate it (28:60–61). In the NT, Paul taught that Jesus Christ became a "curse" for us, so that we might be freed form the curses of the Law (Galatians 3:13).

covenant as a renewal of the covenant made at Mt. Sinai nearly forty years before with the first generation. Here, Moses supposedly updated and renewed this same covenant with the second generation of Israel. The second view sees this covenant as a Palestinian covenant, which guarantees the nation of Israel's right to the land, both at that time and in the future. A third position is that Moses in chaps. 29, 30 anticipated the New Covenant, since he knew Israel would fail to keep the Sinaitic Covenant. The third view seems the best.

OUTLINE
    I. Introduction: The Historical Setting of Moses' Speeches (1:1–4)
    II. The First Address by Moses: A Historical Prologue (1:5–4:43)
        A. A Historical Review of God's Gracious Acts from Horeb to Beth Peor (1:5–3:29)
        B. An Exhortation to Obey the Law (4:1–40)
        C. The Setting Apart of Three Cities of Refuge (4:41–43)
    III. The Second Address by Moses: The Stipulations of the Sinaitic Covenant (4:44–28:68)
        A. Introduction (4:44–49)
        B. The Basic Elements of Israel's Relationship with the Lord (5:1–11:32)
            1. The Ten Commandments (5:1–33)
            2. The total commitment to the Lord (6:1–25)
            3. Separation from the gods of other nations (7:1–26)
            4. A warning against forgetting the Lord (8:1–20)
            5. Illustrations of Israel's rebellion in the past (9:1–10:11)
            6. An admonition to fear and love the Lord and obey His will (10:12–11:32)
        C. The Specific Stipulations for Life in the New Land (12:1–26:19)
            1. Instructions for the life of worship (12:1–16:17)
            2. Instructions for leadership (16:18–18:22)
            3. Instructions for societal order (19:1–23:14)
            4. Instructions from miscellaneous laws (23:15–25:19)
            5. The firstfruits and tithes in the land (26:1–15)
            6. The affirmation of obedience (26:16–19)
        D. The Blessings and Curses of the Covenant (27:1–28:68)
    IV. The Third Address by Moses: Another Covenant (29:1–30:20)
    V. The Concluding Events (31:1–34:12)
        A. The Change of Leadership (31:1–8)
        B. The Future Reading of the Law (31:9–13)
        C. The Song of Moses (31:14–32:47)
            1. The anticipation of Israel's failure (31:14–29)
            2. The witness of Moses' song (31:30–32:43)
            3. The communicating of Moses' song (32:44–47)

D. The Final Events of Moses' Life (32:48–34:12)
    1. The directives for Moses' death (32:48–52)
    2. The blessing of Moses (33:1–29)
    3. The death of Moses (34:1–12)

MEANWHILE, IN OTHER PARTS OF THE WORLD...
Ethiopia becomes an independent power. The Shang dynasty flourishes in China.

ANSWERS TO TOUGH QUESTIONS

1. Is Deuteronomy simply Moses' version of the secular covenants and treaties of his day, or does it represent a unique revelation from God?

The format that Moses used in recording not only the material in Deuteronomy but also the rest of the Pentateuch bears some resemblance to other official documents from a particular time in history. This fact has been used by historians to try to establish a date for the book. It has also been used by those who question God's unique revelation to support the claim that Moses merely copied the style of other nations of his time.

The people whom God enlisted to record His revelation did not shed their personalities, education, or style as they wrote for God. Moses had the equivalent of advanced degrees in the best training Egypt had to offer young princes (Acts 7:22). If we think of the Pentateuch as Moses' God-guided journaling during the wilderness wanderings, it will not seem unusual that his writing style bears similarities to the official and political writings of his day. What sets Moses' writings apart, along with the rest of Scripture, is not so much the style but their authoritative and God-inspired content.

FURTHER STUDY ON DEUTERONOMY

1. What does Moses say about his reasons for taking time to review all that God had done?
2. According to chapter 6, how is the Law to be preserved by each generation?
3. What was the relationship between the Law and the Promised Land?
4. In what ways is God's love revealed throughout this book?
5. Why did Moses die without ever entering the Promised Land?

JOSHUA
G o d ' s   B o l d   W a r r i o r

TITLE
This is the first of the twelve historical books. It gained its name from the exploits of Joshua, the understudy for whom Moses prayed and commissioned as a leader in Israel (Num. 27:12–23). The name *Joshua* means "Jehovah saves," or "the LORD is salvation," and corresponds to the NT name "Jesus." God delivered Israel in Joshua's day when He was personally present as the saving Commander who fought on Israel's behalf (5:14–6:2; 10:42; 23:3,5; Acts 7:45).

AUTHOR AND DATE
Although the author is not named, the most likely candidate is Joshua, who was the key eyewitness to the events recorded (cf. 18:9; 24:26). An assistant whom Joshua groomed could have finished the book by attaching such comments as those concerning Joshua's death (24:29–33). Some have even suggested that this section was written by the high priest Eleazar or by his son, Phinehas. Rahab was still living at the time Joshua 6:25 was penned. The book was completed before David's reign (15:63; cf. 2 Sam. 5:5–9). The most likely writing period is ca. 1405–1385 B.C.

Joshua was born in Egyptian slavery, trained under Moses, and by God's choice rose to his key position of leading Israel into Canaan. Distinguishing features of his life include: (1) service (Ex. 17:10; 24:13; 33:11; Num. 11:28); (2) soldiering (Ex. 17:9–13); (3) scouting (Num. 13–14); (4) supplication (or prayer) by Moses (Num. 27:15–17); (5) the sovereignty of God (Num 27:18ff.); (6) the Spirit's presence (Num. 27:18; Deut. 34:9); (7) separation by Moses (Num. 27:18–23; Deut. 31:7,8,13–15); and (8) selflessness in wholly following the Lord (Num. 32:12).

BACKGROUND AND SETTING
When Moses passed the baton of leadership on to Joshua before he died (Deut. 34), Israel was at the end of its forty-year wilderness wandering period, ca. 1405 B.C. Joshua was approaching 90 years of age when he became Israel's leader. He later died at the age of 110 (24:29), having led Israel to drive out most of the Canaanites and having divided the land among the twelve tribes.

Poised on the plains of Moab, east of the Jordan River and the land which God had promised (Gen. 12:7; 15:18–21), the Israelites awaited God's direction to conquer the Promised Land. They faced peoples on the western side of the Jordan who had become so immersed in sin that God would cause the land, so to speak, to spew out these inhabitants (Lev. 18:24,25). He would give Israel the land by conquest, primarily to fulfill the covenant He had pledged to Abraham and his descendants, but also to pass just judgment on the sinful inhabitants (cf. Gen. 15:16). Long possession of different parts of the land by various peoples had pre-dated even Abraham's day (Gen. 10:15–19; 12:6; 13:7). Its inhabitants had continued on a moral decline in the worship of many gods up to Joshua's time.

THE CONQUEST OF CANAAN

Central and Southern Campaigns

From the military camp at Gilgal, Joshua launched two campaigns, thus conquering central and southern Canaan.

Northern Campaign

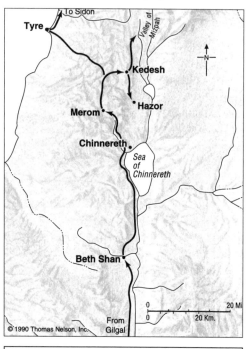

After conquering central and southern Canaan, Joshua took his forces northward to Hazor.

KEY PEOPLE IN JOSHUA

Joshua—led Israel to possess the Promised Land (1–24)

Rahab—prostitute from Jericho; saved from death because of her obedience to God; ancestor of David and Jesus (2; 6:17,22,23,25)

Achan—disobeyed God by stealing from the plunder of Jericho; caused Israel to lose the battle against Ai; stoned as punishment (7; 22:20)

Phinehas—priest and son of Eleazar; acted as intermediary among the tribes of Israel to prevent civil war (22:13,31–34; 24:33)

Eleazar—son of Aaron; succeeded him as high priest; helped Joshua lead Israel (14:1; 17:4; 19:51; 21:1–3; 22:13–33; 24:33)

Joshua's Preparation for Ministry

1. Exodus 17:9,10,13,14	Joshua led the victorious battle against the Amalekites.
2. Exodus 24:13	Joshua, the servant of Moses, accompanied the Jewish leader to the mountain of God (see 32:17).
3. Numbers 11:28	Joshua was the attendant of Moses from his youth.
4. Numbers 13:16	Moses changed his name from Hosea ("salvation") to Joshua ("the LORD saves").
5. Numbers 14:6–10,30,38	Joshua, along with Caleb, spied out the land of Canaan with 10 others. Only Joshua and Caleb urged the nation to possess the land and, thus, only they of the 12 actually entered Canaan.
6. Numbers 27:18	Joshua was indwelt by the Holy Spirit.
7. Numbers 27:18–23	Joshua was commissioned for spiritual service the first time, to assist Moses.
8. Numbers 32:12	Joshua followed the Lord fully.
9. Deuteronomy 31:23	Joshua was commissioned a second time, to replace Moses.
10. Deuteronomy 34:9	Joshua was filled with the spirit of wisdom.

HISTORICAL AND THEOLOGICAL THEMES

A key feature is God's faithfulness to fulfill His promise of giving the land to Abraham's descendants (Gen. 12:7; 15:18–21; 17:8). By God's leading (cf. 5:14–6:2), they inhabited the territories east and west of the Jordan, and so the word "possess" appears nearly twenty times.

Related to this theme is Israel's failure to press their conquest to every part of the land (13:1). Judges 1–2 later describes the tragic results from this sin. Key verses focus on: (1) God's promise of possession of the land (1:3,6); (2) meditation on God's law, which was strategic for His people (1:8); and (3) Israel's actual possession of the land in part (11:23; 21:45; 22:4).

Specific allotment of distinct portions in the land was Joshua's task, as recorded in chaps. 13–22. Levites were placed strategically in forty-eight towns so that God's spiritual services through them would be nearby and accessible to the Israelites, wherever they lived.

God wanted His people to possess the Land: (1) to keep His promise (Gen. 12:7); (2) to set the stage

CHRIST IN . . . JOSHUA

ALTHOUGH THE BOOK OF JOSHUA lacks explicit prophecy about Christ as Messiah, Joshua represents a type of Christ, both in name and in deed. The name *Yeshua* represents Joshua's Hebrew name. This name, meaning "Yahweh is Salvation," is also translated as "Jesus." At one point Joshua received a vision of a "Commander of the army of the Lord" (5:13,14). This Commander represents Christ (before his Incarnation as a man), and He led Joshua, the commander of Israel's army, to victory over the Canaanites.

for later developments in His kingdom plan (cf. Gen. 17:8; 49:8–12), e.g., positioning Israel for events in the periods of the kings and prophets; (3) to punish peoples that were insulting to Him because of extreme sinfulness (Lev. 18:25); and (4) to be a testimony to other peoples (Josh. 2:9–11), as God's covenant heart reached out to all nations (Gen. 12:1–3).

KEY DOCTRINES IN JOSHUA

God's faithfulness in giving the Promised Land to Abraham's descendants (5:14–6:2; 11:23; 21:45; 22:4; Gen. 12:7; 15:18–21; 17:8; Ex. 33:2; Num. 34:2–15; Deut. 12:9,10; 25:19; Heb. 4:8)

GOD'S CHARACTER IN JOSHUA

God is holy—24:19

God is jealous—24:19

God is a promise keeper—22:4; 23:14

God is provident—7:14; 21:45

God is wrathful—10:25; 23:16

KEY WORDS IN

Joshua

Stone: Hebrew ʾ*eben*—4:3,5,9,20; 7:25; 8:31; 10:11,18. The stones that littered the landscape of the ancient Middle East were used in numerous ways. They were the building material for houses, city walls, and fortifications (1 Kin. 5:17; 2 Kin. 12:12). Stones were used for religious purposes, to build sacred pillars (Gen. 35:14) and altars (Deut. 27:5). Stones were also piled up as memorials marking the sites of divine revelation (Gen.28:18,22) or a significant event in the life of an individual (Gen. 31:46) or a nation (4:6). Because a stone was commonly used as a foundation for a structure, God Himself was called the "Stone of Israel" (Gen. 49:24). But Isaiah also described the Lord as a "stone of stumbling" for those Israelites who rejected Him (Is. 8:14). These same images were applied to Jesus Christ in the NT (Is. 28:16; 1 Pet. 2:4–8).

Trumpet: Hebrew *shophar*—6:5,8,9,13,16,20—an animal horn (typically from a ram or a goat) used as a trumpet (6:6; Judg. 7:8). The word can also refer to a metal trumpet (Num. 10:2–10; 1 Chr. 15:28; 2 Chr. 15:14). The *shophar* was a signaling instrument, used in warfare (Judg. 3:27) and for assembling the people together at religious festivals, such as the Day of Atonement (Lev. 25:8; 2 Sam. 6:5; Joel 2:1). A trumpet blast announced God's descent to Mt Sinai to reveal His law (Exodus 19:20). Both the OT and the NT mention a trumpet announcing the Day of the Lord, the day when the Lord will come in judgment (Zeph. 1:16; Matt. 24:31).

Inheritance: Hebrew *nachalah*—13:14,33; 14:3; 17:4; 19:1,9,49: 21:3; 24:32—meaning "possession" or "property," is linked to the promises of God, particularly those involving the Promised Land (Gen. 13:14–17). When this word is used of the Promised Land, it does not merely refer to what a person wills to his children. Rather God, Creator of the world, granted His people a specific parcel of ground. He fixed its boundaries and promised to deliver it to them. However, the concept of Israel's inheritance is more meaningful than a simple association with the land. David and Jeremiah both affirm that God Himself is the real inheritance of His people (Ps. 16:5; Jer. 10:16). God's people can find joy and fulfillment in their relationship with God. Nothing this world can offer as an inheritance compares with God Himself (1 Pet. 1:4).

Rest: Hebrew *shaqat*—1:13; 3:13; 10:20; 13:27; 17:2; 21:44; 22:4; 23:1—means "to be at peace." Rest implies freedom from anxiety and conflict. God promised the Israelites *rest* in the Promised Land (Ex. 33: 14; Deut. 3:1–20; 12:9,10). In the Book of Joshua, the idea of *rest* is related specifically to the conflicts and hostilities Israel had with their neighbors. God promised His people a peaceful place to settle. Obtaining this rest depended on Israel's complete obedience to God's command to drive out the Canaanites (11:23; 14:15). The NT writers also speak of the concept of rest. Christians are told that heaven will bring them rest from death, pain, sin, and all other earthly struggles (Heb. 4:1; Rev. 21:4).

INTERPRETIVE CHALLENGES

Miracles always challenge readers either to believe that the God who created heaven and earth (Gen. 1:1) can do other mighty works, too, or to explain them away. As in Moses' day, miracles in this book were a part of God's purpose, such as: (1) His holding back the Jordan's waters (Josh. 3:7–17); (2) the fall of Jericho's walls (Josh. 6:1–27); (3) the hail-stones (Josh. 10:1–11); and (4) the long day (Josh. 10:12–15).

There are a number of other challenges in Joshua. Many wonder, for example, how God's blessing on the prostitute Rahab, who responded to Him in faith, relate to her telling a lie (Josh. 2)? In short, Rahab was spared not because of her lie, but because she put her faith in God. (For a fuller treatment of this passage, see "Answers to Tough Questions" below.) Another question is why Achan's family members were executed with him (Josh. 7). They were regarded as co-conspirators in what he did because they helped cover up his guilt and withheld information from others. Similarly, family members died in Korah's rebellion (Num. 16), Haman's fall (Esth. 9:13,14), and after Daniel's escape (Dan. 6:24). Some also ask what God meant by "sending the hornet" before Israel (Josh. 24:12). This description, also in Ex. 23:28, is a picturesque figure (cf. also 23:13) portraying God's own fighting to assist Israel (23:3,5,10,18). This awesome force put the enemy to flight, as the feared hornets literally can do (Deut. 7:20,21).

OUTLINE

    I. Entering the Promised Land (1:1–5:15)
    II. Conquering the Promised Land (6:1–12:24)
        A. The Central Campaign (6:1–8:25)
        B. The Southern Campaign (9:1–10:43)
        C. The Northern Campaign (11:1–15)
        D. The Summary of Conquests (11:16–12:24)
    III. Distributing Portions of the Promised Land (13:1–22:34)
        A. Summary of Instructions (13:1–33)
        B. West of the Jordan (14:1–19:51)
        C. Cities of Refuge (20:1–9)
        D. Cities of the Levites (21:1–45)
        E. East of the Jordan (22:1–34)
    IV. Retaining the Promised Land (23:1–24:28)
        A. The First Speech by Joshua (23:1–16)
        B. The Second Speech by Joshua (24:1–28)
    V. Postscript (24:29–33)

MEANWHILE, IN OTHER PARTS OF THE WORLD...

In Egypt, the peaceful reign of Amenhotep III improves and expands Egyptian culture and trade (1420–1385 B.C.).

ANSWERS TO TOUGH QUESTIONS

1. How can we understand the character of God as revealed in the rest of Scripture in comparision with the harsh commands of God to utterly destroy cities and peoples in the conquest of the Promised Land?

When Joshua issued orders for the destruction of Jericho, he was echoing God's very clear commands. Passages like Exodus 23:32,33; 34:11–16 and Deuteronomy 7:1–5; 20:16–18 make it impossible to soften or avoid the truth that God ordered the destruction of entire populations. Those were not just soldiers killing soldiers. Many of the victims were women and children. The challenge for serious and humble Bible students is to face these horrors and the hard lessons they teach without trying to explain them away.

If we do not have a growing awe about the holiness of God and His righteous judgment of sin, our understanding of God's grace and mercy will fade away. Without an acknowledgment that God can and does punish, the possibility of mercy and forgiveness carries little weight. If we do not seek to see the entire scope of God's actions and character, we will tend to gravitate to what we like or don't like and miss the connections. The gaps in our understanding can be partly filled by biblical insights.

Israel's role in applying God's judgment had nothing to do with their own righteousness. But for God's grace, they would easily be in the place of those people who were sentenced to death. "Do not think in your heart, after the LORD your God has cast them out before you, saying, 'Because of my righteousness the LORD has brought me in to possess this land'; but it is because of the wickedness of these nations that the LORD is driving them out from before you" (Deut. 9:4).

God could have used sickness, famine, fire, or flood to clear out the land, but He chose to use the people of Israel. In terrible natural disasters, everyone suffers. It isn't easy to accept that little children shared the fate of their parents, but they often do. And they did as Israel carried out God's judgments. Did God unfairly include these children in punishment, or do the parents and leaders bear responsibility for putting the innocent in harm's way by their rejection of God? Some of these issues will have to be settled beyond death, when the final judgment occurs (Heb. 9:27).

2. Why did God bless Rahab and give her a unique role in history in spite of her lie?

Rahab's life was not spared because of her lie; it was spared because she put her faith in God. Rahab was given a gracious opportunity to side with God by protecting the two Israelite spies, and she acted within her circumstances. She lied daringly and elaborately. Perhaps her initial response was simply a habit of her profession. From the perspective of the king of Jericho, Rahab would have been guilty of treason, not just lying. She had a new allegiance, and she didn't yet know that the God she now wanted to trust had a rule about lying.

The radical change that came into Rahab's life when those spies knocked on her door can be seen in several ways. She risked her life to trust God. The Book of Ruth also reveals that Rahab married and became the great, great-grandmother of King David and one of the ancestors of Jesus. Centuries later, Rahab was one of the women listed in Hebrews 11 because of her faith.

3. How does God's guarantee of success to Joshua carry over to us?

The Book of Joshua begins with God's commissioning of Israel's new leader. God described Joshua's mission—to go in and possess the land (1:2–6). God hinged Joshua's success on three key factors: (1) God's own presence (1:5); (2) Joshua's personal strength and courage (1:7,9); and (3) Joshua's attention to and application of God's Word (1:7,8).

The process of biblical meditation begins with a thoughtful, lingering reading of God's Word. It progresses to familiarity and memorization. In order to "meditate in it day and night" (Joshua 1:8), Joshua needed to spend enough time in the Book of the Law so that the book would eventually get in Joshua. The purpose of God's Word has been achieved when meditation leads us to application—"observe to do according to all that is written in it" (Josh. 1:8).

"Then," God told Joshua, "you will make your way prosperous, and then you will have good success" (1:8). Joshua found that the ultimate measure of prosperity and success was knowing how God wants His people to live and then living that way. God repeatedly assured Joshua of His own presence "wherever you go." What greater measure of success could there be than to honor the ever-present God with our obedience?

FURTHER STUDY ON JOSHUA

1. What character traits in Joshua made him an excellent leader for Israel?
2. What were Joshua's greatest challenges as a leader?
3. Review Numbers 13–14 and compare the attitudes and actions of the people with the next generation that approached the Promised Land in Joshua 1–2.
4. In what ways did God keep His promises to Israel throughout Joshua?
5. How would you apply Joshua 24:15 in your life?

JUDGES
Chosen Servants for Troubled Times

TITLE

The book bears the fitting name "Judges," which refers to unique leaders God gave to His people for preservation against their enemies (2:16–19). Israel's failure to evict the peoples of the land as God had commanded led to the results God had predicted (Joshua 1:27–2:4). The Canaanite nations became thorns to Israel, and the land was in constant turmoil. In desperate times, the people of Israel would acknowledge their slide into sinfulness and cry to God for forgiveness and deliverance. At each occasion, God would send unique leaders (judges) to deliver them (2:16–19). The Hebrew title means "deliverers" or "saviors," as well as judges (cf. Deut. 16:18; 17:9; 19:17). The careers of twelve such judges are included in this book. Eli and Samuel, who appear in subsequent books, raised the final count to fourteen. God Himself is the higher Judge (11:27). The Book of Judges spans about 350 years from Joshua's conquest (ca. 1398 B.C.) until Eli and Samuel judged prior to the establishment of the monarchy (ca. 1043 B.C.).

AUTHOR AND DATE

No author is named in the book, but ancient Jewish tradition identifies Samuel, a key prophet who lived at the time these events took place and could have personally summed up the era (cf. 1 Sam. 10:25). The time was earlier than David's capture of Jerusalem ca. 1004 B.C. (2 Sam. 5:6,7), since Jebusites still controlled the site (Judg. 1:21). Also, the writer deals with a time before a king ruled (17:6; 18:1; 21:25). Since Saul began his reign ca. 1043 B.C., a time shortly after his rule began is probably when Judges was written.

CHRIST IN ... JUDGES

THE BOOK OF JUDGES traces the people of Israel through seven periods of complete rebellion against God. During each period, specific judges are brought forth as deliverers and saviors for the fallen people. These judges illustrate Christ as the final Savior and King of His people (Luke 2:11; John 4:42; Mark 15:2).

BACKGROUND AND SETTING

Judges is a tragic sequel to Joshua. In Joshua, the people were obedient to God in conquering the Promised Land. In Judges, they were disobedient, idolatrous, and often defeated. Judges 1:1–3:6 focuses on the closing days of the Book of Joshua. Judges 2:6–9 gives a review of Joshua's death (cf. Josh. 24:28–31). The account describes seven distinct cycles of Israel's drifting away from the Lord starting even before Joshua's death, with a complete turning away from God afterward. Five basic reasons are evident for these cycles of Israel's moral and spiritual decline:

1. disobedience in failing to drive the Canaanites out of the land (Judg. 1:19, 21, 35)
2. idolatry (2:12)
3. intermarriage with wicked Canaanites (3:5,6)

4. not heeding judges (2:17)

5. turning away from God after the death of the judges (2:19).

A four-part sequence repeatedly occurred in this phase of Israel's history:

1. Israel's departure from God
2. God's punishment in permitting military defeat and enslavement
3. Israel's prayer pleading for deliverance
4. God's raising up "judges," either civil or sometimes local military leaders, who led in shaking off the oppressors.

Fourteen judges arose, six of them military judges (Othniel, Ehud, Deborah, Gideon, Jephthah, and Samson). Two men were of special significance for contrast in spiritual leadership: (1) Eli, judge and high priest (not a good example for the people); and (2) Samuel, judge, priest, and prophet (a good example).

Israel's Judges

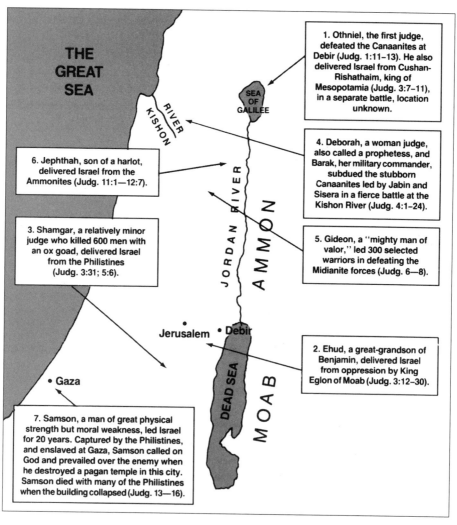

HISTORICAL AND THEOLOGICAL THEMES

Judges is thematic rather than chronological. Most important among its themes is God's power and covenant mercy in graciously delivering the Israelites from the consequences of their failures, which they suffered for their compromise and sin (cf. 2:18,19; 21:25). In seven periods of sin to salvation (cf. Introduction: Outline), God compassionately delivered His people throughout the different geographical areas of tribal inheritances, which He had earlier given through Joshua (Josh. 13–22). The apostasy covered the whole land, as indicated by the fact that each area is specifically identified: southern (3:7–31); northern (4:1–5:31); central (6:1–10:5); eastern (10:6–12:15); and western (13:1–16:31). His power to faithfully rescue shines against the dark backdrop of pitiful human compromise and sometimes bizarre twists of sin, as in the final summary (Judg. 17–21). The last verse (21:25) sums up the account: "In those days there was no king in Israel; everyone did what was right in his own eyes."

KEY PEOPLE IN JUDGES

Othniel—first judge of Israel; victorious over a powerful Mesopotamian king; brought forty years of peace to Israel (1:13–14; 3:7–11)

Ehud—second judge of Israel; brought Israel eighty years of peace by helping to conquer the Moabites (3:15–31)

Deborah—prophet and Israel's only female judge; succeeded Shamgar as fourth judge of Israel (4:4–16; 5)

Gideon—Israel's fifth judge; destroyed the Midianite army (6–8)

Abimelech—Gideon's evil son who declared himself king over Israel; killed sixty-nine of his half brothers (8:31–9:57)

Jephthah—judge of Israel and warrior who conquered the Ammonites (11:1–12:7)

Samson—dedicated to God as a Nazirite from birth; also a judge of Israel sent to overthrow the Philistines (13:24–16:31)

Delilah—Samson's lover who betrayed him to the Philistines for money (16:4–21)

KEY WORDS IN *Judges*

Judge: Hebrew *shaphat*—2:16,18; 10:2; 11:27; 12:9,11; 15:20; 16:31—this Hebrew word for *judge* means "to deliver" or "to rule." The judges of Israel had a wide range of responsibilities. Like their modern counterparts, Old Testament judges could decide controversies and hand down verdicts (Exodus 18:16). These judges were also involved in carrying out their judgment in both defending the righteous (Psalm 26:1) and destroying the wicked (Exodus 7:3). Many judges were God's appointed military leaders who, empowered by God's Spirit (6:34; 15:14), fought Israel's oppressors and thereby delivered the people. Later, Israel's king functioned as the national judge (1 Samuel 8:5). Ultimately, Israel's perfect Judge is God. He alone is capable of flawlessly judging the wicked and delivering the righteous (Isaiah 11:4).

Riddle: Hebrew *chidah*—14:12–19—meaning "a mysterious saying" or "puzzle." In Samson's story, the riddle is used in a contest of wits. Proverbs attributes such puzzles to the wise (Proverbs 1:6). When the Queen of Sheba tested Solomon's wisdom, her questions are described by this same Hebrew word (1 Kin. 10:1; 2 Chron. 9:1). In the Lord's confrontation with Miriam and Aaron, God describes Himself as speaking in "dark sayings" (the same Hebrew word) to the prophets, but to Moses face-to-face (Num. 12:6–8). Perhaps Paul had this last concept in mind when he warned the Corinthians that even someone with the ability to understand all mysteries would not amount to anything if that person did not possess the love of God (1 Cor. 13:2).

The Judges of Israel

Judge and Tribe	Scripture References	Oppressors	Period of Oppression/Rest
(1) Othniel (Judah) Son of Kenaz, younger brother of Caleb	Judges 1:11–15; 3:1–11; Joshua 15:16–19; 1 Chronicles 4:13	Cushan-Rishathaim, king of Mesopotamia	8 years/40 years
(2) Ehud (Benjamin) Son of Gera	Judges 3:12–4:1	Eglon, king of Moab; Ammonites; Amalekites	18 years/80 years
(3) Shamgar (Perhaps foreign) Son of Anath	Judges 3:31; 5:6	Philistines	Not given/Not given
(4) Deborah (Ephraim), Barak (Naphtali) Son of Abinoam	Judges 4:1–5:31 Hebrews 11:32	Jabin, king of Canaan; Sisera commander of the army	20 years/40 years
(5) Gideon (Manasseh) Son of Joash the Abiezrite. Also called: Jerubbaal (6:32; 7:1); Jerubbesheth (2 Samuel 11:21)	Judges 6:1–8:32 Hebrews 11:32	Midianites; Amalekites; "People of the East"	7 years/40 years
(6) Abimelech (Manasseh) Son of Gideon by a concubine	Judges 8:33–9:57; 2 Samuel 11:21	Civil war	Abimelech ruled over Israel 3 years
(7) Tola (Issachar) Son of Puah	Judges 10:1, 2		Judged Israel 23 years
(8) Jair (Gilead-Manasseh)	Judges 10:3–5		Judged Israel 22 years
(9) Jephthah (Gilead-Manasseh) Son of Gilead by a harlot	Judges 10:6–12:7 Hebrews 11:32	Philistines; Ammonites; Civil war with the Ephramites	18 years/ Judged Israel 6 years
(10) Ibzan (Judah or Zebulun) (Bethlehem-Zebulun; see Joshua 19:15)	Judges 12:8–10		Judged Israel 7 years
(11) Elon (Zebulun)	Judges 12:11,12		Judged Israel 10 years
(12) Abdon (Ephraim) Son of Hillel	Judges 12:13–15		Judged Israel 8 years
(13) Samson (Dan) Son of Manoah	Judges 13:1–16:31	Philistines Hebrews 11:32	40 years/ Judged Israel 20 years

KEY DOCTRINES IN JUDGES

God's mercy in delivering Israel (2:16,18,19; Deut. 30:3; Josh. 1:5; Ps. 106:43–45; Luke 1:50; Rom. 11:30–32; 2 Cor. 1:3; Eph. 2:4)

Israel's apostasy (3:7; 4:1; 6:1; 8:33; 10:6; 13:1; 21:25; Num. 31:1–3; Deut. 32:18; 1 Sam. 12:9; 1 Kin. 11:33; Is. 1:4; Ezek. 6:11–14; John 3:18–21; Rom. 7:5,6; Col. 3:25; Titus 3:3)

GOD'S CHARACTER IN JUDGES

God is righteous—5:11
God is wrathful—9:56

INTERPRETIVE CHALLENGES

The most interesting challenges are: (1) how to view men's violent acts against enemies or fellow countrymen, whether with God's approval or without it; (2) God's use of leaders who at times do His will and at times follow their own sinful impulse (Gideon, Eli, Jephthah, Samson); (3) how to view Jephthah's vow and offering of his daughter (11:30–40); and (4) how to resolve God's sovereign will with His providential working in spite of human sin (cf. 14:4).

The chronology of the various judges in different sectors of the land raises questions about how much time passed and how the time totals can fit into the entire time span from the Exodus (ca. 1445 B.C.) to Solomon's fourth year, ca. 967/966 B.C., which is said to be 480 years (1 Kin. 6:1). A reasonable explanation is that the deliverances and years of rest under the judges in distinct parts of the land included overlaps, so that some of them did not run consecutively but rather alongside each other during the 480 years. Paul's estimate of "about 450" years in Acts 13:20 is an approximation.

The Period of the Judges

Events and Judges	Years
Israel serves Cushan-Rishathaim(3:7,8)	8
Peace following Othniel's deliverance (3:7-11)	40
Israel serves Moab (3:12)	18
Peace follows Ehud's deliverance (3:12-30)	80
Shamgar delivers Israel from Philistines (3:31)	1
Israel serves Canaan (4:1-3)	20
Peace following deliverance by Deborah and Barak (4:1–5:31)	40
Israel serves Midian (6:1-6)	7
Peace following Gideon's deliverance (6:1-8:35)	40
Abimelech, king of Israel (9:1-57)	3
Tola's career (10:1,2)	23
Jair's career (10:3-5)	22
Israel serves Ammon and Philistia (10:6-10)	18
Jephthah's career (10:6-12:7)	6
Ibzan's career (12:8-10)	7
Elon's career (12:11,12)	10
Abdon's career (12:13-15)	8
Israel serves Philistia (13:1)	40
Samson's career (12:1-16:31)	20

OUTLINE
I. Introduction and Summary—The Disobedience of Israel (1:1–3:6)
   A. Incomplete Conquest over the Canaanites (1:1–36)
   B. The Decline and Judgment of Israel (2:1–3:6)
II. A Selected History of the Judges—The Deliverance of Israel (3:7–16:31)
   A. First Period: Othniel versus the Mesopotamians (3:7–11)
   B. Second Period: Ehud and Shamgar versus the Moabites (3:12–31)
   C. Third Period: Deborah versus the Canaanites (4:1–5:31)
   D. Fourth Period: Gideon versus the Midianites (6:1–8:32)
   E. Fifth Period: Tola and Jair versus Abimelech's Effects (8:33–10:5)
   F. Sixth Period: Jephthah, Ibzan, Elon, and Abdon versus the
      Philistines and Ammonites (10:6–12:15)
   G. Seventh Period: Samson versus the Philistines (13:1–16:31)
III. Epilogue—The Dereliction of Israel (17:1–21:25)
   A. The Idolatry of Micah and the Danites (17:1–18:31)
   B. The Crime at Gibeah and War against Benjamin (19:1–21:25)

MEANWHILE, IN OTHER PARTS OF THE WORLD...
Prohibition is declared in China, and silk fabrics become widely developed for use in Chinese trade.

ANSWERS TO TOUGH QUESTIONS
1. Men like Gideon, Jephthah, and Samson seem to exhibit as many gross failures as they do successes. Why does God make use of leaders with such obvious weaknesses?

One obvious answer to the question is that as long as God chooses to use people at all, He will end up using people with obvious weaknesses. No one escapes that category. The point is that God uses people in His plans in spite of their obvious weaknesses.

Does this mean that the sins of a leader are somehow to be excused? Of course not. In fact, leaders bear a higher level of accountability. Note, for example, the fact that Moses gave up his opportunity to enter the Promised Land because of an angry outburst (Num. 20:10; Deut. 3:24–27). Jephthah made a rash vow for which his daughter had to bear the primary consequence (Judges 11:29–40). What probably ought to attract our attention to these servants of God is not so much their weaknesses, or even the great accomplishments that God worked through them, but the fact that they remained faithful to God despite their failures.

2. What can we gain by studying the lives of the judges of Israel?

God's Word includes a rich sampling of human experience. Despite the superficial transformation of much of the world, the people who inhabit it remain the same. When we study the lives of the judges we discover ourselves. The shared victories, defeats, mistakes and right choices form a common link across the centuries and turn our attention to the God who was active in their lives. The invitation from the ancients remains silently compelling: If we were to live as boldly for God, surely we would discover each day that same kind of immediate presence of God that was such a part of their experience.

FURTHER STUDY ON JUDGES

1. Who were the twelve judges reviewed in this book, and how well did they carry out their missions of leadership?
2. Which judge do you find most worth imitating?
3. What were the main signs in the lives of the Israelites that indicated their loss of commitment to God and their compromises with the surrounding cultures?
4. Why did God continually rescue the people?
5. How would you illustrate the last verse in Judges to fit the times in which you live: "In those days there was no king in Israel; everyone did what was right in his own eyes" (Judges 21:25)?

R U T H
God's International Family

TITLE
Ancient versions and modern translations consistently entitle this book after Ruth the Moabite heroine, who is mentioned by name twelve times (1:4 to 4:13). Only two OT books receive their names from women—Ruth and Esther. This book also holds another distinction in being the only book in the Old Testament named after an ancestor of Jesus. The OT does not again refer to Ruth, while the NT mentions her just once—in the context of Christ's genealogy (Matt. 1:5; cf. 4:18–22). The name Ruth most likely comes from a Moabite and/or Hebrew word meaning "friendship." Ruth arrived in Bethlehem as a foreigner (2:10), became a maidservant (2:13), married wealthy Boaz (4:13), and was included in the physical lineage of Christ (Matt. 1:5).

AUTHOR AND DATE
Jewish tradition credits Samuel as the author, which is possible since he did not die (1 Sam. 25:1) until after he had anointed David as God's chosen king (1 Sam. 16:6–13). However, neither internal content nor external testimony conclusively identifies the writer. This exquisite story most likely appeared shortly before or during David's reign of Israel (1011–971 B.C.), since David is mentioned (4:17,22) but not Solomon. Goethe reportedly labeled this piece of anonymous literature as "the loveliest complete work on a small scale." What Venus is to statues and the Mona Lisa is to paintings, the Book of Ruth is to literature.

BACKGROUND AND SETTING
Aside from Bethlehem (1:1), Moab (the perennial enemy of Israel which was east of the Dead Sea), stands as the only other mentioned geographic/national entity (1:1,2). This country originated when Lot fathered Moab by an incestuous union with his oldest daughter (Gen. 19:37). Centuries later the Jews encountered opposition from Balak, king of Moab, through the prophet Balaam (Num. 22–25). For eighteen years Moab oppressed Israel during the judges (3:12–30). Saul defeated the Moabites (1 Sam. 14:47) while David seemed to enjoy a peaceful relationship with them (1 Sam. 22:3,4). Later, Moab again troubled Israel (2 Kin.

CHRIST IN . . . RUTH
BOAZ, AS A TYPE OF CHRIST, becomes the kinsman-redeemer of Ruth (see the **Key Words** and **Frequently Asked Questions** below). This account foretells the coming of Jesus as the Redeemer of all believers (1 Pet.1:18,19).

3:5–27; Ezra 9:1). Because of Moab's idolatrous worship of Chemosh (1 Kin. 11:7, 33; 2 Kin. 23:13) and its opposition to Israel, God cursed Moab (Is. 15–16; Jer. 48; Ezek. 25:8–11; Amos 2:1–3).

The story of Ruth occurred in the days "when the judges ruled" Israel (1:1) ca. 1370 to 1041 B.C. (Judg. 2:16–19) and thus bridges time from the judges to Israel's monarchy. God used "a famine in the land" of Judah (1:1) to set in motion this beautiful drama, although the famine does not receive mention in Judges which causes difficulty in dating the events of Ruth. However, by working backward in time from the well known date of David's reign (1011–971 B.C.), the time period of Ruth would most likely be during the judgeship of Jair, ca. 1126–1105 B.C. (Judg. 10:3–5).

Ruth covers about eleven to twelve years according to the following scenario: (1) 1:1–18, ten years in Moab (1:4); (2) 1:19–2:23, several months (mid-April to mid-June) in Boaz's field (1:22; 2:23); (3) 3:1–18, one day in Bethlehem and one night at the threshing floor; and (4) 4:1–22, about one year in Bethlehem.

KEY PEOPLE IN RUTH

Ruth—Naomi's daughter-in-law; later married to Boaz; direct ancestor of Jesus (chaps. 1–4)

Naomi—widow of Elimelech and mother-in-law of Orpah and Ruth; wisely instructed Ruth (chaps. 1–4)

Boaz—prosperous farmer who married Ruth, the Moabite; direct ancestor of Jesus (chaps. 2–4)

The Story of Ruth

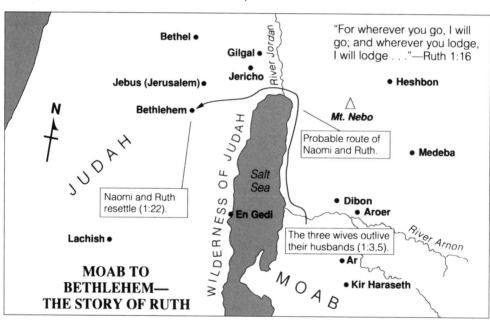

HISTORICAL AND THEOLOGICAL THEMES

All 85 verses of Ruth have been accepted as part of the canon by the Jews. Along with Song of Solomon, Esther, Ecclesiastes, and Lamentations, Ruth stands with the OT books of the Megilloth, or "five scrolls." Rabbis read these books in the synagogue on five special occasions during the year—Ruth being read at Pentecost due to the harvest scenes of Ruth 2–3.

Genealogically, Ruth looks back almost 900 years to events in the time of Jacob (4:11) and forward about 100 years to the coming reign of David (4:17,22). While Joshua and Judges emphasize the legacy of the nation and their land of promise, Ruth focuses on the lineage of David back to the Patriarchal era.

The Family Tree of Ruth

At least seven major theological themes emerge in Ruth. First, Ruth the Moabitess illustrates that God's redemptive plan extended beyond the Jews to Gentiles (2:12). Second, Ruth demonstrates that women are co-heirs with men of God's salvation grace (cf. 1 Pet. 3:7). Third, Ruth portrays the virtuous woman of Proverbs 31:10 (cf. 3:11). Fourth, Ruth describes God's sovereign (1:6; 4:13) and providential care (2:3) of seemingly unimportant people at apparently insignificant times which later prove to be monumentally crucial to accomplishing God's will. Fifth, Ruth along with Tamar (Gen. 38), Rahab (Josh. 2) and Bathsheba (2 Sam. 11–12) stand in Christ's genealogy (4:17, 22; cf. Matt. 1:5). Sixth, Boaz, as a type of Christ, becomes Ruth's kinsman-redeemer (4:1–12). Finally, David's right (and thus Christ's right) to the throne of Israel is traced back to Judah (4:18–22; cf. Gen. 49:8–12).

KEY DOCTRINES IN RUTH

Redemption for both Jews and Gentiles (2:12; 1 Sam. 24:19; Ps. 58:11; Acts 13:46; Rom. 10:11,12; Gal. 3:28; Eph. 2:14)

Women as co-heirs with men of God's salvation grace (2:12; Acts 17:12; Gal. 3:28)

Characteristics of a virtuous woman (3:11; Prov. 12:4; 31:10–31)

David's right (and thus Christ's right) to the throne of Israel (4:18–22; Gen. 49:8–12; Matt. 1:1–7; Luke 3:32)

GOD'S CHARACTER IN RUTH

God is sovereign—1:6; 4:13

God is provident—2:3

Kinsman-Redeemer

O.T. Qualification	Christ's Fulfillment
1. Blood Relationship	Gal. 4:4,5; Heb. 2:16,17
2. Necessary Resources	1 Cor. 6:20; 1 Pet. 1:18,19
3. Willingness to Buy	John 10:15-18; 1 John 3:16

INTERPRETIVE CHALLENGES

Ruth should be understood as a true historical account. The reliable facts surrounding Ruth, in addition to its complete compatibility with Judges plus 1 and 2 Samuel, confirm Ruth's authenticity. However, some individual difficulties require careful attention. First, how could Ruth worship at the tabernacle then in Shiloh (1 Sam. 4:4), since Deuteronomy 23:3 expressly forbids Moabites from entering the assembly for ten generations? Since the Jews entered the land ca. 1405 B.C. and Ruth was not born until ca. 1150 B.C., she then represented at least the eleventh generation (probably later) if the time limitation ended at ten generations. If "ten generations" was an expression meaning "forever" as Nehemiah 13:1 implies, then Ruth would be like the foreigner of Isaiah 56:1–8 who joined himself to the LORD (1:16) thus gaining entrance to the assembly.

Second, are there not immoral overtones to Boaz and Ruth spending the night together before marriage (3:3–18)? Ruth engaged in a common ancient Near Eastern custom by asking Boaz to take her for his wife as symbolically pictured by throwing a garment over the intended woman (3:9), just as Jehovah spread His garment over Israel (Ezek. 16:8). The text does not even hint at the slightest moral impropriety, noting that Ruth slept at his feet (3:14). Thus, Boaz became God's answer to his own earlier prayer for Ruth (2:12).

Third, would not the law stated in Deuteronomy 25:5,6 (if a married man dies and has no sons, his brother must marry the widow to carry on the family) lead to incest and/or polygamy if the nearest relative was already married? God would not design a good plan to involve the grossest of immoralities punishable by death. We should assume that the implementation of Deuteronomy 25:5,6 could involve only the nearest relative who was eligible for marriage as qualified by other demands of the law.

KEY WORDS IN

Ruth

Glean: Hebrew *laqat*—2:2,7,15,17–19,23—used here means "to gather together" or "to pick up." In the Old Testament, people are described as gleaning a variety of objects: stones (Gen.31:46), money (Gen. 47:14), manna (Ex. 16:4,5,26), and even worthless men (Judg. 11:3). The prophet Isaiah used this word to describe how the Lord would "gather up" His people from among all the nations and restore them to their own land (Is. 27:12). The verb occurs thirty-four times in the Old Testament, with twelve instances here in Ruth 2. In this passage, Ruth makes use of the conditions the Lord gave to Moses. God had told the Israelites not to completely harvest their fields; instead they were to leave some unharvested grain so that the poor and strangers in the land could gather it up for their survival (Lev. 19:9,10; 23:22).

Kinsman-Redeemer: Hebrew *ga>al*—2:1,20; 3:9,12,13; 4:1,3,6,14—meaning "kinsman," refers to a "close relative" who acted as a protector or guardian of the family rights. He could be called upon to perform a number of duties: 91) to buy back property that the family had sold; (2) to provide an heir for a deceased brother by marrying that brother's wife and producing a child with her; (3) to buy back a family member who had been sold into slavery due to poverty; and (4) to avenge a relative who had been murdered by killing the murderer. The Scripture calls God the Redeemer or the "close relative" of Israel (Is. 60:16), and Jesus the Redeemer of all believers (1 Pet. 1:18,19).

Fourth, was not marriage to a Moabite woman strictly forbidden by the law? The nations or people to whom marriage was prohibited were those possessing the land that Israel would enter (Ex. 34:16; Deut. 7:1–3; Josh. 23:12), which did not include Moab (cf. Deut. 7:1). Further, Boaz married Ruth, a devout follower of God (1:16–17), not a pagan worshiper of Chemosh—Moab's chief deity (cf. later problems in Ezra 9:1,2 and Neh. 13:23–25).

OUTLINE

     I. Elimelech and Naomi's Ruin in Moab (1:1–5)
     II. Naomi and Ruth's Return to Bethlehem (1:6–22)
     III. Boaz's Reception of Ruth in His Field (2:1–23)
     IV. Ruth's Romance with Boaz (3:1–18)
     V. Boaz's Redemption of Ruth (4:1–12)
     VI. God's Reward of Boaz and Ruth with a Son (4:13–17)
     VII. David's Right to the Throne of Judah (4:18–22)

MEANWHILE, IN OTHER PARTS OF THE WORLD...

Civil war breaks out under the reign of Ramses XI during the twenty-first Dynasty in Egypt (1090 to 945 B.C.).

ANSWERS TO TOUGH QUESTIONS

1. What is the "kinsman-redeemer"?

When Boaz negotiated with another relative about the settlement of Elimelech and Naomi's estate (4:1–12), he referred to a law established by Moses in Deuteronomy 25:5–10. That law set out specific actions to be taken by the surviving family if a married son were to die without a son to inherit or carry on his name. Another (presumably unmarried) man in the family was to marry the widow. The first resulting child would inherit the estate of the man who had died.

Boaz's relative was willing to work out a financial arrangement with Naomi over her estate, but he didn't realize that Ruth was part of the settlement. When Boaz informed the man, he immediately released his right to claim responsibility for the estate. That cleared the way for Boaz and Ruth to marry. The whole exchange demonstrates a commitment to integrity and honor.

FURTHER STUDY ON RUTH

1. In what ways does Naomi's and Ruth's relationship illustrate the best forms of friendship?
2. How does Ruth's story illustrate God's faithfulness?
3. In what ways did Ruth explain and express her faith in God?
4. How did Boaz exhibit wisdom in handling of Naomi's and Ruth's inheritance matters?
5. Describe Naomi's relationship with God throughout the Book of Ruth.
6. What specific illustrations of God's provision can you think of in your own life?

SAMUEL, KINGS, AND CHRONICLES

I. THE KINGSHIP OF GOD (1 Sam. 1:1–7:17; 1 Chr. 1:1–9:44)
    A. Genealogical Tables (1 Chr. 1:1–9:44)
        1. Genealogies of the Patriarchs (1 Chr. 1:1–2:2)
        2. Genealogies of the Tribes of Israel (1 Chr. 2:3–9:44)
    B. The Close of the Theocracy (1 Sam. 1:1–7:17)
        1. The Early Life of Samuel (1 Sam. 1:1–4:1a)
            a. Samuel's birth and infancy (1 Sam. 1:1–2:11)
            b. Samuel at Shiloh (1 Sam. 2:12–4:1a)
        2. The Period of National Disaster (1 Sam. 4:1b–7:2)
            a. Israel's defeat and loss of the ark (1 Sam. 4:1b–11a)
            b. Fall of the house of Eli (1 Sam. 4:11b–22)
            c. The ark of God (1 Sam. 5:1–7:2)
        3. Samuel, the Last of the Judges (1 Sam. 7:3–17)
II. THE KINGSHIP OF SAUL (1 Sam. 8:1–31:13; 1 Chr. 10:1–14)
    A. Establishment of Saul as First King of Israel (1 Sam. 8:1–10:27)
    B. Saul's Reign until His Rejection (1 Sam. 11:1–15:35)
    C. The Decline of Saul and the Rise of David (1 Sam. 16:1–31:13)
        1. David's Early History (1 Sam. 16:1–23)
        2. David's Advancement and Saul's Growing Jealousy (1 Sam. 17:1–20:42)
            a. David and Goliath (1 Sam. 17:1–51)
            b. David at the court of Saul (1 Sam. 18:1–20:42)
        3. David's Life of Exile (1 Sam. 21:1–28:2)
            a. David's flight (1 Sam. 21:1–22:5)
            b. Saul's vengeance on the priests of Nob (1 Sam. 22:6–23)
            c. David rescue of Keilah (1 Sam. 23:1–13)
            d. David's last meeting with Jonathan (1 Sam. 23:14–18)
            e. David's betrayal by the Ziphites (1 Sam. 23:19–24a)
            f. David's escape from Saul in the Wilderness of Maon (1 Sam. 23:24b–28)
            g. David's flight from Saul; David's mercy on Saul's life in the cave (1 Sam. 23:29–24:22)
            h. Samuel's death (1 Sam. 25:1)

    i. David wedding to Abigail (1 Sam. 25:2–44)
    j. David's mercy on Saul's life again (1 Sam. 26:1–25)
    k.David's joining with the Philistines (1 Sam. 27:1–28:2)
   4. Saul's Downfall in War with the Philistines (1 Sam. 28:3–31:13; 1 Chr. 10:1–14)
    a. Saul's fear of the Philistines (1 Sam. 28:3–6)
    b. Saul's visit to the witch of Endor (1 Sam. 28:7–25)
    c. David leaves the Philistines; defeats the Amalakites (1 Sam. 29:1–30:31)
    d. Saul and his sons slain (1 Sam. 31:1–13; 1 Chr. 10:1–14)

III. THE KINGSHIP OF DAVID (2 Sam. 1:1–24:25; 1 Kin. 1:1–2:11; 1 Chr. 10:14–29:30)

 A. David's Victories (2 Sam. 1:1–10:19; 1 Chr. 10:14–20:8)
  1. The Political Triumphs of David (2 Sam. 1:1–5:25; 1 Chr. 10:14–12:40)
   a. David is king of Judah (2 Sam. 1:1–4:12; 1 Chr. 10:1–12:40)
   b. David is king over all Israel (2 Sam. 5:1–5:25)
  2. The Spiritual Triumphs of David (2 Sam. 6:1–7:29; 1 Chr. 13:1–17:27)
   a. The ark of the covenant (2 Sam. 6:1–23; 1 Chr. 13:1–16:43)
   b. The temple and the Davidic Covenant (2 Sam. 7:1–29; 1 Chr. 17:1–27)
  3. The Military Triumphs of David (2 Sam. 8:1–10:19; 1 Chr. 18:1–20:8)
 B. David's Sins (2 Sam. 11:1–27)
  1. David's Adultery with Bathsheba (2 Sam. 11:1–5)
  2. David's Murder of Uriah the Hittite (2 Sam. 11:6–27)
 C. David's Problems (2 Sam. 12:1–24:25; 1 Chr. 21:1–27:34)
  1. David's House Suffers (2 Sam. 12:1–13:36)
   a. Nathan's prophecy against David (2 Sam. 12:1–14)
   b. David's son dies (2 Sam. 12:15–25)
   c. Joab's loyalty to David (2 Sam. 12:26–31)
   d. Amnon's incest (2 Sam. 13:1–20)
   e. Amnon's murder (2 Sam. 13:21–36)
  2. David's Kingdom Suffers (2 Sam. 13:37–24:25; 1 Chr. 21:1–27:34)
   a. Absalom's rebellion (2 Sam. 13:37–17:29)
   b. Absalom's murder (2 Sam. 18:1–33)
   c. David's restoration as king (2 Sam. 19:1–20:26)
   d. David's kingship evaluated (2 Sam. 21:1–23:39)

e. David's numbering of the people (2 Sam. 24:1–24:25; 1 Chr. 21:1–30)

D. David's Preparation and Organization for the Temple (1 Chr. 22:1–27:34)

E. David's Last Days (1 Kin. 1:1–2:11; 1 Chr. 28:1–29:30)

    1. David's Failing Health: Abishag the Shunammite (1 Kin. 1:1–4)

    2. Adonijah's Attempt to Seize the Kingdom (1 Kin. 1:5–9)

    3. Solomon's Anointing as King (1 Kin. 1:10–40; 1 Chr. 29:20–25)

    4. Adonijah's Submission (1 Kin. 1:41–53)

    5. David's Last Words (1 Kin. 2:1–9; 1 Chr. 28:1–29:25)

        a. David's words for Israel (1 Chr. 28:1–8)

        b. David's words for Solomon (1 Kin. 2:1–9; 1 Chr. 28:9–29:19)

    6. David's Death (1 Kin. 2:10,11; 1 Chr. 29:26–30)

IV. THE KINGSHIP OF SOLOMON (1 Kin. 2:12–11:43; 1 Chr. 29:20–30; 2 Chr. 1:1–9:31)

A. Solomon's Kingship Begins (1 Kin. 2:12–4:34; 1 Chr. 29:20–30; 2 Chr. 1:1–17)

    1. Solomon's Kingship Established (1 Kin. 2:12; 1 Chr. 29:20–2 Chr. 1:1)

    2. Solomon's Adversaries Removed (1 Kin. 2:13–46)

    3. Solomon's Wedding to Pharaoh's Daughter (1 Kin. 3:1)

    4. Solomon's Spiritual Condition (1 Kin. 3:2,3)

    5. Solomon's Sacrifice at Gibeon (1 Kin. 3:4; 2 Chr. 1:2–6)

    6. Solomon's Dream and Prayer for Wisdom (1 Kin. 3:5–15; 2 Chr. 1:7–12)

    7. Solomon's Judging of the Harlots with God's Wisdom (1 Kin. 3:16–28)

    8. Solomon's Officers, His Power, Wealth, and Wisdom (1 Kin. 4:1–34; 2 Chr. 1:13–17)

B. Solomon's Splendor (1 Kin. 5:1–8:66; 2 Chr. 2:1–7:22)

    1. Preparations for the Building of the Temple (1 Kin. 5:1–18; 2 Chr. 2:1–18)

    2. The Building of the Temple (1 Kin. 6:1–38; 2 Chr. 3:1–14)

    3. The Building of the Royal Palace (1 Kin. 7:1–12)

    4. The Making of the Vessels for the Temple (1 Kin. 7:13–51; 2 Chr. 3:15–5:1)

    5. The Dedication and Completion of the Temple (1 Kin. 8:1–66; 2 Chr. 5:2–7:22)

C. Solomon's Demise (1 Kin. 9:1–11:43; 2 Chr. 8:1–9:31)

    1. Davidic Covenant Repeated (1 Kin. 9:1–9)

    2. Solomon's Disobedience to the Covenant (1 Kin. 9:10–11:8; 2 Chr. 8:1–9:12)

3. Solomon's Chastening for Breaking the Covenant (1 Kin. 11:9–40; 2 Chr. 9:13–28)

4. Solomon's Death (1 Kin. 11:41–43; 2 Chr. 9:29–31)

V. THE KINGDOM DIVIDED (1 Kin. 12:1–22:53; 2 Kin. 1:1–17:41; 2 Chr. 10:1–28:27)

A. The Kingdom Divides (1 Kin. 12:1–14:31; 2 Chr. 10:1–28:27)

1. The Division's Cause (1 Kin. 12:1–24)

2. Jeroboam, King of Israel (1 Kin. 12:25–14:20; 2 Chr. 10:1–13:22)

3. Rehoboam, King of Judah (1 Kin. 14:21–31; 2 Chr. 10:1–12:16)

B. Judah's Two Kings (1 Kin. 15:1–24; 2 Chr. 13:1–16:14)

1. Abijam, a.k.a. Joram, King of Judah (1 Kin. 15:1–8; 2 Chr. 13:1–22)

2. Asa, King of Judah (1 Kin. 15:9–24; 2 Chr. 14:1–16:14)

C. Israel's Five Kings (1 Kin. 15:25–16:28; 2 Chr.16:1–6)

1. Nadab, King of Israel (1 Kin. 15:25–31)

2. Baasha, King of Israel (1 Kin. 15:32–16:7; 2 Chr. 16:1–6)

3. Elah, King of Israel (1 Kin. 16:8–14)

4. Zimri, King of Israel (1 Kin. 16:15–20)

5. Omri, King of Israel (1 Kin. 16:21–28)

D. Ahab, King of Israel (1 Kin. 16:29–22:40; 2 Chr. 16:1–34)

1. Ahab's Sin (1 Kin. 16:29–34)

2. Elijah the Prophet (1 Kin. 17:1–19:21; 2 Chr. 16:1–34)

3. Wars with Syria (1 Kin. 20:1–43)

4. Naboth Swindled and Killed (1 Kin. 21:1–16)

5. Ahab's Death (1 Kin. 21:17–22:40)

E. Jehoshaphat, King of Judah (1 Kin. 22:41–50; 2 Chr. 17:1–21:3)

F. Ahaziah, King of Israel (1 Kin. 22:51–53; 2 Kin. 1:1–18; 2 Chr. 20:35–37)

G. Jehoram, a.k.a. Joram, King of Israel (2 Kin. 2:1–8:15; 2 Chr. 22:5–7)

H. Jehoram, King of Judah (2 Kin. 8:16–24; 2 Chr. 21:4–20)

I. Ahaziah, King of Judah (2 Kin. 8:25–9:29; 2 Chr. 22:1–9)

J. Jehu, King of Israel (2 Kin. 9:30–10:36; 2 Chr. 22:7–12)

K. Athaliah, Queen of Judah (2 Kin. 11:1–16; 2 Chr. 22:10–23:21)

L. Joash, King of Judah (2 Kin. 11:17–12:21; 2 Chr. 24:1–24:27)

M. Jehoahaz, King of Israel (2 Kin. 13:1–9)

N. Jehoash, a.k.a. Joash, King of Israel (2 Kin. 13:10–25; 2 Chr. 25:17–24)

O. Amaziah, King of Judah (2 Kin. 14:1–22; 2 Chr. 25:1–28)

P. Jeroboam II, King of Israel (2 Kin. 14:23–29)

Q. Uzziah, a.k.a., Azariah, King of Judah (2 Kin. 15:1–7; 2 Chr. 26:1–23)

R. Zechariah, King of Israel (2 Kin. 15:8–12)

S. Shallum, King of Israel (2 Kin. 15:13–15)

T. Menahem, King of Israel (2 Kin. 15:16–22)

U. Pekahiah, King of Israel (2 Kin. 15:23–26)

V. Pekah, King of Israel (2 Kin. 15:27–31)

W. Jotham, King of Judah (2 Kin. 15:32–38; 2 Chr. 27:1–9)

X. Ahaz, King of Judah (2 Kin. 16:1–20; 2 Chr. 28:1–27)

Y. Hoshea, King of Israel (2 Kin. 17:1–41)

VI. **THE SURVIVING KINGDOM OF JUDAH (2 Kin. 18:1–25:30; 2 Chr. 29:1–36:23)**

A. Hezekiah, King of Judah (2 Kin. 18:1–20:21; 2 Chr. 29:1–32:33; Is. 36–39)

B. Manasseh, King of Judah (2 Kin. 21:1–18; 2 Chr. 33:1–20)

C. Amon, King of Judah (2 Kin. 21:19–26; 2 Chr. 33:21–25)

D. Josiah, King of Judah (2 Kin. 22:1–23:30; 2 Chr. 34:1–35:27)

E. Jehoahaz, King of Judah (2 Kin. 23:31–34; 2 Chr. 36:1–4)

F. Jehoiakim, King of Judah (2 Kin. 23:35–24:7; 2 Chr. 36:4–8)

G. Jehoiachin, King of Judah (2 Kin. 24:8–16; 2 Chr. 36:9,10)

H. Zedekiah, King of Judah (2 Kin. 24:17–25:21; 2 Chr. 36:11–21)

I. Gedaliah, Governor of Judah (2 Kin. 25:22–26)

J. Jehoiachin Released in Babylon (2 Kin. 25:27–30)

K. Cyrus Decrees Rebuilding in Jerusalem (2 Chr. 36:22,23)

Chronology of Old Testament Kings and Prophets

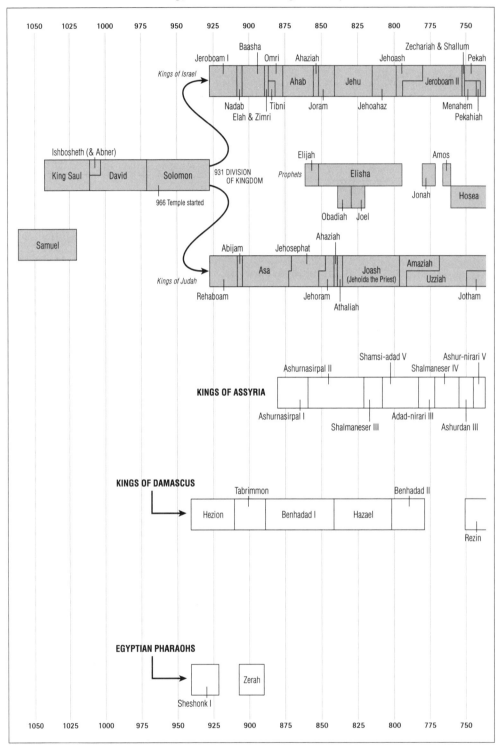

Chronology of Old Testament Kings and Prophets

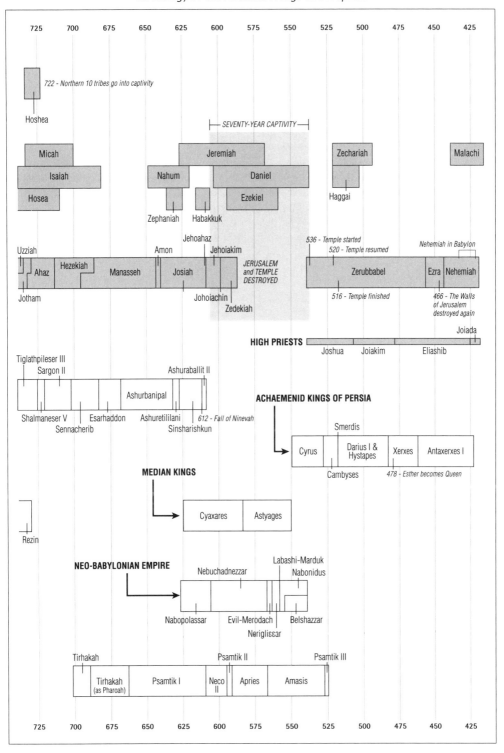

FIRST AND SECOND SAMUEL

Qualifications for a King and the Establishment of David's Line

TITLE

First and Second Samuel were considered as one book in the earliest Hebrew manuscript, and were later divided into the two books by the translators of the Greek version, the Septuagint (LXX), a division followed by the Latin Vulgate (Vg.), English translations, and modern Hebrew Bibles. The earliest Hebrew manuscripts entitled the one book "Samuel" after the man God used to establish the kingship in Israel. Later Hebrew texts and the English versions call the divided book "1 and 2 Samuel." The LXX designated them "The First and Second Books of Kingdoms" and the Vg., "First and Second Kings," with our 1 and 2 Kings being "Third and Fourth Kings."

AUTHOR AND DATE

Jewish tradition ascribed the writing of these books to Samuel himself or to Samuel, Nathan, and Gad (based on 1 Chr. 29:29). But Samuel cannot be the writer because his death is recorded in 1 Samuel 25:1, before the events associated with David's reign even took place. Further, Nathan and Gad were prophets of the Lord during David's lifetime and would not have been alive when the Book of Samuel was written. Though the written records of these three prophets could have been used for information in the writing of 1 and 2 Samuel, the human author of these books is unknown. The work comes to the reader as an anonymous writing, i.e., the human author speaks for the Lord and gives the divine interpretation of the events narrated.

The books of Samuel contain no clear indication of the date of composition. That the author wrote after the division of the kingdom between Israel and Judah in 931 B.C. is clear, due to the many references to Israel and Judah as distinct entities (1 Sam. 11:8; 17:52; 18:16; 2 Sam. 5:5; 11:11; 12:8; 19:42–43; 24:1,9). Also, the statement concerning Ziklag's belonging "to the kings of Judah to this day" in 1 Samuel 27:6 gives clear evidence of a post-Solomonic date of writing. There is no such clarity concerning how late the date of writing could be. However, 1 and 2 Samuel are included in the Former Prophets in the Hebrew canon, along with Joshua, Judges, and 1 and 2 Kings. If the Former Prophets were composed as a unit, then Samuel would have been written during the Babylonian captivity (ca.560–540 B.C.), since 2 Kings concludes during the exile (2 Kin. 25:27–30). However, since Samuel has a different literary style than Kings, it was most likely penned before the Exile during the period of the divided kingdom (ca. 931–722 B.C.) and later made an integral part of the Former Prophets.

BACKGROUND AND SETTING

The majority of the action recorded in 1 and 2 Samuel took place in and around the central highlands in the land of Israel. The nation of Israel was largely concentrated in an area that ran about 90 miles from the hill country of Ephraim in the north

(1 Sam. 1:1; 9:4) to the hill country of Judah in the south (Josh. 20:7; 21:11) and between 15 to 35 miles east to west. This central spine ranges in height from 1,500 to 3,300 feet above sea level. The major cities of 1 and 2 Samuel are to be found in these central highlands: Shiloh, the residence of Eli and the tabernacle; Ramah, the hometown of Samuel; Gibeah, the headquarters of Saul; Bethlehem, the birthplace of David; Hebron, David's capital when he ruled over Judah; and Jerusalem, the ultimate "city of David."

The events of 1 and 2 Samuel took place between the years ca. 1105 B.C., the birth of Samuel (1 Sam. 1:1–28), to ca. 971 B.C., the last words of David (2 Sam. 23:1–7). Thus, the books span about 135 years of history. During those years, Israel was transformed from a loosely knit group of tribes under "judges" to a united nation under the reign of a centralized monarchy. They look primarily at Samuel (ca. 1105–1030 B.C.), Saul, who reigned ca. 1052–1011 B.C., and David, who was king of the united monarchy ca. 1011–971 B.C.

The Kingdom of David

© 1996 Thomas Nelson, Inc.

KEY PEOPLE IN 1 SAMUEL

Eli—high priest and Israel's judge for forty years; trained Samuel to be judge (1:3–28; 2:11–4:18)

Hannah—mother of Samuel; dedicated him to the Lord when he was a baby (1:2–2:11,21)

Samuel—priest, prophet, and greatest judge of Israel; anointed Israel's first two kings (1:20; 2:11,18–26; 3:1–21; 7:3– 13:15; 15:1–16:13; 19:18–24; 25:1; 28:3– 16)

Saul—first king of Israel appointed by God; grew jealous of David and tried to kill him (9:2–11:15; 13:1–19:24; 20:24–33; 21:10,11; 22:6–24:22; 25:44–27:4; 28:3–31:12)

Jonathan—son of Saul; befriended David and protected him against Saul (13:1–14:49; 18:1–23:18; 31:2)

David—greatest king of Israel; also a shepherd, musician, and poet; direct ancestor to Jesus Christ (16:11–30:27)

The Life of David

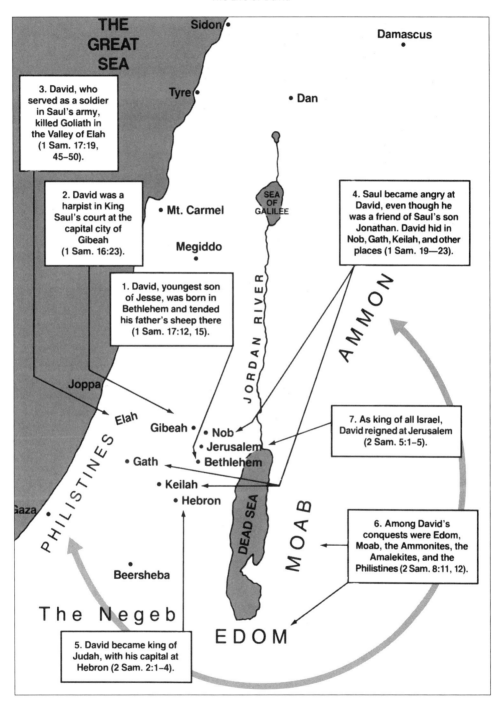

THE GREAT SEA

Sidon

Damascus

3. David, who served as a soldier in Saul's army, killed Goliath in the Valley of Elah (1 Sam. 17:19, 45–50).

Tyre

• Dan

2. David was a harpist in King Saul's court at the capital city of Gibeah (1 Sam. 16:23).

• Mt. Carmel

SEA OF GALILEE

4. Saul became angry at David, even though he was a friend of Saul's son Jonathan. David hid in Nob, Gath, Keilah, and other places (1 Sam. 19—23).

Megiddo

1. David, youngest son of Jesse, was born in Bethlehem and tended his father's sheep there (1 Sam. 17:12, 15).

JORDAN RIVER

AMMON

Joppa

Elah

Gibeah • • Nob
• Jerusalem

7. As king of all Israel, David reigned at Jerusalem (2 Sam. 5:1–5).

PHILISTINES

• Gath • Bethlehem

• Keilah
• Hebron

DEAD SEA

MOAB

Gaza

6. Among David's conquests were Edom, Moab, the Ammonites, the Amalekites, and the Philistines (2 Sam. 8:11, 12).

• Beersheba

The Negeb

EDOM

5. David became king of Judah, with his capital at Hebron (2 Sam. 2:1–4).

The Life and Ministry of Samuel

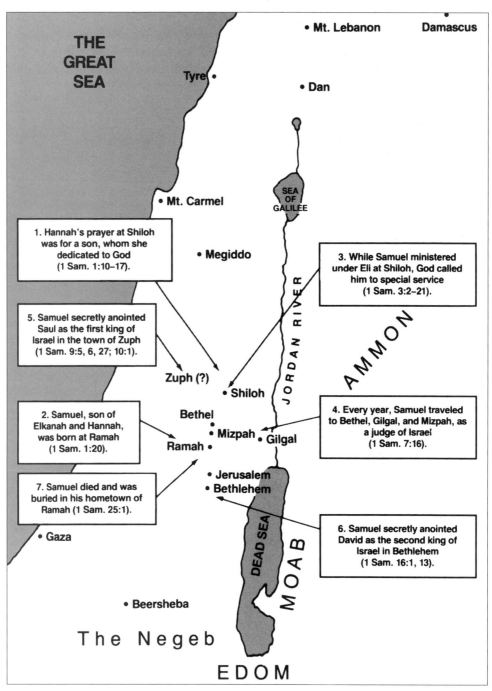

THE
GREAT
SEA

• Mt. Lebanon   Damascus

Tyre •

• Dan

SEA
OF
GALILEE

• Mt. Carmel

1. Hannah's prayer at Shiloh
was for a son, whom she
dedicated to God
(1 Sam. 1:10–17).

• Megiddo

3. While Samuel ministered
under Eli at Shiloh, God called
him to special service
(1 Sam. 3:2–21).

JORDAN RIVER

AMMON

5. Samuel secretly anointed
Saul as the first king of
Israel in the town of Zuph
(1 Sam. 9:5, 6, 27; 10:1).

Zuph (?)

• Shiloh

Bethel

2. Samuel, son of
Elkanah and Hannah,
was born at Ramah
(1 Sam. 1:20).

• Mizpah

Ramah •   • Gilgal

4. Every year, Samuel traveled
to Bethel, Gilgal, and Mizpah, as
a judge of Israel
(1 Sam. 7:16).

• Jerusalem
• Bethlehem

7. Samuel died and was
buried in his hometown of
Ramah (1 Sam. 25:1).

DEAD SEA

MOAB

6. Samuel secretly anointed
David as the second king of
Israel in Bethlehem
(1 Sam. 16:1, 13).

• Gaza

• Beersheba

The Negeb

EDOM

The Philistine Threat

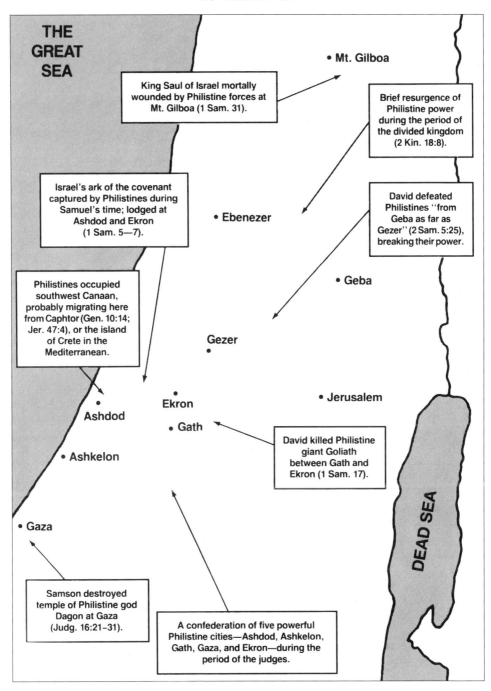

THE GREAT SEA

• Mt. Gilboa

King Saul of Israel mortally wounded by Philistine forces at Mt. Gilboa (1 Sam. 31).

Brief resurgence of Philistine power during the period of the divided kingdom (2 Kin. 18:8).

Israel's ark of the covenant captured by Philistines during Samuel's time; lodged at Ashdod and Ekron (1 Sam. 5—7).

• Ebenezer

David defeated Philistines "from Geba as far as Gezer" (2 Sam. 5:25), breaking their power.

Philistines occupied southwest Canaan, probably migrating here from Caphtor (Gen. 10:14; Jer. 47:4), or the island of Crete in the Mediterranean.

• Geba

Gezer
•

•
Ekron

• Jerusalem

Ashdod

• Gath

David killed Philistine giant Goliath between Gath and Ekron (1 Sam. 17).

• Ashkelon

DEAD SEA

• Gaza

Samson destroyed temple of Philistine god Dagon at Gaza (Judg. 16:21–31).

A confederation of five powerful Philistine cities—Ashdod, Ashkelon, Gath, Gaza, and Ekron—during the period of the judges.

1 Samuel

Hears: Hebrew *shamac*—1:13; 2:23; 4:14; 7:9; 8:18; 17:11; 23:11; 25:24—also means "to listen" or "to obey." This important OT word appears over 1,100 times. It implies that the listener is giving his or her total attention to the one who is speaking. In some cases, the word suggests more than listening and indicates obedience to what has been said. Abraham was blessed not only for hearing but also for obeying God's voice (see Gen. 22:18, where the word is translated "obeyed"). In the third chapter of 1 Samuel, Samuel is listening for God's word and is determined to obey it. This young man is an example of the kind of person God delights to use—one who is always ready to receive His Word and follow it.

King: Hebrew *melek*—2:10; 8:6; 10:24; 15:11; 18:22; 21:11,16; 24:20—may describe a petty ruler of a small city (Joshua 10:3) or a monarch of a vast empire (Esther 1:1–5). An ancient king's jurisdiction included the military (8:20), the economy (1 Kin. 10:26–29), international diplomacy (1 Kin. 5:1–11), and the legal system (2 Sam. 8:15). He often served as a spiritual leader (2 Kin. 23:1–24), although Israel's kings were prohibited from some priestly functions (13:9–14). The Bible presents David as an example of the righteous king who set his heart on faithfully serving God (Acts 13:22). God's promise to give David an everlasting kingdom (2 Sam. 7:16) has been fulfilled in Jesus Christ, whose human ancestry is through the royal family of David (Luke 2:4).

Utterly Destroyed: Hebrew *charam*—15:3,8,9,15,18,20—refers to the "setting apart" of inappropriate things, usually because of defilement associated with idol worship. In the ancient world, anything sacred or defiled was considered inappropriate for common use and was therefore subject to complete destruction. According to Deuteronomy 13:12–15, Israel was to destroy everyone and everything that was wicked enough to be considered corrupted. Violation of this command cost Achan his life (Joshua 7) and Saul his throne (15:9–11). Paul reminds us that we are all wicked, and as a result are defiled and deserve destruction. Yet God in His mercy has chosen to save those who place their trust in Jesus (Rom. 3:10–26).

KEY PEOPLE IN 2 SAMUEL

David—(See above)

Joab—military commander of David's army (2:13–3:39; 8:16; 10:7–12:27; 14:1– 33; 18:2–24:9)

Bathsheba—committed adultery with David; became queen of Israel and mother of Solomon; direct ancestor of Jesus (11:1–26; 12:24)

Nathan—prophet and advisor to David; urged him to repent of his sin (7:2–17; 12:1–25)

Absalom—son of David; attempted to overthrow the throne of Israel (3:3; 13:1–19:10)

HISTORICAL AND THEOLOGICAL THEMES

As 1 Samuel begins, Israel was at a low point spiritually. The priesthood was corrupt (1 Sam. 2:12–17, 22–26), the ark of the covenant was not at the tabernacle (1 Sam. 4:3–7:2), idolatry was practiced (1 Sam. 7:3,4), and the judges were dishonest (1 Sam. 8:2,3). Through the influence of godly Samuel (1 Sam. 12:23) and David (1 Sam. 13:14), these conditions were reversed. Second Samuel concludes with the anger of the Lord being withdrawn from Israel (2 Sam. 24:25).

During the years narrated in 1 and 2 Samuel, the great empires of the ancient world were in a state of weakness. Neither Egypt nor the Mesopotamian powers, Babylon and

KEY WORDS IN

2 Samuel

Ark: Hebrew 'aron—6:2,4,10,12,17; 7:2; 11:11; 15:24—can be translated "chest" (2 Kin. 12:9) or "sarcophagus" (Gen. 50:26), but most often appears in the phrase >aron haberith, which means "ark of the covenant." The ark was a wooden chest overlaid with gold (Ex. 25:10–22), housing the Ten Commandments (Ex. 40:20), Aaron's staff, and a pot of manna (Heb. 9:4). It sat in the Most Holy Place as a reminder of Israel's covenant with God and His presence among them. When the Israelites became careless with the ark (1 Sam. 4:1–11), God allowed it to be captured in order to demonstrate that His covenant relationship with them transcended symbols and superstitions. What He required was continual obedience to His covenant and a contrite heart surrendered to Him (Ps. 51:17; Is. 57:15).

Jerusalem: Hebrew yerushalaim—5:5; 8:7; 11:1; 15:8,29; 16:15; 17:20; 19:19; 24:16—related to the word for "peace." During the reign of King David, Jerusalem was made the political and religious capital of Israel and became central to the unfolding of God's redemptive plan. Jerusalem is described variously in the OT as the city of God (Ps. 87:1–3), the place where God has put His name (2 Kin. 21:4), a place of salvation (Is. 46:13), the throne of God (Jer. 3:17), and a holy city (Is. 52:1). The prophets anticipated a time when Jerusalem would be judged because of its iniquity (Micah 4:10–12), but in pronouncing judgment they could also see its glorious restoration (Is. 40:2; 44:25–28; Dan. 9:2; Zeph. 3:16–20). This vision of a restored Jerusalem included the hope of a New Jerusalem in which God would gather all His people (Is. 65:17–19; Rev. 21:1,2).

Mighty Men: Hebrew gibbor—1:25; 10:7; 16:6; 17:8; 20:7; 23:8,22—emphasizes excellence or unusual quality. In the OT it is used for the excellence of a lion (Prov. 30:30), of good or bad men (Gen. 10:9; 1 Chr.19:8), of giants (Gen. 6:4), of angels (Ps. 103:20), or even God (Deut. 10:17; Neh. 9:32). The Scriptures state that the mighty man is not victorious because of his strength (Ps. 33:16) but because of his understanding and knowledge of the Lord (Jer. 9:23–24). The phrase mighty God is used three times in the OT, including Isaiah's messianic prophecy of the birth of Jesus (Is. 9:6; 10:21; Jer.32:18).

Assyria, were threats to Israel at that time. The two nations most hostile to the Israelites were the Philistines (1 Sam. 4; 7; 13; 14; 17; 23; 31; 2 Sam. 5) to the west and the Ammonites (1 Sam. 11; 2 Sam. 10–12) to the east. The major contingent of the Philistines had migrated from the Aegean Islands and Asia Minor in the 12th century B.C. After being denied access to Egypt, they settled among other preexisting Philistines along the Mediterranean coast of Palestine. The Philistines controlled the use of iron, which gave them a decided military and economic advantage over Israel (1 Sam. 13:19–22). The Ammonites were descendants of Lot (Gen. 19:38) who lived on the Transjordan Plateau. David conquered the Philistines (2 Sam. 8:1) and the Ammonites (2 Sam. 12:29–31), along with other nations that surrounded Israel (2 Sam. 8:2–14).

There are four predominant theological themes in 1 and 2 Samuel. The first is the Davidic Covenant. The books are framed by two references to the "anointed" king in the prayer of Hannah (1 Sam. 2:10) and the song of David (2 Sam. 22:51). This is a reference to the Messiah, the King who will triumph over the nations who are opposed to God (see Gen. 49:8–12; Num. 24:7–9, 17–19). According to the Lord's promise, this Messiah will come through the line of David and establish David's throne forever (2 Sam. 7:12–16). The events of David's life recorded in Samuel foreshadow the actions of David's greater Son (i.e., Christ) in the future.

A second theme is the sovereignty of God, clearly seen in these books. One example is the birth of Samuel in response to Hannah's prayer (1 Sam. 9:17; 16:12,13). Also, in relation to David, it is particularly evident that nothing can obstruct God's plan to have him rule over Israel (1 Sam. 24:20).

CHRIST IN . . . 1 SAMUEL

HANNAH'S PRAYER (2:10) anticipates a future king anointed by God. This anointed one, also called the Messiah, would fulfill God's promise to establish David's throne forever.

Third, the work of the Holy Spirit in empowering men for divinely appointed tasks is evident. The Spirit of the Lord came upon both Saul and David after their anointing as king (1 Sam. 10:10; 16:13). The power of the Holy Spirit brought forth prophecy (1 Sam. 10:6) and victory in battle (1 Sam. 11:6).

Fourth, the books of Samuel demonstrate the personal and national effects of sin. The sins of Eli and his sons resulted in their deaths (1 Sam. 2:12–17,22–25; 3:10–14; 4:17,18). The lack of reverence for the ark of the covenant led to the death of a number of Israelites (1 Sam. 6:19; 2 Sam. 6:6,7). Saul's disobedience resulted in the Lord's judgment, and he was rejected as king over Israel (1 Sam. 13:9,13,14; 15:8,9,20–23). Although David was forgiven for his sin of adultery and murder after his confession (2 Sam. 12:13), he still suffered the inevitable and devastating consequences of his sin (2 Sam. 12:14).

KEY DOCTRINES IN 1 SAMUEL

Davidic covenant—God's promise to David to extend his throne and kingdom forever (2:10; Gen. 49:8–12; Num. 24:7–9,17–19; 2 Kin. 8:19; 2 Chr. 13:5; 21:7; Ps. 89:20–37; Is. 16:5; Acts 15:16–18; Rev. 22:16)

Work of the Holy Spirit—empowers men for divinely appointed tasks (10:6,10; 16:13; Num. 11:25,29; Jud. 14:6; 27:18; Matt. 4:1; 28:19,20; Mark 13:11; Luke 1:35; John 14:16,17; Acts 1:8; 2:4; Rom. 8:5,6; Gal. 5:16–18; James 4:5,6)

Sin—Israel's sin created personal and national consequences (3:10–14; 4:17,18; 6:19; 13:9,13,14; 15:8,9, 20– 23; Gen. 3; Num. 4:15; 15:30, 31; 1 Kin. 11:38; 13:34; 2 Kin. 21:12; Ps. 106:43; Is. 22:14; Jer. 19:3; Ezek. 7:3; 18:30; John 8:34; Rom. 2:5; Heb. 10:4, 26–31)

KEY DOCTRINES IN 2 SAMUEL

Davidic covenant— God's promise to David to extend his throne and kingdom forever (7:12–16; 22:51; see other references for Davidic covenant in 1 Samuel)

Sin—Israel's sin created personal and national consequences (6:6,7; 12:13,14; see other references for Sin in 1 Samuel)

Messiah—foretold to David by Nathan to be the anointed king who will triumph over all nations opposed to God (7:12–16; 22:51; Matt. 1:16,17; 12:22; Mark 1:1; John 7:42; Acts 2:30–33)

GOD'S CHARACTER IN 1 SAMUEL
God is holy—2:2
God is powerful—14:6
God is provident—2:7,8; 6:7–10,12; 30:6
God is righteous—12:7
God is sovereign—9:17; 16:12,13; 24:20
God is wise—2:3
God is wrathful—5:6; 6:19; 7:10; 31:6

GOD'S CHARACTER IN 2 SAMUEL
God is kind—2:6
God is a promise keeper—7:12,13
God is provident—17:14,15
God is true—2:6
God is unequaled—7:22
God is unified—7:22
God is wise—7:20
God is wrathful—6:7; 21:1; 24:1,15,17

CHRIST IN . . . 2 SAMUEL

THE DAVIDIC COVENANT outlined in 2 Samuel 7:12–16 reveals God's promise to extend the kingdom of David for eternity. Christ fulfills this covenant as the Messiah directly descending from the royal line of David. The life of David recorded in 2 Samuel foreshadows Christ's future kingdom.

INTERPRETIVE CHALLENGES

The books of Samuel contain a number of interpretive issues that have been widely discussed: (1) Which of the ancient manuscripts are closest to the original? The standard Hebrew (Masoretic) text has been relatively poorly preserved, and the Septuagint (LXX) often differs from it. Thus, the exact reading of the original copy of the text is in places hard to determine (see 1 Sam. 13:1). The NKJV uses the Masoretic text with significant variant readings in the marginal notes. The Masoretic text will be assumed to represent the original text unless the grammar or context suggests otherwise. This accounts for many of the numerical differences. (2) Is Samuel hesitant about establishing a human kingship in Israel? It is claimed that while 1 Samuel 9–11 presents a positive view of the kingship, 1 Samuel 8 and 12 are strongly opposed to kingship in Israel. It is best, however, to see the book as a balanced perspective of human kingship. While the desire of Israel for a king was acceptable (Deut. 17:15), their reason for wanting a king showed a lack of faith in the Lord. (3) How does one explain the bizarre behavior of the prophets? It is commonly held that 1 and 2 Samuel present the prophets as mystical speakers with bizarre behavior just like the pagan prophets of the other nations. But there is nothing in the text that is inconsistent with seeing the prophets as communicators of divine revelation, at times prophesying with musical accompaniment. (4) How did the Holy Spirit minister before Pentecost? The ministry of the Holy Spirit in 1 Samuel 10:6,10; 11:16; 16:13,14; 19:20, 23; 2 Samuel 23:2 was not describing salvation in the NT sense, but an empowering by the Lord for His service (see also Judg. 3:10; 6:34; 11:29; 13:25; 14:6,19; 15:14). (5) What was the identity of the "distressing spirit from the Lord"? Is it a personal being, i.e., a demon, or a spirit of discontent created by God in the heart (cf. Judg. 9:23)? Traditionally, it has been viewed as a demon. (6) How did Samuel appear in 1 Samuel 28:3–5? It seems best to understand the appearance of Samuel as the Lord allowing the dead Samuel to speak with Saul. (7) What is the identity of David's seed in 2 Samuel 7:12–15? It is usually taken as Solomon. However, the NT refers the words to Jesus, God's Son in Hebrews 1:5.

OUTLINE–1 SAMUEL
I. Samuel: Prophet and Judge to Israel (1:1–7:17)
A. Samuel the Prophet (1:1–4:1a)
1. The birth of Samuel (1:1–28)
2. The prayer of Hannah (2:1–10)
3. The growth of Samuel (2:11–26)
4. The prophesy against Eli's house (2:27–36)
5. The Word of the Lord through Samuel (3:1–4:1a)
B. Samuel the Judge (4:1b–7:17)
1. The saga of the ark (4:1b–7:1)
2. Israel's victory over the Philistines and the judgeship of Samuel (7:2–17)
II. Saul: First King Over Israel (8:1–15:35)
A. The Rise of Saul to the Kingship (8:1–12:25)
1. The demand of Israel for a king (8:1–22)
2. The process of Saul becoming king (9:1–11:13)
3. The warning of Samuel to Israel concerning the king (11:14–12:25)
B. The Decline of Saul in the Kingship (13:1–15:35)
1. The rebuke of Saul (13:1–15)
2. The wars of Saul (13:16–14:52)
3. The rejection of Saul (15:1–35)
III. David and Saul: Transfer of the Kingship in Israel (16:1–31:13)
A. The Introduction of David (16:1–17:58)
1. The anointing of David (16:1–13)
2. David in the court of Saul (16:14–23)
3. David, the warrior of the Lord (17:1–58)
B. David Driven from the Court of Saul (18:1–20:42)
1. The anger and fear of Saul toward David (18:1–30)
2. The defense of David by Jonathan and Michal (19:1–20:42)
C. David's Flight from Saul's Pursuit (21:1–28:2)
1. Saul's killing of the priests at Nob (21:1–22:23)
2. Saul's life spared twice by David (23:1–26:25)
3. David's despair and Philistine refuge (27:1–28:2)
D. The Death of Saul (28:3–31:13)
1. Saul's final night (28:3–25)
2. David's dismissal by the Philistines (29:1–11)
3. David's destruction of the Amalekites (30:1–31)
4. Saul's final day (31:1–13)

OUTLINE–2 SAMUEL
I. The Reign of David as King over Israel (1:1–20:26)
A. David's Appointment to Kingship over Judah (1:1–3:5)
1. The deaths of Saul and Jonathan (1:1–27)
2. David anointed by Judah (2:1–7)
3. David's victories over the house of Saul (2:8–3:1)
4. David's wives/sons in Hebron (3:2–5)

B. David's Appointment to Kingship over Israel (3:6–5:16)
1. The deaths of Abner and Ishbosheth (3:6–4:12)
2. David anointed by all Israel (5:1–5)
3. David's conquest of Jerusalem (5:6–12)
4. David's wives/sons in Jerusalem (5:13–16)

C. David's Triumphal Reign (5:17–8:18)
1. David's victories over the Philistines (5:17–25)
2. David's spiritual victories (6:1–7:29)
3. David's victories over the Philistines, Moabites, Arameans, and Edomites (8:1–18)

D. David's Troubled Reign (9:1–20:26)
1. David's kindness to Mephibosheth (9:1–13)
2. David's sins of adultery and murder (10:1–12:31)
3. David's family troubles (13:1–14:33)
    a. The rape of Tamar (13:1–22)
    b. The murder of Amnon (13:23–39)
    c. The recall and return of Absalom (14:1–33)
4. The rebellions against David (15:1–20:26)
    a. The rebellion of Absalom (15:1–19:43)
    b. The rebellion of Sheba (20:1–26)

II. Epilogue (21:1–24:25)
A. The Lord's Judgment against Israel (21:1–14)
B. David's Heroes (21:15–22)
C. David's Song of Praise (22:1–51)
D. David's Last Words (23:1–7)
E. David's Mighty Men (23:8–39)
F. The Lord's Judgment against David (24:1–25)

MEANWHILE, IN OTHER PARTS OF THE WORLD...

In areas known today as Nevada and California within the United States, the Pinto people group thrives, leaving behind evidence of huts built with reeds, wood, and loam.

The use of wigs becomes popular in Egyptian and Assyrian aristocracy.

Plot Development of 2 Samuel

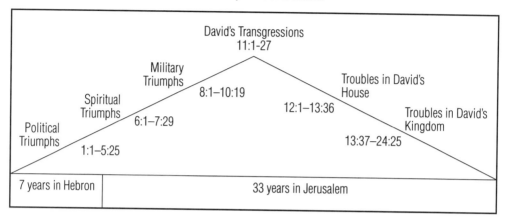

ANSWERS TO TOUGH QUESTIONS

1. If we accept the scholarly view that the surviving ancient manuscripts of 1 and 2 Samuel were relatively poorly preserved, what should be our attitude toward these books as part of God's Word?

Given the challenges involved in hand copying and preserving scrolls, it is a wonder that we have the ancient documents that we do have. Our attitude ought to lean more towards amazement that we have such few discrepancies rather than concern over the difficulties that may puzzle and challenge us.

Many of the discoveries in the science of analyzing ancient manuscripts involve the typical errors that commonly appear when handwritten documents are copied. For example, when two lines of text end with the same word or words, the eye of the copyist tends to skip the second line, deleting it completely. Careful comparisons between manuscripts and reconstruction of the text often reveal these simple errors.

In the case of 1 and 2 Samuel we have two ancient text families: (1) the Masoretic text, in the Hebrew language, and (2) the LXX (Septuagint) text in Greek, which was translated by Jewish scholars in about 100 B.C. Comparing the two, it is true that they differ more often here than they do in other OT books. There are frequent disagreements between the texts when it comes to numbers. In settling these discrepancies, because of the age and language of the Masoretic text it is generally considered a closer version of the original manuscript unless grammar and context indicate a copying error.

A central fact to remember when thinking about the possibility of textual errors in the Scriptures we have is the following: The central doctrines of the Christian faith are never based on a single verse of Scripture, nor do they rely on a disputed section of Scripture. God's plan of salvation and the main outline of Christian teaching can be found throughout Scripture.

2. How do 1 and 2 Samuel help us understand the role of the Holy Spirit in the time of the OT?

First and 2 Samuel illustrate part of the Holy Spirit's role in the OT. The Spirit's specific actions are noted in the following passages: 1 Samuel 10:6,10; 11:6; 16:13,14; 19:20,23; 2 Samuel 23:2. These references offer several conclusions regarding the Holy Spirit's ministry: (1) it was an occasional "coming upon" a chosen person for a particular task or statement; (2) the Spirit's ministry was not controlled by the person(s); (3) the expectation of the Spirit's help could be given and withdrawn; (4) the Holy Spirit inspired certain people to speak or write God's message.

Jesus promised the indwelling presence of the Holy Spirit, not surprise visits. Certainly at times believers might experience a particular empowering by the Holy Spirit for a task, but the picture of the Holy Spirit's ministry changes from the OT of an external visitation by God to the NT picture of a resident presence by God in the life of a believer.

3. Was the rule of kings part of God's plan all along, or did the people's demand for a king bring about a monarchy as a form of divine discipline?

When Israel entered the Promised Land, they encountered Canaanite city-states that were ruled by kings (Josh.12:7–14). Later, during the time of the judges, Israel was enslaved and oppressed by nations led by kings (Judg. 3:8,12; 4:2; 8:5; 11:12). The Book of Judges repeatedly mentions the lack of a king (Judg. 17:6; 18:1; 19:1; 21:25). The idea of having a king like the surrounding nations became a powerful temptation. According to Deuteronomy 17:14, however, God knew this would be their desire and He predicted that He would grant permission. First Samuel 8:4–20 reveals that their motive was actually a rejection of God.

In spite of Samuel's dire warnings about the drawbacks of monarchy, the people offered what they thought were three compelling reasons why they needed a king (1 Sam. 8:20): (1) to be like the other nations; (2) to have a national judge; (3) to have a war champion. Each of these contradicted God's specific purposes: (1) Israel was to be a holy nation, not like any other; (2) God was their ultimate judge; (3) God had fought their battles for them, whereas a king would send them to battle. Israel's problem was not about having a king but rather, it was about replacing God with a human ruler. They exchanged an awesome and powerful Ruler they could not see for one they could see who was utterly capable of failure.

FURTHER STUDY ON 1 SAMUEL

1. In what ways did Samuel's birth and childhood affect his life as a judge and prophet?
2. What remarkable character traits are illustrated in the life of Hannah, Samuel's mother?
3. How did Samuel relate to the first two kings of Israel, and what did that relationship indicate about God's view of kings?
4. To what degree is obedience a central theme of 1 Samuel?
5. How does God's specific call in Samuel's life influence your understanding of God's purposes for your life?

FURTHER STUDY ON 2 SAMUEL

1. What significant character traits of David are illustrated in 2 Samuel?
2. In what ways was he a "man after God's own heart"?
3. What kind of a leader, or king, was David?
4. How does the sequence of events involving David and Bathsheba demonstrate the appeal of sin and its consequences?
5. What prevented the rejection of David by God after his multiple sins?
6. How does David's experience affect your understanding of God's view of you and your sin?

FIRST AND SECOND KINGS
Royal Disappointments and Disasters

TITLE

First and Second Kings were originally one book, called in the Hebrew text, "Kings," from the first word in 1:1. The Greek translation of the OT, the Septuagint (LXX), divided the book in two, and this was followed by the Latin Vulgate (Vg.) version and English translations. The division was for the convenience of copying this lengthy book on scrolls and codexes and was not based on features of content. Modern Hebrew Bibles title the books "Kings A" and "Kings B." The LXX and Vg. connected Kings with the books of Samuel, so that the titles in the LXX are "The Third and Fourth Books of Kingdoms" and in the Vg. "Third and Fourth Kings." The books of 1 and 2 Samuel and 1 and 2 Kings combined are a chronicle of the entire history of Judah's and Israel's kingship from Saul to Zedekiah. First and Second Chronicles provides only the history of Judah's monarchy.

AUTHOR AND DATE

Jewish tradition proposed that Jeremiah wrote Kings, though this is unlikely because the final event recorded in the book (see 2 King 25:27–30) occurred in Babylon in 561 B.C. Jeremiah never went to Babylon, but to Egypt (Jer. 43:1–7), and would have been at least 86 years old by 561 B.C. Actually, the identity of the unnamed author remains unknown. Since the ministry of prophets is emphasized in Kings, it seems that the author was most likely an unnamed prophet of the Lord who lived in exile with Israel in Babylon.

Kings was written between 561–538 B.C. Since the last narrated event (2 Kin. 25:27–30) sets the earliest possible date of completion and because there is no record of the end of the Babylonian captivity in Kings, the release from exile (538 B.C.) identifies the latest possible writing date. This date is sometimes challenged on the basis of "to this day" statements in 1 Kings 8:8; 9:13, 20, 21; 10:12; 12:19; 2 Kings 2:22; 8:22; 10:27; 14:7; 16:6; 17:23, 34, 41;

CHRIST IN . . . 1 KINGS

THE WISDOM OF SOLOMON symbolizes Christ who "became wisdom from God" (1 Cor. 1:30). Yet, in the Book of 1 Kings, Solomon led his kingdom into apostasy by marrying many foreign women (11:1). In contrast, Christ Himself proclaimed that He was "greater than Solomon" (Matt. 12:42). The future kingdom of Christ will not pass away.

21:15. However, it is best to understand these statements as those of the sources used by the author, rather than statements of the author himself.

It is clear that the author used a variety of sources in compiling this book, including "the Book of the acts of Solomon" (1 Kin. 11:41), "the chronicles of the kings of Israel" (1 Kin. 14:19; 15:31; 16:5,14,20,27; 22:39; 2 Kin. 1:18; 10:34; 13:8,12; 14:15,28; 15:11, 15,21,26,31), and "the chronicles of the kings of Judah" (1 Kin. 14:29; 15:7,23; 22:45; 2 Kin. 8:23; 12:19; 14:18; 15:6,36; 16:19; 20:20; 21:17,25; 23:28; 24:5). Further, Isaiah 36:1–39:8 provided information used in 2 Kings 18:9–20:19, and Jeremiah 52:31–34 seems to be the source for 2 Kings 25:27–29. This explanation speculates a single author who was inspired by the Holy Spirit and lived in Babylon during the Exile, using the pre-Exilic source materials at his disposal.

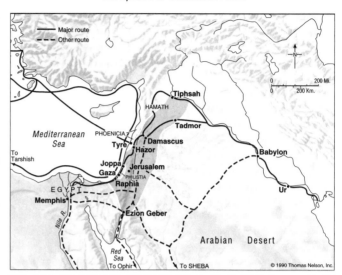

The Spread of Solomon's Fame

BACKGROUND AND SETTING

A distinction must be made between the setting of the books' sources and that of the books' author. The source material was written by both participants in and eyewitnesses of the events. It was reliable information, which was historically accurate concerning the sons of Israel, from the death of David and the accession of Solomon (971 B.C.) to the

Solomon's influence in economic and political affairs was enhanced by the transportation and trade routes that intersected his kingdom.

destruction of the temple and Jerusalem by the Babylonians (586 B.C.). Thus, Kings traces the histories of two sets of kings and two nations of disobedient people, Israel and Judah, both of whom were growing unresponsive to God's law and His prophets and were headed for captivity.

The Book of Kings is not only accurate history but also interpreted history. The author, an exile in Babylon, wished to communicate to his fellow captives both the events of Israel's history as well as the lessons learned through them. Specifically, he taught the exiled people why the Lord's judgment of exile had come. The writer established early in his narrative that the Lord required obedience by the kings to the Mosaic law, if their kingdom was to receive His blessing; disobedience would bring exile (1 Kin. 9:3–9). The sad reality that history revealed was that all the kings of Israel and the majority of the kings of Judah "did evil in the sight of the LORD." These evil kings led their people to sin by refusing to confront idolatry, and even approving of it. Because of the kings' failure, the Lord sent His prophets to confront both the monarchs and the people with their sin and their need to return to Him. Because the message of the prophets was rejected, the prophets foretold that the nation(s) would be carried into exile (2 Kin. 17:13–23; 21:10–15). Like every prophecy uttered by the prophets in Kings, this word from the Lord came to pass (2 Kin. 17:5, 6; 25:1–11). Therefore, Kings interpreted the people's experience of exile and helped them to see why they had suffered God's punishment for idolatry. It also explained that just as God had shown mercy to Ahab (1 Kin. 22:27–29) and Jehoiachin (2 Kin. 25:27–30), so He was willing to show them mercy.

The chief geographical setting of Kings is the whole land of Israel, from Dan to Beersheba (1 Kin. 4:25), including the area east of the Jordan River. Four invading nations

The Divided Kingdom

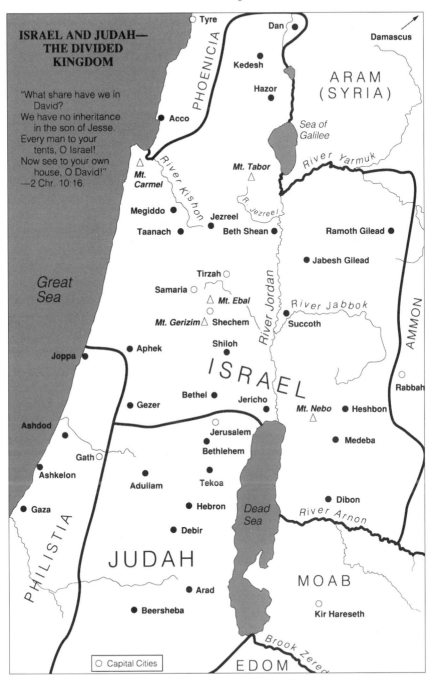

ISRAEL AND JUDAH—THE DIVIDED KINGDOM

"What share have we in David?
We have no inheritance in the son of Jesse.
Every man to your tents, O Israel!
Now see to your own house, O David!"
—2 Chr. 10:16.

Tyre
Dan
Damascus
Kedesh
PHOENICIA
Hazor
ARAM (SYRIA)
Acco
Sea of Galilee
River Kishon
Mt. Carmel
Mt. Tabor
River Yarmuk
R. Jezreel
Megiddo
Jezreel
Taanach
Beth Shean
Ramoth Gilead
Jabesh Gilead
Great Sea
Tirzah
Samaria
Mt. Ebal
River Jordan
River Jabbok
Mt. Gerizim
Shechem
Succoth
AMMON
Shiloh
ISRAEL
Aphek
Joppa
Bethel
Jericho
Rabbah
Gezer
Mt. Nebo
Heshbon
Ashdod
Jerusalem
Medeba
Gath
Bethlehem
Ashkelon
Adullam
Tekoa
Gaza
Hebron
Dead Sea
Dibon
River Arnon
PHILISTIA
Debir
JUDAH
MOAB
Arad
Kir Hareseth
Beersheba
Brook Zered
EDOM

○ Capital Cities

The glory of the united kingdom began to fade with the death of Solomon when his unwise son Rehoboam spoke harshly to the representatives of Israel who requested relief from the heavy taxation of Solomon's time (12:1–24). Rehoboam reigned over Judah to the south and Jeroboam became king of Israel to the north.

The Babylonian Empire

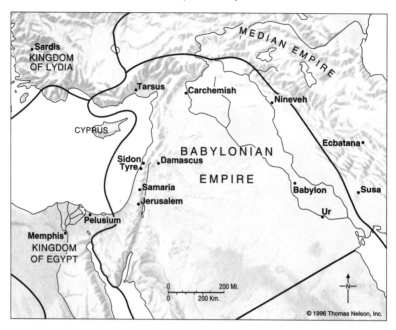

© 1996 Thomas Nelson, Inc.

played a dominant role in the affairs of Israel and Judah from 971 to 561 B.C. In the tenth century B.C., Egypt impacted Israel's history during the reigns of Solomon and Rehoboam (1 Kin. 3:1; 1:14–22, 40; 12:2; 14:25–27). Syria (Aram) posed a great threat to Israel's security during the ninth century B.C., ca. 890–800 B.C. (1 Kin. 15:9–22; 20:1–34; 22:1–4, 29–40; 2 Kin. 6:8–7:20; 8:7–15; 10:32, 33; 12:17,18; 13:22–25). The years from ca. 800–750 B.C. were a half-century of peace and prosperity for Israel and Judah, because Assyria neutralized Syria and did not threaten to the south. This changed during the king-ship of Tiglath-Pileser III (2 Kin. 15:19, 20, 29). From the mid-eighth century to the late seventh century B.C., Assyria terrorized Palestine, finally conquering and destroying Israel (the northern kingdom) in 722 B.C. (2 Kin. 17:4–6) and besieging Jerusalem in 701 B.C. (2 Kin. 18:17–19:37). From 612 to 539 B.C., Babylon was the dominant power in the ancient world. Babylon invaded Judah (the southern kingdom) three times, with the destruction of Jerusalem and the temple occurring in 586 B.C. during that third assault (2 Kin. 24:1–25:21).

KEY PEOPLE IN 1 KINGS

David—king of Israel; appointed his son Solomon to be the next king to rule (1–2:10)

Solomon—son of Bathsheba and David; third king to rule Israel and builder of the tem-ple; God made him the wisest man ever born (1:10–11:43)

Rehoboam—son of Solomon; succeeded him as king of Israel; his evil actions led to the division of Israel into two kingdoms; later became king of the southern kingdom of Judah (11:43–12:24; 14:21–31)

Jeroboam—evil king of the northern ten tribes of Israel; erected idols and appointed non-Levitical priests (11:24–14:20)

The Kings of Israel and Judah

King	Scripture
United Kingdom	
Saul	1 Samuel 9:1–31:13; 1 Chronicles 10:1–14
David	2 Samuel; 1Kings 1:1–2:9; 1 Chronicles 11:1–29:30
Solomon	1 Kings 2:10–11:43; 2 Chronicles 1:1–9:31
Northern Kingdom (Israel)	
Jeroboam I	1 Kings 12:25–14:20
Nadab	1 Kings 15:25–31
Baasha	1 Kings 15:32–16:7
Elah	1 Kings 16:8–14
Zimri	1 Kings 16:15–20
Tibni	1 Kings 16:21,22
Omri	1 Kings 16:21–28
Ahab	1 Kings 16:29–22:40
Ahaziah	1 Kings 22:51–53; 2 Kings 1:1–18
Jehoram (Joram)	2 Kings 2:1–8:15
Jehu	2 Kings 9:1–10:36
Jehoahaz	2 Kings 13:1–9
Jehoash (Joash)	2 Kings 13:10–25
Jeroboam II	2 Kings 14:23–29
Zechariah	2 Kings 15:8–12
Shallum	2 Kings 15:13–15
Menahem	2 Kings 15:16–22
Pekahiah	2 Kings 15:23–26
Pekah	2 Kings 15:27–31
Hoshea	2 Kings 17:1–41
Southern Kingdom (Judah)	
Rehoboam	1 Kings 12:1–14:31; 2 Chronicles 10:1–12:16
Abijam (Abijah)	1 Kings 15:1–8; 2 Chronicles 13:1–22
Asa	1 Kings 15:9–24; 2 Chronicles 14:1–16:14
Jehoshaphat	1 Kings 22:41–50; 2 Chronicles 17:1–20:37
Joram (Jehoram)	2 Kings 8:16–24; 2 Chronicles 21:1–20
Ahaziah	2 Kings 8:25–29; 2 Chronicles 22:1–9
Athaliah (queen)	2 Kings 11:1–16; 2 Chronicles 22:10–23:21
Joash (Jehoash)	2 Kings 11:17–12:21; 2 Chronicles 23:1–24:27
Amaziah	2K ings 14:1–22; 2 Chronicles 25:1–28
Uzziah (Azariah)	2 Kings 15:1–7; 2 Chronicles 26:1–23
Jotham	2 Kings 15:32–38; 2 Chronicles 27:1–9
Ahaz	2 Kings 16:1–20; 2 Chronicles 28:1–27
Hezekiah	2 Kings 18:1–20:21; 2 Chronicles 29:1–32:33
Manasseh	2 Kings 21:1–18; 2 Chronicles 33:1–20
Amon	2 Kings 21:19–26; 2 Chronicles 33:21–25
Josiah	2 Kings 22:1–23:30; 2 Chronicles 34:1–35:27
Jehoahaz	2 Kings 23:31–33; 2 Chronicles 36:1–4
Jehoiakim	2 Kings 23:34–24:7; 2 Chronicles 36:5–8
Jehoiachin	2 Kings 24:8–16; 2 Chronicles 36:9,10
Zedekiah	2 Kings 24:18–25:21; 2 Chronicles 36:11–21

Elijah—prophet of Israel; accomplished extraordinary acts of faith against the prophets of Baal (17:1–19:21; 21:17–28)

Ahab—eighth and most evil king of Israel; committed more evil than any other Israelite king (16:28–17:1; 18:1–19:1; 20:1– 22:40)

Jezebel—married Ahab and became queen of Israel; promoted Baal worship (16:31; 18:4–19; 19:1–2; 21:5–27)

Solomon's Temple

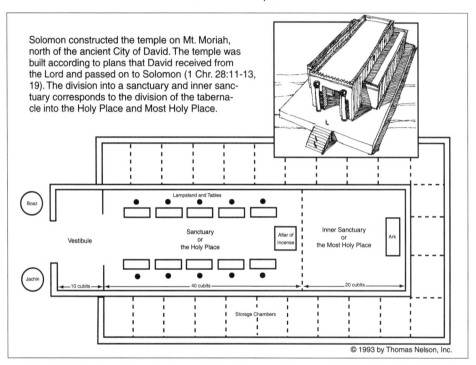

Solomon constructed the temple on Mt. Moriah, north of the ancient City of David. The temple was built according to plans that David received from the Lord and passed on to Solomon (1 Chr. 28:11-13, 19). The division into a sanctuary and inner sanctuary corresponds to the division of the tabernacle into the Holy Place and Most Holy Place.

Boaz

Jachin

Lampstand and Tables

Vestibule

Sanctuary or the Holy Place

Altar of Incense

Inner Sanctuary or the Most Holy Place

Ark

10 cubits — 40 cubits — 20 cubits

Storage Chambers

© 1993 by Thomas Nelson, Inc.

KEY PEOPLE IN 2 KINGS

Elijah—prophet of Israel; escaped death by being carried directly to heaven in a chariot of fire (1:3–2:11; 10:10,17)

Elisha—prophet appointed to be Elijah's successor (2:1–9:3; 13:14–21)

The woman from Shunem—woman who hosted Elisha in her home; Elisha brought her son back to life (4:8–37; 8:1–6)

Naaman—mighty Syrian warrior who suffered from leprosy; healed by Elisha (5:1–27)

Jezebel—evil queen of Israel; attempted to prevent Israel from worshiping God; eventually killed and eaten by dogs (9:7–37)

Jehu—anointed king of Israel; used by God to punish Ahab's family (9:1–10:36; 15:12)

Joash—king of Judah who was saved from death as a child; followed evil advice and was ultimately assassinated by his own officials (11:1–12:21)

Hezekiah—thirteenth king of Judah who remained faithful to God (16:20–20:21)

KEY WORDS IN

1 Kings

Baal: Hebrew *baʿal*—16:31; 18:19,21,26,40; 19:18; 22:53—literally means "master," or "husband." Baal refers to pagan gods of fertility and storms throughout the ancient Middle East. Canaanite literature links Baal with the fertility goddess Asherah, who is mentioned numerous times in the OT (2 Kin. 21:7). Worship of these pagan deities included self-mutilation, ritual prostitution, and infant sacrifice. God punished the Israelites for adopting the worship of Baal and Asherah (Judg. 2:11–15; Jer.19:4–6).

Supplication: Hebrew *techinnah*—8:28,33,45,47,52, 54,59; 9:3—refers to the petitioning of God or a specific person for favor or mercy (Jer. 37:20; 38:26). Solomon uses this word repeatedly in his dedication prayer over the temple (8:23–9:3; 2 Chr. 6:14–42). Supplication is often used in relation to impending distress in the midst of one's enemies (Ps. 55:1–3; 119:70; Jer. 36:7). The Bible describes the supplications of David (Ps. 6:9), Solomon (9:3), and of wicked King Manasseh, who humbled himself before God (2 Chr. 33:12,13).

Name: Hebrew *shem*—1:47; 3:2; 5:5; 7:21; 8:17; 9:3; 11:36; 18:24—most likely means "to mark." In biblical history, a person's name often described personal characteristics such as destiny or position (see 1 Sam. 25:25 for the explanation of Nabal's name, which meant "fool"). Sometimes, God renamed people to reflect a change in their character or status (see Gen. 35:10). The various names of God reveal important aspects of His nature (for example, God Most High, Almighty God, I AM). The name of God should be used with honor and respect (Ex. 20:7). God shared His name with Israel to express His intimate covenantal relationship with them (Ex. 3:13–15).

Gold: Hebrew *zahab*—6:21,28; 7:49; 9:28; 10:14; 12:28; 15:15; 20:3—describes both the substance and the color of gold (1 Kin. 10:16; Zech. 4:12). Gold, usually mentioned with silver, symbolized wealth (Gen. 13:2; 2 Chr. 1:15; Ezek. 16:13). Most references to gold in the OT relate to Solomon's temple and palace (Ex. 25:3; 2 Chr. 2:7; 9:13–27). However precious gold appears, nothing compares to the value of wisdom (Job 28:17), loving favor (Prov. 22:1), and the commandments of the Lord (Ps. 19:9,10; 119:72,127).

Sennacherib—king of Assyria who threatened Judah; his army was destroyed by the Lord (18:13–19:36)

Isaiah—prophet who ministered through the reigns of five kings of Judah (19:2–20:19)

Manasseh—son of Hezekiah; became the fourteenth king of Judah; practiced evil and brought judgment upon Jerusalem (20:21–21:18)

Josiah—sixteenth king of Judah; great-grandson of Hezekiah; remained faithful to God (21:24—23:30)

Jehoiakim—eighteenth king of Judah; practiced evil in the eyes of the Lord (23:34–24:6)

Zedekiah—twentieth king of Judah; captured by the Babylonians as God's punishment for practicing evil (24:17–25:7)

Nebuchadnezzar—king of Babylon allowed by God to conquer Jerusalem (24:1–25:22)

HISTORICAL AND THEOLOGICAL THEMES

Kings concentrates, then, on the history of the sons of Israel from 971 to 561 B.C. First Kings 1:1–11:43 deals with Solomon's accession (or rise to power) and reign (971–931 B.C.). The two divided kingdoms of Israel and Judah (931–722 B.C.) are covered in 1 Kings

KEY WORDS IN

2 Kings

Silver: Hebrew *keseph*—5:5,23; 6:25; 7:8; 12:13; 14:14; 20:13; 23:35—literally referred to as "the pale metal," was the basic unit of money in the OT (1 Kin. 21:6; Isa,55:1). However, there is no reference to silver coins in the OT because silver was valued by weight in ancient times (Is. 46:6; Jer. 32:9–10). Silver, along with gold, was one of the valuable materials used to construct the tabernacle and the temple (Ex. 25:1–9; 2 Chr. 2:7). In Ecclesiastes, Solomon voices a warning about silver: "He who loves silver will not be satisfied" (Eccles. 5:10).

Anger: Hebrew ʻaph—13:3; 17:11; 21:6,15; 22:17; 23:26; 24:20—signifies either "nose," "nostril," or "anger" (Gen. 2:7; Prov. 15:1). This term often occurs with words describing burning. Throughout the OT, figures of speech such as "a burning nose" typically depict anger as the fierce breathing of a person through his nose (Ex. 32:10–12). Most of the OT references using this word describe God's anger (Ps. 103:8; Deut. 4:24,25). The righteous anger of God is reserved for those who break His covenant (Deut.13:17; 29:25–27; Josh.23:16; Judg. 2:20; Ps. 78:38).

High Places: Hebrew *bamah*—12:3; 14:4; 15:4; 17:9; 23:8,15,20—often refers to a sacred area located on high ground such as a hill or ridge. Before the temple was built, the Israelites worshiped the true God at high places (1 Kin. 3:2–4). However, the Israelites began worshiping pagan gods at these sacred sites. Consequently, the term *high places* in the OT became associated with Israel's religious rebellion and apostasy (1 Kin. 14:23; Ps.78:58; Jer. 19:5).

12:1; 2 Kings 17:41. The author arranged the material in a distinctive way in that the narration follows the kings in both the north and the south. For each reign described, there is the following literary framework. Every king is introduced with: (1) his name and relation to his predecessor; (2) his date of accession in relationship to the year of the contemporary ruler in the other kingdom; (3) his age on coming to the throne (for kings of Judah only); (4) his length of reign; (5) his place of reign; (6) his mother's name (for Judah only); and (7) spiritual evaluation of his reign. This introduction is followed by a narration of the events that occurred during the reign of each king. The details of this narration vary widely. Each reign is concluded with: (1) a citation of sources; (2) additional historical notes; (3) notice of death; (4) notice of burial; (5) the name of the successor; and (6) in a few instances, an added postscript (i.e., 1 Kin. 15:32; 2 Kin. 10:36). Second Kings 18:1–25:21 deals with the time when Judah survived alone (722–586 B.C.). Two concluding paragraphs speak of events after the Babylonian exile (2 Kin. 25:22–26, 27–30).

Three theological themes are stressed in Kings. First, the Lord judged Israel and Judah because of their disobedience to His law (2 Kin. 17:7–23). This unfaithfulness on the part of the people was furthered by the spiritual rebellion of the evil kings who led them into idolatry (2 Kin. 17:21,22; 21:11), so the Lord exercised His righteous wrath against His rebellious people. Second, the word of the true prophets came to pass (1 Kin. 13:2,3; 22:15–28; 2 Kin. 23:16; 24:2). This confirmed that the Lord did keep His Word, even His warnings of judgment. Third, the Lord remembered His promise to David (1 Kin. 11:12,13, 34–36; 15:4; 2 Kin. 8:19). Even though the kings of the Davidic line proved themselves to be disobedient to the Lord, He did not bring David's family to an end as He did the families of Jeroboam I, Omri, and Jehu in Israel. Even as the book closes, the line of David still exists (2 Kin. 25:27–30), so there is hope for the coming "seed" of David (see 2 Sam. 7:12–16). The Lord is thus seen as faithful, and His Word is trustworthy.

KEY DOCTRINES IN 1 KINGS

God's judgment of the apostate nations (9:3–9; Deut. 4:26; 28:37; 2 Sam. 14–16; 2 Chr. 7:19,20; Ps. 44:14; 89:30; Jer. 24:9; Hos. 5:11,12; Matt. 23:33–36; John 3:18,19; 12:48; Rom. 2:5,6; 2 Pet. 3:10; Rev. 18:10)

Fulfilled prophecies of God (13:2–5; 22:15–28; Num. 27:17; 2 Kin. 23:15–20; 2 Chr. 18:16; Matt. 9:36; Mark 6:34; John 2:18)

God's faithfulness to His covenant with David (11:12– 13,34–36; 15:4; 2 Sam. 7:12–16; Luke 1:30–33; Acts 2:22–36)

KEY DOCTRINES IN 2 KINGS

God's judgment of the apostate nations (17:7–23; 21:10–15; Judg.6:10; 1 Sam. 3:11; Jer. 6:9; 19:3; Lam. 2:8; Amos 7:7,8; Matt. 23:33–36; John 3:18,19; 12:48; Rom. 2:5–6; 2 Pet. 3:10; Rev. 18:10)

Fulfilled prophecies of God (23:16; 24:2; 1 Kin. 13:2; Jer. 25:9; 32:28; 35:11; Ezek. 19:8)

God's faithfulness to His covenant with David (8:19; 25:27– 30; 2 Sam. 7:12–16; Luke 1:30–33; Acts 2:22–36)

GOD'S CHARACTER IN 1 KINGS

God fills heaven and earth—8:27
God is glorious—8:11
God is merciful—8:23
God is a promise keeper—8:56
God is provident—21:19; 22:30,34, 37,38

GOD'S CHARACTER IN 2 KINGS

God is compassionate—13:23
God is One—19:15
God is wrathful—19:28,35,37; 22:17

INTERPRETIVE CHALLENGES

The major interpretive challenge in Kings concerns the chronology of the kings of Israel and Judah. Though a great deal of chronological data is presented in the Book of Kings, this data is difficult to interpret for two reasons. First, there seems to be internal inconsistency in the information given. For instance, 1 Kings 16:23 states that Omri, king of Israel, began to reign in the thirty-first year of Asa, king of Judah, and that he reigned twelve years. But according to 1 Kings 16:29, Omri was succeeded by his son Ahab in the thirty-eighth year of Asa, giving Omri a reign of only seven years, not twelve. Second, from extra-biblical sources (Greek, Assyrian, and Babylonian), correlated with astronomical data, a reliable series of dates can be calculated from 892 to 566 B.C. Since Ahab and Jehu, kings of Israel, were believed to be mentioned in Assyrian records, 853 B.C. can be fixed as the year of Ahab's death and 841 B.C. as the year Jehu began to reign. With these fixed dates, it is possible to work backward and forward to determine that the date of the division of Israel from Judah was ca. 931 B.C., the fall of Samaria 722 B.C., and the fall of Jerusalem 586 B.C. But when the total years of royal reigns in Kings are added, the number for Israel is 241 years (not the 210 years of 931 to 722 B.C.) and Judah 393 years (not the 346 years of 931 to

CHRIST IN . . . 2 KINGS

ALTHOUGH GREAT JUDGMENT fell on Judah for the nation's disobedience, God still spared the Jewish remnant in Babylonian captivity. This remnant preserved the royal line of David through which Christ would enter the world. Judah's apostasy demanded judgment from the righteous God, yet God remained faithful to His covenant with David. As David's direct descendant, Jesus the Messiah would ultimately free His people from the captivity that held them in sin.

586 B.C.). It is recognized that in both kingdoms there were some co-regencies, i.e., a period in which two kings, usually father and son, ruled at the same time, so the overlapping years were counted twice in the total for both kings. Further, different methods of reckoning the years of a king's rule and even different calendars were used at differing times in the two kingdoms, resulting in the apparent internal inconsistencies. The general accuracy of the chronology in Kings can be demonstrated and confirmed.

A second major interpretive challenge deals with Solomon's relationship to the Abrahamic and Davidic Covenants. First Kings 4:20,21 has been interpreted by some as the fulfillment of the promises given to Abraham (cf. Gen. 15:18–21; 22:17). However, according to Numbers 34:6, the western border of the Land promised to Abraham was the Mediterranean Sea. In 1 Kings 5:1ff, Hiram is seen as the independent king of Tyre (along the Mediterranean), dealing with Solomon as an equal. Solomon's empire was not the fulfillment of the land promise given to Abraham by the Lord, although a great portion of that land was under Solomon's control. Further, the statements of Solomon in 1 Kings 5:5 and 8:20 are his claims to be the promised seed of the Davidic covenant (cf. 2 Sam. 7:12–16). The author of Kings holds out the possibility that Solomon's temple was the fulfillment of the Lord's promise to David. However, while the conditions for the fulfillment of the promise to David are reiterated to Solomon (1 Kin. 6:12), it is clear that Solomon did not meet these conditions (1 Kin. 11:9–13). In fact, none of the historical kings in the house of David met the condition of complete obedience that was to be the sign of the Promised One. According to Kings, the fulfillment of the Abrahamic and Davidic covenants did not take place in Israel's past, thus laying the foundation for the latter prophets (Isaiah, Jeremiah, Ezekiel, and the Twelve) who would point Israel to a future hope under Messiah when the Covenants would be fulfilled (see Is. 9:6,7)

OUTLINE

Since the division of 1 and 2 Kings arbitrarily takes place in the middle of the narrative concerning King Ahaziah in Israel, the following outline is for both 1 and 2 Kings.

    I. The United Kingdom: The Reign of Solomon (1 Kin. 1:1–11:43)

        A. The Rise of Solomon (1 Kin. 1:1–2:46)

        B. The Beginning of Solomon's Wisdom and Wealth (1 Kin. 3:1–4:34)

        C. The Preparations for the Building of the Temple (1 Kin. 5:1–18)

        D. The Building of the Temple and Solomon's House (1 Kin. 6:1–9:9)

        E. The Further Building Projects of Solomon (1 Kin. 9:10–28)

F. The Culmination of Solomon's Wisdom and Wealth (1 Kin. 10:1–29)

G. The Decline of Solomon (1 Kin. 11:1–43)

II. **The Divided Kingdom: The Kings of Israel and Judah (1 Kin. 12:1–2 Kin. 17:41)**

A. The Rise of Idolatry: Jeroboam of Israel/Rehoboam of Judah (1 Kin. 12:1–14:31)

B. Kings of Judah/Israel (1 Kin. 15:1–16:22)

C. The Dynasty of Omri and Its Influence: The Rise and Fall of Baal Worship in Israel and Judah (1 Kin. 16:23–2 Kin. 13:25)

    1. The introduction of Baal worship (1 Kin. 16:23–34)

    2. The opposition of Elijah to Baal worship (1 Kin. 17:1–2 Kin. 1:18)

    3. The influence of Elisha concerning the true God (2 Kin. 2:1–9:13)

    4. The overthrow of Baal worship in Israel (2 Kin. 9:14–10:36)

    5. The overthrow of Baal worship in Judah (2 Kin. 11:1–12:21)

    6. The death of Elisha (2 Kin. 13:1–25)

D. Kings of Judah/Israel (2 Kin. 14:1–15:38)

E. The Defeat and Exile of Israel by Assyria (2 Kin. 16:1–17:41)

III. **The Surviving Kingdom: The Kings of Judah (2 Kin. 18:1–25:21)**

A. Hezekiah's Righteous Reign (2 Kin. 18:1–20:21)

B. Manasseh's and Amon's Wicked Reigns (2 Kin. 21:1–26)

C. Josiah's Righteous Reign (2 Kin. 22:1–23:30)

D. The Defeat and Exile of Judah by Babylon (2 Kin. 23:31–25:21)

IV. **Epilogue: The People's Continued Rebellion and the Lord's Continued Mercy (2 Kin. 25:22–30)**

MEANWHILE, IN OTHER PARTS OF THE WORLD...

The Persian Empire is founded after the overthrow of Lydia, Babylon, and the Medes by King Cyrus the Great (553 to 529 B.C.). King Cyrus the Great later develops a messenger system using horses. Also, the first use of papyrus by the Greeks is recorded.

ANSWERS TO TOUGH QUESTIONS

1. How are the six books—1 and 2 Samuel, 1 and 2 Kings, and 1 and 2 Chronicles—related to one another in recording the history of the kingdom of Israel?

First and 2 Samuel and 1 and 2 Kings provide a chronological account of the kingdom of Israel in its original and divided state. First and 2 Chronicles serve as a special review of the line of David (the kings of Judah).

Those who add up the numbers given for the lengths of reign in these books are sometimes surprised that the math produces inconsistencies. Extra-biblical sources also provide some dating that creates problems when correlated with the text. Two important factors help explain the apparent inconsistencies in these records: (1) a number of cases had co-regencies (fathers and sons sharing the throne) in which each king's years were listed without accounting for the overlap; (2) neither the calendars nor the official reckoning of years was always the same in both kingdoms.

FURTHER STUDY ON 1 KINGS
1. What qualities did the successful kings have in common?
2. What character flaws and bad decisions marked the lives of kings who failed?
3. Why did the kingdom of David divide into the kingdom of Israel and the kingdom of Judah?
4. What role did Elijah fulfill throughout 1 Kings?
5. How does the building and dedication of the temple of God teach us about effective and ineffective ways to honor God?
6. What is the single, most concentrated effort you are carrying out in your life for the glory of God?

FURTHER STUDY ON 2 KINGS
1. In what ways were Elijah and Elisha different, and how did they influence their society?
2. What other prophets are mentioned in 2 Kings?
3. What are God's purposes behind the miracles that occur in 2 Kings?
4. How many kings did Israel and Judah each have and how many were good? How many were evil?
5. What parts of God's character are illustrated and emphasized in 2 Kings?
6. How do you understand and acknowledge God's patience in your own life?

FIRST AND SECOND CHRONICLES

Historical Review and Prelude to Disaster

TITLE

The original title in the Hebrew Bible read, "The annals (i.e., events or happenings) of the days." First and Second Chronicles were comprised of one book until later divided into separate books in the Greek OT translation, the Septuagint (LXX), ca. 200 B.C. The title also changed at that time to the inaccurate title, "the things omitted," i.e., reflecting material not in 1 and 2 Samuel and 1 and 2 Kings. The English title "Chronicles" originated with Jerome's Latin Vulgate translation (ca. A.D. 400), which used the fuller title "The Chronicles of the Entire Sacred History."

The Chronicles' Sources

The inspiration of Scripture (2 Timothy 3:16) was sometimes accomplished through direct revelation from God without a human writer, e.g., the Mosaic law. At other times, God used human sources, as mentioned in Luke 1:1–4. Such was the experience of the chronicler as evidenced by the many contributing sources. Whether the material came through direct revelation or by existing resources, God's inspiration through the Holy Spirit prevented the original human authors of Scripture from any error (2 Peter 1:19–21). Although relatively few scribal errors have been made in copying Scripture, they can be identified and corrected. Thus, the original, inerrant content of the Bible has been preserved.

1. Book of the Kings of Israel/Judah (1 Chronicles 9:1; 2 Chronicles 16:11; 20:34; 25:26; 27:7; 28:26; 32:32; 35:27; 36:8)
2. The Chronicles of David (1 Chronicles 27:24)
3. Book of Samuel (1 Chronicles 29:29)
4. Book of Nathan (1 Chronicles 29:29; 2 Chronicles 9:29)
5. Book of Gad (1 Chronicles 29:29)
6. Prophecy of Ahijah the Shilonite (2 Chronicles 9:29)
7. Visions of Iddo (2 Chronicles 9:29)
8. Records of Shemaiah (2 Chronicles 12:15)
9. Records of Iddo (2 Chronicles 12:15)
10. Annals of Iddo (2 Chronicles 13:22)
11. Annals of Jehu (2 Chronicles 20:34)
12. Commentary on the Book of the Kings (2 Chronicles 24:27)
13. Acts of Uzziah by Isaiah (2 Chronicles 26:22)
14. Letters/Message of Sennacherib (2 Chronicles 32:10–17)
15. Vision of Isaiah (2 Chronicles 32:32)
16. Words of the Seers (2 Chronicles 33:18)
17. Sayings of Hozai (2 Chronicles 33:19)
18. Written instructions of David and Solomon (2 Chronicles 35:4)
19. The Laments (2 Chronicles 35:25)

AUTHOR AND DATE

Neither 1 nor 2 Chronicles contains direct statements regarding the human author, though Jewish tradition strongly favors Ezra the priest (cf. Ezra 7:1–6) as "the chronicler." These records were most likely recorded ca. 450–430 B.C. The genealogical record in 1 Chronicles 1–9 supports a date after 450 B.C. for the writing. The NT does not directly quote either 1 or 2 Chronicles.

BACKGROUND AND SETTING

The immediate historical backdrop included the Jews' three-phase return to the Promised Land from the Babylonian exile: (1) Zerubbabel in Ezra 1–6 (ca. 538 B.C.); (2) Ezra in Ezra 7–10 (ca. 458 B.C.); and (3) Nehemiah in Nehemiah 1–13 (ca. 445 B.C.). Previous history looks back to the Babylonian deportation/Exile (ca. 605–538 B.C.) as predicted/reported by 2 Kings, Esther, Jeremiah, Ezekiel, Daniel, and Habakkuk. The prophets of this restoration era were Haggai, Zechariah, and Malachi.

The Jews had returned from their seventy years of captivity (ca. 538 B.C.) to a land that was markedly different from the one once ruled by King David (ca. 1011–971 B.C.) and King Solomon (971–931 B.C.): (1) there was no Hebrew king, but rather a Persian governor (Ezra 5:3; 6:6); (2) there was no security for Jerusalem, so Nehemiah had to rebuild the wall (Neh. 1–7); (3) there was no temple, so Zerubbabel had to reconstruct a pitiful replacement to the glorious temple Solomon had built (Ezra 3); (4) the Jews no longer dominated the region, but rather were on the defensive (Ezra 4; Neh. 4); (5) they enjoyed few divine blessings beyond the fact of their return; (6) they possessed little of the kingdom's former wealth; and (7) God's divine presence no longer resided in Jerusalem, having departed ca. 597–591 B.C. (Ezek. 8–11).

The Temples of the Bible

The Temple	Date	Description	Reference
The Tabernacle (Mobile Temple)	about 1444 B.C.	Detailed plan received by Moses from the Lord	Ex. 25–30; Ex. 35:30–40:38;
		Constructed by divinely appointed artisans	Lev. 10:1–7
		Desecrated by Nadab and Abihu	
Solomon's Temple	966–586 B.C.	Planned by David	2 Sam. 7:1–29;
		Constructed by Solomon	1 Kin. 8:1–66;
		Destroyed by Nebuchadnezzar	Jer. 32:28–44
Zerubbabel's Temple	516–169 B.C.	Envisioned by Zerubbabel	Ezra 6:1–22;
		Constructed by Zerubbabel and the elders of the Jews	Ezra 3:1–8; 4:1–14; Matt. 24:15
		Desecrated by Antiochus Epiphanes	

Herod's Temple	19 B.C.–A.D. 70.	Zerubbabel's temple restored by Herod the Great Destroyed by the Romans	Mark 13:2, 14–23; Luke 1:11–20; 2:22–38; 2:42–51; 4:21–24; Acts 21:27–33
The Present Temple	Present Age.	Found in the heart of the believer The body of the believer is the Lord's only temple until the Messiah returns	1 Cor. 6:19, 20; 2 Cor. 6:16–18
The Temple of Revelation 11	Tribulation Period.	To be constructed during the Tribulation by the Antichrist To be desecrated and destroyed	Dan. 9:2; Matt. 24:15; Thess. 2:4; Rev. 17:18
Ezekiel's (Millennial) Temple	Millennium.	Envisioned by the prophet Ezekiel To be built by the Messiah during His millennial reign	Ezek. 40:1– 42:20; Zech. 6:12,13
The Eternal Temple of His Presence	The Eternal Kingdom.	The greatest temple of all ("The Lord God Almighty and the Lamb are its temple") A spiritual temple	Rev. 21:22; Rev. 22:1–21

The temple (Gk. *hieron*) is a place of worship, a sacred or holy space built primarily for the national worship of God.

To put it mildly, their future looked bleak compared to their majestic past, especially the time of David and Solomon. The return could best be described as bittersweet, i.e., bitter because their present poverty brought hurtful memories about what was forfeited by God's judgment on their ancestors' sin, but sweet because at least they were back in the land God had given Abraham seventeen centuries earlier (Gen. 12:1–3). The chronicler's selective genealogy and history of Israel, stretching from Adam (1 Chr. 1:1) to the return from Babylon (2 Chr. 26:23), was intended to remind the Jews of God's promises and intentions about: (1) the land; (2) the nation; (3) the line of David; (4) the priests of the Levites; (5) the temple; and (6) true worship, none of which had been annulled because of the Babylonian captivity. All of this was to remind them of their spiritual heritage during the difficult times they faced, and to encourage them to be faithful to God.

KEY PEOPLE IN 1 CHRONICLES

David—king of Israel and ancestor of Jesus Christ; described by God as "a man after My own heart" (2:8–29:30; see Acts 13:22)

David's mighty men—special group of warriors pledged to fight for King David (11:10–28:1)

Nathan—prophet and advisor to David; relayed God's will for Solomon to build the temple (17:1–15)

Solomon—son of David who became the next king of Israel (3:5–29:28)

KEY PEOPLE IN 2 CHRONICLES

Solomon—king of Israel and builder of the Lord's temple; received great wisdom from God (1:1–9:31)

Queen of Sheba—heard of Solomon's reputation for wisdom; visited Jerusalem to test him with hard questions about his success (9:1–12; see Matt. 12:42)

Rehoboam—evil son of Solomon who became the next king of Israel; soon divided the kingdom and later led the southern kingdom of Judah (9:31–13:7)

Asa—king of Judah; tried to accomplish God's purposes through corrupt means (14:1–16:14)

Jehoshaphat—succeeded his father, Asa, as king of Judah; followed God but made several poor choices (17:1–22:9)

Jehoram—wicked son of Jehoshaphat who succeeded him as king of Judah; promoted idol worship and killed his six brothers (21:1–20)

Uzziah—(also called Azariah) succeeded his father, Amaziah, as king of Judah; mostly followed God yet retained a prideful attitude (26:1–23)

Ahaz—succeeded his father, Jotham, as king of Judah; led the people in Baal worship and other idolatry that included the sacrifice of his own children (27:9–29:19)

Hezekiah—succeeded his father, Ahaz, as king of Judah; obeyed God and restored the temple; started religious reform among the people (28:27–32:33)

Manasseh—succeeded his father, Hezekiah, as king of Judah; did evil in the sight of the Lord but repented toward the end of his reign (32:33–33:20)

Josiah—succeeded his father, Amon, as king of Judah; followed the Lord and discovered the Book of the Law of the Lord while restoring the temple (33:25–35:27)

HISTORICAL AND THEOLOGICAL THEMES

First and Second Chronicles, as named by the scholar Jerome, recreate a miniature OT history, with particular emphases on the Davidic covenant and temple worship. In terms of literary similarities, 1 Chronicles is the partner of 2 Samuel, in that both detail the reign of King David. First Chronicles opens with Adam (1:1) and closes with the death of David (29:26–30) in 971 B.C. Second Chronicles begins with Solomon (1:1) and covers the same historical period as 1 and 2 Kings, while focusing exclusively on the kings of the southern kingdom of Judah, thus excluding the history of the northern ten tribes and their rulers, because of their complete wickedness and false worship. It ranges from the reign of Solomon (1:1) in 971 B.C. to the return from Babylon in 538 B.C. (36:23). Over 55 percent of the material in Chronicles is unique, that is, not found in 2 Samuel or 1 and 2 Kings.

The "chronicler" tended to omit what was negative or in opposition to the Davidic kingship; on the other hand, he tended to make unique contributions in validating temple worship and the line of David. Whereas 2 Kings 25 ends dismally with the deportation of Judah to Babylon, 2 Chronicles 36:22–23 concludes hopefully with the Jews' release from Persia and return to Jerusalem.

CHRIST IN . . . 1 CHRONICLES

GOD'S COVENANT WITH DAVID promised him an eternal dynasty: "I will set up your seed after you, who will be of our sons; and I will establish his kingdom. He shall build Me a house, and I will establish his throne forever. I will be his Father, and he shall be My son" (17:11–13). As a fulfillment to this promise, Solomon built the temple for the Lord. The final fulfillment of this covenant will come with the establishment of the eternal kingdom of Christ the Messiah, a direct descendant of David.

These two books were written to the recently returned Jewish exiles as a chronicle of God's intention of future blessing, in spite of the nation's past moral/spiritual failure for which the people paid dearly under God's wrath. First and Second Chronicles could be briefly summarized as follows:

> I. A Selected Genealogical History of Israel (1 Chr. 1–9)
> II. Israel's United Kingdom under Saul (1 Chr. 10), David (1 Chr. 11–29), and Solomon (2 Chr. 1–9)
> III. Judah's Monarchy in the Divided Kingdom (2 Chr. 10–36:21)
> IV. Judah's Release from Their Seventy-Year Captivity (2 Chr. 36:22, 23)

The historical themes are unquestionably linked with the theological in that God's divine purposes for Israel have been and will be played out on the stage of human history. These two books are designed to assure the returning Jews that, in spite of their checkered past and present plight, God will be true to His covenant promises. God has brought them back to the land first given to Abraham, intact as a race of people whose ethnic identity (Jewish) was not obliterated by the deportation and whose national identity (Israel) has been preserved (Gen. 12:1–3; 15:5), although they are still under God's judgment as prescribed by the law of Moses (Deut. 28:15–68). The priestly line of Eleazar's son Phinehas and the Levitical line were still intact so that temple worship could continue in the hopes that

KEY WORDS IN

1 Chronicles

Sons: Hebrew *ben*—1:43; 3:12; 4:25; 5:14; 7:14; 9:4; 11:22; 22:9; 26:28—literally, "to build." The ancient Hebrews considered their children the "builders" of the future generations. *Ben* can refer to a direct son or to one's future descendants (1 Kin. 2:1; 1 Chr. 7:14). Old Testament names such as Benjamin, meaning "Son of my Right Hand," incorporate this Hebrew noun (Gen. 35:18). In the plural, *ben* can be translated as "children" regardless of gender (see Ex. 12:37—"children of Israel"). God Himself uses this term to describe His unique relationship with Israel: "Israel is My son, My firstborn" (Ex. 4:22).

God's presence would one day return (Num. 25:10–13; Mal. 3:1). The promise of a king through David's line was still valid, although yet to come in its fulfillment (2 Sam. 7:8–17; 1 Chr. 17:7–15). Their individual hope of eternal life and restoration of God's blessings forever rested in the New Covenant (Jer. 31:31–34).

Two basic principles enumerated in these two books prevail throughout the OT, namely, obedience brings blessing, disobedience brings judgment. In the Chronicles, when the king obeyed and trusted the Lord, God blessed and protected. But when the king disobeyed and/or put his trust in something or someone other than the Lord, God withdrew His blessing and protection. Three basic failures by the kings of Judah brought God's wrath: (1) personal sin; (2) false worship/idolatry; and/or (3) trust in man rather than God.

CHRIST IN . . . 2 CHRONICLES

In 2 Chronicles, the line of David still remains protected by God. Solomon carries on David's preparation to build the temple to the Lord. In the New Testament, Christ likens Himself to the temple: "Destroy this temple, and in three days I will raise it up" (John 2:19). The temple Solomon built was eventually destroyed. Yet, Christ promises believers an eternal temple in Himself. In Revelation 21:22, the New Jerusalem has no temple for "the Lord God Almighty and the Lamb are its temple."

KEY DOCTRINES IN 1 CHRONICLES

Blessing—when the king obeyed and trusted the Lord, God blessed and protected him (11:4–9; 14:8–14; Ex. 23:22; Deut. 11:27; 1 Sam. 15:22; Pss. 5:12; 106:3; Eccles. 12:13; Is. 30:18; Matt. 5:6; Luke 11:28)

Judgment—when the king disobeyed God and put his trust in something else, God withdrew His blessing (10:1–7; Deut. 28:41; Job 12:23; Ps. 78:32,33; Is. 42:24; Ezek. 39:23; Hos. 4:17; Amos 3:6; 4:10; Mic. 6:9; Mal. 2:2; Matt. 7:22,23; 13:40–42; John 12:48)

The Davidic covenant—God's promise to Israel to restore a king was not abandoned because of the Exile (17:7–15; 2 Sam. 7:1–17; 2 Chr. 3:1,2; Jer. 31:31–34)

KEY DOCTRINES IN 2 CHRONICLES

Wisdom—Solomon learned that the attainment of wisdom was more important than riches, honor, or victory (1:7–12; 1 Kin. 3:9; Prov. 3:15; 16:7,8; Matt. 7:7; James 1:5)

Blessing—when the king obeyed and trusted the Lord, God blessed and protected him (7:13,19,20; 9:13–22; Ex. 23:22; Deut. 11:27; 1 Sam. 15:22; 1 Chr. 11:4–9; 14:8–14; Pss. 5:12; 106:3; Eccles. 12:13; Is. 30:18; Matt. 5:6; Luke 11:28)

Judgment—when the king disobeyed God and put his trust in something else, God withdrew His blessing (7:14,15; Deut.28:41; 1 Chr. 10:1–7; Job 12:23; Ps. 78:32,33; Is. 42:24; Ezek. 39:23; Hos. 4:17; Amos 3:6; 4:10; Mic. 6:9; Mal. 2:2; Matt. 7:22,23; 13:40–42; John 12:48)

The Davidic covenant—God's promise to Israel to restore a king was not abandoned because of the Exile (3:1,2; 2 Sam. 7:1–17; 1 Chr. 17:7–15; Jer. 31:31–34)

GOD'S CHARACTER IN 1 CHRONICLES

God is glorious—16:24
God is holy—16:10
God is merciful—16:34
God is powerful—29:11,12
God is a promise keeper—17:23,26
God is provident—29:12
God is unified—17:20
God is wise—28:9

GOD'S CHARACTER IN 2 CHRONICLES

God is good—30:18
God is great—2:5
God is just—19:7
God is long-suffering—33:10–13
God is powerful—13:4
God is true—6:17

INTERPRETIVE CHALLENGES

First and Second Chronicles present a combination of selective genealogical and historical records and there are no real insurmountable challenges within the two books. A few issues arise, such as: (1) Who wrote 1 and 2 Chronicles? Does the overlap of 2 Chronicles 36:22–23 with Ezra 1:1–3 point to Ezra as author? (2) Does the use of multiple sources taint the inerrancy doctrine of Scripture? (3) How does one explain the variations in the genealogies of 1 Chronicles 1–9 from other OT genealogies? (4) Are the curses of Deuteronomy 28 still in force, even though the seventy-year captivity has concluded? (5) How does one explain the few variations in numbers when comparing Chronicles with parallel passages in Samuel and Kings (see chart, "A Harmony of the Books of Samuel, Kings, and Chronicles").

OUTLINE – 1 CHRONICLES

I. Selective Genealogy (1:1–9:34)

      A. Adam to Just before David (1:1–2:55)

      B. David to the Captivity (3:1–24)

      C. The Twelve Tribes (4:1–9:2)

      D. Jerusalem Dwellers (9:3–34)

KEY WORDS IN

2 Chronicles

Right: Hebrew *yashar*—14:2; 20:32; 24:2; 25:2; 26:4; 27:2; 28:1; 34:2—literally, "to be level" or "to be upright." The Hebrew word *right* refers to being just or righteous. The word is used in many settings to describe the righteousness of God (Deut. 32:4; Ps. 111:7,8), the integrity of one's speech (Job 6:25; Eccles. 12:10), or the lifestyle of a righteous person (Prov. 11:3,6). Often, this word is used to assess the quality of the kings in 1 and 2 Chronicles. David, as Israel's king, exemplified righteousness in his life (1 Kin. 3:6) and became a standard for judging the kings who succeeded him (see 17:3; 34:2).

Passover: Hebrew *pesach*—30:1,15; 35:1,9,11, 13,18,19—literally, "to pass" or "to leap over." The Passover celebration commemorated the day God spared the firstborn children of the Israelites from the death plague brought on Egypt. The Lord "passed over" those who sprinkled the blood from the Passover lamb on their doorposts (Ex. 12). Passover, as specified in the Law of Moses, reminds the Israelites of God's great mercy on them (see Lev. 23:5–8; Num. 28:16–25; Deut. 16:1–8). In the New Testament, Jesus also celebrated the Passover feast with His disciples (Matt. 26:2,18). Christ became the ultimate Passover Lamb when He sacrificed Himself for our sins (John 1:29; 1 Cor. 5:7; 1 Pet. 1:19).

II. David's Ascent (9:35–12:40)1
    A. Saul's Heritage and Death (9:35–10:14)
    B. David's Anointing (11:1–3)
    C. Jerusalem's Conquest (11:4–9)
    D. David's Men (11:10–12:40)

III. David's Reign (13:1–29:30)
    A. The Ark of the Covenant (13:1–16:43)
    B. The Davidic Covenant (17:1–27)
    C. Selected Military History (18:1–21:30)
    D. Temple-Building Preparations (22:1–29:20)
    E. Transition to Solomon (29:21–30)

MEANWHILE, IN OTHER PARTS OF THE WORLD...
The Spartans develop the use of chemicals such as sulfur, pitch, and charcoal in warfare.

OUTLINE – 2 CHRONICLES
I. The Reign of Solomon (1:1–9:31)
    A. Coronation and Beginnings (1:1–17)
    B. Temple Building (2:1–7:22)
    C. Wealth/Achievements (8:1–9:28)
    D. Death (9:29–31)

II. The Reign of the Kings of Judah (10:1–36:21)
    A. Rehoboam (10:1–12:16)
    B. Abijah (13:1–22)
    C. Asa (14:1–16:14)
    D. Jehoshaphat (17:1–21:3)
    E. Jehoram (21:4–20)
    F. Ahaziah (22:1–9)
    G. Athaliah (22:10–23:21)
    H. Joash (24:1–27)
    I. Amaziah (25:1–28)
    J. Uzziah (26:1–23)
    K. Jotham (27:1–9)
    L. Ahaz (28:1–27)
    M. Hezekiah (29:1–32:33)
    N. Manasseh (33:1–20)

O. Amon (33:21–25)
P. Josiah (34:1–35:27)
Q. Jehoahaz (36:1–4)
R. Jehoiakim (36:5–8)
S. Jehoiachin (36:9–10)
T. Zedekiah (36:11–21)
III. **The Return Proclamation of Cyrus (36:22–23)**

MEANWHILE, IN OTHER PARTS OF THE WORLD...
Rivals Athens and Sparta strike up a thirty-year truce (445 to 415 B.C.).

ANSWERS TO TOUGH QUESTIONS
1. Does the use of outside sources affect the claim that Scripture is inerrant? Were these other documents also inspired by God?

First and 2 Chronicles repeatedly quote other sources. Ezra includes many direct quotes from Persian documents. Other Scriptures include extrabiblical references. The answer to this question must reflect not the isolated cases of outside texts, but the numerous places the Bible quotes foreign decrees, pagan leaders, and other secular texts.

The fact that an extrabiblical source is quoted in Scripture does not endorse that entire source as inspired. Biblical content is truth. Sources are not necessarily true because they are in the Bible; facts are in the Bible because they are true. Biblical content remains true even when quoted outside the Bible. Some items of truth that were originally recorded outside Scripture and were available to those whom God inspired to write the Bible were used in Scripture.

These extrabiblical factors have the added effect of reminding us that God's Word was given in real historical situations, lived out and written out by people under God's guidance. These quotes emphasize the Scripture's relationship with reality. God's Word reveals the real God: ultimate reality.

FURTHER STUDY ON 1 CHRONICLES
1. As you read through the historical review of the first nine chapters of 1 Chronicles, what purposes can you discover for this record?
2. What are the highlights and significance of King David's life from the perspective of 1 Chronicles?

3. What happens to the ark of the covenant in 1 Chronicles? What is the background of that event (see 1 Samuel 5–6)?
4. If David was a man after God's own heart, why didn't God allow him to build the great temple in Jerusalem?
5. How is the importance of genuine worship illustrated in 1 Chronicles?
6. In what ways does your own practice of worship match the ideals found in 1 Chronicles?

FURTHER STUDY ON 2 CHRONICLES

1. Whom would you choose as the two or three best examples of a good king from 2 Chronicles?
2. Which kings most influenced the people towards evil during their reigns?
3. What lessons about prayer can be found in 2 Chronicles?
4. What is the context and significance of 2 Chronicles 7:14?
5. By the end of 2 Chronicles, the nation has collapsed and the temple has been destroyed. How did this disaster come about?
6. In what ways are you benefiting right now from good decisions you made a while ago?

EZRA
The Return of the Exiles

TITLE
Even though Ezra's name does not enter the account of Judah's post-Exilic return to Jerusalem until 7:1, the book bears his name ("Jehovah helps") as a title. This is because both Jewish and Christian tradition attribute authorship to this famous scribe-priest. NT writers do not quote the Book of Ezra.

AUTHOR AND DATE
Ezra is most likely the author of both Ezra and Nehemiah, which might have originally been one book. Ezra 4:8–6:18 and 7:12–26 are written in Aramaic. Although Ezra never states his authorship, internal arguments favor him strongly. After his arrival in Jerusalem (ca. 458 B.C.), he changed from writing in the third person to writing in the first person. In the earlier section it is likely that he had used the third person because he was quoting his memoirs. Ezra is believed to possibly be the author of the books of the Chronicles. It would have been natural for the same author to continue the OT narrative by showing how God fulfilled His promise by returning His people to the land after seventy years of captivity. There is also a strong priestly tone in Chronicles, and Ezra was a priestly descendant of Aaron (cf. 7:1–5). The concluding verses of 2 Chronicles (36:22, 23) are virtually identical to the beginning verses of Ezra (1:1–3a), further affirming his authorship of both.

Ezra was a scribe who had access to the myriad of administrative documents found in Ezra and Nehemiah, especially those in the Book of Ezra. Very few people would have been allowed access to the royal archives of the Persian Empire, but Ezra proved to be the exception (cf. Ezra 1:2–4; 4:9–22; 5:7–17; 6:3–12). His role as a scribe of the law is spelled out in 7:10: "For Ezra had prepared his heart to seek the Law of the LORD, and to do it, and to teach statutes and ordinances in Israel." He was a strong and godly man who lived at the time of Nehemiah (cf. Neh. 8:1–9; 12:36). Tradition says he was founder of the Great Synagogue, where the complete OT canon was first formally recognized.

Ezra led the second return from Persia (ca. 458 B.C.), so the completed book was written sometime in the next several decades (ca. 457–444 B.C.).

BACKGROUND AND SETTING
God had originally brought Israel out of the slave markets of Egypt in the Exodus (ca. 1445 B.C.). Hundreds of years later, before the events of Ezra, God told His people that if they chose to break their covenant with Him, He would again allow other nations to take them into slavery (Jer. 2:14–25). In spite of God's repeated warnings from the mouths of His prophets, Israel and Judah chose to reject their Lord and to participate in the worship of foreign gods, in addition to committing the horrible practices that accompanied idolatry (cf. 2 Kin. 17:7–18; Jer. 2:7–13). True to His promise, God brought the Assyrians and Babylonians to issue His punishment upon rebellious Israel and Judah.

In 722 B.C. the Assyrians deported the ten northern tribes and scattered them all over their empire (cf. 2 Kin. 17:24–41; Is. 7:8). Several centuries later, in 605–586 B.C., God used the Babylonians to sack and nearly depopulate Jerusalem. Because Judah persisted in her unfaithfulness to the covenant, God chastened His people with seventy years of captivity (Jer. 25:11), from which they returned to Jerusalem as reported by Ezra and Nehemiah. Cyrus, the Persian, overthrew Babylon in 539 B.C., and the Book of Ezra begins with the decree of Cyrus one year later for the Jews to return to Jerusalem (ca. 538 B.C.), and it chronicles the reestablishment of Judah's national calendar of feasts and sacrifices, including the rebuilding of the second temple (begun in 536 B.C. and completed in 516 B.C.).

As there had been three waves of deportation from Israel into Babylon (605 B.C., 597 B.C., and 586 B.C.), so there were actually three returns to Jerusalem over a nine-decade span. Zerubbabel first returned in 538 B.C. He was followed by Ezra, who led the second return in 458 B.C. Nehemiah did likewise thirteen years later, in 445 B.C. Complete uncontested political autonomy, however, never returned. The prophets Haggai and Zechariah preached during Zerubbabel's time, about 520 B.C. and following.

Post-Exilic Returns to Jerusalem

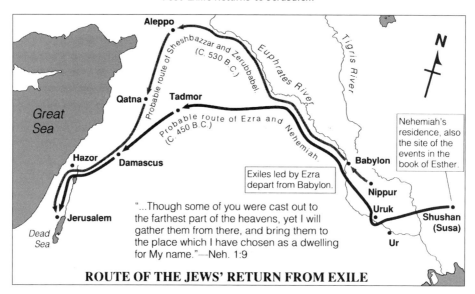

ROUTE OF THE JEWS' RETURN FROM EXILE

KEY PEOPLE IN EZRA

Ezra—scribe and teacher of God's Word who began religious reform among the people; led the second group of exiles from Babylon to Jerusalem (Ezra 7:1–10:16)

Cyrus—Persian king who conquered Babylon; assisted the return of the Israelite exiles to their homeland (Ezra 1:1–6:14)

Zerubbabel—led the first group of Israelite exiles from Babylon to Jerusalem; completed the rebuilding of the temple (Ezra 2:2–5:2)

Haggai—post-Exilic (after the Exile) prophet who encouraged Zerubbabel and the Israelite people to continue rebuilding the temple (Ezra 5:1–2; 6:14)

Zechariah—post-Exilic prophet who encouraged Zerubbabel and the Israelite people to continue rebuilding the temple (Ezra 5:1–2; 6:14)

Darius I—Persian king who supported the rebuilding of the temple by the Israelites (Ezra 4:5–6:14)

Artaxerxes—Persian king who allowed Ezra to return to Jerusalem (Ezra 7:1) and reinstitute temple worship and the teaching of the Law

HISTORICAL AND THEOLOGICAL THEMES

The Jews' return from the Babylonian captivity seemed like a second Exodus, sovereignly patterned in some ways after Israel's first release from Egyptian bondage. The return trip from Babylon involved activities similar to those of the original Exodus: (1) the rebuilding of the temple and the city walls; (2) the reinstitution of the Law, which made Zerubbabel, Ezra, and Nehemiah collectively seem like a second Moses; (3) the challenge of the local enemies; and (4) the temptation to intermarry with non-Jews, resulting in idolatry. Other parallels between the original Exodus and the return from Babylon must have seemed to the returnees like they had been given a fresh start by God.

CHRIST IN . . . EZRA

ISRAEL'S RETURN TO THE LAND of promise illustrates the unconditional forgiveness ultimately offered through Christ. God's protection of His people reinforced His covenant with David to preserve his line. Jesus, a direct descendant from the line of David, would later come to bring salvation to the whole world.

In his account of the return, Ezra drew upon a collection of Persian administrative documents to which he had access as a scribe. The presence of actual royal administrative documents carries a powerful message when accompanied by the resounding line "the hand of the LORD my God was upon him/me"(7:6, 28). The decrees, proclamations, letters, lists, genealogies, and memoranda, many of them written by the Persian administration, attest to the sovereign hand of God in Israel's restoration. The primary message of the book is that God orchestrated the past grim situation (captivity) and would continue to work through a pagan king and his successors to give Judah hope for the future (return). God's administration overrides that of any of the kings of this world, and thus the Book of Ezra is a message of God's continuing covenant grace to Israel.

Another prominent theme which surfaces in Ezra is opposition from the local Samaritan residents whose ancestors had been imported from Assyria (4:2; cf. John 4:4–42). For reasons of spiritual sabotage, Israel's enemies requested to participate in rebuilding the temple (4:1, 2). After being shunned, the enemies hired counselors against the Jews (cf. 4:4, 5). But the Lord, through the preaching of Haggai and Zechariah, rekindled the spirit of the people and their leaders to build, with the words "be strong ... and work; for I am with you" (Hag. 2:4; cf. Ezra 4:24–5:2). The reconstruction resumed (ca. 520 B.C.) and the temple was soon finished, dedicated, and back in service to God (ca. 516 B.C.).

KEY DOCTRINES IN EZRA

    God's sovereignty—the Lord controlled and guarded the path of the Israelites from their exile to their return to the Promised Land (2:1; Gen. 50:20; Job 42:2; Prov. 16:1; Matt. 10:29,30; John 6:37; Rom. 8:28)

GOD'S CHARACTER IN EZRA

God is good—8:18
God is powerful—8:22
God is righteous—9:15
God is wise—7:25
God is wrathful—8:22

INTERPRETIVE CHALLENGES

First, how do the post-Exilic historical books of 1 and 2 Chronicles, Ezra, Nehemiah, and Esther relate to the post-Exilic prophets Haggai, Zechariah, and Malachi? The two books of Chronicles were written by Ezra as a reminder of the promised Davidic kingship, the Aaronic priesthood, and appropriate temple worship. Haggai and Zechariah prophesied in the period of Ezra 4–6, when temple construction was resumed. Malachi wrote during Nehemiah's revisit to Persia (cf. Neh. 13:6).

Second, what purpose does the book serve? Ezra historically reports the first two of three post-Exilic returns to Jerusalem from the Babylonian captivity. The first return (chaps. 1–6) was under Zerubbabel (ca. 538 B.C.), and the second return (chaps. 7–10) was led by Ezra himself (ca. 458 B.C.). Spiritually, Ezra reestablished the importance of the priesthood descended from Aaron by tracing his ancestry to Eleazar, Phinehas, and Zadok (cf. Ezra 7:1–5). He reported on the rebuilding of the second temple (chaps. 3–6). His strategy for dealing with the gross sin of intermarriage with foreigners is presented in chaps. 9–10. Most important, he reports how the sovereign hand of God moved kings and overcame varied opposition to reestablish Israel as Abraham's seed, nationally and individually, in the land promised to Abraham, David, and Jeremiah.

Third, the temple was built during the reign of Cyrus. Mention of Ahasuerus (4:6) and Artaxerxes (4:7–23) might lead one to conclude that the temple could also have been built during their reigns. Such a conclusion, however, disagrees with history. Ezra was not writing about the construction accomplishments of Ahasuerus or Artaxerxes, but rather he continued to chronicle their oppositions after the temple was built, which continued even to Ezra's day. It is apparent,

KEY WORDS IN

Ezra

Jews: Hebrew *yehudi*—4:12,23; 5:1,5; 6:7,8,14—from a root meaning "to praise" or "to give thanks." Jacob used this term during his blessing of his son Judah in Genesis 49:8: "Judah, your brothers will praise you." A Jew may be a person from the tribe of Judah (Numbers 10:14), or an Israelite living in the geographical region known as Judah (see Jer. 7:30). During the post-Exilic period, "Jew" referred to the Israelites as a people group. The use of the term "Jew" is also found in the NT. Jesus is called "the King of the Jews" (Matt. 27:29). Later, Paul clarified that the true Jew is a person marked by "circumcision of the heart" (Rom. 2:28,29).

Remnant: Hebrew *sha'ar*—9:8, 15—literally, "to remain" or "to be left over." A *remnant* refers to the few people who survive after a catastrophe, such as the Flood. In the Bible, the word mostly refers to the diminished Israelite population who survived the Exile (9:8). The prophets also use the word to specifically describe the Israelites who remained faithful to God (Amos 5:14,15). The prophet Isaiah described the Messiah as one day gathering the remnant of Israel from all the nations, even attracting some Gentiles to Himself (Is. 11:10,11,16). The *remnant* therefore points to God's covenant faithfulness in sparing His people. Through the preservation of Israel, all the world would be blessed by the coming of the Messiah (Gen. 12:3).

then, that Ezra 4:1–5 and 4:24–5:2 deal with rebuilding the temple under Zerubbabel, while 4:6–23 is a parenthesis recounting the history of opposition in the times of Ezra and Nehemiah.

Fourth, the interpreter must decide where Esther fits in to the time of Ezra. A careful examination indicates it took place between the events of chaps. 6 and 7.

Fifth, how does divorce in Ezra 10 correlate with the fact that God hates divorce (Mal. 2:16)? Ezra does not establish the norm, but rather deals with a special case in history. It seems to have been decided (Ezra 10:3) on the principle that the lesser wrong (divorce) would be preferable to the greater wrong of the Jewish race being polluted by intermarriage, so that the nation and the messianic line of David would not be ended by being mingled with Gentiles. To solve the problem this way magnifies the mercy of God in that the only other solution would have been to kill all of those involved (husband, wives, and children) by stoning, as was done during the first Exodus at Shittim (Num. 25:1–9).

OUTLINE
I. The First Return under Zerubbabel (1:1–6:22)
    A. Cyrus' Decree to Return (1:1–4)
    B. Treasures to Rebuild the Temple (1:5–11)
    C. Those Who Returned (2:1–70)
    D. Construction of the Second Temple (3:1–6:22)
        1. Building begins (3:1–13)
        2. Opposition surfaces (4:1–5)
        3. Excursus on future opposition (4:6–23)
        4. Construction renewed (4:24–5:2)
        5. Opposition renewed (5:3–6:12)
        6. Temple completed and dedicated (6:13–22)
II. The Second Return under Ezra (7:1–10:44)
    A. Ezra Arrives (7:1–8:36)
    B. Ezra Leads Revival (9:1–10:44)

MEANWHILE, IN OTHER PARTS OF THE WORLD...
The Persian Wars finally cease (490 to 449 B.C.) after the Athenian Cimon, son of Miltiades, defeats the Persians at Salamis.

ANSWERS TO TOUGH QUESTIONS

1. What parts of the OT and what people were active in the events surrounding the return of the Jews from Exile?

Five historical books (1 and 2 Chronicles, Ezra, Nehemiah, and Esther) come from or cover events after the Exile. Three prophetic books (Haggai, Zechariah, and Malachi) come from the same period. The term *post-Exilic* is often used to describe these books and people.

First and second Chronicles provide a summary of history viewed from the final days of the Exile. Ezra and Nehemiah journal the thrilling and difficult days of the return to Judah and the rebuilding of the nation. Haggai and Zechariah were prophets active during the time recorded in Ezra 4–6 when the temple was under reconstruction. Malachi wrote and prophesied during Nehemiah's revisit to Persia (Neh. 13:6).

Although part of the purpose of these books is to confirm God's continued covenant with the house of David and the unbroken kingly line, the emphasis shifts from royalty to other servants of God. A scribe, a cupbearer, and prophets become God's central agents. Even Esther, although a queen, had to rely on God rather than her position and power to accomplish God's role for her in preserving the Jews in Persia.

All of this sets the stage for the mixed expectations that surrounded the birth of Jesus, the fulfillment of God's covenant with David, God's personal involvement in the history of salvation.

2. How does Ezra's handling of the intermarriage and divorce situation fit into the overall pattern of biblical teaching on these important matters?

Ezra 9 and 10 record a critical time in the reestablishment of the Jewish people in their homeland. In the years before Ezra arrived from Persia, many of the returned Jewish men intermarried with pagan women from the area. This practice reflects no circumstances like those we find in the marriages of Rahab or Ruth, Gentiles who became believers in God. The Jewish men who married foreign women upon return from exile failed to take into account the pagan background of these women. Ezra received this news as part of the report when he reached Jerusalem.

For Ezra, this was almost the worst possible news. Intermarriage with pagans had historically played a key role in the repeated downfalls of the nation. These marriages were an act of disobedience to God. Ezra was overwhelmed with shame and distress over the situation (Ezra 9:3–4). His grief was open and convicting. Eventually, the people themselves confessed their error and decided that those who had married pagan women would have to "put away" (divorce) these wives. But God had not changed His mind about divorce. Malachi, who lived in this time period, declared that God hates divorce (Mal. 2:16).

Several important notes can be made about this passage in Ezra. It does not establish that divorce is acceptable under normal circumstances. It is also easy to overlook the fact that while the solution of divorce was a group decision, each of these marriages was examined individually. Presumably, cases in which the women had become believers were treated differently than cases in which the women involved saw questions of faith as a violation of the marriage agreement.

In the humility of the guilty and the care in confronting these issues, a great deal of God's mercy shines through. A strict interpretation of the Law could have led to the death by stoning of all involved. The eagerness to set things right opened the doorway for a solution, even though in some of the cases it involved the grief and sadness of divorce.

FURTHER STUDY ON EZRA
1. What kind of person was Ezra?
2. Describe the attitudes, emotions, and experiences of the first pilgrims who returned to the Promised Land from captivity.
3. What kinds of opposition to rebuilding Jerusalem and the temple did the people face?
4. What role did God's Word play in the lives of those who returned from captivity?
5. In what ways did the returning exiles demonstrate their faith in God?
6. What ruins from your own past have you trusted God to help you rebuild and enjoy once again?

NEHEMIAH
Rebuilding the Walls

TITLE
Nehemiah ("Jehovah comforts") is a famous cupbearer, who never appears in Scripture outside of this book. As with the books of Ezra and Esther, named for his contemporaries (see Introductions to Ezra and Esther), this book recounts selected events of his leadership and was titled after him. Both the Greek Septuagint (LXX) and the Latin Vulgate originally named this book "Second Ezra." Even though the two books of Ezra and Nehemiah are separate in most English Bibles, they may have once been joined together in a single unit as they are currently in the Hebrew texts. NT writers do not quote Nehemiah.

AUTHOR AND DATE
Though much of this book was clearly drawn from Nehemiah's personal diaries and written from his first person perspective (1:1–7:5; 12:27–43; 13:4–31), both Jewish and Christian traditions recognize Ezra as the author. This is based on external evidence that Ezra and Nehemiah were originally one book as reflected in the LXX and Vulgate; it is also based on internal evidence such as the recurrent "hand of the LORD" theme which dominates both Ezra and Nehemiah and the author's role as a priest-scribe. As a scribe, Ezra had access to the royal archives of Persia, which accounts for the countless administrative documents found recorded in the two books, especially in the Book of Ezra. Very few people would have been allowed access to the royal archives of the Persian Empire, but Ezra proved to be the exception (cf. Ezra 1:2–4; 4:9–22; 5:7–17; 6:3–12).

The events in Nehemiah 1 commence late in the year 446 B.C., the 20th year of the Persian king, Artaxerxes (464–423 B.C.). The book follows chronologically from Nehemiah's first term as governor of Jerusalem ca. 445–433 B.C. (Neh. 1–12) to his second term, possibly beginning ca. 424 B.C. (Neh. 13). Nehemiah was written by Ezra sometime during or after Nehemiah's second term, but no later than 400 B.C.

BACKGROUND AND SETTING
True to God's promise of judgment, He brought the Assyrians and Babylonians to deliver His chastisement upon wayward Judah and Israel. In 722 B.C. the Assyrians deported the ten northern tribes and scattered them all over the then known world (2 Kin. 17). Several centuries later, ca. 605–586 B.C., God used the Babylonians to sack, destroy, and nearly depopulate Jerusalem (2 Kin. 25) because Judah had persisted in her unfaithfulness to the covenant. God chastened His people with seventy years of captivity in Babylon (Jer. 25:11).

CHRIST IN . . . NEHEMIAH
THE BOOK OF NEHEMIAH displays the rebuilding of the city of Jerusalem and the revival of the people. However, Israel still awaited the coming of a king. Christ the Messiah completes this restoration of Israel as the long-awaited King of the Jews (Matt. 27:11).

During the Jews' captivity, world empire leadership changed hands from the Babylonians to the Persians (ca. 539 B.C.; Dan. 5), after which Daniel received most of his

Time Line of Nehemiah

Reference	Date	Event
1:1,4	Nov./Dec. 446 B.C. (Kislev)	Nehemiah hears of problems and prays.
2:1,5	Mar./Apr. 445 B.C. (Nisan)	Nehemiah is dispatched to Jerusalem.
3:1; 6:15	July/Aug. 445 B.C. (Ab)	Nehemiah starts the wall.
6:15	Aug./Sept. 445 B.C. (Elul)	Nehemiah completes the wall.
7:73b	Sept./Oct. 445 B.C. (Tishri)	Day of Trumpets celebrated (implied).
8:13–15	Sept./Oct. 445 B.C. (Tishri)	Feast of Tabernacles celebrated.
9:1	Sept./Oct. 445 B.C. (Tishri)	Time of confession.
12:27	Sept./Oct. 445 B.C.(Tishri)	Wall dedicated.
13:6	445–433 B.C.	Nehemiah's first term as governor (Nehemiah 1–12).
13:6	433–424 B.C. (?)	Nehemiah returns to Persia.
No ref.	433–? B.C.	Malachi prophesies in Jerusalem during Nehemiah's absence.
13:1,4,7	424–? B.C.	Nehemiah returns and serves a second term as governor (Nehemiah 13).

prophetic revelation (cf. Dan. 6, 9–12). The Book of Ezra begins with the decree of Cyrus, a Persian king, to return God's people to Jerusalem to rebuild God's house (ca. 539 B.C.), and chronicles the reestablishment of Judah's national calendar of feasts and sacrifices. Zerubbabel and Joshua led the first return (Ezra 1–6) and rebuilt the temple. Esther gives a glimpse of the Jews left in Persia (ca. 483–473 B.C.), when Haman attempted to eliminate the Jewish race. Ezra 7–10 recounts the second return led by Ezra in 458 B.C. Nehemiah chronicles the third return to rebuild the wall around Jerusalem (ca. 445 B.C.). At that time in Judah's history, the Persian Empire dominated the entire Near Eastern world. Its government over Judah, although for the most part relaxed, was mindful of disruptions or any signs of rebellion from its subjects. Rebuilding the walls of conquered cities posed the most glaring threat to the Persian central administration. Only a close confidant of the king himself could be trusted for such an operation. At the most critical juncture in Judah's revitalization, God raised up Nehemiah to exercise one of the most trusted roles in the empire, the King's cupbearer and confidant. Life under the Persian king Artaxerxes (ca. 464–423 B.C.) had its advantages for Nehemiah. Much like Joseph, Esther, and Daniel, he had attained a significant role in the palace of the most powerful king in the world at that time. From this position God could use him to lead the rebuilding of Jerusalem's walls, in spite of the Persian government's control of that city.

Many geographical landmarks in the city of Jerusalem are mentioned in the Book of Nehemiah (3:12–18; 12:27–39). As reconstructed by Zerubbabel, Ezra, and Nehemiah, the postexilic city of Jerusalem was considerably smaller and less grand than the city which fell to Babylon in 586 B.C.

Several other historical notes are of interest. First, Esther was Artaxerxes' stepmother and could have easily influenced him to look favorably upon the Jews, especially Nehemiah. Second, Daniel's prophetic seventy weeks began with the decree to rebuild the city issued by Artaxerxes in 445 B.C. (cf. chaps. 1, 2). Third, the Elephantine papyri

Jerusalem in Nehemiah's Day

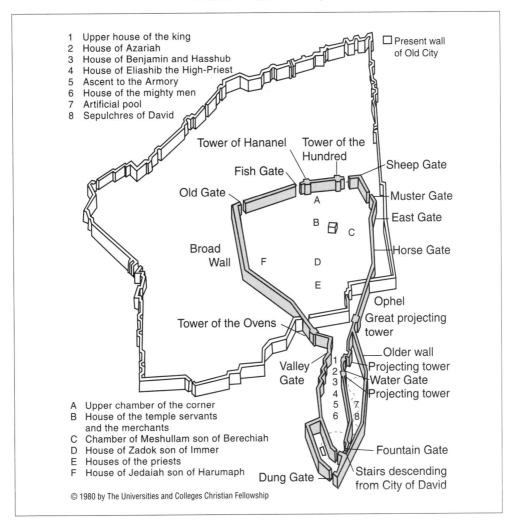

1 Upper house of the king
2 House of Azariah
3 House of Benjamin and Hasshub
4 House of Eliashib the High-Priest
5 Ascent to the Armory
6 House of the mighty men
7 Artificial pool
8 Sepulchres of David

☐ Present wall of Old City

Tower of Hananel
Tower of the Hundred
Fish Gate
Sheep Gate
Old Gate
Muster Gate
East Gate
Broad Wall
Horse Gate
Tower of the Ovens
Ophel
Great projecting tower
Older wall
Valley Gate
Projecting tower
Water Gate
Projecting tower
Fountain Gate
Dung Gate
Stairs descending from City of David

A Upper chamber of the corner
B House of the temple servants and the merchants
C Chamber of Meshullam son of Berechiah
D House of Zadok son of Immer
E Houses of the priests
F House of Jedaiah son of Harumaph

© 1980 by The Universities and Colleges Christian Fellowship

(Egyptian documents), dated to the late 5th century B.C., support the account of Nehemiah by mentioning Sanballat the governor of Samaria (2:19), Jehohanan (6:18; 12:23), and Nehemiah's being replaced as governor of Jerusalem by Bigvai (ca. 410 B.C.; Neh. 10:16). Finally, Nehemiah and Malachi represent the last of the OT canonical writings, both in terms of the time the events occurred (Mal. 1–4; Neh. 13) and the time when they were recorded by Ezra. Thus the next messages from God for Israel do not come until over four hundred years of silence had passed, after which the births of John the Baptist and Jesus Christ were announced (Matt. 1; Luke 1, 2).

With the full OT revelation of Israel's history prior to Christ's incarnation being completed, the Jews had not yet experienced the fullness of God's various covenants and promises to them. While there was a Jewish remnant, as promised to Abraham (cf. Gen. 15:5), it does not appear to be even as large as at the time of the Exodus (Num. 1:46). The Jews neither possessed the land (Gen. 15:7) nor did they rule as a sovereign nation (Gen.

12:2). The Davidic throne was unoccupied (cf. 2 Sam. 7:16), although the High-Priest was of the line of Eleazar and Phinehas (cf. Num. 25:10–13). God's promise to consummate the New Covenant of redemption awaited the birth, crucifixion, and resurrection of Messiah (cf. Heb. 7–10).

KEY PEOPLE IN NEHEMIAH
Nehemiah—influential cupbearer of the Persian king Artaxerxes; led the third group of exiles to Jerusalem to rebuild the city walls (1:1–13:31)
Ezra—led the second group of exiles to Jerusalem; worked with Nehemiah as Israel's priest and scribe (8:1–12:36)
Sanballat—governor of Samaria who attempted to discourage the people and thwart the rebuilding of Jerusalem's wall (2:10–13:28)
Tobiah—Ammonite official who mocked the rebuilding of the wall and discouraged the people (2:10–13:7)

HISTORICAL AND THEOLOGICAL THEMES
Careful attention to the reading of God's Word in order to perform His will is a constant theme. The spiritual revival came in response to Ezra's reading of "the Book of the Law of Moses" (8:1). After the reading, Ezra and some of the priests carefully explained its meaning to the people in attendance (8:8). The next day, Ezra met with some of the fathers of the households, the priests, and Levites, "in order to understand the words of the Law" (8:13). The sacrificial system was carried on with careful attention to perform it "as it is written in the Law" (10:34, 36). So deep was their concern to abide by God's revealed will that they took "a curse and an oath to walk in God's Law … " (10:29). When the marriage reforms were carried out, they acted in accordance with that which "they read from the Book of Moses" (13:1).

A second major theme, the obedience of Nehemiah, is explicitly referred to throughout the book due to the fact that the book is based on the memoirs or first person accounts of Nehemiah. God worked through the obedience of Nehemiah; however, He also worked through the ill-motivated, wicked hearts of His enemies. Nehemiah's enemies failed, not so much as a result of the success of Nehemiah's strategies, but because "God had brought their plot to nothing" (4:15). God used the opposition of Judah's enemies to drive His people

KEY WORDS IN

Nehemiah

Confess: Hebrew *yadah*—1:6; 9:2,3—literally, "to throw" or "to cast off." This Hebrew verb conveys the act of "casting off" sin and acknowledging our rebellion against God's commandments (Neh. 1:6; 9:2; Ps. 32:3; Prov. 28:13; Dan. 9:4). Confession also conveys thanksgiving for God's greatness (1 Kin. 8:33,35). Confession of sin is thanksgiving because it recognizes the grace and goodness of God's forgiveness (2 Chr. 30:22; Dan.9:4).

Awesome: Hebrew *yare*'—1:5,11; 4:14; 6:14,19; 7:2—literally, "to fear." This Hebrew word suggests the virtue that inspires reverence or godly fear. Godly fear is closely related to godly living and respect for God's character (Lev. 19:14; 25:17; Deut. 17:19; 2 Kin. 17:34). Thus while ordinary fear paralyzes a person, godly fear leads to submission and obedience to God. The person who properly fears God follows the will of God (Ps. 128:1) and avoids evil (Job 1:1).

to their knees in the same way that He used the favor of Cyrus to return His people to the Land, to fund their building project, and to even protect the reconstruction of Jerusalem's walls. Not surprisingly, Nehemiah acknowledged the true motive of his strategy to repopulate Jerusalem: "my God put it into my heart" (7:5). It was He who accomplished it.

Another theme in Nehemiah, as in Ezra, is opposition. Judah's enemies started rumors that God's people had revolted against Persia. The goal was to intimidate Judah into forestalling reconstruction of the walls. In spite of opposition from without and heartbreaking corruption and dissension from within, Judah completed the walls of Jerusalem in only 52 days (6:15), experienced revival after the reading of the law by Ezra (8:1ff.), and celebrated the Feast of Tabernacles (8:14ff.; ca. 445 B.C.).

The book's detailed insight into the personal thoughts, motives, and disappointments of Nehemiah makes it easy for the reader to primarily identify with him, rather than "the sovereign hand of God" theme and the primary message of His control and intervention into the affairs of His people and their enemies. But the exemplary behavior of the famous cupbearer is eclipsed by God who orchestrated the reconstruction of the walls in spite of much opposition and many setbacks; the "good hand of God" theme carries through the Book of Nehemiah (1:10; 2:8, 18).

Seven Attempts to Stop Nehemiah's Work

1.	2:19	Sanballat, Tobiah, and Geshem mocked Nehemiah.
2.	4:1–3	Sanballat and Tobiah mocked Nehemiah.
3.	4:7–23	The enemy threatened a military attack.
4.	6:1–4	Sanballat and Geshem attempted to lure Nehemiah outside of Jerusalem to Ono.
5.	6:5–9	Sanballat threatened Nehemiah with false charges.
6.	6:10–14	Shemaiah, Noadiah, and others were paid to prophesy falsely and discredit Nehemiah.
7.	6:17–19	Tobiah had spies in Jerusalem and wrote Nehemiah letters in order to frighten him.

KEY DOCTRINES IN NEHEMIAH

God's Word—reading the Word of God requires careful attention in order to perform His will (8:1,8,13; 10:29,34,36; 13:1; Ezra 7:10; Ps. 119:16,140; Luke 11:28; John 5:39; James 1:25)

Obedience—God worked through the obedience of Nehemiah (7:5; Exod. 19:5; Deut.13:4; 1 Sam. 15:22; Jer. 7:23; Eccles. 12:13; Heb.11:6; 1 Pet. 1:2)

Opposition—despite local opposition and heartbreaking corruption, Judah completed the walls of Jerusalem in only fifty-two days (6:15; 8:1,14; Ps. 7:1; 69:26; Zech. 2:8; Matt. 5:10; Luke 6:22; Rom. 8:35; 2 Tim. 3:12)

GOD'S CHARACTER IN NEHEMIAH

God is glorious—9:5
God is good—1:10; 2:8,18; 9:35
God is kind—9:17

God is long-suffering—9:30
God is merciful—9:17, 27
God is powerful—1:10
God is provident—9:6
God is righteous—9:8
God is unified—9:6
God is wise—9:10

INTERPRETIVE CHALLENGES

First, since much of Nehemiah is explained in relationship to Jerusalem's gates (cf. Neh. 2, 3, 8, 12), one needs to see the map "Jerusalem in Nehemiah's Day" for an orientation. Second, the reader must recognize that the time line of chapters 1–12 encompassed about one year (445 B.C.), followed by a long gap of time (over twenty years) after Neh. 12 and before Neh. 13. Finally, it must be recognized that Nehemiah actually served two governorships in Jerusalem, the first from 445–433 B.C. (cf. Neh. 5:14; 13:6) and the second beginning possibly in 424 B.C. and extending to no longer than 410 B.C.

OUTLINE

I. Nehemiah's First Term as Governor (1:1–12:47)
    A. Nehemiah's Return and Reconstruction (1:1–7:73a)
        1. Nehemiah goes to Jerusalem (1:1–2:20)
        2. Nehemiah and the people rebuild the walls (3:1–7:3)
        3. Nehemiah recalls the first return under Zerubbabel (7:4–73a)
    B. Ezra's Revival and Renewal (7:73b–10:39)
        1. Ezra expounds the law (7:73b–8:12)
        2. The people worship and repent (8:13–9:37)
        3. Ezra and the priests renew the covenant (9:38–10:39)
    C. Nehemiah's Resettlement and Rejoicing (11:1–12:47)
        1. Jerusalem is resettled (11:1–12:26)
        2. The people dedicate the walls (12:27–47)
II. Nehemiah's Second Term as Governor (13:1–31)

MEANWHILE, IN OTHER PARTS OF THE WORLD...

Plato begins to study philosophy under the guidance of Socrates (407 to 399 B.C.).

ANSWERS TO TOUGH QUESTIONS

1. What leadership qualities does Nehemiah illustrate by his life?

Like many biblical leaders, Nehemiah demonstrated an understanding of God's call over his life. Whether as cupbearer to a king or as the rebuilder of Jerusalem, Nehemiah pursued his goals with commitment, careful planning, strategic delegation, creative problem solving, focus on the task at hand, and a continual reliance on God, particularly regarding areas beyond his control. Each of the leadership qualities above can be illustrated from Nehemiah's successful completion of the effort to rebuild the walls of Jerusalem.

First, Nehemiah demonstrated his commitment by his interest and his deep concern over the condition of his fellow Jews in Judah. Next, Nehemiah prayed and planned. He claimed God's promise to bring His people back to the Promised Land, but he didn't assume that he would be part of God's action. He declared himself available (1:11; 2:5).

Even when he arrived in Jerusalem, Nehemiah personally inspected the need before he revealed his plans. Then, he enlisted the help of the local leadership. He challenged them to take responsibility for the common good. He placed before them a very specific goal—to rebuild the wall. Workers were assigned to work on the wall where it ran closest to their own homes. That way they could see the benefit in having the protective barrier rebuilt.

As the work sped forward, Nehemiah did not allow himself to be distracted by attacks of various kings or tricks from enemies. He took threats seriously enough to arm the people but not so seriously that the work came to a halt. At every turn, we find Nehemiah conferring in prayer with God, placing every decision before the ultimate Decider. Nehemiah succeeded because he never lost sight of the true reasons for the work and the source of power with which to do the work.

2. How does Nehemiah fit into the time line of world history?

It is unclear how Nehemiah became King Artaxerxes' cupbearer, but the fact that Esther was the king's stepmother may have inclined the king to consider a Jew for such a trusted position. When Nehemiah carried out his mission to rebuild the walls of Jerusalem, the Persian Empire had been dominant for almost a hundred years. King Cyrus's decree of repatriation given back in 539 B.C. had encouraged a group of Jews to return to Israel under Zerubbabel. Their desperate state almost a century later spurred Nehemiah into action.

Ancient Egyptian documents (Elephantine papyri) dated around the 5th century B.C. independently confirm part of Nehemiah's account. Sanballat the governor of Samaria (2.19), Jehohanan (6:18; 12:23), and Nehemiah himself receive mention.

The events recorded in Nehemiah, along with Malachi's prophecies, make up the final inspired writings of the OT. God chose to remain silent for four hundred years after this time. That silence ended with the announcements of John the Baptist's and Jesus' births.

FURTHER STUDY ON NEHEMIAH

1. What personal character trait impresses you the most about Nehemiah?
2. What leadership characteristics are illustrated by Nehemiah's life?
3. How did Nehemiah use prayer in his leadership role?
4. How did Nehemiah deal with problems?
5. Nehemiah's great work began with a desire. What was it and how did it guide his actions?
6. What are the desires that provide you with a large perspective about your life?

ESTHER

A Queen Who Served God

TITLE

"Esther" serves as the title without variation through the ages. This book and the Book of Ruth are the only OT books named after women. Like Song of Solomon, Obadiah, and Nahum, the NT does not quote or allude to Esther.

"Hadassah" (2:7), meaning "myrtle," was the Hebrew name of Esther, which came either from the Persian word "star," or possibly from the name of the Babylonian love goddess, Ishtar. As the orphaned daughter of her father Abihail, Esther grew up in Persia with her older cousin, Mordecai, who raised her as if she were his own daughter (2:7, 15).

AUTHOR AND DATE

The author remains unknown, although Mordecai, Ezra, and Nehemiah have been suggested. Whoever penned Esther possessed a detailed knowledge of Persian customs, etiquette, and history, plus particular familiarity with the palace at Shushan (1:5–7). He also exhibited intimate knowledge of the Hebrew calendar and customs, while additionally showing a strong sense of Jewish nationalism. Possibly a Persian Jew, who later moved back to Israel, wrote Esther.

Esther appears as the seventeenth book in the literary chronology of the OT and closes the OT historical section. Only Ezra 7–10, Nehemiah, and Malachi report later OT history than Esther. The account in Esther ends in 473 B.C. before Ahasuerus died by assassination (ca. 465 B.C.). Esther 10:2 speaks as though Ahasuerus' reign has been completed, so the earliest possible writing date would be after his reign around mid-5th century B.C. The latest reasonable date would be prior to 331 B.C. when Greece conquered Persia.

BACKGROUND AND SETTING

Esther occurred during the Persian period of world history, ca. 539 B.C. (Dan. 5:30, 31) to ca. 331 B.C. (Dan. 8:1–27). Ahasuerus ruled from ca. 486 to 465 B.C.; Esther covers the 483–473 B.C. portion of his reign. The name Ahasuerus represents the Hebrew transliteration of the Persian name "Khshayarsha," while "Xerxes" represents his Greek name.

The events of Esther occurred during the wider time span between the first return of the Jews after the seventy-year captivity in Babylon (Dan. 9:1–19) under Zerubbabel ca. 538 B.C. (Ezra 1–6) and the second return led by Ezra ca. 458 B.C. (Ezra 7–10). Nehemiah's journey (the third return) from Susa to Jerusalem (Neh. 1–2) occurred later (ca. 445 B.C.).

Esther, along with the Book of Exodus, both chronicle how vigorously foreign powers tried to eliminate the Jewish race and how God sovereignly preserved His people in accordance with His covenant promise to Abraham ca. 2100–2075 B.C. (Gen. 12:1–3; 17:1–8). As a result of God's prevailing, Esther 9, 10 records the beginning of Purim—a new annual festival in the twelfth month (Feb.–Mar.) to celebrate the nation's survival. Purim became one of two festivals given outside of the Mosaic legislation to still be celebrated in Israel (Hanukkah, or the Festival of Lights, is the other, cf. John 10:22).

Jewish Feasts

Feast of	Month on Jewish Calendar	Day Corresponding Month	References
Passover	Nisan 14	Mar.–Apr.	Ex. 12:1–14; Matt. 26:17–20
*Unleavened Bread	Nisan 15–21	Mar.–Apr.	Ex. 12:15–20
*Firstfruits	Nisan 6 or Sivan 16	Mar.–Apr., May–June	Lev. 23:9–14; Num. 28:26
Pentecost (Harvest or Weeks)	Sivan 6 (50 days after barley harvest)	May–June	Deut. 16:9–12; Acts 2:1
Trumpets, Rosh Hashanah	Tishri 1, 2	Sept.–Oct.	Num. 29:1–6
Day of Atonement, Yom Kippur	Tishri 10	Sept.–Oct.	Lev. 23:26–32; Heb. 9:7
*Tabernacles (Booths or Ingathering)	Tishri 15–22	Sept.–Oct.	Neh. 8:13–18; John 7:2
Dedication (Lights), Hanukkah	Chislev 25 (8 days)	Nov.–Dec.	John 10:22
Purium (Lots)	Adar 14, 15	Feb.–Mar.	Esth. 9:18–32

*The three major feasts for which all males of Israel were required to travel to the temple in Jerusalem (Ex. 23:14–19).

KEY PEOPLE IN ESTHER

Esther—replaced Vashti as queen of Persia; saved the Jews against Haman's evil plot (2:7–9:32)

Mordecai—adopted and raised Esther; advisor to Esther as queen; later replaced Haman as second in command under King Xerxes (2:5–10:3)

King Xerxes I—king of Persia; married Esther and made her queen (1:1–10:3)

Haman—second in command under King Xerxes; plotted to kill the Jews (3:1–9:25

The Historical Chronology of Esther

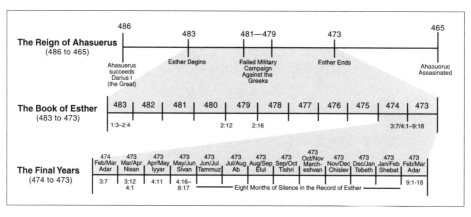

HISTORICAL AND THEOLOGICAL THEMES

All 167 verses of Esther have ultimately been accepted as part of the canon of scripture, although the absence of God's name anywhere has caused some to unnecessarily doubt its authenticity. The Greek Septuagint (LXX) added an extra 107 apocryphal verses which supposedly compensated for this lack. Along with Song of Solomon, Ruth, Ecclesiastes, and Lamentations, Esther stands with the OT books of the Megilloth, or "five scrolls." Rabbis read these books in the synagogue on five special occasions during the year—Esther being read at Purim (cf. 9:20–32).

The historical genesis for the drama played out between Mordecai (a Benjamite descendant of Saul—2:5) and Haman (an Agagite—3:1, 10; 8:3, 5; 9:24) goes back almost 1,000 years, when the Jews exited from Egypt (ca. 1445 B.C.) and were attacked by the Amalekites (Exod. 17:8–16), whose lineage began with Amalek, son of Esau (Gen. 36:12). God pronounced His curse on the Amalekites, which resulted in their total elimination as a people (Exod. 17:14; Deut. 25:17–19). Although Saul (ca. 1030 B.C.) received orders to kill all the Amalekites, including their king Agag (1 Sam. 15:2, 3), he disobeyed (1 Sam. 15:7–9) and incurred God's displeasure (1 Sam. 15:11, 26; 28:18). Samuel finally hacked Agag into pieces (1 Sam. 15:32, 33). Because of his lineage from Agag, Haman carried deep hostility toward the Jews.

CHRIST IN . . . ESTHER

ALTHOUGH ESTHER DOES NOT mention God specifically, His sovereign protection over His people remains apparent throughout the book. God placed Esther in the key position to impede Haman's plan to destroy the Jews. Esther typifies Christ in her willingness to lay down her life to save her people. Esther also represents the position of Christ as Israel's advocate. In all these events, God declares His love for Israel in His constant watch over the Jews: "Behold, He who keeps Israel shall neither slumber nor sleep" (Ps.121:4).

The time of Esther arrived 550 years after the death of Agag, but in spite of such passage of time, neither Haman the Agagite nor Mordecai the Benjamite had forgotten the tribal feud that still smoldered in their souls. This explains why Mordecai refused to bow down to Haman (3:2, 3), and why Haman so viciously attempted to exterminate the Jewish race (3:5, 6, 13). As expected, God's prophecy to extinguish the Amalekites (Exod. 17:14; Deut. 25:17–19) and God's promise to preserve the Jews (Gen. 17:1–8) prevailed.

Because of God's faithfulness to save His people, the festival of Purim (named after the Akkadian word for "lot"—3:7; 9:26), an annual, two day holiday of feasting, rejoicing, sending food to one another, and giving gifts to the poor (9:21, 22), was decreed to be celebrated in every generation, by every family, in every province and city (9:27, 28). Esther later added a new feature of fasting with lamentation (9:31). Purim is not biblically mentioned again, although it has been celebrated throughout the centuries in Israel.

Esther could be compared to a chess game. God and Satan (as invisible players) moved real kings, queens, and nobles. When Satan put Haman into place, it was as if he announced, "Check." God then positioned Esther and Mordecai in order to put Satan into "Checkmate!" Ever since the fall of man (Gen. 3:1–19), Satan has attempted to spiritually sever God's relationship with His human creation and disrupt God's covenant promises with Israel. For example, Christ's line through the tribe of Judah had been murderously reduced to Joash alone, who was rescued and preserved (2 Chr. 22:10–12). Later, Herod slaughtered the infants of Bethlehem, thinking Christ was among them (Matt. 2:16). Satan tempted Christ to denounce God and worship him (Matt. 4:9). Peter, at Satan's insistence, tried to block Christ's journey to Calvary (Matt. 16:22). Finally, Satan entered into Judas who then betrayed Christ to the Jews and Romans (Luke 22:3–6). While God was not mentioned in Esther, He was everywhere apparent as the One who opposed and foiled Satan's diabolical schemes by providential intervention.

In Esther, all of God's unconditional covenant promises to Abraham (Gen. 17:1–8) and to David (2 Sam. 7:8–16) were jeopardized. However, God's love for Israel is nowhere more apparent than in this dramatic rescue of His people from pending elimination.

KEY DOCTRINES IN ESTHER

> Purim as a celebration of God's faithfulness (3:7; 9:21,22, 26–28, 31; Deut. 16:11,14; Neh. 8:10, 12)
>
> God's promise to preserve the Jews (4:14; 8:17; Gen. 17:1–8; 2 Sam. 7:8–16; 2 Chr. 22:10–12; Ps. 121:4; Isai. 65:8–9; Jer. 50:20; Matt. 2:16)

GOD'S CHARACTER IN ESTHER

God is provident—8:5–17

INTERPRETIVE CHALLENGES

The most obvious challenge raised by Esther comes from the fact that God is nowhere mentioned (as in the Book of the Song of Solomon). The skeptic might ask, "Why would God never be mentioned when the Persian king receives over 175 references? Since God's sovereignty prevailed to save the Jews, why does He then not receive appropriate recognition?" It seems satisfying to respond that if God desired to be mentioned, He could just as sovereignly have moved the author to write of Him as He acted to save Israel. This situa-

---

KEY WORDS IN

Esther

Fasting: Hebrew *tsum*—4:3; 4:16—root word simply means "to abstain from food." At times fasting meant abstaining from drinking, bathing, anointing with oil, or sexual intercourse as well. In essence, fasting acknowledges human frailty before God and appeals to His mercy. Fasting was a common practice in the ancient world, associated with mourning for the dead (2 Sam. 12:21,22), intercessory prayer (4:3,16), repentance and contrition for sin (Jer. 36:9; Jon. 3:5), and times of distress (Judg. 20:26; Neh. 1:4). Fasting was required for the Day of Atonement (see the phrase "afflict your souls" in Lev. 16:31). Fasts varied in length from one day (1 Sam. 14:24; Dan. 6:18) to seven days (1 Sam. 31:13) and could even last up to forty days on extraordinary occasions (Exod. 34:28). But no matter what type of fasting was performed, the prophet Isaiah admonished his people to participate in acts of righteousness and social justice with their fasting (Is. 58:3–9).

Pur: Hebrew *pur*—3:7; 9:24,26—in the Book of Esther refers to the Hebrew word for "lot." People cast lots, similar to rolling dice, to make random selections (Neh. 11:1). Lots were also used to apprehend the will of certain gods (Jon. 1:7). In Esther, Haman cast lots to determine the right day to destroy the Jews. God, on the other hand, revealed His sovereign power by choosing that particular day to deliver the Jews. Even today, Jews celebrate the festival of Purim in remembrance of their deliverance (9:28).

tion seems to be more of a problem at the human level than the divine, because Esther is the classic illustration of God's providence as He, the unseen power, controls everything for His purpose. There are no miracles in Esther, but the preservation of Israel through providential control of every event and person reveals God's infinite knowledge and power. Whether He is named is not the issue. He is clearly the main character in the drama.

A second interpretative challenge is the fact that Mordecai and Esther appeared to live a secular lifestyle, and did not seem to have a zeal for holiness. Mordecai kept his and Esther's Jewish heritage secret, unlike Daniel (Dan. 6:5). The law of God was absent, in contrast to Ezra (Ezra 7:10). Nehemiah had a heart for Jerusalem that seemingly eluded the affections of Esther and Mordecai (Neh. 1:1–2:5). (See Answers to Tough Questions for further observations on this issue.)

OUTLINE
    I. **Esther Replaces Vashti (1:1–2:18)**
        A. Vashti's Insubordination (1:1–22)
        B. Esther's Coronation (2:1–18)
    II. **Mordecai Overcomes Haman (2:19–7:10)**
        A. Mordecai's Loyalty (2:19–23)
        B. Haman's Promotion and Decree (3:1–15)
        C. Esther's Intervention (4:1–5:14)
        D. Mordecai's Recognition (6:1–13)
        E. Haman's Fall (6:14–7:10)
    III. **Israel Survives Haman's Genocide Attempt (8:1–10:3)**
        A. Esther and Mordecai's Advocacy (8:1–17)
        B. The Jews' Victory (9:1–19)
        C. Purim's Beginning (9:20–23)
        D. Mordecai's Fame (10:1–3)

MEANWHILE, IN OTHER PARTS OF THE WORLD...
The Chinese complete the construction of the first wall to prevent the Hun people from entering China (356 B.C.).

ANSWERS TO TOUGH QUESTIONS
1. Why isn't God directly mentioned in Esther?
The usual clues about God's presence seem absent. No one refers to the Law of God, sacrifices, worship, or prayer. God does not appear to receive public or private recognition for the preservation of the Jews. When it comes to God, Esther seems strangely silent.

In fact, the silence is so obvious that it becomes an argument. Esther challenges the tendency to demand that God prove His power and presence. Must God be apparent? All too quickly we expect God to demonstrate in unmistakable ways His identity. Yet God has repeatedly resisted human ultimatums. God reveals Himself for His own purposes, not human requirements.

Throughout history, God has more readily operated behind the scenes than in plain sight. The Scriptures are filled with unusual circumstances in which God worked obviously. But Esther comes close to revealing God's standard procedure. God's fingerprints are all over Esther's story. His superficial absence points to a deeper presence. God chose to be subtle, but He was there. The events in Esther give us a model for hope when God works in less than obvious ways in our lives.

2. Why do Esther and Mordecai appear so secular in their lifestyles?
In contrast to their near contemporaries Ezra, Nehemiah, and Daniel, the central people in Esther seem worldly. The lack of references to God is most obvious in Esther and Mordecai's conversations. Are these all subtle indications that Esther and Mordecai were people whose faith had little or no effect on their daily lives?

The Book of Esther does not settle this question. There are several important factors, however, that might hold us back from jumping to conclusions about Esther and Mordecai. Primary among these is the fact that the book has a limited scope. Only a few key events are recorded. Few, if any, details of the inner life of either main character are revealed. Yet the integrity of their actions ought to incline us toward giving them the benefit of the doubt when it comes to faith (4:13–16).

Here are a few other considerations regarding this question: (1) While Mordecai's caution about announcing his and Esther's heritage publicly might be questioned, it must also be pointed out that others were also cautious about this same matter (Nehemiah makes no mention of God in his conversation with Artaxerxes recorded in Nehemiah 2:1–8); (2) Public events such as Passover had fallen out of practice during the captivity, meaning that there were fewer occasions in which faith was practiced in the open (this doesn't mean, however, that the Jews were not a marked people, since they could be identified for the purpose of Haman's law); (3) When it was appropriate, Esther did openly identify her Jewish heritage (7:3–4). These considerations do not remove the charge that Esther and Mordecai seem less devoted to God than, for example, Daniel. But the fact that God did work out His purposes in their lives comes through clearly in the book.

FURTHER STUDY ON ESTHER
1. What insights about the evil of racism can you identify in Esther?
2. Although God is not specifically mentioned in Esther, how do you see Him working?
3. What kind of a person was Esther? How do you know?
4. In what different ways did God arrange for the deliverance and safety of His people?
5. Contrast the characters of Haman and Mordecai.
6. In what ways would you say you are actively involved to make a difference in your own time of history?

JOB
The Righteous Can Suffer

TITLE

As with other books of the Bible, Job bears the name of the narrative's primary character. This name might have been derived from the Hebrew word for "persecution," thus meaning "persecuted one," or from an Arabic word meaning "repent," thus bearing the name "repentant one." The author recounts an era in the life of Job, in which he was tested and the character of God was revealed. NT writers directly quote Job two times (Rom. 11:35; 1 Cor. 3:19), plus Ezekiel 14:14, 20 and James 5:11 show Job was a real person.

AUTHOR AND DATE

The book does not name its author. Job is an unlikely candidate because the book's message rests on Job's ignorance of the events that occurred in heaven as they related to his ordeal. One Jewish Talmudic tradition suggests Moses as author, since the land of Uz (1:1) was adjacent to Midian where Moses lived for forty years, and he could have obtained a record of the story there. Solomon is also a good possibility due to the similarity of content with parts of the Book of Ecclesiastes, as well as the fact that Solomon wrote the other Wisdom books (except Psalms, and he did author Pss. 72; 127). Though he lived long after Job, Solomon could have written about events that occurred long before his own time, in much the same manner as Moses was inspired to write about Adam and Eve. Elihu, Isaiah, Hezekiah, Jeremiah, and Ezra have also been suggested as possible authors, but without support.

The date of the book's writing may be much later than the events recorded therein. This conclusion is based on: (1) Job's age (42:16); (2) his life span of nearly 200 years (42:16), which fits the patriarchal period (Abraham lived 175 years; Gen. 25:7); (3) the social unit being the patriarchal family; (4) the Chaldeans who murdered Job's servants (1:17) were nomads and had not yet become city dwellers; (5) Job's wealth being measured in livestock rather than gold and silver (1:3; 42:12); (6) Job's priestly functions within his family (1:4,5); and (7) a basic silence on matters such as the covenant of Abraham, Israel, the Exodus, and the law of Moses. The events of Job's odyssey appear to be patriarchal. Job, on the other hand, seemed to know about Adam (31:33) and Noah and the Flood (12:15). These cultural/historical features found in the book appear to place the events chronologically at a time probably after Babel (Gen. 11:1–9) but before or during the period of Abraham (Gen. 11:27ff.), making it the most ancient book in the Bible.

Biographical Sketch of Job

1. A spiritually mature man (1:1, 8; 2:3)
2. Father of many children (1:2; 42:13)
3. Owner of many herds (1:3; 42:12)
4. A wealthy and influential man (1:3b)
5. A priest to his family (1:5)
6. A loving, wise husband (2:9)
7. A man of prominence in community affairs (29:7–11)
8. A man of benevolence (29:12–17; 31:32)
9. A wise leader (29:21–24)
10. Grower of crops (31:38–40)

BACKGROUND AND SETTING

This book begins with a scene in heaven that explains everything to the reader (1:6–2:10). Job was suffering because God was contesting with Satan. Job was not aware of this big picture, nor were his friends, so they all struggled to explain suffering from the perspective of their ignorance. Finally Job rested in nothing but faith in God's goodness and the hope of His redemption. That God vindicated his trust is the culminating message of the book. When there are no rational, or even theological, explanations for disaster and pain, trust God.

KEY PEOPLE IN JOB

Job—patient under suffering; his faith was tested by God but he did not sin by blaming God (1:1–42:16)

Eliphaz the Temanite—a friend of Job; believed Job was suffering because of his sin (2:11; 4:1–5:27; 15:1–35; 22:1–30; 42:7–9)

Bildad the Shuhite—another friend of Job; believed Job had not repented of his sin and therefore suffered (2:11; 8:1–22; 18:1–21; 25:1–6; 42:9)

Zophar the Naamathite—a third friend of Job; believed Job deserved to suffer more for his sins (2:11; 11:1–20; 20:1–29; 42:9)

Elihu the Buzite—stood up against Job's three friends; believed God was using suffering to mold Job's character (32:1–37:24)

HISTORICAL AND THEOLOGICAL THEMES

The occasion and events that follow Job's sufferings present significant questions for the faith of believers in all ages. Why does Job serve God? Job is heralded for his righteousness, being compared with Noah and Daniel (Ezek. 14:14–20), and for his spiritual endurance (James 5:11). Several other questions are alluded to throughout Job's ordeal, for instance, "Why do the righteous suffer?" Though an answer to that question may seem important, the book does not set forth such an answer. Job never

CHRIST IN . . . JOB

THE BOOK OF JOB raises many questions over the purpose of suffering. While direct answers are difficult to find in Job, our hope rests in Christ who identifies with our suffering (Heb. 4:15). Ultimately, Job cries out to Christ, the Mediator between God and man (9:33; 25:4; 33:23).

knew the reasons for his suffering and neither did his friends. The righteous sufferer does not appear to learn about any of the heavenly court debates between God and Satan that precipitated his pain. In fact, when finally confronted by the Lord of the universe, Job put his hand over his mouth and said nothing. Job's silent response in no way trivialized the intense pain and loss he had endured. It merely underscored the importance of trusting God's purposes in the midst of suffering because suffering, like all other human experiences, is directed by perfect divine wisdom. In the end, the lesson learned was that one may never know the specific reason for his suffering; but one must trust in Sovereign God. That is the real answer to suffering.

The book treats two major themes and many other minor ones, both in the narrative framework of the prologue (chaps. 1, 2) and epilogue (42:7–17), and in the poetic account of Job's torment that lies in between (3:1–42:6). A key to understanding the first theme of the book is to notice the debate between God and Satan in heaven and how it connects with the three cycles of earthly debates between Job and his friends. God wanted to prove the character of believers to Satan and to all demons, angels, and people. The accusations are by Satan, who indicted God's claims of Job's righteousness as being untested, if not questionable. Satan accused the righteous of being faithful to God only for what they could get. Since Job did not serve God with pure motives, according to Satan, the whole relationship between him and God was a sham. Satan's confidence that he could turn Job against God came, no doubt, from the fact that he had led the holy angels to rebel with him. Satan thought he could destroy Job's faith in God by inflicting suffering on him, thus showing in principle that saving faith could be shattered. God released Satan to make his point if he could, but he failed, as true faith in God proved unbreakable. Even Job's wife told him to curse God (2:9), but he refused; his faith in God never failed (see 13:15). Satan tried to do the same to Peter (see Luke 22:31–34) and was unsuccessful in destroying Peter's faith (see John 21:15–19). When Satan has unleashed all that he can do to destroy saving faith, it stands firm (cf. Rom. 8:31–39). In the end, God proved His point with Satan that saving faith can't be destroyed no matter how much trouble a saint suffers, or how incomprehensible and undeserved it seems.

A Comparison of Satan's Theology with That of Job's Friends

Satan	Friends
IF Job is blessed by God,	THEN he will be faithful.
IF Job is faithful,	THEN he will be blessed.
OR	
IF Job is not blessed by God, (Satan accused God of bribing His followers.)	THEN he will be unfaithful.
IF Job is unfaithful,	THEN he will be punished.

A second and related theme concerns proving the character of God to men. Does this sort of ordeal, in which God and His opponent Satan square off, with righteous Job as the test case, suggest that God is lacking in compassion and mercy toward Job? Not at all. As James says, "You have heard of the perseverance of Job and have seen the end *intended* by the Lord—that the Lord is very compassionate and merciful" (James 5:11). It was to prove the very opposite (42:10–17). Job says, "Shall we indeed accept good from God, and shall we not accept adversity?" (2:10). God's servant does not deny that he has suffered. He does deny that his suffering is a result of sin. Nor does he understand why he suffers. Job simply commits his ordeal with a devout heart of worship and humility (42:5, 6) to a sovereign and perfectly wise Creator—and that was what God wanted him to learn in this conflict with Satan. In the end, God flooded Job with more blessings than he had ever known.

God's Challenge to Job

In the face of God's fearful challenge, Job could only humble himself:	
God's Challenge	**Job's Response**
First, Job's ignorance (38:1-40:2) • He was absent at creation • He cannot explain the forces of nature	Job admits his ignorance and becomes silent (40:3–5)
Second, Job's frailty (40:6-41:34) • He cannot overrule God's ways • He cannot control the forces of nature	Job confesses his presumption and repents (42:2–6)

The major reality of the book is the inscrutable mystery of innocent suffering. God ordains that His children walk in sorrow and pain, sometimes because of sin (cf. Num. 12:10–12), sometimes for chastening (cf. Heb. 12:5–12), sometimes for strengthening (cf. 2 Cor. 12:7–10; 1 Pet. 5:10), and sometimes to give opportunity to reveal His comfort and grace (2 Cor. 1:3–7). But there are times when the compelling issue in the suffering of the saints is unknowable because it is for a heavenly purpose that those on earth can't discern (cf. Exod. 4:11; John 9:1–3).

Job and his friends wanted to analyze the suffering and look for causes and solutions. Using all of their sound theology and insight into the situation, they searched for answers, but found only useless and wrong ideas, for which God rebuked them in the end (42:7). They couldn't know why Job suffered because what happened in heaven between God and Satan was unknown to them. They thought they knew all the answers, but they only intensified the dilemma by their insistent ignorance.

By spreading out some of the elements of this great theme, we can see the following truths in Job's experience:

There are matters going on in heaven with God that believers know nothing about; yet, they affect their lives.

Even the best effort at explaining the issues of life can be useless.

God's people do suffer. Bad things happen all the time to good people, so one cannot judge a person's spirituality by his painful circumstances or successes.

Even though God seems far away, perseverance in faith is a most noble virtue since God is good and one can safely leave his life in His hands.

The believer in the midst of suffering should not abandon God, but draw near to Him, so out of the fellowship can come the comfort—without the explanation.

Suffering may be intense, but it will ultimately end for the righteous and God will bless abundantly.

KEY DOCTRINES IN JOB

Faithfulness in the midst of suffering (2:9; 13:15; Num. 12:10–12; Luke 22:31–34; John 21:15–19; 2 Cor. 1:3–7; 12:7–10; Heb. 12:5–12; 1 Pet. 5:10)

GOD'S CHARACTER IN JOB

God is delivering—33:27,28
God is glorious—37:22
God is invisible—23:8,9
God is just—4:17; 8:3; 34:12; 37:23
God is loving—7:17
God is powerful—5:9; 9:4,10; 26:14; 36:22; 40:9
God is provident—1:21; 26:10; 37:9–13
God is righteous—36:3
God is unsearchable—11:7; 37:23
God is wise—9:4; 11:11; 21:22; 23:10; 28:24; 34:21; 36:4,5; 37:16
God is wrathful—9:13; 14:13; 21:17

INTERPRETIVE CHALLENGES

The most critical interpretive challenge involves the book's primary message. Although often thought to be the pressing issue of the book, the question of why Job suffers is never revealed to Job, though the reader knows that it involves God's proving a point to Satan—a matter completely beyond Job's understanding. James' commentary on Job's case (5:11) draws the conclusion that it was to show God's compassion and mercy, but without apology, offers no explanation for Job's specific ordeal. Readers find themselves, putting their hands over their mouths, figuratively speaking, with no right to question or accuse the all-wise and all-powerful Creator, who will do as He pleases. In so doing, He both proves His points in the spiritual realm to angels and demons and defines His compassion and mercy. Engaging in "theodicy," i.e., man's attempt to defend God's involvement in calamity and suffering, is shown to be appropriate in these circumstances, though in the end, it is apparent that God does not need nor want a humanly crafted defense. The Book of Job expressively illustrates Deut. 29:29, "The secret things belong to the LORD our God … "

KEY WORDS IN Job

Blameless: Hebrew *tam*—1:1,8; 2:3; 8:20; 9:20-22—means "to be complete." This word signifies an individual's integrity: a wholeness and wholesomeness. The word is used as a term of endearment for the Shulamite bride in the Song of Solomon (see "perfect" in 5:2; 6:9). In the OT, blamelessness is frequently associated with the upright (1:1,8; 2:3; Ps. 37:37; Prov. 29:10) in contrast to the wicked (9:22; Ps. 64:2-4). Job's claim to be blameless agrees with God's assessment of him, but it is not a claim to absolute perfection (1:8; 9:21; 14:16,17). The psalmist writes that the future of the blameless man is peace, as was the case for Job (42:10-12; Ps. 37:37).

Affliction: Hebrew *'oni*—10:15; 30:16,27; 36:8,15,21—comes from a root meaning "misery" or "poverty." The image evoked by this word is that of a person bowed down under the weight of a heavy burden. Scripture portrays the Lord as seeing the afflictions that bring pain to His people and hearing the anguished cries of those in distress (as in Gen. 16:11; Exod. 2:23-25). The Lord urges us to place our burdens on Him, for He is strong enough to bear them and loves us so much that He will assist us in our time of need (1 Pet. 5:7). Moreover, since He controls all events, we can be assured that He is accomplishing good out of the temporary difficulties we are now facing (Rom. 8:28). The entire story of Job provides vivid example of this fact (42:10-17; 2 Cor. 12:7-10).

Behold: Hebrew *ra'ah*—19:27; 22:12; 40:11—common term used in reference to the natural function of the eyes and is thus most often translated as "see" (Gen. 48:10; Deut.1:8; 2 Kin. 3:14; Mic. 7:9,10). The word also has a number of metaphorical meanings, such as acceptance (Gen. 7:1; Num. 23:21) and provision (Gen. 22:8,14; 1 Sam.16:1). It can even convey the notion of assurance and salvation, as is the case here. In 42:5 the word means "to see," in the sense of "to come to recognize" or "to experience fully" something previously known or understood.

The nature of Job's guilt and innocence raises perplexing questions. God declared Job perfect, upright, fearing God, and shunning evil (Job 1:1). But Job's comforters raised a critical question based on Job's ordeal: Had not Job sinned? On several occasions Job readily admitted to having sinned (7:21; 13:26). But Job questioned the extent of his sin as compared to the severity of his suffering. God rebuked Job in the end for his demands to be vindicated of the comforters' accusations (Job 38–41). But He also declared that what Job said was correct and what the comforters said was wrong (42:7).

Another challenge comes in keeping separate the assumptions that Job and his comforters brought to Job's ordeal. At the outset, all agreed that God punishes evil, rewards obedience, and no exceptions are possible. Job, due to his suffering, was forced to conclude that exceptions are possible and that the righteous also suffer. He also observed that the wicked prosper. These are more than small exceptions to the rule, thus forcing Job to rethink his simple understanding about God's sovereign interaction with His people. The type of wisdom Job finally comes to embrace was not dependent merely on the promise of reward or punishment. The long disputes between Job and his accusers were attempts to reconcile the their observations about the injustice of God's punishment in Job's life. Such a method is dangerous since the mind of God is too vast to be understood by human rationality. In the end, God offered no explanation to Job, but rather called all parties to a deeper level of trust in the Creator, who rules over a sin-confused world with power and authority directed by perfect wisdom and mercy. Understanding this book requires (1) understanding the nature of wisdom, particularly the difference between man's wisdom and God's, and (2) admitting that Job and his friends lacked the divine wisdom to interpret Job's circumstances accurately, though his friends kept trying while Job learned to be content in God's sovereignty and mercy. The turning point or resolution for this matter is found in Job 28 where the character of divine wisdom is explained: divine wisdom is rare and priceless; man cannot hope to purchase it; and God possesses it all. We may not know what is going on in heaven or what God's purposes are, but we must trust Him. Because of this, the matter of believers suffering takes a back seat to the matter of divine wisdom.

OUTLINE

    I. The Dilemma (1:1–2:13)
        A. Introduction of Job (1:1–5)
        B. Divine Debates with Satan (1:6–2:10)
        C. Arrival of Friends (2:11–13)
    II. The Debates (3:1–37:24)
        A. The First Cycle (3:1–14:22)
            1. Job's first speech expresses despair (3:1–26)
            2. Eliphaz's first speech kindly protests and urges humility and repentance (4:1–5:27)
            3. Job's reply to Eliphaz expresses anguish and questions the trials, asking for sympathy in his pain (6:1–7:21)
            4. Bildad's first speech accuses Job of impugning God (8:1–22)
            5. Job's response to Bildad admits he is not perfect, but may protest what seems unfair (9:1–10:22)

6. Zophar's first speech tells Job to get right with God (11:1–20)
7. Job's response to Zophar tells his friends they are wrong and only God knows and will, hopefully, speak to him (12:1–14:22)

B. The Second Cycle (15:1–21:34)

1. Eliphaz's second speech accuses Job of presumption and disregarding the wisdom of the ancients (15:1–35)
2. Job's response to Eliphaz appeals to God against his unjust accusers (16:1–17:16)
3. Bildad's second speech tells Job he is suffering just what he deserves (18:1–21)
4. Job's response to Bildad cries out to God for pity (19:1–29)
5. Zophar's second speech accuses Job of rejecting God by questioning His justice (20:1–29)
6. Job's response to Zophar says he is out of touch with reality (21:1–34)

C. The Third Cycle (22:1–26:14)

1. Eliphaz's third speech denounces Job's criticism of God's justice (22:1–30)
2. Job's response to Eliphaz is that God knows he is without guilt, and yet in His providence and refining purpose He permits temporary success for the wicked (23:1–24:25)
3. Bildad's third speech scoffs at Job's direct appeal to God (25:1–6)
4. Job's response to Bildad that God is indeed perfectly wise and absolutely sovereign, but not so simple as they thought (26:1–14)

D. The Final Defense of Job (27:1–31:40)

1. Job's first monologue affirms his righteousness and that man can't discover God's wisdom (27:1–28:28)
2. Job's second monologue remembers his past, describes his present, defends his innocence, and asks for God to defend him (29:1–31:40)

E. The Speeches of Elihu (32:1–37:24)

1. Elihu enters into the debate to break the impasse (32:1–22)
2. Elihu charges Job with presumption in criticizing God, not recognizing that God may have a loving purpose, even in allowing Job to suffer (33:1–33)
3. Elihu declares that Job has questioned God's integrity by claiming that it does not pay to lead a godly life (34:1–37)
4. Elihu urges Job to wait patiently for the Lord (35:1–16)
5. Elihu believes that God is disciplining Job (36:1–21)

6. Elihu argues that human observers can hardly expect to understand adequately God's dealings in administering justice and mercy (36:22–37:24)

III. **The Deliverance (38:1–42:17)**
   A. God Interrogates Job (38:1–41:34)
      1. God's first response to Job (38:1–40:2)
      2. Job's answer to God (40:3–5)
      3. God's second response to Job (40:6–41:34)
   B. Job Confesses, Worships, and Is Vindicated (42:1–17)
      1. Job passes judgment upon himself (42:1–6)
      2. God rebukes Eliphaz, Bildad, and Zophar (42:7–9)
      3. God restores Job's family, wealth, and long life (42:10–17)

MEANWHILE, IN OTHER PARTS OF THE WORLD...
The Egyptians discover the use of papyrus and establish the first libraries in Egypt.

ANSWERS TO TOUGH QUESTIONS
1. What kind of relationship did Job have with God?

Job's biography begins with a four-part description of his character: "blameless and upright, and one who feared God and shunned evil" (1:1). He prayed for his children and was concerned about their relationship with God (1:5). He was successful and wealthy, the stereotype of a blessed man. In fact, God adds His own glowing approval of Job, using the same traits that open the book (1:8).

Faced with the sudden, crushing loss of everything—children, servants, herds— Job's initial response was to grieve and recognize God's sovereignty. "'The Lord gave, and the Lord has taken away; Blessed be the name of the Lord.' In all this Job did not sin nor charge God with wrong" (1:21b,22).

Under the harsh judgments of his friends, Job eventually struggled to understand why God seemed unwilling to settle matters. Once God did speak, at least part of Job's problem becomes clear: He confused a relationship with God with familiarity with God. The Lord did not rebuke Job's faith or sincerity; instead, God questioned Job's insistence on an answer for his difficulties. By allowing Job to hear just a little of the extent of his ignorance, God showed Job that there was a great deal he would never understand. As a creature, Job simply had no right to demand an answer from his Creator. Job's final words are filled with humility and repentance: "I have heard of You by the hearing of the ear, but now my eye sees You. Therefore I abhor myself, and repent in dust and ashes" (42:5,6).

Job spent his last days enjoying the same kind of relationship he had earlier with God. He prayed for his friends and raised another family of godly children. He lived a full life.

2. What kind of relationship does Satan have with God in the Book of Job?

Satan may be God's sworn enemy, but they are not equals. Satan is a creature; God is the Creator. Satan was an angel unwilling to serve in his exalted role, and he rebelled against God.

The continual conflict between Satan and God is illustrated when Satan states that righteous people remain faithful to God only because of what they get. They trust in God only as long as God is nice to them. Satan challenged God's claims of Job's righteousness by calling it un-tested, if not questionable. Apparently Satan was convinced that he could destroy Job's faith in God by inflicting suffering on him.

Satan suffered another defeat as God demonstrated through Job's life that saving faith can't be destroyed no matter how much trouble the believer suffers or how incomprehensible and undeserved the suffering seems.

After failing to destroy Job, Satan disappears from the story. He remains God's defeated enemy, still raging against God's inevitable triumph.

3. Why do righteous and innocent people suffer?

Of course no human being is truly righteous or innocent. The Bible clearly states that all have sinned (Rom. 3:23). All sinners deserve to be punished, eternally. That's what makes God's grace so amazing!

In understanding that truth, however, it must be admitted that on a relative human scale, righteous and innocent people exist. That is, some people are more moral and virtuous than others and some are more innocent. Consider, for example, a person who strives to live out the Golden Rule, or another who gives generously to the poor. And certainly most consider small children to have a naive innocence. So this question could be rephrased: "Why do little children and people who live exemplary lives suffer?"

This question reveals the assumption that there is a direct connection between righteousness and innocence on the one hand and pain-free living on the other. There may be a connection, but it is not direct. Indeed, sin eventually does lead to suffering, but suffering is not an in-fallible indicator of sin. Job's friends could not see beyond this point. For them, a person's suffering was always an effect whose only cause could be that person's sin.

The righteous and the innocent do indeed suffer for a variety of reasons: (1) Sometimes righteous actions in a sinful world involve suffering, as when a righteous person sacrifices his or her life for another; (2) Sometimes the sins of others involve the righteous in suffering, as when a child is deeply hurt as a result of his or her parent's actions; (3) The righteous and innocent are not exempt from the painful situations which arise in an imperfect and sinful world, like toothaches and smashed fingers; (4) People sometimes suffer for no specific reason that can be clarified. Job is a perfect illustration of this last experience.

4. Why doesn't God answer all of Job's (and our) questions?

This question assumes that if God answered all our questions, it would be easier to believe. This is not true. Trust goes beyond answers. Sometimes, questions become a way to avoid trust.

In the end, we must trust God more than our capacity to understand God's ways. The lesson from Job's experience does not forbid us from asking questions. Often these questions will lead us to the reasons for our suffering. But Job's experience also warns us that we may not be able to understand all our suffering all the time, or even any of it some of the time.

God doesn't answer all of our questions because we are simply unable to understand many of His answers.

FURTHER STUDY ON JOB

1. What do we learn about the character of Satan from the Book of Job?
2. Summarize the arguments of Job's friends.
3. What does God say to Job's friends?
4. What does God finally say to Job?
5. How does Job change from the righteous man who begins the book to the one who ends the book?
6. How does the Book of Job affect your questions about suffering?

PSALMS
Songbook of a Nation

TITLE

The entire collection of Psalms is entitled "Praises" in the Hebrew text. Later, rabbis often designated it "The Book of Praises." The Septuagint (LXX), the Greek translation of the OT, labeled it "Psalms" (cf. "The Book of Psalms" in the NT: Luke 20:42; Acts 1:20). The Greek verb from which the noun "psalms" comes basically denotes the "plucking or twanging of strings," so that an association with musical accompaniment is implied. The English title derives from the Greek term and its background. The Psalms constituted Israel's ancient, God-breathed (2 Tim. 3:16) "hymnbook," which defined the proper spirit and content of worship.

There are 116 psalms that have superscriptions or "titles." The Hebrew text includes these titles with the verses themselves. When the titles are surveyed individually and studied as a general phenomenon, there are significant indications that they were appended to their respective psalms shortly after composition and that they contain reliable information (cf. Luke 20:42).

These titles convey various kinds of information such as authorship, dedication, historical occasion, liturgical assignment to a worship director, liturgical instructions (e.g., what kind of song it is, whether it is to have a musical accompaniment, and what tune to use), plus other technical instructions of uncertain meaning due to their ancient context. One very tiny, attached Hebrew preposition shows up in the majority of the psalm titles. It may convey different relationships, e.g., "of," "from," "by," "to," "for," "in reference to," "about." Sometimes it occurs more than once, even in short headings, usually supplying "of" or "by" person X, "to" or "for" person Y information. However, this little preposition most frequently indicates the authorship of a psalm, whether "of" David, the accomplished psalmist of Israel, or "by" Moses, Solomon, Asaph, or the sons of Korah.

AUTHOR AND DATE

From the divine perspective, the Psalter points to God as its author. Approaching authorship from the human side one can identify a collection of more than seven composers. King David wrote at least 75 of the 150 psalms; the sons of Korah accounted for 10 (Pss. 42, 44–49, 84, 85, 87); and Asaph contributed 12 (Pss. 50, 73–83). Other penmen included Solomon (Pss. 72, 127), Moses (Ps. 90), Heman (Ps. 88), and Ethan (Ps. 89). The remaining 48 psalms remain anonymous in their authorship, although Ezra is thought to be the author of some. The time range of the Psalms extends from Moses, ca. 1410 B.C. (Ps. 90), to the late sixth or early fifth century B.C. post-Exilic period (Ps. 126), which spans about 900 years of Jewish history.

BACKGROUND AND SETTING

The backdrop for the Psalms is twofold: (1) the acts of God in creation and history, and (2) the history of Israel. Historically, the psalms range in time from the origin of life to the post-Exilic joys of the Jews liberated from Babylon. Thematically, the psalms cover a wide spectrum of topics, ranging from heavenly worship to earthly war. The collected psalms comprise the largest book in the Bible and the most frequently quoted OT book in the NT.

Psalm 117 represents the middle chapter (out of 1,189) in the Bible. Psalm 119 is the largest chapter in the entire Bible. Through the ages, the psalms have retained their original primary purpose, i.e., to engender the proper praise and worship of God

Historical Background to Psalms by David

Psalm	Historical Background	OT Text
Psalm 3	when David fled from Absalom his son	2 Samuel 15:13–17
Psalm 7	concerning the words of Cush a Benjamite	2 Samuel 16:5; 19:16
Psalm 18	the day the Lord delivered David from his enemies/Saul	2 Samuel 22:1–51
Psalm 30	at the dedication of the house of David	2 Samuel 5:11,12; 6:17
Psalm 34	when David pretended madness before Abimelech	1 Samuel 21:10–15
Psalm 51	when Nathan confronted David over sin with Bathsheba	2 Samuel 12:1–14
Psalm 52	when Doeg the Edomite warned Saul about David	1 Samuel 22:9,10
Psalm 54	when the Ziphites warned Saul about David	1 Samuel 23:19
Psalm 56	when the Philistines captured David in Gath	1 Samuel 21:10,11
Psalm 57	when David fled from Saul into the cave	1 Samuel 22:1; 24:3
Psalm 59	when Saul sent men to watch the house in order to kill David	1 Samuel 19:11
Psalm 60	when David fought against Mesopotamia and Syria	2 Samuel 8:3,13
Psalm 63	when David was in the wilderness of Judea	1 Samuel 23:14; or 2 Samuel 15:23–28
Psalm 142	when David was in a cave	1 Samuel 22:1; 24:3

KEY PERSON IN PSALMS

David—king of Israel; called a man after God's own heart by God Himself (Ps. 2–41; 51–70; 72:20; 78:70,71; 86; 89; 96; 101; 103; 105; 108–110; 122; 124; 131–133; 138–145)

HISTORICAL AND THEOLOGICAL THEMES

The basic theme of Psalms is living real life in the real world, where two dimensions operate simultaneously: (1) a horizontal or temporal reality, and (2) a vertical or transcendent reality. Although not commanded to deny the pain of the earthly dimension, the people of God are to live joyfully and dependently on the Person and promises standing behind the heavenly/eternal dimension. All cycles of human troubles and triumphs provide occasions for expressing human complaints, confidence, prayers, or praise, to Israel's sovereign Lord.

CHRIST IN . . . PSALMS

MANY OF THE PSALMS directly anticipate the coming of the Messiah and King through the line of David (2; 18; 20; 21; 24; 47; 110; 132). Since Christ directly descended from the royal life of David, messianic psalms often refer to Christ as a Son of David, or use David as a type of Christ. Some specific messianic prophecies and their fulfillments include 2:7 (and Matt. 3:17; 16:10; Mark 16:6,7); 22:16 (and John 20:25,27; 40:7,8; Heb. 10:7); 68:18 (and Mark 16:19; 69:21; Matt. 27:34); 118:22 (and Matt. 21:42).

In view of this, Psalms presents a broad array of theology, practically couched in day-to-day reality. The sinfulness of man is documented concretely, not only through the behavioral patterns of the wicked, but also by the periodic stumbling of believers. The sovereignty of God is everywhere recognized, but not at the expense of genuine human responsibility. Life often seems to be out of control, and yet all events and situations are understood in the light of divine providence as being right on course according to God's timetable. Assuring glimpses of a future "God's day" bolsters the call for perseverance to the end. This book of praise manifests a very practical theology.

Types of Psalms

Type	Psalms	Act of Worship
Individual and Communal Lament	3–7; 12; 13; 22; 25–28; 35; 38–40; 42–44; 51; 54–57; 59–61; 63; 64; 69–71; 74; 79; 80; 83; 85; 86; 88; 90; 102; 109; 120; 123; 130; 140–143	Express need for God's deliverance
Thanksgiving	8; 18; 19; 29; 30; 32–34; 36; 40; 41; 66; 103–106; 111; 113; 116; 117; 124; 129; 135; 136; 138; 139; 146–148; 150	Make aware of God's blessings; Express thanks
Enthronement	47; 93; 96–99	Describe God's sovereign rule
Pilgrimage	43; 46; 48; 76; 84; 87; 120–134	Establish a mood of worship
Royal	2; 18; 20; 21; 45; 72; 89; 101; 110; 132; 144	Portray Christ the Sovereign Ruler
Wisdom	1; 37; 119	Instruct as to God's will
Imprecatory	7; 35; 40; 55; 58; 59; 69; 79; 109; 137; 139; 144	Invoke God's wrath and judgment against His enemies

©2001 by Thomas Nelson, Inc.

A commonly misunderstood phenomenon in Psalms is the association that often develops between the "one" (the psalmist) and the "many" (the theocratic people). Virtually all of cases of this occur in the psalms of King David. There was an inseparable correlation between the experiences of the ruler and his people; as life and devotion to God went for the king, so it often went for the people. Furthermore, at times this union accounted for the psalmist's apparent connection with Christ in the messianic content of the psalms. The so-called imprecatory (curse pronouncing) psalms in which the psalmist spoke out against his enemies may be better understood with this perspective. As mediator between God and his people, David prayed for judgment on his enemies, since these enemies were not only hurting him, but were primarily hurting God's people. Ultimately, they challenged the King of Kings, the God of Israel.

KEY DOCTRINES IN PSALMS

The sinfulness of man (1:4; 5:4; 32:1–4; 36:1; 51:2; 66:18; 78:17; 106:43; Gen. 6:5; Lev. 15:14; Deut. 31:18; Job 4:17–19; Ps.130:3; Jer. 17:9; John 1:10,11; Rom. 5:15–17; 1 John 1:8)

The law of God (1:1,2; 78:1; 119:97; Exod. 20:1–21; Deut. 5:6-21; Jer. 11:4; Rom. 7:7–14; James 1:25; 1 John 3:4)

GOD'S CHARACTER IN PSALMS

God is accessible—15:1; 16:11; 23:6; 24:3,4; 65:4; 145:18

God is delivering—106:43–45

God is eternal—90:2; 102:25–27; 106:48

God is glorious—8:1; 19:1; 57:5; 63:2; 79:9; 90:16; 93:1; 96:3; 102:16; 104:1,31; 111:3; 113:4; 138:5; 145:5,11,12

God is good—23:6; 25:8; 31:19; 33:5; 34:8; 52:1; 65:4; 68:10; 86:5; 104:24; 107:8; 119:68; 145:9

God is gracious—116:5

God is great—86:10

God is holy—22:3; 30:4; 47:8; 48:1; 60:6; 89:35; 93:5; 99:3,5,9; 145:17

God is immutable—102:26,27

God is just—9:4; 51:4; 89:14; 98:9; 99:3,4

God is kind—17:7; 24:12; 25:6; 26:3; 31:21; 36:7,10; 40:10,11; 42:7,8; 48:9; 63:3; 89:33,49; 92:2; 103:4; 107:43; 117:2; 119:76,88,149; 138:2; 143:8

God is long-suffering—78:38; 86:15

God is merciful—6:2,4; 25:6; 31:7; 32:5; 36:5; 51:1; 52:8; 62:12; 86:5,15; 89:28; 103:4,8,11,17; 106:1; 107:1; 115:1; 118:1–4; 119:64; 130:7; 145:9; 147:11

God is the Most High—83:18

God is omnipresent—139:7

God is omniscient—139:1–6

God is powerful—8:3; 21:13; 29:5; 37:17; 62:11; 63:1,2; 65:6; 66:7; 68:33,35; 79:11; 89:8,13; 106:8; 136:12

God is a promise keeper—89:3,4,35,36; 105:42

God is provident—16:8; 31:15; 33:10; 36:6; 37:28; 39:5; 73:16; 75:6,7; 77:19; 91:3,4,11; 104:5–9,27,28; 119:15; 121:4; 127:1,2; 136:25; 139:1–5,10; 140:7; 145:9,17; 147:9

God is righteous—5:8; 7:9,17; 11:7; 19:9; 22:31; 31:1; 35:24,28; 36:6,10; 40:10; 48:10; 50:6; 51:14; 69:27; 71:2,15,16,19,24; 73:12–17; 85:10; 96:13; 97:2,6; 98:2,9; 103:17; 111:3; 116:5; 119:7,40, 62, 123,137,138,142,144,172; 143:1,11; 145:7,17

God is sovereign—2:4,5; 3:3; 72:5

God is true—9:14; 11:7; 19:9; 25:10; 31:5; 33:4; 57:3,10; 71:22; 85:10; 86:15; 89:14,49; 96:13; 98:3; 100:5; 119:160; 139:2; 146:6

God is unified—83:18; 86:10

God is unsearchable—145:3

God is upright—25:8; 92:15

God is wise—1:6; 44:21; 73:11; 103:14; 104:24; 136:5; 139:2–4,12; 142:3; 147:5

God is wrathful—2:2–5,12; 6:1; 7:11,12; 21:8,9; 30:5; 38:1; 39:10; 58:10,11; 74:1,2; 76:6,8; 78:21,22,49–51,58,59; 79:5; 80:4; 89:30–32; 90:7–9,11; 99:8; 102:9,10

Messianic Prophecies in the Psalms

Prophecy	Psalm	Fulfillment
1. God will announce Christ to be His Son	2:7	Matthew 3:17; Acts 13:33; Hebrews 1:5
2. All things will be put under Christ's feet	8:6	1 Corinthians 15:27; Hebrews 2:8
3. Christ will be resurrected from the grave	16:10	Mark 16:6,7; Acts 13:35
4. God will forsake Christ in His moment of agony	22:1	Matthew 27:46; Mark 15:34
5. Christ will be scorned and ridiculed	22:7,8	Matthew 27:39–43; Luke 23:35
6. Christ's hands and feet will be pierced	22:16	John 20:25,27; Acts 2:23
7. Others will gamble for Christ's clothes	22:18	Matthew 27:35,36
8. Not one of Christ's bones will be broken	34:20	John 19:32,33,36
9. Christ will be hated unjustly	35:19	John 15:25
10. Christ will come to do God's will	40:7,8	Hebrews 10:7
11. Christ will be betrayed by a friend	41:9	John 13:18
12. Christ's throne will be eternal	45:6	Hebrews 1:8
13. Christ will ascend to heaven	68:18	Ephesians 4:8
14. Zeal for God's temple will consume Christ	69:9	John 2:17
15. Christ will be given vinegar and gall	69:21	Matthew 27:34; John 19:28–30
16. Christ's betrayer will be replaced	109:8	Acts 1:20
17. Christ's enemies will bow down to Him	110:1	Acts 2:34,35
18. Christ will be a priest like Melchizedek	110:4	Hebrews 5:6; 6:20; 7:17
19. Christ will be the chief cornerstone	118:22	Matthew 21:42; Acts 4:11
20. Christ will come in the name of the Lord	118:26	Matthew 21:9

INTERPRETIVE CHALLENGES

It is helpful to recognize certain recurring genres or literary types in Psalms. Some of the most obvious are: (1) the wisdom type with instructions for right living; (2) lamentation patterns which deal with the pangs of life (usually arising from enemies without); (3) penitential psalms (mostly dealing with the "enemy" within, i.e., confessing sin); (4) kingship emphases (the king as spiritual role model and mediator); and (5) thanksgiving psalms. A combination of style and subject matter help to identify such types when they appear.

The comprehensive literary characteristic of the psalms is that all of them are poetry par excellence. Unlike most English poetry, which is based on rhyme and meter, Hebrew poetry is essentially characterized by logical parallelisms, which compare or contrast ideas or images within a literary work. Some of the most important kinds of parallelisms are: (1) synonymous (the thought of the first line is restated with similar concepts in the second line, e.g., Ps. 2:1); (2) antithetic (the thought of the second line is contrasted with the first, e.g., Ps. 1:6); (3) climactic (the second and any subsequent lines pick up a crucial word, phrase, or concept and advance it in a stair-step-fashion, e.g., Ps. 29:1, 2); and (4) chiastic or introverted (the logical units are developed in an A . . . B . . . B'. . . A' pattern, e.g., Ps. 1:2).

On a larger scale, some psalms in their development from the first to the last verse employ an acrostic or alphabetical arrangement. Psalms 9, 10, 25, 34, 37, 111, 112, 119, and 145 are recognized as either complete or incomplete acrostics. In the Hebrew text, the

Psalms

Selah: Hebrew *selah*—3:2; 24:10; 39:11; 47:4; 60:4; 76:3; 88:10; 140:3—derived from the verb *salal,* "to lift up." It occurs in thirty-nine psalms and in the "Psalm of Habakkuk" (Habakkuk 3). No one is certain of the exact meaning of this word, that is, what it is to be lifted up. Some think that *Selah* is an emphatic word, marking a point in the psalm for "lifting up" one's thoughts to God. But most scholars think it is simply some form of musical notation, such as a marker of a musical interlude, a pause, or a change of key.

Hope: Hebrew *yachal*—31:24; 42:11; 71:14; 119:49,116; 130:5; 131:3—signifies "to wait with expectation." Almost half of its occurrences are in Psalms, and it is especially frequent in 119. Sometimes the idea of hope is expressed with confidence (Job 13:15; Is. 51:5), and sometimes hope is clearly in vain (Ezek. 13:6). The Bible describes Noah as waiting for seven days to send out the dove (Gen. 8:12), and men as waiting to hear the counsel of Job (Job 29:21). But by far the main object of "expectant waiting" or "hope" is God—His word, His judgment, and His mercy (33:18; 119:43; Mic. 7:7). That hope is not misplaced, for the One in whom we hope is completely faithful to His promises.

Psalm: Hebrew *mizmor*—the titles of chapters 3; 9; 32; 54; 72; 84; 100; 101—derived from the verb *zamar,* "to make music." The word occurs only in the Book of Psalms, and there it appears in fifty-seven of the psalm headings. It may designate a praise song or possibly a song accompanied by a certain type of instrumental music. In thirty-four psalm titles, *mizmor* follows the phrase "To the Chief Musician," perhaps indicating that the psalms were typically songs accompanied by instruments. Frequently the author of the psalm is also identified, such as the sons of Korah (48; 84), Asaph (50; 82), and especially David (23; 29; 51).

Law: Hebrew *torah*—1:2, 19:7; 37:31; 89:30; 119:1,55,174—usually translated "law," the noun *torah* is derived from the verb *yarah,* which means "to teach," and should be understood as carrying the idea of "instruction." The term can refer to any set of regulations, such as the instructions of parents (Prov. 1:8) or of a psalmist (78:1). But usually the word refers to God's Law. The writer of Psalm 119 expressed great love for God's Law because it led him to wisdom and righteousness (119:97–176). In the NT, Paul also praised God's Law because it pointed out his sin and made him realize his desperate need for a Savior (Rom. 7:7).

Truth: Hebrew *'emet*—15:2; 25:10; 30:9; 43:3; 71:22; 108:4; 146:6—signifies truth that conforms to a standard, either to created reality or to God's standards. Truth is often associated with mercy, especially God's mercy (57:3; 117:2; Gen. 24:49). This word is also frequently used in the context of legal language. In secular contexts it is used in speaking of witnesses and judgments (Prov. 14:25; Zech. 8:16), while in the religious contexts it is used in reference to the Law and commandments of God (119:142,151). Truth is precious, and its absence was lamented by the prophets (Is. 59:14; Jer. 9:5; Hos. 4:1). God desires truth in the inward parts of His people (15:2; 51:6); thus it is the basis of a lifestyle that pleases Him (25:5,10; 26:3).

first letter of the first word of every verse begins with a different Hebrew consonant, which advances in alphabetical order until the 22 consonants are exhausted. Such a literary vehicle undoubtedly aided in the memorization of the content and served to indicate that its particular subject matter had been covered from "A to Z." Psalm 119 stands out as the most complete example of this device, since the first letter of each of its 22, 8-verse stanzas comprises the entire Hebrew alphabet.

OUTLINE

The 150 canonical psalms were organized quite early into five "books." Each of these books ends with a doxology (Pss. 41:13; 72:18–20; 89:52; 106:48; 150:6). Jewish tradition appealed to the number 5 and alleged that these divisions echoed the Pentateuch, i.e., the five books of Moses. It is true that there are clusters of psalms, such as (1) those drawn together by an association with an individual or group (e.g., "The sons of Korah," Pss. 42–49; Asaph, Pss. 73–83), (2) those dedicated to a particular function (e.g., "Songs of ascents," Pss. 120–134), or (3) those devoted explicitly to praise worship (Pss. 146–150). But no one configuration key unlocks the "mystery" as to the organizing theme of this five-book arrangement. Thus, there is no identifiable thematic structure to the entire collection of psalms.

MEANWHILE, IN OTHER PARTS OF THE WORLD...

The Chinese compile their first dictionary containing 40,000 characters. The Hebrew alphabet develops beyond earlier Semitic forms.

ANSWERS TO TOUGH QUESTIONS

1. Why are so many uncomfortable expressions in the Psalms, sometimes right in the middle of favorite chapters—for example, Psalms 23 and 139?

Because the Psalms genuinely reflect real life, we should expect that they will be uncomfortable in the same places that life is uncomfortable. According to the best-known Psalm 23, life isn't just about green pastures and still waters; it also includes death and enemies. The psalmists were convinced they knew the only true God. When someone was mistreating them or their people, they would at times cry out for very specific judgment to be applied by God on their enemies. An amazing fact about Psalms is their unblushing record of these cries to God that, if we're honest, echo some of our own deepest hidden complaints before God.

In David's case, the role that he filled as the king and representative of God's people often blurs with his individual self-awareness. At times it is difficult to tell whether he is speaking for himself alone or for the people as a whole. This explains some of the bitterness behind the curse-filled psalms. They unabashedly invoke God's righteous wrath and judgment against his enemies.

2. What are the different kinds of psalms?

The Psalms cover the full breadth of human experience. Some speak in general terms, while others express in very specific terms the shifting events of life. There's a psalm for almost any kind of day.

One way to categorize the Psalms groups them by five general types:

- Wisdom Psalms: instructions for wise living (1; 37; 119)
- Lamentation Psalms: meditations on the pangs of life (3; 17; 120)
- Penitential Psalms: meditations on the pangs of sin (51)
- Kingship Psalms: meditations on God's sovereign rule (2; 21; 144)
- Thanksgiving Psalms: praise and worship offered to God (19; 32; 111)

FURTHER STUDY ON PSALMS

1. Which psalms are you most familiar with, and what impact do they have on your life?
2. What aspects of a healthy relationship with God can you find in Psalm 23?
3. How could you use Psalm 51 to help explain genuine repentance?
4. Read the first and the last psalms (1 and 150) and consider why each of those was chosen for the spot it holds.
5. What is the central theme of Psalm 119, and how does the length of the psalm add to its impact?
6. Which psalm or portion of a psalm do you find most useful for prayer?

PROVERBS
The Way of the Wise

TITLE

The title in the Hebrew Bible is "The Proverbs of Solomon" (1:1), as also in the Greek Septuagint (LXX). Proverbs pulls together 513 of the most important proverbs pondered by Solomon (1 Kin. 4:32; Eccles. 12:9), along with some proverbs of others whom Solomon likely influenced. The word *proverb* means "to be like"; thus Proverbs is a book of comparisons between common, concrete images and life's most profound truths. Proverbs are simple, moral statements (or illustrations) that highlight and teach fundamental realities about life. Solomon sought God's wisdom (2 Chr. 1:8–12) and offered "pithy sayings" designed to make men contemplate (1) the fear of God and (2) living by His wisdom (1:7; 9:10). The sum of this wisdom is personified in the Lord Jesus Christ (1 Cor. 1:30).

AUTHOR AND DATE

Created and compiled by Solomon and other authors from approximately 971 to 686 B.C. The phrase "Proverbs of Solomon" is more a title than an absolute statement of authorship (1:1). While King Solomon, who ruled Israel from 971–931 B.C. and was granted great wisdom by God (see 1 Kin. 4:29–34), is the author of the didactic section (chaps. 1–9) and the proverbs of 10:1–22:16, he is likely only the compiler of the "sayings of the wise" in 22:17–24:34, which are of an uncertain date before Solomon's reign. The collection in chaps. 25–29 was originally composed by Solomon (25:1) but copied and included later by Judah's king Hezekiah (ca. 715–686 B.C.). Chapter 30 reflects the words of Agur and chap. 31 the words of Lemuel, who perhaps was Solomon. Proverbs was not assembled in its final form until Hezekiah's day or after. Solomon authored his proverbs before his heart was turned away from God (1 Kin. 11:1–11), since the book reveals a godly perspective and is addressed to the "naive" and "young" who need to learn the fear of God. Solomon also wrote Psalms 72 and 127, Ecclesiastes, and Song of Solomon. (See "Author and Date" for Ecclesiastes and Song of Solomon.)

Notable Teachers in Scripture

Moses	Renowned as the leader of Israel who first taught God's Law (Deut. 4:5).
Bezalel and Aholiab	Two master craftsmen who were gifted and called to teach others in the construction of the tabernacle (Ex. 35:30–35).
Samuel	The last of Israel's judges before the monarchy, who taught the people "the good and the right way" (1 Sam. 12:23).
David	Prepared his son Solomon to build and staff the temple (1 Chr. 28:9–21).
Solomon	Known for his outstanding wisdom, which he used to teach numerous subjects, including literature, botany, and zoology (1 Kin. 4:29–34).

Ezra	A scribe and priest who was committed not only to keeping the Law himself, but to teaching it to others (Ezra 7:10).
Jesus	Called Rabbi ("teacher," John 1:38; compare Matt. 9:11; 26:18; John 13:13), whose teaching revealed the good news of salvation (Eph. 4:20–21).
Barnabas	One of the teachers among the believers at Antioch (Acts 13:1), who had a lasting impact on Saul after his conversion to the faith (9:26–30).
Gamaliel	A renowned Jewish rabbi who was the teacher of Saul during his youth (Acts 22:3).
Paul	Perhaps the early church's most gifted teacher, known to have taught throughout the Roman world, notably at Antioch (Acts 13:1) and in the school of Tyrannus at Ephesus (19:9).
Priscilla and Aquila	Two believers who taught the way of God to a talented young orator named Apollos (Acts 18:26).
Apollos	A powerful teacher from Alexandria in Egypt, whose teaching paved the way for the gospel at Ephesus (Acts 18:24–26).
Timothy	Pastor-teacher of the church at Ephesus (1 Tim. 1:3; 2 Tim. 4:2).
Titus	Pastor-teacher of a church on the island of Crete (Titus 2:1–15).

BACKGROUND AND SETTING

The book reflects a 3-fold setting as: (1) general wisdom literature; (2) insights from the royal court; and (3) instruction offered in the tender relationship of a father and mother with their children, all designed to produce meditation on God. Since Proverbs is Wisdom literature, by nature it is sometimes difficult to understand (1:6). Wisdom literature is part of the whole of OT truth; the Priest gave the *Law*, the Prophet gave a *Word* from the Lord, and the Sage (or wise man) gave his wise *Counsel* (Jer. 18:18; Ezek. 7:26). In Proverbs, Solomon the Sage gives insight into the "knotty" issues of life (1:6) which are not directly addressed in the Law or the Prophets. Though it is practical, Proverbs is not superficial or external because it contains moral and ethical elements stressing upright living which flow out of a right relationship with God. In 4:1–4, Solomon connected three generations as he entrusted to his son Rehoboam what he learned at the feet of David and Bathsheba. Proverbs is both a pattern for the tender impartation of truth from generation to generation, as well as a vast resource for the content of the truth to be imparted. Proverbs contains the principles and applications of Scripture which the godly characters of the Bible illustrate in their lives.

KEY PEOPLE IN PROVERBS

Solomon—king of Israel, granted great wisdom from God (1 Kin. 4:29-34)
Agur—son of Jakeh, an unknown sage (Prov. 30:1)
Lemuel—king whose mother's teachings are included (Prov. 31); ancient Jewish tradition identifies him as Solomon, but otherwise unknown

HISTORICAL AND THEOLOGICAL THEMES

Solomon came to the throne with great promise, privilege, and opportunity. God had granted his request for understanding (1 Kin. 3:9–12; 1 Chr. 1:10,11), and his wisdom exceeded all others (1 Kin. 4:29–31). However, the shocking reality is that he failed to live out the truth that he knew and even taught his son Rehoboam (1 Kin. 11:1,4,6,7–11), who subsequently rejected his father's teaching (1 Kin. 12:6–11).

Proverbs contains a gold mine of biblical theology, reflecting themes of Scripture brought to the level of practical righteousness (1:3), by addressing man's ethical choices, calling into question how he thinks, lives, and manages his daily life in light of divine truth. More specifically, Proverbs calls man to live as the Creator intended him to live when He made man (Ps. 90:1,2,12).

The recurring promise of Proverbs is that generally the wise (the righteous who obey God) live longer (9:11), prosper (2:20–22), experience joy (3:13–18) and the goodness of God temporally (12:21),

CHRIST IN . . . PROVERBS

THE WRITERS OF PROVERBS desired that believers not only listen to the truth but apply this wisdom to their own lives. Proverbs calls for wisdom to become incarnate (chapt. 8), and indeed it did when "all the treasures of wisdom and knowledge" became flesh in Christ (Col. 2:3). While the OT readers of Proverbs were guided by wisdom through the written word, the NT believers came to know the Word of God in human form. Therefore, Christ not only encompasses Proverbs but also actually "became for us wisdom from God" (1 Cor. 1:30).

while fools suffer shame (3:35) and death (10:21). On the other hand, it must be remembered that this general principle is balanced by the reality that the wicked sometimes prosper (Ps. 73:3,12), though only temporarily (Ps. 73:17–19). Job illustrates that there are occasions when the godly wise are struck with disaster and suffering.

There are a number of important themes addressed in Proverbs, which are offered in random order and address different topics, so that it is helpful to study the proverbs thematically as illustrated.

I. Man's Relationship to God

A. His Trust	Prov. 22:19
B. His Humility	Prov. 3:34
C. His Fear of God	Prov. 1:7
D. His Righteousness	Prov. 10:25
E. His Sin	Prov. 28:13
F. His Obedience	Prov. 6:23
G. Facing Reward	Prov. 12:28
H. Facing Tests	Prov. 17:3
I. Facing Blessing	Prov. 10:22
J. Facing Death	Prov. 15:11

II. Man's Relationship to Himself

A. His Character	Prov. 20:11
B. His Wisdom	Prov. 1:5

C. His Foolishness	Prov. 26:10,11
D. His Speech	Prov. 18:21
E. His Self Control	Prov. 6:9-11
F. His Kindness	Prov. 3:3
G. His Wealth	Prov. 11:4
H. His Pride	Prov. 27:1
I. His Anger	Prov. 29:11
J. His Laziness	Prov. 13:4

III. Man's Relationship to Others

A. His Love	Prov. 8:17
B. His Friends	Prov. 17:17
C. His Enemies	Prov. 19:27
D. His Truthfulness	Prov. 23:23
E. His Gossip	Prov. 20:19
F. As a Father	Prov. 20:7; 31:2-9
G. As a Mother	Prov. 31:10-31
H. As Children	Prov. 3:1-3
I. In Educating Children	Prov. 4:1-4
J. In Disciplining Children	Prov. 22:6

The two major themes which are interwoven and overlapping throughout Proverbs are wisdom and folly. Wisdom, which includes knowledge, understanding, instruction, discretion, and obedience, is built on the fear of the Lord and the Word of God. Folly is everything opposite to wisdom.

KEY DOCTRINES IN PROVERBS

Practical righteousness (1:3; John 14:21)

The benefits of wisdom (2:20–22; 3:13–18; 9:11; 12:21; Job 28:17; Pss. 37:3; 91:10; 1 Pet. 3:13)

Man's relationship to God (1:7; 3:34; 6:23; 10:22; 12:28; 15:11; 22:19; Gen. 4:35; 26:12; Deut. 8:18; Job 28:28; Pss. 19:8; 111:10; Eccles. 12:13; Acts 1:24; James 4:6; 1 Pet. 5:5; 2 Pet. 1:19)

Man's relationship to himself (1:5; 3:3; 6:9–11; 11:4; 13:4; 20:11; 29:11; Exod. 13:9; Deut. 6:8; Jer. 17:1; Ezek. 7:19; Zeph. 1:18; Matt. 7:16; 2 Cor. 3:3)

Man's relationship to others (3:1–3; 4:1–4; 8:17; 17:17; 19:27; 20:19; 23:23; Deut. 8:1; Ruth 1:16; 1 Sam. 2:30; Ps. 34:11; Rom. 16:18)

GOD'S CHARACTER IN PROVERBS

God is merciful—28:13

God is omniscient—5:21

God is provident—3:6; 16:3,9,33; 19:21; 20:24; 21:30,31

God is wise—3:19; 15:11

INTERPRETIVE CHALLENGES

The first challenge is the generally elusive nature of Wisdom literature itself. Like the parables, the intended truths are often veiled from understanding if given only a cursory glance, and thus must be pondered in the heart (1:6; 2:1–4; 4:4–9).

Another challenge is the extensive use of parallelism, which is the placing of truths side by side so that the second line expands, completes, defines, emphasizes, or reaches the logical conclusion, the ultimate end, or, in some cases, the contrasting point of view. Often the actual parallel is only implied. For example, 12:13 contains an unstated, but clearly implied parallel, in that the righteous one comes through trouble because of his virtuous speech (cf. 28:7). In interpreting the Proverbs, one must: (1) determine the parallelism and often complete what is assumed and not stated by the author; (2) identify the figures of speech and rephrase the thought without those figures; (3) summarize the lesson or principle of the proverb in a few words; (4) describe the behavior that is taught; and (5) find examples inside Scripture.

Challenges are also found in the various contexts of Proverbs, all of which affect interpretation and understanding. First, there is the setting in which they were spoken; this is largely the context of the young men in the royal court of the king. Second, there is the setting of the book as a whole and how its teachings are to be understood in light of the rest of Scripture. For example, there is much to be gained by comparing the wisdom Solomon taught with the wisdom Christ personified. Third, there is the historical context in which the principles and truths draw on illustrations from their own day.

A final area of challenge comes in understanding that proverbs are divine guidelines and wise observations, i.e., teaching underlying principles (24:3, 4) which are not always inflexible laws or absolute promises. These expressions of general truth (cf. 10:27; 22:4) generally do have "exceptions," due to the uncertainty of life and unpredictable behavior of fallen men. God does not guarantee uniform outcome or application for each proverb, but in studying them and applying them, one comes to contemplate the mind of God, His character, His attributes, His works, and His blessings. All of the treasures of wisdom and knowledge expressed in Proverbs are hidden in Christ (Col. 2:3).

KEY WORDS IN

Proverbs

Wisdom: Hebrew *chokmah*—1:2; 4:5; 9:10; 14:6; 16:16; 18:4; 23:23; 31:26—can also mean "skill" but is most commonly used to describe daily application of practical wisdom. Proverbs teaches that true wisdom reaches beyond mere knowledge of truth to living a life of moral integrity (8:7–9). Whereas the sinful life leads ultimately to self-destruction; abundant life is found within the wisdom of God (2:6; Job 11:6).

Foolish: Hebrew *'ivvelet*—14:1; 12:23; 14:24; 15:2,14; 19:3; 22:15; 24:9; 27:22—signifies an absence of wisdom. Except for two occurrences in the Psalms, this term occurs only in Proverbs, where the foolishness of fools is frequently contrasted with the wisdom of the wise and prudent (13:16; 14:8,18,24). Foolishness characterizes the speech of fools and the reactions of the impulsive person (12:23; 14:17,29; 15:2,14; 18:13). Foolishness affects the lifestyle of a person, causing his or her heart to fret against God (15:21; 19:3). Indeed, foolishness is often identified with iniquity and sin (5:22,23; 24:9; Ps. 38:4,5). Although Proverbs does not hold out much hope for separating an adult fool from his foolishness, the rod of correction is identified as a remedy for children (22:15; 26:11; 27:22).

MEANWHILE, IN OTHER PARTS OF THE WORLD...
Peking becomes an established city in China, later to be renamed Beijing, the present-day capital city of China.

OUTLINE
   I. Prologue (1:1–7)
      A. Title (1:1)
      B. Purpose (1:2–6)
      C. Theme (1:7)
   II. Praise and Wisdom to the Young (1:8–9:18)
   III. Proverbs for Everyone (10:1–29:27)
      A. From Solomon (10:1–22:16)
      B. From Wise Men (22:17–24:34)
      C. From Solomon Collected by Hezekiah (25:1–29:27)
   IV. Personal Notes (30:1–31:31)
      A. From Agur (30:1–33)
      B. From Lemuel (31:1–31)

ANSWERS TO TOUGH QUESTIONS
1. Some of the proverbs seem unclear or even contradictory. How can we study and apply them if we don't understand them?

More often than not, those proverbs that at first seem unclear or contradictory turn out, instead, to be elusive and deep. Proverbs sometimes do state obvious truths. Their meaning is crystal clear: "A foolish son is a grief to his father, and bitterness to her who bore him" (17:25). But many proverbs require thoughtful meditation: "The lot is cast into the lap, but its every decision is from the Lord" (16:33) or "There is a way that seems right to a man, but its end is the way of death" (16:25). The fact that we may have to search the rest of Scripture or work at thinking ought to make Proverbs dearer to us. If God has chosen this unusual approach to help us grow, why would we hesitate to give our full attention to Proverbs?

Given the context that surrounds Proverbs—the rest of God's Word—a student's failure to grasp a proverb ought not to lead to the conclusion that there's something wrong with the proverb. A better conclusion would be that the student doesn't know enough yet or hasn't paid enough attention. A wise person puts an elusive proverb on hold for further understanding rather than rejecting it as useless. God's further lessons in that person's life may well cast a new light on parts of the Bible that have been difficult to interpret.

2. What are some general, time-tested principles that will help rightly interpret Proverbs?

One of the most common characteristics of Proverbs is the use of parallelism; that is, placing truths side-by-side so that the second statement expands, completes, defines, and emphasizes the first statement. Sometimes a logical conclusion is reached; at other times, a logical contrast is demonstrated.

The following directions will assist a student in gaining greater confidence as he or she interprets these Proverbs:

Determine what facts, principles, or circumstances make up the parallel ideas in that proverb—what two central concepts or persons are being compared or contrasted.

Identify the figures of speech and rephrase the thought without those figures, for example, restate the idea behind "put a knife to your throat" (23:1–3).

Summarize the lesson or principle of the proverb in a few words.

Describe the behavior that is being taught or encouraged.

Think of examples from elsewhere in Scripture that illustrate the truth of that proverb.

3. Many of the proverbs appear to impose absolutes on life situations that prove to be unclear. How do the proverbs apply to specific life decisions and experiences?

Proverbs are divine guidelines and wise observations that teach underlying principles of life (24:3,4). They are not inflexible laws or absolute promises. This is because they are applied in life situations that are rarely clearcut or uncomplicated by other conditions. The consequences of a fool's behavior as described in Proverbs apply to the complete fool. Most people are only occasionally foolish and therefore experience the occasional consequences of foolish behavior. It becomes apparent that the proverbs usually do have exceptions due to the uncertainty of life and the unpredictable behavior of fallen people.

The marvelous challenge and principle expressed in 3:5,6 puts a heavy emphasis on trusting the Lord with "all your heart" and acknowledging Him "in all your ways." Even partly practicing the conditions of those phrases represents a major challenge. Because of God's grace, we don't have to perfectly carry out these conditions in order to experience the truth that "He shall direct your paths."

God does not guarantee uniform outcome or application for each proverb. By studying them and applying them, a believer is allowed to contemplate God's mind, character, attributes, works, and blessings. In Jesus Christ are hidden all the treasures of wisdom and knowledge partly expressed in Proverbs (Colossians 2:3).

FURTHER STUDY ON PROVERBS

1. Using the language of Proverbs, how would you define wisdom?
2. What guidelines does Proverbs offer regarding relationships between people?
3. What recurring themes do you find in Proverbs regarding work?
4. How does God fit in with the teaching of Proverbs?
5. What warnings and guidance does Proverbs offer about speech, or the tongue?
6. Comment on Proverbs 3:5,6 as it relates to your own life.

ECCLESIASTES
Life without God

TITLE

The English title, Ecclesiastes, comes from the Greek and Latin translations of Solomon's book. The Septuagint (LXX) used the Greek term *ekkljsiastjs* for its title. It means "preacher," derived from the word *ekkljsia*, translated "assembly" or "congregation" in the NT. Both the Greek and Latin versions derive their titles from the Hebrew title, *Qoheleth*, which means "one who calls or gathers" the people. It refers to the one who addresses the assembly; hence, the preacher (cf. 1:1,2,12; 7:27; 12:8–10). Along with Ruth, Song of Solomon, Esther, and Lamentations, Ecclesiastes stands with the OT books of the Megilloth, or "five scrolls." Later rabbis read these books in the synagogue on five special occasions during the year—Ecclesiastes being read on Pentecost.

AUTHOR AND DATE

The autobiographical profile of the book's writer unmistakably points to Solomon. Evidence abounds such as: (1) the titles fit Solomon, "son of David, king in Jerusalem" (1:1) and "king over Israel in Jerusalem" (1:12); (2) the author's moral odyssey chronicles Solomon's life (1 Kin. 2–11); and (3) the role of one who "taught the people knowledge" and wrote "many proverbs" (12:9) corresponds to his life. All point to Solomon, the son of David, as the author.

Once Solomon is accepted as the author, the date and occasion become clear. Solomon was writing, probably in his latter years (no later than ca. 931 B.C.), primarily to warn the young people of his kingdom, without omitting others. He warned them to avoid walking through life on the path of human wisdom; he exhorted them to live by the revealed wisdom of God (12:9–14).

BACKGROUND AND SETTING

Solomon's reputation for possessing extraordinary wisdom fits the Ecclesiastes profile. David recognized his son's wisdom (1 Kin. 2:6,9) before God gave Solomon an additional measure. After he received a "wise and understanding heart" from the Lord (1 Kin. 3:7–12), Solomon gained renown for being exceedingly wise by rendering insightful decisions (1 Kin. 3:16–28), a reputation that attracted "all the kings of the earth" to his courts (1 Kin. 4:34). In addition, he composed songs and proverbs (1 Kin. 4:32; cf. 12:9), activity befitting only the ablest of sages. Solomon's wisdom, like Job's wealth, surpassed the wisdom "of all the people of the east" (1 Kin. 4:30; Job 1:3).

CHRIST IN . . . ECCLESIASTES

SOLOMON WROTE ECCLESIASTES as a warning to those who attempt to find joy without God. In fact, living without God is impossible for He has "placed eternity in the hearts [of men]" (3:11). Solomon's pursuit of happiness through experiences and philosophy remained unattainable without God. Christ did not come into the world to make life bearable for humans. He came to provide life "more abundantly" (John 10:9,10). Christ remains the "one Shepherd" who is the source of all wisdom (12:11). Therefore, every pursuit without Christ is futile.

The book is applicable to all who would listen and benefit, not so much from Solomon's experiences, but from the principles he drew as a result. Its aim is to answer some of life's most challenging questions, particularly where they seem contrary to Solomon's expectations. This has led some unwisely to take the view that Ecclesiastes is a book of skepticism. But in spite of amazingly unwise behavior and thinking, Solomon never let go of his faith in God (12:13, 14).

KEY PEOPLE IN ECCLESIASTES
Solomon—king of Israel; God granted Solomon's desire for wisdom, and he became the wisest person ever born (Ecclesiastes 1:1–12:14)

HISTORICAL AND THEOLOGICAL THEMES
As is true with most biblical Wisdom literature, little historical narrative occurs in Ecclesiastes, apart from Solomon's own personal pilgrimage. The kingly sage studied life with high expectations but repeatedly bemoaned its shortcomings, which he acknowledged were due to the curse (Gen. 3:14–19). Ecclesiastes represents the painful autobiography of Solomon who, for much of his life, squandered God's blessings on his own personal pleasure rather than God's glory. He wrote to warn subsequent generations not to make the same tragic error, in much the same manner as Paul wrote to the Corinthians (cf. 1 Cor. 1:18–31; 2:13–16).

The key word is "vanity," which expresses the futile attempt to be satisfied apart from God. This word is used thirty-seven times expressing the many things hard to understand about life.

KEY WORDS IN Ecclesiastes

Vanity: Hebrew *hebel*—1:2; 2:1; 4:4; 6:2,11; 7:15; 8:14; 9:9—basically means "vapor" or "breath," such as the rapidly vanishing vapor of one's warm breath in cool, crisp air. With this word, the preacher described worldly pursuits, such as wealth, honor, fame, and various other pleasures, as similar to desperately grasping at air (2:17). It is absurd and useless. Jeremiah used the same word to denounce idolatry as "worthless" (Jer. 18:15), and Job used it to bemoan the brevity of human life (Job 7:16). But the preacher of Ecclesiastes used the word more than any other OT author. According to him, all of life is vanity unless one recognizes that everything is from the hand of God (2:24–26).

Labor: Hebrew *'amal*—1:3; 2:10,21; 3:13; 4:8; 5:19; 6:7; 10:15—generally means "toil," or work for material gain (Ps. 127:1; Prov. 16:26), but it can also mean "trouble" or "sorrow" (see Job 3:10). The effort required for work and human achievement produces "sorrow" and "troubles" in the sense that it can never satisfy the deeper needs of the human soul (6:7). However, when believers recognize that their work is a gift from God, work can become a joy (5:18–20). Our work is part of God's plan to establish His eternal kingdom. In this sense, we can be assured that our faithful commitment to our work will have eternal consequences and reap eternal rewards (see 1 Cor. 3:8,14; 15:58).

All earthly goals and ambitions when pursued as ends in themselves produce only emptiness. Paul was probably echoing Solomon's dissatisfaction when he wrote, " ... the creation was subjected to futility" (Solomon's "vanity"; Rom. 8:19–21). Solomon's experience with the effects of the curse (see Gen. 3:17–19) led him to view life as "chasing after the wind."

Solomon asked, "What profit has a man from all his labor?" (1:3), a question he repeated in 2:24 and 3:9. The wise king gave over a considerable portion of the book to addressing this dilemma. The impossibility of discovering both the inner workings of God's creation and the personal providence of God in Solomon's life were also deeply troubling to the king, as they were to Job. But the reality of judgment for all, despite many unknowns, emerged as the great certainty. In light of this judgment by God, the only fulfilled life is one lived in proper recognition of God and service to Him. Any other kind of life is frustrating and pointless.

A proper balance of the prominent "enjoy life" theme with that of "divine judgment" tethers the reader to Solomon's God with the sure chord of faith. For a time, Solomon suffered from the imbalance of trying to enjoy life without regard for the fear of Yahweh's judgment holding him on the path of obedience. In the end, he came to grasp the importance of obedience. The tragic results of Solomon's personal experience, coupled with the insight of extraordinary wisdom, make Ecclesiastes a book from which all believers can be warned and grow in their faith (cf. 2:1–26). This book shows that if one perceives each day of existence, labor, and basic provision as a gift from God, and accepts whatever God gives, then that person lives an abundant life (cf. John 10:10). However, one who looks to be satisfied apart from God will live with futility regardless of their accumulations.

KEY DOCTRINES IN ECCLESIASTES

Vanity of life—the futile attempt to be satisfied apart from God (1:2; 12:8; Gen. 3:17–19; Ps. 39:5,6; 62:9; 144:4; Rom. 8:19–21; James 4:14)

The meaning of life (1:3; 2:24; 3:9; 12:13,14; Is. 56:12–57:2; Luke 12:19–21; John 10:10; 1 Cor. 15:32; 1 Tim. 6:17)

Balance in life—there is a time and a season for everything (3:1–8,17; Exod. 15:20; Ps. 126:2; Amos 5:13; Rom. 12:15,16; Heb. 9:27)

The fear of the Lord (12:13,14; Deut. 6:2; 10:12; Mic. 6:8; Matt. 12:36; Acts 17:30,31; Rom. 2:16; 1 Cor. 4:5; 2 Cor. 5:10)

GOD'S CHARACTER IN ECCLESIASTES

God is long-suffering—8:11
God is powerful—3:11

INTERPRETIVE CHALLENGES

The author's declaration that "all is vanity" envelops the primary message of the book (cf. 1:2; 12:8). By stating one of his conclusions in the opening lines, the author of Ecclesiastes challenges readers to pay attention. The word translated "vanity" is used in at least three ways throughout the book. In each case, it looks at the nature of man's activity "under the sun" as: (1) "fleeting," which has in view the vapor-like (cf. James 4:14) or transitory nature of life; (2) "futile" or "meaningless," which focuses on the

The "Vanities" of Ecclesiastes 1:2; 12:8

1. Human wisdom	2:14–16
2. Human effort	2:18–23
3. Human achievement	2:26
4. Human life	3:18–22
5. Human rivalry	4:4
6. Human selfish sacrifice	4:7,8
7. Human power	4:16
8. Human greed	5:10
9. Human accumulation	6:1–12
10. Human religion	8:10–14

cursed condition of the universe and the debilitating effects it has on man's earthly expe-rience; or (3) "incomprehensible" or "enigmatic," which gives consideration to life's unan-swerable questions. Solomon draws upon all three meanings in Ecclesiastes. While the context in each case will determine which meaning Solomon is focusing upon, the most recurring meaning of *vanity* is "incomprehensible" or "unknowable," referring to the mys-teries of God's purposes.

OUTLINE

The book chronicles Solomon's investigations and conclusions regarding man's lifework, which combine all of his activity and its potential outcomes including limited satisfaction. The role of wisdom in experiencing success surfaces repeatedly, particularly when Solomon must acknowledge that God has not revealed all of the details. This leads Solomon to the conclusion that the primary issues of life after the Edenic fall involve divine blessings to be enjoyed and the divine judgment for which all must prepare.

I. Introduction
  A. Title (1:1)
  B. Poem—A Life of Activity That Appears Wearisome (1:2–11)
II. Solomon's Investigation (1:12–6:9)
  A. Introduction—The King and His Investigation (1:12–18)
  B. Investigation of Pleasure-Seeking (2:1–11)
  C. Investigation of Wisdom and Folly (2:12–17)
  D. Investigation of Labor and Rewards (2:18–6:9)
    1. One has to leave them to another (2:18–26)
    2. One cannot find the right time to act (3:1–4:6)
    3. One often must work alone (4:7–16)
    4. One can easily lose all he acquires (5:1–6:9)
III. Solomon's Conclusions (6:10–12:8)
  A. Introduction—The Problem of Not Knowing (6:10–12)
  B. Man Cannot Always Find Out Which Route is the Most Successful for Him to Take Because His Wisdom is Limited (7:1–8:17)
    1. On prosperity and adversity (7:1–14)
    2. On justice and wickedness (7:15–24)
    3. On women and folly (7:25–29)
    4. On the wise man and the king (8:1–17)
  C. Man Does Not Know What Will Come After Him (9:1–11:6)
    1. He knows he will die (9:1–4)
    2. He has no knowledge in the grave (9:5–10)
    3. He does not know his time of death (9:11, 12)
    4. He does not know what will happen (9:13–10:15)
    5. He does not know what evil will come (10:16–11:2)
    6. He does not know what good will come (11:3–6)
    7. Man Should Enjoy Life, But Not Sin, Because Judgment Will Come to All (11:7–12:8)
IV. Solomon's Final Advice (12:9–14)

MEANWHILE, IN OTHER PARTS OF THE WORLD...
Chinese culture advances as written script, brush and ink paintings, and mathematical theories such as multiplication and geometry develop.

ANSWERS TO TOUGH QUESTIONS

1. How does the author's declaration that "all is vanity" relate to the message of the Book of Ecclesiastes?

The word translated "vanity" is used in at least three ways throughout the book (see discussion in Interpretive Challenges). While the context in each of the thirty-seven appearances of "vanity" helps determine the particular meaning Solomon had in mind, his most frequent usage conveyed the idea of "incomprehensible" or "unknowable." He was expressing the human limits when faced with the mysteries of God's purposes. Solomon's final conclusion to "fear God and keep His commandments" (12:13,14) states the only hope of the good life and the only reasonable response of faith and obedience to the sovereign God. God precisely directs all activities under the sun, each in its time according to His perfect plan, while He discloses only as much as His perfect wisdom dictates. All people remain accountable. Those who refuse to take God and His Word seriously are doomed to lives of the severest vanity.

2. When the writer of Ecclesiastes encourages his readers to "enjoy life," does he have any conditions or cautions in mind?

Solomon balanced his enjoyment theme with repeated reminders of divine judgment. Even the best moments in life ought not to cut a person off from awareness of God as Provider to whom all will give an account. Solomon declared that the possibility of enjoyment was based on faith (Eccles. 2:24–26).

Part of Ecclesiastes reports the king's experiment in trying to enjoy life without regard for God's judgment. Solomon discovered that such an effort was in vain. In the end, he came to grasp the importance of obedience. The tragic results of Solomon's personal experience, coupled with the insight of extraordinary wisdom, make Ecclesiastes a book from which all believers can receive warnings and lessons in their faith (2:1–26). This book demonstrates that a person who sees each day of existence, labor, and basic provision as a gift from God, and accepts whatever God gives, will actually live an abundant life. However, anyone who seeks to be satisfied apart from God will live with futility regardless of personal successes.

FURTHER STUDY ON ECCLESIASTES

1. How many different major pursuits did Solomon experiment with in Ecclesiastes?
2. What was Solomon seeking?
3. What conclusions did Solomon reach regarding life's meaning?
4. What insights about time and its uses do you get from chapter 3:1–8?
5. What does the phrase "eternity in their hearts" (3:11) mean in Ecclesiastes?
6. In what specific ways do Solomon's discoveries challenge your life?

SONG OF
SOLOMON
God   Honors   Pure   Marital   Love

TITLE
The Greek Septuagint (LXX) and Latin Vulgate (Vg.) versions follow the Hebrew (Masoretic Text) with literal translations of the first two words in 1:1—"Song of Songs." Several English versions read "The Song of Solomon," thus giving the fuller sense of 1:1. The superlative, "Song of Songs" (cf. "Holy of Holies" in Exod. 26:33,34 and "King of Kings" in Rev. 19:16), indicates that this song is the best among Solomon's 1,005 musical works (1 Kin. 4:32). The word translated "song" frequently refers to music that honors the Lord (cf. 1 Chr. 6:31, 32; Pss. 33:3; 40:3; 144:9).

AUTHOR AND DATE
Solomon, who reigned over the united kingdom forty years (971–931 B.C.), appears seven times by name in this book (1:1,5; 3:7,9,11; 8:11,12). In view of his writing skills, musical giftedness (1 Kin. 4:32), and the authorial, not dedicatory, sense of 1:1, this piece of Scripture could have been penned at any time during Solomon's reign. Since cities to the north and to the south are spoken of in Solomon's descriptions and travels, both the period depicted and the time of actual writing point to the united kingdom before it divided after Solomon's reign ended. Knowing that this portion of Scripture comprises one song by one author, it is best taken as a unified piece of poetic Wisdom literature rather than a series of love poems without a common theme or author.

BACKGROUND AND SETTING
Two people dominate this true-life, dramatic love song. Solomon, whose kingship is mentioned five times (1:4, 12; 3:9, 11; 7:5), appears as "the beloved." The Shulamite maiden (6:13) remains obscure; most likely she was a resident of Shunem, three miles north of Jezreel in lower Galilee. Some suggest she is Pharaoh's daughter (1 Kin. 3:1), although the Song provides no evidence for this conclusion. Others favor Abishag, the Shunammite who cared for King David (1 Kin. 1:1–4, 15). An unknown maiden from Shunem, whose family had possibly been employed by Solomon (8:11), seems most reasonable. She would have been Solomon's first wife (Eccles. 9:9), before he sinned by adding 699 other wives and 300 concubines (1 Kin. 11:3).

CHRIST IN ... SONG OF SOLOMON
THE WORDS OF SOLOMON intimately paint a picture of marriage. Yet, Song of Solomon illustrates the spiritual relationship between God and Israel, His chosen nation, and even the relationship God desires with individuals. Solomon attempts to express the love of the beloved for his bride. This mystery can only be fully revealed in the intimate relationship between Christ and the church (Eph. 5:32).

Minor roles feature several different groups in this book. First, note the not infrequent commentary by "the daughters of Jerusalem" (1:5; 2:7; 3:5; 5:8,16; 8:4), who might be part of Solomon's household staff (cf. 3:10). Second, Solomon's friends join in at 3:6–11; and

Locations in the Song of Solomon

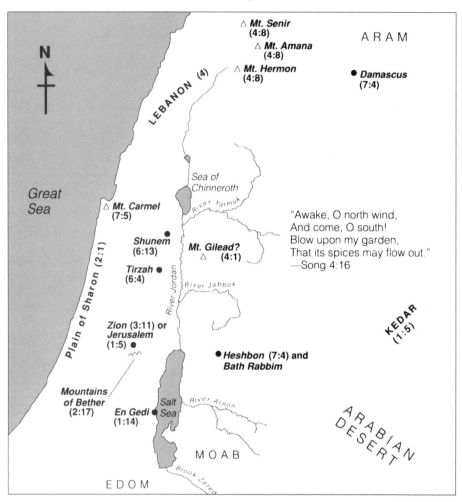

△ Mt. Senir
(4:8)
△ Mt. Amana
(4:8)
△ Mt. Hermon
(4:8)

ARAM

● Damascus
(7:4)

LEBANON (4)

N

Great
Sea

Sea of
Chinneroth

River Yarmuk

△ Mt. Carmel
(7:5)

"Awake, O north wind,
And come, O south!
Blow upon my garden,
That its spices may flow out."
—Song 4:16

Shunem ●
(6:13)

Mt. Gilead?
△   (4:1)

Plain of Sharon (2:1)

Tirzah ●
(6:4)

River Jordan

River Jabbok

KEDAR
(1:5)

Zion (3:11) or
Jerusalem
(1:5) ●

● Heshbon (7:4) and
Bath Rabbim

Mountains
of Bether
(2:17)

En Gedi ●
(1:14)

Salt
Sea

River Arnon

ARABIAN
DESERT

MOAB

Brook Zered

EDOM

third, so do the Shulamite's brothers (8:8, 9). The affirmation of 5:1b would most likely be God's blessing on the couple's union. One can follow the narrative by noticing the suggested parts as indicated in headings throughout the song.

The setting combines both rural and urban scenes. Portions take place in the hill country north of Jerusalem, where the Shulamite lived (6:13) and where Solomon enjoyed prominence as a vinegrower and shepherd (Eccles. 2:4–7). The city section includes the wedding and time afterward at Solomon's abode in Jerusalem (3:6–7:13).

The first spring appears in 2:11–13 and the second in 7:12. Assuming a chronology without gaps, the Song of Solomon took place over a period of time at least one year in length, but probably no longer than two years.

Local Color in the Song of Solomon

1:5	"tents of Kedar"	nomadic tribal tents made of dark goat hair
1:5	"curtains of Solomon	most likely the beautiful curtains of Solomon's palace
1:9	"my filly"	a young female horse
1:12; 4:13,14	"spikenard"	an aromatic oil taken from an Indian herb
1:13; 3:6; 4:6, 14; 5:1,5,13	"myrrh"	an aromatic gum from the bark of a balsam tree made into perfume in either liquid or solid form
1:14; 4:13	"henna blooms"	a common shrub whose white, spring blossoms give off a fragrant scent
1:14	"En Gedi"	a lush oasis just west of the Dead Sea
1:15; 4:1; 5:12	"dove's eyes"	beautiful, deep, smoke gray eyes of the dove
2:1	"rose of Sharon"	probably a bulb flower like crocus, narcissus, iris or daffodil growing in the low country (plain of Sharon), south of Mt. Carmel
2:1,16	"lily of the valleys"	possibly a six petaled flower that grew in the fertile, watered areas
2:3,5; 7:8; 8:5	"apple"	an aromatic, sweet fruit—possibly an apricot
2:5	"cakes of raisins"	a food associated with religious festivals, having possible erotic significance (cf. 2 Sam. 6:19; Hos. 3:1)
2:7,9,17; 3:5; 8:14	"gazelles"	graceful members of the antelope family
2:7; 3:5	"does"	female deer
2:9,17; 8:14	"stag"	a male deer
2:14; 5:2; 6:9	"dove"	a common symbol of love
2:17	"mountains of Bether"	a ravine or rugged hills in an unidentifiable location in Israel
3:6; 4:6,14	"frankincense"	amber resin extracted from trees and used for incense/spice
3:6	"fragrant powders"	various spices
3:7,9	"couch, palanquin"	a sedan chair that transported the king and his bride
3:9; 4:8,11,15; 5:15	"Lebanon"	a beautiful country, north of Israel on the coast, with rich natural resources
4:1; 6:5	"Mount Gilead"	the high plateau east of Galilee and Samaria
4:4	"tower of David"	probably the armory tower of Nehemiah 3:19,25

Local Color in the Song of Solomon

4:8	"top of Amana"	the hill in which the Amana River has its source in Syria
4:8	"top of Senir and Herman"	the Amorite and Hebrew names for the tallest summit in northern Israel (over 9,200 ft., cf. Deut. 3:9)
4:10,14,16; 5:1,13; 6:2; 8:14	"spices"	the sweet smelling oil from the balsam
4:14	"saffron"	the dried, powdered pistils and stamens of a small crocus
4:14	"calamus"	a wild grass with a gingery scent
4:14	"cinnamon"	a spice taken from the bark of a tree
4:14	"aloes"	a spicy drug with a strong scent
5:14	"beryl"	possibly a yellowish or greenish stone such as topaz
5:14	"sapphires"	the azure-blue lapis lazuli which was abundant in the East
6:4	"Tirzah"	a site known for its natural beauty and gardens located seven miles northeast of Shechem in Samaria
6:13	"the dance of the double camp"	literally "the dance of the two companies" which is possibly a dance of unknown origin associated with the place of Mahanaim (cf. Gen. 32:2)
7:4	"the pools in Heshbon"	water reservoirs in the Moabite city of Heshbon near modern Amman
7:4	"the gate of Bath Rabbim"	possibly a gate name in Heshbon
7:4	"the tower of Lebanon"	most likely refers to the white color of the mountain rather than its elevation of 10,000 feet
7:4	"Damascus"	the capital city of Syria to the east of the Lebanon mountains
7:5	"Mount Carmel"	a prominent wooded mountain in northern Israel
7:13	"mandrakes"	a pungently fragrant herb considered to be an aphrodisiac (see Genesis 30:14)
8:11	"Baal Hamon"	an unknown location in the hill country north of Jerusalem

Couples in Love

Solomon and his bride show all of the affection and romance that people universally associate with being in love (Song 2:16). Theirs is one of a number of stories about romantic love told in the Bible.	
Isaac and Rebekah	(Gen. 24:1–67) A father seeks and finds a wife for his son, and the young couple love each other deeply.
Jacob and Rachel	(Gen. 29:1–30) Jacob labors 14 years for his father-in-law in order to gain Rachel as his wife.
Boaz and Ruth	(Ruth 3–4) Legal technicalities bring together a Moabite widow and a wealthy landowner of Bethlehem, and through them a king is descended.
Elkanah and Hannah	(1 Sam. 1–2) A woman is loved by her husband despite being childless, and God eventually blesses her with the birth of a son, who becomes a mighty judge over Israel.
David and Michal	(1 Sam. 18:20–30) Genuine love is manipulated by a jealous king, but instead of ridding himself of his nemesis, the ruler gains a son-in-law.
Solomon and the Shulamite	(Song of Solomon) The commitments and delights of two lovers are told in a beautiful romantic poem.
Hosea and Gomer	(Hos. 1:1–3:5) God calls the prophet Hosea to seek out his adulterous spouse and restore the relationship despite what she has done.
Christ and the Church	(Eph. 5:25–33) Having won His bride's salvation from sin, Christ loves and serves her as His own body, thereby setting an example for human husbands everywhere.

KEY PEOPLE IN SONG OF SOLOMON

King Solomon—the bridegroom; called "beloved" by his wife (1:7–8:12)
The Shulamite woman—the new bride of King Solomon (1:1–8:13)
The daughters of Jerusalem—unidentified virgins who encouraged the Shulamite woman (1:4; 2:14; 3:5,10,11; 5:1,8; 6:1,12; 8:4)

HISTORICAL AND THEOLOGICAL THEMES

All 117 verses in Solomon's Song are recognized by the Jews as a part of their sacred writings. Along with Ruth, Esther, Ecclesiastes, and Lamentations, it is included among the OT books of the Megilloth, or "five scrolls." The Jews read this song at Passover, calling it "the Holy of Holies." Surprisingly, God is not mentioned explicitly except possibly in 8:6. No formal theological themes emerge. The NT never quotes Solomon's Song directly (nor Esther, Obadiah, and Nahum).

Song of Solomon

Beloved: Hebrew *dod*—1:14; 2:8; 4:16; 5:1,6,10; 6:1; 8:14—in Hebrew love poetry, *dod* is a term of endearment used for a male loved one, usually translated "beloved" (Is. 5:1). The writer of the Song of Solomon uses this word thirty-two times. The name David is derived from *dod* and carries the same sense, meaning "beloved one." When *dod* is used in narrative, it means "uncle" or another close male relative (1 Sam. 14:50).

Myrrh: Hebrew *mor*—1:13; 3:6; 4:6,14; 5:1,5,13—describes a taste that is bitter. The word is derived from the verb *marar*, which means "to be bitter." Myrrh is made from the gum or sap of an Arabian balsa tree. The resin was pressed and mixed with oil to make perfume (1:13; 5:1), incense (3:6), and lotion (Esth. 2:12). Naomi took the name Mara as a symbol of the bitterness she had experienced in her life (Ruth 1:20), and the Christ-child was presented with a gift of myrrh by the wise men (see Matt. 2:11). Myrrh was also an embalming spice in NT times and was used on Jesus' body (John 19:39).

In contrast to the two distorted extremes of ascetic abstinence and lustful perversion outside of marriage, Solomon's ancient love song exalts the purity of marital affection and romance. It parallels and enhances other portions of Scripture which portray God's plan for marriage, including the beauty and sanctity of sexual intimacy between husband and wife. The Song rightfully stands alongside other classic Scripture passages which expand on this theme, e.g., Gen. 2:24; Ps. 45; Prov. 5:15–23; 1 Cor. 7:1–5; 13:1–8; Eph. 5:18–33; Col. 3:18, 19; and 1 Pet. 3:1–7. Hebrews 13:4 captures the heart of this song, "Marriage is honorable among all, and the bed undefiled; but fornicators and adulterers God will judge." Thus, the Song of Solomon expands on the ancient marriage instructions of Genesis 2:24 by providing shameless and spiritual music for a lifetime of marital harmony.

KEY DOCTRINES IN SONG OF SOLOMON
The love of God reflected in human love (6:2,3; Gen. 29:20; Lev. 19:18; 2 Chr. 36:15; Matt. 14:14; Luke 15:20–24; Phil.1:8)

God's grace given through marriage (Ruth 1:9; Ezek. 16:6–8; Matt. 1:20; Heb.13:4; 1 Pet. 3:7)

GOD'S CHARACTER IN SONG OF SOLOMON
God is faithful—8:5

God is loving—8:6

God is pure—3:5; 4:1–16

INTERPRETIVE CHALLENGES
The Song of Solomon has suffered strained interpretations over the centuries by those who use the "allegorical" method of interpretation. They claim that this song has no actual historical basis, but rather that it depicts God's love for Israel and/or Christ's love for the church. Another result of this method of interpretation is the misleading idea that Christ is the rose of Sharon and the lily of the valleys (2:1). The "typological" variation admits the historical reality, but concludes that it ultimately pictures Christ's bridegroom love for His bride the church.

MEANWHILE, IN OTHER PARTS OF THE WORLD...
Greek worship of gods and goddesses becomes fully developed. Major deities include Zeus, Hera, Poseidon, Apollo, Ares, Demeter, Athena, Hermes, and Artemis.

Another way to approach Solomon's Song is to take it at face value and interpret it in the normal historical sense, understanding the frequent use of poetic imagery to depict reality. To do so understands that Solomon recounts (1) his own days of courtship, (2) the early days of his first marriage, followed by (3) the maturing of this royal couple through the ups and downs of life. The Song of Solomon expands on the ancient marriage instructions of Genesis 2:24, thus providing spiritual music for a lifetime of marital harmony. It is given by God to demonstrate His intention for the romance and loveliness of marriage, the most precious of human relations and "the grace of life" (1 Pet. 3:7).

OUTLINE
    I. The Courtship: Leaving (1:2–3:5)
        A. The Lovers' Remembrances (1:2–2:7)
        B. The Lovers' Expression of Reciprocal Love (2:8–3:5)
    II. The Wedding: Cleaving (3:6–5:1)
        A. The Kingly Bridegroom (3:6–11)
        B. The Wedding and First Night Together (4:1–5:1a)
        C. God's Approval (5:1b)
    III. The Marriage: Weaving (5:2–8:14)
        A. The First Major Disagreement (5:2–6:3)
        B. The Restoration (6:4–8:4)
        C. Growing in Grace (8:5–14)

ANSWERS TO TOUGH QUESTIONS
1. Should Song of Solomon be interpreted as person-to-person love or as an allegory of God's love for Israel or Christ's love for the church?

Allegorical interpretations of this book tend to be strained. Denying the human and historical setting of this Song creates more discomfort with the subject matter than insight into the nature of Scripture. The idealistic and allegorical language that lovers use might lead one to assume the freedom to allegorize the entire experience, but the lovers themselves would strongly object. The practice of allegorizing the book comes from outside theological and philosophical frameworks, not the content of the book itself.

One form of interpretation similar to allegorizing takes a "typological" approach. It begins by admitting the historical validity of the story. But it also insists that the idealized language of the lovers can ultimately only accurately describe the kind of love that Christ has demonstrated toward His church.

A more satisfying way to approach Solomon's Song takes the story at face value, interprets it in a normal historical sense, and understands the idealized use of poetic language to depict reality. This interpretation affirms Solomon's account of three phases in his relationship with the Shulamite: his early days of courtship, the early days of his marriage, and the maturing of the royal couple through the good and bad days of married life.

FURTHER STUDY ON SONG OF SOLOMON

1. In what ways does the Song of Songs capture the intensity and shamelessness of romantic love?
2. How does the Song of Songs express and encourage commitment?
3. What factors make the Song of Songs' descriptions of sexuality healthy and good in comparison with much that is available in the rest of culture?
4. What insights about expressing enjoyment over the beauty of one's mate can you find in Song of Songs?
5. How would you describe Song of Song's role within the rest of Scripture?

ISAIAH
Announcing the Suffering King

TITLE
The book derives its title from the author, whose name means "The LORD is salvation," and is similar to the names Joshua, Elisha, and Jesus. Isaiah is quoted directly in the NT over sixty-five times, far more than any other OT prophet, and mentioned by name over twenty times.

AUTHOR AND DATE
Isaiah, the son of Amoz, ministered in and around Jerusalem as a prophet to Judah during the reigns of four kings of Judah: Uzziah (called "Azariah" in 2 Kin.), Jotham, Ahaz, and Hezekiah (1:1), from ca. 739–686 B.C. Isaiah evidently came from a family of some rank, because he had easy access to the king (7:3) and intimacy with a priest (8:2). He was married and had two sons who bore symbolic names: "Shear-jashub" ("a remnant shall return," 7:3) and "Maher-shalal-hash-baz" ("hasting to the spoil, hurrying to the prey," 8:3). When called by God to prophesy, in the year of King Uzziah's death (ca. 739 B.C.), he responded with a cheerful readiness, though he knew from the beginning that his ministry would be one of fruitless warning and exhortation (6:9–13). Having been reared in Jerusalem, he was an appropriate choice as a political and religious counselor to the nation.

Isaiah was a contemporary of Hosea and Micah. His writing style has no rival in its versatility of expression, brilliance of imagery, and richness of vocabulary. The early church father Jerome likened him to Demosthenes, the legendary Greek orator. His writing features a range of 2,186 different words, compared to 1,535 in Ezekiel, 1,653 in Jeremiah, and 2,170 in the Psalms. Second Chronicles 32:32 records that he wrote a biography of King Hezekiah also. The prophet lived until at least 681 B.C. when he penned the account of Sennacherib's death (cf. 37:38). Tradition has it that he met his death under King Manasseh (ca. 695–642 B.C.) by being cut in two with a wooden saw (cf. Heb. 11:37).

CHRIST IN . . . ISAIAH

THE BOOK OF ISAIAH presents one of the most startling examples of messianic prophecy in the OT. With vivid imagery, Isaiah depicts the future Christ as the Suffering Servant, who was "led as a lamb to the slaughter" (53:7) and "shall justify many, for He shall bear their iniquities" (53:11).

Other messianic prophecies found in Isaiah with NT fulfillments include 7:14 (Matt. 1:22,23); 9:1–2 (Matt. 4:12–16); 9:6 (Luke 2:11; Eph. 2:14–18); 11:1 (Luke 3:23,32; Acts 13:22,23); 11:2 (Luke 3:22); 28:16 (1 Pet. 2:4–6); 40:3–5 (Matt. 3:1–3); 42:1–4 (Matt. 12:15–21); 42:6 (Luke 2:29–32); 50:6 (Matt. 26:67; 27:26,30); 52:14 (Phil. 2:7–11); 53:3 (Luke 23:18; John 1:11; 7:5); 53:4,5 (Rom. 5:6,8); 53:7 (Matt. 27:12–14; John 1:29; 1 Pet.1:18,19); 53:9 (Matt. 27:57–60); 53:12 (Mark 15:28); 61:1 (Luke 4:17–19,21).

BACKGROUND AND SETTING
During Uzziah's prosperous fifty-two-year reign (ca. 790–739 B.C.), Judah developed into a strong commercial and military state with a port for commerce on the Red Sea and the construction of walls, towers, and fortifications (2 Chr. 26:3–5,8–10,13–15). Yet the period

witnessed a decline in Judah's spiritual status. Uzziah's downfall resulted from his attempt to assume the privileges of a priest and burn incense on the altar (2 Kin. 15:3,4; 2 Chr. 26:16–19). He was judged with leprosy, from which he never recovered (2 Kin. 15:5; 2 Chr. 26:20,21).

His son Jotham (ca. 750–731 B.C.) had to take over the duties of king before his father's death. Assyria began to emerge as a new international power under Tiglath-Pileser (ca. 745–727 B.C.) while Jotham was king (2 Kin. 15:19). Judah also began to incur opposition from Israel and Syria to her north during his reign (2 Kin. 15:37). Jotham was a builder and a fighter like his father, but spiritual corruption still existed in the Land (2 Kin. 15:34,35; 2 Chr. 27:1,2).

Ahaz was 25 when he began to reign in Judah and he reigned until age 41 (2 Chr. 28:1,8; ca. 735–715 B.C.). Israel and Syria formed an alliance to combat the rising Assyrian threat from the E, but Ahaz refused to bring Judah into the alliance (2 Kin. 16:5; Is. 7:6). For this, the northern neighbors threatened to dethrone him, and war resulted (734 B.C.). In panic, Ahaz sent to the Assyrian king for help (2 Kin. 16:7) and the Assyrian king gladly responded, sacking Gaza, carrying all of Galilee and Gilead into captivity, and finally capturing Damascus (732 B.C.). Ahaz's alliance with Assyria led to his introduction of a heathen altar, which he set up in Solomon's temple (2 Kin. 16:10–16; 2 Chr. 28:3). During his reign (722 B.C.), Assyria captured Samaria, capital of the northern kingdom, and carried many of Israel's most capable people into captivity (2 Kin. 17:6,24).

Hezekiah began his reign over Judah in 715 B.C. and continued for twenty-nine years to ca. 686 B.C. (2 Kin. 18:1,2). Reformation was a priority when he became king (2 Kin. 18:4,22; 2 Chr. 30:1). The threat of an Assyrian invasion forced Judah to promise heavy tribute to that eastern power. In 701 B.C. Hezekiah became very ill with a life-threatening disease, but he prayed and God graciously extended his life for fifteen years (2 Kin. 20; Is. 38) until 686 B.C. The ruler of Babylon used the opportunity of his illness and recovery to send congratulations to him, probably seeking to form an alliance with Judah against Assyria at the same time (2 Kin. 20:12 ff.; Is. 39). When Assyria became weak through internal strife, Hezekiah refused to pay any further tribute to that power (2 Kin. 18:7). So in 701 B.C. Sennacherib, the Assyrian king, invaded the coastal areas of Israel, marching toward Egypt on Israel's southern flank. In the process he overran many Judean towns, looting and carrying many people back to Assyria. While besieging Lachish, he sent a contingent of forces to besiege Jerusalem (2 Kin. 18:17–19:8; Is. 36:2–37:8). The side-expedition failed, however, so in a second attempt he sent messengers to Jerusalem demanding an immediate surrender of the city (2 Kin. 19:9ff.; Is. 37:9ff.). With Isaiah's encouragement, Hezekiah refused to surrender, and when Sennacherib's army fell prey to a sudden disaster, he returned to Nineveh and never threatened Judah again.

KEY PEOPLE IN ISAIAH

Isaiah—prophet who ministered throughout the reigns of four kings of Judah; gave both a message of judgment and hope (1–66)

Shear-Jashub—Isaiah's son; name means "a remnant shall return," denoting God's promised faithfulness to His people (7:3; 8:18; 10:21)

Maher-Shalal-Hash-Baz—Isaiah's son; name means "hasting to the spoil, hurrying to the prey," denoting God's coming punishment (8:1,3,18)

HISTORICAL AND THEOLOGICAL THEMES

Isaiah prophesied during the period of the divided kingdom, directing the major thrust of his message to the southern kingdom of Judah. He condemned the empty ritualism of his day (e.g., 1:10–15) and the idolatry into which so many of the people had fallen (e.g., 40:18–20). He foresaw the coming Babylonian captivity of Judah because of this departure from the Lord (39:6,7).

Like certain other Old Testament prophetic books, Isaiah contains a series of oracles against the foreign enemies of Israel and upon unfaithful elements within Israel itself (chs. 13–23). Beginning with Babylon, the future enemy that would destroy Judah (13:1–14:23), Isaiah goes on to prophesy judgment on Assyria (14:24–27), Philistia (14:28–32), Moab (15:1–16:14), Syria and Israel (17:1–11), all nations (17:12–18:7),

God's Judgment on the Nations

	Obadiah	Amos	Isaiah	Jeremiah	Habakkuk	Ezekiel
Ammon		1:13–15 Judgment		49:1–6 Judgment; Restoration		25:1–7 Judgment
Babylon			13:1–14:23 Judgment	50,51 Judgment	2:6–17 Judgment	
Damascus		1:3–5 Judgment	17:1–3 Judgment; Remnant	49:23–27 Judgment		
Edom	1–14 Judgment	1:11,12 Judgment	21:11,12 Judgment	49:7–22 Judgment		25:12–14 Judgment
Egypt			19 Judgment	46:1–26 Judgment		29–32 Judgment
Moab		2:1–3 Judgment	15,16 Judgment; Remnant	48 Judgment; Restoration		25:8–11 Judgment
Philistia		1:6–8 Judgment	14:29–32 Judgment	47 Judgment; Remnant		25:15–17 Judgment
Tyre		1:9,10 Judgment	23 Judgment; Restoration			26–28 Judgment

Egypt (19:1–20:6), Babylon and her allies (21:1–16), Jerusalem and her unfaithful leaders (22:1–25), and the city of Tyre (23:1–18).

Fulfillment of some of his prophesies in his own lifetime provided his credentials for the prophetic office. Sennacherib's effort to take Jerusalem failed, just as Isaiah had said it would (37:6,7,36–38). The Lord healed Hezekiah's critical illness, as Isaiah had predicted (38:5; 2 Kin. 20:7). Long before Cyrus, king of Persia appeared on the scene, Isaiah named him as Judah's deliverer from the Babylonian captivity (44:28; 45:1). Fulfillment of his prophecies of Christ's first coming have given Isaiah further vindication (e.g., 7:14). The pattern of literal fulfillment of his already-fulfilled prophecies gives assurance that prophecies of Christ's second coming will also see literal fulfillment.

Isaiah's Description of Israel's Future Kingdom

Description	Isaiah passages
1. The Lord will restore the faithful remnant of Israel to the Land to inhabit the kingdom at its beginning.	1:9,25–27; 3:10; 4:3; 6:13; 8:10; 9:1; 10:20,22,25,27; 11:11,12,16; 14:1,2; 14:22,26; 26:1–4; 27:12; 28:5; 35:9; 37:4,31,32; 40:2,3; 41:9; 43:5,6; 46:3,4; 49:5,8; 49:12,22; 51:11; 54:7–10; 55:12; 57:13,18; 60:4,9; 61:1–4,7; 65:8–10; 66:8,9,19
2. As the Lord defeats Israel's enemies, He will provide protection for His people.	4:5,6; 9:1,4; 12:1–6; 13:4; 14:2; 21:9; 26:4,5; 27:1–4; 30:30,31; 32:2; 33:16,22; 35:4; 49:8,9; 49:17,18; 52:6; 54:9,10; 55:10,11; 58:12; 60:10,12,18; 62:9; 66:16
3. In her kingdom, Israel will enjoy great prosperity of many kinds.	26:15,19; 27:2,13; 29:18–20; 22:22,23; 30:20; 32:3; 32:15–20; 33:6,24; 35:3,5,6,8–10; 40:11; 42:6,7,16; 43:5,6,8,10,21; 44:5,14; 46:13; 48:6; 49:10; 52:9; 54:2,3; 55:1,12; 58:9,14; 60:5,16,21; 61:4,6–10; 62:5; 65:13–15,18,24; 66:21,22
4. The city of Jerusalem will rise to world preeminence in the kingdom.	2:2–4; 18:7; 25:6; 40:5,9; 49:19–21; 60:1–5,13–15, 17; 62:3,4
5. Israel will be the center of world attention in the kingdom.	23:18; 54:1–3; 55:5; 56:6–8; 60:5–9; 66:18–21
6. Israel's mission in the kingdom will be to glorify the Lord.	60:21; 61:3
7. Gentiles in the kingdom will receive blessing through the channel of faithful Israel.	11:10; 19:18,24,25; 42:6; 45:22,23; 49:6; 51:5; 56:3,6–8; 60:3,7,8; 61:5; 66:19
8. Worldwide peace will prevail in the kingdom under the rule of the Prince of Peace.	2:4; 9:5,6; 11:10; 19:23; 26:12; 32:18; 54:14; 57:19; 66:12
9. Moral and spiritual conditions in the kingdom will reach their highest plane since the Fall of Adam.	27:6; 28:6,17; 32:16; 42:7; 44:3; 45:8; 51:4; 61:11; 65:21,22

10. Governmental leadership in the kingdom will be superlative with the Messiah heading it up.	9:6,7; 11:2,3; 16:5; 24:23; 25:3; 32:1; 32:5; 33:22; 42:1,4; 43:15; 52:13; 53:12; 55:3–5
11. Humans will enjoy long life in the kingdom.	65:20,22
12. Knowledge of the Lord will be universal in the kingdom.	11:9; 19:21; 33:13; 40:5; 41:20; 45:6,14; 49:26; 52:10,13,15; 54:13; 66:23
13. The world of nature will enjoy a great renewal in the kingdom.	12:3; 30:23–26; 32:15; 35:1–4,6,7; 41:18,19; 43:19,20; 44:3,23; 55:1,2,13; 58:10,11
14. "Wild" animals will be tame in the kingdom.	11:6–9; 35:9; 65:25
15. Sorrow and mourning will not exist in the kingdom.	25:8; 60:20
16. An eternal kingdom, as a part of God's new creation, will follow the millennial kingdom.	24:23; 51:6; 51:16; 54:11,12; 60:11,19; 65:17
17. The King will judge overt sin in the kingdom.	66:24

More than any other prophet, Isaiah provides data on the future day of the Lord and the time following. He details numerous aspects of Israel's future kingdom on earth not found elsewhere in the OT or NT, including changes in nature, the animal world, Jerusalem's status among the nations, the Suffering Servant's leadership, and others.

Through a literary device called "prophetic foreshortening," Isaiah predicted future events without outlining the exact sequence of the events or time intervals separating them. For example, nothing in Isaiah reveals the extended period separating the two comings of the Messiah. Also, he does not provide as clear a distinction between the future temporal kingdom and the eternal kingdom as John does in Revelation 20:1–10; 21:1–22:5. In God's program of progressive revelation, details of these relationships awaited a prophetic spokesman of a later time.

Also known as the "evangelical Prophet," Isaiah spoke much about the grace of God toward Israel, particularly in his last twenty-seven chapters. The centerpiece is Isaiah's unrivaled chap. 53, portraying Christ as the slain Lamb of God. Because Isaiah's prophecy hinged on the incarnation and sacrifice of Christ, he is the OT prophet most often quoted in the NT.

KEY DOCTRINES IN ISAIAH

Christ as the Suffering Servant (49:1–57:21; Ps. 68:18; 110:1; Matt. 26:39; John 10:18; Acts 3:13–15; Phi. 2:8,9; Heb. 2:9)

The first coming of the Messiah (7:14; 8:14; 9:2,6,7; 11:1–2; Ezek. 11:16; Matt. 1:23; Luke 1:31; 2:34; John 1:45; 3:16; Rom. 9:33; 1 Pet. 2:8; Rev. 12:5)

The second coming of the Messiah (4:2; 11:2–6,10; 32:1–8; 49:7; 52:13,15; 59:20,21; 60:1–3; 61:2,3; Jer. 23:5; Zech. 3:8; Matt. 25:6; 26:64; Rom. 13:11,12; Phil. 4:5; Rev. 3:11)

Salvation through Christ (9:6,7; 52:13–15; 53:1–12; Is.12:2; Ps.103:11–12; Luke 19:9; John 3:16; Acts 16:31; Rom. 3:21–24; 1 Tim. 1:15)

GOD'S CHARACTER IN ISAIAH

God is accessible—55:3,6
God is eternal—9:6
God is faithful—49:7
God is glorious—2:10; 6:3; 42:8; 48:11; 59:19
God is holy—5:16; 6:3; 57:15
God is just—45:21
God is kind—54:8,10; 63:7
God is Light—60:19
God is long-suffering—30:18; 48:9
God is loving—38:17; 43:3,4; 49:15,16; 63:9
God is merciful—49:13; 54:7,8, 55:3,7
God is powerful—26:4; 33:13; 41:10; 43:13; 48:13; 52:10; 63:12
God is a promise keeper—1:18; 43:2
God is provident—10:5–17; 27:3; 31:5; 44:7; 50:2; 63:14
God is righteous—41:10
God is true—25:1; 38:19; 65:16
God is unequaled—43:10; 44:6; 46:5,9
God is unified—44:6,8,24; 45:5–8,18,21,22; 46:9–11
God is unsearchable—40:28
God is wise—28:29; 40:14,28; 42:9; 44:7; 46:10; 47:10; 66:18
God is wrathful—1:4; 3:8; 9:13,14,19; 13:9; 26:20; 42:24,25; 47:6; 48:9; 54:8; 57:15,16; 64:9

INTERPRETIVE CHALLENGES

Interpretive challenges in a long and significant book such as Isaiah are numerous. The most critical of them focuses on whether Isaiah's prophecies will receive literal fulfillment or not, and on whether the Lord, in His program, has abandoned national Israel and permanently replaced the nation with the church, so that there is no future for national Israel.

On the former issue, literal fulfillment of many of Isaiah's prophecies has already occurred (see Historical and Theological Themes). To contend that those yet unfulfilled will see nonliteral fulfillment is biblically groundless. This fact disqualifies the case for proposing that the church receives some of the promises made originally to Israel. The kingdom promised to David belongs to Israel, not the church. The future exaltation of Jerusalem will be on earth, not in heaven. Christ will reign personally on this earth as we know it, as well as in the new heavens and new earth (Rev. 22:1,3).

Fulfilled Prophecies from Isaiah

The Prophecy	The Fulfillment
The Messiah...	Jesus Christ...
will be born of a virgin (Is. 7:14).	was born of a virgin named Mary (Luke 1:26–31).
will have a Galilean ministry (Is. 9:1, 2).	ministered in Galilee of the Gentiles (Matt. 4:13–16).
will be an heir to the throne of David (Is. 9:7).	was given the throne of His father David (Luke 1:32, 33).
will have His way prepared (Is. 40:3–5).	was announced by John the Baptist (John 1:19–28).
will be spat on and struck (Is. 50:6).	was spat on and beaten (Matt. 26:67).
will be exalted (Is. 52:13).	was highly exalted by God and the people (Phil. 2:9,10).
will be disfigured by suffering (Is. 52:14; 53:2).	was scourged by the soldiers who gave Him a crown of thorns (Mark 15:15–19).
will make a blood atonement (Is. 53:5).	shed His blood to atone for our sins (1 Pet. 1:2).
will be widely rejected (Is. 53:1,3).	was not accepted by many (John 12:37,38).
will bear our sins and sorrows (Is. 53:4,5).	died because of our sins (Rom. 4:25; 1 Pet. 2:24, 25).
will be our substitute (Is. 53:6,8).	died in our place (Rom. 5:6, 8; 2 Cor. 5:21).
will voluntarily accept our guilt and punishment (Is. 53:7,8).	was silent about our sin (Mark 15:4,5; John 10:11; 19:30).
will be buried in a rich man's tomb (Is. 53:9).	was buried in the tomb of Joseph, a rich man from Arimathea (Matt. 27:57–60; John 19:38–42).
will save us who believe in Him (Is. 53:10,11).	provided salvation for all who believe (John 3:16; Acts 16:31).
will die with transgressors (Is. 53:12).	was numbered with the transgressors (Mark 15:27,28; Luke 22:37).
will heal the brokenhearted (Is. 61:1, 2).	healed the brokenhearted (Luke 4:18,19).

On the latter issue, numerous portions of Isaiah support the position that God has not replaced ethnic Israel with an alleged "new Israel." Isaiah has too much to say about God's faithfulness to Israel, that He would not reject the people whom He has created and chosen (43:1). The nation is engraved on the palms of His hands, and Jerusalem's walls are ever before His eyes (49:16). He is bound by His own Word to fulfill the promises He has made to bring them back to Himself and bless them in that future day (55:10–12).

KEY WORDS IN

Isaiah

Light: Hebrew *ʾor*—2:5; 5:30; 10:17; 13:10; 30:26; 45:7; 58:10; 60:20—refers to literal or symbolic light. This Hebrew word often denotes daylight or daybreak (Judg. 16:2; Neh. 8:3), but it can also be symbolic of life and deliverance (Job 33:28,30; Ps. 27:1; 36:9; 49:19; Mic. 7:8,9). In the Bible, light is frequently associated with true knowledge and understanding (42:6; 49:6; 51:4; Job 12:25), and even gladness, good fortune, and goodness (Job 30:26; Ps. 97:11). The Bible describes light as the clothing of God: a vivid picture of His honor, majesty, splendor, and glory (Ps. 104:2; Hab. 3:3,4). A proper lifestyle is characterized by walking in God's light (2:5; Ps. 119:105; Prov. 4:18; 6:20–23).

Blessing: Hebrew *berakah*—19:24,25; 44:3; 51:2; 61:9; 65:8,16; 66:3— comes from a verb expressing several significant ideas, namely "to fill with potency," "to make fruitful," or "to secure victory." The word alludes to God's promise to benefit all nations through Abraham's descendants (Gen. 12:3). When people offer a blessing, they are wishing someone well or offering a prayer on behalf of themselves or someone else (Gen. 49; Deut. 33:1). OT patriarchs are often remembered for the blessings they gave to their children. When God gives a blessing, He gives it to those who faithfully follow Him (Deut. 11:27), providing them with salvation (Ps. 3:8), life (Ps. 133:3), and success (2 Sam. 7:29).

Servant: Hebrew *ʿebed*—20:3; 24:2; 37:35; 42:1; 44:21; 49:5; 53:11—derives from a verb meaning "to serve," "to work," or "to enslave." While *ʿebed* can mean "slave" (Gen. 43:18), slavery in Israel was different than in most places in the ancient Middle East. Slavery was regulated by the law of Moses, which prohibited indefinite slavery and required that slaves be freed on the Sabbath (seventh) year (Exod. 21:2) and the Year of Jubilee, the fiftieth year (Lev. 25:25–28). Sometimes the Hebrew word can refer to the subjects of a king (2 Sam. 10:19). But usually the word is best translated as "servant." God referred to His prophets as "My servants" (Jer. 7:25) and spoke of the coming Messiah as His Servant, the One who would perfectly obey His will (see 42:1–4; 49:1–6; 50:4–9; 52:13–53:12).

Salvation: Hebrew *yeshuʾah*—12:2; 25:9; 33:6; 49:6; 51:8; 59:11; 62:1—describes deliverance from distress and the resultant victory and well-being. The term occurs most often in Psalms and Isaiah, where it is frequently used along with the word *righteousness*, indicating a connection between God's righteousness and His saving acts (45:8; 51:6,8; 56:1; 62:1; Ps. 98:2). This word can be used for a military victory (1 Sam. 14:45), but it is normally used of God's deliverance (Exod. 15:2; Ps. 13:5,6). The expressions *the salvation of the LORD* and *the salvation of our God* speak of God's work on behalf of His people. The expression *the God of my salvation* is more private in nature, referring to the deliverance of an individual (12:2; 52:10; Exod. 14:13; 2 Chr. 20:17; Ps. 88:1; 98:3).

OUTLINE

I. Judgment (1:1–35:10)

    A. Prophecies Concerning Judah and Jerusalem (1:1–12:6)

        1. Judah's social sins (1:1–6:13)

        2. Judah's political entanglements (7:1–12:6)

    B. Oracles of Judgment and Salvation (13:1–23:18)

        1. Babylon and Assyria (13:1–14:27)

        2. Philistia (14:28–32)

        3. Moab (15:1–16:14)

        4. Syria and Israel (17:1–14)

        5. Ethiopia (18:1–7)

        6. Egypt (19:1–20:6)

7. Babylon continued (21:1–10)
8. Edom (21:11, 12)
9. Arabia (21:13–17)
10. Jerusalem (22:1–25)
11. Tyre (23:1–18)
C. Redemption of Israel through World Judgment (24:1–27:13)
1. God's devastation of the earth (24:1–23)
2. First song of thanksgiving for redemption (25:1–12)
3. Second song of thanksgiving for redemption (26:1–19)
4. Israel's chastisements and final prosperity (26:20–27:13)
D. Warnings against Alliance with Egypt (28:1–35:10)
1. Woe to drunken politicians (28:1–29)
2. Woe to religious formalists (29:1–14)
3. Woe to those who hide plans from God (29:15–24)
4. Woe to the pro-Egyptian party (30:1–33)
5. Woe to those who trust in horses and chariots (31:1–32:20)
6. Woe to the Assyrian destroyer (33:1–24)
7. A cry for justice against the nations, particularly Edom (34:1–35:10)
II. Historical Interlude (36:1–39:8)
A. Sennacherib's Attempt to Capture Jerusalem (36:1–37:38)
B. Hezekiah's Sickness and Recovery (38:1–22)
C. Babylonian Emissaries to Jerusalem (39:1–8)
III. Salvation (40:1–66:24)
A. Deliverance from Captivity (40:1–48:22)
1. Comfort to the Babylonian exiles (40:1–31)
2. The end of Israel's misery (41:1–48:22)
B. Sufferings of the Servant of the Lord (49:1–57:21)
1. The Servant's mission (49:1–52:12)
2. Redemption by the Suffering Servant (52:13–53:12)
3. Results of the Suffering Servant's redemption (54:1–57:21)
C. Future Glory of God's People (58:1–66:24)
1. Two kinds of religion (58:1–14)
2. Plea to Israel to forsake their sins (59:1–19)
3. Future blessedness of Zion (59:20–61:11)
4. Nearing of Zion's deliverance (62:1–63:6)
5. Prayer for national deliverance (63:7–64:12)
6. The Lord's answer to Israel's supplication (65:1–66:24)

ANSWERS TO TOUGH QUESTIONS

1. Does Isaiah indicate God's permanent abandonment of the chosen people?

Isaiah's prophecies provide a long view of history, and thus support the future role of Israel in God's plan. God, according to Isaiah, may arrange for harsh punishment of His people, but He has not replaced ethnic Israel with an alleged "new Israel." The

imagery in the NT confirms Isaiah's views. Passages like Romans 11 certainly picture Gentiles being grafted into the tree of God's salvation plan, but the message does not imply complete replacement. God does not forget those who belong to Him.

2. In what ways are Isaiah's prophecies still open to fulfillment, and how?
The literal fulfillment of many of Isaiah's prophecies makes up part of the ancient historical record. Manuscripts like the complete copy of Isaiah found among the Dead Sea scrolls were already well worn when the events of Jesus' life were taking place. The trustworthiness of Isaiah's prophetic statements about the intervening events strongly suggests that his prophecies for the future will also be accurate. To argue that those yet unfulfilled can only be fulfilled figuratively is biblically and historically shortsighted. God's Word remains steadfast. The case for proposing that the church receives some of the promises made originally to Israel rests on shaky ground. The kingdom promised to David still belongs to Israel, not the church. The future exaltation of Jerusalem will be on earth, not in heaven. Christ will reign personally on this earth as we know it, as well as in the new heavens and the new earth (Rev. 22:1,3).

FURTHER STUDY ON ISAIAH
1. Isaiah's call in 6:1–8 represents a memorable event in Scripture. What does it indicate about God's holiness?
2. In the great chapter on salvation (Is. 53), how is God's plan described?
3. What components of Isaiah's character can be found throughout this book?
4. In what ways do Isaiah's prophecies balance hope/salvation with judgment/punishment?
5. What prophecies about the Messiah/Savior stand out for you in Isaiah?
6. How do you understand God's call in your own life (see 6:1–8 again)?

JEREMIAH

The Testimony of Tears

TITLE

This book gains its title from the human author, who begins with "the words of Jeremiah ... " (1:1). Jeremiah recounts more of his own life than any other prophet, telling of his ministry, the reactions of his audiences, testings, and his personal feelings. The name *Jeremiah* means "Jehovah throws," in the sense of laying down a foundation, or "Jehovah establishes, appoints, or sends."

Seven other Jeremiahs appear in Scripture (2 Kin. 23:31; 1 Chr. 5:24; 1 Chr. 12:4; 1 Chr. 12:10; 1 Chr. 12:13; Neh. 10:2; Neh. 12:1), and Jeremiah the prophet is named at least nine times outside of his book (cf. 2 Chr. 35:25; 36:12; 36:21,22; Dan. 9:2; Ezra 1:1; Matt. 2:17; 16:14; 27:9). The Old and New Testaments quote Jeremiah at least seven times: (1) Dan. 9:2 (25:11,12; 29:10); (2) Matt. 2:18 (31:15); (3) Matt. 27:9 (18:2; 19:2,11; 32:6–9); (4) 1 Cor. 1:31 (9:24); (5) 2 Cor. 10:17 (9:24); (6) Heb. 8:8–12 (31:31–34); and (7) Heb. 10:16,17 (31:33,34).

AUTHOR AND DATE

Jeremiah, who served as both a priest and a prophet, was the son of a priest named Hilkiah (not the high priest of 2 Kin. 22:8, who discovered the book of the law). He was from the small village of Anathoth (1:1), today called Anata, about three miles northeast of Jerusalem in Benjamin's tribal inheritance. As an object lesson to Judah, Jeremiah remained unmarried (16:1–4). He was assisted in ministry by a scribe, named Baruch, to whom Jeremiah dictated and who copied and had custody over the writings compiled from the prophet's messages (36:4,32; 45:1). Jeremiah has been known as "the weeping prophet" (cf. 9:1; 13:17; 14:17), living a life of conflict because of his predictions of judgment by the invading Babylonians. He was threatened, tried for his life, put in stocks, forced to flee from Jehoiakim, publicly humiliated by a false prophet, and thrown into a pit.

Jeremiah carried out a ministry directed mostly to his own people in Judah, but which expanded to other nations at times. He appealed to his countrymen to repent and avoid God's judgment via an invader (chaps. 7,26). Once invasion was certain after Judah refused to repent, he pled with them not to resist the Babylonian conqueror in order to prevent total destruction (chap. 27). He also called on delegates of other nations to heed his counsel and submit to Babylon (chap. 27), and he predicted judgments from God on various nations (25:12–38; chaps. 46–51).

Major Trials of Jeremiah

1. Trial By Death Threats (11:18–23)
2. Trial By Isolation (15:15–21)
3. Trial By Stocks (19:14–20:18)
4. Trial By Arrest (26:7–24)
5. Trial By Challenge (28:10–16)
6. Trial By Destruction (36:1–32)
7. Trial By Violence and Imprisonment (37:15)
8. Trial By Starvation (38:1–6)
9. Trial By Chains (40:1)
10. Trial By Rejection (42:1–43:4)

The dates of his ministry, which spanned five decades, are from the Judean king Josiah's thirteenth year, noted in 1:2 (627 B.C.), to beyond the fall of Jerusalem to Babylon in 586 B.C. (Jer. 39,40,52). After 586 B.C., Jeremiah was forced to go with a fleeing remnant of Judah to Egypt (Jer. 43,44). He was possibly still ministering in 570 B.C. A rabbinic note claims that when Babylon invaded Egypt in 568/67 B.C. Jeremiah was taken captive to Babylon. He could have lived even to pen the book's closing scene ca. 561 B.C. in Babylon, when Judah's king Jehoiachin, captive in Babylon since 597 B.C., was allowed liberties in his last days (52:31–34). Jeremiah, if still alive at that time, would have been between 85 and 90 years old.

BACKGROUND AND SETTING

Background details of Jeremiah's times are portrayed in 2 Kings 22–25 and 2 Chronicles 34–36. Jeremiah's messages paint pictures of: (1) his people's sin; (2) the invader God would send; (3) the rigors of siege; and (4) calamities of destruction. Jeremiah's message of impending judgment for idolatry and other sins was preached over a period of forty years (ca. 627–586 B.C. and beyond). His prophecy took place during the reigns of Judah's final five kings (Josiah 640–609 B.C., Jehoahaz 609 B.C., Jehoiakim 609–598 B.C., Jehoiachin 598–597 B.C., and Zedekiah 597–586 B.C.).

Babylon Dominates

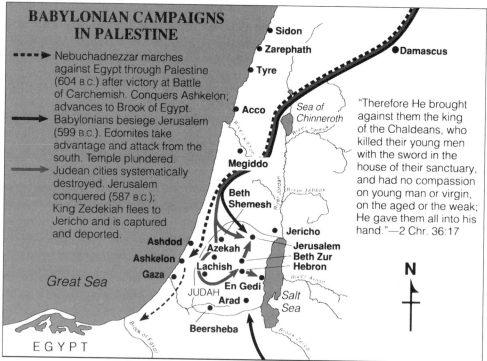

While Joel and Micah had earlier prophesied of Judah's judgment, during Josiah's reign, God's leading prophets were Jeremiah, Habakkuk, and Zephaniah. Later, Jeremiah's contemporaries, Ezekiel and Daniel, played prominent prophetic roles.

The spiritual condition of Judah was one of flagrant idol worship (cf. chap. 2). King Ahaz, preceding his son Hezekiah long before Jeremiah in Isaiah's day, had set up a system of sacrificing children to the god Molech in the Valley of Hinnom just outside Jerusalem (735–715 B.C.). Hezekiah led in reforms and clean-up (Is. 36:7), but his son Manasseh continued to foster child sacrifice along with gross idolatry, which continued into Jeremiah's time (7:31; 19:5; 32:35). Many also worshiped the "queen of heaven" (7:18; 44:19). Josiah's reforms, reaching their apex in 622 B.C., forced a repressing of the worst practices

CHRIST IN . . . JEREMIAH

THE PICTURE OF CHRIST remains interwoven throughout the prophecies of Jeremiah. Christ as the "fountain of living waters" (2:13; John 4:14) stands in stark contrast to the judgment poured over the unrepentant nation of Judah. Jeremiah also portrays Christ as the "balm in Gilead" (8:22), the good Shepherd (23:4), "a righteous Branch" (23:5), "the Lord our righteousness" (23:6), and David the King (30:9).

outwardly, but the deadly cancer of sin was deep and flourished quickly again after a shallow revival. Religious insincerity, dishonesty, adultery, injustice, tyranny against the helpless, and slander prevailed as the norm not the exception.

Politically momentous events occurred in Jeremiah's day. Assyria saw its power wane gradually; then Ashurbanipal died in 626 B.C. Assyria grew so feeble that in 612 B.C. her seemingly invincible capital, Nineveh, was destroyed (cf. the Book of Nahum). The Neo-Babylonian empire under Nabopolassar (625–605 B.C.) became dominant militarily with victories against Assyria (612 B.C.), Egypt (609–605 B.C.), and Israel in 3 phases (605 B.C., as in Dan. 1; 597 B.C., as in 2 Kin. 24:10–16; and 586 B.C., as in Jer. 39,40,52).

KEY PEOPLE IN JEREMIAH

Jeremiah—priest and prophet in the southern kingdom of Judah

King Josiah—sixteenth king of the southern kingdom of Judah; attempted to follow God (1:1–3; 22:11,18)

King Jehoahaz—evil son of Josiah and seventeenth king of the southern kingdom of Judah (22:9–11)

King Jehoiakim—evil son of Josiah and eighteenth king of the southern kingdom of Judah (22:18–23; 25:1–38; 26:1–24; 27:1–11; 35:1–19; 36:1–32)

King Jehoiachin (Coniah)—evil son of Jehoiakim and nineteenth king of the southern kingdom of Judah (13:18–27; 22:24–30)

King Zedekiah—evil uncle of Jehoiachin and twentieth king of the southern kingdom of Judah (21:1–14; 24:8–10; 27:12–22; 32:1–5; 34:1–22; 37:1–21; 38:1–28; 51:59–64)

Baruch—served as Jeremiah's scribe (32:12–16; 36:4–32; 43:3–45:4)

Ebed-Melech—Ethiopian palace official who feared God and helped Jeremiah (38:7–39:16)

King Nebuchadnezzar—greatest king of Babylon; led the people of Judah into captivity (21–52)

The Rechabites—obedient descendants of Jonadab; contrasted to the disobedient people of Israel (35:1–19)

HISTORICAL AND THEOLOGICAL THEMES

The main theme of Jeremiah is judgment upon Judah (chaps. 1–29) with restoration in the future messianic kingdom (23:3–8; 30–33). Whereas Isaiah devoted many chapters to a future glory for Israel (Is. 40–66), Jeremiah gave far less space to this subject. Since God's judgment was imminent he concentrated on current problems as he sought to turn the nation back from the point of no return.

A secondary theme is God's willingness to spare and bless the nation only if the people repent. Though this is a frequent emphasis, it is most graphically portrayed at the potter's shop (18:1–11). A further focus is God's plan for Jeremiah's life, both in his proclamation of God's message and in his commitment to fulfill all of His will (1:5–19; 15:19–21). Other themes include: (1) God's longing for Israel to be tender toward Him, as in the days of first love (2:1–3); (2) Jeremiah's servant tears, as "the weeping prophet" (9:1; 14:17); (3) the close, intimate relationship God had with Israel and that He yearned to keep (13:11); (4) suffering, as in Jeremiah's trials (11:18–23; 20:1–18) and God's sufficiency in all trouble (20:11–13); (5) the vital role that God's Word can play in life (15:16); (6) the place of faith in expecting restoration from the God for whom nothing is too difficult (chap. 32, especially vv. 17,27); and (7) prayer for the coordination of God's will with God's action in restoring Israel to its land (33:3,6–18).

Illustrations of God's Judgment

An Almond Branch (1:11,12)
A Boiling Caldron (1:13–16)
Lions (2:15; 4:7; 5:6; 50:17)
A Scorching Storm Wind (4:11,12; 18:17; 23:19; 25:32)
Wolf (5:6)
Leopard (5:6)
Stripping Away Judah's Branches (5:10)
Fire (5:14)
Making This House (Worship Center) like Shiloh (7:14)
Serpents, Adders (8:17)
Destroying Olive Branches (11:16,17)
Uprooting (12:17)
Linen Sash Made Worthless (13:1–11)
Bottles Filled with Wine and Dashed Against One Another (13:12–14)
A Potter's Jar Shattered (19:10,11; cf. 22:28)
A Hammer [God's Word] Crushing a Rock (23:29)
A Cup of Wrath (25:15)
Zion Plowed as a Field (26:18)
Wearing Yokes of Wood and Iron (27:2; 28:13)
A Hammer [Babylon] (50:23)
A Mountain of Destruction [Babylon] (51:25)

KEY DOCTRINES IN JEREMIAH

Sin—Israel's sin demanded punishment from God (2:1–13,23–37; 5:1–6; 7:16–34; 11:1–17; 17:1–4; 18:1–17; 23:9–40; Exod. 23:33; Deut. 9:16; 1 Kin. 11:39; Ezra 6:17; Job 1:22; Ps. 5:4; Mic. 3:8; Matt. 5:30; Luke 17:1; Rom. 1:29)

Judgment/Punishment (4:3–18; 9:3–26; 12:14–17; 15:1–9; 16:5–13; 19:1–15; 24:8–10; 25:1–38; 39:1–10; 44:1–30; 46:1–51:14; Exod. 12:12; Ps. 1:5; Hos. 5:1; Amos 4:12; John 12:31,32; Rom. 14:10; 2 Thess. 1:7–10)

Restoration of Israel (23:3–8; chaps. 30–33; Deut. 30:1–5; Ps. 71:20,21; Is. 49:6; Nah. 2:2; Acts 1:6–8; 15:16; 1 Pet. 5:10)

GOD'S CHARACTER IN JEREMIAH
God fills heaven and earth—23:24
God is good—31:12,14; 33:9,11
God is holy—23:9
God is just—9:24; 32:19; 50:7
God is kind—31:3
God is long-suffering—15:15; 44:22
God is loving—31:3
God is merciful—3:12; 33:11
God is omnipresent—23:23
God is powerful—5:22; 10:12; 20:11; 37:27
God is a promise keeper—31:33; 33:14
God is righteous—9:24; 12:1
God is sovereign—5:22, 24; 7:1–15; 10:12– 16; 14:22; 17:5–10; 18:5–10, 25:15–38; 27:5–8; 31:1–3; 42:1–22; 51:15–19
God is true—10:10
God is unequaled—10:6
God is wise—10:7,12; 32:19
God is wrathful—3:12,13; 4:8; 7:19,20; 10:10; 18:7,8; 30:11; 31:18–20; 44:3

INTERPRETIVE CHALLENGES
A number of questions arise, such as: How can one explain God's forbidding prayer for the Jews (7:16) and saying that even Moses' and Samuel's advocacy could not avert judgment (15:1)? Did Jeremiah make an actual trek of several hundred miles to the Euphrates River, or did he bury his loin cloth nearby (13:4–7)? Does the curse on Jeconiah's kingly line relate to Christ (22:30)? How is one to interpret the promises of Israel's return to its ancient land (chaps. 30–33)? How will God fulfill the New Covenant in relation to Israel and the church (31:31–34)? See Answers to Tough Questions regarding some of these issues.

A frequent challenge is to understand the prophet's messages in their right time setting, since the Book of Jeremiah is not always chronological, but loosely arranged, moving back and forth in time for thematic effect. Ezekiel, by contrast, usually places his material in chronological order.

OUTLINE
    I. Preparation of Jeremiah (1:1–19)
        A. The Context of Jeremiah (1:1–3)
        B. The Choice of Jeremiah (1:4–10)
        C. The Charge to Jeremiah (1:11–19)
    II. Proclamations to Judah (2:1–45:5)
        A. Condemnation of Judah (2:1–29:32)
            1. First message (2:1–3:5)
            2. Second message (3:6–6:30)
            3. Third message (7:1–10:25)

4. Fourth message (11:1–13:27)

5. Fifth message (14:1–17:18)

6. Sixth message (17:19–27)

7. Seventh message (18:1–20:18)

8. Eight message (21:1–14)

9. Ninth message (22:1–23:40)

10. Tenth message (24:1–10)

11. Eleventh message (25:1–38)

12. Twelfth message (26:1–24)

13. Thirteenth message (27:1–28:17)

14. Fourteenth message (29:1–32)

B. Consolation to Judah—New Covenant (30:1–33:26)

1. The forecast of restoration (30:1–31:40)

2. The faith in restoration (32:1–44)

3. The forecast of restoration—Part 2 (33:1–26)

C. Calamity on Judah (34:1–45:5)

1. Before Judah's fall (34:1–38:28)

2. During Judah's fall (39:1–18)

3. After Judah's fall (40:1–45:5)

III. Proclamations of Judgment on the Nations (46:1–51:64)

A. Introduction (46:1; cf. 25:15–26)

B. Against Egypt (46:2–28)

C. Against Philistia (47:1–7)

D. Against Moab (48:1–47)

E. Against Ammon (49:1–6)

F. Against Edom (49:7–22)

G. Against Damascus (49:23–27)

H. Against Kedar and Hazor [Arabia] (49:28–33)

I. Against Elam (49:34–39)

J. Against Babylon (50:1–51:64)

IV. The Fall of Jerusalem (52:1–34)

A. The Destruction of Jerusalem (52:1–23)

B. The Deportation of Jews (52:24–30)

C. The Deliverance of Jehoiachin (52:31–34)

MEANWHILE, IN OTHER PARTS OF THE WORLD...

Water systems develop that enable water to be brought into certain cities: Jerusalem by means of subterranean water tunnels, Nineveh by means of bucket wells, which were improved under Sennacherib through the construction of aqueducts.

Jeremiah

Heal: Hebrew *rapha*'—3:22; 6:14; 8:11; 15:18; 17:14; 30:17; 51:8—applies literally to the work of a physician. Occasionally it refers to inanimate objects and can best be translated "repair" (1 Kin. 18:30). More commonly, this word connotes the idea of restoring to normal, as in 2 Chronicles 7:14, where God promises to restore the land if His people pray. In the Psalms, God is praised for His role in healing disease (Ps. 103:3), healing the brokenhearted (Ps. 147:3), and healing the soul by providing salvation (Pss. 30:2; 107:20). Isaiah declared that the healing of God's people results from the sacrificial wounds of His Son (Is. 53:5–12).

Shepherd: Hebrew *ro'ah*—6:3; 23:4; 31:10; 43:12; 49:19; 50:44; 51:23—refers to someone who feeds and tends domestic animals. David spoke of God as his Shepherd because God provided, sustained, and guided him (Psalm 23). Kings and other leaders were also seen as shepherds of their people, and the title "shepherd" was frequently applied to kings in the ancient Middle East. David was a true shepherd-king, responsibly leading and protecting his people (2 Sam. 5:1,2). Jeremiah rebuked the leaders of Israel who were false shepherds and failed in their responsibility of caring for the spiritual well-being of God's people (23:1–4).

Prophet: Hebrew *nabi*'—1:5; 6:13; 8:10; 18:18; 23:37; 28:9; 37:3; 51:59—probably comes from the root word meaning "to announce" or "to proclaim" (19:14; Ezek. 27:4). Another possible derivation is from a Hebrew word meaning "to bubble up" or "to pour forth." Prophecy can be compared to the "bubbling up" of the Holy Spirit in a person who delivers a divine message (compare Amos 3:8; Mic. 3:8). In OT times, prophets were heralds or spokesmen who delivered a message for someone else (see 1:5; 2:8; 2 Kin. 17:13; Ezek. 37:7). In the case of the Hebrew prophets, they spoke for God Himself. This is the reason the prophets introduced their messages with "thus says the Lord of hosts" on countless occasions (see 9:7,17).

Word: Hebrew *dabar*—1:2; 5:14; 13:8; 21:11; 24:4; 32:8; 40:1; 50:1—is derived from the verb "to speak," and signifies the word or thing spoken. The phrase *word of the LORD* is used by the prophets at the beginning of a divine message (see 1:13). In the case of prophetic literature, *word* can be a technical term for a prophecy. In the Bible, the word of revelation is associated with prophets (26:5), just as wisdom is associated with wise men and the law with priests (18:18). Jeremiah used *dabar* more than any other prophet in order to clarify the authority given to him by God.

ANSWERS TO TOUGH QUESTIONS

1. How can one explain God's forbidding prayer for the Jews (7:16) and His saying that even Moses and Samuel's intervention would not prevent judgment (15:1)?

General questions about God's willingness or unwillingness to hear someone's prayer must be answered with reference to specific passages. God's direction to Jeremiah not to pray for the people flows from the people's determined attitude of rejection towards God. Jeremiah 7:16 begins with "therefore" and indicates that what follows expresses God's conclusion. The people have no interest in the prayers of Jeremiah, so they are as useless as if God did not hear them.

Later, in Jeremiah 15:1, God describes the desperate sinful condition of His people by stating that even prayers by Moses and Samuel would not stop the consequences that were on the horizon. The spiritual error that God exposes in this passage has to do with the temptation to offer the "right prayer" as a substitute for genuine repentance. The idea that an empty religious ceremony can satisfy the righteous indignation of a holy God was not just an ancient error. Now, as then, God allows people to experience the full results of their behavior as a final opportunity for correction and repentance.

2. Does the curse on Jeconiah's kingly line relate to Christ (22:30)?

Although Jeconiah did have offspring (1 Chr. 3:17,18), he was considered childless in the sense that he had no sons who would reign ("Sitting on the throne … ") because of the curse on his line. That curse continued in his descendants down to Joseph, the husband of Mary. How, then, could Jesus then be the Messiah when His father was under this curse? It was because Joseph was not involved in the blood line of Jesus since He was virgin born (Matt. 1:12). Jesus' blood right to the throne of David came through Mary from Nathan, Solomon's brother, not Solomon (Jeconiah's line) thus bypassing this curse (Luke 3:31, 32). Cf. 36:30.

3. Part of Jeremiah's prophecy includes God's promise of a New Covenant with His people. What is this New Covenant, and how does it relate to Israel, the NT, and the church?

In Jeremiah 31:31–34 God announced the coming establishment of a New Covenant with His people, saying "I will put My law in their minds, and write it on their hearts; and I will be their God, and they shall be My people" (31:33). This covenant will be different than the one that, God says, "I made with their fathers in the day that I took them by the hand to lead them out of the land of Egypt, My covenant which they broke" (verse 32). The fulfillment of this New Covenant would be to individuals as well as to Israel as a nation (verse 36; Rom. 11:16–27). Among the final external indicators of this covenant are (1) a reestablishment of the people in their land (verses 38–40 and chapters 30–33); and (2) a time of ultimate difficulty (30:7).

In principle, this Covenant, also announced by Jesus (Luke 22:20), began to be exercised on behalf of both Jewish and Gentile believers in the church era (1 Cor. 11:25; Heb. 8:7–13; 9:15; 10:14–17; 12:24; 13:20). The idea of a Jewish remnant that appears so often in the OT prophecies, the NT identifies as the "remnant according to the election of grace" (Rom. 11:5). The New Covenant will be finalized for the people of Israel in the last days, including the regathering to their ancient land, Palestine (chapters 30–33). The streams of the Abrahamic, Davidic, and New Covenants will eventually flow as one in the millennial kingdom ruled by the Messiah.

FURTHER STUDY ON JEREMIAH

1. What does the first chapter of Jeremiah indicate about God's plans for individual persons?
2. Jeremiah served as God's prophet for more than forty years. In what ways was he a failure? In what ways was he successful?
3. What does Jeremiah mean when he writes about the New Covenant (chapter 31)?
4. What was Jeremiah's relationship to the kings of his time?
5. How do Jeremiah's prophecies in chapters 46–52 emphasize God's sovereignty in the face of seemingly powerful nations?
6. What does Jeremiah teach you about faithfulness?

LAMENTATIONS
Hope in the Devastation

TITLE
"Lamentations" was derived from a translation of the title as found in the Latin Vulgate (Vg.) translation of the Greek OT, the Septuagint (LXX), and conveys the idea of "loud cries." The Hebrew exclamation *ʾekah* ("How," which expresses "dismay"), used in 1:1; 2:1, and 4:1, gives the book its Hebrew title. However, the rabbis began early to call the book "loud cries" or "lamentations" (cf. Jer. 7:29). No other entire OT book contains only laments, as does this distressful dirge, marking the funeral of the once beautiful city of Jerusalem (cf. 2:15). This book keeps alive the memory of that fall and teaches all believers how to deal with suffering.

AUTHOR AND DATE
The author of Lamentations is not named within the book, but there are internal and historical indications that it was Jeremiah. The LXX introduces Lamentations 1:1, "And it came to pass, after Israel had been carried away captive, . . . Jeremiah sat weeping [cf. 3:48,49, etc.], . . . lamented . . . and said." God had told Jeremiah to have Judah lament (Jer. 7:29), and Jeremiah also wrote laments for Josiah (2 Chr. 35:25).

Jeremiah wrote Lamentations as an eyewitness (cf. 1:13–15; 2:6,9; 4:1–12), possibly with Baruch's secretarial help (cf. Jer. 36:4; 45:1), during or soon after Jerusalem's fall in 586 B.C. It was mid-July when the city fell and mid-August when the temple was burned. Likely, Jeremiah saw the destruction of walls, towers, homes, palace, and temple; he wrote while the event remained painfully fresh in his memory, but before his forced departure to Egypt ca. 583 B.C. (cf. Jer. 43:1–7). The language used in Lamentations closely resembles that used by Jeremiah in his much larger prophetic book (cf. 1:2 with Jer. 30:14; 1:15 with Jer. 8:21; 1:6 and 2:11 with Jer. 9:1,18; 2:22 with Jer. 6:25; 4:21 with Jer. 49:12).

BACKGROUND AND SETTING
The prophetic seeds of Jerusalem's destruction were sown through Joshua 800 years in advance (Josh. 23:15,16). Now, for over forty years, Jeremiah had prophesied of coming judgment and been scorned by the people for preaching doom (ca. 645–605 B.C.). When that judgment came on the disbelieving people from Nebuchadnezzar and the Babylonian army, Jeremiah still responded with great sorrow and compassion toward his suffering and obstinate people. Lamentations relates closely to the Book of Jeremiah, describing the anguish over Jerusalem's receiving God's judgment for unrepentant sins. In the book that bears his name, Jeremiah had predicted the calamity in chaps. 1–29. In Lamentations, he concentrates in more detail on the bitter suffering and heartbreak that was felt over Jerusalem's devastation (cf. Ps. 46:4,5). So critical was Jerusalem's destruction, that the facts are recorded in four separate OT chapters: 2 Kin. 25; Jer. 39:1–11; 52; and 2 Chr. 36:11–21.

All 154 verses have been recognized by the Jews as a part of their sacred canon. Along with Ruth, Esther, Song of Solomon, and Ecclesiastes, Lamentations is included among the OT books of the Megilloth, or "five scrolls," which were read in the synagogue on special occasions. Lamentations is read on the ninth day of Ab (July/Aug.) to remember the date of Jerusalem's destruction by Nebuchadnezzar. Interestingly, this same date later marked the destruction of Herod's temple by the Romans in A.D. 70.

Second Kings, Jeremiah, and Lamentations Compared

	2 Kings 25 (See also 2 Chronicles 36:11–21)	Jeremiah	Lamentations
1. The siege of Jerusalem	1,2	39:1–3; 52:4,5	2:20–22; 3:5,7
2. The famine in the city	3	37:21; 52:6	1:11,19; 2:11,12; 2:19,20; 4:4,5,9,10; 5:9,10
3. The flight of the army and the king	4–7	39:4–7; 52:8–11	1:3,6; 2:2; 4:19,20
4. The burning of the palace, temple, and city	8,9	39:8; 52:13	2:3–5; 4:11; 5:18
5. The breaching of the city walls	10	33:4,5; 52:7	2:7–9
6. The exile of the populace	11,12	28:3,4,14; 39:9,10	1:1,4,5,18; 2:9,14; 3:2,19; 4:22; 5:2
7. The looting of the temple	13–15	51:51	1:10; 2:6,7
8. The execution of the leaders	18–21	39:6	1:15; 2:2,20
9. The vassal status of Judah	22–25	40:9	1:1; 5:8,9
10. The collapse of the expected foreign help	24:7	27:1–11; 37:5–10	4:17; 5:6

© Copyright Moody Press, 1982

KEY PEOPLE IN LAMENTATIONS
Jeremiah—prophet of Judah; mourned the destruction of Jerusalem (1:1–5:22)
People of Jerusalem—people judged by God because of their great sins (1:1–5:22)

HISTORICAL AND THEOLOGICAL THEMES
The chief focus of Lamentations is on God's judgment in response to Judah's sin. This theme can be traced throughout the book (1:5,8,18,20; 3:42; 4:6,13,22; 5:16). A second theme is the hope found in God's compassion (as in 3:22–24,31–33; cf. Ps. 30:3–5). Though the book deals with disgrace, it turns to God's great faithfulness (3:22–25) and closes with grace as Jeremiah moves from lamentation to consolation (5:19–22).

God's sovereign judgment represents a third current in the book. His holiness was so offended by Judah's sin that He ultimately brought the destructive calamity. Babylon was chosen to be His human instrument of wrath (1:5,12,15; 2:1,17; 3:37,38; cf. Jer. 50:23). Jeremiah mentions Babylon more than 150 times from Jer. 20:4 to 52:34, but in Lamentations he never once explicitly names Babylon or its king, Nebuchadnezzar. Only the Lord is identified as the One who dealt with Judah's sin.

Fourth, because the sweeping judgment seemed to be the end of every hope of Israel's salvation and the fulfillment of God's promises (cf. 3:18), much of the book appears in the mode of prayer: (1) 1:11, which represents a wailing confession of sin (cf. v. 18); (2) 3:8, with its anguish when God "shuts out my prayer" (cf. Jer. 7:16; Lam. 3:43–54); (3)

3:55–59, where Jeremiah cries to God for relief, or 3:60–66, where he seeks for recompense to the enemies (which Jer. 50–51 guarantees); and (4) 5:1–22, with its appeal to heaven for restored mercy (which Jer. 30–33 assures), based on the confidence that God is faithful (3:23).

CHRIST IN . . . LAMENTATIONS

THE TEARS OF JEREMIAH flowed from the deep love he had for the people of Israel (3:48-49). In this same way, Christ Himself wept over the city of Jerusalem, crying, "O Jerusalem, Jerusalem, the one who kills the prophets and stones those who are sent to her! How often I wanted to gather your children together, as a hen gathers her chicks under her wings, but you were not willing!" (Matt. 23:37-39; Luke 19:41-44). While Christ must judge those who rebel against Him, He also feels great sorrow over the loss of His beloved people.

A fifth feature relates to Christ. Jeremiah's tears (3:48,49) compare with Jesus' weeping over the same city of Jerusalem (Matt. 23:37–39; Luke 19:41–44). Though God was the judge and executioner, it was a grief to Him to bring this destruction. The statement "In all their affliction, He [God] was afflicted" (Is. 63:9) was true in principle. God will one day wipe away all tears (Is. 25:8; Rev. 7:17; 21:4) when sin shall be no more.

A sixth theme is an implied warning to all who read this book. If God did not hesitate to judge His beloved people (Deut. 32:10), what will He do to the nations of the world who reject His Word?

KEY DOCTRINES IN LAMENTATIONS
God's judgment of Judah's sin (1:5,8,18,20; 3:42; 4:6,13,22; 5:16; Deut. 28:43; Neh. 9:26; Ps. 137:7; Jer. 14:20; 30:14; 52:28; Ezek. 16:37; Dan. 9:5,7,16; Hos. 2:10; Zeph. 3:4; Matt. 23:31)
Hope found in God's compassion (3:22–24,31–33; Ps. 30:3–5; Is. 35:1–10; Jer. 30:1–31:40; Ezek. 37:1–28; Hos. 3:5; 14:1–9; Joel 3:18–21; Amos 9:11–15; Mic. 7:14–20; Zeph. 3:14–20; Zech. 14:1–11; Mal. 4:1–6)

GOD'S CHARACTER IN LAMENTATIONS
God is faithful—3:22–25; 5:19–22
God is good—3:25
God is merciful—3:22–23,32
God is wrathful—1:5,12,15,18; 2:1,17,20–22; 3:37–39

INTERPRETIVE CHALLENGES
Certain details pose initial difficulties. Among them are: (1) imprecatory prayers for judgment on other sinners (1:21–22; 3:64–66); (2) the reason for God shutting out prayer (3:8); and (3) the necessity of judgment that is so severe (cf. 1:1,14; 3:8). See Answers to Tough Questions regarding some of these issues.

OUTLINE
    I. The First Lament: Jerusalem's Devastation (1:1–22)
        A. Jeremiah's Sorrow (1:1–11)
        B. Jerusalem's Sorrow (1:12–22)

II. **The Second Lament: The Lord's Anger Explained (2:1–22)**
   A. The Lord's Perspective (2:1–10)
   B. A Human Perspective (2:11–19)
   C. Jeremiah's Prayer (2:20–22)
III. **The Third Lament: Jeremiah's Grief Expressed (3:1–66)**
   A. His Distress (3:1–20)
   B. His Hope (3:21–38)
   C. His Counsel/Prayer (3:39–66)
IV. **The Fourth Lament: God's Wrath Detailed (4:1–22)**
   A. For Jerusalem (4:1–20)
   B. For Edom (4:21–22)
V. **The Fifth Lament: The Remnant's Prayers (5:1–22)**
   A. To Be Remembered by the Lord (5:1–18)
   B. To Be Restored by the Lord (5:19–22)

ANSWERS TO TOUGH QUESTIONS

1. How does the promise of Christ appear in a book like Lamentations?

Jeremiah serves as one of the strong foreshadowing personalities of Jesus in the OT. Jeremiah's tears over Jerusalem (3:48–49) compare closely with Jesus' weeping over the same city (Matt. 23:37–39; Luke 19:41–44). Jeremiah's grief prepares believers to think about God as the righteous Judge who can execute punishment while at the same time experiencing grief over the suffering of His people. Isaiah described the principle with this statement: "In all their affliction, He [God] was afflicted" (Is. 63:9).

Jeremiah's tears also serve as a reminder of the utter hopelessness of a person without God. Tears point to God's promise to one day remove every cause for tears, and then the tears themselves (Is. 25:8; Rev. 7:17; 21:4) when sin shall be no more.

KEY WORDS IN

Lamentations

Weeps: Hebrew *bakah*—1:2,16—describes the act of wailing, which expresses emotions ranging from grief to happiness. While the word is often associated with lamentation, the "bitter wailing" of ancient people who were mourning their dead (2 Sam.1:12), it is also used with expressions of joy (Gen. 29:11). The ancients wept when saying farewell (Ruth 1:9), over impending doom (Jer. 9:1), to express their joy over the rebuilt temple (Ezra 3:12), and at the burial of an individual (Gen. 50:1). In Lamentations, Jeremiah weeps over the sins of the people, the sins that would eventually result in the destruction of Jerusalem (1:1,16).

Renew: Hebrew *chadash*—5:21—can mean "to renew" (Ps. 51:10) or "to repair" (Is. 61:4). As an adjective, the word identifies something new in contrast to something old (such as the "old harvest" versus the "new harvest;" see Lev. 26:10), or something different when compared to the status quo (such as "a new spirit;" see Ezek. 11:19; 18:31). The Bible teaches that God alone is the One who makes things new, whether a new song in the heart of the faithful (Ps. 40:3), a new phase in His plan of redemption (Is. 42:9; 43:19), a new name (Is. 62:2), or a new heaven and earth (Is. 65:17).

MEANWHILE, IN OTHER PARTS OF THE WORLD...

Pythagoras, the famous mathematician and creator of the Pythagorean Theorem, is born in 581 B.C.

2. What appears to be God's purpose in including a book like Lamentations in the Bible?

The Book of Lamentations presents an implied warning to every reader. Through Jeremiah's words, we see consequences from within. The sorrow and sadness that flow from judgment offer a deterrent. If God did not hesitate to judge His beloved people (Deut. 32:10), what will He do to the nations and peoples of the world who reject His Word?

3. What lessons can we find in Jeremiah's bold call for judgment on the enemies of Judah (1:21–22; 3:64–66) and his report that God has shut out his prayers (3:8)?

The prayers of the prophets and psalmists often sound harsh to us. The boldness of their expressions remind us that it is often a good thing that God has not promised to answer our prayers as we have prayed them. We may express our real desires and real emotions in prayer, but we would be foolish to think that God would limit Himself to our perceptions. Jeremiah's call for retribution was partially answered in the fall of Babylon (Is. 46–47; Jer. 50–51; Dan. 5). God will exercise justice in His time. All accounts will be settled ultimately at the Great White Throne (Rev. 20:11–15).

Jeremiah's description of his prayer life offers a vivid picture of how he felt rather than what God was actually doing. God's negative response to Jeremiah's prayers was not because Jeremiah was guilty of personal sin; rather, it was due to Israel's perpetual sin without repentance. Jeremiah knew that, yet he prayed, wept, and longed to see repentance from his people.

FURTHER STUDY ON LAMENTATIONS

1. How does Lamentations compare and contrast with Jeremiah?
2. How does Lamentations 3:22–32 fit with the rest of the book?
3. What powerful feelings does Jeremiah express in Lamentations?
4. What unique role does Lamentations fill within Scripture?
5. In what ways could Lamentations help you during times of grief?

EZEKIEL
Reflections of God's Glory

TITLE

The book has always been named for its author, Ezekiel (1:3; 24:24), who is nowhere else mentioned in Scripture. His name means "strengthened by God," which, indeed, he was for the prophetic ministry to which God called him (3:8,9). Ezekiel stands like a lonely pillar in the center of the Bible. The location and the loneliness that surrounded his ministry required the truth of his name. Ezekiel uses visions, prophecies, parables, signs, and symbols to proclaim and dramatize the message of God to His exiled people.

AUTHOR AND DATE

If the "thirtieth year" of 1:1 refers to Ezekiel's age, he was 25 when taken captive and 30 when called into ministry. Thirty was the age when priests commenced their office, so it was a notable year for Ezekiel. His ministry began in 593/92 B.C. and extended at least twenty-two years until 571/70 B.C. (cf. 25:17). He was a contemporary of both Jeremiah (who was about twenty years older) and Daniel (who was the same age), whom he names in 14:14,20; 28:3 as an already well-known prophet. Like Jeremiah (Jer. 1:1) and Zechariah (cf. Zech. 1:1 with Neh. 12:16), Ezekiel was both a prophet and a priest (1:3). Because of his priestly background, he was particularly interested in and familiar with the temple details; so God used him to write much about them (8:1–11:25; 40:1–47:12).

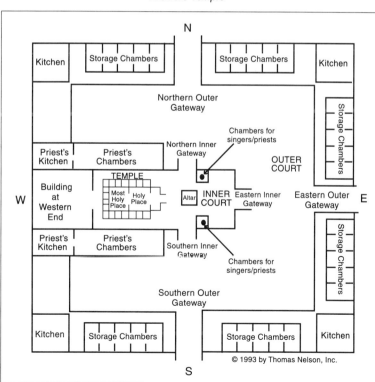

Ezekiel's Temple

The author received his call to prophesy in 593 B.C. (1:2), in Babylon ("the land of the Chaldeans"), during the fifth year of King Jehoiachin's captivity, which began in 597 B.C. Frequently, Ezekiel dates his prophecies from 597 B.C. (8:1; 20:1; 24:1; 26:1; 29:1; 30:20; 31:1; 32:1,17; 33:21; 40:1). He also dates the message in 40:1 as 573/72, the 14th year after 586 B.C., i.e., Jerusalem's final fall. The last dated utterance of Ezekiel was in 571/70 B.C. (29:17). Interestingly, neither Ezekiel nor his book are mentioned anywhere else in Scripture.

Prophecies in chaps. 1–28 are in chronological order. In 29:1, the prophet regresses to a year earlier than in 26:1. But from 30:1 on (cf. 31:1; 32:1,17), he is close to being strictly chronological.

Chapter 40 presents a detailed plan for a new temple complex in Jerusalem. Some interpret this prophecy as an exact blueprint of a physical temple to be constructed in or near Jerusalem during a future millennial (thousand-year) period. A more preferable interpretation views Ezekiel's restored temple not as a blueprint, but as a vision that stresses the purity and spiritual vitality of the ideal place of worship and those who will worship there. Thus, it is not intended to refer to an earthly, physical fulfillment, but expresses the truth found in the name of the new city: THE LORD IS THERE (48:35). For a fuller treatment of these issues, see Answers to Tough Questions

Ezekiel and his wife (who is mentioned in 24:15–27) were among 10,000 Jews taken captive to Babylon in 597 B.C. (2 Kin. 24:11–18). They lived in Tel-Abib (3:15) on the bank of the Chebar River, probably southeast of Babylon. Ezekiel writes of his wife's death in exile (Ezek. 24:18), but the book does not mention Ezekiel's death, which rabbinical tradition suggests occurred at the hands of an Israelite prince whose idolatry he rebuked around 560 B.C.

CHRIST IN . . . EZEKIEL

EZEKIEL CONTAINS SEVERAL PASSAGES illustrating Israel's triumph through the work of the Messiah. Christ is pictured as "one of the highest branches of the high cedar" (17:22–24). This messianic prophecy demonstrates Christ's royal lineage connected to David. The branch, used consistently in Scripture to depict the Messiah, shows Christ as a "young twig, a tender one" who will be planted on the mountain of Israel (34:23,24; 37:24,25; Is. 4:2; Jer. 23:5; 33:15; Zech. 3:8; 6:12). On this height, Ezekiel pictures Christ as growing into a "majestic cedar" able to protect Israel in its shadow.

Christ also appears as the Shepherd over His sheep (34:11–31). However, Ezekiel also describes the Shepherd's judgment on those who abuse the people of Israel (34:17–24; see Matt. 25:31–46).

BACKGROUND AND SETTING

From the historical perspective, Israel's united kingdom lasted more than 110 years (ca. 1043–931 B.C.), through the reigns of Saul, David, and Solomon. Then the divided kingdom, Israel (north) and Judah (south), extended from 931 B.C. to 722/21 B.C. Israel fell to Assyria in 722/21 B.C. leaving Judah, the surviving kingdom for 135 years, which fell to Babylon in 605–586 B.C.

In the more immediate setting, several features were strategic. Politically, Assyria's vaunted military might crumbled after 626 B.C., and the capital, Nineveh, was destroyed in 612 B.C. by the Babylonians and Medes (cf. Nahum). The neo-Babylonian empire had flexed its muscles since Nabopolassar took the throne in 625 B.C., and Egypt, under

Pharaoh Necho II, was determined to conquer what she could. Babylon smashed Assyria in 612–605 B.C., and registered a decisive victory against Egypt in 605 B.C. at Carchemish, leaving, according to the Babylonian Chronicle, no survivors. Also in 605 B.C., Babylon, led by Nebuchadnezzar, began the conquest of Jerusalem and the deportation of captives, among them Daniel (Dan. 1:2). In Dec., 598 B.C., he again besieged Jerusalem, and on Mar. 16, 597 B.C. took possession. This time, he took captive Jehoiachin and a group of 10,000, including Ezekiel (2 Kin. 24:11–18). The final destruction of Jerusalem and the conquest of Judah, including the third deportation, came in 586 B.C.

Religiously, King Josiah (ca. 640–609 B.C.) had instituted reforms in Judah (cf. 2 Chr. 34). Tragically, despite his effort, idolatry had so dulled the Judeans that their awakening was only "skin deep" overall. The Egyptian army killed Josiah as it crossed Palestine in 609 B.C., and the Jews plunged on in sin toward judgment under Jehoahaz (609 B.C.), Jehoiakim [Eliakim] (609–598 B.C.), Jehoiachin (598–597 B.C.), and Zedekiah (597–586 B.C.).

Domestically, Ezekiel and the 10,000 lived in exile in Babylonia (2 Kin. 24:14), more as colonists than captives, being permitted to farm tracts of land under somewhat favorable conditions (Jer. 29). Ezekiel even had his own house (3:24; 20:1).

Prophetically, false prophets deceived the exiles with assurances of a speedy return to Judah (13:3,16; Jer. 29:1). From 593–585 B.C., Ezekiel warned that their beloved Jerusalem

---

KEY WORDS IN

Ezekiel

Son of Man: Hebrew *ben ʾadam*—2:1; 3:17; 12:18; 20:46; 29:18; 39:17; 44:5; 47:6—used over one hundred times referring to Ezekiel. It serves both to emphasize the difference between God the Creator and His creatures, and to mark the prophet Ezekiel as a representative member of the human race. Ezekiel's life was a living parable or object lesson to the Hebrew captives in Babylon (compare 1:3; 3:4–7). In word and deed, Ezekiel was a "sign" to the house of Israel (12:6). Jesus adopted the title Son of Man because He, too, is a representative person—the "last Adam" who became a life-giving spirit (see Matt. 8:20; 1 Cor. 15:45). The title Son of Man also alludes to Daniel's vision of the heavenly being, who is "like the Son of Man" (Dan.l 7:13). Thus the title highlights the mystery of the Incarnation, the fact that Christ is both divine and human. As the God-man, Jesus became a glorious sign for all of sinful humanity (Luke 2:34).

Idols: Hebrew *gillulim*—6:4; 8:10; 14:6; 20:24; 23:30; 36:18; 44:10—related to a verb which means "to roll" (Gen. 29:3; Josh. 10:18). The word refers to "shapeless things" like stones or tree logs of which idols were made (6:9; 20:39; 22:3; 1 Kin. 21:26). The prophet Ezekiel uses this Hebrew term for *idols* nearly forty times, always contemptuously, as these false gods had led Israel away from the true God (14:5). The word *gillulim* may be related to a similar Hebrew expression meaning "dung pellets." Later Jewish commentators mocked the *gillulim* as the "dung idols," idols worthless as dung.

Glory: Hebrew *kabod*—1:28; 3:23; 9:3; 10:18; 31:18; 43:2; 44:4—derived from a Hebrew verb that is used to describe the weight or worthiness of something. It can refer to something negative. For example, in reference to Sodom, it depicts the severe degree of sin that had reached the point of making that city worthy of complete destruction (Gen. 18:20). But usually the word is used to depict greatness and splendor (Gen. 31:1). The noun form is translated *honor* in some instances (1 Kin. 3:13). God's glory is described in the OT as taking the form of a cloud (Exod. 24:15–18) and filling the temple (1 Kin. 8:11). The appropriate response to God's glory is to reverence Him by bowing before Him, as Ezekiel did (3:23; 43:3).

would be destroyed and their exile prolonged, so there was no hope of immediate return. In 585 B.C., an escapee from Jerusalem, who had evaded the Babylonians, reached Ezekiel with the first news that the city had fallen in 586 B.C., about 6 months earlier (33:21). That dashed the false hopes of any immediate deliverance for the exiles, so the remainder of Ezekiel's prophecies related to Israel's future restoration to its homeland and the final blessings of the messianic kingdom.

KEY PEOPLE IN EZEKIEL
Ezekiel—prophet to the people of Israel in Babylonian captivity (1:1–48:35)
Israel's leaders—led the people of Israel into idolatry (7:26–8:12; 9:5,6; 11; 14:1–3; 20:1–3; 22:23–29)
Ezekiel's wife—unnamed woman whose death symbolized the future destruction of Israel's beloved temple (24:15–27)
Nebuchadnezzar—king of Babylon used by God to conquer Tyre, Egypt, and Judah (26:7–14; 29:17–30:10)

HISTORICAL AND THEOLOGICAL THEMES
The "glory of the Lord" is central to Ezekiel, appearing in 1:28; 3:12,23; 10:4,18; 11:23; 43:4,5; 44:4. The book includes graphic descriptions of the disobedience of Israel and Judah, despite God's kindness (chap. 23; cf. chap. 16). It shows God's desire for Israel to bear fruit that He can bless; however, selfish indulgence had left Judah ready for judgment, like a torched vine (chap. 15). References are plentiful to Israel's idolatry and its consequences, such as Pelatiah dropping dead (11:13), a symbolic illustration of overall disaster for the people.

Ezekiel's Sign Experiences

(see Ezekiel 24:24,27)
1. Ezekiel was housebound, tied up, and mute (3:23–27).
2. Ezekiel used a clay tablet and an iron plate as illustrations in his preaching (4:1–3).
3. Ezekiel had to lie on his left side for 390 days and his right side for 40 days (4:4–8).
4. Ezekiel had to eat in an unclean manner (4:9–17).
5. Ezekiel had to shave his head and beard (5:1–4).
6. Ezekiel had to pack his bags and dig through the wall of Jerusalem (12:1–14).
7. Ezekiel had to eat his bread with quaking and drink water with trembling (12:17–20).
8. Ezekiel brandished a sharp sword and struck his hands together (21:8–17).
9. Ezekiel portrayed Israel in the smelting furnace (22:17–22).
10. Ezekiel had to cook a pot of stew (24:1–14).
11. Ezekiel could not mourn at the death of his wife (24:15–24).
12. Ezekiel was mute for a season (24:25–27).
13. Ezekiel put two sticks together and they became one (37:15–28).

Many picturesque scenes illustrate spiritual principles. Among these are Ezekiel eating a scroll (chap. 2); the faces on four angels representing aspects of creation over which God rules (1:10); a "barbershop" scene (5:1–4); graffiti on temple walls reminding readers of what God really wants in His dwelling place, namely holiness and not ugliness (8:10); and sprinkled hot coals depicting judgment (10:2,7).

Chief among the theological themes are God's holiness and sovereignty. These are conveyed by frequent contrast of His bright glory against the despicable backdrop of Judah's sins (1:26–28; often in chaps. 8–11; and 43:1–7). Closely related is God's purpose of glorious triumph so that all may "know that I am the LORD." This divine "trademark," God's signature authenticating His acts, is mentioned more than 60 times, usually with a judgment (6:7; 7:4), but occasionally after the promised restoration (34:27; 36:11,38; 39:28).

Another feature involves God's angels carrying out His program behind the scenes (1:5–25; 10:1–22). A further important theme is God's holding each individual accountable for pursuing righteousness (18:3–32).

Ezekiel also stresses sinfulness in Israel (2:3–7; 8:9,10) and other nations (throughout chaps. 25–32). He deals with the necessity of God's wrath to deal with sin (7:1–8; 15:8); God's frustration of man's devices to escape from besieged Jerusalem (12:1–13; cf. Jer. 39:4–7); and God's grace pledged in the Abrahamic covenant (Gen. 12:1–3) being fulfilled by restoring Abraham's people to the land of the covenant (chaps. 34,36–48; cf. Gen. 12:7). God promises to preserve a remnant of Israelites through whom He will fulfill His restoration promises and keep His inviolate Word.

KEY DOCTRINES IN EZEKIEL

The work of angels—who carry out God's program behind the scenes in many ways by demonstrating God's glory (1:5–25; 10:1–22), destroying evil (Gen. 19:12–13), and worshiping God (Deut. 32:43; Is. 6:2–4; Rev. 4:6–8)

The sinfulness of Israel (2:3–7; 5:6; 8:9,10; 9:9; 1 Sam. 8:7,8; 2 Kin. 21:16; Pss. 10:11; 94:7; Is. 6:9; 29:15; Jer. 3:25; Mic. 3:1–3; 7:3; John 3:20,21; Acts 13:24; Rev. 2:14)

GOD'S CHARACTER IN EZEKIEL

God is glorious—1:28; 3:12,23; 9:3; 10:4,18,19; 11:23; 43:4,5; 44:4
God is holy—1:26–28; 8–11; 43:1–7
God is just—18:25,29; 33:17,20
God is long-suffering—20:17
God is provident—28:2–10
God is wrathful—7:19

INTERPRETIVE CHALLENGES

Ezekiel uses extensive symbolic language, as did Isaiah and Jeremiah. This raises the question as to whether certain portions of Ezekiel's writings are to be taken literally or figuratively. Other challenges include how individual judgment can be worked out in chap. 18, when the wicked elude death in 14:22,23 and some of the godly die in an invasion, 21:3,4; how God would permit a faithful prophet's wife to die (24:15–27); when some of the judgments on other nations will occur (chaps. 25–32); whether the temple in chaps. 40–46 will be a literal one and in what form; and how promises of Israel's future relate to God's program with the church. See Answers to Tough Questions regarding some of these issues.

OUTLINE

The book can be largely divided into sections about condemnation/retribution and then consolation/restoration. A more detailed look divides the book into four sections. First, are prophecies on the ruin of Jerusalem (chaps. 1–24). Second, are prophecies of retribution on nearby nations (chaps. 25–32), with a glimpse at God's future restoration of Israel (28:25,26). Thirdly, there is a transition chapter (33), which gives instruction concerning a last call for Israel to repent. Finally, the fourth division includes rich expectations involving God's future restoration of Israel (chaps. 34–48).

    I. Prophecies of Jerusalem's Ruin (1:1–24:27)
        A. Preparation and Commission of Ezekiel (1:1–3:27)
            1. Divine appearance to Ezekiel (1:1–28)
            2. Divine assignment to Ezekiel (2:1–3:27)
        B. Proclamation of Jerusalem's Condemnation (4:1–24:27)
            1. Signs of coming judgment (4:1–5:4)
            2. Messages concerning judgment (5:5–7:27)
            3. Visions concerning abomination in the city and temple
               (8:1–11:25)
            4. Explanations of judgment (12:1–24:27)
    II. Prophecies of Retribution to the Nations (25:1–32:32)
        A. Ammon (25:1–7)
        B. Moab (25:8–11)
        C. Edom (25:12–14)
        D. Philistia (25:15–17)
        E. Tyre (26:1–28:19)
        F. Sidon (28:20–24) (Digression): The Restoration of Israel (28:25, 26)
        G. Egypt (29:1–32:32)
    III. Provision for Israel's Repentance (33:1–33)
    IV. Prophecies of Israel's Restoration (34:1–48:35)
        A. Regathering of Israel to the Land (34:1–37:28)
            1. Promise of a True Shepherd (34:1–31)
            2. Punishment of the nations (35:1–36:7)
            3. Purposes of restoration (36:8–38)
            4. Pictures of restoration—dry bones and two sticks (37:1–28)

B. Removal of Israel's Enemies from the Land (38:1–39:29)
    1. Invasion of Gog to plunder Israel (38:1–16)
    2. Intervention of God to protect Israel (38:17–39:29)
C. Reinstatement of True Worship in Israel (40:1–46:24)
    1. New temple (40:1–43:12)
    2. New worship (43:13–46:24)
D. Redistribution of the Land in Israel (47:1–48:35)
    1. Position of the river (47:1–12)
    2. Portions for the tribes (47:13–48:35)

MEANWHILE, IN OTHER PARTS OF THE WORLD...
Aesop, a former Phrygian slave, writes his famous fables. Greek settlers bring the olive tree to Italy.

ANSWERS TO TOUGH QUESTIONS

1. When reading Ezekiel, it is sometimes difficult to decide whether the language he uses is descriptive of a literal event or symbolic of an idea or principle. Can we use some examples in Ezekiel to demonstrate the difference?

Ezekiel's life offered his audience a sequence of experiences and actions that became teachable moments. Some of these were scenes in visions that held special significance. For example, the first three chapters of the book report extended visions in which the prophet saw a whirlwind, heavenly creatures, and an edible scroll; he also received his call to the prophetic ministry.

In addition, Ezekiel carried out certain unusual or highly symbolic actions that were intended to picture a message or convey a warning. In 4:1–3, the prophet was directed to carve on a clay tablet and then use an iron plate as a sign about the danger facing Jerusalem. Other acted-out sermons followed: symbolic sleeping postures (4:4–8), siege bread making and baking (4:9–17), and haircutting and burning (5:1–4). God instructed Ezekiel to respond even to the tragedies in his life in such a way that a message was communicated to the people. The prophet learned of his wife's impending death but was told by God that his loss would provide an important lesson the people needed to hear. Just as Ezekiel was not allowed to mourn, the people would not be allowed to mourn when they finally faced the "death" of Jerusalem. "Thus Ezekiel is a sign to you; according to all that he has done you shall do; and when this comes, you shall know that I am the Lord GOD" (24:24).

The unique nature of Ezekiel's approach creates a striking contrast between the clarity of his message and the willful rejection of that message by the people. His ministry removed every excuse.

2. Is there a contradiction between 18:1–20, in which individual responsibility for sin is emphasized, and 21:1–7, in which God applies judgment to both the "righteous and wicked" (verse 4)?

The specific subject of these two passages is quite different. The first deals with the personal consequences and responsibilities that are part of each person's life. No amount of blaming others or offering excuses can remove a person's accountability before God. The second passage deals with the corporate consequences of living in a fallen world. When God chose to use Babylon as a weapon of punishment, He did so fully aware that some people who honored Him would suffer and die as a result. A person's connection with a society means that the good and evil that fall on that society may fall on members who have not directly contributed to the cause.

The principles in 18:1–20 prevail in the end because they describe the way in which God will eventually settle moral accounts. Each person will be held responsible for his or her own life. Only those "in Christ" can face that event with hope.

3. Is the temple in chapters 40-46 a literal temple?

The temple mentioned here could not be the heavenly temple since Ezekiel was taken to Israel to see it (v. 2). It could not be Zerubbabel's temple since the glory of God was not present then. It could not be the eternal temple since the Lord and the Lamb are its temple (cf. Rev. 21:22). Therefore, the temple mentioned must be the earthly millennial temple built with all of the exquisite details that are yet to be outlined.

The Holy District

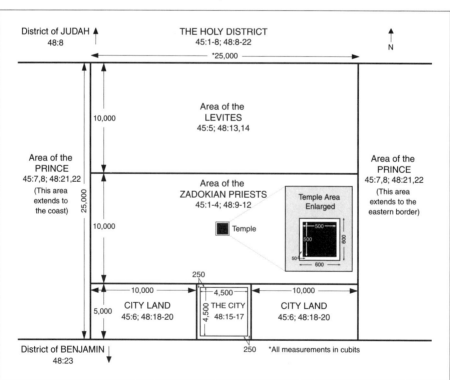

FURTHER STUDY ON EZEKIEL

1. What memorable visions were given to Ezekiel as part of his prophetic role?
2. How does Ezekiel illustrate and describe God's holiness?
3. What differences are there between the false hopes being offered to the people by Ezekiel's contemporaries and the promises of restoration he preached?
4. What scathing words of judgment did Ezekiel have for leaders?
5. How does Ezekiel emphasize the importance of true worship throughout his book?

DANIEL
Portrait of a Godly Man

TITLE

According to Hebrew custom, the title is drawn from the prophet who throughout the book received revelations from God. Daniel bridges the entire seventy years of the Babylonian captivity (ca. 605–536 B.C.; cf. 1:1 and 9:1–3). Nine of the twelve chapters relate revelation through dreams/visions. Daniel was God's mouthpiece to the Gentile and Jewish world, declaring God's current and future plans.

AUTHOR AND DATE

Several verses indicate that the writer is Daniel (8:15,27; 9:2; 10:2,7; 12:4,5), whose name means "God is my Judge." He wrote in the first person from 7:2 on, and is to be distinguished from the other three men named Daniel in the OT (cf. 1 Chr. 3:1; Ezra 8:2; Neh. 10:6). As a teenager, possibly about 15 years old, Daniel was kidnapped from his noble family in Judah and deported to Babylon to be brainwashed into Babylonian culture for the task of assisting in dealing with the imported Jews. There he spent the remainder of a long life (85 years or more). He made the most of the exile, successfully exalting God by his character and service. He quickly rose to the role of statesman by official royal appointment and served as a confidant of kings as well as a prophet in two world empires, i.e., the Babylonian (2:48) and the Medo-Persian (6:1,2). Christ confirmed Daniel as the author of this book (cf. Matt. 24:15).

Daniel lived beyond the time described in Dan. 10:1 (ca. 536 B.C.). It seems most probable that he wrote the book shortly after this date but before ca. 530 B.C. Daniel 2:4b–7:28, which prophetically describes the course of Gentile world history, was originally and appropriately written in Aramaic, the contemporary language of international business. Ezekiel, Habakkuk, Jeremiah, and Zephaniah were Daniel's prophetic contemporaries.

BACKGROUND AND SETTING

The book begins in 605 B.C. when Babylon conquered Jerusalem and exiled Daniel, his three friends, and others. It continues to the eventual demise of Babylonian supremacy in 539 B.C., when Medo-Persian armies conquered Babylon (5:30,31), and goes even beyond that to 536 B.C. (10:1). After Daniel was transported to Babylon, the Babylonian victors conquered Jerusalem in two further stages (597 B.C. and 586 B.C.). In both takeovers, they deported more Jewish captives. Daniel passionately remembered his home, particularly the temple at Jerusalem, almost seventy years after having been taken away from it (6:10).

Daniel's background is alluded to in part by Jeremiah, who names three of the last five kings in Judah before captivity (cf. Jer. 1:1–3): Josiah (ca. 641–609 B.C.), Jehoiakim (ca. 609–597 B.C.) and Zedekiah (597–586 B.C.). Jehoahaz (ca. 609 B.C.) and Jehoiachin (ca. 598–597 B.C.) are not mentioned (see Jeremiah: Background and Setting). Daniel is also mentioned by Ezekiel (cf. 14:14,20; 28:3) as being righteous and wise. He is alluded to by the writer of Hebrews as one of "the prophets: who through faith . . . stopped the mouths of lions" (Heb. 11:32,33).

The long-continued sin of the Judeans without national repentance eventually led to God's judgment for which Jeremiah, Habakkuk, and Zephaniah had given fair warning. Earlier, Isaiah and other faithful prophets of God had also trumpeted the danger. When Assyrian power had ebbed by 625 B.C., the Neo-Babylonians conquered: (1) Assyria with its capital Nineveh in 612 B.C.; (2) Egypt in

CHRIST IN . . . DANIEL

IN DANIEL, Christ is portrayed as a stone that "became a great mountain and filled the whole earth" (2:35). Daniel's prophecies describe Christ's kingdom as standing forever and "consuming all [other] kingdoms" (2:44). Christ is called the coming Messiah who shall be cut off (9:25,26). Daniel identifies the date of His coming, which corresponds to the date of the triumphal entry of Jesus into Jerusalem.

Daniel also describes Christ as "One like the Son of Man" (7:13). This title was used by Christ Himself (Matt. 16:26; 19:28; 26:64) and demonstrates the humanity of Jesus. However, Daniel describes the Son of Man as one who approaches Almighty God and is given universal authority.

the following years; and (3) Judah in 605 B.C., when they overthrew Jerusalem in the first of three steps (also 597 B.C., 586 B.C.). Daniel was one of the first groups of deportees, and Ezekiel followed in 597 B.C.

Israel of the northern kingdom had earlier fallen to Assyria in 722 B.C. With Judah's captivity, the judgment was complete. In Babylon, Daniel received God's word concerning successive stages of Gentile world domination through the centuries until the greatest Conqueror, Messiah, would put down all Gentile lordship. He then would defeat all foes and raise His covenant people to blessing in His glorious millennial kingdom.

KEY PEOPLE IN DANIEL

Daniel—also called Belteshazzar; Israelite captive who became a royal advisor (1:1–12:13)

Nebuchadnezzar—great king of Babylon; went temporarily insane for not acknowledging God's sovereign position (1:1–4:37)

Shadrach—also called Hananiah; exiled Jew placed in charge of the province of Babylon; saved by God from the "fiery furnace" (1:7; 2:49; 3:8–30)

Meshach—also called Mishael; exiled Jew placed in charge of the province of Babylon; saved by God from the "fiery furnace" (1:7; 2:49; 3:8–30)

Abed-Nego—also called Azariah; exiled Jew placed in charge of the province of Babylon; saved by God from the "fiery furnace" (1:7; 2:49; 3:8–30)

Belshazzar—successor of Nebuchadnezzar as king of Babylon; also used Daniel as an interpreter (5:1–30)

Darius—Persian successor of Belshazzar as ruler of Babylon; his advisors tricked him into sending Daniel to the lions' den (5:31–6:28)

HISTORICAL AND THEOLOGICAL THEMES

Daniel was written to encourage the exiled Jews by revealing God's program for them, both during and after the time of Gentile power in the world. Prominent above every other theme in the book is God's sovereign control over the affairs of all rulers and nations, and their final replacement with the True King. The key verses are 2:20–22,44 (cf. 2:28,37; 4:34,35; 6:25–27). God had not suffered defeat in allowing Israel's fall (Dan. 1), but was providentially working His sure purposes toward an eventual full display of His King, the exalted Christ. He sovereignly allowed Gentiles to dominate Israel, i.e., Babylon (605–539 B.C.), Medo-Persia (539–331 B.C.), Greece (331–146 B.C.), Rome (146 B.C.–A.D. 476), and all the way to the Second Advent of Christ. These stages in Gentile power are set forth in chaps. 2 and 7. This same theme also embraces Israel's experience both in defeat and finally in her kingdom blessing in chaps. 8–12 (cf. 2:35,45; 7:27). A key aspect within the over-arching theme of God's kingly control is Messiah's coming to rule the world in glory over all men (2:35,45; 7:13,14,27). He is like a stone in chap. 2, and like a son of man in chap. 7. In addition, He is the Anointed One (Messiah) in chap. 9:26. Chapter 9 provides the chronological framework from Daniel's time to Christ's kingdom.

A second theme woven into the fabric of Daniel is the display of God's sovereign power through miracles. Daniel's era is one of six in the Bible with a major focus on miracles by which God accomplished His purposes. Other periods include: (1) the Creation and Flood (Gen. 1–11); (2) the patriarchs and Moses (Gen. 12–Deut.); (3) Elijah and Elisha (1 Kin. 19–2 Kin. 13); (4) Jesus and the apostles (Gospels, Acts); and (5) the time of the Second Advent (Revelation). God, who has everlasting dominion and ability to work according to His will (4:34,35), is capable of miracles, all of which would be lesser displays of power than was exhibited when He acted as Creator in Genesis 1:1. Daniel chronicles the God-enabled recounting and interpreting of dreams which God used to reveal His will (chaps. 2,4,7). Other miracles included: (1) His writing on the wall and Daniel's interpreting it (chap. 5); (2) His protection of the three men in a blazing furnace (chap. 3); (3) His provision of safety for Daniel in a lions' den (chap. 6); and (4) supernatural prophecies (chaps. 2; 7; 8; 9:24–12:13).

KEY WORDS IN

Daniel

Interpretation: Aramaic *peshar*—2:6,30; 4:7,18; 5:7,15,17; 7:16—literally means "to untie" or "to loose." In other words, Daniel could unravel the mysteries of dreams and visions: He could explain or solve them. Yet he was always quick to give God the credit for his ability (2:28).

Vision: Hebrew *chazon*—8:1,13,15,26; 9:21, 24; 11:14—dream or a vision, derived from a common Hebrew verb meaning "to see." Dreams and visions were often recognized by the ancients as revelations from the gods, or from God Himself in the case of the Hebrews (Is. 1:1). Daniel received a visionary message from God that spoke about the future of the kingdoms of Persia and Greece. His dream was encoded in symbols that required the interpretive assistance of the angel Gabriel (8:15–27). The author of Proverbs insists that revelation from God is essential to the well-being of a society. Without God's law revealed in Scripture, the foundation of a society crumbles (see Prov. 29:18).

KEY DOCTRINES IN DANIEL

God's sovereign control (2:20-22,44; 1 Kin. 3:9,10; 4:29; Ps. 31:15; Esther 1:13; Job 12:18,22; Heb. 4:13; James 1:5)

Miracles of God (6:16–23; Ex. 4:3,4; 14:21,22; Josh. 6:6–20; 1 Kin. 18:36,38; Matt. 9:5–13; Luke 17:14; John 2:6–10; 3:2; Acts 14:13; 19:11)

The promised Messiah (2:35,45; 7:13,14,27; 9:26; Is. 28:16; Ezek. 1:26; Matt. 16:16–20; 24:30; Luke 20:18; John 3:35,36; 1 Cor. 15:27; Eph. 1:22; Phil. 2:9–11)

GOD'S CHARACTER IN DANIEL
God is merciful—9:9
God is powerful—3:17; 4:35
God is provident—4:29–31,37
God is righteous—9:7,16
God is true—4:37
God is wise—2:20–22
God is wrathful—9:16

INTERPRETIVE CHALLENGES
The main challenges center on interpreting passages about future tribulation and kingdom promises. Though the use of Imperial Aramaic and archeology have confirmed the early date of writing, some skeptical interpreters, unwilling to acknowledge supernatural prophecies that came to pass (there are over 100 in chap. 11 alone that were fulfilled), place these details in the intertestamental times, between the last events of the OT and the first events of the NT (ca. 424–26 B.C.). They see these prophecies, not as miraculously foretelling the future, but as simply the observations of a later writer, who is recording events of his own day. Thus, they date Daniel in the days of Antiochus IV Epiphanes (175–164 B.C., chap. 8; 11:21–45). According to this scheme, the expectation of Christ as the "stone" and "Son of Man" (chaps. 2,7) turned out to be a mistaken notion that did not actually come to pass, or the writer was being intentionally deceptive.

However, interpreted literally, Daniel's work and that of the other prophets teach a future seven-year judgment period (cf. 7:21,22; 11:36–45; 12:1), and a literal 1,000-year kingdom (cf. Rev. 20) after Christ's second coming, when He will reign over Israelites and Gentiles (7:27). This will be an era before and distinct from the absolutely perfect, ultimate state of the new heaven and the new earth, with its capital, the New Jerusalem (Rev. 21,22). The literal interpretation of prophecy leads to the premillennial perspective of the end times.

Many other aspects of interpretation challenge readers: such as, interpreting numbers (1:12,20; 3:19; 9:24–27); identifying the one like a Son of Man (7:13,14); determining whether chap. 8:19-23 is Antiochus of the past or Antichrist of the far future; explaining the "seventy sevens" in 9:24–27; and deciding whether Antiochus of 11:21–35 is still meant in 11:36–45, or whether it is the future Antichrist.

OUTLINE
    I. The Personal Background of Daniel (1:1–21)
        A. Conquest of Jerusalem (1:1,2)
        B. Conscription of Jews for Training (1:3–7)
        C. Courage of Four Men during Trials (1:8–16)
        D. Choice of Four Men for Royal Positions (1:17–21)
    II. The Prophetic Course of Gentile Dominion (2:1–7:28)
        A. Dilemmas of Nebuchadnezzar (2:1–4:37)
        B. Debauchery and Demise of Belshazzar (5:1–31)
        C. Deliverance of Daniel (6:1–28)
        D. Dream of Daniel (7:1–28)

III. The Prophetic Course of Israel's Destiny (8:1–12:13)
 A. Prophecy of the Ram and Male Goat (8:1–27)
 B. Prophecy of the Seventy Weeks (9:1–27)
 C. Prophecy of Israel's Humiliation and Restoration (10:1–12:13)

MEANWHILE, IN OTHER PARTS OF THE WORLD...
Confucius, the Chinese philosopher, is born and later spreads his philosophies around Asia.

ANSWERS TO TOUGH QUESTIONS

1. How can those who believe in the miraculous nature of Daniel's prophecies and other miracles answer those skeptics who actually doubt Daniel's authorship and early date because the predictions are so astonishingly accurate?

Confidence in the divine origin of Scripture does not rely on blind faith. There are reasonable explanations and acceptable corroborating evidence that point to the trustworthiness of the Bible. Daniel's use of what is now called Imperial Aramaic in writing the book points to an early date. The Dead Sea scrolls offer evidence that also pushes back the date for Daniel.

When accurate prophecy and possible miracles are discounted by definition as unacceptable, proving Daniel's value becomes challenging. But the problem has little to do with lack of evidence and much to do with willful unbelief. Skeptical interpreters, unwilling to acknowledge supernatural prophecies in Daniel that came to pass (over a hundred in chap. 11 alone that were fulfilled) attempt to replace miraculous foresight with simple observation. They assume that the writer of Daniel was actually living in the time of Antiochus and reported current events in prophetic form. That is, the writer wrote as though he was predicting certain events, when, in reality, he was writing after the events had occurred. For scholars like these, no amount of fulfilled prophecy will be enough to convince. They actually become a reminder to believers that people are not argued into the kingdom of God. The most compelling evidence needs the assistance of God's Spirit in bringing resistant people to genuine faith.

2. Who was the fourth person in the fiery furnace of 3:19–25?

The delivery of Shadrach, Meshach, and Abed-Nego from the flames was an astonishing, miraculous event. The furnace was real, and the flames were hot. The guards who carried the young men close enough to cast them into the furnace were killed. Why complicate this miracle with a fourth person in the furnace? Because the king himself noticed the discrepancy between the number he had thrown into the flames and the number he saw strolling about. The truth usually includes unexpected complications.

The king concluded the fourth person was a heavenly being. He identified the visitor in two different ways: "like the Son of God" (3:25) and "angel" (3:28). When he commanded the three friends to exit the furnace, the king did not extend an invitation to God's special servant.

Viewed from the context of all of Scripture, the fourth person could possibly have been the second person of the Godhead (Jesus Christ) in a preincarnate appearance. For other, similar, Old Testament instances, see Exodus 3:2, Joshua 5:13–15, and Judges 6:11 and following. While the term *angel* is used in these reports, the person had a special connection with the Lord. He wasn't just any angel, but the Angel of the Lord. His presence may be startling, but He does not have the stunning and awe-inspiring appearance of an angel. The king saw four men in the furnace. The One who appeared miraculously he identified as the Son of God. It may well have been an inspired exclamation.

3. Why is the Book of Daniel often called the Old Testament equivalent of the New Testament Book of Revelation?

The books of Daniel and Revelation complement one another in many ways. Written about six hundred years apart, they both deal with God's plan in history. Though much of Daniel's prophetic vision had already come true by the time John wrote Revelation, there are two specific ways in which John's work complements Daniel's:

Both books deal in part with final events and offer parallel prophetic views of the closing days of the original universe and God's design of the new heaven, earth, and kingdom.

Revelation confirms the understanding of prophecy that suggests fulfillment can often happen in stages or waves. For instance, many of the prophecies given to Daniel were fulfilled to some degree in the historic events preceding the life of Christ, but will be ultimately and completely fulfilled in the final events of history.

FURTHER STUDY ON DANIEL

1. Develop a biographical sketch of Daniel. What kind of person was he?
2. How would you hold Daniel up as an example for young people?
3. How did Daniel balance responsibility as a government official and his relationship with God?
4. What do Daniel's friends teach us about faith?
5. What prophetic visions in Daniel most pique your curiosity to learn more?
6. What does Daniel teach us about God?

HOSEA
U n c o n d i t i o n a l   L o v e   a n d   C o m p a s s i o n

TITLE

The title is derived from the main character and author of the book. The meaning of his name, "salvation," is the same as that of Joshua (cf. Num. 13:8,16) and Jesus (Matt. 1:21). Hosea is the first of the twelve minor prophets. "Minor" refers to the brevity of the prophecies, as compared to the length of the works of Isaiah, Jeremiah, and Ezekiel.

AUTHOR AND DATE

The Book of Hosea is the sole source of information about the author. Little is known about him, and even less about his father, Beeri (1:1). Hosea was probably a native of the northern kingdom of Israel, since he shows familiarity with the history, circumstances, and topography of the north (cf. 4:15; 5:1,13; 6:8,9; 10:5; 12:11,12; 14:6). This would make him and Jonah the only writing prophets from the northern kingdom. Although he addressed both Israel (the northern kingdom) and Judah (the southern kingdom), he identified the king of Israel as "our king" (7:5).

Hosea had a lengthy period of ministry, prophesying ca. 755–710 B.C., during the reigns of Uzziah (790–739 B.C.), Jotham (750–731 B.C.), Ahaz (735–715 B.C.), and Hezekiah (715–686 B.C.) in Judah, and Jeroboam II (793–753 B.C.) in Israel (1:1). His long career spanned the last six kings of Israel from Zechariah (753–752 B.C.) to Hoshea (732–722 B.C.). The overthrow of Zechariah (the last of the dynasty of Jehu) in 752 B.C. is depicted as yet future (1:4). Thus he followed Amos' preaching in the north, and was a contemporary of Isaiah and Micah as well, both of whom prophesied in Judah. Second Kings 14–20 and 2 Chronicles 26–32 record the historical period of Hosea's ministry.

BACKGROUND AND SETTING

Hosea began his ministry to Israel (also called Ephraim, after its largest tribe) during the final days of Jeroboam II, under whose guidance Israel was enjoying both political peace and material prosperity, but moral corruption and spiritual bankruptcy. Upon Jeroboam II's death (753 B.C.), however, anarchy prevailed and Israel declined rapidly. Until her overthrow by Assyria twenty years later, four of Israel's six kings were assassinated by their successors. Prophesying during the days surrounding the fall of Samaria, Hosea focuses on Israel's moral waywardness (cf. the Book of Amos) and her breach of the convenantal relationship with the Lord, announcing that judgment was imminent.

Circumstances were not much better in the southern kingdom. Usurping the priestly function, Uzziah had been struck with leprosy (2 Chr. 26:16–21); Jotham condoned idolatrous practices, opening the way for Ahaz to encourage Baal worship (2 Chr.

CHRIST IN . . . HOSEA

HOSEA PICTURES THE RELATIONSHIP between a faithful husband (Hosea, God) and an unfaithful bride (Gomer, Israel). The presence of Christ permeates the Book of Hosea as the Lover and redeemer of His people, just as Hosea acted as the redeemer of his wife, Gomer. Hosea also depicts Christ's position as Savior of His people: "And you shall know no God but Me; for there is no savior besides Me" (13:4).

27:1–28:4). Hezekiah's revival served only to slow Judah's acceleration toward a fate similar to that of her northern sister. Weak kings on both sides of the border repeatedly sought out alliances with their heathen neighbors (7:11; cf. 2 Kin. 15:19; 16:7) rather than seeking the Lord's help.

KEY PEOPLE IN HOSEA

Hosea—prophet to the northern kingdom of Israel; his marriage reflected God's relationship with Israel (1:1–14:9)

Gomer—prostitute who became Hosea's wife (1:3–9)

Their children—Jezreel, Lo-Ruhamah, Lo-Ammi; the name of each child illustrated God's relationship with Israel (1:3–2:1)

HISTORICAL AND THEOLOGICAL THEMES

The theme of Hosea is God's loyal love for His covenant people, Israel, in spite of their idolatry. Thus Hosea has been called the St. John (the apostle of love) of the OT. The Lord's true love for His people is unending and will tolerate no rival. Hosea's message contains much condemnation, both national and individual, but at the same time, he poignantly portrays the love of God toward His people with passionate emotion. Hosea was instructed by God to marry a certain woman, and experience with her a domestic life which was a dramatization of the sin and unfaithfulness of Israel. The marital life of Hosea and his wife, Gomer, provide the rich metaphor which clarifies the themes of the book: sin, judgment, and forgiving love.

KEY WORDS IN

Hosea

Stumble: Hebrew *kashal*—4:5; 5:5—literally means "to totter," "to trip and fall," or "to stumble." The prophets frequently used this word to describe the spiritual life of the Hebrews. For example, Hosea likens both false prophets and their followers to those who stumble in the dark. They are stumbling over the sin of idolatry and falling to their ruin (4:5; 5:5; Is. 3:8). Isaiah warns that those who rely on their own strength will stumble and fall (Is. 40:30), but those who are led by the Lord will not stumble (Is. 63:13). In fact, the Lord will provide strength to those who have stumbled in the past and now call upon Him (1 Sam. 2:4).

Commit Harlotry: Hebrew *zanah*—2:5; 3:3; 4:15—refers to having illicit sexual relations, especially involving prostitution. Two forms of prostitution were practiced in the ancient world: common prostitution and ritual, or "religious," prostitution, which involved pagan fertility rites. Both forms were strictly forbidden in God's Law (Lev. 19:29; Deut. 23:17). The OT frequently uses prostitution as an image of the sin of idolatry. Israel was pledged to serve one God (Exodus 20:3), so idolatry was like marital unfaithfulness against the Lord. Hosea actually married a prostitute as a living symbol of God's patience with Israel's infidelities (see chap. 1).

KEY DOCTRINES IN HOSEA

God's unconditional love for His covenant people (6:1–3; 11:1–12; Deut. 7:7; Job 7:17; Is. 49:15,16; John 3:16; Titus 3:4)

GOD'S CHARACTER IN HOSEA

God is accessible—14:2
God is good—3:5
God is kind—2:19

God is loving—11:4
God is merciful—2:23; 14:3–4
God is provident—2:8–9

INTERPRETIVE CHALLENGES

That the faithless wife, Gomer, is symbolic of faithless Israel is without doubt; but questions remain. First, some suggest that the marital scenes in chaps. 1–3 should be taken only as allegory. However, there is nothing in the narrative, presented in simple prose, which would question its literal occurrence. Much of its impact would be lost if not literal. When nonliteral elements within the book are introduced, they are prefaced with "saw" (5:13; 9:10,13), the normal Hebraic means of introducing nonliteral scenes. Furthermore, there is no account of a prophet ever making himself the subject of an allegory or parable.

Second, what are the moral implications of God's command for Hosea to marry a prostitute? It appears best to see Gomer as chaste at the time of marriage to Hosea, only later having become an immoral woman. See Answers to Tough Questions for further discussion of this issue.

A third question arises concerning the relationship between chap. 1 and chap. 3 and whether the woman of chap. 3 is Gomer or another woman. There are a number of factors that suggest that the woman of chap. 3 is Gomer. In 1:2, God's command is to "Go, take;" in 3:1, however, His command is to "Go again, love," suggesting that Hosea's love was to be renewed to the same woman. Furthermore, within the analogy of chap. 1, Gomer represents Israel. As God renews His love toward faithless Israel, so Hosea is to renew his love toward faithless Gomer. For Hosea 3 to denote a different woman would confuse the analogy.

OUTLINE

    I. Adulterous Wife and Faithful Husband (1:1–3:5)
        A. Hosea and Gomer (1:1–11)
        B. God and Israel (2:1–23)
        C. Both Parties Reconciled (3:1–5)
    II. Adulterous Israel and Faithful Lord (4:1–14:9)
        A. Adulterous Israel Found Guilty (4:1–6:3)
        B. Adulterous Israel Put Away (6:4–10:15)
        C. Adulterous Israel Restored to the Lord (11:1–14:9)

MEANWHILE, IN OTHER PARTS OF THE WORLD...
The city of Rome is founded (753 B.C.).

ANSWERS TO TOUGH QUESTIONS

1. Did God instruct Hosea to actually marry a prostitute?

Some interpreters try to ease the question by suggesting that the marital scenes in the first three chapters of Hosea are merely an allegory of God's relationship to His people. Nothing in the account encourages such an interpretation. The language of God's command in the original text provides some support for the chastity of Gomer at the time of her marriage to Hosea. The words "take yourself a wife of harlotry" (1:2) can be understood prophetically (looking to the future). Thus, Gomer would have taken up immoral behavior after marriage. This explanation fits better with God's description of Israel coming out of Egypt as a "young woman" (2:15; 9:10), who then wandered away from God (11:1). The moral power behind Hosea's action in taking back Gomer after her adultery (chapter 3) depends on the purity of their original union, which she violated. Had Hosea married an acknowledged prostitute, he would have had no grounds for offense over her adultery.

FURTHER STUDY ON HOSEA

1. As you read through Hosea, how many different word pictures for God can you find?
2. In how many different ways dids Hosea depict God's love for His people?
3. What was the significance of the names of each of Hosea and Gomer's children?
4. On a scale of increasing difficulty, how would you rate God's command to Hosea to marry a prostitute?
5. How would you describe the most difficult action God has asked you to take?

JOEL
The Day of the Lord

TITLE
The Greek Septuagint (LXX) and Latin Vulgate (Vg.) versions follow the Hebrew Masoretic Text (MT), titling this book after Joel the prophet, the recipient of the message from God (1:1). The name means "the LORD is God" and refers to at least a dozen men in the OT. Joel is referred to only once in the NT (Acts 2:16–21).

AUTHOR AND DATE
The author identified himself only as "Joel the son of Pethuel" (1:1). The prophecy provides little else about the man. Even the name of his father is not mentioned elsewhere in the OT. Although he displayed a profound zeal for the temple sacrifices (1:9; 2:13–16), his familiarity with pastoral and agricultural life and his separation from the priests (1:13,14; 2:17) suggest he was not a Levite. Extrabiblical tradition records that he was from the tribe of Reuben, from the town of Bethom or Bethharam, located northeast of the Dead Sea on the border of Reuben and Gad. The context of the prophecy, however, hints that he was a Judean from the Jerusalem vicinity, since the tone of a stranger is absent.

Dating the book relies solely on canonical position, historical allusions, and linguistic elements. Because of: (1) the lack of any mention of later world powers (Assyria, Babylon, or Persia); (2) the fact that Joel's style is like that of Hosea and Amos rather than of the post-Exilic prophets; and (3) the verbal parallels with other early prophets (Joel 3:16/Amos 1:2; Joel 3:18/Amos 9:13), a late ninth century B.C. date, during the reign of Joash (ca. 835–796 B.C.), seems most convincing. Nevertheless, while the date of the book cannot be known with certainty, the impact on its interpretation is minimal. The message of Joel is timeless, forming doctrine which could be repeated and applied in any age.

BACKGROUND AND SETTING
Tyre, Sidon, and Philistia had made frequent military incursions into Israel (3:2ff.). An extended drought and massive invasion of locusts had stripped every green thing from the land and brought severe economic devastation (1:7–20), leaving the southern kingdom weak. This physical disaster gives Joel the illustration for God's judgment. As the locusts were a judgment on sin, God's future judgments during the Day of the Lord will far exceed them. In that day, God will judge His enemies and bless the faithful. No mention is made of specific sins, nor is Judah rebuked for idolatry. Yet, possibly due to a calloused indifference, the prophet calls them to a genuine repentance, admonishing them to "rend your heart, and not your garments" (2:13).

KEY PEOPLE IN JOEL
Joel—prophet to the people of Judah during the reign of Joash (1:1–3:21)
The people of Judah—the southern kingdom punished for their sins by a locust plague (1:2; 2:1; 3:1–2,19–21)

HISTORICAL AND THEOLOGICAL THEMES

The theme of Joel is the Day of the Lord. It permeates all parts of Joel's message, making it the most sustained treatment in the entire OT (1:15; 2:1; 2:11; 2:31; 3:14). The phrase is employed nineteen times by eight different OT authors (Is. 2:12; 13:6,9; Ezek. 13:5; 30:3; Joel 1:15; 2:1,11,31; 3:14; Amos 5:18 [2x], 20; Obad. 15; Zeph. 1:7,14 [2x]; Zech. 14:1; Mal. 4:5). The phrase does not have reference to a chronological time period, but to a general period of wrath and judgment uniquely belonging to the Lord. It is exclusively the day that unveils His character—mighty, powerful, and holy, thus terrifying His enemies. The Day of the Lord does not always refer to an eschatological event (relating to the end times); on occasion it has a

CHRIST IN . . . JOEL

JOEL'S PROPHECY described God pouring out His Spirit on the people so that one day, "Your sons and your daughters shall prophesy, your old men shall dream dreams, your young men shall see visions" (2:28-32). Peter quotes from this passage in Joel as the prophecy previewed and sampled at the Day of Pentecost (Acts 2:16-21). The final fulfillment of Joel's prophecy will come in the millennial kingdom of Christ when God's Spirit is poured out on all creation.

near historical fulfillment, as seen in Ezek. 13:5, where it speaks of the Babylonian conquest and destruction of Jerusalem. As is common in prophecy, the near fulfillment is an historic event upon which to comprehend the more distant, eschatological fulfillment.

The Day of the Lord is frequently associated with seismic disturbances (e.g., 2:1–11; 2:31; 3:16), violent weather (Ezek. 13:5ff.), clouds and thick darkness (e.g., 2:2; Zeph. 1:7ff.), cosmic upheaval (2:3,30), and as a "great and very terrible" (2:11) day that would "come as destruction from the Almighty" (1:15). The latter half of Joel depicts time subsequent to the Day of the Lord in terms of promise and hope. There will be a pouring out of the Spirit on all flesh, accompanied by prophetic utterances, dreams, visions (2:28,29), as well as the coming of Elijah, an epiphany bringing restoration and hope (Mal. 4:5,6). As a result of the Day of the Lord there will be physical blessings, fruitfulness, and prosperity (2:21ff.; 3:16–21). It is a day when judgment is poured out on sinners that subsequently leads to blessings on the penitent, and reaffirmation of God's covenant with His people.

KEY DOCTRINES IN JOEL

The Day of the Lord—a general period of wrath and judgment from the Lord; the day in which God unveils His character (1:15; 2:1-11, 31; 3:16; Is. 2:12; 13:6; Ezek. 13:5; Zeph. 1:14; Mal. 4:5,6; Acts 2:20; 1 Cor. 5:5; 2 Cor. 1:14; 2 Pet.3:10).

GOD'S CHARACTER IN JOEL

God is accessible—2:12
God is longsuffering—2:13
God is merciful—2:13
God is wrathful—2:12–14

INTERPRETIVE CHALLENGES

It is preferable to view chap. 1 as describing an actual invasion of locusts that devastated the land. In chap. 2, a new level of description meets the interpreter. Here the prophet is projecting something beyond the locust plague of chap. 1, elevating the level of description to new heights, with increased intensity that is focused on the plague and the immediate necessity for true repentance. The prophet's choice of similes, such as "like the appearance of horses" (2:4) and "like mighty men" (2:7), suggests that he is still using the actual locusts to illustrate an invasion that can only be the massive overtaking of the final Day of the Lord.

A second issue confronting the interpreter is Peter's quotation in Acts 2:16–21 from Joel 2:28–32. See Answers to Tough Questions regarding this issue.

OUTLINE

Following 1:1, the contents of the book are arranged under three basic categories. In the first section (1:2–20) the prophet describes the contemporary Day of the Lord. The land is suffering massive devastation caused by a locust plague and drought. The details of the calamity (1:2–12) are followed by a summons to communal penitence and reformation (1:13–20).

> ### KEY WORDS IN
> # Joel
>
> **Spirit:** Hebrew *ruach*—2:28—related to a verb meaning "to breathe" or "to blow." It can signify breath (Job 9:18; 19:17), wind (Gen. 8:1; Ex. 10:13), air (Eccles. 1:14; Is. 26:18), the breath of life (whether animal or human, see Gen. 6:17; 7:15), disposition or mood (Gen. 41:8; Ezek. 21:7), an evil or distressing spirit (1 Sam.16:14–16), or the Spirit of God (Gen. 1:2; Ps. 51:11). The spirit of life is the gift of God to all creatures (Job 12:10; 33:4; Eccles. 12:7). The endowment of God's Holy Spirit is a special gift to believers, which brings spiritual life (Ps. 51:10,11; 143:10), power (Judg.6:34), wisdom and understanding (Is. 11:2), and divine revelation that leads to a better understanding of God's Word and His perfect ways (2:28; Is. 61:1,2).

The second section (2:1–17) provides a transition from the historical plague of locusts described in chap. 1 to the eschatological Day of the Lord in 2:18–3:21. Employing the contemporary infestation of locusts as a backdrop, the prophet, with an increased level of intensity, paints a vivid and forceful picture of the impending visitation of the Lord (2:1–11) and, with powerful and explicit terminology, tenaciously renews the appeal for repentance (2:12–17).

In the third section (2:18–3:21), the Lord speaks directly, assuring His people of His presence among them (2:27; 3:17,21). This portion of the book assumes that the repentance solicited (2:12–17) had occurred and describes the Lord's zealous response (2:18,19a) to their prayer. Joel 2:18–21 forms the transition in the message from lamentation and woe to divine assurances of God's presence and the reversal of the calamities, with 2:19b, 20 introducing the essence and nature of that reversal. The Lord then gives three promises to assure the penitents of His presence: material restoration through the divine healing of their land (2:21–27), spiritual restoration through the divine outpouring of His Spirit (2:28–32), and national restoration through the divine judgment on the unrighteous (3:1–21).

> ### I. Day of the Lord Experienced: Historical (1:1–20)
> A. Source of the Message (1:1)
> B. Command to Contemplate the Devastation (1:2–4)
> C. Completeness of the Devastation (1:5–12)
> D. Call to Repent in Light of the Devastation (1:13–20)

II. **Day of the Lord Illustrated: Transitional (2:1–17)**
   A. Alarm Sounds (2:1)
   B. Army Invades (2:2–11)
   C. Admonition to Repent (2:12–17)
III. **Day of the Lord Described: Eschatological (2:18–3:21)**
   A. Introduction (2:18–20)
   B. Material Restoration (2:21–27)
   C. Spiritual Restoration (2:28–32)
   D. National Restoration (3:1–21)

MEANWHILE, IN OTHER PARTS OF THE WORLD...
The caste system develops in India, beginning centuries of racial segregation.

ANSWERS TO TOUGH QUESTIONS

1. Does Joel's account mean the land of Israel was actually overrun with locusts?

Insect plagues such as the one reported by Joel are well known in many parts of the world. Joel described at length the different stages of life, or the different types of locusts (1:4). The vivid details included by Joel increase the usefulness of the event as a teaching tool, but they also emphasize the fact that the prophet saw before his eyes the devastated remains of his nation.

Joel's prophetic vision of the Day of the Lord elevated the tragedy of the locusts to become an illustration of the final devastation. In the prophet's similes, the locusts are "like the appearance of horses" (2:4) and "like mighty men" (2:7), but the underlying message announces the coming Day when real horses and men will arrive on the scene bringing God's judgment.

2. When Peter quoted Joel 2:28–32 at the beginning of his sermon in Acts 2:16–21, how did his interpretation relate to the ultimate fulfillment of that prophecy?

Some have viewed the events of Acts 2 and the destruction of Jerusalem in A.D. 70 as the fulfillment of the Joel passage. Others have reserved its ultimate fulfillment for the final Day of the Lord. It appears likely that the initial pouring out of the Holy Spirit at Pentecost was not a fulfillment but a preview and sample of the Spirit's power and work. The full outpouring of the Holy Spirit will come in the Messiah's kingdom after the Day of the Lord. That was the ultimate vision in Joel's prophecy.

FURTHER STUDY ON JOEL

1. What are the details of Joel's description of the plague of locusts?
2. How did Joel use the phrase *day of the Lord?*
3. How do the locusts illustrate the ways God judges nations?
4. What principles of grace and mercy did Joel include in his messages?
5. What does Peter's use of Joel's prophecy teach you about the ministry of the Holy Spirit (Joel 2; Acts 2)?

AMOS
The Necessity of True Justice and Worship

TITLE
As with each of the Minor Prophets, the title comes from the name of the prophet to whom God gave His message (1:1). The name *Amos* means "burden" or "burden-bearer." He is not to be confused with Amoz ("stout, strong"), the father of Isaiah (Is. 1:1).

AUTHOR AND DATE
Amos was from Tekoa, a small village 10 mi. south of Jerusalem. He was the only prophet to give his occupation before declaring his divine commission. He was not of priestly or noble descent, but worked as a "sheepbreeder" (1:1; cf. 2 Kin. 3:4) and a "tender of sycamore fruit" (7:14) and was a contemporary of Jonah (2 Kin. 14:25), Hosea (Hos. 1:1), and Isaiah (Is. 1:1). The date of writing is mid-8th century B.C., during the reigns of Uzziah, king of Judah (ca. 790–739 B.C.) and Jeroboam II, king of Israel (ca. 793–753 B.C.), two years before a memorable earthquake (1:1; cf. Zech. 14:5, ca. 760 B.C.).

BACKGROUND AND SETTING
Amos was a Judean prophet called to deliver a message primarily to the northern tribes of Israel (7:15). Politically, it was a time of prosperity under the long and secure reign of Jeroboam II who, following the example of his father Joash (2 Kin. 13:25), significantly "restored the territory of Israel" (2 Kin. 14:25). It was also a time of peace with both Judah (cf. 5:5) and her more distant neighbors; the ever-present menace of Assyria was subdued earlier that century because of Nineveh's repentance at the preaching of Jonah (Jon. 3:10). Spiritually, however, it was a time of rampant corruption and moral decay (4:1; 5:10–13; 2 Kin. 14:24).

CHRIST IN . . . AMOS
THE REFERENCES TO CHRIST in the Book of Amos point to the permanent restoration of Israel. The Lord speaks through Amos, declaring, "I will plant them in their land, and no longer shall they be pulled up from the land I have given them" (9:15). Israel's complete restoration and recovery of the land will only be fulfilled during the second advent of Christ the Messiah.

KEY PEOPLE IN AMOS
Amos—Judean prophet who warned Israel of God's judgment (1:1–9:15)
Amaziah—king of southern kingdom of Judah; son of Joash (7:10–17)
Jeroboam II—wicked king of Israel after his father, Jehoash (7:7–13)

HISTORICAL AND THEOLOGICAL THEMES
Amos addresses Israel's two primary sins: (1) an absence of true worship, and (2) a lack of justice. In the midst of their ritualistic performance of worship, they were not pursuing the Lord with their hearts (4:4,5; 5:4–6) nor following His standard of justice with her neighbors (5:10–13; 6:12). This apostasy, evidenced by continual, willful rejection of the prophetic message of Amos, is promised divine judgment. Because of His covenant,

however, the Lord will not abandon Israel altogether, but will bring future restoration to the righteous remnant (9:7–15).

KEY DOCTRINES IN AMOS

Genuine worship of God (4:4,5; 5:4–6; Num. 28:3; Deut.4:29; 14:28; Lev. 7:13; 2 Chr. 15:2; Jer. 29:13; Is. 55:3,6,7; John 4:20–24; Rom. 1:25; Rev. 4:10–11)

Justice—God gave Israel a standard of fairness with their neighbors (5:10–13; 6:12; Deut. 16:20; 1 Kin. 22:8; Prov. 31:9; Is. 29:21; 56:1; 59:15; 66:5; Jer. 17:16–18; Col. 4:1; 1 Thess. 2:10)

Future restoration of the faithful remnant of Israel (9:7–15; Is. 27; 42–44; 65; 66; Jer. 30–33; Ezekiel 36; 37; 40–48; Dan. 9:20–27; 12:1–3; Hos. 2:14–23; 14:4–7; Joel 3:19–21; Obad. 17,21; Mic. 7:14–20; Zeph. 3:14–20; Hag. 2:20–23; Zech. 13; 14; Mal. 4:1–3)

GOD'S CHARACTER IN AMOS

God is holy—4:2

God is provident—3:6

INTERPRETIVE CHALLENGES

Is the prophecy in Amos 9:11 fulfilled yet? In 9:11, the Lord promised that He "will raise up the tabernacle of David, which has fallen down." In the NT the Jerusalem Council convened to discuss whether Gentiles should be allowed into the church without requiring circumcision, James quotes this passage (Acts 15:15,16) to support Peter's report of how God had opened the gospel to the Gentiles. Some have thus concluded that the passage was fulfilled in Jesus, the greater Son of David, through whom the dynasty of David was reestablished. The Acts reference, however, is best seen as an illustration of Amos' words and not the fulfillment. See Answers to Tough Questions for further discussion.

The Ultimate Restoration of Israel

1. Is. 27; 42–44; 65; 66	8. Obad. 17,21
2. Jer. 30–33	9. Micah 7:14–20
3. Ezek. 36; 37; 40–48	10. Zeph. 3:14–20
4. Dan. 9:20–27; 12:1–3	11. Hag. 2:20–23
5. Hosea 2:14–23; 14:4–7	12. Zech. 13;14
6. Joel 3:18–21	13. Mal. 4:1–3
7. Amos 9:11–15	

OUTLINE

I. Judgments Against the Nations (1:1–2:16)
    A. Introduction (1:1, 2)
    B. Against Israel's Enemies (1:3–2:3)
    C. Against Judah (2:4, 5)
    D. Against Israel (2:6–16)

II. Condemnations Against Israel (3:1–6:14)
    A. Sin of Irresponsibility (3:1–15)
    B. Sin of Idolatry (4:1–13)
    C. Sin of Moral/Ethical Decay (5:1–6:14)

III. Visions of Judgment and Restoration (7:1–9:15)
    A. The Lord Will Spare (7:1–6)
        1. Vision of locusts (7:1–3)
        2. Vision of fire (7:4–6)
    B. The Lord Will No Longer Spare (7:7–9:10)
        1. Vision of the plumb line (7:7–9)
        2. Historical interlude (7:10–17)
        3. Vision of the fruit basket (8:1–14)
        4. Vision of the altar (9:1–10)
    C. The Lord Will Restore (9:11–15)

MEANWHILE, IN OTHER PARTS OF THE WORLD...
The Greeks begin to settle the area known today as Spain. Greek art also develops.

ANSWERS TO TOUGH QUESTIONS

1. Since Amos 9:11 was quoted as prophecy in the NT, to what degree has it been fulfilled?

This verse promises that the Lord "will raise up the tabernacle of David, which has fallen down." The apostle James quoted the same promise in Acts 15:15–16 during the first Jerusalem Council discussion. At stake was whether Gentiles should be allowed into the church without being circumcised. James apparently thought of this passage because it makes the point that part of God's plan all along was to include the Gentiles. Some, however, have concluded that James's usage indicates the complete fulfillment of Amos's prophecy. They assign the phrase above to Jesus as the greater Son of David, through whom the dynasty of David was reestablished.

> **KEY WORDS IN**
> ## *Amos*
> **Seek:** Hebrew *darash*—5:4–6,14—describes the act of seeking, inquiring, or asking. The people of Israel began to worship the false gods of Bethel and Gilgal (5:4). Yet, Amos encourages the people to seek the one, true God. Throughout history, none of those who have sought God in need of safety or forgiveness has been disappointed by Him (Ps. 34:4; 77:2; 1 Chr. 16:11; 2 Chr. 30:19).

It seems better to see James's use as an illustration of Amos's words rather than a fulfillment. The original prophecy contains the key phrase "on that day" (9:11), indicating along with the details of the passage that the prophet was speaking of the Messiah's return at the second advent to sit upon the throne of David. The establishment of the church by the apostles and the inclusion of the Gentiles set the stage for that eventual fulfillment. The temporal allusions to a future time ("On that day," 9:11), when Israel will "possess the remnant of Edom, and all the Gentiles" (9:12), when the Lord "will plant them in their land, and no longer shall they be pulled up from the land I have given them" (9:15), all make it clear that the prophet is speaking of Messiah's return at the Second Advent to sit upon the throne of David (cf. Is. 9:7), not the establishment of the church by the apostles.

FURTHER STUDY ON AMOS

1. How does a passage like Amos 5:21–24 get applied or overlooked by Christians in today's world?
2. How does Amos make the point that every person must give an account to God for his or her life?
3. What does Amos have to say to Christians who live in prosperous times?
4. How does Amos's message attack those who would live superficial spiritual lives?
5. To what degree do you seek to live your life by God's standard of justice?

OBADIAH

God's Judgment of Israel's Enemies

TITLE
The book is named after the prophet who received the vision (1:1). Obadiah means "servant of the LORD" and occurs twenty times in the OT, referring to at least twenty other OT individuals. Obadiah is the shortest book in the OT and is not quoted in the NT.

AUTHOR AND DATE
Nothing is known for certain about the author. Other OT references to men of this name do not appear to be referring to this prophet. His frequent mentions of Jerusalem, Judah, and Zion suggest that he belonged to the southern kingdom (cf. vv. 10–12,17,21). Obadiah was probably a contemporary of Elijah and Elisha.

The date of writing is equally difficult to determine, though we know it is tied to the Edomite assault on Jerusalem described in vv. 10–14. Obadiah apparently wrote shortly after the attack. There were foursignificant invasions of Jerusalem in OT history: (1) by Shishak, king of Egypt, ca. 925 B.C. during the reign of Rehoboam (1 Kin. 14:25,26; 2 Chr. 12); (2) by the Philistines and Arabians between 848–841 B.C. during the reign of Jehoram of Judah (2 Chr. 21:8–20); (3) by Jehoash, king of Israel, ca. 790 B.C. (2 Kin. 14; 2 Chr. 25); and (4) by Nebuchadnezzar, king of Babylon, in the fall of Jerusalem in 586 B.C. Of these four, only the second and the fourth are possible fits with historical data. Number two is preferable, since Obadiah's description does not indicate the total destruction of the city, which took place under Nebuchadnezzar's attack. Also, although the Edomites were involved in Nebuchadnezzar's destruction of Jerusalem (Ps. 137; Lam. 4:21), it is significant that Obadiah does not mention the Babylonians by name (as with all the other prophets who wrote about Jerusalem's fall), nor is there any reference to the destruction of the temple or the deportation of the people; in fact, the captives appear to have been taken to the southwest, not east to Babylon (cf. v. 20).

BACKGROUND AND SETTING
The Edomites trace their origin to Esau, the firstborn (twin) son of Isaac and Rebekah (Gen. 25:24–26), who struggled with Jacob even while in the womb (Gen. 25:22). Esau's name means "hairy," because "he was like a hairy garment all over" (Gen. 25:25). He is also called Edom, meaning "red," owing to the sale of his birthright in exchange for some "red stew" (Gen. 25:30). He showed a disregard for the covenant promises by marrying two Canaanite women (Gen. 26:34) and later the daughter of Ishmael (Gen. 28:9). He loved the out-of-doors and, after having his father's blessing stolen from him by Jacob, was destined to remain a man of the open spaces (Gen. 25:27; 27:38–40). Esau settled in a region of mostly rugged mountains south of the Dead Sea (Gen. 33:16; 36:8,9; Deut. 2:4,5) called Edom (Gr., "Idumea"), the forty miles wide area which stretches approximately 100 miles south to the Gulf of Aqabah. The fabled King's Highway, an essential caravan route linking North Africa with Europe and Asia, passes along the eastern plateau (Num. 20:17). The struggle and birth of Jacob and Esau (Gen. 25) form the ultimate background to the prophecy of Gen. 25:23, "two nations are in your womb." Their respective

descendants, Israel and Edom, were perpetual enemies. When Israel came out from Egypt, Edom denied their brother Jacob passage through their land, located south of the Dead Sea (Num. 20:14–21). Nevertheless, Israel was instructed by God to be kind to Edom (Deut. 23:7,8). Obadiah, having received a vision from God, was sent to describe their crimes and to pronounce total destruction upon Edom because of their treatment of Israel.

The Edomites opposed Saul (ca. 1043–1011 B.C.) and were subdued under David (ca. 1011–971 B.C.) and

CHRIST IN . . . OBADIAH

IN OBADIAH, Christ acts as both Judge over Israel's enemies (vv. 15,16), and Savior of His chosen nation (vv. 17–20). Israel's final triumph comes only through Christ Himself.

Solomon (ca. 971–931 B.C.). They fought against Jehoshaphat (ca. 873–848 B.C.) and successfully rebelled against Jehoram (ca. 853–841 B.C.). They were again conquered by Judah under Amaziah (ca. 796–767 B.C.), but they regained their freedom during the reign of Ahaz (ca. 735–715 B.C.). Edom was later controlled by Assyria and Babylon; and in the fifth century B.C. the Edomites were forced by the Nabateans to leave their territory. They moved to the area of southern Palestine and became known as Idumeans.

Herod the Great, an Idumean, became king of Judea under Rome in 37 B.C. In a sense, the enmity between Esau and Jacob was continued in Herod's attempt to murder Jesus. The Idumeans participated in the rebellion of Jerusalem against Rome and were defeated along with the Jews by Titus in A.D. 70. Ironically, the Edomites applauded the destruction of Jerusalem in 586 B.C. (cf. Ps. 137:7) but died trying to defend it in A.D. 70. After that time they were never heard of again. As Obadiah predicted, they would be "cut off forever" (v. 10); "and no survivor shall remain of the house of Esau" (v. 18).

KEY WORDS IN

Obadiah

Pride: Hebrew *zadon*—verse 3—literally means "to act proudly or presumptuously" (Deut. 18:22; 1 Sam.17:28). The OT writers used this noun to characterize the prideful nation of Edom (v. 3; Jer. 49:16). Pride comes when humans think they can live without God. However, this godlessness only leads to shame and ultimate destruction (Prov. 11:2; 13:10; Jer. 49:16; Ezek. 7:10–12).

KEY PEOPLE IN OBADIAH

The Edomites—the nation originating from Esau, despised and judged by God (vv. 1–16)

HISTORICAL AND THEOLOGICAL THEMES

The book is a case study of Genesis 12:1–3, with two interrelated themes: (1) the judgment of Edom by God for cursing Israel. This was apparently told to Judah, thereby providing reassurance to Judah that the Day of the Lord (v. 15) would bring judgment upon Edom for her pride and for her participation in Judah's downfall; (2) Judah's restoration. This would even include the territory of the Edomites (vv. 19–21; Is. 11:14). Obadiah's blessing includes the near fulfillment of Edom's demise (vv. 1–15) under the assault of the Philistines and Arabians (2 Chr. 21:8–20) and the far fulfillment of the nation's judgment in the first century A.D. and Israel's final possession of Edom (vv. 15–21).

KEY DOCTRINES IN OBADIAH

The judgment of God on Edom and the nations (vv. 1–16; Pss. 83:5–18; 137:7; Is. 11:14; 21:11,12; 34:5; 63:1–6; Jer. 49:7–22; Lam. 4:21,22; Ezek. 25:12–14; 35:1–15; Joel 3:19; Amos 1:11,12; 9:11,12; Mal. 1:2–5)

God's covenant mercy on Israel (vv. 17–21; Ps. 22:28; Is.14:1,2; Dan. 2:44; Joel 2:32; Amos 9:8; James 5:20; Rev. 11:15)

GOD'S CHARACTER IN OBADIAH

God is judging—vv. 1–16
God is restoring—vv. 17–21

INTERPRETIVE CHALLENGES

The striking similarity between Obadiah 1–9 and Jeremiah 49:7–22 brings up the question: Who borrowed from whom? Assuming there was not a third common source, it appears that Jeremiah borrowed, where appropriate, from Obadiah, since the shared verses form one unit in Obadiah, while in Jeremiah they are scattered among other verses.

God's Judgment on Edom

> More than any other nation mentioned in the OT, Edom is the supreme object of God's wrath.
>
> • Pss. 83:5–18; 137:7
> • Is. 11:14; 21:11,12; 34:5; 63:1–6
> • Jer. 49:7–22
> • Lam. 4:21,22
> • Ezek. 25:12–14; 35:1–15
> • Joel 3:19
> • Amos 1:11,12; 9:11,12
> • Mal. 1:2–5

OUTLINE

I. God's Judgment on Edom (1–14)
    A. Edom's Punishment (1–9)
    B. Edom's Crimes (10–14)
II. God's Judgment on the Nations (15,16)
III. God's Restoration of Israel (17–21)

MEANWHILE, IN OTHER PARTS OF THE WORLD...

Homer writes the classic Greek epics the *Iliad* and the *Odyssey*.

ANSWERS TO TOUGH QUESTIONS

1. Why did God include such a short book in Scripture?

First, Obadiah is not the shortest book in the Bible. Two others, in fact, are shorter: 2 John (13 verses) and 3 John (14 verses). These short books should not be overlooked because of their length. God manages to communicate a great deal in a small amount of space.

Second, Obadiah and other short books offer highly concentrated views of single issues. The prophet may have had years of ministry and dozens of messages, but he had one vision. God gave him a powerful warning to deliver, and even the echoes of its truth can offer hope today. In Obadiah's closing words, "And the kingdom shall be the LORD'S" (v. 21b).

FURTHER STUDY ON OBADIAH

1. What were God's specific charges against the Edomites?
2. How did God describe His own attitude toward Israel in Obadiah?
3. What illustrations of pride does Obadiah include?
4. How do the warnings in Obadiah about pride apply at the personal level in your life?

JONAH
The Reluctant Missionary

TITLE

Following the lead of the Hebrew Masoretic text (MT), the title of the book is derived from the principal character, Jonah (meaning "dove"), the son of Amittai (1:1). Both the Septuagint (LXX) and the Latin Vulgate (Vg.) ascribe the same name.

AUTHOR AND DATE

The book makes no direct claim regarding authorship. Throughout the book, Jonah is repeatedly referred to in the third person, causing some to search for another author. It was not an uncommon OT practice, however, to write in the third person (e.g., Ex. 11:3; 1 Sam. 12:11). Furthermore, the autobiographical information revealed within its pages clearly points to Jonah as the author. The firsthand accounts of such unusual events and experiences would be best recounted from the hand of Jonah himself. Nor should the introductory verse suggest otherwise, since other prophets such as Hosea, Joel, Micah, Zephaniah, Haggai, and Zechariah have similar openings.

According to 2 Kings 14:25, Jonah came from Gath-hepher near Nazareth. The context places him during the long and prosperous reign of Jeroboam II (ca. 793–758 B.C.), making him a prophet to the northern tribes just prior to Amos during the first half of the eighth century B.C., ca. 760 B.C. The Pharisees were wrong when they said "no prophet has arisen out of Galilee" (John 7:52), because Jonah was a Galilean. An unverifiable Jewish tradition says Jonah was the son of the widow of Zarephath whom Elijah raised from the dead (1 Kin. 17:8–24).

BACKGROUND AND SETTING

As a prophet to the ten northern tribes of Israel, Jonah shares a background and setting with Amos. The nation enjoyed a time of relative peace and prosperity. Both Syria and Assyria were weak, allowing Jeroboam II to enlarge the northern borders of Israel to where they had been in the days of David and Solomon (2 Kin. 14:23–27). Spiritually, however, it was a time of poverty; religion was ritualistic and increasingly idolatrous, and justice had become perverted. Peacetime and wealth had made her bankrupt spiritually, morally, and ethically (cf. 2 Kin. 14:24; Amos 4:1ff; 5:10–13). As a result, God was to punish her by bringing destruction and captivity from the Assyrians in 722 B.C. Nineveh's repentance may have been aided by the two plagues (765 and 759 B.C.) and a solar eclipse (763 B.C.), preparing them for Jonah's judgment message.

KEY PEOPLE IN JONAH

Jonah—reluctant missionary to the Ninevites; needed to be swallowed by a giant fish in order to comply with God's command (1:1–9:9)

The captain and crew of Jonah's getaway ship—tried to avoid killing Jonah; threw Jonah overboard to stop the storm (1:5–16)

HISTORICAL AND THEOLOGICAL THEMES

Jonah, though a prophet of Israel, is not remembered for his ministry in Israel, which could explain why the Pharisees erringly claimed in Jesus' day that no prophet had come from Galilee (cf. John 7:52). Rather, the book relates the account of his call to preach repentance to Nineveh and his refusal to go. Nineveh, the capital of Assyria and infamous for its cruelty, was an historical nemesis of Israel and Judah. The focus of this book is on that Gentile city, which was founded by Nimrod, great-grandson of Noah (Gen. 10:6–12). Perhaps the largest

CHRIST IN . . . JONAH

JONAH ATTAINS NOTORIETY as the only prophet whom Jesus Christ identified with Himself (Matt. 12:39–41). Just as Jonah remained three days and three nights in the belly of the whale, Christ uses this experience as an example of the three days and three nights He would be "in the heart of the earth" after His crucifixion.

city in the ancient world (1:2; 3:2,3; 4:11), it was nevertheless destroyed about 150 years after the repentance of the generation in the time of Jonah's visit (612 B.C.), as Nahum prophesied (Nah. 1:1ff.). Israel's political distaste for Assyria, coupled with a sense of spiritual superiority as the recipient of God's covenant blessing, produced a recalcitrant attitude in Jonah toward God's request for missionary service. Jonah was sent to Nineveh in part to shame Israel by the fact that a pagan city repented at the preaching of a stranger, whereas Israel would not repent though preached to by many prophets. He was soon to learn that God's love and mercy extends to all of His creatures (4:2,10,11), not just His covenant people (cf. Gen. 9:27; 12:3; Lev. 19:33,34; 1 Sam. 2:10; Is. 2:2; Joel 2:28–32).

The Book of Jonah reveals God's sovereign rule over man and all creation. Creation came into being through Him (1:9) and responds to His every command (1:4,17; 2:10; 4:6,7; cf. Mark 4:41). Jesus employed the repentance of the Ninevites to rebuke the Pharisees, thereby illustrating the hardness of the Pharisees' hearts and their unwillingness to repent (Matt. 12:38–41; Luke 11:29–32). The heathen city of Nineveh repented at the preaching of a reluctant prophet, but the Pharisees would not repent at the preaching of the greatest of all prophets, in spite of overwhelming evidence that He was actually their Lord and Messiah. Jonah is a picture of Israel, who was chosen and commissioned by God to be His witness (Is. 43:10–12; 44:8), who rebelled against His will (Ex. 32:1–4; Judg. 2:11–19; Ezek. 6:1–5; Mark 7:6–9), but who

KEY WORDS IN

Jonah

Prepared: Hebrew *manah*—1:17; 4:6–8—describes God's sovereign power to bring about His will. Literally, *manah* signifies the power to appoint or ordain. God's great power in the Book of Jonah in the *preparing* of the fish, the plant, and the worm, illustrated His sovereignty over all His creation. God used these created animals to reveal to Jonah His mercy and love for all people. Through all of Jonah's plans, Jonah's path was carefully guided by God (see 4:6–8).

Slow to Anger: Hebrew *'erek 'appayim*—4:2—idiom meaning "the nose burns" or "the nose becomes hot" characterizing the heavy breathing of an angry person (Gen. 30:2; Ex. 4:14). In the OT, the word for anger was directly related to the nose. Thus, when the Old Testament writers describe God as "slow to anger," they literally say "long of nose" (Pss. 86:15; 103:8). The Hebrew idiom for "slow to anger" reveals God's great mercy and patience (Ps. 145:8; Joel 2:13).

has been miraculously preserved by God through centuries of exile and dispersion to finally preach His truth (Jer. 30:11; 31:35–37; Hos. 3:3–5; Rev. 7:1–8; 14:1–3).

KEY DOCTRINES IN JONAH
The mercy of God towards all nations (4:2,10,11; Ex. 34:6; Num. 14:18; Ps. 86:5,15; Joel 2:13; 1 Tim. 2:4; 2 Pet. 3:9)

God's sovereign rule (1:4,9,17; 2:10; 4:6,7; Job 42:2; Pss. 107:25; 146:6; Neh. 9:6; Matt. 10:29,30; Acts 17:24; Rom. 8:28)

GOD'S CHARACTER IN JONAH
God is merciful—4:2,10–11
God is provident—1:4,15
God is wrathful—4:2

INTERPRETIVE CHALLENGES
The primary challenge is whether the book is to be interpreted as historical narrative or as allegory/parable. The grand scale of the miracles, such as being kept alive three days and nights in a big fish, has led some skeptics and critics to deny their historical validity and substitute spiritual lessons, either to the constituent parts (allegory) or to the book as a whole (parable). But however grandiose and miraculous the events may have been, the narrative must be viewed as historical. Centered on an historically identifiable OT prophet who lived in the eighth century B.C., the account of whom has been recorded in narrative form, there is no alternative but to understand Jonah as historical. Furthermore, Jesus did not teach the story of Jonah as a parable but as an actual account firmly rooted in history (Matt. 12:38–41; 16:4; Luke 11:29–32).

Ten Miracles in Jonah

1.	1:4	"the LORD sent out a great wind on the sea"
2.	1:7	"the lot fell on Jonah"
3.	1:15	"the sea ceased from its raging"
4.	1:17	"the LORD had prepared a great fish"
5.	1:17	"to swallow Jonah (alive)"
6.	2:10	"the LORD spoke to the fish...it vomited Jonah onto dry *land*"
7.	3:10	"God saw their works...they turned from their evil way"
8.	4:6	"the LORD God prepared a plant"
9.	4:7	"God prepared a worm"
10.	4:8	"God prepared a vehement east wind"

OUTLINE
I. **Running from God's Will (1:1–17)**
  A. The Commission of Jonah (1:1,2)
  B. The Flight of Jonah (1:3)
  C. The Pursuit of Jonah (1:4–16)
  D. The Preservation of Jonah (1:17)
II. **Submitting to God's Will (2:1–10)**
  A. The Helplessness of Jonah (2:1–3)
  B. The Prayer of Jonah (2:4–7)

C. The Repentance of Jonah (2:8,9)
D. The Deliverance of Jonah (2:10)
III. Fulfilling God's Will (3:1–10)
A. The Commission Renewed (3:1,2)
B. The Prophet Obeys (3:3,4)
C. The City Repents (3:5–9)
D. The Lord Relents (3:10)
IV. Questioning God's Will (4:1–11)
A. The Prophet Displeased (4:1–5)
B. The Prophet Rebuked (4:6–11)

MEANWHILE, IN OTHER PARTS OF THE WORLD...
The first authenticated solar eclipse in Chinese history was documented on September 6, 775 B.C.

ANSWERS TO TOUGH QUESTIONS

1. Were Jonah's adventures some kind of mythical story, or did the prophet actually experience those amazing miracles?

Those who have a problem with the idea of miracles have a great problem with Jonah. The miracles in this book happen on a grand scale: a relentless storm, survival inside a large fish, repentance by the leader of a recognized world power. These are not for the timid in faith. Some skeptics and critics simply deny Jonah's historical validity. Others attempt to offer substitute spiritual lessons by making parts of Jonah allegorical or interpreting the whole book as a parable.

Two factors speak strongly in favor of taking Jonah at face value: (1) The role of the miracles in Jonah offended the central character. Those miracles made him look cowardly, mean, and bitter. Given the constant tension between the prophet and the mission God had given to him, the greatest miracle of all is probably that Jonah eventually recorded these God-glorifying and prophet-humiliating historical events. (2) Jesus referred to Jonah several times as a historical person, not a parable (see Matt. 12:38–44; 16:4; Luke 11:29–32).

2. Why did God care about what happened to Nineveh?

That was precisely Jonah's question. He certainly did not care about Nineveh. He hoped and prayed that God would carry out His intention to overthrow the city. But Jonah also knew that God usually gives warnings as opportunities. Jonah did not want Nineveh to have another chance.

Jonah hated Nineveh and its reputation. He resented the suffering that had befallen his own people through the rulers of Nineveh. He failed to identify with the people of Nineveh, seeing them simply as a faceless enemy. God offered Jonah a priceless lesson in compassion. He stirred up Jonah's sense of outrage through a plant and then explained to the prophet that He had the divine right to exercise compassion on the many thousands in Nineveh who were ignorant of their own condition (4:1–11).

FURTHER STUDY ON JONAH

1. Why didn't Jonah want to go to Nineveh?
2. Describe the ups and downs of Jonah's attitude throughout this book.
3. Why did God rescue Jonah in spite of the prophet's blatant disobedience?
4. What insights does the Book of Jonah give about God's love?
5. In what specific ways can you identify with Jonah? What would you like to avoid about his experiences?

MICAH
Who Is Like God?

TITLE
The name of the book is derived from the prophet who, having received the word of the Lord, was commissioned to proclaim it. Micah, whose name is shared by others in the OT (e.g., Judg. 17:1; 2 Chr. 13:2; Jer. 36:11), is a shortened form of Micaiah (or Michaiah) and means "Who is like the LORD?" In 7:18, Micah uses a play on his own name, saying "Who is a God like You?"

AUTHOR AND DATE
The first verse establishes Micah as the author. Beyond that, little is known about him. His parentage is not given, but his name suggests a godly heritage. He traces his roots to the town of Moresheth (1:1,14), located in the foothills of Judah, approximately 25 mi. southwest of Jerusalem, on the border of Judah and Philistia, near Gath. From a productive agricultural area, he was like Amos, a country resident removed from the national politics and religion, yet chosen by God (3:8) to deliver a message of judgment to the princes and people of Jerusalem.

Micah places his prophecy during the reigns of Jotham (750–731 B.C.), Ahaz (731–715 B.C.), and Hezekiah (715–686 B.C.). His indictments of social injustices and religious corruption renew the theme of Amos (mid-eighth century B.C.) and his contemporaries, Hosea in the north (ca. 755–710 B.C.) and in the south Isaiah (ca. 739–690 B.C.). This fits that which is known about the character of Ahaz (2 Kin. 16:10–18) and his son Hezekiah prior to his sweeping spiritual reformations (2 Chr. 29; 31:1). His references to the imminent fall of Samaria (1:6) clearly position him before 722 B.C., at approximately 735–710 B.C.

BACKGROUND AND SETTING
Because the northern kingdom was about to fall to Assyria during Micah's ministry in 722 B.C., Micah dates his message with the mention of Judean kings only. While the northern kingdom of Israel was an occasional recipient of his words (cf. 1:5–7), his primary attention was directed toward the southern kingdom in which he lived. The economic prosperity and the absence of international crises that marked the days of Jeroboam II (793–753 B.C.), during which the borders of Judah and Israel rivaled those of David and Solomon (cf. 2 Kin. 14:23–27), were slipping away. Syria and Israel invaded Judah, temporarily taking the wicked Ahaz captive (cf. 2 Chr. 28:5–16; Is. 7:1,2). After Assyria had overthrown Syria and Israel, the good king Hezekiah withdrew his allegiance to Assyria, causing Sennacherib to besiege Jerusalem in 701 B.C. (cf. 2 Kin. 18,19; 2 Chr. 32). The Lord then sent His angel to deliver Judah (2 Chr. 32:21). Hezekiah was used by God to lead Judah back to true worship.

After the prosperous reign of Uzziah, who died in 739 B.C., his son Jotham continued the same policies, but failed to remove the centers of idolatry. Outward prosperity was only a facade masking rampant social corruption and religious syncretism. Worship of the Canaanite fertility god Baal was increasingly integrated with the OT sacrificial system, reaching epidemic proportions under the reign of Ahaz (cf. 2 Chr. 28:1–4). When Samaria fell, thousands of refugees swarmed into Judah, bringing their religious syncretism with them. But while Micah (like Hosea) addressed this issue, it was the disintegration of personal and social values to which he delivered his most stinging rebukes and stern warnings (e.g., 7:5,6). Assyria was the dominant power and a constant threat to Judah, so Micah's prediction that Babylon, then under Assyrian rule, would conquer Judah (4:10) seemed remote. Thus, as the prophet Amos was to Israel, Micah was to Judah.

KEY PEOPLE IN MICAH

The people of Israel—the northern kingdom which was about to fall into Assyrian captivity (1:2–7:20)

HISTORICAL AND THEOLOGICAL THEMES

Primarily, Micah proclaimed a message of judgment to a people persistently pursuing evil. Similar to other prophets (cf. Hos. 4:1; Amos 3:1), Micah presented his message in lawsuit/courtroom terminology (1:2; 6:1,2). The prophecy is arranged in 3 oracles or cycles, each beginning with the admonition to "hear" (1:2; 3:1; 6:1). Within each oracle, he moves from doom to hope—doom because they have broken God's law given at Sinai; hope because of God's unchanging covenant with their forefathers (7:20). One-third of the book targets the sins of his people; another third looks at the punishment of God to come; and another third promises hope for the faithful after the judgment. Thus, the theme of the inevitability of divine judgment for sin is coupled together with God's immutable commitment to His covenant promises. The combination of God's (1) absolute consistency in judging sin and (2) unbending commitment to His covenant through the remnant of His people provides the hearers with a clear disclosure of the character of the Sovereign of the universe. Through divine intervention, He will bring about both judgment on sinners and blessing on those who repent.

CHRIST IN . . . MICAH

MICAH PROVIDES ONE OF THE MOST significant prophecies in the Bible referring to Christ's birthplace and eternality: "But you, Bethlehem Ephrathah, though you are little among the thousands of Judah, yet out of you shall come forth to Me the One to be Ruler in Israel, whose goings forth are from the old, from everlasting" (5:2). This passage was used by the scribes and chief priest to answer Herod's query about the birthplace of Jesus (Matthew 2:6). Micah 7:6 was also used by Jesus to explain the nature of His coming (Matthew 10:35,36).

KEY DOCTRINES IN MICAH

God's judgment of sin (1:2–2:5; 1 Chron. 16:33; Ps. 96:13; Eccl. 3:17; Matt. 7:22–23; John 12:48; Rom. 2:12; 2 Tim. 4:1; Rev. 20:12)

God's covenant with Israel's forefathers (7:20; Gen. 15:7–18; 17:2–14,19,21; 26:3,4; 28:13,14; Ex. 6:4; 2 Sam. 23:5; 1 Chron. 16:16,17; Ps. 89:3,4; Luke 1:72–75; Acts 3:25; Gal. 3:16)

GOD'S CHARACTER IN MICAH

God is long-suffering—7:1
God is merciful—7:18,20
God is provident—5:2

God is righteous—6:4,5; 7:9
God is true—7:20
God is unified—7:18
God is wrathful—7:9,11

INTERPRETIVE CHALLENGES

The verbal similarity between Micah 4:1–3 and Isaiah 2:2–4 raises the question of who quoted whom. Interpreters are divided, with no clear-cut answers on either side. Because the two prophets lived in close proximity to each other, prophesying during the same period, this similarity is understandable. God gave the same message through two preachers. The introductory phrase, "in the latter days" (4:1), removes these verses from the context of Israel's return from exile and places it within the timeframe surrounding the Second Advent of Christ and the beginning of the Millennium.

Apart from Is. 2:2–4, three other passages from Micah are quoted elsewhere in Scripture. Micah 3:12 is quoted in Jer. 26:18, thereby saving Jeremiah's life from King Jehoiakim's death sentence. Micah 5:2 is quoted by the chief priests and scribes (Matt. 2:6) in response to Herod's query about the birthplace of the Messiah. Micah 7:6 is employed by Jesus in Matt. 10:35,36 when commissioning His disciples.

KEY WORDS IN

Micah

Complaint: Hebrew *rib*—6:2—can mean "dispute" or "quarrel" in the sense of a feud (Judg. 12:2), "controversy" or "strife" (Prov. 17:14; 18:6) prompted by a rebellious spirit (Numbers 20:13; Proverbs 17:14; 18:6), or even a "legal case" or "lawsuit" (Job 31:13,35; Jeremiah 11:20). The prophets frequently used this word as a technical, legal term in contexts pertaining to the Lord's covenant relationship with Israel (Jer. 25:31; Josh. 4:1; 12:2). In this chapter, Micah was informing Judah that God had registered a formal, legal complaint against His people. He was ordering them to stand trial for violating covenant stipulations forbidding idolatry and requiring social justice (6:2–16).

Compassion: Hebrew *raham*—7:19—translated here as *compassion,* means "to love from the womb" and is also frequently translated *mercy* (Is. 14:1). The noun form of this verb means "womb," and consequently this verb depicts the tender love of a mother for her own helpless child (1 Kin. 3:26). "From the womb" speaks of the depth of emotion associated with this expression of love. God loves His people with a deep compassion and love that is almost beyond description. God used a form of this Hebrew word to reveal His character and name to Moses: "And the Lord passed before him and proclaimed: 'The LORD, the LORD God, merciful and gracious, longsuffering, and abounding in goodness and truth'" (Ex. 34:6).

OUTLINE
I. Superscription (1:1)
II. God Gathers to Judge and Deliver (1:2–2:13)
    A. Samaria and Judah Punished (1:2–16)
    B. Oppressors Judged (2:1–5)
    C. False Prophets Renounced (2:6–11)
    D. Promise of Deliverance (2:12,13)
III. God Judges Rulers and Comes to Deliver (3:1–5:15)
    A. The Contemporary Leaders Are Guilty (3:1–12)
    B. The Coming Leader Will Deliver and Restore (4:1–5:15)
IV. God Brings Indictments and Ultimate Deliverance (6:1–7:20)
    A. Messages of Reproof and Lament (6:1–7:6)
    B. Messages of Confidence and Victory (7:7–20)

MEANWHILE, IN OTHER PARTS OF THE WORLD...
The Celtic people begin to move southward from the country
known today as Scotland to settle the rest of Great Britain.

ANSWERS TO TOUGH QUESTIONS

1. How is a book like Micah used in the New Testament?
Twice in the Book of Matthew, passages from Micah play a significant part in events. In Matthew 2:6, the chief priests and scribes quote 5:2 in response to Herod's query about the birthplace of the Messiah. Later, in Matthew 10:35–36, Jesus quotes 7:6 while commissioning His disciples. The people in the New Testament were intimately familiar with the Old Testament prophets. Their writing and thinking were permeated with the phrases as well as the predictions that God had given to those messengers of old.

FURTHER STUDY ON MICAH

1. If the religious scholars of Jesus' day knew the prophecy about the Messiah and Bethlehem, why didn't they believe Jesus was the Savior?
2. Does Micah 6:6–8 teach that we can please God and gain eternal favor by being good?
3. What is the purpose of living to please God?
4. How did Micah confront the national and personal oppression that was rampant in his day?
5. How did Micah confront false faith in his own society? What would he say about today?

NAHUM
Postponed Judgment Applied

TITLE

The book's title is taken from the prophet of God's oracle against Nineveh, the capital of Assyria. *Nahum* means "comfort" or "consolation" and is a short form of Nehemiah ("comfort of Yahweh"). Nahum is not quoted in the NT, although there may be an allusion to 1:15 in Romans 10:15 (cf. Is. 52:7).

AUTHOR AND DATE

The significance of the writing prophets was not their personal lives; it was their message. Thus, background information about the prophet from within the prophecy is rare. Occasionally one of the historical books will shed additional light. In the case of Nahum, nothing is provided except that he was an Elkoshite (1:1), referring either to his birthplace or his place of ministry. Attempts to identify the location of Elkosh have been unsuccessful. Suggestions include Al Qosh, situated in northern Iraq (thus Nahum would have been a descendant of the exiles taken to Assyria in 722 B.C.), Capernaum ("town of Nahum"), or a location in southern Judah (cf. 1:15). His birthplace or locale is not significant to the interpretation of the book.

With no mention of any kings in the introduction, the date of Nahum's prophecy must be implied by historical data. The message of judgment against Nineveh portrays a nation of strength, intimating a time not only prior to her fall in 612 B.C. but also probably before the death of Ashurbanipal in 626 B.C., after which Assyria's power fell rapidly. Nahum's mention of the fall of north Amon, also called Thebes (3:8–10), in 663 B.C. (at the hands of Ashurbanipal) appears to be fresh in their minds and there is no mention of

> ## CHRIST IN ... NAHUM
>
> NAHUM'S PORTRAYAL OF GOD'S ATTRIBUTES also describes the person of Christ in His future coming. Christ first came to earth as the promised Messiah drawing the faithful unto Himself. Nahum depicts God's protection of the faithful revealing, "The LORD is good, a stronghold in the day of trouble" (1:7). However, the second coming of Christ will bring judgment as Christ takes "vengeance on His adversaries" (1:2).

the rekindling that occurred ten years later, suggesting a mid-seventh-century B.C. date during the reign of Manasseh (ca. 695–642 B.C.; cf. 2 Kin. 21:1–18).

BACKGROUND AND SETTING

A century after Nineveh repented at the preaching of Jonah, she returned to idolatry, violence, and arrogance (3:1–4). Assyria was at the height of her power, having recovered from Sennacherib's defeat (701 B.C.) at Jerusalem (cf. Is. 37:36–38). Her borders extended all the way into Egypt. Esarhaddon had recently transplanted conquered peoples into Samaria and Galilee in 670 B.C. (cf. 2 Kin. 17:24; Ezra 4:2), leaving Syria and Palestine very weak. But God brought Nineveh down under the rising power of Babylon's king Nabopolassar and his son, Nebuchadnezzar (ca. 612 B.C.). Assyria's demise turned out just as God had prophesied.

KEY PEOPLE IN NAHUM

The people of Nineveh—Assyrians who returned to evil and were destined for destruction (2:1–3:19)

HISTORICAL AND THEOLOGICAL THEMES

Nahum forms a sequel to the Book of Jonah, who prophesied over a century earlier. Jonah recounts the remission of God's promised judgment toward Nineveh, while Nahum depicts the later execution of God's judgment. Nineveh was proud of her invulnerable city, with her walls reaching 100 feet high and with a moat 150 feet wide and 60 feet deep; but Nahum established the fact that the sovereign God (1:2–5) would bring vengeance upon those who violated His law (1:8,14; 3:5–7). The same God would bring judgment against evil that was also redemptive, bestowing His loving-kindnesses upon the faithful (cf. 1:7,12, 13,15; 2:2). The prophecy brought comfort to Judah and all who feared the cruel Assyrians. Nahum said Nineveh would end "with an overflowing flood" (1:8); and it happened when the Tigris River overflowed to destroy enough of the walls to let the Babylonians through. Nahum also predicted that the city would be hidden (3:11). After its destruction in 612 B.C., the site was not rediscovered until 1842 A.D.

> ### KEY WORDS IN
> # *Nahum*
>
> **Jealous:** Hebrew *qanno*ʾ—1:2—related to a root word that can mean "to be eager, zealous for" (1 Kin. 19:10,14), or even "to be furious" (Zech. 8:2). One of God's names is Jealous (Ex. 34:14). When the expression "the LORD your God is a jealous God" is used in the OT, it is usually associated with an injunction against idol worship (Ex. 20:5; Deut. 4:24; 5:9; 6:15). God's jealousy for His people is a claim for exclusive allegiance rooted in His holiness (Josh.24:19) and His role as their Creator and Redeemer (Pss. 95:6,7; 96:2–5). We tend to associate jealousy with a self-serving emotion that usually results from feelings of inadequacy. God's jealousy, in contrast, proceeds from His holiness. Because He alone is the Holy One (see Is. 6:3; 40:25), He will tolerate no rival (Ex. 20:5).

KEY DOCTRINES IN NAHUM

God's judgment—the sovereign God would bring vengeance upon those who violated His law (1:8,14; 3:5–7; Ex. 20:5; Deut. 28:41; Job 12:23; Ezek. 39:23; Joel 3:19; Amos 3:6; Acts 17:31; Rom. 2:16; Rev. 6:17)

God's loving-kindness toward the faithful (1:7,12,13,15; 2:2; Num. 6:22–27; Ps. 46:1; Is. 33:2–4; 37:3–7,29–38; Matt. 11:28,29; 19:13,14; 2 Tim. 2:24; Titus 3:4; 1 John 4:11)

GOD'S CHARACTER IN NAHUM

God is good—1:7
God is jealous—1:2
God is powerful—1:3
God is provident—1:4
God is sovereign—1:2–5
God is wrathful—1:2,3,6

INTERPRETIVE CHALLENGES

Apart from the uncertain identity of Elkosh (cf. Author and Date), the prophecy presents no real interpretive difficulties. The book is a straightforward prophetic announcement of judgment against Assyria and her capital Nineveh for cruel atrocities and idolatrous practices.

OUTLINE

    I. Superscription (1:1)
    II. Destruction of Nineveh Declared (1:2–15)
        A. God's Power Illustrated (1:2–8)
        B. God's Punishment Stated (1:9–15)
    III. Destruction of Nineveh Detailed (2:1–13)
        A. The City Is Assaulted (2:1–10)
        B. The City Is Discredited (2:11–13)
    IV. Destruction of Nineveh Demanded (3:1–19)
        A. The First Charge (3:1–3)
        B. The Second Charge (3:4–7)
        C. The Third Charge (3:8–19)

MEANWHILE, IN OTHER PARTS OF THE WORLD...
Japan becomes a recognized nation (660 B.C.).

FURTHER STUDY ON NAHUM

1. How is the entire Book of Nahum an example of God's patience?
2. What were God's charges against the city of Nineveh?
3. Why did God call Himself a jealous God?
4. What examples of God's sovereignty are included in Nahum?
5. What is your own perspective on the possibility of God's judgment on your life?

HABAKKUK
The Just Shall Live by Faith

TITLE

This prophetic book takes its name from its author and possibly means "one who embraces" (1:1; 3:1). By the end of the prophecy, this name becomes appropriate as the prophet clings to God regardless of his confusion about God's plans for his people.

AUTHOR AND DATE

As with many of the Minor Prophets, nothing is known about the prophet except that which can be inferred from the book. In the case of Habakkuk, internal information is virtually nonexistent, making it impossible to establish any certain conclusions about his identity and life. His simple introduction as "the prophet Habakkuk" may imply that he needed no introduction since he was a well-known prophet of his day. It is certain that he was a contemporary of Jeremiah, Ezekiel, Daniel, and Zephaniah.

The mention of the Chaldeans (1:6) suggests a late-seventh-century B.C. date, shortly before Nebuchadnezzar commenced his military march through Nineveh (612 B.C.), Haran (609 B.C.), and Carchemish (605 B.C.), on his way to Jerusalem (605 B.C.). Habakkuk's bitter lament (1:2–4) may reflect a time period shortly after the death of Josiah (609 B.C.), days in which the godly king's reforms (cf. 2 Kin. 23) were quickly overturned by his successor, Jehoiakim (Jer. 22:13–19).

CHRIST IN . . . HABAKKUK

ALTHOUGH HABAKKUK NEVER MENTIONS Christ's name, he rejoices in the saving ministry of Jesus as the "God of my salvation" (3:18). Habakkuk also foreshadows Christ's coming salvation: "You went forth for the salvation of Your people; For salvation with Your Anointed" (3:13). The Old and New Testaments clearly point to Christ as the Anointed One (Ps. 28:8; Dan. 9:25,26; Acts 4:27; 10:38; Heb. 1:9).

BACKGROUND AND SETTING

Habakkuk prophesied during the final days of the Assyrian Empire and the beginning of Babylonia's world rulership under Nabopolassar and his son Nebuchadnezzar. When Nabopolassar ascended to power in 626 B.C., he immediately began to expand his influence to the north and west. Under the leadership of his son, the Babylonian army overthrew Nineveh in 612 B.C., forcing the Assyrian nobility to take refuge first in Haran and then Carchemish. Nebuchadnezzar pursued them, overrunning Haran in 609 B.C. and Carchemish in 606 B.C.

The Egyptian king Necho, traveling through Judah in 609 B.C. to assist the fleeing Assyrian king, was opposed by King Josiah at Megiddo (2 Chr. 35:20–24). Josiah was killed in the ensuing battle, leaving his throne to a succession of three sons and a grandson. Earlier, as a result of discovering the Book of the Law in the temple (622 B.C.), Josiah had instituted significant spiritual reforms in Judah (2 Kin. 22,23), abolishing many of the idolatrous practices of his father Amon (2 Kin. 21:20–22) and grandfather Manasseh (2 Kin. 21:11–13). Upon his death, however, the nation quickly reverted to her evil ways (cf. Jer. 22:13–19), causing Habakkuk to question God's silence and apparent lack of punitive action (1:2–4) to purge His covenant people.

KEY PEOPLE IN HABAKKUK

Habakkuk—the last prophet sent to Judah before its fall into Babylonian captivity (1:1–3:19)

The Chaldeans—Babylonians raised up by God to punish Judah (1:6–11; 2:2–20)

HISTORICAL AND THEOLOGICAL THEMES

The opening verses reveal a historical situation similar to the days of Amos and Micah. Justice had essentially disappeared from the land; violence and wickedness were pervasive, existing unchecked. In the midst of these dark days, the prophet cried out for divine intervention (1:2–4). God's response—that He was sending the Chaldeans to judge Judah (1:5–11)—creates an even greater theological dilemma for Habakkuk. Why didn't God flush out the evil from His people and restore their righteousness? How could God use the Chaldeans to judge a people more righteous than they (1:12–2:1)? God's answer that He would judge the Chaldeans also (2:2–20), did not fully satisfy the prophet's theological dilemma; in fact, it only intensified it. In Habakkuk's mind, the issue crying for resolution is no longer God's righteous response toward evil (or lack thereof), but the vindication of God's character and covenant with His people (1:13). Like Job, the prophet argued with God, and through that experience he achieved a deeper understanding of God's sovereign character and a firmer faith in Him (cf. Job 42:5,6; Is.55:8,9). Ultimately, Habakkuk realized that God was not to be worshiped merely because of the temporal blessings He bestowed, but for His own sake (3:17–19).

> **KEY WORDS IN**
>
> ## Habakkuk
>
> **Image:** Hebrew *pesel*—2:18—related to a verbal root meaning "to hew out stone" or "to cut or carve wood" (see Ex. 34:4). A *pesel* is an image or idol in the likeness of a human being or animal made from stone, wood, or metal. God prohibited the Hebrews from making such idols at Mt. Sinai (Ex. 20:4). God intended the lack of images among the Hebrews to be one distinguishing feature of their true religion. Tragically, Israel followed the example of their pagan neighbors and worshiped carved images (Judg. 18:30; 2 Chr. 33:7). The psalmist describes such images as worthless and those who worship them as shameful (Ps. 97:7). Both Isaiah (Is. 40:19,20; 44:9–20) and Hab. (2:18,19) mock those who would put their trust in images made with mere human hands. They have no capacity to see, hear, speak, or do anything for their devotees.

KEY DOCTRINES IN HABAKKUK

The nature of God's judgment—God used the Babylonians to judge the people of Judah (1:5–11; 2:2–20; Deut. 28:49,50; 2 Kin. 24:2; 2 Chr. 36:17; Jer. 4:11–13; Ezek. 7:24; 21:31; Mic. 4:10; Acts 17:31; Rom. 2:16; Rev. 6:17)

Proper worship of God—God is not to be worshiped merely because of temporal blessings but for His own sake (3:17–19; Deut. 28:1–14; Ps. 97:12; Is. 12:2; 41:16; 61:10; Luke 1:47; Phil. 4:4; Rev. 4:10–11)

Justification by faith—Humans are saved through faith in God alone and not through works (2:4; Gen. 15:6; Lev. 18:5; Is. 45:25; 50:8,9; Zech. 3:4,5; John 3:36; Rom. 1:17; 5:1; Gal. 3:11; Col. 1:22,23; Heb. 3:12–14; 10:38)

GOD'S CHARACTER IN HABAKKUK
God is glorious—2:14
God is wrathful—3:2

INTERPRETIVE CHALLENGES
The queries of the prophet represent some of the most fundamental questions of life, with the answers providing crucial foundation stones on which to build a proper understanding of God's character and His sovereign ways in history. The core of his message lies in the call to trust God (2:4), "the just shall live by his faith."

The NT references to this verse ascribe unusual importance theologically to Habakkuk. The writer of Hebrews quotes Habakkuk 2:4 to emphasize the believer's need to remain strong and faithful in the midst of affliction and trials (Heb. 10:38). The apostle Paul, on the other hand, employs the verse twice (Rom. 1:17; Gal. 3:11) to highlight the doctrine that Christians are justified by faith. Though these different uses might indicate an interpretive conflict, such is not the case. All of these references point beyond a single act of faith to include the continuity of faith. Faith in the Scriptures is not a one-time act but a way of life. The true believer, declared righteous by God, will persevere in faith throughout his or her life (Col. 1:22,23; Heb. 3:12–14). The believer will trust the sovereign God, who only does what is right.

OUTLINE
I. Superscription (1:1)
II. The Prophet's Perplexities (1:2–2:20)
    A. Habakkuk's First Complaint (1:2–4)
    B. God's First Response (1:5–11)
    C. Habakkuk's Second Complaint (1:12–2:1)
    D. God's Second Response (2:2–20)
III. The Prophet's Prayer (3:1–19)
    A. Petition for God's Mercy (3:1,2)
    B. Praise of God's Power (3:3–15)
    C. Promise of God's Sufficiency (3:16–19)

MEANWHILE, IN OTHER PARTS OF THE WORLD...
The Temple of Artemis, one of the seven wonders of the world, is built in Ephesus.

ANSWERS TO TOUGH QUESTIONS

1. In what ways do God's answers to Habakkuk's deep questions offer help to modern people reading his book?

God's answers to the prophet's searching questions give a proper understanding of God's character and sovereign actions in history. Ultimately, Habakkuk demonstrates that life's meaning does not rest in finely argued intellectual answers, but in trusting God. The prophet echoes the theme of genuine holy living: "The just shall live by his faith" (2:4). Those who read the prophet today will find a fellow traveler who may well lead them to trusting the God he came to trust.

2. What impact does Habakkuk have on the NT?

The writers of the NT quoted Habakkuk in a way that gave him importance. The writer of Hebrews quoted 2:4 to amplify the believer's need to remain strong in the midst of affliction (Heb. 10:38). The apostle Paul, on the other hand, employed that same verse twice (Rom. 1:17; Gal. 3:11) to accentuate the doctrine of justification by faith.

FURTHER STUDY ON HABAKKUK

1. How did God answer Habakkuk's first question: *Why aren't things fair, God?*
2. How did God answer the prophet's second question: *Why don't you do something when things aren't fair, God?*
3. When you experience struggles and doubt, how do you resolve them?
4. In what ways is the Book of Habakkuk a tribute to the sovereignty of God?
5. For Habakkuk, what was the ultimate source of hope in this world?

ZEPHANIAH
Shelter in the Midst of Judgment

TITLE
As with each of the twelve Minor Prophets, the prophecy bears the name of its author, which is generally thought to mean "the LORD hides" (cf. 2:3).

AUTHOR AND DATE
Little is known about the author, Zephaniah. Three other OT individuals share his name. He traces his genealogy back four generations to King Hezekiah (ca. 715–686 B.C.), standing alone among the prophets descended from royal blood (1:1). Royal genealogy would have given him the ear of Judah's king, Josiah, during whose reign he preached.

The prophet himself dates his message during the reign of Josiah (640–609 B.C.). The moral and spiritual conditions detailed in the book (cf. 1:4–6; 3:1–7) seem to place the prophecy prior to Josiah's reforms, when Judah was still languishing in idolatry and wickedness. It was in 628 B.C. that Josiah tore down all the altars to Baal, burned the bones of false prophets, and broke the carved idols (2 Chr. 34:3–7); and in 622 B.C. the Book of the Law was found (2 Chr. 34:8–35:19). Consequently, Zephaniah most likely prophesied from 635–625 B.C., and was a contemporary of Jeremiah.

BACKGROUND AND SETTING
Zephaniah prophesied during a time of almost universal upheaval. Politically, the imminent transfer of Assyrian world power to the Babylonians weakened Nineveh's hold on Judah, bringing an element of independence to Judah for the first time in fifty years. King Josiah's desire to retain this newfound freedom from taxation and subservience undoubtedly led him to interfere later with Egypt's attempt to interdict the fleeing king of Nineveh in 609 B.C. (cf. 2 Chr. 35:20–27). Spiritually, the reigns of Hezekiah's son Manasseh (ca. 695–642 B.C.), extending over four decades, and his grandson Amon (ca. 642–640 B.C.), lasting only two years, were marked by wickedness and spiritual rebellion (2 Kin. 21; 2 Chr. 33). The early years of Josiah's reign were also characterized by the evil from his fathers (2 Kin. 23:4). In 622 B.C., however, while repairing the house of the Lord, Hilkiah, the high priest, found the Book of the Law (2 Kin. 22:8). Upon reading it, Josiah initiated extensive reforms (2 Kin. 23). It was during the early years of Josiah's reign, prior to the great revival, that this eleventh-hour prophet, Zephaniah, prophesied and no doubt had an influence on the sweeping reforms Josiah brought to the nation. But the evil kings before Josiah had had such an effect on Judah that it never recovered. The effects of half a century of evil leadership left a nation steeped in sin, and King Josiah's reforms resulted in little more than surface changes. Even the discovery of the Law of God in the temple rubble after Zephaniah's time had little long-term effect on the attitudes of the people. Josiah's reforms were too late and didn't outlast his life.

KEY PEOPLE IN ZEPHANIAH

Zephaniah—prophet who warned Judah of coming judgment and also future hope (1:1–3:20)

The people of Judah—led by King Josiah to repent but eventually fell into Babylonian captivity (1:2–2:3; 3:1–20)

HISTORICAL AND THEOLOGICAL THEMES

Zephaniah's message on the Day of the Lord warned Judah that the final days were near, through divine judgment at the hands of Nebuchadnezzar, ca. 605–586 B.C. (1:4–13). Yet, it also looks beyond to the far fulfillment in the judgments of Daniel's seventieth week (1:18; 3:8). The expression "Day of the Lord" is employed by the author more often than by any other OT writer, and is described as a day that is near (1:7), and as a day of wrath, trouble, dis-

CHRIST IN . . . ZEPHANIAH

EVEN THOUGH ZEPHANIAH explicitly portrays the judgment of God, Christ is present as the "Mighty One" who will bring salvation to the earth (3:17). Christ Himself made allusions to Zephaniah (1:3, see Matt. 13:41; and 1:15, see Matt. 24:29), further connecting the prophecies of Zephaniah and the second coming of Christ.

tress, devastation, desolation, darkness, gloominess, clouds, thick darkness, trumpet, and alarm (1:15,16,18). Yet even within these oracles of divine wrath, the prophet exhorted the people to seek the Lord, offering a shelter in the midst of judgment (2:3), and proclaiming the promise of eventual salvation for His believing remnant (2:7; 3:9–20).

KEY DOCTRINES IN ZEPHANIAH

The Day of the Lord (1:7,14–16,18; 3:8; Is. 2:12; 13:6,9; Ezek. 13:5; 20:3; Joel 1:15; 2:1,11,31; 3:14; Amos 5:18–20; Obad. 1–21; Zech. 14:1; Mal. 4:5)

God's grace in the midst of judgment (2:3; 3:14–20; Ps. 45:2; Is. 26:20; Joel 2:14; Amos 5:14,15; Zech. 12:10; Rom. 5:21; 2 Cor. 12:9; Heb. 4:16)

Salvation for the believing remnant (2:7; 3:9–20; Is. 35:4; 45:17; Jer. 29:14; Mic. 5:7,8; Zech. 9:16; John 3:16; Luke 1:68; Acts 5:31; Rom. 11:26)

KEY WORDS IN

Zephaniah

Meek: Hebrew *'anav*—2:3—may be translated *humble* (Ps. 34:2) or *meek* (Ps. 37:11; see also Matt. 5:5) and is derived from a verb meaning "to be afflicted" or "to be bowed down" (Ps. 116:10). Forms of this word occur twice in 2:3: first translated as *meek* and then as *humility*. The word frequently refers to the poor or oppressed (see Prov. 14:21; Amos 2:7). But it also signifies strength of character in enduring suffering without resentment. Such character is rooted in a strong faith in God and His goodness and a steadfast submission to the will of God.

GOD'S CHARACTER IN ZEPHANIAH

God is judging—1:2,3; 2:2; 3:6,7
God is just—3:5
God is loving—3:17
God is wrathful—1:14–18

INTERPRETIVE CHALLENGES

The book presents an unambiguous denunciation of sin and warning of imminent judgment on Judah. Some scholars have referred the phrase "I will restore to the peoples a pure language" (3:9) to the restoration of a universal language, similar to the days prior to confusion of languages at the Tower of Babel (Gen. 11:1–9). They point out that the same word for *language* is also used in Genesis 11:7. It is better, however, to understand the passage as pointing to a purification of heart and life. See Answers to Tough Questions for further discussion.

OUTLINE
I. Superscription (1:1)
II. The Lord's Judgment (1:2–3:8)
    A. On the Whole Earth (1:2, 3)
    B. On Judah (1:4–2:3)
    C. On the Surrounding Nations (2:4–15)
        1. Philistia (2:4–7)
        2. Moab/Ammon (2:8–11)
        3. Ethiopia (2:12)
        4. Assyria (2:13–15)
    D. On Jerusalem (3:1–7)
    E. On All Nations (3:8)
III. The Lord's Blessing (3:9–20)
    A. For the Nations (3:9, 10)
    B. For Judah (3:11–20)

MEANWHILE, IN OTHER PARTS OF THE WORLD...
In India, Brahminic religion develops with the completion of the Vedas, sacred writings of religion, education, and philosophy.

ANSWERS TO TOUGH QUESTIONS

1. How much validity can be given to the interpretation of 3:9, "I will restore to the peoples a pure language," as a prophetic anticipation of God's restoration of a universal language?

    Although some have taken this phrase to refer to an undoing of God's decision to confuse the languages at the Tower of Babel (Gen. 11:1–9), the context of the phrase does not lend much support to that interpretation. Although it is true that the word *language* in Zephaniah is identical to the one used in Genesis, the overall context indicates that Zephaniah had in mind a purification of heart and life (Zeph. 3:13).

Throughout the OT, the word *language* is most often translated "lip." When combined with "pure," the reference to speech refers to an inward cleansing from sin (Is. 6:5) that is demonstrated in speech (Matt.12:34). This kind of speech is purified by the removal of the names of false gods from their lips (Hos. 2:17). It is unlikely that Zephaniah had in mind a single world language.

FURTHER STUDY ON ZEPHANIAH
1. Why did God indicate such a strong reaction towards idol worship?
2. What aspects did Zephaniah reveal about what he calls the "day of joy"?
3. In the Book of Zephaniah, what did mercy have to do with judgment?
4. In what ways were the lives of the people being offensive to God?
5. As you read God's indictment of the people, think about ways in which people today practice the same attitudes toward God.

HAGGAI
God Will Have His Temple

TITLE

The prophecy bears the name of its author. Because his name means "festal one," it is suggested that Haggai was born on a feast day. Haggai is the second shortest book in the OT (Obadiah is shorter) and is quoted by the NT once (cf. Heb. 12:26).

AUTHOR AND DATE

Little is known about Haggai apart from this short prophecy. He is mentioned briefly in Ezra 5:1 and 6:14, on both occasions in conjunction with the prophet Zechariah. The lists of refugees in Ezra mention nothing of Haggai; there are no indications of his parentage or tribal ancestry, nor does history provide any record of his occupation. He is the only person in the OT with the name, although similar names occur (cf. Gen. 46:16; Num. 26:15; 2 Sam. 3:4; 1 Chr. 6:30). Furthermore, Haggai 2:3 may suggest that he too had seen the glory of Solomon's temple before it was destroyed, making him at least 70 years of age when writing his prophecy.

There is no ambiguity or controversy about the date of the prophecy. The occasion of each of his four prophecies is clearly specified (1:1; 2:1; 2:10; 2:20), occurring within a four-month span of time in the second year (ca. 520 B.C.) of Persian king Darius Hystaspes (ca. 521–486 B.C.). Haggai most likely had returned to Jerusalem from Babylon with Zerubbabel eighteen years earlier in 538 B.C.

BACKGROUND AND SETTING

In 538 B.C., as a result of the proclamation of Cyrus the Persian (cf. Ezra 1:1–4), Israel was allowed to return from Babylon to her homeland under the civil leadership of Zerubbabel and the spiritual guidance of Joshua, the high priest (cf. Ezra 3:2). About 50,000 Jews returned. In 536 B.C., they began to rebuild the temple (cf. Ezra 3:1–4:5) but opposition from neighbors and indifference by the Jews caused the work to be abandoned (cf. Ezra 4:1–24). Sixteen years later Haggai and Zechariah were commissioned by the Lord to stir up the people to not only rebuild the temple, but also to reorder their spiritual priorities (cf. Ezra 5:1–6:22). As a result, the temple was completed four years later (ca. 516 B.C.; cf. Ezra 6:15).

CHRIST IN . . . HAGGAI

THE BOOK OF HAGGAI reveals Zerubbabel's significant place in the messianic line of David. His position, illustrated by a signet ring (2:23; see Key Words), continued the royal line of David through which Christ would come. Zerubbabel's name is found in both the ancestries of Mary (Luke 3:27) and Joseph (Matt. 1:12), demonstrating his importance in grafting both branches of Christ's lineage together.

KEY PEOPLE IN HAGGAI

Haggai—prophet of Judah after the return from the Babylonian exile; urged the people to rebuild the temple (1:3–2:23)

Zerubbabel—led the Jews out of Babylonian exile; stood as the official representative of the Davidic dynasty; called the signet ring (1:1–2:23)

The Temples of the Bible

Identification	Date	Description	References
The Tabernacle (mobile Temple)	about 1444 B.C.	Detailed plan received by Moses from the Lord Constructed by divinely appointed artisans Desecrated by Nadab and Abihu	Exodus 25–30; 35:30–40:38; Leviticus 10:1–7
Solomon's Temple	966–586 B.C. Constructed by Solomon Destroyed by Nebuchadnezzar	Planned by David Jeremiah 32:28–44	2 Samuel 7:1–29; 1 Kings 8:1–66;
Zerubbabel's Temple	516–169 B.C.	Envisioned by Zerubbabel Constructed by Zerubbabel and the elders of the Jews Desecrated by Antiochus Epiphanes	Ezra 6:1–22; 3:1–8; 4:1–14
Herod's Temple	19 B.C.–A.D. 70	Zerubbabel's temple restored by Herod the Great Destroyed by the Romans	Mark 13:2,4–23; Luke 1:11–20; 2:22–38;2:42–51; 4:21–24; Acts 21:27–33
The Present Temple	Present Age	Found in the heart of the believer The body of the believer is the Lord's only temple until the Messiah returns	1 Corinthians 6:19,20; 2 Corinthians 6:16–18
The Temple of Revelation 11	Tribulation Period	To be constructed during the Tribulation by the Antichrist To be desecrated and destroyed	Daniel 9:2; Matthew 24:15; 2 Thessalonians 2:4; Revelation 17:1
Ezekiel's (Millennial) Temple	Millennium	Envisioned by the prophet Ezekiel To be built by the Messiah during His millennial reign	Ezekiel 40:1–42:20; Zechariah 6:12,13
The Eternal Temple of His Presence	The Eternal Kingdom	The greatest temple of all ("The Lord God Almighty and the Lamb are its temple") A spiritual temple	Revelation 21:22; 22:1–21

The temple (Gr. *hieron) is a* place of worship, a sacred or holy space built primarily for the national worship of God.

Jeshua—high priest of Judah; coleader with Zerubbabel (1:1–2:4)

The people of Judah—encouraged by Haggai to complete the rebuilding of the temple (1:2,12; 2:2)

HISTORICAL AND THEOLOGICAL THEMES

The primary theme is the rebuilding of God's temple, which had been lying in ruins since its destruction by Nebuchadnezzar in 586 B.C. By means of five messages from the Lord, Haggai exhorted the people to renew their efforts to build the house of the Lord. He motivated them by noting that the drought and crop failures were caused by misplaced spiritual priorities (1:9–11).

But to Haggai, the rebuilding of the temple was not an end in itself. The temple represented God's dwelling place, His manifest presence with His chosen people. The destruction of the temple by Nebuchadnezzar followed the departure of God's dwelling glory (cf. Ezek. 8–11); to the prophet, the rebuilding of the temple invited the return of God's presence to their midst. Using the historical situation as a springboard, Haggai reveled in the supreme glory of the ultimate messianic temple yet to come (2:7), encouraging them with the promise of even greater peace (2:9), prosperity (2:19), divine rulership (2:21,22), and national blessing (2:23) during the Millennium.

KEY WORDS IN

Haggai

Signet Ring: Hebrew *chotham*—2:23—derived from a verbal root meaning "to affix a seal," "to seal up," or "to fasten by sealing." The signet in OT times was an engraved stone set in a gold or silver finger ring, bracelet, or armband (see Song of Sol. 8:6). When pressed upon wax or soft clay, the ring left the impression of the personal insignia of the bearer (see Ex. 28:11,21,36; 39:6, 14,30). The signet ring was like an identification card or badge in the ancient world (Gen. 38:18). It symbolized status or position and the binding nature of the authority attached to items sealed by the ring (1 Kin. 21:8; Job 38:14). Haggai's comparison of Zerubbabel to a signet ring (2:23) has messianic implications, since Zerubbabel would overturn the curse of Jeremiah on King Jehoiachin's dynasty and restore royal authority to the line of King David (Jeremiah 22:24–30).

KEY DOCTRINES IN HAGGAI

God's presence in the temple (1:7,8; 2:7–9; 1 Kin. 8:10,11; 2 Chr. 5:13,14; Ezek. 43:5; 1 Cor. 6:19,20; 2 Cor. 6:16–18; Rev. 21:22; 22:1–21)

Obedience by the people who feared God (1:12–15; Deut. 11:8; 1 Chr. 24:19; 2 Chr. 19:9; Ezra 5:2; Prov. 15:33; Col. 2:6,7; 3:22)

GOD'S CHARACTER IN HAGGAI

God is glorious—2:1–9

INTERPRETIVE CHALLENGES

The most prominent ambiguity within the prophecy is the phrase "the Desire of All Nations" (2:7). Although many translations exist, there are essentially only two interpretations. Some contend that it refers to Jerusalem (cf. Is. 60:11; 61:6). More likely, however, this is a reference to the Messiah, a Deliverer for whom all the nations ultimately long. See Answers to Tough Questions for further discussion.

Outline and Chronology

	Year	Month	Day
I. Rebuke for Disobedience 1:1-11	2	6	1
II. Remnant Responds and Rebuilds 1:12-15	2	6	24
III. Return of God's Glory 2:1-9	2	7	21
IV. Religious Questions 2:10-19	2	9	24
V. Reign of the Lord 2:20-23	2	9	24

MEANWHILE, IN OTHER PARTS OF THE WORLD...
Forsaking worldly comforts, Buddha leaves his home to begin his study of philosophy. In 521 B.C., he preaches his first sermon in the holy city of Barnares.

ANSWERS TO TOUGH QUESTIONS
1. What exactly did Haggai mean when he used the phrase "the Desire of All Nations" (2:7)?

A number of translations of the original phrase have been offered, but only two interpretations seem possible. Pointing to "The silver is Mine, and the gold is Mine" (2:8), as well as to references such as Isaiah 60:5 and Zechariah 14:14, some argue that Haggai had the city of Jerusalem in mind, to which the wealth of the nations will be brought during the Millennium. The preferable interpretation, however, sees this as a reference to the Messiah Himself, the Deliverer for whom all the nations ultimately long. Not only is this interpretation supported by the ancient rabbis and the early church, but the mention of "glory" in the latter part of the verse also suggests a personal reference to the Messiah (cf. Is. 40:5; 60:1; Luke 2:32).

FURTHER STUDY ON HAGGAI
1. What approaches and arguments did Haggai use to get the people to rebuild the temple?
2. Illustrate from Haggai the concept of priorities.
3. What did God do to provide a warning and incentive for the people to work?
4. What special message did God have Haggai deliver to Zerubbabel the leader of the Israelites?
5. What long-term tasks have you undertaken in your life to accomplish for God?

ZECHARIAH
Preparations for the Coming Messiah

TITLE

The universal tradition of both Jews and Christians endorses the prophet Zechariah as author. His name, common to more than twenty-nine OT men, means "The LORD remembers." This book is second only to Isaiah in the breadth of the prophet's writings about Messiah.

AUTHOR AND DATE

Like Jeremiah and Ezekiel, Zechariah was also a priest (Neh. 12:12–16) According to tradition, he was a member of the Great Synagogue, a council of 120 members originated by Nehemiah and presided over by Ezra. This council later developed into the ruling elders of the nation, called the Sanhedrin. He was born in Babylon and joined his grandfather, Iddo, in the group of exiles who first returned to Jerusalem under the leadership of Zerubbabel and Joshua the high priest (cf. Neh. 12:4). Because he is occasionally mentioned as the son of his grandfather (cf. Ezra 5:1; 6:14; Neh. 12:16), it is thought that his father, Berechiah, died at an early age before he could succeed his father into the priesthood.

Zechariah's opening words are dated from 520 B.C., the second year of Darius I (cf. 1:1). The Persian emperor Cyrus had died and was succeeded by Cambyses (ca. 530–521 B.C.) who conquered Egypt. He had no son, he killed himself, and Darius rose to the throne by quelling a revolution. He was a contemporary of Haggai, and began his prophesying two months after him (cf. Haggai Background and Setting). He is called a young man in 2:4, suggesting that Zechariah was younger than Haggai. The length of his ministry is uncertain; the last dated prophecy (7:1) came approximately two years after the first, making them identical in time with Haggai's prophecy (520–518 B.C.). Chapters 9–14 are generally thought to come from a later period of his ministry. Differences in style and references to Greece indicate a date of ca. 480–470 B.C., after Darius I (ca. 521–486 B.C.) and during Xerxes' reign (ca. 486–464 B.C.), the king who made Esther queen of Persia. According to Matthew 23:35, he was murdered between the temple and the altar, a fate similar to an earlier Zechariah (cf. 2 Chr. 24:20,21), who had been stoned to death.

CHRIST IN . . . ZECHARIAH

THE BOOK OF ZECHARIAH abounds with passages prophesying the coming Messiah. Christ is portrayed as "My Servant the Branch" (3:8), "a priest on His throne" (6:13), and as "[Him] whom they pierced" (12:10). Zechariah accurately depicts Christ as both humble and triumphant. Christ is the King who provides salvation but comes "lowly and riding on a donkey" (9:9).

BACKGROUND AND SETTING

The historical background and setting of Zechariah are the same as that of his contemporary, Haggai (cf. Haggai Background and Setting). In 538 B.C., Cyrus the Persian freed the captives from Israel to resettle their homeland (cf. Ezra 1:1–4) and about 50,000 returned from Babylon. They immediately began to rebuild the temple (cf. Ezra 3:1–4:5), but opposition from neighbors, followed by indifference from within, caused the work to be abandoned (cf. Ezra 4:24). Sixteen years later (cf. Ezra 5:1,2), Zechariah and Haggai were commissioned by the Lord to stir up the people to rebuild the temple. As a result, the temple was completed four years later in 516 B.C. (Ezra 6:15).

KEY PEOPLE IN ZECHARIAH

Zechariah—prophet of Judah after the Exile; encouraged Judah to finish building the temple (1:1–14:20)

Zerubbabel—leader of the Judean exiles; carried out the work on the temple (4:6–10)

Joshua—Israel's high priest after the remnant returned to Israel (3:1–10; 6:11–13)

The Jews rebuilding the temple—who returned to Jerusalem after the Exile to obey God (1:16; 4:9; 6:15; 8:13)

HISTORICAL AND THEOLOGICAL THEMES

Zechariah joined Haggai in rousing the people from their indifference, challenging them to resume the building of the temple. Haggai's primary purpose was to rebuild the temple; his preaching has a tone of rebuke for the people's indifference, sin, and lack of trust in God. He was used to start the revival, while Zechariah was used to keep it going strong with a more positive emphasis, calling the people to repentance and reassuring them regarding future blessings. Zechariah sought to encourage the people to build the temple in view of the promise that someday Messiah would come to inhabit it. The

KEY WORDS IN

Zechariah

Angel: Hebrew *malʾak*—1:9,13; 2:3; 3:1,5; 4:1; 5:5; 6:5; 12:8—may refer to angelic beings (4:1,5; Gen. 19:1; Ps. 91:11), human messengers (Gen. 32:3; Deut. 2:26), or ambassadors (Is. 30:4; Ezek. 17:15). A special use is the manifestation of the Godhead known as the "Angel of God" or the "Angel of the Lord" in the OT (1:11; 3:6; see Gen. 16:7-13; 21:17; 22:15; Ex. 14:19). In the OT, prophets (Hag. 1:13) and priests (Mal. 2:7) function as messengers from God. In Zechariah, angels bring revelations from God about the future and interpret the meaning of dreams and visions (1:14; 6:4,5). Jesus identified the messenger who prepared the way for the Day of the Lord, forecast in Malachi 3:1, as John the Baptist (Matt. 11:10,11).

Branch: Hebrew *tsemach*—3:8; 6:12—means "shoot" or "twig." This is one title for the coming Messiah, the "Branch," who would shoot up from the royal stock of David, a dynasty that had been interrupted with the Babylonian exile (Is. 11:1). Many of the prophets promised that a king from David's line would reign in righteousness (Jer. 23:5,6) and as a priest would reestablish true worship of the Lord (6:12,13). In His ministry, Jesus Christ fulfilled these predictions by taking on both a royal (see John 12:13-15; 1 Tim. 6:13-16) and a priestly role (see Heb. 4:14).

people were not just building for the present, but with the future hope of Messiah in mind. He encouraged the people, still downtrodden by the Gentile powers (1:8–12), with the reality that the Lord remembers His covenant promises to them and that He would restore and bless them. Thus the name of the book (which means "The LORD remembers") contains in seed form the theme of the prophecy.

This "apocalypse of the Old Testament," as it is often called, relates both to Zechariah's immediate audience as well as to the future. This is borne out in the structure of the prophecy itself, since in each of the three major sections (chaps. 1–6; 7–8; 9–14), the prophet begins historically and then moves forward to the time when Messiah returns to His temple to set up His earthly kingdom.

Of all the books in the OT, this book is the most messianic (with references to Christ, the Messiah) and the most apocalyptic in its discussion of the end times. Primarily, it is a prophecy about Jesus Christ, focusing on His coming glory as a means to comfort Israel (cf. 1:13,17). While the book is filled with visions, prophecies, signs, celestial visitors, and the voice of God, it is also practical, dealing with issues like repentance, divine care, salvation, and holy living. Prophecy was soon to be silent for more than 400 years until John the Baptist, so God used Zechariah to bring a rich, abundant outburst of promise for the future to sustain the faithful remnant through those silent years.

Zechariah's Visions

The visions of Zechariah had historical meaning for his day, but they also have meaning for all time. God will save His people and bring judgment on the wicked.	
Vision	**Significance**
Man and horses among the myrtle trees (1:8)	The Lord will again be merciful to Jerusalem (1:14,16,17).
Four horns, four craftsmen (1:18-20)	Those who scattered Judah are cast out (1:21).
Man with measuring line (2:1)	God will be a protective wall of fire around Jerusalem (2:3-5).
Cleansing of Joshua (3:4)	The Servant, the Branch, comes to save (3:8,9).
Golden lampstand and olive trees (4:2,3)	The Lord empowers Israel by His Spirit (4:6).
Flying scroll (5:1)	Dishonesty is cursed (5:3).
Woman in the basket (5:6,7)	Wickedness will be removed (5:9).
Four chariots (6:1)	The spirits of heaven execute judgment on the whole earth (6:5,7).

KEY DOCTRINES IN ZECHARIAH

Repentance—true repentance involves more than mere words; actions must also change (1:1–6; 7:8–14; Is. 31:6; 44:22; Jer. 3:12; 18:11; Ezek. 18:30; Mic. 7:19; Mal. 3:7–10; Luke 15:20; James 4:8; 1 Cor. 10:11; 2 Cor. 6:6; Rev. 21:3)

Divine care—the coming glory of Jesus Christ will be a comfort to Israel (1:13,17; Ps. 23:4; Is. 30:26; 40:1,2; 51:3; Jer. 29:10; 50:4; Hos. 6:1; 14:4; 2 Cor. 1:3–7; Phil. 2:1,2; 2 Thess. 2:16,17)

Messiah's rejection at the first coming (9:1–11:17; 13:7–9; Ps. 22:1–18; Is. 52:13–15; 53:1–12; Acts 2:23; 1 Pet. 1:18–20)

Messiah's acceptance at the second coming (12:1–14:21; Jer. 33:15,16; Dan. 7:13,14; Rom. 14:11; Phil. 2:10; Rev. 16:15)

Holy living (7:1–7; Lev. 20:7; Is. 1:10–15; 58:3–9; Eccles. 3:12; Eph. 5:1; Phil. 1:21; Col. 3:12; 2 Tim. 3:16,17)

GOD'S CHARACTER IN ZECHARIAH
God is good—9:17

INTERPRETIVE CHALLENGES
While there are numerous challenges to the reader, two passages within the prophecy are especially difficult to understand. In 11:8, the Good Shepherd "dismissed the three shepherds in one month." The presence of the definite article points to familiarity, so that the Jews would have understood the identity of these shepherds without further reference. It is not so easy for modern readers to understand. Numerous alternatives concerning their identity have been suggested. One of the oldest, and probably the correct view identifies them as three orders of leaders: the priests, elders, and scribes of Israel. During His earthly ministry, Jesus also confronted the hypocrisy of Israel's religious leaders (cf. Matt. 23), disowning them with scathing denunciations, followed by destruction of the whole nation in A.D. 70. Since His coming, the Jewish people have had no other prophet, priest, or king.

Considerable discussion also surrounds the identity of the individual who possessed "wounds between your arms" (13:6). Some have identified him with Christ, the wounds supposedly referring to His crucifixion. But Christ could neither have denied that He was a prophet, nor could He have claimed that He was a farmer, or that He was wounded in the house of His friends. Obviously, it is a reference to a false prophet (cf. vv. 4,5) who was wounded in his idolatrous worship. The zeal for the Lord will be so great in the kingdom of Messiah that idolaters will make every attempt to hide their true identity, but their scars will be the telltale evidence of their iniquity.

OUTLINE
    I. Call to Repentance (1:1–6)
    II. Eight Night Visions of Zechariah (1:7–6:15)
        A. Man Among the Myrtle Trees (1:7–17)
        B. Four Horns and Four Craftsmen (1:18–21)
        C. Man with Measuring Line (2:1–13)
        D. Cleansing of High Priest (3:1–10)
        E. Gold Lampstand and Two Olive Trees (4:1–14)
        F. Flying Scroll (5:1–4)
        G. Woman in Basket (5:5–11)
        H. Four Chariots (6:1–8)
        I. Appendix: Coronation of Joshua the High-Priest (6:9–15)
    III. Four Messages of Zechariah (7:1–8:23)
        A. Question about Fasting (7:1–3)
        B. Four Responses (7:4–8:23)
            1. Rebuke for wrong motives (7:4–7)
            2. Repentance required (7:8–14)
            3. Restoration of favor (8:1–17)
            4. Fasts become feasts (8:18–23)
    IV. Two Burdens of Zechariah (9:1–14:21)
        A. Messiah's Rejection at First Advent (9:1–11:17)
        B. Messiah's Acceptance at Second Advent (12:1–14:21)

MEANWHILE, IN OTHER PARTS OF THE WORLD...

Two philosophers of worldwide significance were born within one year of each other (550 and 551 B.C.) and died within one year of each other (480 and 479 B.C.): Guatama Buddha, the originator of Buddhism, and Confucius, the renowned Chinese philosopher.

ANSWERS TO TOUGH QUESTIONS

1. Why is Zechariah sometimes called the "apocalypse of the Old Testament"?

Zechariah's message functions in much the same way as that of the Book of Revelation (the Apocalypse of the New Testament). His prophecies related both to Zechariah's immediate audience as well as to future generations. This conclusion is borne out in the structure of the prophecy itself. In each of the three major sections (chaps. 1–6; 7–8; 9–14), the prophet begins historically and then moves forward to the time of the Second Advent, when Messiah returns to His temple to set up His earthly kingdom.

The prophet reminded the people that Messiah had both an immediate and a long-term commitment to His people. Thus Zechariah's words were "good and comforting" (1:13), both to the exiles of his own day as well as to the remnant of God's chosen people in that future day. It is this dual function of speaking to the present and to the future that has caused some to give Zechariah this title of "apocalypse of the Old Testament."

FURTHER STUDY ON ZECHARIAH

1. How do you apply the well-known verse Zechariah 4:6 in your life?
2. To what historical event did Zechariah 12:10 refer?
3. In what ways did Zechariah speak about God's jealousy?
4. How did Zechariah add his voice to Haggai's to encourage the people to rebuild the temple?
5. What does Zechariah have to say about future events beyond the time of Christ?

MALACHI
Final Prophetic Words

TITLE

The title is derived from the prophecy's author, Malachi. With this last work in the Minor Prophets, God closes the OT canon historically and prophetically.

AUTHOR AND DATE

Some have suggested that the book was written anonymously, noting that the name *Malachi*, meaning "my messenger" or "the LORD's messenger," could be a title rather than a proper name. It is pointed out that the name occurs nowhere else in the OT, nor is any background material provided about the author. However, since all other prophetic books have historically identified their author in the introductory heading, this suggests that Malachi was indeed the name of the last OT writing prophet in Israel. Jewish tradition identifies him as a member of the Great Synagogue that collected and preserved the Scriptures.

Looking at internal evidence exclusively, the date of the prophecy points to the late fifth century B.C., most likely during Nehemiah's return to Persia ca. 433–424 B.C. (cf. Neh. 5:14; 13:6). Sacrifices were being made at the second temple (1:7–10; 3:8), which was finished in 516 B.C. (cf. Ezra 6:13–15). Many years had passed since then as the priests had increasingly become complacent and corrupt (1:6–2:9). Malachi's reference to "governor" (1:8) speaks of the time of Persian dominance in Judah when Nehemiah was revisiting Persia (Neh. 13:6), while his emphasis on the law (4:4) coincides with a similar focus by Ezra and Nehemiah (cf. Ezra 7:14,25,26; Neh. 8:18). They shared other concerns as well, such as marriages to foreign wives (2:11–15; cf. Ezra 9,10; Neh. 13:23–27), withholding of tithes (3:8–10; cf. Neh. 13:10–14), and social injustice (3:5; cf. Neh. 5:1–13). Nehemiah came to Jerusalem in 445 B.C. to rebuild the wall, and returned to Persia in 433 B.C. He later returned to Israel (ca.

> ## CHRIST IN ... MALACHI
>
> THE LAST PROPHETIC WORDS from the OT still reveal hope in the coming of Christ the Messiah. Malachi speaks of two messengers: the messenger that will precede Christ, whom the NT identifies as John the Baptist (see Matthew 3:3; 11:10,14; 17:12; Mark 1:2; Luke 1:17; 7:26,27; John 1:23), and Christ, "the Messenger of the covenant" (3:1). The Book of Malachi closes the OT and marks the beginning of four hundred years of prophetic silence. However, Malachi leaves readers with the striking proclamation, "Behold, He is coming" (3:1).

424 B.C.) to deal with the sins Malachi described (Neh. 13:6). So it is likely that Malachi was written during the period of Nehemiah's absence, almost a century after Haggai and Zechariah began to prophesy. Similar to Revelation 2–3, in which Christ writes about the conditions of the churches, here God writes through Malachi to impress upon Israel His thoughts about the nation.

BACKGROUND AND SETTING

Only 50,000 exiles had returned to Judah from Babylon (538–536 B.C.). The temple had been rebuilt under the leadership of Zerubbabel (516 B.C.) and the sacrificial system renewed. Ezra had returned in 458 B.C., followed by Nehemiah in 445 B.C. After being back in the land of Palestine for only a century, the ritual of the Jews' religious routine led to hard-heartedness toward God's great love for them and to widespread departure from His law by both people and priest. Malachi rebuked and condemned these abuses, forcefully indicting the people and calling them to repentance. When Nehemiah returned from Persia the second time (ca. 424 B.C.), he vigorously rebuked them for these abuses in the temple and priesthood, for the violation of the Sabbath rest, and for the unlawful divorce of their Jewish wives so they could marry Gentile women (cf. Neh. 13).

As over two millennia of OT history since Abraham concluded, none of the glorious promises of the Abrahamic, Davidic, and New Covenants had been fulfilled in their ultimate sense. Although there had been a few high points in Israel's history, e.g., Joshua, David, and Josiah, the Jews had seemingly lost all opportunity to receive God's favor. Less than 100 years after returning from captivity, they had already sunk to a depth of sin greater than what had brought on the Assyrian and Babylonian deportations. Beyond this, the long anticipated Messiah had not arrived and did not seem to be in sight.

So, Malachi wrote the capstone prophecy of the OT in which he delivered God's message of judgment on Israel for their continuing sin, and God's promise that one day in the future, when the Jews would repent, Messiah would be revealed and God's covenant promises would be fulfilled. There were over 400 years of divine silence, with only Malachi's words ringing condemnation in their ears, before another prophet arrived with a message from God. That was John the Baptist preaching, "Repent, for the Kingdom of heaven is at hand!" (Matt. 3:2). Messiah had come.

KEY WORDS IN

Malachi

Day: Hebrew *yom*—3:2,17; 4:1,3,5—has a variety of uses in the OT. It can refer to the daylight hours in contrast to the night (Amos 5:8), or to a twenty-four-hour day, such as a certain day of the month (Gen. 7:11). It may also refer to a time period, such as the "time" or harvest (Prov. 25:13), or even to a year (2 Sam. 13:23). The word is used in the significant phrase "the Day of the LORD" (see Is. 2:12; Ezek. 13:5; Joel 1:15; Zeph. 1:14). For the prophets, the Day of the Lord would be the future day when God would decisively triumph over all His foes. That day would be a day of great rejoicing and blessing for God's faithful servants (Is. 2), whereas for God's enemies it will be a day of "darkness" (Amos 5:18).

Try: Hebrew *bachan*—3:10—means "to try" or "to put to the test" (Job 23:10; Ps. 139:23; Zech. 13:9). The word can mean "to test" in the sense of separating or discriminating one thing from another (Job 34:3). When this word is used to depict God's "testing" of people, it means the proving of individuals in such a way that his or her faith becomes more established (see Ps. 66:10–12; Jer. 17:10; 20:12). Malachi's challenge to the Israelites to *try* God is a rare instance in which people are encouraged to test the faithfulness of the Lord (3:10). This word for *try* can be contrasted with another Hebrew verb for testing, *nasah*. That word is frequently used in a negative sense, to describe the way Israel was testing God with their unbelief (Ex. 17:7; Ps. 78:18; 95:9). The law of Moses warned the Israelites not to tempt God (Deut. 6:16; Ps. 95:9); it was a mark of spiritual adultery (Matt. 12:38,39). According to James, God tests people in order to grant them the crown of life, but He tempts no one (James 1:12–14).

KEY PEOPLE IN MALACHI

Malachi—prophet to Judah; last of the OT prophets until John the Baptist (1:1–4:6)

The priests—revealed their unfaithfulness by marrying foreign wives and giving false interpretation of the Law (1:7,8; 2:1–9)

The people of Judah—married foreign wives and fell into idolatry (2:11–17)

HISTORICAL AND THEOLOGICAL THEMES

The Lord repeatedly referred to His covenant with Israel (cf. 2:4,5,8,10,14; 3:1), reminding them, from His opening words, of their unfaithfulness to His love/marriage relationship with them (cf. 1:2–5). God's love for His people pervades the book. Apparently the promises by the former prophets of the coming Messiah who would bring final deliverance and age-long blessings, and the encouragement from the recent promises (ca. 500 B.C.) of Haggai and Zechariah, had only made the people and their leaders more resolute in their complacency. They thought that this love relationship could be maintained by formal ritual alone, no matter how they lived. In a penetrating rebuke of both priests (1:6–2:9) and people (2:10–16), the prophet reminds them that the Lord's coming, which they were seeking (3:1), would be in judgment to refine, purify, and purge (3:2,3). The Lord not only wanted outward compliance to the law, but an inward acceptance as well (cf. Matt. 23:23). The prophet assaults the corruption, wickedness, and false security by directing his judgments at their hypocrisy, infidelity, compromise, divorce, false worship, and arrogance.

Malachi set forth his prophecy in the form of a dispute, employing the question-and-answer method. The Lord's accusations against His people were frequently met by cynical questions from the people (1:2,6,7; 2:17; 3:7,8,13). At other times, the prophet presented himself as God's advocate in a lawsuit, posing rhetorical questions to the people based on their defiant criticisms (1:6,8,9; 2:10,15; 3:2).

Malachi indicted the priests and the people on at least six counts of willful sin: (1) repudiating God's love (1:2–5); (2) refusing God His due honor (1:6–2:9); (3) rejecting God's faithfulness (2:10–16); (4) redefining God's righteousness (2:17–3:5); (5) robbing God's riches (3:6–12); and (6) reviling God's grace (3:13–15). There are three interludes in which Malachi rendered God's judgment: (1) to the priests (2:1–9); (2) to the nation (3:1–6); and (3) to the remnant (3:16–4:6).

KEY DOCTRINES IN MALACHI

The Lord's covenant with Israel (2:4,5,8,10,14; 3:1; Num. 3:44–48; 18:8–24; 25:12; Deut. 33:8–11; Ezek. 34:25)

Israel's unfaithfulness (1:2–5; Josh. 7:1; 1 Chr. 5:25; Ezra 9:4; Ps. 78:8; Is. 1:21; Ezek. 44:10; Hos. 1:2; Matt. 25:29; Luke 12:46; Rom. 3:3; 2 Tim. 2:13)

The coming of the Lord (3:1–3; Is. 40:3; 63:9; Jer. 10:10; Joel 2:11; Nah. 1:6; Hab. 2:7; Matt. 11:10; Mark 1:2; Luke 1:76; 7:27; John 1:23; 2:14,15)

GOD'S CHARACTER IN MALACHI

God is loving—1:2,3

The Coming of Christ

Malachi's Prophecy	Confirmed in the New Testament
As Messenger of the covenant, Christ comes to His temple (3:1) and purifies His people (3:3).	Christ cleanses the temple (John 2:14-17) and sacrifices His people (Heb. 13:12).
His coming brings judgment (4:1).	Those whose names are not in the Book of Life are cast into the lake of fire (Rev. 20:11-15).
As the Sun of Righteousness, Christ heals His people (4:2).	Christ heals the multitude; ultimately all sickness will pass away (Matt. 12:15; Rev. 21:4).
His forerunner prepares for the coming of the Lord (3:1, 4:5).	John the Baptist announces Christ (Matt. 11:10-14).

INTERPRETIVE CHALLENGES

The meaning of Elijah being sent "before the coming of the great and dreadful day of the LORD" (4:5) has been debated. Was this fulfilled in John the Baptist or is it yet to be fulfilled? Will Elijah be reincarnated? It seems best to view Malachi's prophecy as a reference to John the Baptist and not to a literal returned Elijah. See Answers to Tough Questions for further discussion.

OUTLINE

    I. The Condemnation of Israel's Sins (1:1–2:16)
        A. Reminder of God's Love for Israel (1:1–5)
        B. Rebuke of the Priests (1:6–2:9)
            1. Contempt for God's altar (1:6–14)
            2. Contempt for God's glory (2:1–3)
            3. Contempt for God's law (2:4–9)
        C. Rebuke of the People (2:10–16)
    II. The Declaration of Israel's Judgment and Blessing (2:17–4:6)
        A. Coming of a Messenger (2:17–3:5)
        B. Challenge to Repent (3:6–12)
        C. Criticism by Israel Against the Lord (3:13–15)
        D. Consolation to the Faithful Remnant (3:16–4:6)

MEANWHILE, IN OTHER PARTS OF THE WORLD...

The Greeks begin building the temple of Zeus at Olympia and a marble temple in honor of Apollo at Delphi.

ANSWERS TO TOUGH QUESTIONS

1. In what ways does John the Baptist fulfill Malachi's final prophecy in which God promises to send Elijah "before the coming of the great and dreadful day of the LORD" (4:5)?

The identity and meaning of Malachi's "Elijah" has been debated. Was this prophecy fulfilled in John the Baptist, or is it yet to be fulfilled? Could God have been announcing the reincarnation of Elijah? Evidence seems to weigh in favor of seeing Malachi's prophecy fulfilled by John the Baptist. Not only did the angel announce that John the Baptist would "go before Him in the spirit and power of Elijah" (Luke 1:17), but John himself stated that he was not Elijah (John 1:21). We conclude that John was like Elijah: (1) internally in "spirit and power," and (2) externally in rugged independence and nonconformity. To the Jews who received the Messiah, John would be the Elijah spoken of (Matt. 11:14; 17:9–13). But, since the Jews as a whole refused the King, then another Elijah-like prophet would be sent in the future, perhaps as one of the two witnesses (Rev. 11:1–19).

FURTHER STUDY ON MALACHI

1. What makes Malachi significant as the last OT prophet?
2. When God speaks in Malachi 3:6, what conclusions does God want people to reach?
3. What different aspects of the subject of sin did Malachi address in his prophecies?
4. What do we learn about God's love in Malachi?
5. In what ways has God's love left an indelible mark on your life?

OLD TESTAMENT

Book	Approximate Writing Date	Author
Job	Unknown	Anonymous
Genesis	1445–1405 B.C.	Moses
Exodus	1445–1405 B.C.	Moses
Leviticus	1445–1405 B.C.	Moses
Numbers	1445–1405 B.C.	Moses
Deuteronomy	1445–1405 B.C.	Moses
Psalms	1410–450 B.C.	Multiple Authors
Joshua	1405–1385 B.C.	Joshua
Judges	about 1043 B.C.	Samuel
Ruth	about 1030–1010 B.C.	Samuel (?)
Song of Solomon	971–965 B.C.	Solomon
Proverbs	971–686 B.C.	Solomon primarily
Ecclesiastes	940–931 B.C.	Solomon
1 Samuel	931–722 B.C.	Anonymous
2 Samuel	931–722 B.C.	Anonymous
Obadiah	850–840 B.C.	Obadiah
Joel	835–796 B.C.	Joel
Jonah	about 775 B.C.	Jonah
Amos	about 750 B.C.	Amos
Micah	735–710 B.C.	Micah
Hosea	750–710 B.C.	Hosea
Isaiah	700–681 B.C.	Isaiah
Nahum	about 650 B.C.	Nahum
Zephaniah	635–625 B.C.	Zephaniah
Habakkuk	615–605 B.C.	Habakkuk
Ezekiel	590–570 B.C.	Ezekiel
Lamentations	586 B.C.	Jeremiah
Jeremiah	586–570 B.C.	Jeremiah
1 Kings	561–538 B.C.	Anonymous
2 Kings	561–538 B.C.	Anonymous
Daniel	536–530 B.C.	Daniel
Haggai	about 520 B.C.	Haggai
Zechariah	480–470 B.C.	Zechariah
Ezra	457–444 B.C.	Ezra
1 Chronicles	450–430 B.C.	Ezra (?)
2 Chronicles	450–430 B.C.	Ezra (?)
Esther	450–331 B.C.	Anonymous
Malachi	433–424 B.C.	Malachi
Nehemiah	424–400 B.C.	Ezra

Introduction to the

INTERTESTAMENTAL PERIOD

Over 400 years separated the final events (Neh. 13:4–30) and final prophecy (Mal. 1:1–4:6) recorded in the OT from the beginning actions (Luke 1:5–25) narrated in the NT (ca. 424–26 B.C.). Because there was no prophetic word from God during this time, this period is sometimes called "the four hundred silent years." However, the history of these years followed the pattern predicted in Daniel (Dan. 2:24,45; 7:1–28; 8:1–27; 11:1–35) with exact precision. Though the voice of God was silent, the hand of God was actively directing the course of events during these centuries.

JEWISH HISTORY

As predicted by Daniel, control of the land of Israel passed from the empire of Medo-Persia to Greece and then to Rome (Dan. 2:39,40; 7:5–7). For about 200 years, the Persian Empire ruled the Jews (539–332 B.C.). The Persians allowed the Jews to return, rebuild, and worship at the temple in Jerusalem (2 Chr. 36:22,23; Ezra 1:1–4). For about 100 years after the close of the OT canon, Judea continued to be a Persian territory under the governor of Syria, with the high priest exercising a measure of civil authority. The Jews were allowed to observe their religious beliefs without any official governmental interference.

Between 334 B.C. and 331 B.C., Alexander the Great defeated the Persian king, Darius III, in three decisive battles that gave him control of the lands of the Persian Empire. The land of Israel thus passed into Greek control in 332 B.C. (Dan. 8:5–7,20,21; 11:3). Alexander permitted the Jews in Judea to observe their laws and granted them an exemption from taxes during their sabbatical years. However, Alexander sought to bring Greek culture, called "Hellenism," to the lands he had conquered. He wished to create a world united by Greek language and thinking. This policy, carried on by Alexander's successors, was as dangerous to the religion of Israel as the cult of Baal had been, because the Greek way of life was attractive, sophisticated, and humanly appealing, but utterly ungodly.

Upon Alexander's death in 323 B.C., a struggle ensued among his generals as his empire was divided (Dan. 8:22; 11:4). Ptolemy I Sater, founder of the Ptolemies of Egypt, took control of Israel, even though an agreement in 301 B.C. assigned it to Seleucus I Nicator, founder of the Seleucids of Syria. This caused continuing contention between the Seleucid and Ptolemaic dynasties (Dan. 11:5). The Ptolemies ruled Judea from 301 B.C. to 198 B.C. (Dan. 11:6–12). Under the Ptolemies, the Jews had comparative religious freedom in a setting of economic oppression.

In 198 B.C., Antiochus III the Great defeated Ptolemy V Epiphanes and took control of Palestine (Dan. 11:13–16). Judea was under Seleucid rule until 143 B.C. (Dan. 11:17–35). Early Seleucid toleration of Jewish religious practices came to an end in the reign of Antiochus IV Epiphanes (175–164 B.C.). Antiochus desecrated and plundered the temple of Jerusalem in 170 B.C. In 167 B.C., Antiochus ordered Hellenization in Palestine and forbade the Jews from keeping their laws, observing the Sabbath, keeping festivals, offering sacrifices, and circumcising their children. Copies of the Torah were ordered destroyed, idolatrous altars were set up, plus the Jews were commanded by Antiochus to offer unclean sacrifices and to eat swine's flesh. Antiochus was the first pagan monarch to persecute the Jews for their faith (Dan. 8:9–14,23–25; 11:21–35).

An aged priest, Mattathias, and his five sons led the Jewish resistance against Antiochus and his Seleucid successors. This was known as the Maccabean Revolt because Judas Maccabeus (lit. "Hammer") was the first leader among the five sons. After a twenty-four-year war (166–142 B.C.), the Jews were able to gain their independence from Syria because of the growing Roman pressure on the Seleucids. The descendants of Mattathias founded the Hasmonean dynasty, a name derived from Hashmon, an ancestor of the Maccabees.

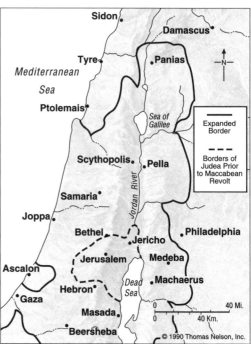

Expansion Under the Maccabees

The Hasmoneans took over the office of high priest, although they did not belong to the line of Zadok (Num. 25:10–13; Ezek. 40:46; 48:11). Quickly, the Hasmoneans began to follow Hellenistic ways, the very practices they had at first resisted. The Greek influence continued in Palestine from 142 B.C. to 63 B.C. through this native dynasty.

The Hasmonean dynasty ended in 63 B.C. when Pompey, a general of Rome, inter-vened in a clash between two claimants to the high priesthood, Aristobulus II and Hyrcanus II. The land thus passed into Roman control (Dan. 2:40; 7:7). Continuing unrest led the Romans to make Herod the Great king of Judea. He was an Idumean by birth, a Jewish convert, and thoroughly Greco-Roman in outlook. He ruled Palestine from 37 B.C. to 4 B.C. and was the "king of the Jews" when Jesus was born (Matt. 2:1,2).

JEWISH DEVELOPMENTS

Diaspora. The dispersion of Israel began in the two exiles, i.e., Israel in Assyria (2 Kin. 17:23) and Judah in Babylon (2 Kin. 25:21). The majority of Israelites did not return to Judea after the exile and so became colonists, no longer captives, in the Persian Empire. The geographical movement of Israelites continued in the Greek and Roman Empires so that by the first century A.D., Jews were found throughout the Mediterranean basin and Mesopotamia. The majority of Israelites lived outside of Palestine during the later intertes-tamental period.

Scribes and Rabbis. Believing the Exile had come because of a lack of knowledge of and obedience to the Torah, the Israelite exiles devoted themselves to the study of the OT. The scribes became experts in and were considered authorities on the interpretation of the Scriptures during the intertestamental period. The rabbis were the teachers who passed on the scribal understanding of the Scriptures to the people of Israel.

Synagogue. With the destruction of the temple in 586 B.C., the synagogue became the place of education and worship for the Jews in exile. Since the majority of Jews did not return to Palestine after the Exile, synagogues continued to function in the Diaspora and also became established in Palestine, even after the reconstruction of the temple by Zerubbabel in 516 B.C.

Septuagint. With the emphasis placed on using the Greek language from ca. 330 B.C. on, the Jews of the Diaspora became predominately Greek-speakers. According to Jewish legend, in ca. 250 B.C., Ptolemy Philadelphus brought together seventy-two scholars who translated the OT into Greek in seventy-two days. Thus, the Latin word for *seventy,* "Septuagint" (LXX), was the name attached to this translation. Probably translated over the period from 250 B.C. to 125 B.C. in Alexandria, Egypt, the Septuagint was the most important and widely used Greek translation of the OT.

Pharisees. This religious party probably began as the "holy ones" associated with the Maccabees in the endeavor to rid the land of Hellenistic elements. When the Maccabees turned themselves to Hellenism once it was in power, these holy ones "separated" (the possible source of the name, Pharisee) from the official religious establishment of Judea. The Pharisees interpreted the law strictly in accordance with a developing oral tradition and sought to make their understanding binding upon all Jews. Though few in number, the Pharisees enjoyed the favor of the majority of the people in Palestine.

Sadducees. Probably from the name "Zadok," the high priestly line, these Hellenized, aristocratic Jews became the guardians of the temple policy and practices. Except for the Torah (the first five books of the OT), the Sadducees rejected the OT as Scripture, as well as any teaching they believed was not found in the Torah e.g., the resurrection from the dead (Acts 23:6–8).

Roman Control of Palestine

© 1990 Thomas Nelson, Inc.

Chronology of the Intertestamental Period

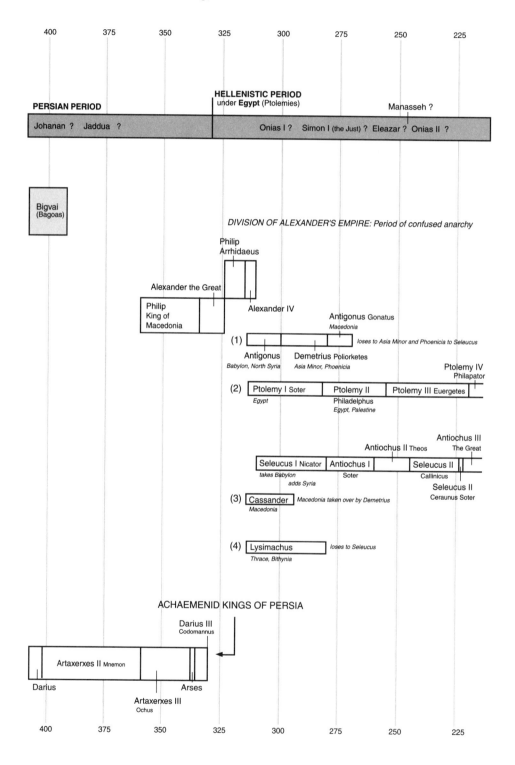

400   375   350   325   300   275   250   225

HELLENISTIC PERIOD
under **Egypt** (Ptolemies)

PERSIAN PERIOD

Manasseh ?

Johanan ?   Jaddua ?

Onias I ?   Simon I (the Just) ?   Eleazar ?   Onias II ?

Bigvai
(Bagoas)

DIVISION OF ALEXANDER'S EMPIRE: Period of confused anarchy

Philip
Arrhidaeus

Alexander the Great

Philip
King of
Macedonia

Alexander IV

Antigonus Gonatus
Macedonia

(1)   *loses to Asia Minor and Phoenicia to Seleucus*

Antigonus   Demetrius Poliorketes
Babylon, North Syria   *Asia Minor, Phoenicia*

Ptolemy IV
Philapator

(2)   Ptolemy I Soter   Ptolemy II   Ptolemy III Euergetes
Egypt   Philadelphus
Egypt, Palestine

Antiochus III
Antiochus II Theos   The Great

Seleucus I Nicator   Antiochus I   Seleucus II
takes Babylon   Soter   Callinicus
adds Syria

Seleucus II
Ceraunus Soter

(3)   Cassander   *Macedonia taken over by Demetrius*
Macedonia

(4)   Lysimachus   *loses to Seleucus*
Thrace, Bithynia

ACHAEMENID KINGS OF PERSIA

Darius III
Codomannus

Artaxerxes II Mnemon

Darius   Arses

Artaxerxes III
Ochus

400   375   350   325   300   275   250   225

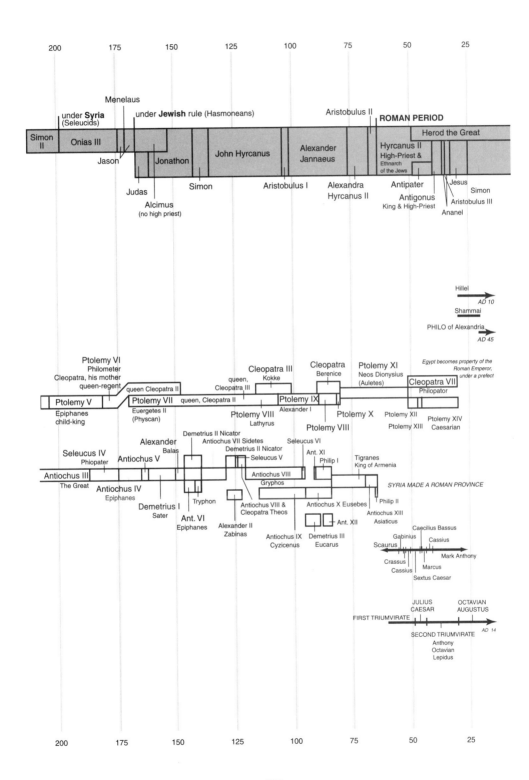

Book	Approximate Writing Date	Author
James	A.D. 44–49	James
Galatians	A.D. 49–50	Paul
Matthew	A.D. 50–60	Matthew
Mark	A.D. 50–60	Mark
1 Thessalonians	A.D. 51	Paul
2 Thessalonians	A.D. 51–52	Paul
1 Corinthians	A.D. 55	Paul
2 Corinthians	A.D. 55–56	Paul
Romans	A.D. 56	Paul
Luke	A.D. 60–61	Luke
Ephesians	A.D. 60–62	Paul
Philippians	A.D. 60–62	Paul
Colossians	A.D. 60–62	Paul
Philemon	A.D. 60–62	Paul
Acts	A.D. 62	Luke
1 Timothy	A.D. 62–64	Paul
Titus	A.D. 62–64	Paul
1 Peter	A.D. 64–65	Peter
2 Timothy	A.D. 66–67	Paul
2 Peter	A.D. 67–68	Peter
Hebrews	A.D. 67–69	Unknown
Jude	A.D. 68–70	Jude
John	A.D. 80–90	John
1 John	A.D. 90–95	John
2 John	A.D. 90–95	John
3 John	A.D. 90–95	John
Revelation	A.D. 94–96	John

Introduction to the
GOSPELS

The English word "gospel" derives from the Anglo-Saxon word *godspell*, which can mean either "a story about God," or "a good story." The latter meaning is in harmony with the Greek word translated "gospel," *euangellion*, which means "good news." In secular Greek, *euangellion* referred to a good report about an important event. The four gospels are the good news about the most significant events in all of history—the life, sacrificial death, and resurrection of Jesus of Nazareth.

The gospels are not biographies in the modern sense of the word, since they do not intend to present a complete life of Jesus (cf. John 20:30; 21:25). Apart from the birth narratives, they give little information about the first thirty years of Jesus' life. While Jesus' public ministry lasted over three years, the gospels focus much of their attention on the last week of His life (cf. John 12–20). Though they are completely accurate historically, and present important biographical details of Jesus' life, the primary purposes of the gospels are theological and apologetic (John 20:31). They provide authoritative answers to questions about Jesus' life and ministry, and they strengthen believers' assurance regarding the reality of their faith (Luke 1:4).

Although many false gospels were written, the church from earliest times has accepted only Matthew, Mark, Luke, and John as inspired Scripture. While each gospel has its unique perspective and audience (see the discussion of the "Synoptic Problem" in Mark: Interpretive Challenges), Matthew, Mark, and Luke in particular share a common point of view, not shared by John. Because of that, these three are known as the synoptic (from a Greek word meaning "to see together," or "to share a common point of view") gospels. One example of this shared vision is the common focus of all three on Christ's Galilean ministry, while John focuses on His ministry in Judea. Also, the synoptic gospels contain numerous parables, while John records none. John and the synoptic gospels record only two common events (Jesus' walking on the water, and the feeding of the 5,000) prior to Passion Week. These differences between John and the synoptic gospels, however, are not contradictory, but complementary.

As already noted, each gospel writer wrote from a unique perspective and for a different audience. As a result, each gospel contains distinctive elements. Taken together, the four gospels form a unified testimony about Jesus Christ.

Matthew wrote primarily to a Jewish audience, presenting Jesus of Nazareth as Israel's long-awaited Messiah and rightful King. His genealogy, unlike Luke's, focuses on Jesus' royal descent from Israel's greatest king, David. Interspersed throughout Matthew are OT quotes presenting various aspects of Jesus' life and ministry as the fulfillment of OT messianic prophecy. Matthew alone uses the phrase "kingdom of heaven," avoiding the parallel phrase "kingdom of God" because of the unbiblical connotations it had in first-century Jewish thought. Matthew wrote his gospel, then, to strengthen the faith of Jewish Christians, and it remains today a useful tool for explaining the gospel to a Jewish audience.

Mark targeted a Gentile audience and in particular, a Roman one (see Mark: Background and Setting). Mark is the gospel of action; the frequent use of "immediately" and "then" keeps his narrative moving rapidly along. Jesus appears in Mark as the Servant (cf. Mark 10:45) who came to suffer for the sins of many. Mark's fast-paced approach would especially appeal to the practical, action-oriented Romans.

Luke addressed a broader Gentile audience. As an educated Greek (see Luke: Author and Date), Luke wrote using the most sophisticated literary Greek of any NT writer. He was a careful researcher (Luke 1:1–4) and an accurate historian. Luke portrays Jesus as the Son of Man (a title appearing twenty-six times), the answer to the needs and hopes of the human race, who came to seek and save lost sinners (Luke 9:56; 19:10).

John, the last gospel written, emphasizes the deity of Jesus Christ (e.g., 5:18; 8:58; 10:30–33; 14:9). John wrote to strengthen the faith of believers and to appeal to unbelievers to come to faith in Christ. The apostle clearly stated his purpose for writing in 20:31: ". . . these are written that you may believe that Jesus is the Christ, the Son of God, and that believing you may have life in His name."

Taken together, the four gospels weave a complete portrait of the God-Man, Jesus of Nazareth. In Him were blended perfect humanity and deity, making Him the only sacrifice for the sins of the world, and the worthy Lord of those who believe.

The Roman Empire in the New Testament Era

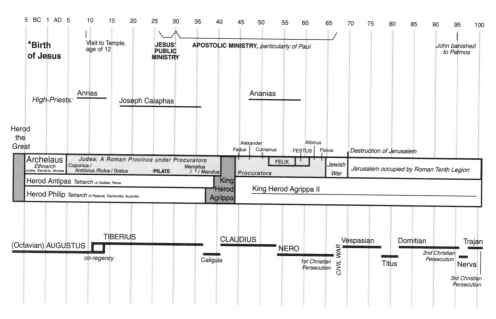

A H a r m o n y o f

THE GOSPELS

<table>
<tr><td></td><td>Matt.</td><td>Mark</td><td>Luke</td><td>John</td></tr>
<tr><td>**Part One: A Preview of Who Jesus Is**</td><td></td><td></td><td></td><td></td></tr>
<tr><td>Luke's purpose for writing a gospel</td><td></td><td></td><td>1:1–4</td><td></td></tr>
<tr><td>John's prologue: from pre-incarnation to crucifixion</td><td></td><td></td><td></td><td>1:1–18</td></tr>
<tr><td>Jesus' legal lineage through Joseph and natural
   lineage through Mary</td><td>1:1-17</td><td></td><td>3:23b-38</td><td></td></tr>
<tr><td></td><td></td><td></td><td></td><td></td></tr>
<tr><td>**Part Two: The Early Years of John the Baptist**</td><td></td><td></td><td></td><td></td></tr>
<tr><td>John's birth foretold to Zacharias</td><td></td><td></td><td>1:5–25</td><td></td></tr>
<tr><td>Jesus' birth foretold to Mary</td><td></td><td></td><td>1:26–38</td><td></td></tr>
<tr><td>Mary's visit to Elizabeth</td><td></td><td></td><td>1:39–45</td><td></td></tr>
<tr><td>Mary's song of joy</td><td></td><td></td><td>1:46–56</td><td></td></tr>
<tr><td>John's birth</td><td></td><td></td><td>1:57–66</td><td></td></tr>
<tr><td>Zacharias' prophetic song</td><td></td><td></td><td>1:67–79</td><td></td></tr>
<tr><td>John's growth and early life</td><td></td><td></td><td>1:80</td><td></td></tr>
<tr><td></td><td></td><td></td><td></td><td></td></tr>
<tr><td>**Part Three: The Early Years of Jesus Christ**</td><td></td><td></td><td></td><td></td></tr>
<tr><td>Circumstances of Jesus' birth explained to Joseph</td><td>1:18–25</td><td></td><td></td><td></td></tr>
<tr><td>Birth of Jesus</td><td></td><td></td><td>2:1–7</td><td></td></tr>
<tr><td>Witness of the shepherds</td><td></td><td></td><td>2:8–20</td><td></td></tr>
<tr><td>Circumcision of Jesus</td><td></td><td></td><td>2:21</td><td></td></tr>
<tr><td>Jesus presented in the temple</td><td></td><td></td><td>2:22–38</td><td></td></tr>
<tr><td>Return to Nazareth</td><td></td><td></td><td>2:39</td><td></td></tr>
<tr><td>Visit of the Magi</td><td>2:1–12</td><td></td><td></td><td></td></tr>
<tr><td>Flight into Egypt</td><td>2:13–18</td><td></td><td></td><td></td></tr>
<tr><td>New home in Nazareth</td><td>2:19–23</td><td></td><td></td><td></td></tr>
<tr><td>Growth and early life of Jesus</td><td></td><td></td><td>2:40</td><td></td></tr>
<tr><td>Jesus' first Passover in Jerusalem</td><td></td><td></td><td>2:41–50</td><td></td></tr>
<tr><td>Jesus' adolescence and early manhood</td><td></td><td></td><td>2:51–52</td><td></td></tr>
<tr><td></td><td></td><td></td><td></td><td></td></tr>
<tr><td>**Part Four: The Public Ministry of
John the Baptist**</td><td></td><td></td><td></td><td></td></tr>
<tr><td>His ministry launched</td><td></td><td>1:1</td><td>3:1–2</td><td></td></tr>
<tr><td>His person, proclamation, and baptism</td><td>3:1–6</td><td>1:2–6</td><td>3:3–6</td><td></td></tr>
<tr><td>His messages to the Pharisees, Sadducees,
   multitudes, tax-gatherers, and soldiers</td><td>3:7–10</td><td></td><td></td><td></td></tr>
<tr><td>His description of the Christ</td><td>3:11–12</td><td>1:7–8</td><td>3:15–18</td><td></td></tr>
<tr><td></td><td></td><td></td><td></td><td></td></tr>
<tr><td>**Part Five: The End of John's Ministry and
the Beginning of Christ's (largely in Judea)**</td><td></td><td></td><td></td><td></td></tr>
<tr><td>Jesus' baptism by John</td><td>3:13–17</td><td>1:9–11</td><td>3:21–23a</td><td></td></tr>
<tr><td>Jesus' temptation in the wilderness</td><td>4:1–11</td><td>1:12–13</td><td>4:1–13</td><td></td></tr>
<tr><td>John's self-indentification to the priests and Levites</td><td></td><td></td><td></td><td>1:19–28</td></tr>
<tr><td>John's identification of Jesus as the Son of God</td><td></td><td></td><td></td><td>1:29–34</td></tr>
<tr><td>Jesus' first followers</td><td></td><td></td><td></td><td>1:35–51</td></tr>
<tr><td>First miracle, water becomes wine</td><td></td><td></td><td></td><td>2:1–11</td></tr>
<tr><td>Visit at Capernaum with His disciples</td><td></td><td></td><td></td><td>2:12</td></tr>
</table>

	Matt.	Mark	Luke	John
First cleansing of the temple at the Passover				2:13–22
An early response to Jesus' miracle				2:23–25
Nicodemus' interview with Jesus				3:1–21
John superseded by Jesus				3:22–36
Jesus' departure from Judea	4:12	1:14a	3:19;20; 4:14a	4:1–4
Discussion with a Samaritan woman				4:5–26
Challenge of a spiritual harvest				4:27–38
Evangelization of Sychar				4:39–42
Arrival in Galilee				4:43–45

Part Six: The Ministry of Christ in Galilee
OPPOSITION AT HOME AND A NEW

	Matt.	Mark	Luke	John
Nature of the Galilean ministry	4:17	1:14b–15	4:14b–15	
Child at Capernaum healed by Jesus while at Cana				4:46–54
Ministry and rejection at Nazareth			4:16–31	
Move to Capernaum	4:13–16			
DISCIPLES CALLED AND MINISTRY THROUGHOUT GALILEE				
First call of the four	4:18–22	1:16–20		
Teaching in the synagogue of Capernaum authenticated by healing a demoniac		1:21–28	4:31b–37	
Peter's mother-in-law and others healed	8:14–17	1:29–34	4:38–41	
Tour of Galilee with Simon and others	4:23–24	1:35–39	4:42–44	
Second call of the four			5:1–11	
Cleansing of a leper followed by much publicity	8:2–4	1:40–45	5:12–16	
Forgiving and healing of a paralytic	9:1–8	2:1–12	5:17–26	
Call of Matthew	9:9	2:13–14	5:27,28	
Banquet at Matthew's house	9:10–13	2:15–17	5:29–32	
Changed conditions with the Messiah present explained by three illustrations	9:14–17	2:18–22	5:33–39	
SABBATH CONTROVERSIES AND WITHDRAWAL				
A lame man healed in Jerusalem on the Sabbath				5:1–9
Effort to kill Jesus for breaking the Sabbath and saying He was equal with God				5:10–18
Discourse demonstrating the Son's equality with the Father				5:19–47
Controversy over disciples' picking grain on the Sabbath	12:1–8	2:23–28	6:1–5	
Healing of a man's withered hand on the Sabbath	12:9–14	3:1–6	6:6–11	
Withdrawal to the Sea of Galilee with a great multitude from many places	12:15–21; 4:25	3:7–12		
APPOINTMENT OF THE TWELVE AND SERMON ON THE MOUNT				
Twelve apostles named		3:13–19	6:12–16	
Setting of the Sermon	5:1,2		6:17–19	
Blessings of those who inherit the kingdom and woes to those who do not	5:3–12		6:20–26	
Responsibility while awaiting the kingdom	5:13–16			
Law, righteousness, and the kingdom	5:17–20			
Six contrasts in interpreting the law	5:21–48		6:27–30,32–36	
Three hypocritical practices to be avoided	6:1–18			

	Matt.	Mark	Luke	John
Three prohibitions against avarice, harsh judgement, and unwise exposure of sacred things	6:19–7:6		6:37–42	
Application and conclusion	7:7–27		6:31,43–49	
Reaction of the multitudes	7:28,29			
GROWING FAME AND EMPHASIS ON REPENTANCE				
A certain centurion's faith and the healing of his servant	8:1,5–13		7:1–10	
A widow's son raised at Nain			7:11–17	
John the Baptist's relationship to the kingdom	11:2–19		7:18–35	
Woes upon Chorazin and Bethsaida for failure to repent	11:20–30			
Christ's feet anointed by a sinful, but contrite, woman			7:36–50	
FIRST PUBLIC REJECTION BY JEWISH LEADERS				
A tour with the twelve and other followers			8:1–3	
Blasphemous accusation by the scribes and Pharisees	12:22–37	3:20–30		
Request for a sign refused	12:38–45			
Announcement of new spiritual ties	12:46–50	3:31–35	8:19–21	
PARABOLIC MYSTERIES ABOUT THE KINGDOM				
The setting of the parables	13:1–3a	4:1,2	8:4	
The parable of the soils	13:3b–23	4:3–25	8:5–18	
The parable of the seed's spontaneous growth		4:26–29		
The parable of the tares	13:24–30			
The parable of the mustard tree		13:31–32	4:30–32	
The parable of the leavened loaf	13:33–35	4:33–34		
To the Disciples in the House				
The parable of the tares explained	13:36–43			
The parable of the hidden treasure	13:44			
The parable of the pearl of great price	13:45–46			
The parable of the dragnet	13:47–50			
The parable of the householder	13:51,52			
CONTINUING OPPOSITION				
Departure across the sea and calming the storm	13:53; 8:18,23–27		4:35–41	8:22–25
Healing the Gerasene demoniacs and resultant opposition	8:28–34	5:1–20	8:26–39	
Return to Galilee, healing of woman who touched Christ's garment, and raising of Jairus' daughter	9:18–26	5:21–43	8:40–56	
Three miracles of healing and another blasphemous accusation	9:27–34			
Final visit to unbelieving Nazareth	13:54–58	6:1–6a		
FINAL GALILEAN CAMPAIGN				
Shortage of workers	9:35–38	6:6b		
Commissioning of the twelve	10:1–42	6:7–11	9:1–5	
Workers sent out	11:1	6:12,13	9:6	
Antipas' mistaken identification of Jesus	14:1,2	6:14–16	9:7–9	
Earlier imprisonment and beheading of John the Baptist	14:3–12	6:17–29		
Return of the workers		6:30	9:10a	

Part Seven: The Ministry of Christ Around Galilee
LESSON ON THE BREAD OF LIFE

	Matt.	Mark	Luke	John
Withdrawal from Galilee	14:13–14	6:31–34	9:10b–11	6:1–3
Feeding the 5,000	14:15–21	6:35–44	9:12–17	6:4–13

	Matt.	Mark	Luke	John
A premature attempt to make Jesus king blocked	14:22,23	6:45,46		6:14,15
Walking on the water during a storm at sea	14:24–33	6:47–52		6:16–21
Healings at Gennesaret	14:34–36	6:53–56		
Discourse on the true bread of life				6:22–59
Defection among the disciples				6:60–71
LESSON ON THE LEAVEN OF THE PHARISEES, SADDUCESS, AND HERODIANS				
Conflict over the tradition of ceremonial defilement	15:1–20	7:1–23		7:1
Ministry to a believing Gentile woman in Tyre and Sidon	15:21–28	7:24–30		
Healings in Decapolis	15:29–31	7:31–37		
Feeding the 4,000 in Decapolis	15:32–38	8:1–9		
Return to Galilee and encounter with the Pharisees and Sadducees	15:39–16:4	8:10–12		
Warning about the error of the Pharisees, Sadducees, and Herodians	16:5–12	8:13–21		
Healing a blind man at Bethsaida		8:22–26		
LESSON OF MESSIAHSHIP LEARNED AND CONFIRMED				
Peter's identification of Jesus as the Christ, and first prophecy of the church	16:13–20	8:27–30	9:18–21	
First direct prediction of the rejection, crucifixion, and resurrection	16:21–26	8:31–37	9:22–25	
Coming of the Son of Man and judgment	16:27–28	8:38–9:1	9:26–27	
Transfiguration of Jesus	17:1–8	9:2–8	9:28–36a	
Command to keep transfiguration a secret	17:9	9:9–10	9:36b	
Elijah, John the Baptist, and the Son of Man's coming	17:10–13	9:11–13		
LESSONS ON RESPONSIBILITY TO OTHERS				
Healing of the demoniac boy, and faithfulessness rebuked 9:37–43a		17:14–20,[21]		9:14–29
Second prediction of the resurrection	17:22,23	9:30–32	9:43b–45	
Payment of the temple tax	17:24–27			
Rivalry over greatness dispelled	18:1–5	9:33–37	9:46–48	
Warning against causing believers to stumble	18:6–14	9:38–50	9:49–50	
Treatment and forgiveness of a sinning brother	18:15–35			
JOURNEY TO JERUSALEM FOR THE FEAST OF TABERNACLES (BOOTHS)				
Ridicule by the Lord's half-brothers				7:2–9
Journey through Samaria			9:51–56	7:10
Complete commitment required of followers	8:19–22		9:57–62	

Part Eight: The Later Judean Ministry of Christ
TEACHINGS AT THE FEAST OF TABERNACLES (BOOTHS)

	Matt.	Mark	Luke	John
Mixed reaction to Jesus' teaching and miracles				7:11–31
Frustrated attempt to arrest Jesus				7:32–52
[Jesus' forgiveness of an adulteress]				[7:53–8:11]
Conflict over Jesus' claim to be the light of the world				8:12–20
Invitation to believe in Jesus				8:21–30
Relationship to Abraham, and attempted stoning				8:31–59
PRIVATE LESSONS ON LOVING SERVICE AND PRAYER				
Commissioning of the seventy			10:1–16	
Return of the seventy			10:17–24	

	Matt.	Mark	Luke	John
Story of the good Samaritan			10:25–37	
Jesus' visit with Mary and Martha			10:38–42	
Lesson on how to pray and parable of the importunate friend			11:1–13	
SECOND DEBATE WITH THE SCRIBES AND PHARISEES				
A third blasphemous accusation and a second debate			11:14–36	
Woes against the scribes and Pharisees while eating with a Pharisee			11:37–54	
Warning the disciples about hypocrisy			12:1–12	
Warning about greed and trust in wealth			12:13–34	
Warning against being unprepared for the Son of Man's coming			12:35–48	
Warning about the coming division			12:49–53	
Warning against failing to discern the present time			12:54–59	
Two alternatives: repent or perish			13:1–9	
Opposition from a synagogue official for healing a woman on the Sabbath			13:10–21	
TEACHING AT THE FEAST OF DEDICATION				
Healing of a man born blind				9:1–7
Reaction of the blind man's neighbors				9:8–12
Examination and excommunication of the blind man by the Pharisees				9:13–34
Jesus' identification of Himself to the blind man				9:35–38
Spiritual blindness of the Pharisees				9:39–41
Allegory of the Good Shepherd and the thief				10:1–18
Further division among the Jews				10:19–21
Another attempt to stone or arrest Jesus for blasphemy				10:22–39
Part Nine: The Ministry of Christ in and around Perea				
PRINCIPLES OF DISCIPLESHIP				
From Jerusalem to Perea				10:40–42
Question about salvation and entering the kingdom			13:22–30	
Anticipation of His coming death and lament over Jerusalem			13:31–35	
Healing of a man with dropsy while eating with a Pharisaic leader on the Sabbath			14:1–24	
Cost of discipleship			14:25–35	
Parables in defense of associations with sinners			15:1–32	
Parable to teach the proper use of money			16:1–13	
Story to teach the danger of wealth			16:14–31	
Four lessons on discipleship			17:1–10	
RAISING OF LAZARUS AND A BRIEF TOUR THROUGH SAMARIA AND GALILEE				
Sickness and death of Lazarus				11:1–16
Lazarus raised from the dead				11:17–44
Decision of the Sanhedrin to put Jesus to death				11:45–54
Healing of ten lepers while passing through Samaria and Galilee			17:11–21	
Instructions regarding the Son of Man's coming			17:22–37	

	Matt.	Mark	Luke	John
TEACHING WHILE ON FINAL JOURNEY TO JERUSALEM				
Two parables on prayer: the importunate widow and the Pharisee and the publican			18:1–14	
Conflict with the Pharisaic teaching on divorce	19:1–12	10:1–12		
Example of little children in relation to the kingdom	19:13–15	10:13–16	18:15–17	
Riches and the kingdom	19:16–30	10:17–31	18:18–30	
Parable of the landowner's sovereignty	20:1–16			
Third prediction of the resurrection	20:17–19	10:32–34	18:31–34	
Warning against ambitious pride	20:20–28	10:35–45		
Healing of blind Bartimaeus and his companion	20:29–34	10:46–52	18:35–43	
Salvation of Zacchaeus			19:1–10	
Parable to teach responsibility while the kingdom is delayed			19:11–28	

Part Ten: The Formal Presentation of Christ to Israel and the Resulting Conflict
TRIUMPHAL ENTRY AND THE FIG TREE

	Matt.	Mark	Luke	John
Arrival at Bethany				11:55–12:1
Mary's anointing of Jesus for burial	26:6–13	14:3–9		12:2–11
Triumphal entry into Jerusalem	21:1–11, 14–17	11:1–11	19:29–44	12:12–19
Cursing of the fig tree having leaves but no figs	21:18,19a	11:12–14		
Second cleansing of the temple	21:12,13	11:15–18	19:45–48	
Request of some Greeks and necessity of the Son of Man's being lifted up				12:20–36a
Departure from the unbelieving multitude and Jesus' response				12:36b–50
Withered fig tree and the lesson on faith	21:19b–22	11:19–25,[26]		
OFFICIAL CHALLENGE OF CHRIST'S AUTHORITY				
A question by the chief priests, scribes, and elders	21:23–27	11:27–33	20:1–8	
Faithful discharge of responsibility taught by 3 parables	21:28–22:14	12:1–12	20:9–19	
A question by the Pharisees and Herodians	22:15–22	12:13–17	20:20–26	
A question by the Sadducees	22:23–33	12:18–27	20:27–40	
A question by a Pharisee scribe	22:34–40	12:28–34		
CHRIST'S RESPONSE TO HIS ENEMIES' CHALLENGES				
Christ's relationship to David as Son and Lord	22:41–46	12:35–37	20:41–44	
Seven woes against the scribes and Pharisees	23:1–36	12:38–40	20:45–47	
Lament over Jerusalem	3:37–39			
A poor widow's gift of all she had			12:41–44	21:1–4

Part Eleven: Prophecies in Preparation for the Death of Christ
THE OLIVET DISCOURSE: PROPHECIES ABOUT THE TEMPLE AND THE RETURN OF CHRIST

	Matt.	Mark	Luke	John
Setting of the discourse	24:1–3	13:1–4	21:5–7	
Beginning of birth pangs	24:4–14	13:5–13	21:8–19	
Abomination of desolation and subsequent distress	24:15–28	13:14–23	21:20–24	
Coming of the Son of Man	24:29–31	13:24–27	21:25–27	
Signs of nearness, but unknown time	24:32–41	13:28–32	21:28–33	

	Matt.	Mark	Luke	John
Five parables to teach watchfulness and faithfulness	24:42–25:30	13:33–37	21:34–36	
Judgment at the Son of Man's coming	25:31–46			
ARRANGEMENTS FOR BETRAYAL				
Plot by the Sanhedrin to arrest and kill Jesus	26:1–5	14:1,2	21:37–22:2	
Judas' agreement to betray Jesus	26:14–16	14:10–11	22:3–6	
THE LAST SUPPER				
Preparation for the Passover meal	26:17–19	14:12–16	22:7–13	
Beginning of the Passover meal	26:20	14:17	22:14–16	
Washing the disciples' feet				13:1–20
Indentification of the betrayer	26:21–25	14:18–21	22:21–23	13:21–30
Dissension among the disciples over greatness			22:24–30	
First prediction of Peter's denial			22:31–38	13:31–38
Conclusion of the meal and the Lord's Supper instituted (1 Cor. 11:23–26)	26:26–29	14:22–25	22:17–20	
DISCOURSE AND PRAYERS FROM THE UPPER ROOM TO GETHSEMANE				
Questions about His destination, the Father, and the Holy Spirit answered				14:1–31
The Vine and the branches				15:1–17
Opposition from the world				15:18–16:4
Coming and ministry of the Spirit				16:5–15
Prediction of joy over His resurrection				16:16–22
Promise of answered prayer and peace				16:23–33
Jesus' prayer for His disciples and all who will believe				17:1–26
Second prediction of Peter's denial	16:30–35	14:26–31	22:39,40a	18:1
Jesus' 3 agonizing prayers in Gethsemane	26:36–46	14:32–42	22:40b–46	

Part Twelve: The Death of Christ

	Matt.	Mark	Luke	John
BETRAYAL AND ARREST				
Jesus betrayed, arrested, and forsaken	26:47–56	14:43–52	22:47–53	18:2–12
TRIAL				
First Jewish phase, before Anna				18:13–24
Second Jewish phase, before Caiaphas and the Sanhedrin	26:57–68	14:53–65	22:54	
Peter's denials	26:69–75	14:66–72	22:55–65	18:25–27
Third Jewish phase, before the Sanhedrin	27:1	15:1a	22:66–71	
Remorse and suicide of Judas Iscariot (Acts 1:18–19)	27:3–10			
First Roman phase, before Pilate	27:2,11–14	15:1b–5	23:1–5	18:28–38
Second Roman phase, before Herod Antipas			23:6–12	
Third Roman phase, before Pilate	27:15–26	15:6–15	23:13–25	18:39–19:16
CRUCIFIXION				
Mockery by the Roman soldiers	27:27–30	15:16–19		
Journey to Golgotha	27:31–34	15:20–23	23:26–33a	19:17
First 3 hours of crucifixion	27:35–44	15:24–32	23:33b–43	19:18–27
Last 3 hours of crucifixion	27:45–50	15:33–37	23:44–45a, 46	19:28–30
Witnesses of Jesus' death	27:51–56	15:38–41	23:45b,47–49	
BURIAL				
Certification of death and procurement of the body	27:57,58	15:42–45	23:50–52	19:31–38
Jesus' body placed in a tomb	27:59,60	15:46	23:53,54	19:39–42
Tomb watched by the women and guarded by the soldiers	27:61–66	15:47	23:55,56	

	Matt.	Mark	Luke	John
Part Thirteen: The Resurrection and Ascension of Christ				
THE EMPTY TOMB				
The tomb visited by the women	28:1	16:1		
The stone rolled away	28:2–4			
The tomb found to be empty by the women	28:5–8	16:2–8	24:1–8	20:1
The tomb found the be empty by Peter and John			24:9–11, [12]	20:2–10
THE POST-RESURRECTION APPEARANCES				
Appearance to Mary Magdalene		[16:9–11]		20:11–18
Appearance to the other women	28:9–10			
Report of the soldiers to the Jewish authorities	28:11–15			
Appearance to two disciples traveling to Emmaus		[16:12,13]	24:13–32	
Report of the two disciples to the rest (1 Cor. 15:5a)			24:33–35	
Appearance to the 10 assembled disciples		[16:14]	24:36–43	20:19–25
Appearance to the 11 assembled disciples (1 Cor. 15:5b)				20:26–31
Appearance to the 7 disciples while fishing				21:1–25
Appearance to the 11 in Galilee (1 Cor. 15:6)	28:16–20	[16:15–18]		
Appearance to James, His brother (1 Cor. 15:7)				
Appearance to the disciples in Jerusalem (Acts 1:3–8)			24:44–49	
THE ASCENSION				
Christ's parting blessing and departure (Acts 1:9–12)		[16:19,20]	24:50–53	

The Ministries of the Apostles

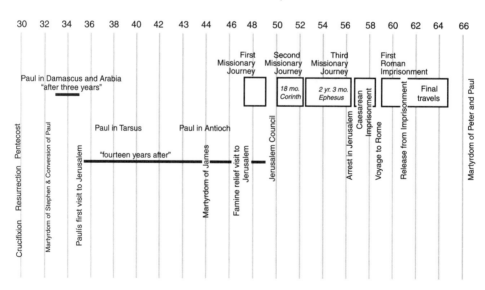

A Brief Overview of Christ's Life

6 B.C.	
	BIRTH OF CHRIST
	DEATH OF HEROD THE GREAT
1 B.C.	
A.D. 1	
	GROWTH AND EARLY LIFE
A.D. 5	
	FIRST PASSOVER IN JERUSALEM
A.D. 10	
A.D. 15	
	ADOLESCENCE AND EARLY MANHOOD
A.D. 20	
A.D. 25	
	BAPTISM OF CHRIST
	MINISTRY, DEATH, AND RESURRECTION
A.D. 30	

A Brief Overview of Christ's Ministry

26 winter	
	PUBLIC MINISTRY OF JOHN
spring	
summer	Baptism of Christ
fall	The temptation
27 winter	
	END OF JOHN'S MINISTRY AND BEGINNING OF CHRIST'S
spring	First Passover in His public ministry
summer	Nicodemus' interview with Christ
fall	Challenge of a spiritual harvest
28 winter	
	Disciples called
spring	Second Passover (not mentioned in the gospels)
summer	MINISTRY IN GALILEE
	Feast of Tabernacles; Sabbath controversies
fall	Sermon on the Mount
29	First public rejection; parabolic ministry begun
winter	Final Galilean campaign
	Third Passover
spring	The Bread of Life
	MINISTRY AROUND GALILEE
summer	Lesson of Messiahship learned and confirmed
	Feast of Tabernacles
fall	LATER JUDEAN MINISTRY
30	Feast of Dedication
winter	MINISTRY IN AND AROUND PEREA
spring	PASSION WEEK
	RESURRECTION AND ASCENSION
summer	

The Ministry of Jesus Christ

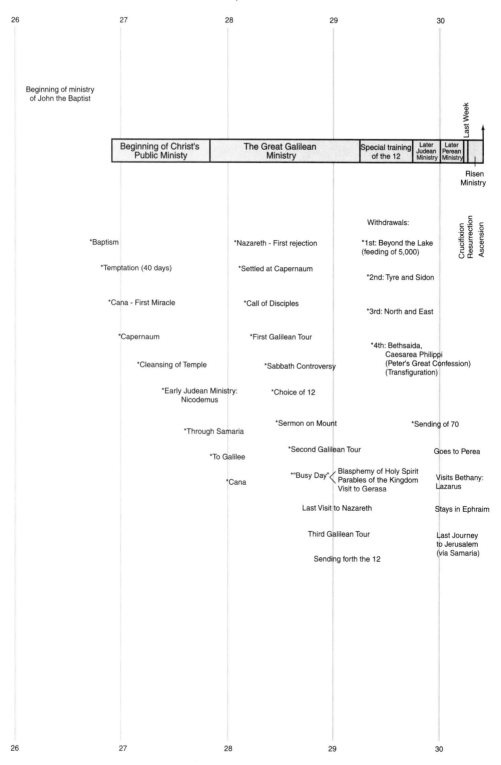

Christ's Passion Week

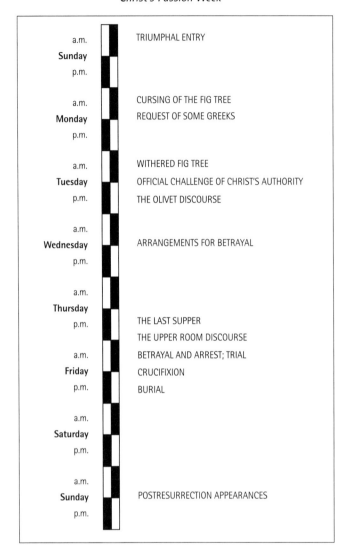

a.m.		TRIUMPHAL ENTRY
Sunday		
p.m.		
a.m.		CURSING OF THE FIG TREE
Monday		REQUEST OF SOME GREEKS
p.m.		
a.m.		WITHERED FIG TREE
Tuesday		OFFICIAL CHALLENGE OF CHRIST'S AUTHORITY
p.m.		THE OLIVET DISCOURSE
a.m.		
Wednesday		ARRANGEMENTS FOR BETRAYAL
p.m.		
a.m.		
Thursday		
p.m.		THE LAST SUPPER
		THE UPPER ROOM DISCOURSE
a.m.		BETRAYAL AND ARREST; TRIAL
Friday		CRUCIFIXION
p.m.		BURIAL
a.m.		
Saturday		
p.m.		
a.m.		
Sunday		POSTRESURRECTION APPEARANCES
p.m.		

MATTHEW
J e s u s   I s   t h e   P r o m i s e d   M e s s i a h

TITLE

Matthew, meaning "gift of the Lord," was the other name of Levi (9:9), the tax collector who left everything to follow Christ (Luke 5:27,28). Matthew was one of the twelve apostles (10:3; Mark 3:18; Luke 6:15; Acts 1:13). In his own list of the Twelve, he explicitly calls himself a "tax collector" (10:3). Nowhere else in Scripture is the name Matthew associated with "tax collector"; the other evangelists always employ his former name, Levi, when speaking of his sinful past. This is evidence of humility on Matthew's part. As with the other three gospels, this work is known by the name of its author.

AUTHOR AND DATE

The acceptance of this gospel into the canon of Scripture and Matthew's authorship went unchallenged in the early church. Eusebius (ca. A.D. 265–339) quotes Origen (ca. A.D. 185–254):

> Among the four gospels, which are the only indisputable ones in the Church of God under heaven, I have learned by tradition that the first was written by Matthew, who was once a publican, but afterwards an apostle of Jesus Christ, and it was prepared for the converts from Judaism (*Ecclesiastical History,* 6:25).

It is clear that this gospel was written at a relatively early date—prior to the destruction of the temple in A.D. 70. Some scholars have proposed a date as early as A.D. 50. For a further discussion of some of the issues related to the authorship and dating of this gospel, especially "The Synoptic Problem," see the Introduction to Mark.

BACKGROUND AND SETTING

The Jewish flavor of Matthew's gospel is noteworthy. This is evident even in the opening genealogy, which Matthew traces back only as far as Abraham. In contrast, Luke, aiming to show Christ as the Redeemer of humanity, goes all the way back to Adam. Matthew's somewhat narrower purpose is to show that Christ is the King and Messiah of Israel. This gospel quotes from OT prophetic passages more than sixty times, emphasizing how Christ is the fulfillment of all those promises.

The probability that Matthew's audience was predominantly Jewish is further evident from several facts: Matthew usually cites Jewish custom without explaining it, in contrast to the other gospels (cf. Mark 7:3; John 19:40). He constantly refers to Christ as "the Son of David" (1:1; 9:27; 12:23; 15:22; 20:30; 21:9,15; 22:42,45). Matthew even guards Jewish sensitivities about speaking the name of God by referring to "the kingdom of heaven" where the other evangelists speak of "the kingdom of God." All the book's major themes are rooted in the OT and set in light of Israel's messianic expectations.

Matthew's use of Greek may suggest that he was writing as a Palestinian Jew to Hellenistic Jews elsewhere. He wrote as an eyewitness of many of the events he described, giving firsthand testimony about the words and works of Jesus of Nazareth.

His purpose is clear: to demonstrate that Jesus is the Jewish nation's long-awaited Messiah. His extensive quoting of the OT is specifically designed to show the tie between the Messiah of promise and the Christ of history. This purpose is never out of focus for Matthew, and he even offers many incidental details from the OT prophecies as proofs of Jesus' messianic claims (e.g., 2:17,18; 4:13–15; 13:35; 21:4,5; 27:9,10).

KEY PEOPLE IN MATTHEW

Jesus—the promised Messiah and King of the Jews (1:1–28:20)

Mary—the mother of Jesus the Messiah (1:1–2:23; 13:55)

Joseph—husband of Mary and descendant of David; carried the royal line to Jesus (1:16–2:23)

John the Baptist—prophet and forerunner who announced the coming of Christ (3:1–15; 4:12; 9:14; 11:2–19; 14:1–12)

The twelve disciples—Simon Peter, Andrew, James, John, Philip, Bartholomew, Thomas, Matthew, James (son of Alphaeus), Thaddaeus, Simon, Judas Iscariot; twelve men chosen by Jesus to aid His ministry on earth (4:18–22; 5:1; 8:18–27; 9:9–28:20)

Religious leaders—comprised of Pharisees and Sadducees; two religious groups who joined together in their hatred of Jesus (3:7–10; 5:20; 9:11–34; 12:10–45; 15:1–20; 16:1–12; 19:1–9; 21:23–28:15)

Caiaphas—high priest and leader of the Sadducees; held an illegal trial that led to Jesus' death (26:3,4,57–68)

Pilate—Roman governor who ordered the crucifixion of Jesus in place of Barabbas (27:1–65)

Mary Magdalene—devoted follower of Jesus; first person to see Jesus after His resurrection (27:56–28:11)

HISTORICAL AND THEOLOGICAL THEMES

Since Matthew is concerned with setting forth Jesus as Messiah, the King of the Jews, an interest in the OT kingdom promises runs throughout this gospel. Matthew's signature phrase "the kingdom of heaven" occurs thirty-two times in this book (and nowhere else in all of Scripture).

CHRIST IN . . . MATTHEW

MATTHEW WRITES PRIMARILY to the Jews defending Jesus as the King and Messiah of Israel. He supports the fulfillment of Christ as the Messiah by quoting OT prophetic passages more than sixty times in his gospel. Matthew demonstrates the royalty of Jesus by constantly referring to him as "the Son of David" (1:1; 9:27; 12:23; 15:22; 20:30; 21:9,15; 22:42,45).

The opening genealogy is designed to document Christ's credentials as Israel's king, and the rest of the book completes this theme. Matthew shows that Christ is the heir of the kingly line. He demonstrates that He is the fulfillment of dozens of OT prophecies regarding the king who would come. He offers evidence after evidence to establish Christ's kingly prerogative. All other historical and theological themes in the book revolve around this one.

Matthew records five major discourses: the Sermon on the Mount (chaps. 5–7); the commissioning of the apostles (chap. 10); the parables about the kingdom (chap. 13); a discourse about the childlikeness of the believer (chap. 18); and the discourse on His second coming (chaps. 24,25). Each discourse ends with a variation of this phrase: "when Jesus had ended these sayings" (7:28; 11:1; 13:53; 19:1; 26:1). That becomes a pattern signaling a new narrative portion. A long opening section (chaps. 1–4) and a short conclusion (28:16–20), bracket the rest of the gospel, which naturally divides into five sections, each with a discourse and a narrative section. Some have seen a parallel between these five sections and the five books of Moses in the OT.

The conflict between Christ and the Pharisees is another common theme in Matthew's gospel. But Matthew is keen to show the error of the Pharisees for the benefit of his Jewish audience—not for personal reasons or to build himself up. Matthew omits, for example, the parable of the Pharisee and the tax collector, even though that parable would have put him in a favorable light.

Matthew also mentions the Sadducees more than any of the other gospels. Both Pharisees and Sadducees are regularly portrayed negatively, and held up as warning beacons. Their doctrine is a "leaven" that must be avoided (16:11,12). Although these two groups were doctrinally at odds with one another, they were united in their hatred of Christ. To Matthew, they epitomized all in Israel who rejected Christ as King.

The rejection of Israel's Messiah is another constant theme in this gospel. In no other gospel are the attacks against Jesus portrayed as strongly as here. From the flight into

KEY WORDS IN

Matthew

Jesus: Greek *Iēsous*—1:1; 4:23; 8:22; 11:4; 19:1; 24:1; 26:52; 27:37—equivalent to the Hebrew name Yeshua (Joshua), literally, "The Lord shall save." In the OT times, the name Jesus was a common Jewish name (Luke 3:29; Col. 4:11). However, the meaning of this name expresses the redemptive work of Jesus on earth. The messenger angel sent to Joseph affirmed the importance of Jesus' name: "for He will save His people from their sins" (1:21). After Jesus sacrificed Himself for the sins of His people and rose from the dead, the early apostles proclaimed Jesus as the one and only Savior (Acts 5:31; 13:23).

Christ: Greek *Christos*—1:1,18; 2:4; 11:2; 16:20; 23:8; 26:68; 27:22—literally, "the Anointed One." Many speak of Jesus Christ without realizing that the title *Christ* is actually a confession of faith. *Messiah*, the Hebrew equivalent for Christ, was used in the OT to refer to prophets (1 Kin. 19:16), priests (Lev. 4:5,16), and kings (1 Sam. 24:6,10), in the sense that all of them were anointed with oil. This anointing symbolized a dedication to ministry by God. Jesus Christ, as the Anointed One, would be the ultimate Prophet, Priest, and King (Isai. 61:1; John 3:34). With his dramatic confession, "You are the Christ, the Son of the living God" (16:16), Peter declared his faith in Jesus as the promised Messiah.

Blessed: Greek *makarios*—5:3–5,11; 16:17; 24:46—literally, "fortunate" or "happy." This term appears in classical Greek literature, in the Septuagint (the Greek translation of the OT), and in the NT to describe the kind of happiness that comes only from God. In the NT, *makarios* is usually written passively: God is the One who is blessing or favoring the person.

The Kingdom of Heaven: Greek *hē basileia tōn ouranōn*—3:2; 4:17; 5:3,10; 10:7; 25:1—literally, "the kingdom of God." To show respect and honor, the Jews avoided saying the name of God out loud. Instead, they often used the word *heaven* as an alternate way to refer to God. The word *heaven* also points to the kingdom of Jesus. Jesus proclaimed His kingdom as residing in the hearts of His people. This spiritual kingdom required internal repentance, not just external submission. It provided deliverance from sin rather than the political deliverance many Jews desired.

Egypt to the scene at the cross, Matthew paints a more vivid portrayal of Christ's rejection than any of the other evangelists. In Matthew's account of the crucifixion, for example, no thief repents, and no friends or loved ones are seen at the foot of the cross. In death He is forsaken even by God (27:46). The shadow of rejection is never lifted from the story.

Yet Matthew portrays Him as a victorious King who will one day return "on the clouds of heaven with power and great glory" (24:30).

KEY DOCTRINE IN MATTHEW

Jesus is the Messiah—also called the Christ; prophesied in the OT as the awaited One who would die for the sins of the world (2:17,18; 4:13–15; 13:35; 21:4,5; 27:9,10; Gen. 49:10; Deut. 18:15–18; 2 Sam. 7:12–14; Is. 52:13–53:12; Dan. 9:26; Mic. 5:2–5; Mark 1:1; Luke 23:2,3; John 4:26; Acts 18:28)

GOD'S CHARACTER IN MATTHEW

God is accessible—6:6; 27:51
God is good—5:45; 19:17
God is holy—13:41
God is long-suffering—23:37; 24:48–51
God is perfect—5:48
God is powerful—6:13; 10:28; 19:26; 22:29
God is provident—6:26,33,34; 10:9,29,30
God is unequaled—19:17
God is unified—4:10; 19:17
God is wise—6:8,18; 10:29,30; 24:36
God is wrathful—10:28; 25:41

INTERPRETIVE CHALLENGES

One challenge is Matthew's timeline. A comparison of the gospels reveals that Matthew freely places things out of order. In general, Matthew presents a topical or thematic approach to the life of Christ using Jesus' five discourses:

- The Sermon on the Mount (chaps. 5–7)
- The commissioning of the apostles (chapt. 10)
- The parables of the kingdom (chapt. 13)
- The childlikeness of the believer (chapt. 18)
- The discourse on His second coming (chapts. 24–25).

Matthew makes no attempt to follow a strict chronology. He was dealing with themes and broad concepts, not laying out a timeline. Mark's and Luke's gospels follow a chronological order more closely. The prophetic passages present a particular interpretive challenge. Jesus' Olivet discourse, for example, contains some details that evoke images of the violent destruction of Jerusalem in A.D. 70. Jesus' words in 24:34 have led some to conclude that all these things were fulfilled—albeit not literally—in the Roman conquest of that era, forcing the interpreter to read into these passages unwarranted spiritualized, allegorical meanings. The proper approach is to analyze the grammar and historical context. This yields a consistently futuristic interpretation of crucial prophecies. See Answers to Tough Questions for further discussion.

The Parables of Jesus

Parable	Matthew	Mark	Luke
1. Lamp Under a Basket	5:14–16	4:21,22	8:16,17; 11:33–36
2. A Wise Man Builds on Rock and a Foolish Man Builds on Sand	7:24–27		6:47–49
3. Unshrunk (New) Cloth on an Old Garment	9:16	2:21	5:36
4. New Wine in Old Wineskins	9:17	2:22	5:37,38
5. The Sower	13:3–23	4:2–20	8:4–15
6. The Tares (Weeds)	13:24–30		
7. The Mustard Seed	13:31,32	4:30–32	13:18,19
8. The Leaven	13:33		13:20,21
9. The Hidden Treasure	13:44		
10. The Pearl of Great Price	13:45,46		
11. The Dragnet	13:47–50		
12. The Lost Sheep	18:12–14		15:3–7
13. The Unforgiving Servant	18:23–35		
14. The Workers in the Vineyard	20:1–16		
15. The Two Sons	21:28–32		
16. The Wicked Vinedressers	21:33–45	12:1–12	20:9–19
17. The Wedding Feast	22:2–14		
18. The Fig Tree	24:32–44	13:28–32	21:29–33
19. The Wise and Foolish Virgins	25:1–13		
20. The Talents	25:14–30		
21. The Growing Seed		4:26–29	
22. The Absent Householder		13:33–37	
23. The Creditor and Two Debtors			7:41–43
24. The Good Samaritan			10:30–37
25. A Friend in Need			11:5–13
26. The Rich Fool			12:16–21
27. The Watchful Servants			12:35–40
28. The Faithful Servant and the Evil Servant			12:42–48
29. The Barren Fig Tree			13:6–9
30. The Great Supper			14:16–24
31. Building a Tower and a King Making War			14:25–35
32. The Lost Coin			15:8–10
33. The Lost Son			15:11–32
34. The Unjust Steward			16:1–13
35. The Rich Man and Lazarus			16:19–31
36. Unprofitable Servants			17:7–10
37. The Persistent Widow			18:1–8
38. The Pharisee and the Tax Collector			18:9–14
39. The Minas (Pounds)			19:11–27

OUTLINE

I. (Prologue) The King's Advent (1:1–4:25)
   A. His Birth (1:1–2:23)
      1. His ancestry (1:1–17)
      2. His arrival (1:18–25)
      3. His adoration (2:1–12)
      4. His adversaries (2:13–23)
   B. His Entry into Public Ministry (3:1–4:25)
      1. His forerunner (3:1–12)
      2. His baptism (3:13–17)
      3. His temptation (4:1–11)
      4. His earliest ministry (4:12–25)

II. The King's Authority (5:1–9:38)
   A. Discourse 1: The Sermon on the Mount (5:1–7:29)
      1. Righteousness and happiness (5:1–12)
      2. Righteousness and discipleship (5:13–16)
      3. Righteousness and the Scriptures (5:17–20)
      4. Righteousness and morality (5:21–48)
      5. Righteousness and practical religion (6:1–18)
      6. Righteousness and mundane things (6:19–34)
      7. Righteousness and human relations (7:1–12)
      8. Righteousness and salvation (7:13–29)
   B. Narrative 1: The Authenticating Miracles (8:1–9:38)
      1. A leper cleansed (8:1–4)
      2. The centurion's servant healed (8:5–13)
      3. Peter's mother-in-law healed (8:14,15)
      4. Multitudes healed (8:16–22)
      5. The winds and sea rebuked (8:23–27)
      6. Two demoniacs delivered (8:28–34)
      7. A paralytic pardoned and healed (9:1–8)
      8. A tax collector called (9:9–13)
      9. A question answered (9:14–17)
      10. A girl raised from the dead (9:18–26)
      11. Two blind men given sight (9:27–31)
      12. A mute speaks (9:32–34)
      13. Multitudes viewed with compassion (9:35–38)

III. The King's Agenda (10:1–12:50)
   A. Discourse 2: The Commissioning of the Twelve (10:1–42)
      1. The Master's men (10:1–4)
      2. The sending of the disciples (10:5–23)
      3. Hallmarks of discipleship (10:24–42)
   B. Narrative 2: The Mission of the King (11:1–12:50)
      1. Jesus' identity affirmed for John's disciples (11:1–19)
      2. Woes pronounced on the impenitent (11:20–24)

3. Rest offered to the weary (11:25–30)
4. Lordship asserted over the Sabbath (12:1–13)
5. Opposition fomented by the Jewish leaders (12:14–45)
6. Eternal relationships defined by spiritual ancestry (12:46–50)

IV. The King's Adversaries (13:1–17:27)
   A. Discourse 3: The Kingdom Parables (13:1–52)
      1. The soils (13:1–23)
      2. The wheat and tares (13:24–30,34–43)
      3. The mustard seed (13:31,32)
      4. The leaven (13:33)
      5. The hidden treasure (13:44)
      6. The pearl of great price (13:45,46)
      7. The dragnet (13:47–50)
      8. The householder (13:51,52)
   B. Narrative 3: The Kingdom Conflict (13:53–17:27)
      1. Nazareth rejects the King (13:53–58)
      2. Herod murders John the Baptist (14:1–12)
      3. Jesus feeds the 5,000 (14:13–21)
      4. Jesus walks on water (14:22–33)
      5. Multitudes seek healing (14:34–36)
      6. The Scribes and Pharisees challenge Jesus (15:1–20)
      7. A Syro-phoenician woman believes (15:21–28)
      8. Jesus heals multitudes (15:29–31)
      9. Jesus feeds the 4,000 (15:32–39)
      10. The Pharisees and Sadducees seek a sign (16:1–12)
      11. Peter confesses Christ (16:13–20)
      12. Jesus predicts His death (16:21–28)
      13. Jesus reveals His glory (17:1–13)
      14. Jesus heals a child (17:14–21)
      15. Jesus foretells His betrayal (17:22,23)
      16. Jesus pays the temple tax (17:24–27)

V. The King's Administration (18:1–23:39)
   A. Discourse 4: The Childlikeness of the Believer (18:1–35)
      1. A call for childlike faith (18:1–6)
      2. A warning against offenses (18:7–9)
      3. A parable about a lost sheep (18:10–14)
      4. A pattern for church discipline (18:15–20)
      5. A lesson about forgiveness (18:21–35)
   B. Narrative 4: The Jerusalem Ministry (19:1–23:39)
      1. Some kingly lessons (19:1–20:28)
        a. On divorce (19:1–10)
        b. On celibacy (19:11,12)
        c. On children (19:13–15)

d. On surrender (19:16–22)

e. On who may be saved (19:23–30)

f. On equality in the kingdom (20:1–16)

g. On His death (20:17–19)

h. On true greatness (20:20–28)

2. Some kingly deeds (20:29–21:27)

    a. He heals two blind men (20:29–34)

    b. He receives adoration (21:1–11)

    c. He cleanses the temple (21:12–17)

    d. He curses a fig tree (21:18–22)

    e. He answers a challenge (21:23–27)

3. Some kingly parables (21:28–22:14)

    a. The two sons (21:28–32)

    b. The wicked vinedressers (21:33–46)

    c. The wedding feast (22:1–14)

4. Some kingly answers (22:15–46)

    a. The Herodians: on paying taxes (22:15–22)

    b. The Sadducees: on the resurrection (22:23–33)

    c. The Scribes: on the first and great commandment (22:34–40)

    d. The Pharisees: on David's greater Son (22:41–46)

5. Some kingly pronouncements (23:1–39)

    a. Woe to the scribes and Pharisees (23:1–36)

    b. Woe to Jerusalem (23:37–39)

VI. The King's Atonement (24:1–28:15)

A. Discourse 5: The Olivet Discourse (24:1–25:46)

1. The destruction of the temple (24:1,2)

2. The signs of the times (24:3–31)

3. The parable of the fig tree (24:32–35)

4. The lesson of Noah (24:36–44)

5. The parable of the two servants (24:45–51)

6. The parable of the ten virgins (25:1–13)

7. The parable of the talents (25:14–30)

8. The judgment of the nations (25:31–46)

B. Narrative 5: The Crucifixion and Resurrection (26:1–28:15)

1. The plot to kill the King (26:1–5)

2. Mary's anointing (26:6–13)

3. Judas' betrayal (26:14–16)

4. The Passover (26:17–30)

5. The prophecy of Peter's denial (26:31–35)

6. Jesus' agony (26:36–46)

7. Jesus' arrest (26:47–56)

8. The trial before the Sanhedrin (26:57–68)

9. Peter's denial (26:69–75)

10. Judas' suicide (27:1–10)
11. The trial before Pilate (27:11–26)
12. The soldiers' mocking (27:27–31)
13. The crucifixion (27:32–56)
14. The burial (27:57–66)
15. The resurrection (28:1–15)

VII. (Epilogue) The King's Assignment (28:16–20)

Christ's Trials, Crucifixion, and Resurrection

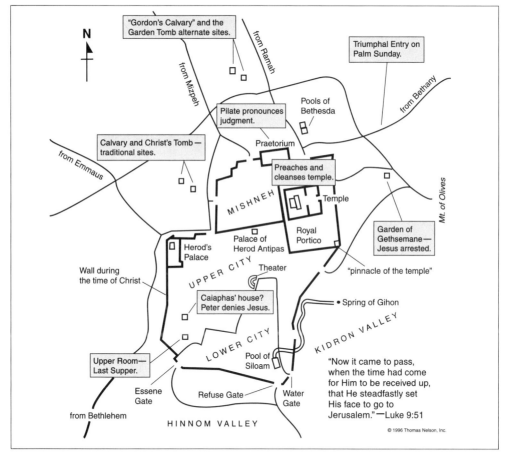

MEANWHILE, IN OTHER PARTS OF THE WORLD...

The first recorded sumo wrestling match takes place in Japan in 23 B.C.

ANSWERS TO TOUGH QUESTIONS

1. The first three gospels share many similarities in wording. Who copied from whom?

It is true that even a cursory reading of Matthew, Mark, and Luke reveals many striking similarities. Compare, for example, Matthew 9:2–8; Mark 2:3–12; and Luke 5:18–26. But there are also significant differences in the way each writer views the life, ministry, and teaching of Jesus. The question about how to explain these similarities and differences is known as the "synoptic problem" (*syn* means "together" and *optic* means "seeing"). For a lengthy discussion of the synoptic problem, see Mark: Interpretive Challenges.

2. Why are three similar gospels necessary?

Careful examination of the gospels, noting the viewpoints of the authors and the details they include, yields two important conclusions: (1) The differences between the gospels highlight their independence and their value as part of a complete picture; (2) The similarities affirm their common subject and message. The accounts are never contradictory, but complementary. When seen together, they present a fuller understanding of Christ.

3. How should Jesus' prophetic statements, many of which are found in Matthew 24 and 25, be interpreted?

The Olivet discourse (Matthew 24–25) contains some details that suggest images of the destruction of Jerusalem in A.D. 70. Jesus' words in 24:34 have led some to conclude that all these things were fulfilled—albeit not literally—in the Roman conquest of that era. This view is known as "preterism." But it is a serious error. The preterist interpreter has to read into these passages allegorical meanings that don't fit normal exegetical study methods. The approach that honors the language and history behind the biblical texts is called the grammatical-historical hermeneutical approach, which involves examining the grammar used and historical context to derive the intended meaning of the passage. This makes better sense and yields a consistent, futuristic interpretation of crucial prophecies.

4. Why is Jesus' genealogy in Matthew different from the one in Luke?

The genealogies of Jesus recorded by Matthew and Luke have two significant differences: (1) Matthew's genealogy traces the line of descent through Joseph, while Luke traces Jesus' ancestry through Mary; and (2) Matthew begins his genealogy with Abraham, since his concern has to do with the Jewish connection with Christ and God's plan of salvation; and Luke's genealogy begins with Adam and sees Christ's role in the salvation of mankind.

5. Does Matthew include any material not found in the other gospels?

Matthew includes nine events in Jesus' life that are unique to his gospel:

- Joseph's dream (1:20–24)
- Visit of the wise men (2:1–12)
- Flight into Egypt (2:13–15)
- Herod kills the children (2:16–18)
- Judas repents (27:3–10; but see Acts 1:18,19)

- The dream of Pilate's wife (27:19)
- Other resurrections (27:52)
- The bribery of the soldiers (28:11–15)
- The Great Commission (28:19,20)

FURTHER STUDY ON MATTHEW

1. In what special ways did Matthew choose to introduce Jesus' biography?
2. Choose one or two of the kingdom parables from Matthew 13. What central idea was Jesus teaching with those parables?
3. In the section called the Sermon on the Mount (Matthew 5–7), how many different subjects did Jesus speak about?
4. How did Matthew reveal Jesus as the King in his gospel?
5. What reasons can you come up with for why Matthew referred so often to the OT in his gospel?
6. How does the gospel of Matthew inform your relationship with Jesus Christ?

MARK

Jesus Is the Suffering Servant

TITLE

Mark, for whom this gospel is named, was a close companion of the apostle Peter and a recurring character in the Book of Acts, where he is known as "John whose surname was Mark" (Acts 12:12,25; 15:37,39). It was to John Mark's mother's home in Jerusalem that Peter went when released from prison (Acts 12:12).

John Mark was a cousin of Barnabas (Col. 4:10), who accompanied Paul and Barnabas on Paul's first missionary journey (Acts 12:25; 13:5). But he deserted them along the way in Perga and returned to Jerusalem (Acts 13:13). When Barnabas wanted Paul to take John Mark on the second missionary journey, Paul refused. The friction that resulted between Paul and Barnabas led to their separation (Acts 15:38–40).

But John Mark's earlier indecisiveness evidently gave way to great strength and maturity, and in time he proved himself even to the apostle Paul. When Paul wrote the Colossians, he instructed them that if John Mark came, they were to welcome him (Col. 4:10). Paul even listed Mark as a fellow worker (Philem. 24). Later, Paul told Timothy to "Get Mark and bring him with you, for he is useful to me for ministry" (2 Tim. 4:11).

John Mark's restoration to useful ministry may have been, in part, due to the ministry of Peter. Peter's close relationship with Mark is evident from his description of him as "Mark my son" (1 Pet. 5:13). Peter, of course, was no stranger to failure himself, and his influence on the younger man was no doubt instrumental in helping him out of the instability of his youth and into the strength and maturity he would need for the work to which God had called him.

AUTHOR AND DATE

Unlike the epistles, the gospels do not name their authors. The early church fathers, however, unanimously affirm that Mark wrote this second gospel. Papias, bishop of Hieropolis, writing about A.D. 140, noted:

> And the presbyter [the Apostle John] said this: Mark having become the interpreter of Peter, wrote down accurately whatsoever he remembered. It was not, however, in exact order that he related the sayings or deeds of Christ. For he neither heard the Lord nor accompanied Him. But afterwards, as I said, he accompanied Peter, who accommodated his instructions to the necessities [of his hearers], but with no intention of giving a regular narrative of the Lord's sayings. Wherefore Mark made no mistake in thus writing some things as he remembered them. For of one thing he took especial care, not to omit anything he had heard, and not to put anything fictitious into the statements. [*From the Exposition of the Oracles of the Lord* (6)]

Justin Martyr, writing about A.D. 150, referred to the gospel of Mark as "the memoirs of Peter," and suggested that Mark wrote his gospel while in Italy. This agrees with the uniform voice of early tradition, which regarded this gospel as having been written in Rome, for the benefit of Roman Christians. Irenaeus, writing about A.D. 185, called Mark "the disciple and interpreter of Peter," and recorded that the second gospel consisted of what Peter preached about Christ. The testimony of the church fathers differs as to whether this gospel was written before or after Peter's death (ca. A.D. 67–68).

Evangelical scholars have suggested dates for the writing of Mark's gospel ranging from A.D. 50 to 70. A date before the destruction of Jerusalem and the temple in A.D. 70 is required by the comment of Jesus in 13:2. Luke's gospel was clearly written before Acts (Acts 1:1–3). The date of the writing of Acts can probably be fixed at about A.D. 63, because that is shortly after the narrative ends (see Acts: Author and Date). It is therefore likely, though not certain, that Mark was written at an early date, probably sometime in the A.D. 50s.

BACKGROUND AND SETTING

Whereas Matthew was written to a Jewish audience, Mark seems to have targeted Roman believers, particularly Gentiles. When employing Aramaic terms, Mark translated them for his readers (3:17; 5:41; 7:11,34; 10:46; 14:36; 15:22, 34). On the other hand, in some places he used Latin expressions instead of their Greek equivalents (5:9; 6:27; 12:15,42; 15:16,39). He also reckoned time according to the Roman system (6:48; 13:35) and carefully explained Jewish customs (7:3,4; 14:12; 15:42). Mark omitted Jewish elements, such as the genealogies found in Matthew and Luke. This gospel also makes fewer references to the OT, and includes less material that would be of particular interest to Jewish readers—such as that which is critical of the Pharisees and Sadducees (Sadducees are mentioned only once, in 12:18). When mentioning Simon the Cyrene (15:21), Mark identifies him as the father of Rufus, a prominent member of the church at Rome (Rom. 16:13). All of this supports the traditional view that Mark was written for a Gentile audience initially at Rome.

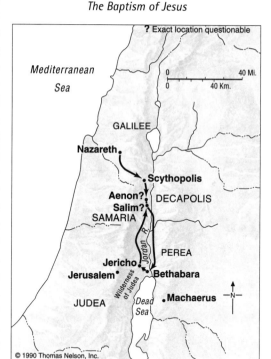

The Baptism of Jesus

KEY PEOPLE IN MARK

Jesus—the Servant who offered Himself as a sacrifice for the sins of the world (1:1–16:19)

The twelve disciples—Simon Peter, Andrew, James, John, Philip, Bartholomew, Thomas, Matthew, James (son of Alphaeus), Thaddaeus, Simon, Judas Iscariot; twelve men chosen by Jesus to aid His ministry on earth (1:16–16:20)

Pilate—Roman governor who ordered the crucifixion of Jesus in place of Barabbas (15:1–45)

The Jewish religious leaders—comprised of Pharisees and Sadducees; two religious groups who joined together in their hatred of Jesus (3:22; 11:27–15:32)

HISTORICAL AND THEOLOGICAL THEMES

Mark presents Jesus as the suffering Servant of the Lord (10:45). His focus is on the deeds of Jesus more than His teaching, particularly emphasizing service and sacrifice. Mark omits the lengthy discourses found in the other gospels, often relating only brief excerpts to give the gist of Jesus' teaching. Mark also omits any account of Jesus' ancestry and birth, beginning where Jesus' public ministry began, with His baptism by John in the wilderness.

Mark demonstrated the humanity of Christ more clearly than any of the other evangelists, emphasizing Christ's human emotions (1:41; 3:5; 6:34; 8:12; 9:36), His human limitations (4:38; 11:12; 13:32), and other small details that highlight the human side of the Son of God (e.g., 7:33,34; 8:12; 9:36; 10:13–16).

KEY DOCTRINES IN MARK

The humanity of Christ—Jesus humbled Himself and became a man in order to reconcile humanity to God (1:41; 3:5; 4:38; 6:34; 8:12; 9:36; 11:12; 13:32; Is. 50:6; 53:7; Mic. 5:2; Luke 2:4–7; John 1:14; Rom. 1:3,4; 8:3; Phil. 2:6–11; Col. 2:9; Heb. 4:15; 5:7)

Servanthood—Jesus was the perfect example of true servanthood, even unto death (8:34–37; 9:35; 10:43–45; Zech. 9:9; Matt. 20:28; 21:5; Luke 22:27; John 13:5; 2 Cor. 8:9; Phil. 2:7)

GOD'S CHARACTER IN MARK

God is accessible—15:38

God is unified—2:7; 12:29

INTERPRETIVE CHALLENGES

Three significant questions confront the interpreter of Mark: (1) What is the relationship of Mark to Luke and Matthew? (see below "The Synoptic Problem") (2) How should one interpret the passages that discuss the end times? (3) Were the last twelve verses of chap. 16 originally part of Mark's gospel? (See Answers to Tough Questions for discussions on 2 and 3.)

CHRIST IN . . . MARK

OMITTING ALL ACCOUNTS of Jesus' ancestry and birth, Mark emphasizes Jesus' role as the Suffering Servant of the Lord (10:45). More than any other gospel, Mark focuses on the humble deeds of Jesus over His teachings.

THE SYNOPTIC PROBLEM

Even a cursory reading of Matthew, Mark, and Luke reveals both striking similarities (cf. 2:3–12; Matt. 9:2–8; Luke 5:18–26) and significant differences, as each views the life, ministry, and teaching of Jesus. The question of how to explain those similarities and differences is known as the "Synoptic Problem" (*syn* means "together"; *optic* means "seeing").

The Life of Jesus

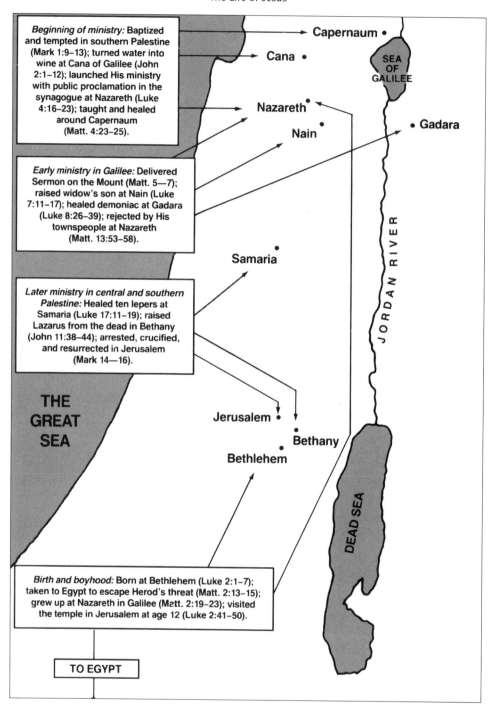

Beginning of ministry: Baptized and tempted in southern Palestine (Mark 1:9–13); turned water into wine at Cana of Galilee (John 2:1–12); launched His ministry with public proclamation in the synagogue at Nazareth (Luke 4:16–23); taught and healed around Capernaum (Matt. 4:23–25).

Early ministry in Galilee: Delivered Sermon on the Mount (Matt. 5—7); raised widow's son at Nain (Luke 7:11–17); healed demoniac at Gadara (Luke 8:26–39); rejected by His townspeople at Nazareth (Matt. 13:53–58).

Later ministry in central and southern Palestine: Healed ten lepers at Samaria (Luke 17:11–19); raised Lazarus from the dead in Bethany (John 11:38–44); arrested, crucified, and resurrected in Jerusalem (Mark 14—16).

Birth and boyhood: Born at Bethlehem (Luke 2:1–7); taken to Egypt to escape Herod's threat (Matt. 2:13–15); grew up at Nazareth in Galilee (Matt. 2:19–23); visited the temple in Jerusalem at age 12 (Luke 2:41–50).

Capernaum •

Cana •

SEA OF GALILEE

Nazareth

• Gadara

Nain

JORDAN RIVER

Samaria

THE GREAT SEA

Jerusalem •

• Bethany

Bethlehem

DEAD SEA

TO EGYPT

The modern solution—even among evangelicals—has been to assume that some form of common literary dependence exists between the synoptic gospels. The most commonly accepted theory to explain such an alleged literary dependence is known as the "Two-Source" theory. According to that hypothesis, Mark was the first gospel written, and Matthew and Luke then used Mark as a source in writing their gospels. Proponents of this view imagine a non-existent, second source, labeled Q (from the German word *Quelle*, "source"), and argue that this is the source of the material in Matthew and Luke that does not appear in Mark. They advance several lines of evidence to support their scenario.

First, most of Mark is paralleled in Matthew and Luke. Since it is much shorter than Matthew and Luke, the latter must be expansions of Mark. Second, the three gospels follow the same general chronological outline, but when either Matthew or Luke departs from Mark's chronology, the other agrees with Mark. Put another way, Matthew and Luke do not both depart from Mark's chronology in the same places. That, it is argued, shows that Matthew and Luke used Mark for their historical framework. Third, in passages common to all three gospels, Matthew's and Luke's wording seldom agrees when it differs from Mark's. Proponents of the "Two-Source" theory see that as confirmation that Matthew and Luke used Mark's gospel as a source.

But those arguments do not prove that Matthew and Luke used Mark's gospel as a source. In fact, the weight of evidence is strongly against such a theory:

(1) The nearly unanimous testimony of the church until the nineteenth century was that Matthew was the first gospel written. Such an impressive body of evidence cannot be ignored.

(2) Why would Matthew, an apostle and eyewitness to the events of Christ's life, depend on Mark (who was not an eyewitness)—even for the account of his own conversion?

(3) A significant statistical analysis of the synoptic gospels has revealed that the parallels between them are far less extensive and the differences more significant than is commonly acknowledged. The differences, in particular, argue against literary dependence between the gospel writers.

(4) Since the gospels record actual historical events, it would be surprising if they did not follow the same general historical sequence. For example, the fact that 3 books on American history all had the Revolutionary War, the Civil War, World War I, World War II, the Vietnam War, and the Gulf War in the same chronological order would not prove that the authors had read each others' books. General agreement in content does not prove literary dependency.

(5) The passages in which Matthew and Luke agree against Mark (see argument 3 in favor of the "Two-Source" theory) amount to about one-sixth of Matthew and one-sixth of Luke. If they used Mark's gospel as a source, there is no satisfactory explanation for why Matthew and Luke would so often both change Mark's wording in the same way.

(6) The "Two-Source" theory cannot account for the important section in Mark's gospel (6:45–8:26) which Luke omits. That omission suggests Luke had not seen Mark's gospel when he wrote.

(7) There is no historical or manuscript evidence that the Q document ever existed; it is purely an invention of modern skeptics. Worse yet, it is a way to deny the verbal inspiration of the gospels.

The Miracles of Jesus

Miracle	Matthew	Mark	Luke	John
1. Cleansing a Leper	8:2	1:40	5:12	
2. Healing a Centurion's Servant (of paralysis)	8:5		7:1	
3. Healing Peter's Mother-in-Law	8:14	1:30	4:38	
4. Healing the Sick at Evening	8:16	1:32	4:40	
5. Stilling the Storm	8:23	4:35	8:22	
6. Demons Entering a Herd of Swine	8:28	5:1	8:26	
7. Healing a Paralytic	9:2	2:3	5:18	
8. Raising the Ruler's Daughter	9:18,23	5:22,35	8:40,49	
9. Healing the Hemorrhaging Woman	9:20	5:25	8:43	
10. Healing Two Blind Men	9:27			
11. Curing a Demon-Possessed, Mute Man	9:32			
12. Healing a Man's Withered Hand	12:9	3:1	6:6	
13. Curing a Demon-Possessed, Blind and Mute Man	12:22		11:14	
14. Feeding the Five Thousand	14:13	6:30	9:10	6:1
15. Walking on the Sea	14:25	6:48		6:19
16. Healing the Gentile Woman's Daughter	15:21	7:24		
17. Feeding the Four Thousand	15:32	8:1		
18. Healing the Epileptic Boy	17:14	9:17	9:38	
19. Temple Tax in the Fish's Mouth	17:24			
20. Healing Two Blind Man	20:30	10:46	18:35	
21. Withering the Fig Tree	21:18	11:12		
22. Casting Out an Unclean Spirit		1:23	4:33	
23. Healing a Deaf-Mute		7:31		
24. Healing a Blind Man at Bethsaida		8:22		
25. Escape from the Hostile Multitude			4:30	
26. Catch of Fish			5:1	
27. Raising of a Widow's Son at Nain			7:11	
28. Healing the Infirm, Bent Woman			13:11	
29. Healing the Man with Dropsy			14:1	
30. Cleansing the Ten Lepers			17:11	
31. Restoring a Servant's Ear			22:51	
32. Turning Water into Wine				2:1
33. Healing the Nobleman's Son (of fever)				4:46
34. Healing an Infirm Man at Bethesda				5:1
35. Healing the Man Born Blind				9:1
36. Raising of Lazarus				11:43
37. Second Catch of Fish				21:1

(8) Any theory of literary dependence between the gospel writers overlooks the significance of their personal contacts with each other. Mark and Luke were both companions of Paul (cf. Philem. 24); the early church (including Matthew) met for a time in the home of Mark's mother (Acts 12:12); and Luke could easily have met Matthew during Paul's two-year imprisonment at Caesarea. Such contacts make theories of mutual literary dependence unnecessary.

The simplest solution to the Synoptic Problem is that no such problem exists! Because critics cannot prove literary dependence between the gospel writers, there is no need to explain it. The traditional view that the gospel writers were inspired by God and wrote independently of each other—except that all three were moved by the same Holy Spirit (2 Pet. 1:20)—remains the only plausible view.

As the reader compares the various viewpoints in the gospels, it becomes clear how well they harmonize and lead to a more complete and unified picture of the whole event or message. The accounts are not contradictory, but complementary, revealing a fuller understanding when brought together.

OUTLINE
   I. Prologue: In the Wilderness (1:1–13)
      A. John's Message (1:1–8)
      B. Jesus' Baptism (1:9–11)
      C. Jesus' Temptation (1:12, 13)
   II. Beginning His Ministry: In Galilee and the Surrounding Regions (1:14–7:23)
      A. He Announces His Message (1:14,15)
      B. He Calls His Disciples (1:16–20)
      C. He Ministers in Capernaum (1:21–34)
      D. He Reaches Out to Galilee (1:35–45)
      E. He Defends His Ministry (2:1–3:6)
      F. He Ministers to Multitudes (3:7–12)
      G. He Commissions the Twelve (3:13–19)
      H. He Rebukes the Scribes and Pharisees (3:20–30)
      I. He Identifies His Spiritual Family (3:31–35)
      J. He Preaches in Parables (4:1–34)
         1. The sower (4:1–9)
         2. The reason for parables (4:10–12)
         3. The parable of the sower explained (4:13–20)
         4. The lamp (4:21–25)
         5. The seed (4:26–29)
         6. The mustard seed (4:30–34)
      K. He Demonstrates His Power (4:35–5:43)
         1. Calming the waves (4:35–41)
         2. Casting out demons (5:1–20)
         3. Healing the sick (5:21–34)
         4. Raising the dead (5:35–43)

L. He Returns to His Hometown (6:1–6)

M. He Sends out His Disciples (6:7–13)

N. He Gains a Powerful Enemy (6:14–29)

O. He Regroups with the Disciples (6:30–32)

P. He Feeds the Five Thousand (6:33–44)

Q. He Walks on Water (6:45–52)

R. He Heals Many People (6:53–56)

S. He Answers the Pharisees (7:1–23)

III. Broadening His Ministry: In Various Gentile Regions (7:24–9:50)

A. Tyre and Sidon: He Delivers a Gentile Woman's Daughter (7:24–30)

B. Decapolis: He Heals a Deaf-Mute (7:31–37)

C. The Eastern Shore of Galilee: He Feeds the Four Thousand (8:1–9)

D. Dalmanutha: He Disputes with the Pharisees (8:10–12)

E. The Other Side of the Lake: He Rebukes the Disciples (8:13–21)

F. Bethsaida: He Heals a Blind Man (8:22–26)

G. Caesarea Philippi and Capernaum: He Instructs the Disciples (8:27–9:50)

1. Peter confesses Jesus as Christ (8:27–30)

2. He predicts His death (8:31–33)

3. He explains the cost of discipleship (8:34–38)

4. He reveals His glory (9:1–10)

5. He clarifies Elijah's role (9:11–13)

6. He casts out a stubborn spirit (9:14–29)

7. He again predicts His death and resurrection (9:30–32)

8. He defines kingdom greatness (9:33–37)

9. He identifies true spiritual fruit (9:38–41)

10. He warns would-be stumbling blocks (9:42–50)

IV. Concluding His Ministry: The Road to Jerusalem (10:1–52)

A. He Teaches on Divorce (10:1–12)

B. He Blesses the Children (10:13–16)

C. He Confronts the Rich Young Ruler (10:17–27)

D. He Confirms the Disciples' Rewards (10:28–31)

E. He Prepares the Disciples for His Death (10:32–34)

F. He Challenges the Disciples to Humble Service (10:35–45)

G. He Heals a Blind Man (10:46–52)

V. Consummating His Ministry: Jerusalem (11:1–16:20)

A. Triumphal Entry (11:1–11)

B. Purification (11:12–19)

1. Cursing the fig tree (11:12–14)

2. Cleansing the temple (11:15–19)

C. Teaching in Public and in Private (11:20–13:37)

1. Publicly: in the temple (11:20–12:44)

a. Prelude: the lesson of the cursed fig tree (11:20–26)

b. Concerning His authority (11:27–33)

c. Concerning His rejection (12:1–12)

d. Concerning paying taxes (12:13–17)

e. Concerning the resurrection (12:18–27)

f. Concerning the greatest commandment (12:28–34)

g. Concerning the Messiah's true sonship (12:35–37)

h. Concerning the scribes (12:38–40)

i. Concerning true giving (12:41–44)

2. Privately: on the Mount of Olives (13:1–37)

a. The disciples' question about the end times (13:1)

b. The Lord's answer (13:2–37)

D. Arrangements for Betrayal (14:1,2,10,11)

E. Anointing, the Last Supper, Betrayal, Arrest, Trial [Jewish Phase] (14:3–9; 12–72)

1. The anointing: Bethany (14:3–9)

2. The Last Supper: Jerusalem (14:12–31)

3. The prayer: Gethsemane (14:32–42)

4. The betrayal: Gethsemane (14:43–52)

5. The Jewish trial: Caiaphas' house (14:53–72)

F. Trial (Roman Phase), Crucifixion (15:1–41)

1. The Roman trial: Pilate's Praetorium (15:1–15)

2. The crucifixion: Golgotha (15:16–41)

G. Burial in Joseph of Arimathea's Tomb (15:42–47)

H. Resurrection (16:1–8)

I. Postscript (16:9–20)

MEANWHILE, IN OTHER PARTS OF THE WORLD...

The Han dynasty begins in China, creating the country's largest ethnic group.

Mark

Faith: Greek *pistis*—2:5; 4:40; 5:34,36; 10:52; 11:22—"trust" or "belief." To have faith is to relinquish trust in oneself and transfer that trust to someone or something else. The woman who had a hemorrhage for years had first put her trust in physicians. Then as she reached for Jesus' robe, she believed and trusted Jesus to cure her. After she was healed, Jesus declared her faith had made her well (see Matt. 8:10; 9:22,29; 15:28; Luke 7:50; 8:48). Within the Epistles, the word *pistis* sometimes refers to the content of one's faith and beliefs—God's revelation in the Scripture (see Gal. 1:23).

Gospel: Greek *euangelion*—1:1,14,15; 13:10; 14:9; 16:15—literally, "good news" or "good message." Messengers bringing news of victory in battle originally used this Greek term. In the NT it points to the Good News of salvation: Jesus Christ came to earth to abolish the power of sin in the lives of His people by offering Himself as a perfect sacrifice on the cross. Christ commands believers to share this Good News with the rest of the world. This Good News is Christ's life-giving message to a dying world (16:15).

Scribes; Chief Priests: Greek *grammateus*—2:6; 3:22; 8:31; 9:14; 11:18; 12:38; 15:31—literally, "writer." Originally, scribes functioned as transcribers of the Law and readers of the Scripture. Later they acted as lawyers and religious scholars by interpreting both civil and religious law. The Greek word for *chief priests* translates as "the leading priests." This group included the high priest and other priests who were experts in the Scriptures. Ironically, these priests did not realize that by mocking Jesus they were fulfilling Isaiah's prophecy regarding the Messiah: "He was despised and rejected by men, a Man of sorrows and acquainted with grief" (Is. 53:3).

ANSWERS TO TOUGH QUESTIONS

1. How did Mark come to write one of the gospels if he wasn't one of the original disciples?

Although Mark was not one of the original apostles of Jesus, he was involved in many of the events recorded in the NT. He traveled as a close companion of the apostle Peter and appears repeatedly throughout the Book of Acts, where he is known as "John whose surname was Mark" (Acts 12:12,25; 15:37,39). When Peter was miraculously freed from prison, his first action was to go to John Mark's mother's home in Jerusalem (Acts 12:12). John Mark's restoration to useful ministry and preparation for writing his gospel was due, in part, to his extended close relationship with Peter (1 Pet. 5:13). Mark's gospel represents primarily Peter's version of the life of Jesus.

2. How should one interpret the end times passages in Mark?

Jesus' great sermon in Mark 13 is known as the Olivet Discourse because he delivered it on the Mt. of Olives. Here he predicted the coming destruction of the temple, which prompted a question from the disciples about the character of the end times. When Jesus talks about "the end," he means the consummation of the present age. Among other thigns, He predicts the great tribulation in the future, and his coming again in power and glory.

3. Were the last twelve verses of chapter 16 originally part of Mark's gospel?

The external evidence strongly suggests that Mark 16:9–20 were not originally part of Mark's gospel. While the majority of Greek manuscripts contain these verses, the ear-

The Plan of Herod's Temple

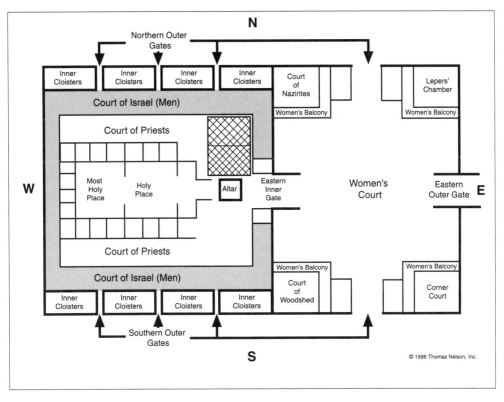

liest and most reliable ones do not. A shorter ending also existed, but it is not includ-ed in some texts. Further, some manuscripts that include the passage note that it was missing from older Greek copies, while others have scribal marks indicating the pas-sage was considered doubtful. The fourth-century church fathers Eusebius and Jerome noted that almost all Greek manuscripts available to them lacked verses 9–20.

The internal evidence from this brief passage also weighs heavily against Mark's authorship. The grammatical transition between verses 8 and 9 is abrupt and awk-ward. The vocabulary in these verses does not match with the rest of Mark. Even the events and people mentioned in these verses appear in awkward fashion. For example, Mary Magdalene is introduced as if she was a new person on the scene rather than someone Mark has mentioned three times (verse 1; 15:40,47). Clearly, Mark 16:9–20 represents an early attempt to complete Mark's gospel.

While for the most part summarizing truths taught elsewhere in Scripture, these verses should always be compared with the rest of Scripture, and no doctrines should be formulated based solely on them. Further, in spite of all these considerations of the likely unreliability of this section, it is possible to be wrong on the issue. Therefore, it is good to consider the meaning of this passage and leave it in the text, just as is done with the other text with a similar history, John 7:53–8:11.

4. Does Mark include any material not found in the other gospels?

There are three passages found in Mark that are only recorded in his gospel:

> The parable of the growing seed (4:26–29)
> A deaf and mute man is healed (7:31–37)
> A blind man is healed (8:22–26)

FURTHER STUDY ON MARK

1. In what different ways did Mark illustrate Jesus' attitude of servanthood in his gospel?
2. What answer did Jesus expect when He asked His disciples, "Who do you say that I am?" (Mark 8:29)?
3. How did Jesus reveal His identity as the Son of God in the gospel of Mark?
4. What role do miracles play in demonstrating Jesus' special identity in Mark?
5. How did Mark make it clear in his gospel that those who believe in Jesus have a responsibility to pass on the Good News to others?

LUKE

Jesus Is the Son of Man

TITLE

As with the other three Gospels, the title is derived from the author's name. According to tradition, Luke was a Gentile. The apostle Paul seems to confirm this, distinguishing Luke from those who were "of the circumcision" (Col. 4:11,14). That would make Luke the only Gentile to pen any books of Scripture. He is responsible for a significant portion of the NT, having written both this gospel and the Book of Acts (see Author and Date).

AUTHOR AND DATE

The gospel of Luke and the Book of Acts clearly were written by the same individual (cf. 1:1–4; Acts 1:1). Although he never identified himself by name, it is clear from his use of "we" in many sections of Acts that he was a close companion of the apostle Paul (Acts 16:10–17; 20:5–15; 21:1–18; 27:1–28:16). Luke is the only person, among the colleagues Paul mentions in his own letters (Col. 4:14; 2 Tim. 4:11; Philem. 24), who fits the profile of the author of these books. That accords perfectly with the earliest tradition of the church, which unanimously attributed this gospel to Luke.

Very little is known about Luke. He almost never included personal details about himself, and nothing definite is known about his background or his conversion. Both Eusebius and Jerome identified him as a native of Antioch (which may explain why so much of the Book of Acts centers on Antioch—cf. Acts 11:19–27; 13:1–3; 14:26; 15:22,23,30–35; 18:22,23). Luke was a frequent companion of the apostle Paul, at least from the time of Paul's Macedonian vision (Acts 16:9,10) right up to the time of Paul's martyrdom (2 Tim. 4:11).

The apostle Paul referred to Luke as a physician (Col. 4:14). Luke's interest in medical phenomena is evident in the high profile he gave to Jesus' healing ministry (e.g., 4:38–40; 5:15–25; 6:17–19; 7:11–15; 8:43–47,49–56; 9:2,6,11; 13:11–13; 14:2–4; 17:12–14; 22:50, 51). In Luke's day, physicians did not have a unique vocabulary of technical medical terminology; so when Luke discusses healings and other medical issues, his language is not markedly different from that of the other gospel writers.

Luke and Acts appear to have been written at about the same time—Luke first, then Acts. Combined, they make a two-volume work addressed to "Theophilus" (1:3; Acts 1:1; see Background and Setting) giving a sweeping history of the founding of Christianity, from the birth of Christ to Paul's imprisonment under house arrest in Rome (Acts 28:30, 31).

The Book of Acts ends with Paul still in Rome, which leads to the conclusion that Luke wrote these books from Rome during Paul's imprisonment there (ca. A.D. 60–62). Luke records Jesus' prophecy of the destruction of Jerusalem in A.D. 70 (19:42–44; 21:20–24) but makes no mention of the fulfillment of that prophecy, either here or in Acts. Luke made it a point to record such prophetic fulfillments (cf. Acts 11:28), so it is extremely unlikely he wrote these books after the Roman invasion of Jerusalem. Acts also includes no mention of the great persecution that began under Nero in A.D. 64. In addition, many scholars set the date of James' martyrdom at A.D. 62, and if that was before Luke completed his history, he certainly would have mentioned it. So, the most likely date for this gospel is A.D. 60 or 61.

BACKGROUND AND SETTING

Luke dedicated his works to "most excellent Theophilus" (lit. "lover of God"—1:3; cf. Acts 1:1). This title, which may be a nickname or a pen name, is accompanied by a formal address ("most excellent")—possibly signifying that "Theophilus" was a well-known Roman dignitary, perhaps one of those who had turned to Christ in "Caesar's household" (Phil. 4:22).

It is almost certain, however, that Luke envisioned a much broader audience for his work than this one man. The dedications at the outset of Luke and Acts are like the formal dedication in a modern book. They are not exclusively the address of an epistle.

Luke expressly stated that his knowledge of the events recorded in his gospel came from the reports of those who were eyewitnesses (1:1,2)—strongly implying that he himself was not an eyewitness. It is clear from his prologue that his aim was to give an ordered account of the events of Jesus' life, but this does not mean he always followed a strict chronological order in all instances.

By acknowledging that he had compiled his account from various other sources, Luke was not disclaiming divine inspiration for his work. The process of inspiration never bypasses or overrides the personalities, vocabularies, and styles of the human authors of Scripture. The unique traits of the human authors are always indelibly stamped on all the books of Scripture. Luke's research is no exception to this rule. The research itself was orchestrated by divine Providence. And in his writing, Luke was moved by the Spirit of God (2 Pet. 1:21). Therefore, his account is infallibly true.

CHRIST IN . . . LUKE

LUKE, A PHYSICIAN HIMSELF, presents Jesus as the Great Physician (5:31,32; 15:4–7,31,32; 19:10). Luke examines Jesus' interaction with tax collectors, women, children, Gentiles, and Samaritans, demonstrating His unique ministry to the outcasts of society. Luke also describes Jesus as the Son of Man, emphasizing His offer of salvation to the world.

KEY PEOPLE IN LUKE

Jesus—the Son of Man who lived a perfect life to reconcile sinful men and women to God (1:26–24:53)

Elizabeth—godly wife of Zechariah and mother of John the Baptist (1:5–60)

Zechariah—Jewish priest and father of John the Baptist (1:4–79)

John the Baptist—prophet and forerunner who announced the coming of Christ (1:13–80; 3:2–9:9)

Mary—the virgin mother of Jesus (1:26–2:51)

The twelve disciples—Simon Peter, Andrew, James, John, Philip, Bartholomew, Thomas, Matthew, James (son of Alphaeus), Thaddaeus, Simon, Judas Iscariot; twelve men chosen by Jesus to aid His ministry on earth (1:2; 5:30–12:55; 16:1–24:53)

Herod the tetrarch—son of Herod the Great; had John the Baptist executed and participated in the trials of Jesus (3:1–20; 9:7–9; 23:6–16)

Pilate—Roman governor who ordered the crucifixion of Jesus in place of Barabbas (3:1; 13:1; 23:1–52)

Mary Magdalene—devoted follower of Jesus; first person to see Jesus after His resurrection (8:2; 24:10)

HISTORICAL AND THEOLOGICAL THEMES

Luke's style is that of a scholarly, well-read author. He wrote as a meticulous historian, often giving details that helped identify the historical context of the events he described (1:5; 2:1,2; 3:1,2; 13:1–4).

His account of the nativity is the fullest in all the gospel records—and (like the rest of Luke's work) more polished in its literary style. He included in the birth narrative a series of praise psalms (1:46–55; 1:68–79; 2:14; 2:29–32; 34,35). He alone reported the unusual circumstances surrounding the birth of John the Baptist, the annunciation to Mary, the manger, the shepherds, and Simeon and Anna (2:25–38).

A running theme in Luke's gospel is Jesus' compassion for Gentiles, Samaritans, women, children, tax collectors, sinners, and others who were often marginalized by society. Every time he mentions a tax collector (3:12; 5:27; 7:29; 15:1; 18:10–13; 19:2), it is in a positive sense. Yet, Luke did not ignore the salvation of those who were rich and respectable—e.g., 23:50–53. From the outset of Jesus' public ministry (4:18) to the Lord's final words on the cross (23:40–43), Luke underscored this theme of Christ's ministry to the pariahs of society. Again and again he showed how the Great Physician ministered to those most aware of their need (cf. 5:31,32; 15:4–7; 31,32; 19:10).

The high profile Luke accords to women is particularly significant. From the nativity account, where Mary, Elizabeth, and Anna are given prominence (chaps. 1; 2), to the events of resurrection morning, where women again are major characters (24:1,10), Luke emphasized the

KEY WORDS IN

Luke

Baptize: Greek *baptizō*—3:7,16,12,21; 7:29,30; 12:50—literally, "to dip" or "to immerse." People came to John to be immersed by him in the Jordan River. The baptism of Gentile proselytes to Judaism was common to the Jews, but this kind of baptism for Jews was new and strange to them. John called them to be baptized as a public renunciation of their old way of life. Their baptism also symbolized the preparation of their hearts for the coming of the Messiah. Paul connected baptism with the believers' identification with Christ. Just as a cloth soaked in dye absorbs the color of the dye, so a person immersed in Christ should take on the nature of Christ.

Mammon: Greek *mamōnas*—16:9,11, 13—literally, "wealth," "money," or "property." In Luke 16, this word is used for "riches." *Mammon* is also considered an idol or god of the human heart that is in conflict with the true God. The Bible proclaims it is impossible to serve this god of the world and the true God at the same time.

Paradise: Greek *paradeisos*—23:43—literally, "garden" or "park." The Septuagint uses this word literally in Ecclesiastes 2:5 and Song of Solomon 4:13, although the term also refers to the Garden of Eden (see Gen. 2:8). Later, Paradise was described as the place of the righteous dead in Sheol (Luke 16:19–31). When Jesus spoke to the thief on the cross, He assured him that he would that day reside with Him in Paradise (23:42). This seems to indicate that this word refers to a pleasant place for the righteous among the dead. Revelation 2:7 speaks of Paradise as the restitution of an Edenic paradise, an everlasting home for believers (compare Gen. 2 and Rev. 22).

central role of women in the life and ministry of our Lord (e.g., 7:12–15,37–50; 8:2,3, 43–48; 10:38–42; 13:11–13; 21:2–4; 23:27–29,49,55,56).

New Testament Women

Mary, the virgin mother of Jesus, has a place of honor among the women of the New Testament. She is an enduring example of faith, humility, and service (Luke 1:26–56).

Other notable women of the New Testament include the following:

Name	Description	Biblical Reference
Anna	Recognized Jesus as the long-awaited Messiah	Luke 2:36-38
Bernice	Sister of Agrippa before whom Paul made his defense	Acts 25:13
Candace	A queen of Ethiopia	Acts 8:27
Chloe	Woman who know of divisions in the church at Corinth	1 Cor. 1:11
Claudia	Christian of Rome	2 Tim. 4:21
Damaris	Woman of Athens converted under Paul's ministry	Acts 17:34
Dorcas (Tabitha)	Christian in Joppa who was raised from the dead by Peter	Acts 9:36-41
Drusilla	Wife of Felix, governor of Judea	Acts 24:24
Elizabeth	Mother of John the Baptist	Luke 1:5,13
Eunice	Mother of Timothy	2 Tim. 1:5
Herodias	Queen who demanded the execution of John the Baptist	Matt. 14:3-10
Joanna	Provided for the material needs of Jesus	Luke 8:3
Lois	Grandmother of Timothy	2 Tim. 1:5
Lydia	Converted under Paul's ministry in Philippi	Acts 16:14
Martha and Mary	Sisters of Lazarus; friends of Jesus	Luke 10:38-42
Mary Magdalene	Woman from whom Jesus cast out demons	Matt. 27:56-61; Mark 16:9
Phoebe	A servant, perhaps a deaconess, in the church at Cenchrea	Rom. 16:1,2
Priscilla	Wife of Aquila; laborer with Paul at Corinth and Ephesus	Acts 18:2,18,19
Salome	Mother of Jesus' disciples James and John	Matt. 20:20-24
Sapphira	Held back goods from the early Christian community	Acts 5:1
Susanna	Provided for the material needs of Jesus	Luke 8:3

Several other recurring themes form threads through Luke's gospel. Examples of these are human fear in the presence of God; forgiveness (3:3; 5:20–25; 6:37; 7:41–50; 11:4; 12:10; 17:3,4; 23:34; 24:47); joy; wonder at the mysteries of divine truth; the role of the Holy Spirit (1:15,35,41,67; 2:25–27; 3:16,22; 4:1,14,18; 10:21; 11:13; 12:10,12); the temple in Jerusalem (1:9–22; 2:27–38,46–49; 4:9–13; 18:10–14; 19:45–48; 20:1–21:6; 21:37, 38; 24:53); and Jesus' prayers.

Starting with 9:51, Luke devoted ten chapters of his narrative to a travelogue of Jesus' final journey to Jerusalem. Much of the material in this section is unique to Luke. This is the heart of Luke's gospel, and it features a theme Luke stressed throughout: Jesus' relentless progression toward the cross. This was the very purpose for which Christ had come to earth (cf. 9:22,23; 17:25; 18:31–33; 24:25,26,46), and He would not be deterred. The saving of sinners was His whole mission (19:10).

KEY DOCTRINES IN LUKE
Human fear in the presence of God—this response is normal and appropriate when confronted with the mighty work of God (1:30,65; 2:9,10; 5:10,26; 7:16; 8:25,37,50; 9:34,45; 12:5; 23:40; Lev. 19:14,32; 25:17,36,43; Deut. 25:18; Judg. 6:22; 2 Sam. 23:3; 2 Chr. 20:29; 26:5; Prov. 1:7; Neh. 5:15; 13:22; Mark 16:5; Acts 9:31; 1 Tim. 5:20)

The mysteries of divine truth—wonderment surrounds the mysteries of Christ's words and works (1:21,63; 2:18,19,33,47,48; 5:9; 8:25; 9:43–45; 11:14; 20:26; 24:12,41; Job 11:7; Dan. 2:47; Matt. 13:35; Mark 4:10–20; Rom. 11:25; 1 Cor. 2:7; 4:1; Eph. 5:32; Col. 1:25–27; 4:3; 1 Tim. 3:16; Rev. 10:7)

Forgiveness—its place in human life (3:3; 5:20–25; 6:37; 7:41–50; 11:4; 12:10; 17:3,4; 23:34; 24:47; Gen. 50:20,21; Ps. 7:4; Prov. 19:11; Matt. 6:1,15; 18:22; Mark 11:25; 2 Cor. 2:5–11; James 2:13; 1 Pet. 4:8)

The role of the Holy Spirit—the Spirit in our lives (1:15,35,41,67; 2:25–27; 3:16,22; 4:1,14,18; 10:21; 11:13; 12:10,12; Gen. 1:2; Job 26:13; Ps. 104:30; Ezek. 37:11–14; Zech. 4:7; Matt. 12:28; John 14:16; 15:26; Acts 1:8; 8:29; Rom. 8:11; 15:19; 1 Cor. 2:4,13; 1 Thess. 1:5; 1 Pet. 3:18)

Christ's death on the cross—the very purpose for which Christ came to earth (9:22–23; 17:25; 18:31–33; 24:25,26,46; Is. 53:7–9; Acts 13:29; 1 Cor. 1:18; 5:7; Gal. 5:11; 6:14; Eph. 5:2; Phil. 2:8; Col. 2:14; Heb. 10:1,1,12)

GOD'S CHARACTER IN LUKE
God is accessible—23:45
God is holy—1:49
God is long-suffering—13:6–9
God is merciful—1:50, 78
God is powerful—11:20; 12:5
God is a promise keeper—1:38,45,54,55,69–73
God is provident—2:1–4; 21:18,32,33; 22:35
God is wise—16:15

INTERPRETIVE CHALLENGES

Luke, like Mark, and in contrast to Matthew, appears to target a Gentile readership (for a discussion of the Synoptic Problem, see Introduction to Mark: Interpretive Challenges). He identified locations that would have been familiar to all Jews (e.g., 4:31; 23:51; 24:13), suggesting that his audience went beyond those who already had knowledge of Palestinian geography. He usually preferred Greek terminology over Hebraisms (e.g., "Calvary" instead of "Golgotha" in 23:33). The other gospels all use occasional Semitic terms such as "Abba" (Mark 14:36), "rabbi" (Matt. 23:7, 8; John 1:38,49), and "hosanna" (Matt. 21:9; Mark 11:9,10; John 12:13)—but Luke either omitted them or used Greek equivalents.

Luke quoted the OT more sparingly than Matthew, and when citing OT passages, he nearly always employed the Septuagint (LXX), a Greek translation of the Hebrew Scriptures. Furthermore, most of Luke's OT citations are allusions rather than direct quotations, and many of them appear in Jesus' words rather than Luke's narration (2:23,24; 3:4–6; 4:4,8,10–12,18,19; 7:27; 10:27; 18:20; 19:46; 20:17,18,37,42,43; 22:37).

Luke, more than any of the other gospel writers, highlighted the universal scope of the gospel invitation. He portrayed Jesus as the Son of Man, rejected by Israel, and then offered to the world. As noted above (see Historical and Theological Themes), Luke repeatedly related accounts of Gentiles, Samaritans, and other outcasts who found grace in Jesus' eyes. This emphasis is precisely what we would expect from a close companion of the "apostle of the Gentiles" (Rom. 11:13).

Yet some critics have claimed to see a wide gap between Luke's theology and that of Paul. It is true that there is almost no terminology in Luke's gospel that is uniquely Pauline. Luke wrote with his own style. Yet the underlying theology is perfectly in harmony with that of the apostle's. The centerpiece of Paul's doctrine was justification by faith. Luke also highlighted and illustrated justification by faith in many of the incidents and parables he related, chiefly the account of the Pharisee and the publican (18:9–14); the familiar story of the Prodigal Son (15:11–32); the incident at Simon's house (7:36–50); and the salvation of Zacchaeus (19:1–10).

OUTLINE

I. **The Prelude to Christ's Ministry (1:1–4:13)**
    A. Preamble (1:1–4)
    B. The Birth of Jesus (1:5–2:38)
        1. The annunciation to Zacharias (1:5–25)
        2. The annunciation to Mary (1:26–38)
        3. The visitation (1:39–45)
        4. The Magnificat (1:46–56)
        5. The birth of the forerunner (1:57–80)
        6. The nativity (2:1–38)
    C. The Boyhood of Jesus (2:39–52)
        1. In Nazareth (2:39,40)
        2. In the temple (2:41–50)
        3. In His family (2:51,52)
    D. The Baptism of Jesus (3:1–4:13)

1. The preaching of John the Baptist (3:1–20)
2. The testimony of heaven (3:21,22)
3. The genealogy of the Son of Man (3:23–38)
4. The temptation of the Son of God (4:1–13)

II. The Ministry in Galilee (4:14–9:50)

    A. The Commencement of His Ministry (4:14–44)

        1. Nazareth (4:14–30)

        2. Capernaum (4:31–42)

            a. A demon cast out (4:31–37)

            b. Multitudes healed (4:38–42)

        3. The cities of Galilee (4:43,44)

    B. The Calling of His Disciples (5:1–6:16)

        1. Four fishermen (5:1–26)

            a. Fishing for men (5:1–11)

            b. Healing infirmities (5:12–16)

            c. Pardoning sins (5:17–26)

        2. Levi (5:27–6:11)

            a. The gospel: not for the righteous, but for sinners (5:27–32)

            b. The wineskins: not old, but new (5:33–39)

            c. The Sabbath: not for bondage, but for doing good (6:1–11)

        3. The twelve (6:12–16)

    C. The Continuation of His Work (6:17–9:50)

        1. Preaching on the plateau (6:17–49)

            a. Beatitudes (6:17–23)

            b. Woes (6:24–26)

            c. Commandments (6:27–49)

        2. Ministering in the cities (7:1–8:25)

            a. He heals a centurion's servant (7:1–10)

            b. He raises a widow's son (7:11–17)

            c. He encourages John the Baptist's disciples (7:18–35)

            d. He forgives a sinful woman (7:36–50)

            e. He gathers loving disciples (8:1–3)

            f. He teaches the multitudes with parables (8:4–21)

            g. He stills the winds and waves (8:22–25)

        3. Traveling in Galilee (8:26–9:50)

            a. He delivers a demoniac (8:26–39)

            b. He heals a woman (8:40–48)

            c. He raises a girl (8:49–56)

            d. He sends out the Twelve (9:1–6)

            e. He confounds Herod (9:7–9)

            f. He feeds the multitude (9:10–17)

        g. He predicts His crucifixion (9:18–26)

        h. He unveils His glory (9:27–36)

        i. He casts out an unclean spirit (9:37–42)

        j. He instructs His disciples (9:43–50)

III. The Journey to Jerusalem (9:51–19:27)

    A. Samaria (9:51–10:37)

        1. A village turns Him away (9:51–56)

        2. He turns away the half-hearted (9:57–62)

        3. He sends out the seventy (10:1–24)

        4. He gives the parable of the Good Samaritan (10:25–37)

    B. Bethany and Judea (10:38–13:35)

        1. Mary and Martha (10:38–42)

        2. The Lord's prayer (11:1–4)

        3. The importance of importunity (11:5–13)

        4. The impossibility of neutrality (11:14–36)

        5. Woes upon Pharisees and lawyers (11:37–54)

        6. Lessons along the way (12:1–59)

           a. Against hypocrisy (12:1–12)

           b. Against worldly materialism (12:13–21)

           c. Against worry (12:22–34)

           d. Against unfaithfulness (12:35–48)

           e. Against love of ease (12:49–53)

           f. Against unpreparedness (12:54–56)

           g. Against division (12:57–59)

        7. Questions answered (13:1–30)

           a. About the justice of God (13:1–9)

           b. About the Sabbath (13:10–17)

           c. About the kingdom (13:18–21)

           d. About the few who are saved (13:22–30)

        8. Christ's lament (13:31–35)

    C. Perea (14:1–19:27)

        1. Guest of a Pharisee (14:1–24)

           a. He tests them about the Sabbath (14:1–6)

           b. He teaches them about humility (14:7–14)

           c. He tells them about the heavenly banquet (14:15–24)

        2. Teacher of multitudes (14:25–18:34)

           a. The cost of discipleship (14:25–35)

           b. The parable of the lost sheep (15:1–7)

           c. The parable of the lost coin (15:8–10)

           d. The parable of the lost son (15:11–32)

           e. The parable of the unjust steward (16:1–18)

           f. The rich man and Lazarus (16:19–31)

           g. A lesson about forgiveness (17:1–4)

   h. A lesson about faithfulness (17:5–10)

   i. A lesson about thankfulness (17:11–19)

   j. A lesson about readiness (17:20–37)

   k. The parable of the persistent widow (18:1–8)

   l. The parable of the Pharisee and the publican (18:9–14)

   m. A lesson about childlikeness (18:15–17)

   n. A lesson about commitment (18:18–30)

   o. A lesson about the plan of redemption (18:31–34)

  3. Friend of sinners (18:35–19:10)

   a. He opens blind eyes (18:35–43)

   b. He seeks and saves the lost (19:1–10)

  4. Judge of all the earth (19:11–27)

   a. The end of a long journey (19:11)

   b. The parable of the minas (19:12–27)

IV. The Passion Week (19:28–23:56)

 A. Sunday (19:28–44)

  1. The triumphal entry (19:28–40)

  2. Christ weeps over the city (19:41–44)

 B. Monday (19:45–48)

  1. He cleanses the temple (19:45,46)

  2. He teaches the Passover crowds (19:47,48)

 C. Tuesday (20:1–21:38)

  1. He contends with the Jewish rulers (20:1–8)

  2. He teaches the Passover crowds (20:9—21:38)

   a. The parable of the wicked vinedressers (20:9–19)

   b. An answer to the Pharisees about paying taxes (20:20–26)

   c. An answer to the Sadducees about the resurrection (20:27–40)

   d. A question for the scribes about messianic prophecy (20:41–47)

   e. The lesson of the widow's mites (21:1–4)

   f. A prophecy about the destruction of Jerusalem (21:5–24)

   g. Some signs of the times (21:25–38)

 D. Wednesday (22:1–6)

  1. The plot against Jesus (22:1,2)

  2. Judas joins the conspiracy (22:3–6)

 E. Thursday (22:7–53)

  1. Preparation for Passover (22:7–13)

  2. The Lord's Supper (22:14–38)

   a. The New Covenant instituted (22:14–22)

   b. Disputes among the disciples (22:23–30)

          c. Peter's denial predicted (22:31–34)

          d. God's provision promised (22:35–38)

      3. The agony in the garden (22:39–46)

      4. Jesus' arrest (22:47–53)

   F. Friday (22:54–23:55)

      1. Peter's denial (22:54–62)

      2. Jesus mocked and beaten (22:63–65)

      3. The trial before the Sanhedrin (22:66–71)

      4. The trial before Pilate (23:1–25)

          a. The indictment (23:1–5)

          b. The hearing before Herod (23:6–12)

          c. Pilate's verdict (23:13–25)

      5. The crucifixion (23:26–49)

      6. The burial (23:50–55)

   G. The Sabbath (23:56)

V. The Consummation of Christ's Ministry (24:1–53)

   A. The Resurrection (24:1–12)

   B. The Road to Emmaus (24:13–45)

   C. The Ascension (24:46–53)

MEANWHILE, IN OTHER PARTS OF THE WORLD...
Mark Antony and Cleopatra are defeated by Octavian in the Battle of Actium in 30 B.C. and commit suicide. As a result, Egypt becomes a Roman province.

ANSWERS TO TOUGH QUESTIONS

1. What do we know about Luke himself?

According to tradition and limited internal evidence, Luke was a Gentile. The apostle Paul seems to confirm this, distinguishing Luke from those who were "of the circumcision" (Col. 4:11,14). Both Eusebius and Jerome identified him as a native of Antioch. Luke was a frequent companion of Paul, who referred to Luke as a physician (Col. 4:14). For more on Luke, see Author and Date above.

2. What is the relationship of Luke to Matthew and Mark?

Even a cursory reading of the first three gospel reveals many striking similarities. Compare Luke 5:18-26, Matthew 9:2-8, and Mark 2:3-12. Significant differences can also be found, however, in the way each writer handles many details about Jesus. The question about how to explain these similarities and differences is known as the "Synoptic Problem." See the discussion of the Synoptic Problem in Mark: Interpretive Challenges.

3. What passages in Luke are unique to his gospel?

- Luke included twelve events or major passages not found in the other gospels:
- Events preceding the birth of John the Baptist and Jesus (1:5–80)
- Scenes from Jesus' childhood (2:1–52)
- Herod imprisons John the Baptist (3:19,20)
- The people of Nazareth reject Jesus (4:16–30)
- The first disciples are called (5:1–11)
- A widow's son is raised (7:11–17)
- A woman anoints Jesus' feet (7:36–50)
- Certain women minister to Christ (8:1–3)
- Events, teaching, and miracles during the months leading up to Christ's death (10:1–18:14)
- Christ abides with Zacchaeus (19:1–27)
- Herod tries Christ (23:6–12)
- Some of Jesus' final words before His ascension (24:44–49)

FURTHER STUDY ON LUKE

1. What evidence would you point to in the gospel of Luke that would indicate he was a physician?
2. How can you tell the writer of Luke's gospel was a historian?
3. What details about Jesus' birth and early life do you find particularly significant? Why?
4. How does Jesus particularly demonstrate compassion in the gospel of Luke?
5. In what ways did Luke note and acknowledge the presence of the Holy Spirit throughout his gospel?
6. What aspects of Luke's resurrection account make it clear that he recognized the historical importance of the events he was recording?

JOHN

Jesus Is the Son of God

TITLE

The title of the fourth gospel continues the pattern of the other gospels, being identified originally as "According to John." Like the others, the phrase "The Gospel" was added later.

AUTHOR AND DATE

Although the author's name does not appear in the gospel, early church tradition strongly and consistently identified him as the apostle John. The early church father Irenaeus (ca. A.D. 130–200) was a disciple of Polycarp (ca. A.D. 70–160), who was a disciple of the apostle John, and he testified on Polycarp's authority that John wrote the gospel during his residence at Ephesus in Asia Minor when he was advanced in age (*Against Heresies* 2.22.5; 3.1.1). Subsequent to Irenaeus, all the church fathers assumed John to be the gospel's author. Clement of Alexandria (ca. A.D. 150–215) wrote that John, aware of the facts set forth in the other gospels and being moved by the Holy Spirit, composed a "spiritual gospel" (see Eusebius' *Ecclesiastical History* 6.14.7).

Reinforcing early church tradition are significant internal characteristics of the gospel. While the synoptic gospels (Matthew, Mark, Luke) identify the apostle John by name approximately twenty times (including parallels), he is not directly mentioned by name in the gospel of John. Instead, the author prefers to identify himself as the disciple "whom Jesus loved" (13:23; 19:26; 20:2; 21:7,20). The absence of any mention of John's name directly is remarkable when one considers the important part played by other named disciples in this gospel. Yet, the recurring designation of himself as the disciple "whom Jesus loved," a deliberate avoidance by John of his personal name, reflects his humility and celebrates his relation to his Lord Jesus. No mention of his name was necessary since his original readers clearly understood that he was the gospel's author. Also, through a process of elimination based primarily on analyzing the material in chaps. 20, 21, this disciple "whom Jesus loved" narrows down to the apostle John (e.g., 21:24; cf. 21:2). Since the gospel's author is exacting in mentioning the names of other characters in the book, if the author had been someone other than John the apostle, he would not have omitted John's name.

The gospel's anonymity strongly reinforces the arguments favoring John's authorship, for only someone of his well known and preeminent authority as an apostle would be able to write a gospel that differed so markedly in form and substance from the other gospels and have it receive unanimous acceptance in the early church. In contrast, other gospels produced from the mid-second century onward were falsely ascribed to apostles or other famous persons closely associated with Jesus, yet universally rejected by the church.

John and James, his older brother (Acts 12:2), were known as "the sons of Zebedee" (Matt. 10:2–4), and Jesus gave them the name "Sons of Thunder" (Mark 3:17). John was an apostle (Luke 6:12–16) and one of the three most intimate associates of Jesus (along with Peter and James—cf. Matt. 17:1; 26:37), being an eyewitness to and participant in Jesus' earthly ministry (1 John 1:1–4). After Christ's ascension, John became a "pillar" in

Palestine

the Jerusalem church (Gal. 2:9). He ministered with Peter (Acts 3:1; 4:13; 8:14) until he went to Ephesus (tradition says before the destruction of Jerusalem), from where he wrote this gospel and from where the Romans exiled him to Patmos (Rev. 1:9). Besides the gospel that bears his name, John also authored 1, 2, and 3 John and the Book of Revelation (Rev. 1:1).

Though probably written in the great city of Ephesus in the province of Asia Minor, across the Aegean Sea from Greece, the gospel of John is set exclusively in the seemingly insignificant area of faraway Palestine. Nevertheless, John shows that the events described in the book are of universal significance, and he writes in order that those who read his work "may believe that Jesus is the Christ" and that they "may have life in His name" (20:31).

Because the writings of some church fathers indicate that John was actively writing in his old age and that he was already aware of the synoptic gospels, many date the gospel sometime after their composition, but prior to John's writing of 1–3 John or Revelation. John wrote his gospel ca. A.D. 80–90, about fifty years after he witnessed Jesus' earthly ministry.

BACKGROUND AND SETTING

Strategic to John's background and setting is the fact that, according to tradition, John was aware of the synoptic gospels. Apparently, he wrote his gospel in order to make a unique contribution to the record of the Lord's life ("a spiritual gospel") and, in part, to be supplementary as well as complementary to Matthew, Mark, and Luke.

The gospel's unique characteristics reinforce this purpose: First, John supplied a large amount of unique material not recorded in the other gospels. Second, he often supplied information that helps the understanding of the events in the synoptics. For example, while the synoptics begin

CHRIST IN . . . JOHN

UNQUESTIONABLY, THE GOSPEL OF JOHN stands as a proclamation of the divinity of Jesus Christ. John reveals the nature of Jesus in his first sentence: "In the beginning was the Word, and the Word was with God, and the Word was God" (1:1). Whereas the gospel of Mark focuses on Jesus as the Son of Man, the message of John is that "Jesus is the Christ, the Son of God" (20:31). Notably, Jesus asserts Himself as God in seven explicit statements designating Himself as "I am" (6:35; 8:12; 10:7,9; 10:11,14; 11:25; 14:6; 15:1,5).

with Jesus' ministry in Galilee, they imply that Jesus had a ministry prior to that (e.g., Matt. 4:12; Mark 1:14). John supplies the answer with information on Jesus' prior ministry in Judea (chap. 3) and Samaria (chap. 4). In Mark 6:45, after the feeding of the 5,000, Jesus compelled his disciples to cross the Sea of Galilee to Bethsaida. John recorded the reason. The people were about to make Jesus king because of His miraculous multiplying of food, and He was avoiding their ill-motivated efforts (6:26). Third, John is the most theological of the gospels, containing, for example, a heavily theological introduction (1:1–18), larger amounts of instructional material in proportion to narrative (e.g., 3:13–17), and the largest amount of teaching on the Holy Spirit (e.g., 14:16,17,26; 16:7–14). Although John was aware of the synoptics and fashioned his gospel with them in mind, he did not depend upon them for information. Rather, under the inspiration of the Holy Spirit, he utilized his own memory as an eyewitness in composing the gospel (1:14; 19:35; 21:24).

The Seven Signs

Turns water into wine (John 2:1–12)	Jesus is the Source of life.
Heals a nobleman's son (John 4:46–54)	Jesus is Master over distance.
Heals a lame man at the pool of Bethesda (John 5:1–17)	Jesus is Master over time.
Feeds 5,000 (John 6:1–14)	Jesus is the Bread of life.
Walks on water, stills a storm (John 6:15–21)	Jesus is Master over nature.
Heals a man blind from birth (John 9:1–41)	Jesus is the Light of the world.
Raises Lazarus from the dead (John 11:17–45)	Jesus has power over death.

KEY WORDS IN

John

The Word: Greek *ho logos*—1:1,14; 2:22; 5:24; 8:43; 15:3; 17:14,17—used to speak of the Creator of the universe, even the creative energy that generated the universe. In the OT, the term logos may also be connected with wisdom as a personification or attribute of God (see Prov. 8). In both Jewish and Greek usage, the Logos was associated with the idea of beginnings—the world began with the Word (Gen. 1:3). John specifically used this word to identify the Son of God as divine. Jesus is the image of the invisible God (Col. 1:15), and the very substance of God (Heb. 1:3). In the Godhead, the Son functions as the revelation of God and is God in reality.

Born Again: Greek *gennaō anōthen*—3:3,7—literally, "again" or "from above." Jesus spoke of a birth that was either a new birth, or a heavenly birth, or both. Most likely Jesus was speaking of a heavenly birth because He described this birth using an analogy of the wind, coming from some unknown, heavenly source. Nicodemus clearly understood Jesus to be speaking of a second natural birth—being born again. Jesus explained this birth in 3:6–8 by contrasting being born of the flesh and being born of the Spirit.

I AM: Greek *egō eimi*—6:36; 8:58; 10:7,14; 15:1; 18:5—literally, "self-identity in self-sufficiency." In one breath, Jesus proclaimed that He existed for all eternity and that He is God. Jesus Christ, the Son of God, unlike any human, never had a beginning. He is the eternal God. Jesus clearly states His deity by using the words "I AM" to refer to Himself. In Exodus 3:14, God reveals His identity as "I AM WHO I AM." Thus, Jesus claimed before His judges to be the ever-existing, self-existent God.

Believe: Greek *pisteuō*—1:7; 5:44; 6:64; 7:5; 10:26; 11:48; 13:19; 20:31—literally, "to place one's trust in another." True belief in Jesus requires one to completely trust Him for salvation (3:15–16). When Jesus walked the earth, many people believed in His miraculous powers, but they would not put their faith in Jesus Himself (6:23–26). Others wanted to believe in Jesus only as a political defender of Israel (Mark 15:32). However, we must be careful to believe and trust in the Jesus presented in the Scriptures—the Son of God who humbly sacrificed Himself to deliver us from the bondage of sin (Gal. 1:3,4; Phil. 2:5–8).

John's gospel is the only one of the four that contains a precise statement regarding the author's purpose (20:30,31). He declares, "these are written that you may believe that Jesus is the Christ, the Son of God, and that believing you may have life in His name" (20:31). The primary purposes, therefore, are two-fold: evangelistic (to convert non-believers) and apologetic (to explain and defend the truth). Reinforcing the evangelistic purpose is the fact that the word "believe" occurs approximately 100 times in the gospel (the synoptics use the term less than half as much). John composed his gospel to provide reasons for saving faith in his readers and, as a result, to assure them that they would receive the divine gift of eternal life (1:12).

The apologetic purpose is closely related to the evangelistic purpose. John wrote to convince his readers of Jesus' true identity as the incarnate God-Man whose divine and human natures were perfectly united into one person who was the prophesied Christ ("Messiah") and Savior of the world (e.g., 1:41; 3:16; 4:25,26; 8:58). He organized his whole gospel around eight "signs" or proofs that reinforce Jesus' true identity leading to faith. The first half of his work revolves around seven miraculous signs selected to reveal Christ's person and engender belief: (1) water made into wine; (2) the healing of the royal official's son; (3) the healing of the lame man; (4) the feeding of multitude; (5) walking on water; (6) healing of the blind man; and 7) the raising of Lazarus. The eighth sign is the miraculous catch of fish (21:6–11) after Jesus' resurrection.

KEY PEOPLE IN JOHN

Jesus—the Word of God who came into the world; both fully God and fully human (1:1–21:25)

John the Baptist—prophet and forerunner who announced the coming of Christ (1:6–42; 3:23–27; 4:1; 5:33; 10:40–41)

The disciples—Simon Peter, Andrew, James, John, Philip, Bartholomew, Thomas, Matthew, James (son of Alphaeus), Thaddaeus, Simon, Judas Iscariot; twelve men chosen by Jesus to aid His ministry on earth (1:53–21:14)

Mary—sister of Lazarus; believed and anointed Jesus before His death (11:1–12:11)

Martha—sister of Lazarus; known for her hospitality; grew in faith when Jesus raised her brother from the dead (11:17–45)

Lazarus—raised from the dead by Jesus, his friend (11:1–12:17)

Mary, Jesus' mother—demonstrated her servanthood to Jesus; entrusted to the care of John at Jesus' death (2:1–12; 19:25–27)

Pilate—Roman governor who ordered the crucifixion of Jesus in place of Barabbas (18:29–19:38)

Mary Magdalene—devoted follower of Jesus; first person to see Jesus after His resurrection (19:25–20:18)

HISTORICAL AND THEOLOGICAL THEMES

In accordance with John's evangelistic and apologetic purposes, the overall message of the gospel is found in 20:31: "Jesus is the Christ, the Son of God." The book, therefore, centers on the person and work of Christ. Three predominant words ("signs," "believe," and "life") in 20:30,31 receive constant reemphasis throughout the gospel to enforce the theme of salvation in Him, which is first set forth in the prologue (1:1–18; cf. 1 John 1:1–4) and re-expressed throughout the gospel in varying ways (e.g., 6:35, 48; 8:12; 10:7, 9; 10:11–14; 11:25; 14:6; 17:3). In addition, John provides the record of how men responded to Jesus Christ and the salvation that He offered. Summing up, the gospel focuses on: (1) Jesus as the Word, the Messiah, and Son of God; (2) who brings the gift of salvation to mankind; (3) who either accept or reject the offer.

The "I AM" Statements

Twenty-three times in all we find our Lord's meaningful "I AM" (ego eimi, Gk.) in the Greek text of this gospel (4:26; 6:20,35,41,48,51; 8:12,18,24,28,58; 10:7,9,11,14; 11:25; 13:19; 14:6; 15:1,5; 18:5,6,8). In several of these He joins His "I AM" with seven tremendous metaphors which are expressive of His saving relationship toward the world.

"I AM the Bread of life" (6:35,41,48,51)

"I AM the Light of the world" (8:12)

"I AM the Door of the sheep" (10:7,9)

"I AM the Good Shepherd" (10:11,14)

"I AM the Resurrection and the Life" (11:25)

"I AM the Way, the Truth, the Life" (14:6)

"I AM the true Vine" (15:1,5).

John also presents certain contrasting sub-themes that reinforce his main theme. He uses dualism (life and death, light and darkness, love and hate, from above and from below) to convey vital information about the person and work of Christ and the need to believe in Him (e.g., 1:4,5,12,13; 3:16–21; 12:44–46; 15:17–20). There are also seven emphatic "I AM" statements identifying Jesus as God and Messiah.

KEY DOCTRINES IN JOHN
The divinity of Jesus Christ—who Jesus really is (6:35; 8:12; 10:7,9; 10:11,14; 11:25; 14:6; 15:1,5; 20:28–31; Is. 9:6; 40:9; Jer. 23:5,6; Zech. 13:7; Matt. 1:23; Mark 2:7–10; Rom. 9:5; 1 Cor. 1:30; Phil. 2:6; Col. 2:9; Titus 2:13; 1 John 5:20; Rev. 22:13)

Salvation through Jesus Christ—how people should respond to Jesus (1:1–18; 6:35,48; 8:12; 10:7,9; 10:11–14; 11:25; 14:6; 17:3; Gen. 3:15; Pss. 3:8; 37:39; Is. 45:2–22; 49:6; 59:16; 63:9; Luke 1:69; Acts 4:12; 16:31; Rom. 5:8; 10:9; Eph. 2:8; 5:23; 2 Tim. 1:10; Heb. 2:10; 5:9; 1 Pet. 1:5; 1 John 1:1–4)

GOD'S CHARACTER IN JOHN
God is accessible—1:51; 10:7,9; 14:6

God is glorious—1:14

God is invisible—1:18; 5:37

God is loving—3:16; 15:9,10; 16:27; 17:23,26

God is righteous—17:25

God is spirit—4:24

God is true—17:3,17

God is unified—10:30; 14:9–11; 17:3

God is wrathful—3:14–18,36

INTERPRETIVE CHALLENGES
Because John composed his record in a clear and simple style, one might tend to underestimate the depth of this gospel. Since John's gospel is a "spiritual" gospel (see Author and Date), the truths he conveys are profound. The reader must prayerfully and meticulously explore the book, in order to discover the vast richness of the spiritual treasures that the apostle, under the guidance of the Holy Spirit (14:26; 16:13), has lovingly deposited in his gospel.

The chronological reckoning between John's gospel and the synoptics presents a challenge, especially in relation to the time of the Last Supper (13:2). While the synoptics portray the disciples and the Lord at the Last Supper as eating the Passover meal on Thursday evening and Jesus being crucified on Friday, John's gospel states that the Jews did not enter into the Praetorium (the Roman governor's headquarters) early Friday morning, "lest they should be defiled, but that they might eat the Passover" (18:28). So, the disciples had eaten the Passover on Thursday evening, but the Jews had not. In fact, John (19:14) states that Jesus' trial and crucifixion were on Preparation Day for the Passover and not after the eating of the Passover, so that with the trial and crucifixion on Friday, Christ was actually sacrificed at the same time the Passover lambs were being slain (19:14). The question is, "Why did the disciples eat the Passover meal on Thursday?"

Titles of Jesus

The two most popular titles or names Christians use in speaking of our Lord are *Jesus*, a translation of the Hebrew word *Joshua*, which means "YAHWEH Is Salvation" and *Christ*, a translation of the Greek term *Christos*, meaning "Anointed One" or "Messiah". Following are some other significant names or titles for Christ used in the New Testament. Each title expresses a distinct truth about Jesus and his relationship to believers.

Name or Title	Significance	Biblical Reference
Adam, Last Adam	First of the new race of the redeemed	1 Cor. 15:45
Alpha and Omega	The beginning and ending of all things	Rev. 21:6
Bread of Life	The one essential food	John 6:35
Chief Cornerstone	A sure foundation for life	Eph. 2:20
Chief Shepherd	Protector, sustainer, and guide	1 Pet. 5:4
Firstborn from the Dead	Leads us into resurrection and eternal life	Col. 1:18
Good Shepherd	Provider and caretaker	John 10:11
Great Shepherd of the Sheep	Trustworthy guide and protector	Heb. 13:20
High Priest	A perfect sacrifice for our sins	Heb. 3:1
Holy One of God	Sinless in His nature	Mark 1:24
Immanuel (God With Us)	Stands with us in all of life's circumstances	Matt. 1:23
King of Kings, Lord of Lords	The Almighty, before whom every knee will bow	Rev. 19:16
Lamb of God	Gave His life as a sacrifice on our behalf	John 1:29
Light of the World	Brings hope in the midst of darkness	John 9:5
Lord of Glory	The power and presence of the living God	1 Cor. 2:8
Mediator between God and Men	Brings us into God's presence redeemed and forgiven	1 Tim. 2:5
Only Begotten of the Father	The unique, one-of-a-kind Son of God	John 1:14
Prophet	Faithful proclaimer of the truths of God	Acts 3:22
Savior	Delivers from sin and death	Luke 1:47
Seed of Abraham	Mediator of God's covenant	Gal. 3:16
Son of Man	Identifies with us in our humanity	Matt. 18:11
The Word	Present with God at the creation	John 1:1

The answer lies in a difference among the Jews in the way they reckoned the beginning and ending of days. From Josephus, the Mishna, and other ancient Jewish sources we learn that the Jews in northern Palestine calculated days from sunrise to sunrise. That area included the region of Galilee, where Jesus and all the disciples, except Judas, had grown up. Apparently most, if not all, of the Pharisees used that system of reckoning. But Jews in the southern part, which centered in Jerusalem, calculated days from sunset to sunset. Because all the priests necessarily lived in or near Jerusalem, as did most of the Sadducees, those groups followed the southern scheme.

That variation doubtlessly caused confusion at times, but it also had some practical benefits. During Passover time, for instance, it allowed for the feast to be celebrated legitimately on two adjoining days, thereby permitting the temple sacrifices to be made over a total period of four hours rather than two. That separation of days may also have had the effect of reducing both regional and religious clashes between the two groups.

On that basis the seeming contradictions in the gospel accounts are easily explained. Being Galileans, Jesus and the disciples considered Passover day to have started at sunrise on Thursday and to end at sunrise on Friday. The Jewish leaders who arrested and tried Jesus, being mostly priests and Sadducees, considered Passover day to begin at sunset on Thursday and end at sunset on Friday. By that variation, decided long ahead of time by God's sovereign provision, Jesus could thereby legitimately celebrate the last Passover meal with His disciples and yet still be sacrificed on Passover day.

Once again one can see how God sovereignly and marvelously provides for the precise fulfillment of His redemptive plan. Jesus was anything but a victim of men's wicked schemes, much less of blind circumstance. Every word He spoke and every action He took were divinely directed and secured. Even the words and actions by others against Him were divinely controlled. See, for example, 11:49–52; 19:11.

OUTLINE

I. The Incarnation of the Son of God (1:1–18)
    A. His Eternality (1:1,2)
    B. His Pre-incarnate Work (1:3–5)
    C. His Forerunner (1:6–8)
    D. His Rejection (1:9–11)
    E. His Reception (1:12,13)
    F. His Deity (1:14–18)

II. The Presentation of the Son of God (1:19–4:54)
    A. Presentation by John the Baptist (1:19–34)
        1. To the religious leaders (1:19–28)
        2. At Christ's baptism (1:29–34)
    B. Presentation to John's Disciples (1:35–51)
        1. Andrew and Peter (1:35–42)
        2. Philip and Nathanael (1:43–51)
    C. Presentation in Galilee (2:1–12)
        1. First sign: water to wine (2:1–10)
        2. Disciples believe (2:11,12)

D. Presentation in Judea (2:13–3:36)
    1. Cleansing the temple (2:13–25)
    2. Teaching Nicodemus (3:1–21)
    3. Preaching by John the Baptist (3:22–36)
E. Presentation in Samaria (4:1–42)
    1. Witness to the Samaritan woman (4:1–26)
    2. Witness to the disciples (4:27–38)
    3. Witnesses to the Samaritans (4:39–42)
F. Presentation in Galilee (4:43–54)
    1. Reception by the Galileans (4:43–45)
    2. Second sign: healing the nobleman's son (4:46–54)

III. The Opposition to the Son of God (5:1–12:50)
A. Opposition at the Feast in Jerusalem (5:1–47)
    1. Third sign: healing the paralytic (5:1–9)
    2. Rejection by the Jews (5:10–47)
B. Opposition During Passover (6:1–71)
    1. Fourth sign: feeding the 5,000 (6:1–14)
    2. Fifth sign: walking on water (6:15–21)
    3. Bread of Life discourse (6:22–71)
C. Opposition at the Feast of Tabernacles (7:1–10:21)
D. Opposition at the Feast of Dedication (10:22–42)
E. Opposition at Bethany (11:1–12:11)
    1. Seventh sign: raising of Lazarus (11:1–44)
    2. Pharisees plot to kill Christ (11:45–57)
    3. Mary anointing Christ (12:1–11)
F. Opposition in Jerusalem (12:12–50)
    1. The triumphal entry (12:12–22)
    2. The discourse on faith and rejection (12:23–50)

IV. The Preparation of the Disciples by the Son of God (13:1–17:26)
A. In the Upper Room (13:1–14:31)
    1. Washing feet (13:1–20)
    2. Announcing the betrayal (13:21–30)
    3. Discourse on Christ's departure (13:31–14:31)
B. On the Way to the Garden (15:1–17:26)
    1. Instructing the disciples (15:1–16:33)
    2. Interceding with the Father (17:1–26)

V. The Execution of the Son of God (18:1–19:37)
A. The Rejection of Christ (18:1–19:16)
    1. His arrest (18:1–11)
    2. His trials (18:12–19:16)
B. The Crucifixion of Christ (19:17–37)

VI. The Resurrection of the Son of God (19:38–21:23)
A. The Burial of Christ (19:38–42)
B. The Resurrection of Christ (20:1–10)

C. The Appearances of Christ (20:11–21:23)
    1. To Mary Magdalene (20:11–18)
    2. To the disciples without Thomas (20:19–25)
    3. To the disciples with Thomas (20:26–29)
    4. Statement of purpose for the gospel (20:30,31)
    5. To the disciples (21:1–14)
    6. To Peter (21:15–23)
VII. Conclusion (21:24,25)

MEANWHILE, IN OTHER PARTS OF THE WORLD...
Music develops in Asia as the Chinese octave is subdivided into sixty different musical notes.

ANSWERS TO TOUGH QUESTIONS

1. How do scholars conclude that the expression "whom Jesus loved" was John's way of referring to himself in the gospel of John?

Three obvious clues about John's gospel help identify the unnamed disciple who called himself the disciple "whom Jesus loved" (13:23; 19:26; 20:2; 21:7,20):

- Early church fathers invariably identify the apostle John as the author of this gospel.
- John is frequently mentioned by the other gospel writers as an active participant among the disciples of Jesus.
- John's name is absent from the fourth gospel.

If four people take a trip together and each carries a camera, the group shots each person takes will naturally not include them. In fact, someone else could probably guess who took which pictures by which member of the group was absent. The gospel of John functions this way. John's absence by name shouts his presence. As for his signature phrase, the words "whom Jesus loved" convey both a sense of the apostle's humility and the depth of his relationship to Jesus. The phrase doesn't mean that John thought of himself as the only disciple Jesus loved. It simply expresses with disarming honesty the wonder of this disciple over the fact that the Lord loved him!

2. What makes the gospel of John so different from the other three gospels?

Clement of Alexandria (about A.D. 150–215), one of the early church fathers, may have been the first to describe John's biography of Jesus as a "spiritual gospel." Apparently, John wrote his gospel in order to make a unique contribution to the records of the Lord's life and to be supplementary as well as complementary to Matthew, Mark, and Luke. (See Background and Setting for further discussion.)

3. The timing of events in parts of the gospel of John seems to differ from the other gospels. How can we explain those apparent differences?

The chronological reckoning between John's gospel and the synoptic gospels of Matthew, Mark, and Luke does present a challenge in the accounts of the Last Supper (13:2). The synoptics portray the disciples and the Lord at the Last Supper as eating the Passover meal on Thursday evening and Jesus being crucified on Friday. John states that Jesus' trial and crucifixion were on the day of preparation for the Passover (19:14) and *not* after the eating of the Passover. The question then becomes, "Why did the disciples eat the Passover meal on Thursday?" The answer lies in the fact that there were two distinct ways the Jews in Jesus' day reckoned the beginning and ending of days. Jews in northern Palestine calculated days from sunrise to sunrise. The Jews in southern Israel calculated days from sunset to sunset. The double calendar easily explains the apparent contradictions in the gospel accounts. See Interpretive Challenges for further discussion.

FURTHER STUDY ON JOHN

1. How would you describe the difference in style and approach between John and the other three gospels?
2. What were John's purposes in the first eighteen verses of his gospel?
3. Compare the use of the word *believe* in John 3:16 with the same word in other verses in John. What kind of belief does God require?
4. Summarize Jesus' teaching on the Holy Spirit in John 14:15–31 and 16:5–16.
5. How have you responded to Jesus' question in John 11:25–26?
6. As in each of the gospels, the Resurrection of Jesus is the climax of John's gospel. Why is that event so crucial in Christianity?

ACTS
C h r i s t   B u i l d s   H i s   C h u r c h

TITLE
The Book of Acts may originally have had no title. The Greek manuscripts title it "Acts," and many add "of the Apostles." The Greek word translated "Acts" (*praxeis*) was often used to describe the achievements of great men. Acts does feature the notable figures in the early years of the church, especially Peter (chaps. 1–12) and Paul (chaps. 13–28). But the book could more properly be called "The Acts of the Holy Spirit through the Apostles," since His sovereign, all-powerful work was far more significant than that of any man. It was the Spirit's directing, controlling, and empowering ministry that strengthened the church and caused it to grow in numbers, spiritual power, and influence.

AUTHOR AND DATE
Since Luke's gospel was the first book addressed to Theophilus (Luke 1:3), and Acts was also addressed to Theophilus, it is logical to conclude that Luke is also the author of Acts, although he is not named in either book. The writings of the early church Fathers such as Irenaeus, Clement of Alexandria, Tertullian, Origen, Eusebius, and Jerome affirm Luke's authorship, and so does the Muratorian Canon (ca. A.D. 170). Because Theophilus is a relatively obscure figure, mentioned only three times in the NT (Col. 4:14; 2 Tim. 4:11, Philem. 24), it is unlikely that anyone would have forged a work to make it appear to be Luke's. A forger surely would have attributed his work to a more prominent person.

Luke was Paul's close friend, traveling companion, and personal physician (Col. 4:14). He was a careful researcher (Luke 1:1–4) and an accurate historian, displaying an intimate knowledge of Roman laws and customs, as well as the geography of Palestine, Asia Minor, and Italy. In writing Acts, Luke drew on written sources (15:23–29; 23:26–30), and also no doubt interviewed key figures, such as Peter, John, and others in the Jerusalem church. Paul's two-

CHRIST IN . . . ACTS

THE BOOK OF ACTS gives the account of Jesus' ministry being passed on to His disciples. Their mission was to proclaim the resurrected Christ and fulfill the Great Commission given to them by Jesus (Matt. 28:19,20). The disciples acted as witnesses to the salvation brought about by Christ (4:12; 10:43).

year imprisonment at Caesarea (24:27) gave Luke ample opportunity to interview Philip and his daughters (who were considered important sources of information on the early days of the church). Finally, Luke's frequent use of the first person plural pronouns "we" and "us" (16:10–17; 20:5–21:18; 27:1–28:16) reveals that he was an eyewitness to many of the events recorded in Acts.

Some believe Luke wrote Acts after the fall of Jerusalem (A.D. 70; his death was probably in the mid-eighties). It is more likely, however, that he wrote much earlier, before the end of Paul's first Roman imprisonment (ca. A.D. 60–62). That date is the most natural explanation for the abrupt ending of Acts—which leaves Paul awaiting trial before Caesar. Surely Luke, who devoted more than half of Acts to Paul's ministry, would have given the outcome of that trial, and described Paul's subsequent ministry, second imprisonment (cf. 2 Tim. 4:11), and death, if those events had happened before he wrote Acts. Luke's silence about such notable events as the martyrdom of James, head of the Jerusalem church (A.D. 62 according to the Jewish historian Josephus), the persecution under Nero (A.D. 64), and the fall of Jerusalem (A.D. 70) also suggests he wrote Acts before those events transpired.

BACKGROUND AND SETTING

As Luke makes clear in the prologue to his gospel, he wrote to give Theophilus (and the others who would read his work) a "narrative of those things" (Luke 1:1) that Jesus had accomplished during His earthly ministry. Accordingly, Luke wrote in his gospel "an orderly account" (Luke 1:3) of those momentous events. Acts continues that record, noting what Jesus accomplished through the early church. Beginning with Jesus' ascension, through the birth of the church on the Day of Pentecost, to Paul's preaching at Rome, Acts chronicles the spread of the gospel and the growth of the church (cf. 1:15; 2:41,47; 4:4; 5:14; 6:7; 9:31; 12:24; 13:49; 16:5; 19:20). It also records the mounting opposition to the gospel (cf. 2:13; 4:1–22; 5:17–42; 6:9–8:4; 12:1–5; 13:6–12,45–50; 14:2–6,19,20; 16:19–24; 17:5–9; 19:23–41; 21:27–36; 23:12–21; 28:24).

Theophilus, whose name means "lover of God," is unknown to history apart from his mention in Luke and Acts. Whether he was a believer whom Luke was instructing, or a pagan whom Luke sought to convert is not known. Luke's address of him as "most excellent Theophilus" (Luke 1:3) suggests he was a Roman official of some importance (cf. 24:3; 26:25).

KEY WORDS IN

Acts

Spirit: Greek to *pneuma*—2:4; 5:9; 8:39; 10:19; 11:12; 16:7; 19:21; 23:9—derived from the verb *pneuō*, meaning "to breathe" or "to blow." It is sometimes used to refer to the wind and sometimes to life itself (see John 3:8; Rev. 13:15). It can refer to the life of angels (Heb. 1:14), demons (Luke 4:33), and human beings (7:59). Yet this word is also used for the Spirit of God (see 1 Cor. 2:11), that is, the Holy Spirit (Matt. 28:19), the third Person of the Trinity, the One who lives inside believers (see James 4:5; 1 John 4:13). This same Spirit is called "the Spirit of Jesus Christ" (Phil. 1:19); manuscripts have the title *the Spirit of Jesus* in 16:7. This title emphasizes the unity of action between Jesus and the Spirit that permeates this book and its companion volume, the gospel of Luke. During the days of Jesus' earthly ministry, the disciples were directed by Jesus; now, after His resurrection and ascension, by the Spirit of Jesus.

Grace: Greek *charis*—4:33; 11:23; 13:43; 14:26; 15:11; 18:27; 20:32—probably equivalent to the Hebrew word *chesed*, meaning "loving-kindness," a word frequently used by the psalmists to describe God's character. In the New Testament, the word *charis* usually signifies divine favor or goodwill, but it also means "that which gives joy" and "that which is a free gift." This is a noteworthy occurrence of the word *grace* because while it was one of Paul's favorite words for God's free gift of salvation, here we see Luke using it in the same way.

Together: Greek *epi to auto*—1:15; 2:1,44— an expression meaning "toward the same thing" or "in the same place"; it conveys the idea of united purpose or collective unity. In the early church it acquired a special meaning, indicating the union of the Christian body. All the members of the church not only gathered together regularly, but they also shared all things in common and were committed to each other and Christ with united fervor.

KEY PEOPLE IN ACTS

Peter—one of the twelve disciples of Jesus; called "the Rock" (1:13–12:18; 15:7–14)

John—one of the twelve disciples of Jesus; called "the disciple whom Jesus loved" (1:13; 3:1–4:31; 8:14–25; see John 21:20)

James—one of the twelve disciples; first disciple to die for his faith in Christ (1:13; 12:1,2)

Stephen—appointed as a manager of food distribution in the early church; martyred for his faith in Christ (6:3–8:2; 22:20)

Philip—appointed as a manager of food distribution in the early church; one of the first missionaries to Samaria (1:13; 6:5; 8:1–40; 21:8)

Paul—New Testament writer and missionary; originally named Saul; early persecutor of Christians before his conversion (7:58–8:3; 9:1–30; 11:25–30; 12:25–28:30)

Barnabas—name means "Son of Encouragement"; traveled as a missionary with Paul and then with John Mark (4:36; 9:27; 11:22–15:39)

Cornelius—Roman officer; one of the first Gentile Christians (10:1–48)

Timothy—Paul's assistant; later became a pastor in Ephesus (16:1–20:4)

Lydia—believer and hostess to Paul and Silas; seller of purple cloth (16:13–40)

Silas—served as a missionary; involved in the ministries of Paul and Timothy and Peter (15:22–18:5)

Apollos—Alexandrian preacher who ministered in Achaia; instructed by Aquila and Priscilla (18:24–19:1)

Felix—Roman governor of Judea; kept Paul in prison for two years (23:24–25:14)

Festus—succeeded Felix as governor; reviewed Paul's case with Herod Agrippa II (24:27–26:32)

Herod Agrippa II—reviewed Paul's case with Festus; responded to the gospel with sarcasm (25:13—26:32)

Luke—medical physician who traveled with Paul; author of the Book of Acts (16:10–28:31)

HISTORICAL AND THEOLOGICAL THEMES

As the first work of church history ever penned, Acts records the initial response to the Great Commission (Matt. 28:19,20). It provides information on the first three decades of the church's existence—material found nowhere else in the NT. Though not primarily concerned with teaching doctrine, Acts nonetheless emphasizes that Jesus of Nazareth was Israel's long-awaited Messiah, shows that the gospel is offered to all men (not merely the Jewish people), and stresses the work of the Holy Spirit (mentioned more than fifty times). Acts also makes frequent use of the OT: e.g., 2:17–21 (Joel 2:28–32); 2:25–28 (Ps. 16:8–11); 2:35 (Ps. 110:1); 4:11 (Ps. 118:22); 4:25,26 (Ps. 2:1,2); 7:49,50 (Is. 66:1,2); 8:32,33 (Is. 53:7,8); 28:26,27 (Is. 6:9,10).

Acts abounds with transitions: from the ministry of Jesus to that of the apostles; from the Old Covenant to the New Covenant; from Israel as God's witness nation to the church (composed of both Jews and Gentiles) as God's witness people. The Book of Hebrews sets forth the theology of the transition from the Old Covenant to the New Covenant; Acts depicts the New Covenant's practical outworking in the life of the church.

KEY DOCTRINES IN ACTS

The establishment of the church—the history of how the faith spread (2:1; 4:23, 24,32–37; 9:31; Matt. 16:18; Rom. 12:5; 1 Cor. 10:17; 12:12; Gal. 3:28; Eph. 4:15–16; 1 Tim. 3:15; Rev. 19:8)

The work of the Holy Spirit—how the Spirit of God directed the church and individual believers (1:8; 2:2–4,16–18,38; 4:8; 8:29; 11:12; 13:2; 16:6; 21:11; Gen. 6:3; Num. 11:25–27; Neh. 9:30; Is. 48:16; Zech. 7:12; John 15:26; Rom. 8:16,26; 1 Cor. 2:4,9,10; Heb. 2:4; 1 John 3:24; 4:13; Rev. 2:7,11,29)

GOD'S CHARACTER IN ACTS

God is accessible—14:27

God is glorious—7:2,55

God is good—14:17

God is just—17:31

God is Most High—7:48

God is a promise keeper—1:4; 2:33,39; 7:17; 13:2,23,32; 26:6,7

God is provident—1:26; 3:17,18; 12:5; 17:26; 27:22,31,32

God is righteous—17:31

God is wise—15:18

INTERPRETIVE CHALLENGES

Because Acts is primarily a historical narrative, not a theological work like Romans or Hebrews, it contains relatively few interpretive challenges. Those that exist mainly concern the book's transitional nature (see Historical and Theological Themes) and involve the role of signs and wonders.

OUTLINE

Prologue (1:1–8)

    I. The Witness to Jerusalem (1:9–8:3)

        A. The Anticipation of the Church (1:9–26)

        B. The Founding of the Church (2:1–47)

        C. The Growth of the Church (3:1–8:3)

            1. Apostles: Preaching, healing, and enduring persecution (3:1–5:42)

            2. Deacons: Praying, teaching, and enduring persecution (6:1–8:3)

    II. The Witness to Judea and Samaria (8:4–12:25)

        A. The gospel to the Samaritans (8:4–25)

        B. The Conversion of a Gentile (8:26–40)

        C. The Conversion of Saul (9:1–31)

        D. The gospel to Judea (9:32–43)

        E. The gospel to the Gentiles (10:1–11:30)

        F. The Persecution by Herod (12:1–25)

III. The Witness to the Ends of the Earth (13:1–28:31)
A. Paul's First Missionary Journey (13:1–14:28)
B. The Jerusalem Council (15:1–35)
C. Paul's Second Missionary Journey (15:36–18:22)
D. Paul's Third Missionary Journey (18:23–21:16)
E. Paul's Jerusalem and Caesarean Trials (21:17–26:32)
F. Paul's Journey to Rome (27:1–28:31)

MEANWHILE, IN OTHER PARTS OF THE WORLD...
The Romans learn from the Gauls to use soap for cleaning purposes.

ANSWERS TO TOUGH QUESTIONS

1. How can Luke's authorship of Acts of the Apostles be defended when his own name is not mentioned in the book?

The gospel of Luke and Acts of the Apostles share numerous marks of common human authorship. They are addressed to the same person—Theophilus (Luke 1:3; Acts 1:1). They are parallel in style. The second book claims to be an extension of the first. Lack of the author's name within a text is not an unusual challenge in establishing the authorship of a Bible book. Many books of the Bible come to us without obvious human authorship. In most cases, however, internal and external clues lead us to reasonable confidence in identifying the authors. One benefit created by initial anonymity involves recognizing that the Bible books originated by the inspiration of the Holy Spirit. It may take some effort to discover whom God used in writing one of those books, but the original Author is not in question. See Author and Date for further discussion of Luke's authorship.

2. What can we learn from the Book of Acts about the Holy Spirit's special role in our lives?

One caution we must exercise in studying the Book of Acts has to do with the difference between *description* and *prescription*. The difference plays an important role in interpreting the historical biblical books. The Bible's description of an event does not imply that the event or action can, should, or will be repeated.

The arrival of the Holy Spirit as the promised Helper (John 14:17), which Acts describes as a startling event (2:1–13), had some partial and selected repetitions (8:14–19; 10:44–48; 19:1–7). These were special cases in which believers are reported to have received or been filled with the Holy Spirit. In each of these cases, the sound and the tongues as of fire that were present in the original event (2:1–13) were absent, but the people spoke in tongues they did not know (but others recognized). These events should not be taken as the basis for teaching that believers today should expect the same evidence—tongues—to accompany the filling of the Holy Spirit. Even in Acts itself, genuine conversions did not necessarily lead to extraordinary filling by the Holy Spirit. For example, a crowd of three thousand people believed and were baptized on that same Day of Pentecost (2:41) that started so dramatically with the gift of tongues, yet no mention of tongues is made with regard to the new converts. So, why in some cases did tongues accompany the confirmation of faith? This likely demonstrated that believers were being drawn from very different groups into the church. Each new group received a special welcome from the Holy Spirit. Thus, Samaritans (8:14–19), Gentiles (10:44–48), and believers from the Old Covenant (19:1–7) were added to the church, and the unity of the church was established. To demonstrate that unity, it was necessary to have some replication in each instance of what had occurred at Pentecost with the believing Jews, such as the presence of the apostles and the coming of the Spirit manifested through speaking in the languages of Pentecost.

3. How does the baptism with the Holy Spirit (1 Cor. 12:13) relate to the Holy Spirit's activities in the Book of Acts?

Acts describes a number of occasions in which the Holy Spirit "fell on" or "filled" or "came upon" people (2:4; 10:44; 19:6). Peter identifies these actions by God as a fulfillment of Joel's prophecy (Joel 2:28–32). Viewed from the perspective of the entire NT, these experiences were neither the same nor replacements for what John the Baptist (Mark 1:8) and Paul described as the baptism with the Holy Spirit (1 Cor. 12:13). The baptism with the Spirit is the one-time act by which God places believers into His body. The filling, on the other hand, is a repeated reality of Spirit-controlled behavior that God commands believers to maintain (Eph. 5:18). Peter and others who experienced that special filling on Pentecost day (2:4) were filled with the Spirit again (4:8,31; 6:5; 7:55) and so boldly spoke the Word of God. That was just the beginning. The fullness of the Spirit affects all areas of life, not just speaking boldly (Eph. 5:18–33).

FURTHER STUDY ON ACTS

1. What event from the Book of Acts would you most like to have attended yourself? Why?
2. How did the church begin? How did it grow?
3. What different kinds of opposition did the early Christians face?
4. In what different ways did those Christians share their faith?
5. How was the Holy Spirit acknowledged and welcomed in the early church?
6. In what ways are you continuing to carry the gospel to your Jerusalem, Judea, Samaria, and the ends of the earth (Acts 1:8)?

The Career of the Apostle Paul

Origin:	Tarsus in Cilicia (Acts 22:3) Tribe of Benjamin (Phil. 3:5)
Training:	Learned tentmaking (Acts 18:3) Studied under Gamaliel (Acts 22:3)
Early Religion:	Hebrew and Pharisee (Phil. 3:5) Persecuted Christians (Acts 8:1-3; Phil. 3:6)
Salvation:	Met the risen Christ on the road to Damascus (Acts 9:1-8) Received the infilling of the Holy Spirit on the street called Straight (Acts 9:17)
Called to Missions:	Church work at Antioch was instructed by the Holy Spirit to send out Paul to the work (Acts 13:1-3) Carried the gospel to the Gentiles (Gal. 2:7-10)
Roles:	Spoke up for the church at Antioch at the council of Jerusalem (Acts 15:1-35) Opposed Peter (Gal. 2:11-21) Disputed with Barnabas about John Mark (Acts 15:36-41)
Achievements:	Three extended missionary journeys (Acts 13-20) Founded numerous churches in Asia Minor, Greece and possibly Spain (Rom. 15:24,28) Wrote letters to numerous churches and various individuals which now make up one-fourth of our New Testament
End of Life:	Following arrest in Jerusalem, was sent to Rome (Acts 21:27; 28:16-31) According to Christian tradition, released from prison allowing further missionary work in Macedonia; rearrested, imprisoned again in Rome, and beheaded outside of the city

Paul's First and Second Journeys

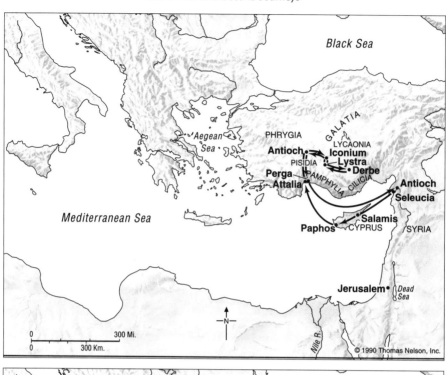

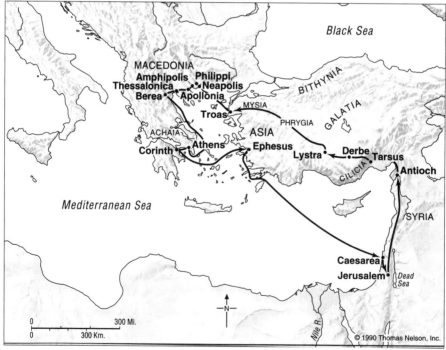

Paul's Third and Fourth Journeys

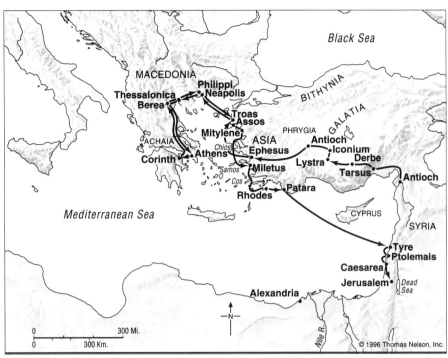

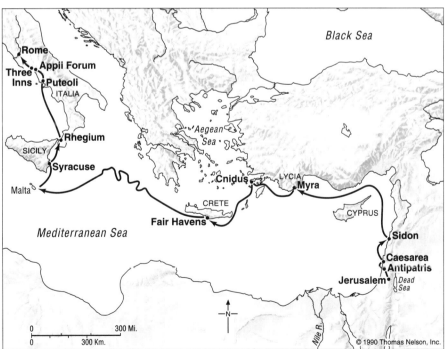

Major Sermons in Acts

Several important sermons and speeches are recorded in the Book of Acts. Over twenty are included with the majority coming from Peter (7 total) and Paul (11 total). Below are listed the more significant, together with the theme and text location.

Speech	Theme	Biblical Reference
Peter to crowds at Pentecost	Peter's explanation of the meaning of Pentecost	Acts 2:14-40
Peter to crowds at the temple	The Jewish people should repent for crucifying the Messiah	Acts 3:12–26
Peter to the Sanhedrin	Testimony that a helpless man was healed by the power of Jesus	Acts 4:5-12
Stephen to the Sanhedrin	Stephen's rehearsal of Jewish history, accusing the Jews of killing the Messiah	Acts 7
Peter to Gentiles	Gentiles can be saved in the same manner as Jews	Acts 10:28-47
Peter to church at Jerusalem	Peter's testimony of his experiences at Joppa and a defense of his ministry to the Gentiles	Acts 11:4–18
Paul to synagogue at Antioch	Jesus was the Messiah in fulfillment of Old Testament prophecies	Acts 13:16-41
Peter to Jerusalem council	Salvation by grace available to all	Acts 15:7–11
Peter to Jerusalem council	Gentile converts do not require circumcision	Acts 15:13-21
Paul to Ephesian elders	Remain faithful in spite of false teachers and persecution	Acts 20:17–35
Paul to crowd at Jerusalem	Paul's statement of his conversion and his mission to the Gentiles	Acts 22:1-21
Paul to Sanhedrin	Paul's defense, declaring himself a Pharisee and a Roman citizen	Acts 23:1–6
Paul to King Agrippa	Paul's statement of his conversion and his zeal for the gospel	Acts 26
Paul to the Jewish leaders at Rome	Paul's statement about his Jewish heritage	Acts 28:17–20

The Ministry of the Apostles

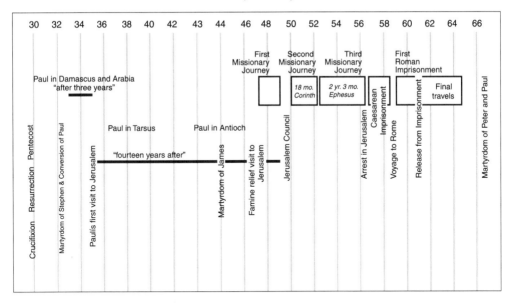

Ministries of the Holy Spirit

Baptismal Medium	1 Corinthians 12:13
Calls to Ministry	Acts 13:2–4
Channel of Divine Revelation	2 Samuel 23:2; Nehemiah 9:30; Zechariah 7:12; John 14:17
Empowers	Exodus 31:1,2; Judges 13:25; Acts 1:8
Fills	Luke 4:1; Acts 2:4; Ephesians 5:18
Guarantees	2 Corinthians 1:22; 5:5; Ephesians 1:14
Guards	2 Timothy 1:14
Helps	John 14:16,26; 15:26; 16:7
Illuminates	1 Corinthians 2:10–13
Indwells	Romans 8:9–11; 1 Corinthians 3:16; 6:19
Intercedes	Romans 8:26,27
Produces Fruit	Galatians 5:22,23
Provides Spiritual Character	Galatians 5:16,18,25
Regenerates	John 3:5,6,8
Restrains/Convicts of Sin	Genesis 6:3; John 16:8–10; Acts 7:51
Sanctifies	Romans 15:16; 1 Corinthians 6:11; 2 Thessalonians 2:13
Seals	2 Corinthians 1:22; Ephesians 1:14; 4:30
Selects Overseers	Acts 20:28
Source of Fellowship	2 Corinthians 13:14; Philippians 2:1
Source of Liberty	2 Corinthians 3:17,18
Source of Power	Ephesians 3:16
Source of Unity	Ephesians 4:3,4
Source of Spiritual Gifts	1 Corinthians 12:4–11
Teaches	John 14:26; Acts 15:28; 1 John 2:20,27

The Nations of Pentecost

Pentecost, a Jewish feast also known as the Feast of Weeks, marked the completion of the barley harvest. On this annual holiday about 50 days after the resurrection of Jesus, Jewish people from throughout the Roman Empire were gathered in the city of Jerusalem to observe this great religious holiday. When the Holy Spirit was poured out on the apostles, they began to speak with "other tongues," and these people from other nations understood them perfectly (Acts 2:5–13). This map shows the different regions of the Roman Empire represented in Jerusalem on the Day of Pentecost.

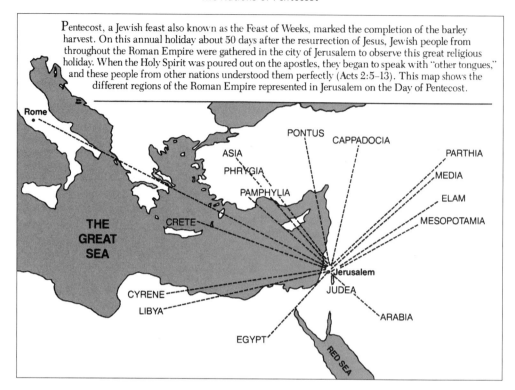

ROMANS
S u m m a r y   o f   C h r i s t i a n   D o c t r i n e

TITLE
This epistle's name comes from its original recipients: the members of the church in Rome, the capital of the Roman Empire (1:7).

AUTHOR AND DATE
No one disputes that the apostle Paul wrote Romans. Like his namesake, Israel's first king (*Saul* was Paul's Hebrew name; *Paul* his Greek name), Paul was from the tribe of Benjamin (Phil. 3:5). He was also a Roman citizen (Acts 16:37; 22:25). Paul was born about the time of Christ's birth, in Tarsus (Acts 9:11), an important city (Acts 21:39) in the Roman province of Cilicia, located in Asia Minor (modern Turkey). He spent much of his early life in Jerusalem as a student of the celebrated rabbi Gamaliel (Acts 22:3). Like his father before him, Paul was a Pharisee (Acts 23:6), a member of the strictest Jewish sect (cf. Phil. 3:5).

Miraculously converted while on his way to Damascus (ca. A.D. 33–34) to arrest Christians in that city, Paul immediately began proclaiming the gospel message (Acts 9:20). After narrowly escaping from Damascus with his life (Acts 9:23–25; 2 Cor. 11:32, 33), Paul spent three years in Nabatean Arabia, south and east of the Dead Sea (Gal. 1:17, 18). During that time, he received much of his theological teaching as direct revelation from the Lord (Gal. 1:11,12).

More than any other individual, Paul was responsible for the spread of Christianity throughout the Roman Empire. He made three missionary journeys through much of the Mediterranean world, tirelessly preaching the gospel he had once sought to destroy (Acts 26:9). After he returned to Jerusalem bearing an offering for the needy in the church there, he was falsely accused by some Jews (Acts 21:27–29), savagely beaten by an angry mob (Acts 21:30,31), and arrested by the Romans. Though two Roman governors, Felix and Festus, as well as Herod Agrippa, did not find him guilty of any crime, pressure from the Jewish leaders kept Paul in Roman custody. After two years, the apostle exercised his right as a Roman citizen and appealed his case to Caesar. After a harrowing trip (Acts 27–28), including a violent, two-week storm at sea that culminated in a shipwreck, Paul reached Rome. Eventually released for a brief period of ministry, he was arrested again and suffered martyrdom at Rome in ca. A.D. 65–67 (cf. 2 Tim. 4:6).

Though physically unimpressive (cf. 2 Cor. 10:10; Gal. 4:14), Paul possessed an inner strength granted him through the Holy Spirit's power (Phil. 4:13). The grace of God proved sufficient to provide for his every need (2 Cor. 12:9, 10), enabling this noble servant of Christ to successfully finish his spiritual race (2 Tim. 4:7).

Paul wrote Romans from Corinth, as the references to Phoebe (Rom. 16:1, Cenchrea was Corinth's port), Gaius (Rom. 16:23), and Erastus (Rom. 16:23)—all of whom were associated with Corinth—indicate. The apostle wrote the letter toward the close of his third missionary journey (most likely in A.D. 56), as he prepared to leave for Palestine with an offering for the poor believers in the Jerusalem church (Rom. 15:25). Phoebe was given the great responsibility of delivering this letter to the Roman believers (16:1,2).

The City of Rome

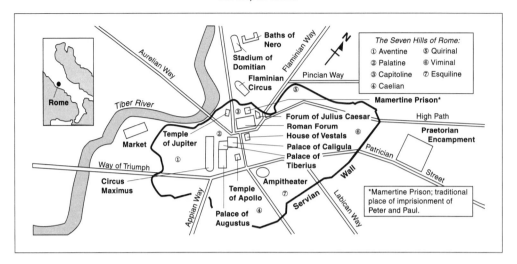

BACKGROUND AND SETTING

Rome was the capital and most important city of the Roman Empire. It was founded in 753 B.C., but is not mentioned in Scripture until NT times. Rome is located along the banks of the Tiber River, about fifteen miles from the Mediterranean Sea. Until an artificial harbor was built at nearby Ostia, Rome's main harbor was Puteoli, some 150 miles away. In Paul's day, the city had a population of over one million people, many of whom were slaves. Rome boasted magnificent buildings, such as the Emperor's palace, the Circus Maximus, and the Forum, but its beauty was marred by the slums in which so many lived. According to tradition, Paul was martyred outside Rome on the Ostian Way during Nero's reign (A.D. 54–68).

Some of those converted on the Day of Pentecost probably founded the church at Rome (cf. Acts 2:10). Paul had long sought to visit the Roman church, but had been prevented from doing so (1:13). In God's providence, Paul's inability to visit Rome gave the world this inspired masterpiece of gospel doctrine.

Paul's primary purpose in writing Romans was to teach the great truths of the gospel of grace to believers who had never received apostolic instruction. The letter also introduced him to a church where he was personally unknown, but hoped to visit soon for several important reasons: to edify the believers (1:11); to preach the gospel (1:15); and to get to know the Roman Christians, so they could encourage him (1:12; 15:32), better pray for him (15:30), and help him with his planned ministry in Spain (15:28).

Unlike some of Paul's other epistles (e.g., 1, 2 Cor., Gal.), his purpose for writing was not to correct incorrect theology or rebuke ungodly living. The Roman church was doctrinally sound, but, like all churches, it was in need of the rich theological teaching and practical instruction this letter provides.

KEY PEOPLE IN ROMANS
Paul—apostle and author of the Book of Romans (1:1–16:22)
Phoebe—deaconess of the church at Cenchrea; trusted by Paul to deliver his letter (the Book of Romans) to the Roman believers (16:1–2)

HISTORICAL AND THEOLOGICAL THEMES
Since Romans is primarily a work of theological teaching, it contains little historical material. Paul does use such familiar OT figures as Abraham (chap. 4), David (4:6–8), Adam (5:12–21), Sarah (9:9), Rebekah (9:10), Jacob and Esau (9:10–13), and Pharaoh (9:17) as illustrations. He also recounts some of Israel's history (chaps. 9–11). Chapter 16 provides insightful glimpses into the nature and character of the first-century church and its members.

The overarching theme of Romans is the righteousness that comes from God: the glorious truth that God justifies guilty, condemned sinners by grace alone through faith in Christ alone. Chapters 1–11 present the theological truths of that doctrine, while chaps. 12–16 detail its practical outworking in the lives of individual believers and the life of the whole church. Some specific theological topics include principles of spiritual leadership (1:8–15); God's wrath against sinful mankind (1:18–32); principles of divine judgment (2:1–16); the universality of sin (3:9–20); an explanation and defense of justification by faith alone (3:21–4:25); the security of salvation (5:1–11); the transference of Adam's sin to all humanity (5:12–21); sanctification (chaps. 6–8); sovereign election (chap. 9); God's plan for Israel (chap. 11); spiritual gifts and practical godliness (chap. 12); the believer's responsibility to human government (chap. 13); and principles of Christian liberty (14:1–15:12).

Kingdom-Style Mentoring

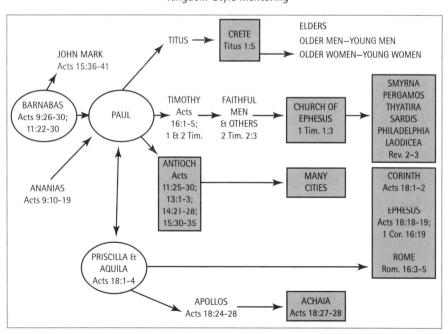

KEY DOCTRINES IN ROMANS

Mankind's sinfulness—Sin separates every human from God; only Jesus Christ can reconcile God and man (3:9–20; Gen. 3:6,7; 18:20; Ex. 32:31; Deut. 9:7; 1 Kin. 8:46; 14:16; Ps. 38:18; Prov. 20:9; Eccl. 7:20; Jer. 2:22; Rom. 5:12; 2 Cor. 5:21; Heb. 4:15; 7:26)

Justification by faith—Complete freedom from judgment and the bondage of sin comes by faith alone in Jesus Christ (1:16,17; 3:21–4:25; 5:1–2,18; Lev. 18:5; Is. 45:25; 50:8; 53:11; Jer. 23:6; Hab. 2:4; John 5:24; Acts 13:39; 1 Cor. 6:11; Gal. 2:14–21; 3:11; 5:4; Titus 3:7; James 2:10)

Sanctification—Through Christ's atonement, believers are glorified and set apart for the service of God (6:1–8:39; 15:16; Ps. 4:3; Ezek. 37:28; Acts 20:32; 26:18; 2 Cor. 6:17; Eph. 5:26,27; 1 Thess. 4:3,4; 5:23; 2 Thess. 2:13; 2 Tim. 2:21; Heb. 2:11; 13:12; 1 Pet. 1:2; Jude 1:1)

Reconciliation—The sacrifice of Jesus Christ renews the relationship between God and man (5:1,10–11; Lev. 8:15; 16:20; Dan. 9:24; Is. 53:5; Matt. 5:24–26; 2 Cor. 5:18–20; Eph. 2:14–16; Col. 1:20–22; 2:14; Heb. 2:17)

GOD'S CHARACTER IN ROMANS

God is accessible—5:2
God is eternal—1:20
God is forgiving—3:25
God is glorious—3:23; 6:4
God is good—2:4
God is incorruptible—1:23
God is just—2:11; 3:4,26
God is longsuffering—2:4,5; 3:25; 9:22
God is loving—5:5,8; 8:39; 9:11–13
God is merciful—9:15,18
God is powerful—1:16,20; 9:21,22
God is a promise keeper—1:1,2; 4:13,16,20; 9:4,8; 15:8
God is provident—8:28; 11:33
God is reconciling—5:1,10
God is righteous—2:5; 3:25,26
God is unsearchable—11:33
God is wise—11:33; 16:27
God is wrathful—1:18; 2:5,6,8; 3:5,6; 5:9; 9:18,20,22

INTERPRETIVE CHALLENGES

As the preeminent doctrinal work in the NT, Romans naturally contains a number of difficult passages. Paul's discussion of the tainting of humanity through Adam's sin (5:12–21) is one of the deepest, most profound theological passages in all of Scripture. The nature of mankind's union with Adam, and how his sin was transferred to the human race has always been the subject of intense debate (see Answers to Tough Questions). Bible students also disagree on whether 7:7–25 describes Paul's experience as a believer or unbeliever, or whether it is merely a literary device not intended to be autobiographical at all (see Answers to Tough Questions). The closely related doctrines of election (8:28–30) and the sovereignty of God (9:6–29) have confused many believers (see Answers

CHRIST IN . . . ROMANS

THE BOOK OF ROMANS, functioning primarily as a doctrinal work, presents Christ as the Redeemer of mankind. Paul declares that faith in Christ alone bridges the chasm between the almighty God and sinful humanity. Thus, man is justified through the work of Christ on the cross.

to Tough Questions). Other questions include whether chaps. 9–11 teach that God has a future plan for the nation of Israel and the issue of believer's obedience to human government (13:1–7).

OUTLINE

     I. Greetings and Introduction (1:1–15)
     II. Theme (1:16,17)
     III. Condemnation: The Need of God's Righteousness (1:18–3:20)
          A. Unrighteous Gentiles (1:18–32)
          B. Unrighteous Jews (2:1–3:8)
          C. Unrighteous Mankind (3:9–20)
     IV. Justification: The Provision of God's Righteousness (3:21–5:21)
          A. The Source of Righteousness (3:21–31)
          B. The Example of Righteousness (4:1–25)
          C. The Blessings of Righteousness (5:1–11)
          D. The Imputation of Righteousness (5:12–21)
     V. Sanctification: The Demonstration of God's Righteousness (6:1–8:39)
     VI. Restoration: Israel's Reception of God's Righteousness (9:1–11:36)
     VII. Application: The Behavior of God's Righteousness (12:1–15:13)
     VIII. Conclusion, Greetings, and Benediction (15:14–16:27)

ANSWERS TO TOUGH QUESTIONS

1. Who was Paul the apostle, and why does he seem to have two names?

Paul (Greek name) the apostle was also known as Saul, which was his Hebrew name. Along with his double name, Paul was also able to exercise dual citizenship as a Jewish descendant from the tribe of Benjamin (Phil. 3:5) and as a Roman (Acts 16:37; 22:25). Paul was born about the time of Christ's birth, in Tarsus, located in modern Turkey (Acts 9:11).

More than any other individual, Paul was responsible for the spread of Christianity throughout the Roman Empire. He made three missionary journeys along the north side of the Mediterranean Sea, tirelessly preaching the gospel he had once tried to destroy (Acts 26:9). Eventually he was arrested in Jerusalem (Acts 21:27–31), appealed for a hearing before Caesar, and finally reached Rome (chapters 27–28). Later, he was released for a short time of ministry, then arrested again and martyred at Rome in about A.D. 65 to 67. (See Author and Date above for further discussion.)

Romans

Justification: Greek *dikaiōsis*—4:25; 5:18—derived from the Greek verb *dikaiō*, meaning "to acquit" or "to declare righteous," used by Paul in 4:2,5; 5:1. It is a legal term used of a favorable verdict in a trial. The word depicts a courtroom setting, with God presiding as the Judge, determining the faithfulness of each person to the law. In the first section of Romans, Paul makes it clear that no one can withstand God's judgment (3:9–20). The law was not given to justify sinners but to expose their sin. To remedy this deplorable situation, God sent His Son to die for our sins in our place. When we believe in Jesus, God imputes His righteousness to us, and we are declared righteous before God. In this way, God demonstrates that He is both a righteous Judge and the One who declares us righteous, our Justifier (3:26).

Reconciliation: Greek *katallagē*—5:11; 11:15—basically means "change" or "exchange." In the context of relationships between people, the term implies a change in attitude on the part of both individuals, a change from enmity to friendship. When used to describe the relationship existing between God and a person, the term implies the change of attitude on the part of both a person and God. The need for change in the sinful ways of a human being is obvious, but some argue that no change is needed on the part of God. Yet inherent in the doctrine of justification is the changed attitude of God toward the sinner. God declares a person who was formerly His enemy to be righteous before Him.

Hope: Greek *elpis*—4:18; 5:2; 8:20,24; 12:12; 15:4,13—denotes "confident expectation" or "anticipation," not "wishful thinking" as in common parlance. The use of the word *hope* in this context is unusual and ironic, for it suggests that the Gentiles, who know nothing or little about the Messiah, were anticipating His coming. However, we need only think of Cornelius (Acts 10) to realize that some Gentiles had anticipated the coming of the Jewish Messiah. Jesus was sent not only for the salvation of the Jews, but also for the Gentiles. Since God is the Author of our salvation, we can call Him the God of hope for He has given us hope (15:13).

Law: Greek *nomos*—2:12,27; 3:27; 4:15; 7:1,7,23; 9:31; 13:10—means an inward principle of action, either good or evil, operating with the regularity of a law. The term also designates a standard for a person's life. The apostle Paul described three such laws. The first is called "the law of sin" which was operating through his flesh, causing him to sin. Paul, like all other believers, needed another law to overcome "the law of sin." This is "the law of the Spirit of life in Christ Jesus," which makes us "free from the law of sin and death" (8:2). By following this "law," believers can actually fulfill the righteous requirements of "God's law" (8:4). God's law is the standard for human action that corresponds to the righteous nature of God.

2. When Paul writes in Romans 5:12 that "through one man sin entered the world, and death through sin, and thus death spread to all men, because all sinned," what does he mean?

Paul's discussion of the perpetuation of Adam's sin (5:12–21) is one of the deepest, most significant theological passages in all of Scripture. It establishes the basis for Paul's teaching that one man's (Christ's) death can provide salvation for many. To prove his point, he uses Adam to develop the principle that it is possible for one man's actions to inevitably affect many other people.

In this passage, the word *sin* does not refer to a particular sin, but to the inherent propensity to sin that invaded the human realm through Adam. People became sinners by nature. Adam passed on to all his descendants that inherently sinful nature he possessed as a result of his first disobedience. He caught the infection; the rest of us inherit it. The sin nature is present from the moment of conception (Ps. 51:5), making it impossible for any person to live in a way that pleases God.

When Adam sinned, his sin transformed his inner nature and brought spiritual death and depravity that was then passed on to his descendants (all of humanity). Because all humanity existed in the loins of Adam, and have through procreation inherited his fallenness and depravity, it can be said that all sinned in him. Therefore, humans are not sinners because they sin, but, rather, they sin because they are sinners.

3. In verses like Romans 5:12 and 6:23, to what kind of death is Paul referring?
The word *death* has three distinct manifestations in biblical terminology:

- Spiritual death or separation from God (Eph. 1:1–2,4,18)
- Physical death (Heb. 9:27)
- Eternal death (also called the second death), which includes not only eternal separation from God, but eternal torment in the lake of fire (Rev. 20:11–15)

When sin entered the human race through Adam, all these aspects of death came with it. Adam was not originally subject to death, but through his sin, death became a grim certainty for him and his posterity. The death referred to in Romans 6:23 includes the first and third descriptions above. That verse establishes two unquestionable truths: (1) spiritual death and eternal separation from God make up the paycheck for every person's slavery to sin; and (2) eternal life is a free gift God gives undeserving sinners who believe in His Son (Eph. 2:8,9).

4. In Romans 7:7–25, what is Paul's actual perspective? Is he describing his own experience as a believer or unbeliever, or is his style simply a literary device?
Paul uses the personal pronoun *I* throughout this passage, using his own experience as an example of what is true of unredeemed humanity (7:7–12) and of true Christians (7:13–25). Some interpret this chronicle of Paul's inner conflict as describing his life before Christ. They point out that Paul describes the person as "sold under sin" (7:14), as having "nothing good" in him (7:18), and as a "wretched man" trapped in a "body of death" (7:24). Those descriptions seem to contradict Paul's earlier description of the believer (6:2,6–7,11,17–18,22).

MEANWHILE, IN OTHER PARTS OF THE WORLD...
Buddhism is introduced into China by the emperor MingTi.

It is correct, however, to understand Paul here to be speaking about a believer. This person desires to obey God's law and hates sin (7:15,19,21). He is humble, recognizing that nothing good dwells in his humanness (7:18). He sees sin in himself, but not as all that is there (7:17,20–22). And he serves Jesus Christ with his mind (7:25). Paul has already established that none of those attitudes ever describe the unsaved (1:18–21,32; 3:10–20). Paul's use of the present tense verbs in 7:14–25 strongly supports the idea that he was describing his current experience as a Christian.

Even those who agree that Paul was speaking as a genuine believer, however, still find room for disagreement. Some see a carnal, fleshly Christian under the influence of old habits. Others see a legalistic Christian, frustrated by his feeble attempts in his own power to please God by keeping the Mosaic Law. But the personal pronoun *I* refers to the apostle Paul, a standard of spiritual health and maturity. This leads to the conclusion that Paul, in 7:7–25, must be describing all Christians—even the most spiritual and mature—who, when they honestly evaluate themselves against the righteous standard of God's law, realize how far short they fall. Notice, particularly, Paul's honesty and transparency in the four laments (7:14–17,18–20,21–23, 24–25).

5. Explain the process Paul refers to in Romans 8:28–30 and 9:6–29. What do words like *called, foreknew, predestined,* and *elect* tell us about our standing with God?

With these words, God reveals in human terms His divine role in the process of salvation. Paul's description offends the human spirit because it minimizes our role. Yet only those who see their own helplessness in the face of sin can come to see how gracious God has been in acting and choosing ahead of time. We never surprise God; He always anticipates us! "But God demonstrates His own love toward us, in that while we were still sinners, Christ died for us" (Rom. 5:8).

The word *called* refers not only to God's general invitation to believe the gospel, but also His drawing to Himself all those He has chosen for salvation.

The term *foreknew* (8:29) does not simply refer to God's omniscience—that in eternity past He knew who would come to Christ. Rather, it speaks of a predetermined choice by God to set His love on us and establish an intimate relationship. The term *election* (9:11) refers to the same action on God's part (1 Pet. 1:1,2,20). Salvation is not initiated by human choice. Even faith is a gift of God (Rom. 1:16; John 6:37; Eph. 2:8,9).

The term *predestined* (8:29) literally means "to mark out, appoint, or determine beforehand." Those God chooses, He destines for His chosen end, that is, likeness to His Son (Eph. 1:4–5,11). The goal of God's predestined purpose for His own is that they would be made like Jesus Christ.

The reality and security of our standing with God rests ultimately in His character and decision, not ours. Paul summarized his teaching about the believer's security in Christ with a blaze of questions and answers that haunt believers. They reach their peak with "Who shall separate us from the love of Christ" (8:35)? Paul's answer is an almost poetic expression of praise for God's grace in bringing salvation to completion for all who are chosen and believe. It is a hymn of security.

FURTHER STUDY ON ROMANS

1. What major themes did Paul introduce in the first chapter of Romans?
2. How did Paul discuss the subject of sin both personally and in relation to the world at large?
3. In what ways do the following verses (3:23; 5:8; 6:23; 10:9–10) outline the gospel mentioned in Romans 1:16?
4. How do the last five chapters of Romans differ from the first eleven?
5. What key words have you had to take time to understand in your study of Romans?
6. Summarize what Paul writes about the character and work God in Romans.
7. In what ways has the message of Romans made a difference in your own life?

FIRST
CORINTHIANS
Discipline for an
Undisciplined Church

TITLE

The letter is named for the city of Corinth, where the church to whom it was written was located. With the exception of personal epistles addressed to Timothy, Titus, and Philemon, all of Paul's letters bear the name of the city where the church addressed existed.

AUTHOR AND DATE

As indicated in the first verse, the epistle was written by the apostle Paul, whose authorship cannot be seriously questioned. Pauline authorship has been universally accepted by the church since the first-century, when 1 Corinthians was penned. Internally, the apostle claimed to have written the epistle (1:1,13; 3:4–6; 4:15; 16:21). Externally, this correspondence has been acknowledged as genuine since A.D. 95 by Clement of Rome, who was writing to the Corinthian church. Other early Christian leaders who authenticated Paul as author include Ignatius (ca. A.D. 110), Polycarp (ca. A.D. 135), and Tertullian (ca. A.D. 200).

This epistle was most likely written in the first half of A.D. 55 from Ephesus (16:8,9, 19) while Paul was on his third missionary journey. The apostle intended to remain on at Ephesus to complete his three-year stay (Acts 20:31) until Pentecost (May/June) A.D. 55 (16:8). Then he hoped to winter (A.D. 55–56) at Corinth (16:6; Acts 20:2). His departure for Corinth was anticipated even as he wrote (4:19; 11:34; 16:8).

BACKGROUND AND SETTING

The city of Corinth was located in southern Greece, in what was the Roman province of Achaia, about forty-five miles west of Athens. This lower part, the Peloponnesus, is connected to the rest of Greece by a four-mile-wide isthmus, which is bounded on the east by the Saronic Gulf and on the west by the Gulf of Corinth. Corinth is near the middle of the isthmus and is prominently situated on a high plateau. For many centuries, all north-south land traffic in that area had to pass through or near this ancient city. Since travel by sea around the Peloponnesus involved a 250-mile voyage that was dangerous and obviously time consuming, most captains carried their ships on skids or rollers across the isthmus directly past Corinth. Corinth understandably prospered as a major trade city, not only for most of Greece but for much of the Mediterranean area, including North Africa, Italy, and Asia Minor. A canal across the isthmus was begun by the emperor Nero during the first-century A.D., but was not completed until near the end of the nineteenth century.

The Isthmian games, one of the two most famous athletic events of that day (the other being the Olympian games), was hosted by Corinth, causing more people-traffic. Even by the pagan standards of its own culture, Corinth became so morally corrupt that its very name became synonymous with debauchery and moral depravity. To "corinthianize" came to represent gross immorality and drunken debauchery. In 6:9,10, Paul lists some of the specific sins for which the city was noted and which formerly had characterized many believers in the church there. Tragically, some of the worst sins were still found among some church members. One of those sins, incest, was condemned even by most pagan Gentiles (5:1).

Like most ancient Greek cities, Corinth had an acropolis (lit. "a high city"), which rose 2,000 feet and was used both for defense and for worship. The most prominent edifice on the acropolis was a temple to Aphrodite, the Greek goddess of love. Some 1,000 priestesses, who were "religious" prostitutes, lived and worked there and came down into the city in the evening to offer their services to male citizens and foreign visitors.

The church in Corinth was founded by Paul on his second missionary journey (Acts 18:1ff.). As usual, his ministry began in the synagogue, where he was assisted by two Jewish believers, Priscilla and Aquila, with whom he lived for a while and who were fellow tradesmen. Soon after, Silas and Timothy joined them and Paul began preaching even more intensely in the synagogue. When most of the Jews resisted the gospel, he left the synagogue, but not before Crispus, the leader of the synagogue, his family, and many other Corinthians were converted (Acts 18:5–8).

CHRIST IN . . . 1 CORINTHIANS

PAUL'S LETTER TO THE CORINTHIANS helped the believers mature in their understanding of Christ and corrected some of the false teachings that had flourished. Paul stressed the reality of Christ's death and resurrection to people who had begun to deny the resurrection of the dead (15:12–28). Sanctification through Christ is also portrayed as an ongoing process by which believers strive for godliness in their daily lives (1:2,30).

After ministering in Corinth for over a year and a half (Acts 18:11), Paul was brought before a Roman tribunal by some of the Jewish leaders. Because the charges were strictly religious and not civil, the proconsul, Gallio, dismissed the case. Shortly thereafter, Paul took Priscilla and Aquila with him to Ephesus. From there he returned to Israel (vv. 18–22).

Unable to fully break with the culture from which it came, the church at Corinth was exceptionally factional, showing its carnality and immaturity. After the gifted Apollos had ministered in the church for some time, a group of his admirers established a clique and had little to do with the rest of the church. Another group developed that was loyal to Paul, another claimed special allegiance to Peter (Cephas), and still another to Christ alone (see 1:10–13; 3:1–9).

The most serious problem of the Corinthian church was worldliness, an unwillingness to divorce the culture around them. Most of the believers could not consistently separate themselves from their old, selfish, immoral, and pagan ways. It became necessary for Paul to write to correct this, as well as to command the faithful Christians not only to break fellowship with the disobedient and unrepentant members, but to put those members out of the church (5:9–13).

Before he wrote this inspired letter, Paul had written the church other correspondence (see 5:9), which was also corrective in nature. Because a copy of that letter has never been discovered, it has been referred to as "the lost epistle." There was another non-canonical letter after 1 Corinthians, usually called "the severe letter" (2 Cor. 2:4).

KEY PEOPLE IN 1 CORINTHIANS

Paul—author of the letters to the Corinthian church (1:1–16:24)

Timothy—fellow missionary sent by Paul to assist the Corinthian church (4:17; 16:10,11)

Members of Chloe's household—informed Paul of the divisions among the Corinthian Christians (1:11)

HISTORICAL AND THEOLOGICAL THEMES

Although the major thrust of this epistle is correcting behavior rather than teaching doctrine, Paul gives decisive teaching on many doctrines that directly relate to the matters of sin and righteousness. In one way or another, wrong living always stems from wrong belief. Sexual sins for example, including divorce, are inevitably related to disobeying God's plan for marriage and the family (7:1–40). Proper worship is determined by such things as recognition of God's holy character (3:17), the spiritual identity of the church (12:12–27) and pure partaking of the Lord's Supper (11:17–34). It is not possible for the church to be edified faithfully and effectively unless believers understand and exercise their spiritual gifts (12:1–14:40). The importance of the doctrine of the Resurrection, of course, cannot be overestimated because if there is no resurrection of the dead, then Christ is not risen. And if Christ is not risen, then preaching is empty and so is faith (15:13,14).

In addition to those themes, Paul deals briefly with God's judgment of believers, which if rightly understood, will produce right motives for godly living (see 3:13–15). The right understanding of idols and of false gods, in general, was to help the immature Corinthians think maturely about such things as eating meat that had been sacrificed to idols (8:1–11:1). The right understanding and expression of genuine, godly love was mandatory for right use the gifts and even for right knowledge about all the things of God (13:1–13).

So Paul deals with the Cross, divine wisdom and human wisdom, the work of the Spirit in illumination, carnality, eternal rewards, the transformation of

---

KEY WORDS IN

1 Corinthians

Resurrection: Greek *anastasis*—15:12,13,21,42—literally, "resurrection out from among the dead ones." This is the wording in the first half of 15:12 and in other verses (see Acts 17:31; 1 Pet. 1:3). When Scripture speaks of the resurrection in general, commonly the phrase is "a resurrection of dead ones." This is the wording in the second half of 15:12 (see also 15:13,42). In Romans 1:4, Christ's resurrection is spoken of as "a resurrection of dead ones." The same terminology is used in 15:21, where the Greek text literally reads: "For since through a man death came, so also through a Man came a resurrection of dead persons." This shows that Christ's resurrection included the resurrection of believers to eternal life. When He arose, many arose with Him, for they were united with Him in His resurrection (see Rom. 6:4,5; Eph. 2:6; Col. 3:1).

Spiritual Gifts: Greek *charisma*—12:4,9,28,30–31—closely akin to the word *charis,* which means "grace" or "favor"; *charisma* denotes "that which is graciously given." Paul used the term *charisma* synonymously with the Greek term *ta pneumatika*—literally, "the spiritual things"—because the things graciously given are spiritual gifts. These gifts were given by the Lord to various individuals in the church so as to enliven the meetings and to edify the believers in the church body. Each and every member has been gifted with at least one kind of *charisma,* whether it be the gift of teaching, prophesying, exercising faith, healing, performing miracles, discerning spirits, speaking in tongues, interpreting tongues, or other gifts.

salvation, sanctification, the nature of Christ, union with Him, the divine role for women, marriage and divorce, Spirit baptism, indwelling and gifting, the unity of the church in one body, the theology of love, and the doctrine of resurrection. All these establish foundational truth for godly behavior.

KEY DOCTRINES IN 1 CORINTHIANS

Sexual sin—disobedience to God's plan for marriage and the family (6:13,18; 7:1–40; 2 Sam. 11:1–4; Prov. 2:16–19; Matt. 5:32; 19:9; Mark 7:21; Acts 15:20; Rom. 13:13; Gal. 5:19; Eph. 5:5; Col. 3:5; Heb. 12:16; Jude 1:4,7)

Proper worship—God deserves our wholehearted worship and praise. Proper worship includes recognition of God's holy character (3:17); pure partaking of the Lord's Supper (11:17–34); and spiritual identification with the church (12:12–27; Matt. 2:1,2; 2:11; 28:16,17; John 4:20–24; 9:30–38; Rom. 1:25; Heb. 1:6; Rev. 4:10,11)

Spiritual gifts—divine enablements for ministry that the Holy Spirit gives in some measure to all believers (12:1–14:40; Is. 35:4–6; Joel 2:28,29; Matt. 7:22,23; 12:28; 24:24; Acts 2:1–4; 8:17–20; 10:44–46; 19:6; 1 Thess. 5:20; 2 Thess. 2:9; 1 Tim. 4:14; 2 Tim. 1:6; Rev. 13:13,14)

Resurrection of Jesus—central to the hope of Christians; without the Resurrection, faith in Christ would be useless (15:4,12–28; Pss. 2:7; 16:10; Is. 26:19; Matt. 20:19; Mark 9:9; 14:28; Luke 24:45,46; John 2:19–22; 10:18; Acts 1:3; 2:24; 3:15; 13:33–35; Rom. 1:4; 4:25; 6:4; 8:11,34; Eph. 1:20; Phil. 3:10; Col. 2:12; 2 Tim. 2:8; 1 Pet. 1:3,21; 3:18; Rev. 1:18)

GOD'S CHARACTER IN 1 CORINTHIANS

God is faithful—1:9; 10:13
God is glorious—11:7
God is holy—6:9–10
God is powerful—1:18,24; 2:5; 3:6–8; 6:14
God is unified—8:4,6
God is wise—1:24; 2:7
God is wrathful—10:22

INTERPRETIVE CHALLENGES

By far the most controversial issue for interpretation is that of the sign gifts discussed in chaps. 12–14, particularly the gifts of miracles and speaking in tongues. Many believe that all the gifts are permanent, so that the gift of speaking in tongues will cease (13:8) only when the gifts of prophecy and of knowledge cease, namely, when that which is perfect has come (13:10). Those who maintain that tongues and miracles are still valid spiritual gifts in the church today believe they should be exercised with the same power by which they were exercised in NT times by the apostles. Others believe the miraculous sign gifts have ceased. (This controversy is discussed further in Answers to Tough Questions below.)

The issue of divorce is a troubling one for many. Chapter 7 addresses the subject, but calls for careful interpretation to yield consistent biblical doctrine on the matter. Advocates of Universalism, the idea that all people will eventually be saved, use 15:22 in support of that view, claiming that, just as every human being died spiritually because of Adam's sin, they will all be saved through Christ's righteousness. (See Answers to Tough Questions for further discussion on these issues.)

From chapter 15, the obscure phrase "baptized for the dead" (v. 29) is used to defend the notion that a dead person can be saved by being baptized vicariously through a living Christian. There have been over forty suggested explanations for this baptism. Regardless of how that particular verse is interpreted, many other texts clearly show the false idea that dead people have the opportunity to be saved.

A much less serious issue concerns the meaning of 6:4, which pertains to Christians taking other Christians to court before unbelievers. This is a difficult verse to translate, as suggested by the widely varying English renderings. But the basic meaning is clear: when Christians have earthly quarrels and disputes among themselves, it is inconceivable that they would turn to those least qualified (unbelievers) to resolve the matter. The most legally untrained believers, who know the Word of God and are obedient to the Spirit, are far more competent to settle disagreements between believers than the most experienced unbeliever, void of God's truth and Spirit.

Appearances of the Risen Christ

Central to Christian faith is the bodily resurrection of Jesus. By recording the Resurrection appearances, the New Testament leaves no doubt about this event.

- In or around Jerusalem

  To Mary Magdalene (John 20:11–18)

  To the other women (Matt. 28:8–10)

  To Peter (Luke 24:34)

  To ten disciples (Luke 24:36–43; John 20:19–25)

  To the Eleven, including Thomas (John 20:26–29)

  At His ascension (Luke 24:50–53; Acts 1:4–12)

- To the disciples on the Emmaus road (Luke 24:13–35)

- In Galilee (Matt. 28:16–20; John 21:1–24)

- To five hundred people (1 Cor. 15:6)

- To Paul on the road to Damascus (Acts 9:1–6; 18:9,10; 22:1–8; 23:11; 26:12–18; 1 Cor. 15:8)

© 1996 Thomas Nelson, Inc.

OUTLINE

I. Introduction: The Calling and Benefits of Sainthood (1:1–9)
II. Disunity in the Church (1:10–4:21)
    A. The Need for Unity (1:10–3:23)
    B. The Need for Servanthood (4:1–21)
III. Immorality in the Church (5:1–6:20)
IV. Marriage in the Church (7:1–40)
V. Liberty in the Church (8:1–11:1)
VI. Worship in the Church (11:2–14:40)
    A. Roles of Men and Women in the Church (11:2–16)
    B. The Lord's Supper (11:17–34)
    C. Spiritual Gifts (12:1–14:40)
VII. The Hope of the Church: Resurrection (15:1–58)
VIII. A Charge to the Church (16:1–24)
    A. Stewardship (16:1–4)
    B. Personal Plans and Greetings (16:5–24)

MEANWHILE, IN OTHER PARTS OF THE WORLD...

Roman emperor Claudius I is poisoned by his fourth wife, Agrippina. Nero, the son of Agrippina by another marriage, succeeds Claudius as emperor.

ANSWERS TO TOUGH QUESTIONS

1. What factors made it difficult for the gospel to take root in a healthy way in the city of Corinth?

The mind-set of the Corinthians made it almost impossible for the church to fully break with the surrounding culture. The congregation continually behaved in a factional way, showing its carnality and immaturity. After the gifted Apollos had ministered in the church for a while, some of his admirers established a clique that had little to do with the rest of the church. Another group, loyal to Paul, developed; another claimed special allegiance to Peter (Cephas); and still another to Christ alone (1:10–13; 3:1–9). Instead of the church having a significant impact on the city, the city had too much impact on the church.

Paul knew that this church would never become a faithful witness for Christ until they understood that those who claimed to be members of the church but continued to be disobedient and unrepentant before God must be removed from the local body (5:9–13). The Corinthians seem to have been unwilling to pay the price of obedience.

2. How does Paul's teaching in 1 Corinthians help resolve the controversy over the gifts discussed in chapters 12–14?

Three chapters in this letter are devoted to the subject of spiritual gifts in the church. By far the most controversial issue for interpretation is that of the sign gifts, particularly the gifts of miracles and speaking in tongues. Paul knew that the subject was controversial but vital to a healthy church. The atmosphere of false religions that abounded in Corinth caused counterfeit spiritual manifestations that had to be confronted. Paul informed the church and challenged the believers in Corinth to regulate their behavior by the truth and the Spirit.

The categories of giftedness in these verses do not refer to natural talents, skills, or abilities. Believers and unbelievers alike possess such resources. These gifts are sovereignly and supernaturally bestowed by the Holy Spirit on all believers (12:7,11), enabling them to spiritually edify each other and thus honor the Lord.

The varieties of spiritual gifts fall roughly into two general types: (1) speaking gifts and (2) serving gifts (12:8–10; Rom. 12:6–8; 1 Pet. 4:10,11). The speaking or verbal gifts (prophecy, knowledge, wisdom, teaching, and exhortation) and the serving, nonverbal gifts (leadership, helps, giving, mercy, faith, and discernment) are all permanent and will operate throughout the church age. Their purpose is to build up the church and glorify God. The list here and in Romans 12:3–8 is best seen as representative of categories of giftedness from which the Holy Spirit draws to give each believer whatever kind or combination He chooses (12:11). Some believers may be gifted in similar ways to others, but each is personally unique because the Spirit suits each gift to the individual.

A special category made up of miracles, healing, languages, and the interpretation of languages served as a set of temporary sign gifts limited to the apostolic age and have, therefore, ceased. Their purpose was to authenticate the apostles and their message as the true Word of God. Once God's Word was complete and became self-authenticating, they were no longer required.

3. How does Paul address the issue of divorce for the Corinthian church?

Paul taught about divorce in the context of answering a number of questions that the church had sent to him. The first of those questions had to do with marriage, an area of trouble due to the moral corruption of the surrounding culture, which tolerated fornication, adultery, homosexuality, polygamy, and having concubines.

The apostle reminded the believers that his teaching was based on what Jesus had already made clear during His earthly ministry (Matt. 5:31,32; 19:5–8). Jesus Himself based His teaching on the previously revealed Word of God (Gen. 2:24; Mal. 2:16).

Paul's departure point for teaching affirmed God's prohibition of divorce. He wrote that in cases where a Christian has already divorced another Christian except for adultery (7:10–11), neither partner is free to marry another person. They should reconcile or at least remain unmarried.

Paul then added some helpful direction on the issue of marital conflicts created in cases where one spouse becomes a believer (7:12–16). First, the believing spouse lives under orders to make the best of the marriage, seeking to win his or her spouse to

Christ. If the unbelieving spouse decides to end the marriage, Paul's response is "let him depart" (7:15). This term refers to divorce (7:10–11). When an unbelieving spouse cannot tolerate the partner's faith and wants a divorce, it is best to let that happen in order to preserve peace in the family (Rom. 12:18). Therefore, the bond of marriage is broken only by death (Rom. 7:2), adultery (Matt. 19:9), or an unbeliever's departure.

When the bond of marriage is broken in any of those ways, a Christian is free to marry another believer (7:15). Throughout Scripture, whenever legitimate divorce occurs, remarriage is an assumed option. When divorce is permitted, so is remarriage.

In general, conversion and obedience to Christ should lead us to greater faithfulness and commitment in every relationship. This extended passage (7:1–24) plainly repeats the basic principle that Christians should willingly accept the marital condition and social situations into which God has placed them and be content to serve Him there until He leads them elsewhere.

4. What difference would it make if the resurrection of Jesus never really happened?
Jesus' resurrection is the least optional part of the Christian faith. It is the most important among the essential beliefs Christians hold. The apostle Paul identified at least six disastrous consequences that would be unavoidable if the resurrection of Jesus was proved to be a hoax:

- The preaching of Christ would be senseless and meaningless (15:14).
- Faith in Christ would be useless since He would still be dead (15:14).
- All the witnesses and preachers of the Resurrection would be liars (15:15).
- No one would be redeemed (saved) from sin (15:17).
- All former believers would have died as fools (15:18).
- Christians would be the most pitiable people in the world (15:19).

At the center of Christianity stands the risen Christ, victorious, and coming again.

5. Does 1 Corinthians 15:22 actually teach Universalism—the idea that all people will eventually be saved?
Some people, under a misguided notion of fairness and a woefully inadequate view of God, attempt to see in this verse a basis for their belief in *universalism* (salvation of everyone without regard to faith). The two uses of the word *all* in 15:22 are alike only in the sense that they both apply to descendants. The second *all* applies only to believers. The immediate context (verse 23) limits the second *all* to "those who are Christ's." Many other passages clearly teach against Universalism by affirming the eternal punishment of unbelievers (Matt. 5:29; 10:28; 25:41,46; Luke 16:23; 2 Thess. 1:9; Rev. 20:15).

FURTHER STUDY ON 1 CORINTHIANS

1. People were choosing sides and allegiances in the Corinthian church. How did Paul respond?

2. In handling questions about convictions regarding "meat offered to idols," what principles of Christian behavior did Paul explain and apply?

3. What kinds of immorality did Paul have to confront in the Corinthian church, and how did he do that?

4. Chapters 11–14 deal with many matters that affect corporate worship. What are the central teachings from these chapters, and how have you seen them applied or ignored in your church?

5. In what ways is Paul's description of the resurrection of Jesus and his explanation of its significance different from that of the gospels?

6. How has the resurrection of Jesus Christ affected your life?

SECOND CORINTHIANS
Words from a Caring Shepherd

TITLE

This is the second NT epistle the apostle Paul wrote to the Christians in the city of Corinth (see Author and Date, 1 Corinthians).

AUTHOR AND DATE

That the apostle Paul wrote 2 Corinthians is uncontested; the lack of any motive for a forger to write this highly personal, biographical epistle has led even the most critical scholars to affirm Paul as its author.

Several considerations establish a feasible date for the writing of this letter. Extrabiblical sources indicate that July, A.D. 51 is the most likely date for the beginning of Gallio's role as proconsul (cf. Acts 18:12). Paul's trial before him at Corinth (Acts 18:12–17) probably took place shortly after Gallio assumed office. Leaving Corinth (probably in A.D. 52), Paul sailed for Palestine (Acts 18:18), thus concluding his second missionary journey. Returning to Ephesus on his third missionary journey (probably in A.D. 52), Paul ministered there for about two-and-a-half years (Acts 19:8,10). The apostle wrote 1 Corinthians from Ephesus toward the close of that period (1 Cor. 16:8), most likely in A.D. 55. Since Paul planned to stay in Ephesus until the following spring (cf. the reference to Pentecost in 1 Cor. 16:8), and 2 Corinthians was written after he left Ephesus (see Background and Setting), the most likely date for 2 Corinthians is late A.D. 55 or very early A.D. 56.

BACKGROUND AND SETTING

Paul's association with the important commercial city of Corinth (see 1 Corinthians: Background and Setting) began on his second missionary journey (Acts 18:1–18), when he spent 18 months (Acts 18:11) ministering there. After leaving Corinth, Paul heard of immorality in the Corinthian church and wrote a letter (since lost) to confront that sin, referred to in 1 Corinthians 5:9. During his ministry in Ephesus, he received further reports of trouble in the Corinthian church in the form of divisions among them (1 Cor. 1:11). In addition, the Corinthians wrote Paul a letter (1 Cor. 7:1) asking for clarification of some issues. Paul responded by writing the letter known as 1 Corinthians. Planning to remain at Ephesus a little longer (1 Cor. 16:8,9), Paul sent Timothy to Corinth (1 Cor. 4:17; 16:10,11). Disturbing news reached the apostle (possibly from Timothy) of further difficulties at Corinth, including the arrival of self-styled false apostles.

To create the platform to teach their false gospel, these false apostles began by assaulting the character of Paul. They had to convince the people to turn from Paul to them if they were to succeed in preaching demon doctrine. Temporarily abandoning the work at Ephesus, Paul went immediately to Corinth. The visit (known as the "painful visit," 2:1) was not a successful one from Paul's perspective; someone in the Corinthian church (possibly one of the false apostles) even openly insulted him (2:5–8,10; 7:12). Saddened by the

Corinthians' lack of loyalty to defend him, seeking to spare them further reproof (cf. 1:23), and perhaps hoping time would bring them to their senses, Paul returned to Ephesus. From Ephesus, Paul wrote what is known as the "severe letter" (2:4) and sent it with Titus to Corinth (7:5–16). Leaving Ephesus after the riot sparked by Demetrius (Acts 19:23–20:1), Paul went to Troas to meet Titus (2:12,13). But Paul was so anxious for news of how the Corinthians had responded to the "severe letter" that he could not minister there though the Lord had opened the door (2:12; cf. 7:5). So he left for Macedonia to look for Titus (2:13). To Paul's immense relief and joy, Titus met him with the news that the majority of the Corinthians had repented of their rebellion

CHRIST IN . . . 2 CORINTHIANS

PAUL'S SECOND LETTER to the Corinthians reveals Jesus Christ as the One who comforts the persecuted (1:5; 12:9), fulfills the promises of God (1:20), remains Lord over humanity (4:5), and perfectly reconciles believers to God (5:19). Paul declares believers to be new creations reconciled by Christ's atonement for sin "that we might become the righteousness of God in Him" (5:21).

against Paul (7:7). Wise enough to know that some rebellious attitudes still smoldered under the surface, and could erupt again, Paul wrote (possibly from Philippi, cf. 11:9 with Phil. 4:15; also, some early manuscripts list Philippi as the place of writing) the Corinthians the letter called 2 Corinthians. In this letter, though the apostle expressed his relief and joy at their repentance (7:8–16), his main concern was to defend his apostleship (chaps. 1–7), encourage the Corinthians to resume preparations for the collection for the poor at Jerusalem (chaps. 8, 9), and confront the false apostles head on (chaps. 10–13). He then went to Corinth, as he had written (12:14; 13:1,2). The Corinthians' participation in the Jerusalem offering (Rom. 15:26) implies that Paul's third visit to that church was successful.

KEY PEOPLE IN 2 CORINTHIANS
Paul—author of the letters to the Corinthian church (1:1–13:14)
Timothy—fellow missionary sent by Paul to assist the Corinthian church (1:1–19)
Titus—Gentile man who helped collect money for the church in Jerusalem; trusted by Paul to deliver his letters to Corinth (2:13; 7:6–8:24; 12:18)
False apostles—false teachers in the Corinthian church who had disguised themselves as believers (11:13–15)

HISTORICAL AND THEOLOGICAL THEMES
Second Corinthians complements the historical record of Paul's dealings with the Corinthian church recorded in Acts and 1 Corinthians. It also contains important biographical data on Paul throughout.

Although an intensely personal letter, written by the apostle in the heat of battle against those attacking his credibility, 2 Corinthians contains several important theological themes. It portrays God the Father as a merciful comforter (1:3; 7:6), the Creator (4:6), the One who raised Jesus from the dead (4:14; cf. 13:4), and who will raise believers as well (1:9). Jesus Christ is the One who suffered (1:5), who fulfilled God's promises (1:20), who was the proclaimed Lord (4:5), who manifested God's glory (4:6), and the One who in His incarnation became poor for believers (8:9; cf. Phil. 2:5–8). The letter portrays the Holy Spirit as God (3:17,18) and the guarantee of believers' salvation (1:22; 5:5). Satan is identified as the "god of this age" (4:4; cf. 1 John 5:19), a deceiver (11:14), and the leader of human and angelic deceivers (11:15). The end times include both the believer's glorification (4:16–5:8) and his judgment (5:10). The glorious truth of God's sovereignty in salvation is the theme of 5:14–21, while 7:9,10 sets forth man's response to God's offer of salvation—genuine repentance. Second Corinthians also presents the clearest, most concise summary of how sinners are reconciled to God—through the substitutionary atonement of Christ—to be found anywhere in Scripture (5:21), and defines the mission of the church to proclaim reconciliation (5:18–20). Finally, the nature of the New Covenant receives its fullest exposition, outside the Book of Hebrews, in chapt. 3:6–16).

KEY WORDS IN

2 Corinthians

Service: Greek *leitourgia*—9:12—indicates "public ministry" or "official duty." The related word *leitourgos* is used frequently in Greek literature to designate a man who performed some public service (see Rom. 13:6). In general, it means a public servant or administrator. Paul used *leitourgia* in connection with the service of those who labored to benefit the church.

Apostle: Greek *apostolos*—1:1; 11:5,13; 12:11-12—simply means "sent ones." Out of Jesus' many disciples, He selected twelve to be His apostles. These were the men who were sent by Jesus to take His message to the world and then raise up churches. Paul also became an apostle by the appointment of the risen Christ, who encountered Paul on the road to Damascus (see Acts 9). Paul's apostleship was accompanied by a great deal of suffering; and then, to add to it, some false teachers in the Corinthian church doubted his authority. Thus in 2 Corinthians, Paul repeatedly defended the genuineness of His apostleship.

KEY DOCTRINES IN 2 CORINTHIANS

Reconciliation with God—the sacrifice of Jesus Christ renews the relationship between God and man (5:17–21; Rom. 5:1,10,11; Lev. 8:15; 16:20; Dan. 9:24; Is. 53:5; Matt. 5:24–26; Eph. 2:14–16; Col. 1:20–22; 2:14; Heb. 2:17)

Christ's substitutionary atonement for sin—Christ's work upon the cross paid the penalty for sin (5:21; Is. 53; Dan. 9:24–27; Zech. 13:1,7; John 1:29,36; 11:50–51; Acts 4:10; Rom. 3:25; 5:8–11; Gal. 1:4; 1 Thess. 1:10; 1 Tim. 2:5,6; 1 Pet. 1:11,20; 1 John 2:2; 4:10; Rev. 13:8)

Guarantee of believers' salvation—God adopts faithful believers as His own children (1:22; 5:5; Pss. 3:8; 37:39; Is. 45:21,22; 59:16; 63:9; Jer. 3:23; Mark 16:16; Acts 4:12; 16:31; Rom. 10:9; Eph. 2:8; 1 Thess. 5:9; 1 Tim. 2:4; Heb. 5:9; 1 Pet. 1:5)

The nature of Satan—the original rebel among God's creatures (4:4; 11:14,15; Gen. 3:1,14; Job 1:6; Zech. 3:1; Matt. 4:3–10; 13:19; Luke 10:18; Eph. 2:2; 6:11,12; 1 Thess. 2:18; 2 Thess. 2:9; 1 Tim. 3:6; 1 Pet. 5:8; 2 Pet. 2:4; 1 John 3:8; 5:19)

Judgment—God's righteous response to sin (5:9–11; Gen. 19:29; Deut. 32:39; Is. 1:9; Matt. 12:36,37; Rom. 1:18–2:16; 2 Pet. 2:5,6)

GOD'S CHARACTER IN 2 CORINTHIANS
God is comforting—1:3; 7:6
God is glorious—4:6
God is loving—9:7; 13:11
God is merciful—1:3
God is powerful—6:7; 9:8; 13:4
God is a promise keeper—1:20; 6:18; 7:1
God is reconciling—5:18,19
God is spirit—3:17
God is true—1:20

INTERPRETIVE CHALLENGES
The main challenge confronting the interpreter is the relationship of chaps. 10–13 to chaps. 1–9, and the obvious change in tone. See a discussion of this topic in Answers to Tough Questions. The identity of Paul's opponents at Corinth has produced various interpretations, as has the identity of the brother who accompanied Titus to Corinth (8:18,22). Also, there is some speculation as to whether the offender mentioned in 2:5–8 is the incestuous man of 1 Corinthians 5. Finally, it is difficult to explain Paul's vision (12:1–5) and to identify specifically his "thorn in the flesh," the "messenger of Satan [sent] to buffet [him]" (12:7). (See Answers to Tough Questions below.)

OUTLINE
I. Paul's Greeting (1:1–11)
II. Paul's Ministry (1:12–7:16)
    A. Paul's Plans (1:12–2:4)
    B. The Offender's Punishment (2:5–11)
    C. Titus' Absence (2:12,13)
    D. The Ministry's Nature (2:14–6:10)
        1. The triumph of the ministry (2:14–17)
        2. The commendation of the ministry (3:1–5)
        3. The basis of the ministry (3:6–18)
        4. The theme of the ministry (4:1–7)
        5. The trials of the ministry (4:8–18)
        6. The motivation of the ministry (5:1–10)
        7. The message of the ministry (5:11–21)
        8. The conduct of the ministry (6:1–10)
    E. The Corinthians Exhorted (6:11–7:16)
        1. To open their hearts to Paul (6:11–13)
        2. To separate themselves from unbelievers (6:14–7:1)
        3. To be assured of Paul's love (7:2–16)
III. Paul's Collection (8:1–9:15)
    A. The Patterns of Giving (8:1–9)
        1. The Macedonians (8:1–7)
        2. Jesus Christ (8:8,9)

B. The Purpose of Giving (8:10–15)
C. The Procedures of Giving (8:16–9:5)
D. The Promise of Giving (9:6–15)

IV. Paul's Apostleship (10:1–12:13)
A. Apostolic Authority (10:1–18)
B. Apostolic Conduct (11:1–15)
C. Apostolic Suffering (11:16–33)
D. Apostolic Credentials (12:1–13)

V. Paul's Visit (12:14–13:14)
A. Paul's Unselfishness (12:14–18)
B. Paul's Warnings (12:19–13:10)
C. Paul's Benediction (13:11–14)

MEANWHILE, IN OTHER PARTS OF THE WORLD...
Nero is declared Roman emperor at age seventeen. During Nero's reign, two-thirds of Rome burns to the ground.

ANSWERS TO TOUGH QUESTIONS

1. What does Paul mean when he writes about being "in Christ" and someone being "a new creation" (5:17)?

Paul uses the phrase *in Christ* when he writes about various aspects of our relationship with Jesus Christ as Lord and Savior. These two words comprise a brief but profound statement of the significance of the believer's redemption (salvation), which includes the following:

- The believer's security in Christ, who bore in His body God's judgment against sin
- The believer's acceptance in (through) Christ, with whom God alone is well pleased
- The believer's future assurance in Him, who is the resurrection to eternal life and the sole guarantor of the believer's inheritance in heaven
- The believer's participation in the divine nature of Christ, the everlasting Word (2 Pet. 1:4)

All of the changes that Christ brings to the believer's life result in a state that can be rightly called "a new creation." The terms describe something created at a qualitatively new level of excellence. They parallel other biblical concepts like *regeneration* and *new birth* (John 3:3; Eph. 2:1–3; Titus 3:5; 1 Pet. 1:23; 1 John 2:29; 3:9; 5:4). The expression includes the Christian's forgiveness of sins paid for in Christ's substitution-ary death (Gal. 6:15; Eph. 4:24).

2. Why does the tone of 2 Corinthians change so abruptly between 9:15 and 10:1?

Even a casual reader usually notices the sudden change in tone that occurs between the ninth and tenth chapters of 2 Corinthians. This apparent difference has prompt-ed various explanations of the relationship between chapters 1–9 and 10–13.

Some have argued that chapters 10–13 were actually part of the "severe letter" that Paul mentions in 2:4. Based on this theory, these four chapters belong chrono-logically before chapters 1–9. Chapters 10–13 cannot, however, have been written before chapters 1–9 because they refer to Titus's visit as a past event (see 8:6; 12:18). Further, the offender whose defiance prompted Paul's "severe letter" (2:5–8) is nowhere mentioned in chapters 10–13.

Others agree that chapters 10–13 belong after chapters 1–9 but suggest that they form a separate letter. They assume that Paul, after sending chapters 1–9 to the Corinthians, received reports of new trouble at Corinth and wrote chapters 10–13 in response. A variation of this view proposes that Paul paused after writing chapters 1–9, then heard bad news from Corinth before he resumed writing chapters 10–13. Although this view preserves the unity of 2 Corinthians, Paul gives no indication in the last four chapters that he received fresh news from Corinth.

The best interpretation sees 2 Corinthians as a unified letter with two distinct sec-tions. Chapters 1–9 are addressed to the repentant majority (see 2:6) and chapters 10–13 to the minority still influenced by the false teachers. The following facts sup-port this view: (1) no ancient authorities (Greek manuscripts, early church fathers, or early translations) indicate that chapters 10–13 ever circulated as a separate letter; (2) the overall differences in tone between the two sections have been exaggerated (compare 6:11; 7:2 with 11:11; 12:14); and (3) chapters 10–13 do form a logical con-clusion to chapters 1–9, as Paul prepared the Corinthians for his promised visit (1:15–16; 2:1–3).

3. To what was Paul referring by the phrase "thorn in the flesh" (12:7)?

Paul began his account about the thorn in the flesh by indicating the reason it was given to him—"lest I should be exalted"—in other words, to keep him humble. As with Job, Satan was the immediate cause, but God was the ultimate cause behind Paul's thorn. This is why the thorn was not removed in spite of Paul's pleas (12:8). God had a purpose in allowing Paul to suffer in this way—to show him that "My grace is sufficient for you" (12:9).

Paul's use of the word *messenger* (Greek, *angellos*, or angel) from Satan suggests the thorn in the flesh (literally, "a stake for the flesh") was a demon, not a physical ill-ness. Of the 188 uses of the Greek word *angellos* in the NT, at least 180 refer to angels. This particular angel was from Satan, a demon afflicting Paul.

Perhaps the best explanation for this demon is that he was indwelling the ring-leader of the Corinthian conspiracy, the leader of the false apostles. Through them he was tearing apart Paul's beloved church and thus driving a painful stake through Paul. Added support for this view comes from the context of chapters 10–13, in which Paul engages his enemies (the false prophets). The verb translated "buffet" always refers to ill-treatment from other people (Matt. 26:67; Mark 14:65; 1 Cor. 4:11; 1 Pet. 2:20). Finally, the OT frequently describes Israel's enemies as thorns (Num. 33:55; Josh. 23:13; Judg. 2:3; Ezek. 28:24).

FURTHER STUDY ON 2 CORINTHIANS

1. Based on his comments throughout this letter, what was Paul's relationship with the church in Corinth?
2. What principles of church discipline did Paul explain and apply in this letter?
3. What aspects of his own spiritual struggle and growth did Paul write about in this letter?
4. In 2 Corinthians 4, how did Paul explain the limits of ministry and the reasons behind the effectiveness of the gospel?
5. How do Paul's comments about the collection from the Asian churches for the church in Jerusalem help you understand some of the principles of giving among Christians?
6. In his response to those who are challenging his apostolic authority, what were Paul's central concerns?
7. In what ways can you identify with Paul's lessons about the thorn in the flesh (12:7)?

The Agora of Corinth

GALATIANS
Freed and Justified by Faith

TITLE

Galatians derives its title (*pros Galatas*) from the region in Asia Minor (modern Turkey) where the churches addressed were located. It is the only one of Paul's epistles specifically addressed to churches in more than one city (1:2; cf. 3:1; 1 Cor. 16:1).

AUTHOR AND DATE

There is no reason to question the internal claims that the apostle Paul wrote Galatians (1:1; 5:2). Paul was born in Tarsus, a city in the province of Cilicia, not far from Galatia. Under the famous rabbi, Gamaliel, Paul received a thorough training in the OT Scriptures and in the rabbinic traditions at Jerusalem (Acts 22:3). A member of the ultra-traditional sect of the Pharisees (Acts 23:6), he was one of first-century Judaism's rising stars (1:14; cf. Phil. 3:5,6).

The course of Paul's life took a sudden and startling turn when, on his way to Damascus from Jerusalem to persecute Christians, he was confronted by the risen, glorified Christ. That dramatic encounter turned Paul from Christianity's chief persecutor to its greatest missionary. His three missionary journeys and trip to Rome turned Christianity from a faith that included only a small group of Palestinian Jewish believers into an Empire-wide phenomenon. Galatians is one of thirteen inspired letters he addressed to Gentile congregations or his fellow workers. For further biographical information on Paul, see Romans: Author and Date.

In chap. 2, Paul described his visit to the Jerusalem Council of Acts 15, so he must have written Galatians after that event. Since most scholars date the Jerusalem Council about A.D. 49, the most likely date for Galatians is shortly thereafter.

BACKGROUND AND SETTING

In Paul's day, the word *Galatia* had two distinct meanings. In a strict ethnic sense, Galatia was the region of central Asia Minor inhabited by the Galatians. They were a Celtic people who had migrated to that region from Gaul (modern France) in the third century B.C. The Romans conquered the Galatians in 189 B.C. but allowed them to have some measure of independence until 25 B.C. when Galatia became a Roman province, incorporating some regions not inhabited by ethnic Galatians (e.g., parts of Lycaonia, Phrygia, and Pisidia). In a political sense, *Galatia* came to describe the entire Roman province, not merely the region inhabited by the ethnic Galatians.

Paul founded churches in the southern Galatian cities of Antioch, Iconium, Lystra, and Derbe (Acts 13:14–14:23). These cities, although within the Roman province of Galatia, were not in the ethnic Galatian region. There is no record of Paul's founding churches in that northern, less populated region.

Those two uses of the word *Galatia* make it more difficult to determine who the original recipients of the epistle were. Some interpret *Galatia* in its strict racial sense and argue that Paul addressed this epistle to churches in the northern Galatian region, inhabited by the ethnic descendants of the Gauls. Although the apostle apparently crossed the border into the fringes of ethnic Galatia on at least two occasions (Acts 16:6; 18:23), Acts does not record that he founded any churches or engaged in any evangelistic ministry there.

Because neither Acts nor Galatians mentions any cities or people from northern (ethnic) Galatia, it is reasonable to believe that Paul addressed this epistle to churches located in the southern part of the Roman province, but outside of the ethnic Galatian region. Acts records the apostle's founding of such churches at Pisidian Antioch (13:14–50), Iconium (13:51–14:7; cf. 16:2), Lystra (14:8–19; cf. 16:2), and Derbe (14:20,21; cf. 16:1). In addition, the churches Paul addressed had apparently been established before the Jerusalem Council (2:5), and the churches of southern Galatia fit that criterion, having been founded during Paul's first missionary journey before the Council met. Paul did not visit northern (ethnic) Galatia until after the Jerusalem Council (Acts 16:6).

Paul wrote Galatians to counter false teachers who were undermining the central Christian doctrine of justification by faith. Ignoring the express decree of the Jerusalem Council (Acts 15:23–29), these false teachers spread their harmful teaching that Gentiles must first become Jewish proselytes and submit to all the Mosaic law before they could become Christians (see 1:7; 4:17,21; 5:2–12; 6:12,13). Shocked by the Galatians' openness to this heresy (cf. 1:6), Paul wrote this letter to defend justification by faith, and to warn these churches of the dire consequences of abandoning that essential Christian belief. Galatians is the only epistle Paul wrote that does not contain any kind of commendation or praise for its readers. That obvious omission reflects how urgently he felt about confronting the lies being spread and defending the essential doctrine of justification.

The Cities of Galatia

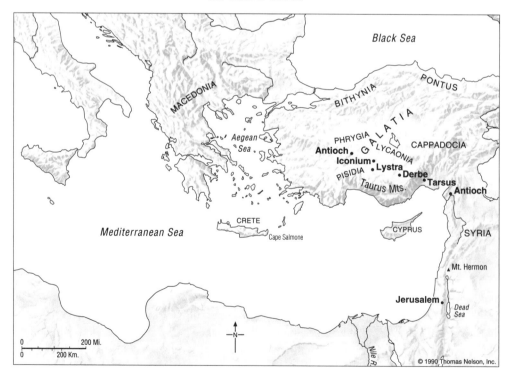

KEY PEOPLE IN GALATIANS

Paul—urged the Galatians to remember their freedom from the law through Christ Jesus (1:1–6:18)

Peter—leader of the church in Jerusalem; confronted by Paul for looking to the law for salvation (1:18–2:21)

Barnabas—traveled with Paul as a missionary; allowed Paul to correct several of his misguided beliefs (2:1–13)

Titus—Gentile believer and close friend to Paul; later served on the island of Crete (2:1–3)

Abraham—Paul used Abraham's life to exemplify God's salvation through faith alone (3:6–4:22)

False teachers—persuasive teachers who attempted to lure the people away from Paul's teaching (4:17–20)

HISTORICAL AND THEOLOGICAL THEMES

Galatians provides valuable historical information about Paul's background (chaps. 1, 2), including his three-year stay in Nabatean Arabia (1:17,18), which Acts does not mention; his fifteen-day visit with Peter after his stay in Arabia (1:18,19); his trip to the Jerusalem Council (2:1–10); and his confrontation of Peter (2:11–21).

As already noted, the central theme of Galatians (like that of Romans) is justification by faith. Paul defends that doctrine (which is the heart of the gospel) both in its theological (chaps. 3, 4) and practical (chaps. 5,

CHRIST IN . . . GALATIANS

THE BOOK OF GALATIANS deals with the freedom that Christ gives to believers. The Galatians were tempted by Jewish legalists to trade away that freedom and return to slavery under the law (2:4). Paul's letter urges believers to "not be entangled again with a yoke of bondage" but to hold to their position of liberty in Jesus Christ (5:1).

6) consequences. He also defends his position as an apostle (chaps. 1, 2) since, as had happened in Corinth, false teachers were attempting to gain a hearing for their heretical teaching by undermining Paul's credibility. The main theological themes of Galatians are strikingly similar to those of Romans, e.g., the inability of the law to justify (2:16; cf. Rom. 3:20); the believer's deadness to the law (2:19; cf. Rom. 7:4); the believer's crucifixion with Christ (2:20; cf. Rom. 6:6); Abraham's justification by faith (3:6; cf. Rom. 4:3); that believers are Abraham's spiritual children (3:7; cf. Rom. 4:10,11) and therefore blessed (3:9; cf. Rom. 4:23,24); that the law brings not salvation but God's wrath (3:10; cf. Rom. 4:15); that the just shall live by faith (3:11; cf. Rom. 1:17); the universality of sin (3:22; cf. Rom. 11:32); that believers are spiritually baptized into Christ (3:27; cf. Rom. 6:3); believers' adoption as God's spiritual children (4:5–7; cf. Rom. 8:14–17); that love fulfills the law (5:14; cf. Rom. 13:8–10); the importance of walking in the Spirit (5:16; cf. Rom. 8:4); the warfare of the flesh against the Spirit (5:17; cf. Rom. 7:23,25); and the importance of believers bearing one anothers' burdens (6:2; cf. Rom. 15:1).

Law and Grace

THE FUNCTION		THE EFFECT	
Of Law	*Of Grace*	*Of Law*	*Of Grace*
Based on works (3:10)	Based on faith (3:11,12)	Works put us under a curse (3:10)	Justifies us by faith (3:3,24)
Our guardian (3:23, 4:2)	Centered in Christ (3:24)	Keeps us for faith (3:23)	Christ lives in us (2:20)
Our tutor (3:24)	Our certificate of freedom (4:30,31)	Brings us to Christ (3:24)	Adopts us as sons and heirs (4:7)

The law functions to (1) declare our guilt, (2) drive us to Christ, and (3) direct us in a life of obedience. However, the law is powerless to save.

KEY DOCTRINES IN GALATIANS

Justification by faith—complete freedom from judgment and from the bondage of sin comes by faith alone in Jesus Christ (2:14–21; 3:11; 5:4; Lev. 18:5; Is. 45:25; 50:8; 53:11; Jer. 23:6; Hab. 2:4; John 5:24; Acts 13:39; Rom. 1:16,17; 3:21–4:25; 5:1,2,18; 1 Cor. 6:11; Titus 3:7; James 2:10)

The law—believers are freed from the bondage of the law (2:20,21; 5:1; Jer. 31:33; Rom. 2:12; 6:14; 7:4–6; Gal. 3:10–13; Heb. 8:10)

The role of the Holy Spirit—the Spirit remains in constant battle against the desires of the flesh (5:16,17; John 14:16; Rom. 5:3–5; 7:23,25; 8:4–6; Phil. 3:3; 1 Pet. 3:18)

GOD'S CHARACTER IN GALATIANS

God is merciful—6:16
God is powerful—2:8
God is a promise keeper—3:16–19,21,22,29; 4:4

INTERPRETIVE CHALLENGES

First, Paul described a visit to Jerusalem and a subsequent meeting with Peter, James, and John (2:1–10). There is a question to be resolved in that text, as to whether that was his visit to the Jerusalem Council (Acts 15), or his earlier visit bringing famine relief to the Jerusalem church (Acts 11:27–30). Second, those who teach baptismal regeneration (the false doctrine that baptism is necessary for salvation) support their view from 3:27. Third, others have used this epistle to support their attacks on the biblical roles of men and women, claiming that the spiritual equality taught in 3:28 is incompatible with the traditional concept of authority and submission. Fourth, those who reject the doctrine of eternal security argue that the phrase "you have fallen from grace" (5:4) describes believers who lost their salvation. (See Answers to Tough Questions for further discussion on these issues.)

Fifth, there is disagreement whether Paul's statement, "see with what large letters I have written to you with my own hand!" (6:11), refers to the entire letter or merely the concluding verses. A good translation of the Greek verb indicates that Paul wrote the

---

KEY WORDS IN

Galatians

Elements: Greek *stoicheia*—4:3,9—can mean (1) "elementary or rudimentary principles" or (2) "elemental spirits." The word literally means things placed in line or in a row, like an alphabet. It was used to speak of rudimentary principles (Heb. 5:12) or basic elements of the universe, whether physical (2 Pet. 3:10) or spiritual. If Paul was thinking of elementary principles, he meant that people are in bondage to the basic elements of religion (see Col. 2:20); if he meant spirits, he was saying that people are in bondage to the "elemental spirits," meaning certain gods or demons. Elementary *principles* suits the overall context of Galatians, whereas *spirits* accords with 4:8–10. In either case, Paul was saying that people were in bondage until Christ came.

Flesh: Greek *sarx*—1:16; 2:20; 4:13,14; 5:17; 6:12,13—in Greek literature, the word *sarx* usually meant nothing more than the human body. It was also used this way in the New Testament (see John 1:14; Rev. 17:16; 19:18,21). However, Paul often used the word to denote the entire fallen human being—not just the sinful body but the entire being, including the soul and mind, as affected by sin. Thus Paul often pitted the *flesh* against the *Spirit* as being two completely opposing forces. The unbeliever can live only in the flesh, but the believer can live in the flesh or in the Spirit. Paul repeatedly encourages believers to overcome the deeds of the flesh by living in the Spirit.

---

entire letter by his own hand, not by merely penning a brief statement at the end of dictation to a secretary, as he did other times. Finally, many claim that Paul erased the line between Israel and the church when he identified the church as the "Israel of God" (6:16). But by "Israel of God" Paul means all Jewish believers in Christ, i.e., those who are both physical and spiritual descendants of Abraham.

OUTLINE
I. Personal: The Preacher of Justification (1:1–2:21)
  A. Apostolic Chastening (1:1–9)
  B. Apostolic Credentials (1:10–2:10)
  C. Apostolic Confidence (2:11–21)
II. Doctrinal: The Principles of Justification (3:1–4:31)
  A. The Experience of the Galatians (3:1–5)
  B. The Blessing of Abraham (3:6–9)
  C. The Curse of the Law (3:10–14)
  D. The Promise of the Covenant (3:15–18)
  E. The Purpose of the Law (3:19–29)
  F. The Sonship of Believers (4:1–7)
  G. The Futility of Ritualism (4:8–20)
  H. The Illustration from Scripture (4:21–31)
III. Practical: The Privileges of Justification (5:1–6:18)
  A. Freedom from Ritual (5:1–6)
  B. Freedom from Legalists (5:7–12)
  C. Freedom in the Spirit (5:13–26)
  D. Freedom from Spiritual Bondage (6:1–10)
  E. Conclusion (6:11–18)

MEANWHILE, IN OTHER PARTS OF THE WORLD...
The Goths, traveling from present-day Sweden, establish a kingdom along the basin of the Vistula, the longest river in Poland.

ANSWERS TO TOUGH QUESTIONS

1. How do the events mentioned in Galatians match the chronology of Acts?

A comparison of the references in Acts (11:27–30; 15:2,12,22,35) and Galatians (1:18; 2:1–10) seems to indicate at least three visits by Paul to Jerusalem, including his trip to participate in the Jerusalem Council. Other visits occurred after the Council (Acts 18:18–22; 21:15–17). The visit mentioned in Galatians 1:18 records Paul's first direct contact with the apostles in Jerusalem after his own conversion. Chapter 2:1 mentions a fourteen-year gap, after which Paul returned again to Jerusalem, most likely as a participant in the Jerusalem Council (Acts 15), called to resolve the issue of Gentile salvation.

Linguistically, the word *again* (2:1) need not refer to the next visit; it can just as easily mean "once again" or "another time" without respect to how many visits took place in between. And in fact, Paul did visit Jerusalem at least once during that fourteen-year period to deliver famine relief to the church there (Acts 11:27–30; 12:24,25). He simply did not mention that intervening visit in Galatians probably because it was not significant in his defense of his apostolic authority.

2. Galatians 3:27 seems to read as if baptism is necessary for salvation. What did Paul mean in that verse?

Paul's use of the term *baptized* in this verse does not refer to water baptism, which cannot save. Paul used the word here in a metaphorical manner to speak of being "immersed," or "placed into" Christ. The larger context here refers to faith and to the spiritual miracle of union with Him in His death and resurrection, not to an outward ceremony. The phrase that immediately follows, "put on Christ," pictures the result of the believer's spiritual union with Christ. Paul was emphasizing the fact that we have been united with Christ through salvation. Before God, we have put on Christ, His death, resurrection, and righteousness. Practically we need to "put on Christ" before our family, friends, neighbors, and coworkers in our conduct (Rom. 13:14).

3. How does Paul's statement about gender, race, and status equality in 3:28 affect other biblical teachings about roles?

This passage is sometimes quoted by those who wish to challenge the traditional concepts of authority and submission, particularly as they affect marriage. This verse does not deny that God's plan has included certain racial, social, and sexual distinctions among Christians, but it affirms that those do not imply spiritual inequality before

God. In other words, the great doctrine of spiritual equality is not incompatible with the God-ordained roles of headship and submission in the church, society, and home. Even Jesus Christ, though fully equal with the Father, assumed a submissive role during His incarnation (Phil. 2:5–8).

4. What does the phrase "you have fallen from grace" (5:4) mean in relation to the doctrine of eternal security?

Paul uses two terms in this verse that imply separation, loss, and breakdown: "estranged from Christ" and "fallen from grace." The Greek word for *estranged* means "to be separated" or "to be severed." The word for *fallen* means "to lose one's grasp of something." The context clarifies Paul's meaning. Any attempt to be justified by the law equates to a rejection of salvation by grace alone through faith alone. Those who were once exposed to the gracious truth of the gospel and then turn their backs on Christ (Heb. 6:4–6) and seek to be justified by the law are separated from Christ and lose all prospects of God's gracious salvation. Their desertion of Christ and the gospel only proves that their faith was never genuine (Luke 8:13,14; 1 John 2:19).

FURTHER STUDY ON GALATIANS

1. How did Paul explain the relationship of the law to works of righteousness in Galatians?
2. Why did Paul call the Galatians "foolish"?
3. What did Paul tell the Galatians about faith? How does that description fit your own understanding of faith in your relationship with God?
4. When Paul discussed the concept of "freedom" with the Galatians, to what was he referring?
5. Paul discussed at length the effects of the Holy Spirit's presence in a Christian's life (5:16–26). What are those effects, and to what degree have you experienced them?

EPHESIANS
The Body of Christ Is Blessed

TITLE

The letter is addressed to the church in the city of Ephesus, capital of the Roman province of Asia (Asia Minor, modern Turkey). Because the name Ephesus is not mentioned in every early manuscript, some scholars believe the letter was an encyclical, intended to be circulated and read among all the churches in Asia Minor and was simply sent first to believers in Ephesus.

AUTHOR AND DATE

There is no indication that the authorship of Paul should be in question. He is indicated as author in the opening salutation (1:1; 3:1). The letter was written from prison in Rome (Acts 28:16–31) sometime between A.D. 60–62 and is, therefore, often referred to as a prison epistle (along with Philippians, Colossians, and Philemon). It may have been composed at nearly the same time as Colossians and initially sent with that epistle and Philemon by Tychicus (Eph. 6:21,22; Col. 4:7,8). See Philippians: Author and Date for a discussion of the city from which Paul wrote.

BACKGROUND AND SETTING

It is likely that the gospel was first brought to Ephesus by Priscilla and Aquila, an exceptionally gifted couple (see Acts 18:26), who were left there by Paul on his second missionary journey (Acts 18:18,19). Located at the mouth of the Cayster River, on the east side of the Aegean Sea, the city of Ephesus was perhaps best known for its magnificent temple of Artemis, or Diana, one of the seven wonders of the ancient world. It was also an important political, educational, and commercial center, ranking with Alexandria in Egypt, and Antioch of Pisidia, in southern Asia Minor.

The fledgling church begun by Priscilla and Aquila was later firmly established by Paul on his third missionary journey (Acts 19) and he served as their pastor for some three years. After Paul left, Timothy pastored the congregation for perhaps a year and a half, primarily to counter the false teaching of a few influential men

The City of Ephesus

"But now in Christ Jesus you who once were far off have been brought near by the blood of Christ."—Eph. 2:13

Ephesus

Gymnasium of Vedius
Stadium
To temple of Diana
Temple
Arcadiane Street
(Wall excavated)
Harbor Baths
Mt. Pion
(Ancient harbor, now filled in)
Great Theater*
Eastern Gymnasium
Agora
Temple of Serapis
Odeum
Magnesian Gate
Library of Celsus
Fountain Temple of
Temple of Trajan Hestia Boulaea
*"Great Theater—Site of the riotous assembly (Acts 19:29 ff).
Wall of Lysimachus
Mt. Koressos
(Probable wall)

© 1996 Thomas Nelson, Inc.

(such as Hymenaeus and Alexander), who were probably elders in the congregation there (1 Tim. 1:3,20). Because of those men, the church at Ephesus was plagued by "fables and endless genealogies" (1:4) and by such fleshly and unscriptural ideas as the forbidding of marriage and abstaining from certain foods (4:3). Although those false teachers did not rightly understand Scripture, they taught their ungodly interpretations with confidence (1:7), which produced in the church harmful "disputes rather than godly edification which is in faith" (1:4). Thirty years or so later, Christ gave to the apostle John a letter for this church, indicating its people had left their first love for Him (Rev. 2:1–7).

KEY PEOPLE IN EPHESIANS

Paul—instructed the church at Ephesus about their position as the body of Christ and their relationship with God (1:1–6:24)

Tychicus—sent by Paul to encourage the believers of Ephesus (6:21,22)

HISTORICAL AND THEOLOGICAL THEMES

The first three chapters are theological, emphasizing NT doctrine, whereas the last three chapters are practical and focus on Christian behavior. Perhaps, above all, this is a letter of encouragement and admonition, written to remind believers of their immeasurable blessings in Jesus Christ; and not only to be thankful for those blessings, but also to live in a manner worthy of them. Despite, and partly even because of, a Christian's great blessings in Jesus Christ, he is sure to be tempted by Satan to self-satisfaction and complacency. It was for that reason that, in the last chapter, Paul reminds believers of the full and sufficient spiritual armor supplied to them through God's Word and by His Spirit (6:10–17) and of their need for vigilant and persistent prayer (6:18).

> # CHRIST IN . . . EPHESIANS
>
> IN THE BOOK OF EPHESIANS, Paul explains the unique relationship between Jesus and the church as His body. Christ is the head of the church uniting believers together and strengthening the body (4:15,16). Paul also focuses on the believer's position as being "in Christ" (1:1,3–7,11–13; 2:5–6,10,13,21; 3:6,12).

A key theme of the letter is the mystery (meaning a heretofore unrevealed truth) of the church, which is "that the Gentiles should be fellow heirs, of the same body, and partakers of His promise in Christ through the gospel" (3:6), a truth completely hidden from the OT saints (cf. 3:5,9). All believers in Jesus Christ, the Messiah, are equal before the Lord as His children and as citizens of His eternal kingdom, a marvelous truth that only believers of this present age possess. Paul also speaks of the mystery of the church as the bride of Christ (5:32; cf. Rev. 21:9).

A major truth emphasized is that of the church as Christ's present spiritual, earthly body, also a distinct and formerly unrevealed truth about God's people. This metaphor depicts the church, not as an organization, but as a living organism composed of mutually related and interdependent parts. Christ is head of the body and the Holy Spirit is its lifeblood, as it were. The body of Christ functions through the faithful use of its members' various spiritual gifts, sovereignly and uniquely bestowed by the Holy Spirit on each believer.

Other major themes include the riches and fullness of blessing to believers. Paul writes of "the riches of His [God's] grace (1:7), "the unsearchable riches of Christ" (3:8), and "the riches of His glory" (3:16). Paul admonishes believers to "be filled with all the fullness of God" (3:19), to "come to the unity of the faith and of the knowledge of the Son of God, to a perfect man, to the measure of the stature of the fullness of Christ" (4:13), and to "be filled with the Spirit" (5:18). Their riches in Christ are based on His grace (1:2,6,7; 2:7), His peace (1:2), His will (1:5), His pleasure and purpose (1:9), His glory (1:12,14), His calling and inheritance (1:18), His power and strength (1:19; 6:10), His love (2:4), His workmanship (2:10), His Holy Spirit (3:16), His offering and sacrifice (5:2), and His armor (6:11, 13). The word "riches" is used five times in this letter; "grace" is used twelve times; "glory" eight times; "fullness" or "filled" six times; and the key phrase "in Christ" (or "in Him") some twelve times.

KEY DOCTRINES IN EPHESIANS

The mystery of the church, the body of Christ— all believers in Jesus Christ are equal before the Lord as His children and citizens of His eternal kingdom (1:22,23; 3:6; 5:32; Col. 1:24; Rev. 21:9)

The blessings of Jesus Christ—all believers receive the unsearchable riches in Christ through His grace and inheritance (1:2,5–9; 2:7; 3:8, 16,19; 4:13; 5:18; 6:10–13; Gen. 24:31; 26:29; Pss. 36:8; 63:5; 91:5–10; Is. 12:2; 40:11; Matt. 25:34; John 17:21; Eph. 3:12; 2 Pet. 1:4; Rev. 13:8)

GOD'S CHARACTER IN EPHESIANS

God is accessible—2:13,18; 3:12
God is glorious—1:12; 3:16
God is kind—2:7
God is loving—2:4–5
God is merciful—2:4
God is powerful—1:19; 3:7,20; 6:10
God is a promise keeper—1:13; 2:12; 3:6
God is reconciling—2:14,17
God is unified—4:6
God is wise—1:8; 3:10
God is wrathful—5:6

KEY WORDS IN

Ephesians

Purpose; Counsel; Will: Greek *prothesis*—1:9,11; 3:11; Greek *boulē*—1:11; Greek *thelēma*—1:1,5,9,11; 5:17; 6:6—three key words, all related conceptually, appear in 1:11. One of these words *(thelēma)* has been used by Paul twice before (1:1,9). The word conveys the idea of desire, even a heart's desire, for the word primarily expresses emotion instead of volition. Thus God's will is not so much God's intention, as it is His heart's desire. The word *prothesis* denotes an intention or a plan; it literally means "a laying out beforehand," like a blueprint. This plan was created in God's counsel, a translation of the Greek word *boulē*, which means the result of deliberate determination. But behind the plan and the counsel was not just a mastermind but a heart of love.

New Man: Greek *kainos anthrōpos*—2:15; 4:24—word for *new* does not mean something more recent in time, but something having a different quality or nature. Thus the *new man* is the new humanity created in Christ, of which all believers partake, both individually and corporately. Since Paul has already spoken of the new man created in Christ in terms of a new, unified, corporate humanity (2:14,15), the new man in this verse must also be thought of corporately (see Col. 3:9–11). In the immediate context, Paul is exhorting each believer to put on his or her new human nature.

INTERPRETIVE CHALLENGES

The general theology of Ephesians is direct, unambiguous, and presents no ideas or interpretations whose meanings are seriously contended. There are, however, some texts that require careful thought to rightly interpret, namely: (1) 2:8, in which one must decide if the salvation or the faith is the gift; (2) 4:5, in which the type of baptism must be discerned; and (3) 4:8, in its relationship to Psalm 68:18.

OUTLINE

I. Salutation (1:1,2)

II. God's Purpose for the Church (1:3–3:13)
- A. Predestination in Christ (1:3–6a)
- B. Redemption in Christ (1:6b-10)
- C. Inheritance in Christ (1:11–14)
- D. Resources in Christ (1:15–23)
- E. New Life in Christ (2:1–10)
- F. Unity in Christ (2:11–3:13)

III. God's Fullness for the Church (3:14–21)

IV. God's Plan for Faithful Living in the Church (4:1–6)

V. God's Son Endows and Builds the Church (4:7–16)

VI. God's Pattern and Principles for Members of the Church (4:17–32)

VII. God's Standards for Faithfulness in the Church (5:1–21)
- A. Walking in Love (5:1–7)
- B. Living in Light (5:8–14)
- C. Walking in Wisdom and Sobriety (5:15–18a)
- D. Filled with God's Spirit (5:18b-21)

VIII. God's Standards for Authority and Submission in the Church (5:22–6:9)
- A. Husbands and Wives (5:22–33)
- B. Parents and Children (6:1–4)
- C. Employers and Employees (6:5–9)

IX. God's Provision for His Children's Spiritual Battles (6:10–17)
- A. The Believer's Warfare (6:10–13)
- B. The Believer's Armor (6:14–17)

X. God's Appeal for Prayer in the Church (6:18–20)

XI. Benediction (6:21–24)

MEANWHILE, IN OTHER PARTS OF THE WORLD...

Jewish historian Josephus is training to become an invaluable resource on the historical background of much of the Bible.

ANSWERS TO TOUGH QUESTIONS

1. Why does Paul use the word *mystery* so often in his letter to the Ephesians?

Paul actually uses the word *mystery* six times in this letter (1:9; 3:3,4,9; 5:32; 6:19). By comparison, the word appears twice in Romans, once in 1 Corinthians, four times in Colossians, once in 1 Timothy, and nowhere else. Contrary to our use of mystery as a series of clues to be figured out, Paul's use of the word points to mystery as a heretofore unrevealed truth that has been made clear. The word *mystery* preserves the sense that the revealed truth has such awesome implications that it continues to amaze and humble those who accept it.

Ephesians introduces various aspects of the "mystery." Paul explained his use of the word in 3:4–6 by saying that "the Gentiles should be fellow heirs, of the same body, and partakers of His promise in Christ through the gospel." When the unsearchable riches of Christ are preached among the Gentiles, one result is an understanding of the "fellowship of the mystery" (3:9). And when God's plan for human marriage is used to explain the unique relationship between Christ and His bride, the church, Paul reminded his readers that the real subject is a great mystery (5:32). And finally, Paul asked the Ephesians to pray for him that he would be able "boldly to make known the mystery of the gospel" (6:19). The gospel is not mysterious because it is hard to understand. It is mysterious because it is unexpected, unmerited, and free. Though Paul didn't use the word in this passage, his summary of the mystery for the Ephesians can be found in 2:8,9: "For by grace you have been saved through faith, and that not of yourselves; it is the gift of God, not of works, lest anyone should boast."

2. How do grace, faith, and works make up the process of salvation that Paul describes in 2:8–10?

Paul describes the effective process of salvation as something God graciously accomplishes through faith. The word *that* in verse 8—"and that not of yourselves"—refers to the entire previous statement of salvation, not only the grace but also the faith. Although individuals are required to believe for salvation, even that faith is part of the gift of God that saves and cannot be exercised by one's own power. God's grace accomplishes the crucial action in every aspect of salvation.

Even *works*, which cannot produce salvation, are also part of God's gift. As with salvation, a believer's sanctification and good works are appointed by God before time. Opportunities, strength, and will to do good works are subsequent to God's ordained decision and a result of it. They are God-empowered fruits and evidence that grace has accomplished salvation through faith (see John 15:8; Phil. 2:12,13; 2 Tim. 3:17; Titus 2:14; James 2:16–26).

3. Paul describes a number of leadership roles in 4:11. How do we understand these roles in the church today?

Christ possesses the authority and sovereignty to assign the spiritual gifts (4:7,8) to those He has called into service in His church. He gives not only gifts but also gifted people. This passage uses five terms to describe these roles: apostles, prophets, evangelists, pastors, and teachers.

Apostles is a NT term used particularly of the twelve disciples who had seen the risen Christ (Acts 1:22), including Matthias, who replaced Judas. Later, Paul was uniquely set apart as the apostle to the Gentiles (Gal. 1:15–17). Those apostles were chosen directly by Christ, so as to be called "apostles of Christ" (Gal. 1:1; 1 Pet. 1:1). They were given three basic responsibilities:

- To lay the foundation of the church (2:20)
- To receive, declare, and write God's Word (3:5; Acts 11:28; 21:10,11)
- To confirm that Word through signs, wonders, and miracles (2 Cor. 12:12; Acts 8:6,7; Heb. 2:3,4)

The term *apostle* is used in more general ways of others in the early church, including Barnabas (Acts 14:4), Silas, and Timothy (1 Thess. 2:6), and others (Rom. 16:7; Phil. 2:25).

Prophets were not ordinary believers who had the gift of prophecy but those who had been especially commissioned by the early church. The office of prophet seems to have been exclusively for work within local congregations. They sometimes spoke practical, direct revelation for a church about God (Acts 11:21–28), or they expounded revelation already given (implied in Acts 13:1). Since the offices of apostle and prophet ceased with the completion of the NT, the ongoing leadership needs of the church have been met by other offices.

Evangelists proclaimed the good news of salvation in Jesus Christ to unbelievers (Acts 21:8; 2 Tim. 4:5). The related verb translated "to preach the gospel" is used fifty-four times and the related noun translated "gospel" is used seventy-six times in the NT.

The phrase *pastors and teachers* is best understood in context as a single office of leadership in the church. The Greek word translated "and" can mean "in particular" (1 Tim. 5:17). Pastor is the equivalent of "shepherd," so the words *pastor* and *teacher*, and the two functions together define the teaching shepherd. This person is identified as one who is under the "great Pastor" Jesus (Heb. 13:20,21; 1 Pet. 2:25). One who holds this office is also called an "elder" and "bishop" (Acts 20:28; 1 Tim. 3:1–7; Titus 1:5–9; 1 Pet. 5:1,2).

4. How do the principles of submission and love establish God's expectation of Christian marriage as described in 5:21–33?

The section that begins with a call to wise living (5:15) leads up to Paul's general counsel about submission (5:21). This last verse serves to introduce the next section (5:22–6:9), which spells out the godly expectations for various relationships. Here Paul stated unequivocally that every Spirit-filled Christian is to be a humble, submissive Christian. This is foundational to all the relationships in this section. No believer is inherently superior to any other believer. In their standing before God, all believers are equal in every way (3:28).

Having established the foundational principle of submission (5:21), Paul applied it first to the wife. The command is unqualified and applicable to every Christian wife, no matter what her own abilities, education, knowledge of Scripture, spiritual maturity, or any other qualities might be in relation to those of her husband. The submission is not the husband's to command but for the wife to willingly and lovingly offer. The phrase *your own husband* limits the wife's submission to the one man that God has placed over her.

The Spirit-filled wife recognizes that her husband's role in giving leadership is not only God-ordained but also a reflection of Christ's own loving, authoritative headship of the church. As the Lord delivered His church from the dangers of sin, death, and hell, so the husband provides for, protects, preserves, and loves his wife, leading her to blessing as she submits (Titus 1:4; 2:13; 3:6).

Paul has much more to say to the man who has been placed in the role of authority within marriage. That authority comes with supreme responsibilities for husbands in regard to their wives. Husbands are to love their wives with the same sacrificial love that Christ has for His church. Christ gave everything He had, including His own life, for the sake of His church, and that is the standard of sacrifice for a husband's love of his wife.

The clarity of God's guidelines makes it certain that problems in marriage must always be traced in both directions so that each partner clearly understands his or her roles and responsibilities. Failure to love is just as often the source of marital trouble as failure to submit.

5. Why does Paul insist in 6:10–17 that Christians must be prepared for spiritual battle?

The true believer described in chapters 1 to 3, who lives the Spirit-controlled life described in 4:1–6:9, can be sure to encounter spiritual warfare. So, Paul closed his letter with warnings about upcoming battles and instructions about victorious living. The Lord provides His saints with sufficient armor to combat and defeat the adversary. Ephesians 6:10–13 briefly sets forth the basic truths regarding the believer's necessary spiritual preparation as well as truths about the enemy, the battle, and the victory. Verses 14–17 specify the six most necessary pieces of spiritual armor with which God equips His children to resist and overcome Satan's assaults. The spiritual equipment parallels the standard military equipment worn by soldiers in Paul's day:

- Belt of truth—The soldier wore a tunic of loose fitting clothing. Since ancient combat was largely hand-to-hand, the tunic was a potential hindrance and danger. The belt cinched up the loose material. The belt that pulls together all the spiritual loose ends is "truth" or, better, "truthfulness."
- Breastplate of righteousness—A tough, sleeveless piece of leather or heavy material covered the soldier's full torso, protecting his heart and other vital organs. Because righteousness, or holiness, is such a distinctive characteristic of God Himself, it is easy to understand why it is the Christian's chief protection against Satan and his schemes.
- Boots of the gospel—Roman soldiers wore boots with nails in them to grip the ground in combat. The gospel of peace pertains to the good news that through Christ believers are at peace with God, and He is on their side (Rom. 5:6–10).

- Shield of faith—This Greek word usually refers to the large shield that pro-tected the soldier's entire body. The believer's continual trust in God's Word and promise is "above all" absolutely necessary to protect him or her from temptations to every sort of sin.
- Helmet of salvation—The helmet protected the head, always a major tar-get in battle. This passage is speaking to those who are already saved; there-fore, it does not refer to attaining salvation. Rather, since Satan seeks to destroy a believer's assurance of salvation with his weapons of doubt and discouragement, the believer must be as conscious of his or her confident status in Christ as he or she would be aware of a helmet on the head.
- Sword of the Spirit—A sword was the soldier's only weapon. In the same way, God's Word is the only weapon that a believer needs, infinitely more powerful than any of Satan's devices.

FURTHER STUDY ON EPHESIANS

1. In what ways did Paul explain his description of the church as a mystery in Ephesians?
2. When Paul described the church as the body of Christ in chapter 4, what processes and relationships did he highlight?
3. In chapter 5, how did Paul use marriage as a pattern for understanding the relationship between Christ and the church?
4. What are the components of the armor of God that Paul described in chapter 6? In what ways do you use those components in your spiritual life?
5. In what ways do Paul's guidelines for family living and work relationships affect your way of life?
6. To what degree does Ephesians 2:8–10 represent your own relationship with Christ?

PHILIPPIANS
Christ Is the Source of
Joy and Strength

TITLE
Philippians derives its name from the Greek city where the church to which it was addressed was located. Philippi was the first town in Macedonia where Paul established a church.

AUTHOR AND DATE
The unanimous testimony of the early church was that the apostle Paul wrote Philippians. Nothing in the letter would have motivated a forger to write it.

The question of when Philippians was written cannot be separated from that of where it was written. The traditional view is that Philippians, along with the other Prison Epistles (Ephesians, Colossians, Philemon), was written during Paul's first imprisonment at Rome (ca. A.D. 60–62). The most natural understanding of the references to the "palace guard" (1:13) and the "saints … of Caesar's household" (4:22) is that Paul wrote from Rome, where the emperor lived. The similarities between the details of Paul's imprisonment given in Acts and in the Prison Epistles also argue that those epistles were written from Rome (e.g., Paul was guarded by soldiers, Acts 28:16; cf. 1:13,14; was permitted to receive visitors, Acts 28:30; cf. 4:18; and had the opportunity to preach the gospel, Acts 28:31; cf. 1:12–14; Eph. 6:18–20; Col. 4:2–4).

Some have held that Paul wrote the Prison Epistles during his two-year imprisonment at Caesarea (Acts 24:27). But Paul's opportunities to receive visitors and proclaim the gospel were severely limited during that imprisonment (cf. Acts 23:35). The Prison Epistles express Paul's hope for a favorable verdict (1:25; 2:24; cf. Philem. 22). In Caesarea, however, Paul's only hope for release was either to bribe Felix (Acts 24:26), or agree to stand trial at Jerusalem under Festus (Acts 25:9). In the Prison Epistles, Paul expected the decision in his case to be final (1:20–23; 2:17,23). That could not have been true at Caesarea, since Paul could and did appeal his case to the emperor.

Another alternative has been that Paul wrote the Prison Epistles from Ephesus. But at Ephesus, like Caesarea, no final decision could be made in his case because of his right to appeal to the emperor. Also, Luke was with Paul when he wrote Colossians (Col. 4:14), but he apparently was not with the apostle at Ephesus. Acts 19, which records Paul's stay in Ephesus, is not in one of the "we sections" of Acts (Acts: Author and Date). The most telling argument against Ephesus as the point of origin for the Prison Epistles, however, is that there is no evidence that Paul was ever imprisoned at Ephesus.

In light of the serious difficulties faced by both the Caesarean and Ephesian views, there is no reason to reject the traditional view that Paul wrote the Prison Epistles—including Philippians—from Rome.

Paul's belief that his case would soon be decided (2:23,24) points to Philippians being written toward the close of the apostle's two-year Roman imprisonment (ca. A.D. 61).

BACKGROUND AND SETTING

Originally known as Krenides ("The Little Fountains") because of the numerous nearby springs, Philippi ("city of Philip") received its name from Philip II of Macedon (the father of Alexander the Great). Attracted by the nearby gold mines, Philip conquered the region in the fourth century B.C. In the second century B.C., Philippi became part of the Roman province of Macedonia.

The city existed in relative obscurity for the next two centuries until one of the most famous events in Roman history brought it recognition and expansion. In 42 B.C., the forces of Antony and Octavian defeated those of Brutus and Cassius at the Battle of Philippi, thus ending the Roman Republic and ushering in the Empire. After the battle, Philippi became a Roman colony (cf. Acts 16:12), and many veterans of the Roman army settled there. As a colony, Philippi had autonomy from the provincial government and the same rights granted to cities in Italy, including the use of Roman law,

CHRIST IN ... PHILIPPIANS

PHILIPPIANS PRESENTS one of the most poignant testimonies of the life lived in Christ. Paul intimately describes his relationship with his Lord with the words "to live is Christ and to die is gain" (1:21). Paul's selflessness leads not to feelings of loss but only to joy and peace in Jesus Christ (4:4-7). Therefore, he encourages believers to seek Christlikeness (2:5).

exemption from some taxes, and Roman citizenship for its residents (Acts 16:21). Being a colony was also the source of much civic pride for the Philippians, who used Latin as their official language, adopted Roman customs, and modeled their city government after that of Italian cities. Acts and Philippians both reflect Philippi's status as a Roman colony.

Paul's description of Christians as citizens of heaven (3:20) was appropriate, since the Philippians prided themselves on being citizens of Rome (cf. Acts 16:21). The Philippians may well have known some of the members of the palace guard (1:13) and Caesar's household (4:22).

The church at Philippi, the first one founded by Paul in Europe, dates from the apostle's second missionary journey (Acts 16:12–40). Philippi evidently had a very small Jewish population. Because there were not enough men to form a synagogue (the requirement was for 10 Jewish men who were heads of a household), some devout women met outside the city at a place of prayer (Acts 16:13) alongside the Gangites River. Paul preached the gospel to them and Lydia, a wealthy merchant dealing in expensive purple dyed goods (Acts 16:14), became a believer (16:14,15). It is likely that the Philippian church initially met in her spacious home.

Satanic opposition to the new church immediately arose in the person of a demon-possessed, fortune-telling slave girl (Acts 16:16,17). Not wanting even agreeable testimony from such an evil source, Paul cast the demon out of her (Acts 16:18). The apostle's act enraged the girl's masters, who could no longer sell her services as a fortune-teller (Acts 16:19). They hauled Paul and Silas before the city's magistrates (Acts 16:20) and inflamed the civic pride of the Philippians by claiming the two preachers were a threat to Roman customs (Acts 16:20,21). As a result, Paul and Silas were beaten and imprisoned (Acts 16:22–24).

The two preachers were miraculously released from prison that night by an earthquake, which unnerved the jailer and opened his heart and that of his household to the gospel (Acts 16:25–34). The next day the magistrates, panicking when they learned they had illegally beaten and imprisoned two Roman citizens, begged Paul and Silas to leave Philippi.

Paul apparently visited Philippi twice during his third missionary journey, once at the beginning (cf. 2 Cor. 8:1–5), and again near the end (Acts 20:6). About four or five years after his last visit to Philippi, while a prisoner at Rome, Paul received a delegation from the Philippian church. The Philippians had generously supported Paul in the past (4:15,16), and had also contributed abundantly for the needy at Jerusalem (2 Cor. 8:1–4). Now, hearing of Paul's imprisonment, they sent another contribution to him (4:10), and along with it Epaphroditus to minister to Paul's needs. Unfortunately Epaphroditus suffered a near-fatal illness (2:26,27), either while en route to Rome, or after he arrived. Accordingly, Paul decided to send Epaphroditus back to Philippi (2:25,26) and wrote the letter to the Philippians to send back with him.

Paul had several purposes in composing this epistle. First, he wanted to express in writing his thanks for the Philippians' gift (4:10–18). Second, he wanted the Philippians to know why he decided to return Epaphroditus to them, so they would not think his service to Paul had been unsatisfactory (2:25,26). Third, he wanted to inform them about his circumstances at Rome (1:12–26). Fourth, he wrote to exhort them to unity (2:1,2; 4:2). Finally, he wrote to warn them against false teachers (3:1–4:1).

KEY WORDS IN

Philippians

Supply: Greek *epichorēgia*–1:19–used to describe what a choir manager would provide to all the members of a Greek choir who performed in Greek drama. In short, he took care of all their living expenses. The word came to mean a full supply of any kind. The Philippians' prayer would generate the Spirit's *supply*. Paul was looking forward to getting a full supply of Jesus Christ's Spirit as a result of the Philippians' prayers.

Form of God: Greek *morphē theou*–2:6–morphē, the word for *form*, was generally used to express the way in which a thing exists and appears according to what it is in itself. Thus, the expression *form of God* may be correctly understood as the essential nature and character of God. To say, therefore, that Christ existed in *the form of God* is to say that apart from His human nature, Christ possessed all the characteristics and qualities belonging to God because He is, in fact, God.

Virtue: Greek *aretē*–4:8–a rare word in the NT but generously used in Greek writings to denote moral excellence. Peter in his first letter used the word to describe the excellent nature or "excellencies" of God (see 1 Pet. 2:9, where the word is translated *praises*). Such excellence is said to have been possessed by various people, but it is a quality that comes from God. Only those who are given divine power can be morally excellent on this earth (2 Pet. 1:3).

KEY PEOPLE IN PHILIPPIANS

Paul—wrote to the Philippians about the joy and strength found in Christ (1:1–4:23)

Timothy—missionary of both Jewish and Gentile descent; prepared by Paul to carry on his ministry in Philippi (1:1–2:23)

Epaphroditus—faithful worker from Philippi; sent to Paul with supportive money (2:25–30; 4:18)

Euodia—faithful worker rebuked by Paul for her unreconciled relationship with Syntyche, another sister in the church (4:2,3)

Syntyche—faithful worker rebuked by Paul for her unreconciled relationship with Euodia (4:2,3)

HISTORICAL AND THEOLOGICAL THEMES

Since it is primarily a practical letter, Philippians contains little historical material (there are no OT quotes), apart from the momentous treatment of Paul's spiritual autobiography (3:4–7). There is, likewise, little direct theological instruction, also with one big exception. The magnificent passage describing Christ's humiliation and exaltation (2:5–11) contains some of the most profound and crucial teaching on the Lord Jesus Christ in all the Bible. The major theme of pursuing Christlikeness, as the most defining element of spiritual growth and the one passion of Paul in his own life, is presented in 3:12–14. In spite of Paul's imprisonment, the dominant tone of the letter is joyful (1:4,18,25,26; 2:2,16–18,28; 3:1,3; 4:1,4,10).

KEY DOCTRINES IN PHILIPPIANS

Humility of Christ—Christ came into the world to serve and sacrifice Himself for humankind (2:5–8; Pss. 22:6; 69:9; Is. 50:6; 53:3,7; Zech. 9:9; Matt. 11:29; 13:55; Luke 2:4–7,51; 9:58; John 5:41; 13:14,15; Rom. 15:3; 2 Cor. 8:9; Heb. 2:16; 4:15; 5:7)

Submission to Christ—believers should pursue Christlikeness (1:21; 3:7–14; Gen. 43:14; Judg. 10:15; 1 Sam. 3:18; 2 Sam. 15:26; Job 2:10; Pss. 37:7; 46:10; Matt. 6:10; Acts 7:59; Heb. 12:6; 2 Pet. 1:14)

Christ's provision for believers—God supplies the needs of His children (4:13,19; Neh. 9:19; Ps. 146:7–9; Matt. 9:36; John 7:37; 2 Cor. 9:12; 12:9,10; Heb. 4:16)

GOD'S CHARACTER IN PHILIPPIANS

God is glorious—2:11

God is merciful—2:27

God is provident—1:12

INTERPRETIVE CHALLENGES

The major difficulty connected with Philippians is determining where it was written (see Author and Date). The text itself presents only one significant interpretive challenge: the identity of the "enemies of the cross." As he had done in many of his contacts with churches he had founded (Acts 20:28–31), Paul warned the Philippians about the dangers of false teachers. Paul's language implies that these teachers did not openly claim to oppose Christ, His work on the cross, or salvation by grace alone through faith alone, but they did not pursue Christlikeness through godly living. Their faith was a fraud. Apparently, they had been posing as friends of Christ and possibly had even reached positions of leadership in the church. Their lives displayed their true allegiance.

OUTLINE

I. Paul's Greeting (1:1–11)
II. Paul's Circumstances (1:12–26)
III. Paul's Exhortations (1:27–2:18)
    A. To Stand Firm Amid Persecution (1:27–30)
    B. To Be United by Humility (2:1–4)
    C. To Remember the Example of Christ (2:5–11)
    D. To Be Light in a Dark World (2:12–18)
IV. Paul's Companions (2:19–30)
    A. Timothy (2:19–24)
    B. Epaphroditus (2:25–30)
V. Paul's Warnings (3:1–4:1)
    A. Against Legalism (3:1–16)
    B. Against Lawlessness (3:17–4:1)
VI. Paul's Admonition (4:2–9)
VII. Paul's Thankfulness (4:10–20)
VIII. Paul's Farewell (4:21–23)

MEANWHILE, IN OTHER PARTS OF THE WORLD...

Buddhist monks move from India into China bringing with them chants. Later, these chants were incorporated into Chinese music.

ANSWERS TO TOUGH QUESTIONS

1. What can we learn about Jesus from the great eulogy in 2:6–11?

This is a classic passage in the NT, summarizing the divinity, character, and incarnation of Jesus Christ. It stands so clearly as a unit that it was probably sung as a hymn in the early church.

This meditation begins by focusing on the eternal nature of Christ (2:6). The common Greek term for *being* is not used here. Instead, Paul chose another term that stresses the essence of a person's nature—his or her continuous state or condition. Also, of the two Greek words for *form*, Paul chose the one that specifically denotes the essential, unchanging character of something—what it is in and of itself. The fundamental doctrine of the deity of Christ has always included these crucial characteristics (see also John 1:1,3–4,14; 8:58; Col. 1:15–17; Heb. 1:3). Although Christ had all the rights, privileges, and honors of deity—for which He was eternally and continually worthy—His attitude was not to cling to His position but to willingly give it up for a time.

Next, the passage describes the process that Christ underwent in order to carry out the Incarnation. First, He "made Himself of no reputation" or better, "emptied Himself" (2:7). The Greek root word used here, *kenosis*, is now used as the theological term for the doctrine of Christ's self-emptying in His incarnation. This step did not mean that Jesus emptied Himself of deity. Jesus did, however, renounce or set aside His privileges in several areas:

- Heavenly glory (John 17:5)
- Independent authority—during His incarnation Christ completely submitted Himself to the will of His Father (Matt. 26:39; John 5:30; Heb. 5:8)
- Divine prerogatives—Christ set aside the voluntary display of His divine attributes and submitted Himself to the Spirit's direction (Matt. 24:36; John 1:45–49)
- Eternal riches (2 Cor. 8:9)
- A favorable relationship with God—Christ felt the Father's wrath for human sin while on the cross (Matt. 27:46).

Next, Christ took on the "form of a bondservant" and the "likeness of men" (2:7). The same Greek word for *form* occurs here as in verse 6. Christ became more than just God in a human body; He took on all the essential attributes of humanity (Luke 2:52; Gal. 4:4; Col. 1:22), even to the extent that He identified with basic human needs and weaknesses (Heb. 2:14,17; 4:15). He became the God-man: fully divine and fully human.

Next, Christ carried out the full purposes and implications of His divine action. He experienced every aspect of life as a human being. This included the ultimate obedience of dying as a criminal, following God's plan for Him (Matt. 26:39; Acts 2:23).

Christ's utter humiliation (2:5–8) is inseparably linked to His exaltation by God (2:9–11). Jesus was honored in at least six distinct ways: (1) His resurrection; (2) His coronation (His position at the right hand of God); (3) His role of interceeding on our behalf (Acts 2:32,33; 5:30,31; Eph. 1:20,21; Heb. 4:15; 7:25,26); (4) His ascension (Heb. 4:14); (5) His acknowledged role as the ultimate and perfect substitute for sin; and (6) His given title and name as Lord, which identifies Him fully as the divine and sovereign ruler (Is. 45:21–23; Mark 15:2; Luke 2:11; John 13:13; 18:37; 20:28; Acts 2:36; 10:36; Rom. 14:9–11; 1 Cor. 8:6; 15:57; Rev. 17:14; 19:16). Scripture repeatedly affirms Jesus' rightful title as the God-man.

2. How do the words *joy* and *rejoice* capture Paul's central message to this group of believers?

Paul uses the word *joy* four times in this letter (1:4,25; 2:2; 4:1). The word *rejoice* appears in the text nine times (1:18 twice, 26; 2:17,18; 3:1; 4:4 twice, 10). In the early chapters, these terms are used primarily to describe Paul's own experience of life in Christ. The beginning of chapter 3, however, is a transition point, shifting to a section of spiritual direction. Paul's expression "rejoice in the Lord" (3:1) is the first time in this letter for the phrase "in the Lord," signifying the reason and the sphere in which the believers' joy exists. Unrelated to the circumstances of life, the believers' joy flows from an indisputable, unchanging relationship with the sovereign Lord.

The theme of joy reaches a peak in 4:4 with the double command, "Rejoice in the Lord always. Again I will say, rejoice!" The verses that follow spell out the external behavior and the internal attitudes that characterize a person whose joy is genuine. Paul also included God's promise to supply both His presence and His peace to those who live rejoicing in the Lord.

FURTHER STUDY ON PHILIPPIANS

1. Read Philippians 2:5–11 and then put it into your own words, describing how Christ's actions affect your life.
2. In Philippians 3, to what did Paul compare all his achievements when measured against what it means to know Christ?
3. In how many different ways can you identify Paul's emphasis on joy in this letter?
4. What guidelines does Paul offer in chapter 4 that relate to your prayer life and your thought life? How many of them do you practice?
5. What did Paul mean by Philippians 4:13, and to what degree have you experienced the truth of his discovery?

COLOSSIANS
Man Is Completed through God the Son

TITLE
Colossians is named for the city of Colosse, where the church it was addressed to was located. It was also to be read in the neighboring church at Laodicea (4:16).

AUTHOR AND DATE
Paul is identified as author at the beginning (1:1; cf. v. 23; 4:18), as customarily in his epistles. The testimony of the early church, including such key figures as Irenaeus, Clement of Alexandria, Tertullian, Origen, and Eusebius, confirms that the opening claim is genuine. Additional evidence for Paul's authorship comes from the book's close parallels with Philemon, which is universally accepted as having been written by Paul. Both were written (ca. A.D. 60–62) while Paul was a prisoner in Rome (4:3,10,18; Philem. 9,10,13,23); plus the names of the same people (e.g., Timothy, Aristarchus, Archippus, Mark, Epaphras, Luke, Onesimus, and Demas) appear in both epistles, showing that both were written by the same author at about the same time. For biographical information on Paul, see Romans: Author and Date.

BACKGROUND AND SETTING
Colosse was a city in Phrygia, in the Roman province of Asia (part of modern Turkey), about 100 miles east of Ephesus in the region of the seven churches of Revelation 1–3. The city lay alongside the Lycus River, not far from where it flowed into the Maender River. The Lycus Valley narrowed at Colosse to a width of about two miles, and Mt. Cadmus rose 8,000 feet above the city.

Colosse was a thriving city in the fifth century B.C. when the Persian king Xerxes (Ahasuerus, cf. Esth. 1:1) marched through the region. Black wool and dyes (made from the nearby chalk deposits) were important products. In addition, the city was situated at the junction of the main north-south and east-west trade routes. By Paul's day, however, the main road had been rerouted through nearby Laodicea, thus bypassing Colosse and leading to its decline and the rise of the neighboring cities of Laodicea and Hierapolls.

> ## CHRIST IN . . . COLOSSIANS
> THE MESSAGE OF COLOSSIANS affirms the believer's perfect completion in Christ (1:28). Paul stressed the deity of Jesus against those who attacked the Person of Christ with "philosophy and empty deceit" (2:8,9). Accepting the fullness of Christ as God allows believers to come to fullness of life in Him (2:10).

Although Colosse's population was mainly Gentile, there was a large Jewish settlement dating from the days of Antiochus the Great (223–187 B.C.). Colosse's mixed population of Jews and Gentiles manifested itself both in the composition of the church and in the heresy that plagued it, which contained elements of both Jewish legalism and pagan mysticism.

The church at Colosse began during Paul's three-year ministry at Ephesus (Acts 19). Its founder was not Paul, who had never been there (2:1); but Epaphras (1:5–7), who apparently was saved during a visit to Ephesus, then likely started the church in Colosse when he returned home. Several years after the Colossian church was founded, a dangerous heresy arose to threaten it—one not identified with any particular historical system. It contained elements of what later became known as Gnosticism: that God is good, but matter is evil, that Jesus Christ was merely one of a series of emanations descending from God and being less than God (a belief that led them to deny His true humanity), and that a secret, higher knowledge above Scripture was necessary for enlightenment and salvation. The Colossian heresy also embraced aspects of Jewish legalism, e.g., the necessity of circumcision for salvation, observance of the ceremonial rituals of the OT law (dietary laws, festivals, Sabbaths), and other fleshly laws. It also called for the worship of angels and mystical experience. Epaphras was so concerned about this heresy that he made the long journey from Colosse to Rome (4:12,13), where Paul was a prisoner.

This letter was written from prison in Rome (Acts 28:16–31) sometime between A.D. 60–62 and is, therefore, referred to as a Prison Epistle (along with Ephesians, Philippians, and Philemon). It may have been composed at nearly the same time as with Ephesians and initially sent with that epistle and Philemon by Tychicus (Eph. 6:21,22; Col. 4:7,8). See Philippians: Author and Date for a discussion of the city from which Paul wrote. He wrote this letter to warn the Colossians against the heresy they faced, and sent the letter to them with Tychicus, who was accompanying the runaway slave Onesimus back to his master, Philemon, a member of the Colossian church (4:7–9; see Philemon: Background and Setting). Epaphras remained behind in Rome (cf. Philem. 23), perhaps to receive further instruction from Paul.

KEY PEOPLE IN COLOSSIANS
Paul—urged the church at Colosse to flee from false doctrines which deny Christ's deity (1:1–4:18)
Timothy—fellow missionary who traveled with Paul (1:1)
Tychicus—sent to the church at Colosse to bring letters and news from Paul (4:7–9)
Onesimus—faithfully served with Paul before returning to Colosse to reconcile with Philemon, his former master (see the Book of Philemon) (4:9)
Aristarchus—Thessalonian who traveled with Paul on his third missionary journey (4:10)
Mark—cousin of Barnabas who accompanied Paul and Barnabas on the first missionary journey (4:10)
Epaphras—founder of the Colossian church (1:7,8; 4:12,13)

HISTORICAL AND THEOLOGICAL THEMES
Colossians contains teaching on several key areas of theology, including the deity of Christ (1:15–20; 2:2–10), reconciliation (1:20–23), redemption (1:13,14; 2:13,14; 3:9–11), election (3:12), forgiveness (3:13), and the nature of the church (1:18,24,25; 2:19; 3:11,15). Also, as noted above, it refutes the heretical teaching that threatened the Colossian church (chap. 2).

The Glories of Christ

"Not that we are sufficient of ourselves to think of anything as *being* from ourselves, but our sufficiency is from God..." (2 Cor. 3:5)

One of the great tenets of Scripture is the claim that Jesus Christ is completely sufficient for all matters of life and godliness (2 Pet. 1:3,4)! He is sufficient for creation (Col. 1:16,17), salvation (Heb. 10:10–12), sanctification (Eph. 5:26,27), and glorification (Rom. 8:30). So pure is He that there is no blemish, stain, spot of sin, defilement, lying, deception, corruption, error, or imperfection (1 Pet. 1:18–20).

So complete is He that there is no other God besides Him (Is. 45:5); He is the only begotten Son (John 1:14,18); all the treasures of wisdom and knowledge are in Him (Col. 2:3); the fullness of the Godhead dwells bodily in Him (Col. 2:9); He is heir of all things (Heb. 1:2); He created all things and all things were made by Him, through Him, and for Him (Col. 1:16); He upholds all things by the word of His power (Col. 1:17; Heb. 1:3); He is the firstborn of all creation (Col. 1:15); He is the exact representation of God (Heb. 1:3).

He is the only Mediator between God and man; He is the Sun that enlightens; the Physician that heals; the Friend that comforts; the Pearl that enriches; the Ark that supports; and the Rock to sustain under the heaviest of pressures; He is seated at the right hand of the throne of the Majesty on high (Heb. 1:3; 8:1); He is better than the angels (Heb. 1:4–14); better than Moses; better than Aaron; better than Joshua; better than Melchizedek; better than all the prophets; greater than Satan (Luke 4:1–12); and stronger than death (1 Cor. 15:55).

He has no beginning and no end (Rev. 1:17,18); He is the spotless Lamb of God; He is our Peace (Eph. 2:14); He is our Hope (1 Tim. 1:1); He is our Life (Col. 3:4); He is the living and true Way (John 14:6); He is the Strength of Israel (1 Sam. 15:29); He is the Root and Offspring of David, the Bright and Morning Star (Rev. 22:16); He is Faithful and True (Rev. 19:11); He is the Author and Finisher of our faith (Heb. 12:1,2); He is the Captain of our Salvation (Heb. 2:10); He is the Champion; He is the Elect One (Is. 42:1); He is the Apostle and High-Priest of our confession (Heb. 3:1); He is the Righteous Servant (Is. 53:11).

He is the Lord of Hosts, the Redeemer—the Holy One of Israel, the God of the whole earth (Is. 54:5); He is the Man of Sorrows (Is. 53:3); He is the Light; He is the Son of Man (Matt. 20:28); He is the Vine; He is the Bread of Life; He is the Door; He is Lord (Phil. 2:10–13); He is Prophet, Priest and King (Heb. 1:1–3); He is our Sabbath rest (Heb. 4:9); He is our Righteousness (Jer. 23:6); He is the Wonderful Counselor, the Mighty God, the Everlasting Father, the Prince of Peace (Is. 9:6); He is the Chief Shepherd (1 Pet. 5:4); He is Lord God of hosts; He is Lord of the nations; He is the Lion of Judah; the Living Word; the Rock of Salvation; the Eternal Spirit; He is the Ancient of Days; Creator and Comforter; Messiah; and He is the great I AM (John 8:58)!

KEY DOCTRINES IN COLOSSIANS

The deity of Christ—Jesus did not only come from God; He is the one, true God and Messiah (1:15–20; 2:2–10; Pss. 24:7,10; 45:6,7; Is. 7:14; 8:13,14; 9:6; 40:3,11; Jer. 23:5,6; Zech. 13:7; Matt. 1:23; 3:3; 12:8; 26:63–67; Mark 2:7,10; John 1:1,14,18; 3:16; Acts 10:36; Rom. 9:5; Titus 2:13; Heb. 13:20; 1 Pet. 2:8)

Reconciliation—the sacrifice of Jesus Christ renews the relationship between God and man (1:20–22; 2:14; Lev. 8:15; 16:20; Dan. 9:24; Is. 53:5; Matt. 5:24–26; Rom. 5:1,10,11; 2 Cor. 5:18–20; Eph. 2:14–16; Heb. 2:17)

Redemption—Jesus Christ bought our salvation for a price, His own death on the cross (1:13,14; 2:13,14; 3:9–11; Is. 43:1; 44:21–23; Matt. 20:28; Luke 1:68; Acts 20:28; 1 Cor. 1:30; 6:20; 7:23; Gal. 3:13; 4:4,5; Heb. 9:12; 1 Pet. 1:19; Rev. 5:9)

Election—the life and future of each believer was intimately known by God before time began (3:12; Matt. 20:16; John 6:44; 13:18; 15:16; Acts 22:14; Rom. 8:29; 9:11,15,16; 1 Cor. 1:27; Eph. 1:4,5,11; 1 Thess. 1:4; 2 Thess. 2:13; Titus 1:1; 1 Pet. 1:2)

Forgiveness—we are to forgive others in the same merciful manner God forgives us (3:13; Ps. 7:4; Prov. 19:11; Matt. 18:22; Mark 11:25; Luke 6:36; 17:4; 23:34; Rom. 12:19; Eph. 4:32; 1 Pet. 4:8)

The nature of the church as the body of Christ—all believers in Jesus Christ are equal before the Lord as His children and citizens of His eternal kingdom (1:18,24,25; 2:19; 3:11,15; Eph. 1:22,23; 3:6; 5:32; Rev. 21:9)

The Preeminence of Christ

```
                      CHRIST

            THE UNIVERSAL GOVERNMENT
          The visible image of God (1:15)
          The agent of creation (1:16)
              The Sustainer (1:17)
          The head of the church (1:18)

              IN RECONCILIATION
          Pleases the Father (1:19,20)
      Reconciles us through His death (1:21,22)
      Lives in us as our hope of glory (1:27)

           IN WISDOM AND KNOWLEDGE
       The source of all the treasures (2:2,3)
     Worldly philosophy does not conform to Him (2:8)

            IN PERSONAL OBSERVANCE
          We are alive in Him (2:11-13)
      No need for legalism and ritualism (2:16–23)

             IN CHRISTIAN LIVING
              He is our life (3:3)
    We can avoid immorality and can bless others (3:5–14)
```

GOD'S CHARACTER IN COLOSSIANS
God is accessible—1:21,22
God is invisible—1:15
God is just—3:25
God is powerful—1:11; 2:12
God is reconciling—1:20
God is wrathful—3:6

INTERPRETIVE CHALLENGES
Those cults that deny Christ's deity have seized upon the description of Him as "the first-born over all creation" (1:15) as proof that He was a created being. Paul's statement that believers will be "holy, and blameless, and above reproach" if they "continue in the faith"

Titles of Christ

Name or Title	Significance	Biblical Reference
Adam, Last Adam	First of the new race of the redeemed	1 Corinthians 15:45
Alpha and Omega	The beginning and ending of all things	Revelation 21:6
Bread of Life	The one essential food	John 6:35
Chief Cornerstone	A sure foundation for life	Ephesians 2:20
Chief Shepherd	Protector, sustainer, and guide	1 Peter 5:4
Firstborn from the Dead	Leads us into resurrection and eternal life	Colossians 1:18
Good Shepherd	Provider and caretaker	John 10:11
Great Shepherd of the Sheep	Trustworthy guide and protector	Hebrews 13:20
High Priest	A perfect sacrifice for our sins	Hebrews 3:1
Holy One of God	Sinless in His nature	Mark 1:24
Immanuel (God With Us)	Stands with us in all life's circumstances	Matthew 1:23
King of Kings, Lord of Lords	The Almighty, before whom every knee will bow	Revelation 19:16
Lamb of God	Gave His life as a sacrifice on our behalf	John 1:29
Light of the World	Brings hope in the midst of darkness	John 9:5
Lord of Glory	The power and presence of the living God	1 Corinthians 2:8
Mediator between God and Men	Brings us into God's presence redeemed and forgiven	1 Timothy 2:5
Only Begotten of the Father	The unique, one-of-a-kind Son of God	John 1:14
Prophet	Faithful proclaimer of the truths of God	Acts 3:22
Savior	Delivers from sin and death	Luke 1:47
Seed of Abraham	Mediator of God's covenant	Galatians 3:16
Son of Man	Identifies with us in our humanity	Matthew 18:11
The Word	Present with God at the creation	John 1:1

(1:22,23) has led some to teach that believers can lose their salvation. (See Answers to Tough Questions for further discussion on these issues.)

Some have argued for the existence of purgatory based on Paul's statement, "I ... fill up in my flesh what is lacking in the afflictions of Christ" (1:24). Paul was experiencing the persecution intended for Christ. In spite of His death on the cross, Christ's enemies had not gotten their fill of inflicting injury on Him. So they turned their hatred on those who preached the gospel (cf. John 15:18,24; 16:1–3). It was in that sense that Paul filled up what was lacking in Christ's afflictions.

Also, there are others who see support in Colossians for baptismal regeneration (2:12). Circumcision symbolized man's need for cleansing of the heart (cf. Deut. 10:16; 30:6; Jer. 4:4; 9:26; Acts 7:51; Rom. 2:29) and was the outward sign of that cleansing of sin that comes by faith in God (Rom. 4:11; Phil. 3:3). At salvation, believers undergo a spiritual "circumcision" "by putting off the body of the sins of the flesh" (cf. Rom. 6:6; 2 Cor. 5:17;

Phil 3:3; Titus 3:5). This is the new birth, the new creation in conversion. The outward affirmation of the already accomplished inner transformation is now the believer's baptism by water (Acts 2:38).

Finally, the identity of the "epistle from Laodicea" (4:16) has also prompted much discussion. The letter to the Colossians was to be publicly read in the churches in Colosse and in Laodicea. The epistle from Laodicea was a separate letter from Paul, usually identified as the epistle to the Ephesians. The oldest manuscripts of Ephesians do not contain the words "in Ephesus," indicating that in all likelihood it was a circular letter intended for several churches in the region. Tychicus may have delivered Ephesians to the church at Laodicea first.

OUTLINE

I. Personal Matters (1:1–14)
    A. Paul's Greeting (1:1,2)
    B. Paul's Thankfulness (1:3–8)
    C. Paul's Prayer (1:9–14)

II. Doctrinal Instruction (1:15–2:23)
    A. About Christ's Deity (1:15–23)
    B. About Paul's Ministry (1:24–2:7)
    C. About False Philosophy (2:8–23)

III. Practical Exhortations (3:1–4:18)
    A. Christian Conduct (3:1–17)
    B. Christian Households (3:18–4:1)
    C. Christian Speech (4:2–6)
    D. Christian Friends (4:7–18)

MEANWHILE, IN OTHER PARTS OF THE WORLD...

An ambassador from the king of Nu, a country formerly located on the island of modern-day Japan, arrives in China to give homage to the Han emperor Guang Wudi.

ANSWERS TO TOUGH QUESTIONS

1. How does a passage like 1:15–20, which describes Christ as the "firstborn over all creation," fit with the biblical doctrine of Christ's deity?

This passage, 1:15–20, includes a powerful defense of Christ's deity. Apparently, a central component of the heresy that threatened the Colossian church was the denial of the deity of Christ. Ironically, throughout the centuries some cults have used the phrase "firstborn over all creation" (1:15) to undermine Christ's deity. The assumption is that if Jesus was born at creation, then He is more like us than He is God.

Colossians

Jesus Christ: Greek *Iēsous Christos*—1:1–4,28; 2:6; 3:17. Many people believe *Jesus Christ* refers to the first and last names of Jesus. However, *Jesus* is a human name, which means "the Lord saves" (see Matt. 1:21). The title *Christ* describes a unique position: Jesus is "the Anointed One." He serves as the perfect King, Prophet, and High Priest of humanity. The name *Jesus Christ* was used prolifically after Jesus revealed Himself as the promised Messiah. Paul indicated the supremacy of Jesus Christ by using this combined name to begin his letter to the Colossians.

First Born: Greek *prōtotokos*—1:15,18—literally, "first in time" or "first in place." In this context, *prōtotokos* should be translated as preeminent or "first in place." Therefore, Jesus Christ is the "chief born" who reigns over all creation (see Ex. 4:22; Deut. 21:16,17; Psalm 89:23). This title reveals the humanity of the Son as the foremost creature of all creation. However, this designation in no way suggests that Christ Himself was created by God. The next verse clearly declares Christ as the Creator of all things. Thus, Christ cannot be a created being. Instead He is the eternal Son of God and the second Person of the Godhead.

Perfect: Greek *teleios*—1:28; 4:12—literally, "end," "limit," or "fulfillment." Paul uses *teleios* to describe the completion or perfection of believers in Christ (Col. 1:28; 4:12). Christians move towards "perfection" and godliness when their faith matures through trials (James 1:4). Christians are made more complete by expressing God's love to others (3:14; 1 John 4:12). Just as Paul pressed on towards the goal of perfection in his Christian walk (Phil. 3:12–14), so we too should make perfection in Christ our goal. For humanity, the goal of perfection will be completed when "that which is perfect" comes (1 Cor. 13:10).

The Greek word for firstborn, however, can refer to one who was born first chronologically, but it most often refers to preeminence in position or rank (Heb. 1:6; Rom. 8:9). *Firstborn* in this context clearly means highest in rank, not first created (Ps. 89:27; Rev. 1:5) for several reasons:

- Christ cannot be both "first begotten" and "only begotten" (see John 1:14,18; 3:16,18; 1 John 4:9); and, when the firstborn is one of a class, the class is in the plural form (1:18; Rom. 8:29), but "creation," the class here, is in a singular form.
- If Paul were teaching that Christ was a created being, he would be agreeing with the heresy that he was writing to refute.
- It is impossible for Christ to be both created and the Creator of everything (1:16). Thus, Jesus is the firstborn in the sense that He has the preeminence (1:18) and that he possesses the right of inheritance "over all creation" (Heb. 1:2; Rev. 5:1–7,13).

2. What does the conditional statement "if indeed you continue in the faith" (1:22,23) have to do with whether or not believers can lose their salvation?

The Christian doctrine that deals with this question is often called "the perseverance of the saints." Scripture, as here, sometimes calls us to hold fast to our faith (Heb. 10:23; Rev. 3:11) or warns us against falling away (Heb. 10:26–29). Such admonitions do not negate the many promises that true believers will persevere (John 10:28,29;

Rom. 8:38,39; 1 Cor. 1:8,9; Phil. 1:6). Rather, the warnings and pleas are among the means God uses to secure our perseverance in the faith. Conditional statements like the one in 1:22 and 23 simply underscore the point that those who do fall away from Christ give conclusive proof that they were never truly believers to begin with (1 John 2:19). To say that God secures our perseverance is not to say that we are passive in the process, however. God keeps us "through faith" (1 Pet. 1:5)—our faith.

3. **What were the Prison Epistles, and what prison was Paul in when he wrote them?**
Four of Paul's letters are grouped as the Prison Epistles: Ephesians, Philippians, Colossians, and Philemon. Each of them includes clear internal references to the writer's prison surroundings (Eph. 3:1; 4:1; 6:20; Phil. 1:7,13,14,17; Col. 4:3,10,18; Phil. 1,9,10,13,23). The similarities between the details of Paul's imprisonment given in Acts and in the Prison Epistles support the traditional position that the letters were written from Rome. Among these details are these:

- Paul was guarded by soldiers (Acts 28:16; Phil. 1:13,14).
- Paul was permitted to receive visitors (Acts 28:30; Phil. 4:18).
- Paul had the opportunity to preach the gospel (Acts 28:31; Eph. 6:18–20; Phil. 1:12–14; Col. 4:2–4).

Caesarea and Ephesus have also been suggested as Paul's possible location when he wrote at least some of these letters. Paul was imprisoned in Caesarea for two years (Acts 24:27), but his opportunities to receive visitors and proclaim the gospel were severely limited during that time (Acts 23:35). The Prison Epistles express Paul's hope for a favorable verdict (Phil. 1:25; 2:24; Phil. 23). In Caesarea, however, Paul's only hope for release was to either bribe Felix (Acts 24:26) or agree to stand trial at Jerusalem under Festus (Acts 25:9). In the Prison Epistles, Paul expected the decision in his case to be final (Phil. 1:20–23; 2:17,23). That could not have been true at Caesarea, since Paul could and did appeal his case to the emperor.

Ephesus has been the other suggested location. Most of the same difficulties faced by the Caesarea suggestion face those who support Ephesus. The most telling argument against Ephesus as the point of origin for the Prison Epistles, however, is that there is no evidence that Paul was ever imprisoned at Ephesus.

In light of the serious difficulties faced by both the Caesarean and Ephesian views, no reason remains for rejecting the traditional view that Paul wrote the Prison Epistles from Rome while awaiting a hearing before the emperor on his appeal for justice as a Roman citizen.

FURTHER STUDY ON COLOSSIANS
1. Based on his counterarguments, what false teaching was Paul refuting in Colossians?
2. What particular themes about the character of Jesus Christ did Paul emphasize in Colossians?
3. How did Paul spell out the requirements of a genuine disciple of Christ in Colossians?
4. In the last chapter of Colossians, what kind of help did Paul ask of the Colossian Christians?
5. In what different ways do you rely on other Christians to encourage your efforts to follow Christ?

FIRST
THESSALONIANS
Christ   Will   Come   Again

TITLE
In the Greek NT, 1 Thessalonians is listed literally as "To the Thessalonians." This represents the apostle Paul's first canonical correspondence to the church in the city of Thessalonica (cf. 1:1).

AUTHOR AND DATE
The apostle Paul identified himself twice as the author of this letter (1:1; 2:18). Silvanus (Silas) and Timothy (3:2,6), Paul's traveling companions on the second missionary journey when the church was founded (Acts 17:1–9), were also mentioned in Paul's greeting (1:1). Though Paul was the single inspired author, most of the first person plural pronouns (we, us, our) refer to all three men. However, during Timothy's visit back to Thessalonica, they refer only to Paul and Silvanus (3:1,2,6). Paul commonly used such editorial plurals because the letters came with the full support of his companions.

Paul's authorship has not been questioned until recently by radical critics. Their attempts to undermine Pauline authorship have failed in light of the combined weight of evidence favoring Paul such as: (1) the direct assertions of Paul's authorship (1:1; 2:18); (2) the letter's perfect correlation with Paul's travels in Acts 16–18; (3) the multitude of intimate details regarding Paul; and (4) the confirmation by multiple, early historical verifications starting with Marcion's canon in A.D. 140.

The first of Paul's two letters written from Corinth to the church at Thessalonica is dated ca. A.D. 51. This date has been archeologically verified by an inscription in the temple of Apollos at Delphi (near Corinth), which dates Gallio's service as proconsul in Achaia to A.D. 51–52 (Acts 18:12–17). Since Paul's letter to the churches of Galatia was probably written ca. A.D. 49–50, this was his second piece of canonical correspondence.

BACKGROUND AND SETTING
Thessalonica (modern Salonica) lies near the ancient site of Therma on the Thermaic Gulf at the northern reaches of the Aegean Sea. This city became the capital of Macedonia (ca. 168 B.C.) and enjoyed the status of a "free city" which was ruled by its own citizenry (Acts 17:6) under the Roman Empire. Because it was located on the main east-west highway, Via Egnatia, Thessalonica served as the hub of political and commercial activity in Macedonia, and became known as "the mother of all Macedonia." The population in Paul's day reached 200,000 people.

Paul had originally traveled 100 miles from Philippi via Amphipolis and Apollonia to Thessalonica on his second missionary journey (A.D. 50; Acts 16:1–18:22). As his custom was upon arrival, he sought out the synagogue in which to teach the local Jews the gospel (Acts 17:1,2). On that occasion, he dialogued with them from the OT concerning Christ's death and resurrection in order to prove that Jesus of Nazareth was truly the promised Messiah (Acts 17:2,3). Some Jews believed and soon after, Hellenistic proselytes and some wealthy women of the community also were converted (Acts 17:4). Mentioned among these new believers were Jason (Acts 17:5), Gaius (Acts 19:29), Aristarchus (Acts 20:4), and Segundus (Acts 20:4).

Because of their effective ministry, the Jews had Paul's team evicted from the city (Acts 17:5–9), so they went south to evangelize Berea (Acts 17:10). There Paul had a similar experience to Thessalonica with conversions followed by hostility, so the believers sent Paul away. He headed for Athens, while Silvanus and Timothy remained in Berea (Acts 17:11–14). They rejoined Paul in Athens (cf. Acts 17:15,16 with 3:1), from which Timothy was later dispatched back to Thessalonica (3:2). Apparently, Silas afterwards traveled from Athens to Philippi while Paul journeyed on alone to Corinth (Acts 18:1). It was after Timothy and Silvanus rejoined Paul in Corinth (Acts 18:5), that he wrote 1 Thessalonians in response to Timothy's good report of the church.

Paul undoubtedly had multiple reasons for writing, all coming out of his supreme concern for the flock from which he had been separated. Some of Paul's purposes clearly included: (1) encouraging the church (1:2–10); (2) answering false allegations (2:1–12); (3) comforting the persecuted flock (2:13–16); (4) expressing his joy in their faith (2:17–3:13); (5) reminding them of the importance of moral purity (4:1–8); (6) condemning the sluggard lifestyle (4:9–12); (7) correcting a wrong understanding of prophetic events (4:13–5:11); (9) defusing tensions within the flock (5:12–15); and (9) exhorting the flock in the basics of Christian living (5:16–22).

Communities with Christian Churches

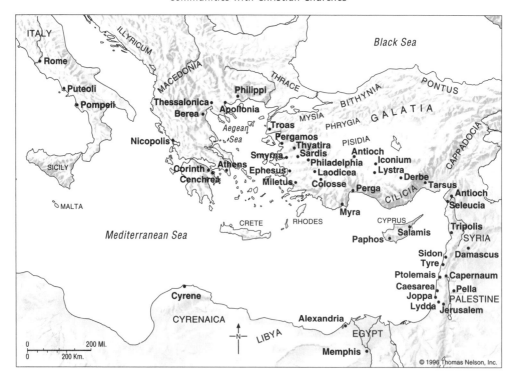

KEY PEOPLE IN 1 THESSALONIANS

Paul—wrote to the church at Thessalonica to confirm the second coming of Christ and commend them for their faithfulness (1:1–5:28)

Timothy—attested to the faithfulness of the church at Thessalonica (1:1–3:10)

Silas—traveled with Paul as a missionary (1:1)

HISTORICAL AND THEOLOGICAL THEMES

Both letters to Thessalonica have been referred to as "the eschatological epistles," perhaps because of their treatment of end times issues. However, in light of their more extensive focus upon the church, they would better be categorized as the "church epistles." Five major themes are woven together in 1 Thessalonians: (1) an apologetic theme with the historical correlation between Acts and 1 Thessalonians; (2) an ecclesiastical (or church-related) theme with the portrayal of a healthy, growing church; (3) a pastoral theme with the example of shepherding activities and attitudes; (4) an eschatological theme with the focus on future events as the church's hope; and (5) a missionary theme with the emphasis on gospel proclamation and church planting.

CHRIST IN . . . 1 THESSALONIANS

FIRST THESSALONIANS discusses the believer's hope in Christ, particularly in His second coming (1:10; 2:19; 3:13; 4:16; 5:23). Paul instructs believers to prepare for the Day of the Lord, for it shall come "as a thief in the night" (5:2). However, this Day is not to be feared by believers, for Christ obtains our salvation and guards against the wrath of God.

KEY DOCTRINES IN 1 THESSALONIANS

Sanctification—through Christ's atonement, believers are glorified and set apart for the service of God (3:12,13; 4:3,4,16–18; 5:23; Ps. 4:3; Ezek. 7:28; Acts 20:32; 26:18; Rom. 6:1–8:39; 15:16; 2 Cor. 6:17; Eph. 5:26,27; 2 Thess. 2:13; 2 Tim. 2:21; Heb. 2:11; 13:12; 1 Pet. 1:2; Jude 1:1)

Christ's second coming—Christ's return will mark the judgment of all mankind (1:10; 2:19; 3:13; 4:16; 5:23; Ps. 50:3,4; Dan. 7:13; Matt. 24:36; 25:31; Mark 13:32; John 14:3; 1 Cor. 1:8; Titus 2:13; 2 Pet. 3:12; Jude 1:14; Rev. 1:7)

GOD'S CHARACTER IN 1 THESSALONIANS

God is faithful—5:24

God is wrathful—1:10; 2:16

INTERPRETIVE CHALLENGES

Primarily the challenges for understanding this epistle involve the sections that are eschatological in nature, relating to the end times: (1) the coming wrath (1:10; 5:9); (2) Christ's return (2:19; 3:13; 4:15; 5:23); (3) the rapture of the church (4:13–18); and (4) the meaning and time of the Day of the Lord (5:1–11). See Answers to Tough Questions.

OUTLINE
    I. Paul's Greeting (1:1)
    II. Paul's Personal Thoughts (1:2–3:13)
        A. Thanksgiving for the Church (1:2–10)
        B. Reminders for the Church (2:1–16)
        C. Concerns for the Church (2:17–3:13)
    III. Paul's Practical Instructions (4:1–5:22)
        A. On Moral Purity (4:1–8)
        B. On Disciplined Living (4:9–12)
        C. On Death and the Rapture (4:13–18)
        D. On Holy Living and the Day of the Lord (5:1–11)
        E. On Church Relationships (5:12–15)
        F. On the Basics of Christian Living (5:16–22)
    IV. Paul's Benediction (5:23, 24)
    V. Paul's Final Remarks (5:25–28)

MEANWHILE, IN OTHER PARTS OF THE WORLD...

Caractacus, a Welsh chieftain, is taken captive by Roman invaders after being betrayed by Cartimandua, the queen of the Yorkshire Brigantes.

ANSWERS TO TOUGH QUESTIONS

1. How did Paul answer the Thessalonians' concerns about the fate of those Christians who had already died?

The statement in 4:13–18 provides an enduring and powerful answer to some of the recurring questions that trouble Christians when they face the death of loved ones in Christ. The Thessalonians had the same practical concerns. Even though Paul's ministry in Thessalonica was brief, it is clear that the people came to believe in and hope for the reality of their Savior's return (1:3,9,10; 2:19; 5:1–2; 2 Thess. 2:1,5). They were living in expectation of that coming, eagerly awaiting Christ. They knew that His return was the climactic event in redemptive history and anticipated their participation in it. Verse 13 (see also 2 Thess. 2:1–3) indicates that the believers were agitated about those who might miss Christ's return. Based on Paul's answers, their major questions seem to have been: "What happens to the Christians who die before He comes? Do they miss His return?"

Clearly, the Thessalonians had an imminent view of Christ's return. Evidently they had interpreted Paul's teaching to mean that Christ would definitely come back very soon, during their lifetime. Quite naturally, they became confused as they were being persecuted, an experience from which they assumed they would be delivered by the Lord's return.

Paul's answer begins with a note about grief. It does not say that Christians shouldn't "sorrow" over the death of another Christian. Instead, Paul's point is that sorrow for the Christian is hopeful, not hopeless. Then the letter offers a series of promises that affect those who "fall asleep in Christ"—believers who die. As Jesus died and rose again, so too will those who have died in Christ (4:14 and John 14:1–3; 1 Cor. 15:51–58). These texts describe the rapture of the church (including dead Christians) which will occur when Jesus comes to collect His redeemed and take them back to heaven.

Those who are alive and those who have died will experience the Lord's return at the same time (4:15). Apparently, the Thessalonians were informed fully about the Day of the Lord judgment (5:1,2) but not the preceding event—the rapture of the church. Until Paul revealed it as the revelation from God to him, it had been a secret, with the only prior mention being Jesus' teaching in John 14:1–3. Because Paul didn't know God's timing, he lived and spoke as if this event could happen in his lifetime. As with all early Christians, he believed it was near (Rom. 13:11; 1 Cor. 6:14; 10:11; 16:22; Phil. 3:20,21; 1 Tim. 6:14; Titus 2:13).

"The Lord Himself will descend" (4:16). This fulfills the pledge by Jesus in John 14:1–3. Until then, He remains in heaven (1:10; Heb. 1:1–3). Believers who have died will rise first, in time to participate in Christ's return (4:16; 1 Cor. 15:52). Those alive at the Rapture will accompany those dead who rise first (4:17) and "meet the Lord in the air."

Paul assured the Thessalonians, and all believers, that Jesus will not have any of His own miss out on His return. The final verse of the chapter reveals Paul's central intent in the passage—to encourage those Christians whose loved ones have died. The comfort here is based on the following:

KEY WORDS IN

1 Thessalonians

Sanctification: Greek *hagiasmos*—4:3–4—literally, "set apart"—refers to a process whereby God sets aside that which is holy. However, sanctification is perfect only in principle; it is not yet attained by humanity. But though we still remain in a fallen world, we stand in relation to God as though we were already made perfect (Hebrews 10:10). Christ's one and only sacrifice sanctified us (made us holy), and that sanctification has the lasting result that it continues to work in us, making us holy (Heb. 10:14).

Spirit; Soul; Body: Greek *pneuma*—4:8; 5:19,23—literally, "spirit"; Greek *psuchē*—5:23—literally, "life"; Greek *sōma*—5:23—literally, "body." First Thessalonians 5:23 is the only place in the NT where the being of a person is delineated into three portions. Yet in this passage, all three make up a whole person. The spirit enables a person to contact and be regenerated by the divine Spirit (John 3:6; Rom. 8:16). The *psuchē*, which is translated *soul*, speaks of a person's personality or essence. Finally the NT writers identify the *body* as a physical entity separate from one's soul or spirit. As this verse indicates, God works from the inside out, sanctifying our entire being for eternal life.

Coming: Greek *parousia*—2:19; 3:13; 4:15; 5:23—literally, "presence," commonly used in the NT to describe the visitation of important people such as royalty. Thus the word points to a unique and distinct "coming." This term is used in the NT to designate the second coming of Christ. This glorious coming will reveal Christ as King over all.

- The dead will be resurrected and will participate in the Lord's coming for His own.
- When Christ comes the living will be reunited forever with their loved ones.
- All believers, both the living and the dead, will be with the Lord eternally (4:17,18).

2. What did Paul mean by the "times and seasons" (5:1), and why did he find no need to write the church about them?

Chapter 5 begins with Paul's shifting the specific subject from his discussion of the blessings of the rapture of believers (4:13–18) to the judgment of unbelievers (5:1–11). The two terms *times* and *seasons* refer to the measurement of time and the character of the times respectively (Dan. 2:21; Acts 1:7). Instead of writing to them about this subject, Paul needed only to remind them of what they had already been taught.

Apparently, the Thessalonians knew all God intended believers to know about coming judgment, and once Paul had taught them what they needed to know about the Rapture (4:13–18), his remaining duty was to encourage. Paul exhorted them to live godly lives in the light of coming judgment on the world, rather than to be distracted by probing into issues of prophetic timing. They could not know the timing of God's final judgment, but they knew well that it would come unexpectedly (5:2).

3. How does Paul add his voice to the rest of Scripture in using the expression "the Day of the Lord" (5:2)?

Nineteen indisputable uses of *the Day of the Lord* occur in the OT and four in the NT (Acts 2:20; 1 Thess. 5:2; 2 Thess. 2:2; 2 Pet.3:10). The OT prophets used *Day of the Lord* to describe:

- Near historical judgments (Is. 13:6–12; Ezek. 30:2–19; Joel 1:15; 3:14; Amos 5:18–20; Zeph. 1:14–18)
- Far eschatological divine judgments (Joel 2:30–32; Zech. 14:1; Mal. 4:1,5). Six times it is referred to as the "day of doom" and four times "day of vengeance."

The NT calls it a day of "wrath," day of "visitation," and the "Great Day of God Almighty" (Rev. 16:4).

These are terrifying judgments from God (Joel 2:30,31; 2 Thess. 1:7) for the overwhelming sinfulness of the world. The future Day of the Lord, which unleashes God's wrath, falls into two parts: the end of the seven-year tribulation period (Rev. 19:11–21) and the end of the Millennium. These two are actually one thousand years apart. Peter refers to the end of the one-thousand-year period in connection with the final Day of the Lord (2 Pet. 3:10; Rev. 20:7–15).

Here the reference to the Day of the Lord refers to the conclusion of the tribulation period. The descriptive phrase "a thief in the night" is never used in Scripture to refer to the rapture of the church. It is used of Christ's coming in judgment on the Day of the Lord at the end of the seven-year tribulation that is distinct from the rapture of the church (4:15), which occurs immediately prior to this seven-year period. It is also used of the judgment that concludes the Millennium (2 Pet. 3:10). As a thief comes unexpectedly and without warning, so will the Day of the Lord come in both its final phases.

FURTHER STUDY ON 1 THESSALONIANS

1. What did Paul teach about the second coming of Christ in 1 Thessalonians?
2. How did Paul use his own experiences to encourage the Thessalonians?
3. What comments and counsel did Paul record about the persecution of Thessalonian believers?
4. What encouraging statements did Paul have to make about the faith of the Thessalonians?
5. What evidence from your life demonstrates that you are prepared for Christ's second coming?

SECOND
THESSALONIANS
*Comfort, Correction, and
Confrontation*

TITLE

In the Greek NT, 2 Thessalonians is listed as "To the Thessalonians." This represents the apostle Paul's second canonical correspondence to the fellowship of believers in the city of Thessalonica (cf. 1:1).

AUTHOR AND DATE

Paul, as in 1 Thessalonians, identified himself twice as the author of this letter (1:1; 3:17). Silvanus (Silas) and Timothy, Paul's co-laborers in founding the church, were present with him when he wrote. Evidence, both within this letter and with regard to vocabulary, style, and doctrinal content, strongly supports Paul as the only possible author. The time of this writing was surely a few months after the first epistle, while Paul was still in Corinth with Silas and Timothy (1:1; Acts 18:5) in late A.D. 51 or early A.D. 52 (see 1 Thessalonians: Author and Date).

BACKGROUND AND SETTING

For the history of Thessalonica, see 1 Thessalonians: Background and Setting. Some have suggested that Paul penned this letter from Ephesus (Acts 18:18–21), but his eighteen-month stay in Corinth provided ample time both for the Thessalonian epistles to be authored (Acts 18:11).

Apparently, Paul had stayed appraised of the happenings in Thessalonica through correspondence and/or couriers. Perhaps the bearer of the first letter brought Paul back an update on the condition of the church, which had matured and expanded (1:3); but pressure and persecution had also increased. The seeds of false doctrine concerning the Lord had been sown, and the people

CHRIST IN . . . 2 THESSALONIANS

PAUL'S SECOND LETTER to the Thessalonians describes the effects of Christ's second coming. While 1 Thessalonians reveals the expectation of Christ's return, 2 Thessalonians describes the glorification of believers on that day and God's judgement of unbelievers (1:10,12; 2:8–12).

were behaving disorderly. So Paul wrote to his beloved flock who were: (1) discouraged by persecution and needed incentive to persevere; (2) deceived by false teachers who confused them about the Lord's return; and (3) disobedient to divine commands, particularly by refusing to work. Paul wrote to address those three issues by offering: (1) comfort for the persecuted believers (1:3–12); (2) correction for the falsely taught and frightened believers (2:1–15); and (3) confrontation for the disobedient and undisciplined believers (3:6–15).

KEY PEOPLE IN 2 THESSALONIANS

Paul—wrote to give guidance on how to maintain a healthy church with an effective testimony (1:1–3:18)

Silas—traveled with Paul as a missionary (1:1)

Timothy—traveled with Paul as a missionary (1:1)

HISTORICAL AND THEOLOGICAL THEMES

Although chaps. 1 and 2 contain much prophetic material because the main issue was a
serious misunderstanding generated by false teachers about the coming Day of the Lord, it
is still best to call this "a pastoral letter." The emphasis is on how to maintain a healthy
church with an effective testimony in proper response to sound eschatology and obedience
to the truth.

Discussion of future and end times, or eschatology, dominates the theological issues.
One of the clearest statements on personal eschatology for unbelievers is found in 1:9.
Church discipline is the major focus of 3:6–15, which needs to be considered along with
Matthew 18:15–20; 1 Corinthians 5:1–13; Galatians 6:1–5, and 1 Timothy 5:19,20 for
understanding the complete biblical teaching on this theme.

A Comparison of Emphases in 1 and 2 Thessalonians

1 THESSALONIANS	2 THESSALONIANS
• Addresses how the Thessalonians were evangelized as they received the Word of God	• Addresses how the Thessalonians are being edified, noting their progress in faith, love, and patience
• The imminency and importance of the Lord's return is emphasized	• Misunderstandings about the Lord's return are corrected
• The saints are comforted and encouraged	• The saints are assured of God's judgment on His enemies

KEY DOCTRINES IN 2 THESSALONIANS

Church discipline—clear guidelines about godly conduct are necessary for a healthy
church (3:6–15; Matt. 18:15–20; 1 Cor. 5:1–13; Gal. 6:1–5; 1 Tim. 5:19,20)

Eternal reward and retribution—each human after death will either be with God forever (eternal reward) or absent from God's presence and glory forever (eternal punishment) (1:5–12; Matt. 8:12; 22:13; 25:30; Luke 16:24–26; Rom. 2:7; 2 Cor. 5:10; Col.
3:24; Heb. 11:6; Rev. 20:14,15; 22:5)

GOD'S CHARACTER IN 2 THESSALONIANS

God is good—1:11

God is loving—2:16

God is righteous—1:6

God is wrathful—1:8

INTERPRETIVE CHALLENGES

Eternal reward and retribution are discussed in 1:5–12 in such general terms that it is difficult to precisely identify some of the details with regard to exact timing. Matters concerning the Day of the Lord (2:2), the restrainer (2:6,7), and the lawless one (2:3,4,8–10) provide challenging prophetic material to interpret. See Answers to Tough Questions.

OUTLINE

      I. Paul's Greeting (1:1,2)
      II. Paul's Comfort for Affliction (1:3–12)
          A. By Way of Encouragement (1:3, 4)
          B. By Way of Exhortation (1:5–12)
      III. Paul's Correction for Prophetic Error (2:1–17)
          A. Prophetic Crisis (2:1,2)
          B. Apostolic Correction (2:3–12)
          C. Pastoral Comfort (2:13–17)
      IV. Paul's Concern for the Church (3:1–15)
          A. Regarding Prayer (3:1–5)
          B. Regarding Undisciplined Living (3:6–15)
      V. Paul's Benediction (3:16–18)

MEANWHILE, IN OTHER PARTS OF THE WORLD...

Lake Fucino, located in central Italy, is drained for cultivation under the direction of Claudius.

ANSWERS TO TOUGH QUESTIONS

1. How does Paul expand on some of his teaching about the Day of the Lord in 2:1–5?
    The Christians in Thessalonica had a persistent problem with the tension between an attitude of expectation for the Lord's soon return and the realities of daily living that required hard work and commitment. False teachers were fanning the flames of confusion. The idea that the Day of the Lord had already arrived conflicted with what Paul had previously taught them about the Rapture. Whoever was telling them they were already in the Day of the Lord claimed that the message had come from Paul. Thus the lie was given supposed apostolic authority. The results were shock, fear, and alarm. This error, which so upset the Thessalonians, Paul corrected in 2:1–12. He showed that the Day of the Lord hadn't come and couldn't come until certain realities were in place, most especially, "the man of sin" (verse 3).

    Verse 3 refers to "the falling away." Paul had in mind the apostasy (abandonment of beliefs). This is clearly a unique and specifically identifiable event, the consummate act of rebellion, an event of final magnitude. The key to identifying the event depends on the identity of the main person involved. Paul calls him the "man of sin." This figure is also called "the prince who is to come" (Dan. 9:26) and "the little horn" (Dan. 7:8). John calls him "the beast" (Rev. 13:2–10,18), but most know him as the Antichrist. The "falling away" is referring to the very act of ultimate apostasy that reveals the final Antichrist and sets the course for the events that usher in the Day of the Lord. Apparently, he will be seen as supportive of religion so that God and Christ will not appear as his enemies until the apostasy. He exalts himself and opposes God by moving into the temple, the place for worship of God, declaring himself to be God and demanding the world's worship (verse 4). In this act of Satanic self-deification, he commits the great apostasy in defiance of God. The seven-year tribulation that follows under the reign of the Antichrist (Dan. 7:25; 11:36–39; Matt. 24:15–21; Rev. 13:1–8) culminates with the Day of the Lord.

> ## KEY WORDS IN
> # 2 Thessalonians
>
> **Destruction:** Greek *olethros*–1:9–does not mean annihilation or extinction, in which one would cease to exist, but rather the loss of everything good and worthwhile. In 1 Corinthians, Paul uses the word to speak of the immediate consequences of sin (1 Cor. 5:5). Yet, in 1 Thessalonians 1:91, he uses the same word to describe the eternal consequences of sin (see also 1 Tim. 6:9). The punishment for sin is not annihilation, but eternal separation from the love of Christ. Just as eternal life belongs to believers, endless suffering awaits those who rebel against Christ.
>
> **The Lawless One:** Greek *ho anomos*–2:8–literally, "without law," points to a man consumed with rebellion. This evil figure is also called "the Antichrist" (1 John 4:2,3) and "the beast" (Rev. 13:1). He stands in direct defiance to Jesus Christ, the embodiment of righteousness. Yet, in the end, this man will be conquered by the sovereign Ruler of the universe.

This section of Paul's letter continues to emphasize that the Thessalonians did not need to be agitated or troubled, thinking that they had missed the Rapture and thus were in the Day of Judgment. They were destined for glory, not judgment, and would not be included with those deceived and judged in that Day.

2. How does Paul's teaching on church discipline in 3:6–15 fit with other major passages of Scripture on this subject?

Paul addressed a particular issue of church discipline with the Thessalonians in 3:6–15. Helpful parallel passages that should be consulted in studying this one include Matthew 18:15–20; 1 Corinthians 5:1–13; Galatians 6:1–5; and 1 Timothy 5:19,20.

This passage (3:6–15) gives specific direction on the nature of the church's response to someone who deliberately refuses to follow God's Word, expecting to benefit from fellowship with God's people while being unwilling to participate in a meaningful way. In Paul's words, "If anyone will not work, neither shall he eat" (3:10). These were fellow-believers acting in a parasitic way, sapping the generosity of other believers. Paul had already addressed this pattern in his first letter (1 Thess. 4:11).

This passage offers an emphatic command, a personal confrontation, and a compassionate caution. First, verses 6 and 14 instruct the rest of the church to "withdraw" and "not keep company" with such a person. In other words, Paul was commanding the church to not fellowship with blatantly disobedient Christians in order to produce shame (verse 14) and, hopefully, repentance. Second, Paul was giving the sluggards a direct command to "work in quietness and eat their own bread" (verse 12), removing any excuse that they had not been warned about discipline. Third, Paul added two crucial words of caution. He reminded the believers that genuinely needy people deserved help. He urged them, "Do not grow weary in doing good" (verse 13). He also cautioned them to limit their disciplinary withdrawal. "Yet do not count him as an enemy, but admonish him as a brother" (verse 15). While an unrepentant pattern of sin should be handled decisively, they should continually remember that the person being disciplined is a brother or sister in the Lord. All further warnings to this person about his or her sin should be done with love and concern, praying for this fellow believer's restoration.

FURTHER STUDY ON 2 THESSALONIANS

1. In what ways does the message of 2 Thessalonians compare and contrast with Paul's message in 1 Thessalonians?
2. Outline Paul's description of final events.
3. What kind of outlook and attitude did Paul expect Christians to have in the light of Christ's coming?
4. How would you describe your attitude to the possibility of being persecuted for being a Christian?

FIRST TIMOTHY
The Youthful Minister

TITLE

This is the first of two inspired letters Paul wrote to his beloved son in the faith. Timothy received his name, which means "one who honors God," from his mother (Eunice) and grandmother (Lois), devout Jews who became believers in the Lord Jesus Christ (2 Tim. 1:5). They taught Timothy the OT Scriptures from his childhood (2 Tim. 3:15). His father was a Greek (Acts 16:1), who may have died before Timothy met Paul.

Timothy was from Lystra (Acts 16:1–3), a city in the Roman province of Galatia (part of modern Turkey). Paul led Timothy to Christ (1:2,18; 1 Cor. 4:17; 2 Tim. 1:2), undoubtedly during his ministry in Lystra on his first missionary journey (Acts 14:6–23). When he revisited Lystra on his second missionary journey, Paul chose Timothy to accompany him (Acts 16:1–3). Although Timothy was very young (probably in his late teens or early twenties, since about fifteen years later Paul referred to him as a young man, 4:12), he had a reputation for godliness (Acts 16:2). Timothy was to be Paul's disciple, friend, and co-laborer for the rest of the apostle's life, ministering with him in Berea (Acts 17:14), Athens (Acts 17:15), Corinth (Acts 18:5; 2 Cor. 1:19), and accompanying him on his trip to Jerusalem (Acts 20:4). He was with Paul in his first Roman imprisonment and went to Philippi (2:19–23) after Paul's release. In addition, Paul frequently mentions Timothy in his epistles (Rom. 16:21; 2 Cor. 1:1; Phil. 1:1; Col. 1:1; 1 Thess. 1:1; 2 Thess. 1:1; Philem. (1). Paul often sent Timothy to churches as his representative (1 Cor. 4:17; 16:10; Phil. 2:19; 1 Thess. 3:2), and 1 Timothy finds him on another assignment, serving as pastor of the church at Ephesus (1:3). According to Heb. 13:23, Timothy was imprisoned somewhere and released.

AUTHOR AND DATE

Many post-modernist critics delight in attacking the plain statements of Scripture and, for no good reason, deny that Paul wrote the Pastoral Epistles (1, 2 Tim., Titus). Ignoring the testimony of the letters themselves (1:1; 2 Tim. 1:1; Titus 1:1) and that of the early church (which is as strong for the Pastoral Epistles as for any of Paul's epistles, except Rom. and 1 Cor.), these critics maintain that a devout follower of Paul wrote the Pastoral Epistles in the second century. As proof, they offer five lines of supposed evidence: (1) The historical references in the Pastoral Epistles cannot be harmonized with the chronology of Paul's life given in Acts; (2) The false teaching described in the Pastoral Epistles is the fully-developed Gnosticism of the second century; (3) The church organizational structure in the Pastoral Epistles is that of the second century, and is too well developed for Paul's day; (4) The Pastoral Epistles do not contain the great themes of Paul's theology; (5) The Greek vocabulary of the Pastoral Epistles contains many words not found in Paul's other letters, nor in the rest of the NT.

While it is unnecessary to dignify with an answer such unwarranted attacks by unbelievers, occasionally such an answer does enlighten. Thus, in reply to the critics' arguments, it can be pointed out that: (1) This contention of historical incompatibility is valid only if Paul was never released from his Roman imprisonment mentioned in Acts. But he was released, since Acts does not record Paul's execution, and Paul himself expected to be released (Phil. 1:19,25,26; 2:24; Philem. 22). The historical events in the Pastoral Epistles do not fit into the chronology of Acts because they happened after the close of the Acts narrative, which ends with Paul's first imprisonment in Rome. (2) While there are similarities between the heresy of the Pastoral Epistles and second-century Gnosticism (see Colossians: Background and Setting for discussion on Gnosticism), there are also important differences. Unlike second-century Gnosticism, the false teachers of the Pastoral Epistles were still within the church (cf. 1:3–7) and their teaching was based on Judaistic legalism (1:7; Titus 1:10,14; 3:9). (3) The church organizational structure mentioned in the Pastoral Epistles is, in fact, consistent with that established by Paul (Acts 14:23; Phil. 1:1). (4) The Pastoral Epistles do mention the central themes of Paul's theology, including the

CHRIST IN . . . 1 TIMOTHY

PAUL'S LETTER TO TIMOTHY describes the person of Christ as "manifested in the flesh, justified in the Spirit, seen by angels, preached among the Gentiles, believed on in the world, received up in glory" (3:16). Paul also speaks of the actions of Christ as the ransom and Savior of humanity (2:6; 4:10). Paul reminds Timothy to keep faith in Christ (1:14) and to "fight the good fight of faith" (6:12).

inspiration of Scripture (2 Tim. 3:15–17); election (2 Tim. 1:9; Titus 1:1,2); salvation (Titus 3:5–7); the deity of Christ (Titus 2:13); His work as mediator (2:5), and substitutionary atonement (sacrifice for our sins) (2:6). (5) The different subject matter in the Pastoral Epistles required a different vocabulary from that in Paul's other epistles. Certainly a pastor today would use a different vocabulary in a personal letter to a fellow pastor than he would in a work of systematic theology.

The idea that a "pious forger" wrote the Pastoral Epistles faces several further difficulties: (1) The early church did not approve of such practices and surely would have exposed this as a ruse, if there had actually been one (cf. 2 Thess. 2:1,2; 3:17). (2) Why forge three letters that include similar material and no deviant doctrine? (3) If a counterfeit, why not invent an itinerary for Paul that would have harmonized with Acts? (4) Would a later, devoted follower of Paul have put the words of 1:13,15 into his master's mouth? (5) Why would he include warnings against deceivers (2 Tim. 3:13; Titus 1:10), if he himself were one?

The evidence seems clear that Paul wrote 1 Timothy and Titus shortly after his release from his first Roman imprisonment (ca. A.D. 62–64), and 2 Timothy from prison during his second Roman imprisonment (ca. A.D. 66–67), shortly before his death.

BACKGROUND AND SETTING

After being released from his first Roman imprisonment (cf. Acts 28:30), Paul revisited several of the cities in which he had ministered, including Ephesus. Leaving Timothy behind there to deal with problems that had arisen in the Ephesian church, such as false doctrine (1:3–7; 4:1–3; 6:3–5), disorder in worship (2:1–15), the need for qualified leaders (3:1–14), and materialism (6:6–19), Paul went on to Macedonia, from where he wrote Timothy this letter to help him carry out his task in the church (cf. 3:14,15).

KEY PEOPLE IN 1 TIMOTHY
Paul—encouraged Timothy in his ministry in Ephesus (1:1–6:21)
Timothy—name means "one who honors God"; served as the pastor of the church at Ephesus (1:2–6:21)

HISTORICAL AND THEOLOGICAL THEMES
First Timothy is a practical letter containing pastoral instruction from Paul to Timothy (cf. 3:14,15). Since Timothy was well versed in Paul's theology, the apostle had no need to give him extensive doctrinal instruction. This epistle does, however, express many important theological truths, such as the proper function of the law (1:5–11), salvation (1:14–16; 2:4–6); the attributes of God (1:17); the Fall (2:13,14); the person of Christ (3:16; 6:15,16); election (6:12); and the second coming of Christ (6:14,15).

KEY DOCTRINES IN 1 TIMOTHY
Salvation—comes through Jesus Christ alone (1:14–16; 2:4–6; Gen. 3:15; Pss. 3:8; 37:39; Is. 45:21,22; 49:6; 59:16; 63:9; Luke 1:69; John 1:1–18; 6:35,48; 8:12; 10:7,9; 10:11–14; 11:25; 14:6; 17:3; Acts 4:12; 16:31; Rom. 5:8; 10:9; Eph. 2:8; 5:23; 2 Tim. 1:10; Heb. 2:10; 5:9; 1 Pet. 1:5; 1 John 1:1–4)
The Fall—sin entered all mankind through the disobedience of the first two humans (2:13,14; Gen. 3:6,11,12; 6:5; Job 15:14; 25:4; Ps. 51:5; Is. 48:8; Jer. 16:12; Matt. 15:19; Rom. 5:12,15,19; 2 Cor. 11:3)
The person of Christ—Christ is fully God and fully man (3:16; 6:15,16; Is. 7:14; Matt. 4:11; John 1:14; Rom. 1:3,4; Acts 1:9; 1 John 4:2,3; 5:6)
Election—before time began, God intimately knew the life and future of His children (6:12; Deut. 7:6; Matt. 20:16; John 6:44; 13:18; 15:16; Acts 22:14; Eph. 1:4; 1 Thess. 1:4; Titus 1:1)
The second coming of Christ—Christ's return will mark the judgment of all mankind (6:14,15; Ps. 50:3,4; Dan. 7:13; Matt. 24:36; 25:31; Mark 13:32; John 14:3; 1 Cor. 1:8; 1 Thess. 1:10; 2:19; 3:13; 4:16; 5:23; Titus 2:13; 2 Pet. 3:12; Jude 1:14; Rev. 1:7)

GOD'S CHARACTER IN 1 TIMOTHY
God is eternal—1:17
God is immortal—1:17; 6:16
God is invisible—1:17
God is long-suffering—1:16
God is merciful—1:2,13
God is a promise keeper—4:8
God is unified—2:5
God is wise—1:17

INTERPRETIVE CHALLENGES
There is disagreement over the identity of the false teachers (1:3) and the genealogies (1:4) involved in their teaching (see Answers to Tough Questions). Also, the exact meaning of "delivered to Satan" (1:20) has been a source of debate. In this context, Paul put

both men out of the church, thus ending their influence and removing them from the protection and insulation of God's people. They were no longer in the environment of God's blessing but under Satan's control. In some instances God has turned believers over to Satan for positive purposes, such as revealing the genuineness of saving faith, keeping them humble and dependent on Him, enabling them to strengthen others, or offering God praise (cf. Job. 1:1–22; Matt. 4:1–11; Luke 22:31–33; 2 Cor. 12:1–10; Rev. 7:9–15). God hands some people over to Satan for judgment, such as King Saul (1 Sam. 16:12–16; 28:4–20), Judas (John 13:27), and the sinning member in the Corinthian church.

The letter contains key passages in the debate over the extent of the atonement (2:4–6; 4:10), and if all will be saved. For more on this discussion, see Answers to Tough Questions.

In chapters 2-3, Paul's teaching on the role of women (2:9–15) has generated much discussion, particularly his declaration that they are not to assume leadership roles in the church (2:11,12). It's important to be aware of the issues that Paul was addressing. Women in the church were living impure and self-centered lives (cf. 5:6,11–15; 2 Tim. 3:6), and that practice carried over into the worship service, where they became distractions. Because of the centrality of worship in the life of the church, Paul calls on Timothy to confront the problem. How women can be saved by bearing children (2:15) has also confused many. The word "saved" would be better translated in this context, "preserved." Paul is not advocating that women are eternally saved from sin through childbearing or that they maintain their salvation by having babies, both of which would be clear contradictions of the NT teaching of salvation by grace alone through faith alone (Rom. 3:19,20). Paul is teaching that even though a woman bears the stigma of being the initial instrument who led the race into sin, it is women, through childbearing, who may be preserved or freed from that stigma by raising a generation of godly children (cf. 5:10). Because mothers have a unique bond and intimacy with their children, and often spend far more time

KEY WORDS IN

1 Timothy

Ransom: Greek *antilutron*—2:6—literally, "ransom"—actually composed of two words: *anti* meaning "substitution," and *lutron* meaning "ransom of a slave or prisoner." The *antilutron* is a payment given in substitution for a slave. The slave's owner accepts the payment for the release of their slave. Galatians 3:13 shows how Christ paid the ransom for sinners under the curse of the law. Christ's sacrifice on the cross redeemed us from the bondage of sin.

Bishop: Greek *episkopos*—3:1-2—literally, "one who oversees." In the NT, elders functioned as overseers of their congregations (Acts 20:17,28). Elders were responsible to maintain the internal affairs of the church. To accomplish this task, several elders held positions of responsibility in any given congregation (see Acts 14:23; Titus 1:5-7). After NT times, the term elder was replaced with *bishop,* and it became customary for only one bishop to oversee each congregation.

Idle Babblings: Greek *kenophōnia*—6:20—literally, "empty words." Paul uses this term to express a total void of spiritual meaning. In other words, human achievement amounts to nothing if it does not come from the will of God. In Paul's time, Judaizers were trying to entice believers by using clever-sounding philosophies. Paul described their hollow talk as *idle babblings* (see 6:20; Eph. 5:6; Col. 2:8; 2 Tim. 2:16). On the other hand, the teaching of Paul and the apostles was not futile; it would last throughout eternity because it originated in God's unchanging will (Matt. 5:18; 1 Cor. 15:12-15).

with them than do fathers, they have far greater influence in their lives and thus a unique responsibility and opportunity for rearing godly children.

Finally, whether the fact that an elder must be "the husband of one wife" excludes divorced or unmarried men has been disputed, as well as whether Paul refers to deacons' wives or deaconesses (3:11). This says nothing about marriage or divorce. The issue is not the elder's marital status, but his moral and sexual purity. This qualification heads the list, because it is in this area that leaders are most prone to fail. In 3:11, Paul likely refers here not to deacons' wives, but to the women who serve as deacons

Those who believe Christians can lose their salvation cite 4:1 as support for their view. The Greek word for "depart" is the source of the English word "apostatize," and refers to someone moving away from an original position. These are professing or nominal Christians who associate with those who truly believe the gospel, but defect after believing lies and deception, thus revealing their true nature as unconverted.

There is a question about the identity of the widows in 5:3–16. Are they needy women ministered to by the church, or an order of older women ministering to the church? This section refers to needy women and supports the mandate of Scripture that women who have lost the support of their husbands are to be cared for (cf. Ex. 22:22–24; Deut. 27:19; Is. 1:17). God's continual compassion for widows only reinforces this command (cf. Ps. 68:5; 146:9; Mark 12:41–44; Luke 7:11–17).

Finally, does "double honor" accorded to elders who rule well (5:17,18) refer to money or to greater acknowledgment from their congregations? This expression does not mean such men should receive exactly twice as much money as others, but because they have earned such respect, they should be paid more generously.

OUTLINE

    I. Greeting (1:1,2)
    II. Instructions Concerning False Doctrine (1:3–20)
        A. The False Doctrine at Ephesus (1:3–11)
        B. The True Doctrine of Paul (1:12–17)
        C. The Exhortation to Timothy (1:18–20)
    III. Instructions Concerning the Church (2:1–3:16)
        A. The Importance of Prayer (2:1–8)
        B. The Role of Women (2:9–15)
        C. The Qualifications for Leaders (3:1–13)
        D. The Reason for Paul's Letter (3:14–16)
    IV. Instructions Concerning False Teachers (4:1–16)
        A. The Description of False Teachers (4:1–5)
        B. The Description of True Teachers (4:6–16)
    V. Instructions Concerning Pastoral Responsibilities (5:1–6:2)
        A. The Responsibility to Sinning Members (5:1,2)
        B. The Responsibility to Widows (5:3–16)
        C. The Responsibility to Elders (5:17–25)
        D. The Responsibility to Slaves (6:1,2)

VI. Instructions Concerning the Man of God (6:3–21)

A. The Peril of False Teaching (6:3–5)
B. The Peril of Loving Money (6:6–10)
C. The Proper Character and Motivation of a Man of God (6:11–16)
D. The Proper Handling of Treasure (6:17–19)
E. The Proper Handling of Truth (6:20, 21)

MEANWHILE, IN OTHER PARTS OF THE WORLD...

Pit houses, circular dwellings composed of mud, were constructed by the Mogollon tribe in the Southeast region of present-day United States.

ANSWERS TO TOUGH QUESTIONS

1. When Paul writes, "This is a faithful saying," is he quoting other Scripture?

Paul used this phrase a number of times in the Pastoral Epistles (1:15; 3:1; 4:9; 2 Tim. 2:11; Titus 3:8). The statement that follows in each case summarizes a key doctrine. The added phrase "worthy of all acceptance" gives the statement added emphasis. Apparently, these sayings were well known in the churches as concise expressions of cardinal gospel truth. In their travels together, Timothy and Titus would have heard Paul expand on these statements many times.

These sayings do not quote other Scripture directly but summarize biblical teaching. For example, the saying in 1:15 that "Christ Jesus came into the world to save sinners" is based on Jesus' statements recorded in Matthew 9:13 and Luke 19:10. Naturally, their usage by Paul under the inspiration of the Holy Spirit confirmed that these sayings were God's Word.

2. If 2:4–6 states that God "desires all men to be saved," why isn't everyone saved? How far does salvation extend?

The Greek word for *desires* is not the word usually used to express God's will of decree (His sovereign eternal purpose). Rather, it expresses God's will of desire. There is a distinction between God's *desire* and His eternal saving *purpose*, which must transcend His desires. God does not want people to sin. He hates sin with all His being (see Pss. 5:4; 45:7). Thus, He hates its consequences—eternal wickedness in hell. God does not want people to remain wicked forever in eternal remorse and hatred of Him. Yet God, for His own glory, and to manifest that glory in wrath, chose to endure "vessels . . . prepared for destruction" for the supreme fulfillment of His will (see Rom. 9:22). In His eternal purpose, He chose only the elect out of the world (see John 17:6) and passed over the rest, leaving them to the consequences of their sin, unbelief, and rejection of Christ (see Rom. 1:18–32). Ultimately, God's choices and action are determined by His sovereign, eternal purpose, not His desires.

Paul describes Christ's role in salvation with the phrase "a ransom for all" (2:6). Jesus Himself used similar wording when He described His purpose to be "a ransom for many" (Matt. 20:28). The all is qualified by the many. Not all will be ransomed (though His death would be sufficient), but only the many who believe by the work of the Holy Spirit and for whom the actual atonement was made. The "for all" should be taken in two senses:

- Temporal benefits of the atonement that accrue to people universally (for example, daily experiences of God's compassion and grace)
- Christ's death was sufficient to cover the sins of all people.

Yet the substitutionary aspect of His death is applied only to the elect. Christ's death is therefore unlimited in its sufficiency but limited in its application. The fact that not all are saved has no bearing on Christ's ability to save but rather rests in humanity's profound sinfulness and God's sovereign plan.

3. What specific instructions did Paul give Timothy that would apply to a young person?

A young person seeking to live as a disciple of Jesus Christ can find essential guidelines in 4:12–16, where Paul listed five areas (verse 12) in which Timothy was to be an example to the church:

- In "word" or speech—see also Matthew 12:34–37; Ephesians 4:25,29,31
- In "conduct" or righteous living—see also Titus 2:10; 1 Peter 1:15; 2:12; 3:16
- In "love" or self-sacrificial service for others—see also John 15:13
- In "faith" or faithfulness or commitment, not belief—see also 1 Corinthians 4:2
- In "purity" and particularly sexual purity—see also 4:2

The verses that follow hold several other building blocks to a life of discipleship:

- Timothy was to be involved in the public reading, study, and application of Scripture (4:13).
- Timothy was to diligently use his spiritual gift that others had confirmed and affirmed in a public way (4:14).
- Timothy was to be committed to a process of progress in his walk with Christ (4:15).
- Timothy was to "take heed" to pay careful attention to "yourself and to the doctrine" (4:16).

The priorities of a godly leader should be summed up in Timothy's personal holiness and public teaching. All of Paul's exhortations in verses 6–16 fit into one or the other of those two categories. By careful attention to his own godly life and faithful preaching of the Word, Timothy would continue to be the human instrument God would use to bring the gospel and to save some who heard him. Though salvation is God's work, it is His pleasure to do it through human instruments.

4. What are the characteristics of a false teacher?

Paul provided for Timothy a helpful profile of false teachers by identifying three primary characteristics in 6:3. False teachers reveal themselves in these ways: (1) they "teach otherwise"—a different doctrine, or any teaching that contradicts God's revelation in Scripture (see Gal. 1:6–9); (2) they do "not consent to wholesome words"—they do not agree with sound, healthy teaching, specifically the teaching contained in Scripture (see 2 Pet. 3:16); (3) they reject "doctrine which accords with godliness"—teaching not based on Scripture will always result in an unholy life. Instead of godliness, the lives of false teachers will be marked by sin (see 2 Pet. 2:10–22; Jude 4,8–16).

5. What directions did Paul give Timothy about dealing with people who are wealthy?

Paul counseled Timothy (6:17–19) concerning what to teach those who are rich in material possessions—that is, those who have more than the mere essentials of food, clothing, and shelter. Paul had already made the case (6:6–8) that Christians should be satisfied and sufficient, and not to seek for more than what God has already given them, for He is the source of true contentment. Instead of condemning wealthy people or commanding them to get rid of their wealth, Paul called them to be good stewards of their God-given resources (see also Deut. 8:18; 1 Sam. 2:7; 1 Chr. 29:12; 2 Cor. 3:5; 9:8; Phil. 4:11–13,19).

Those who have an abundance face a constant temptation to look down on others and act superior—haughty (6:17). Paul reminded Timothy that riches and pride often go together; thus, the wealthier a person becomes, the more he or she is tempted to be proud (see Prov. 18:23; 28:11; James 2:1–4). In fact, those who have much tend to trust in their wealth (see Prov. 23:4,5). But God provides far more security than any earthly investment can ever give (see Eccl. 5:18–20; Matt. 6:19–21).

FURTHER STUDY ON 1 TIMOTHY

1. What clues about Timothy's youthfulness and relationship with Paul are found in this letter?
2. What duties did Paul give to Timothy?
3. How did Paul describe the kind of leaders Timothy should seek to appoint in the church?
4. In chapter 4, Paul gave Timothy several guidelines for personal discipline. What are these?
5. What relationships did Paul highlight in describing how the church should function within a community?
6. In what ways do you identify with Timothy?

SECOND TIMOTHY

Final Words

TITLE

This epistle is the second of two inspired letters Paul the apostle wrote to his son in the faith, Timothy (1:2; 2:1). For biographical information on Timothy, see 1 Timothy: Title. It is titled, as are the other personal letters of Paul to individuals (1 Timothy, Titus, and Philemon), with the name of the addressee (1:2).

AUTHOR AND DATE

The issue of Paul's authorship of the Pastoral Epistles is fully discussed in the introductin to 1 Timothy: Author and Date. Paul wrote 2 Timothy, the last of his inspired letters, shortly before he was killed for his faith (ca. A.D. 67).

BACKGROUND AND SETTING

Paul was released from his first Roman imprisonment for a short period of ministry during which he wrote 1 Timothy and Titus. Second Timothy, however, finds Paul once again in a Roman prison (1:16; 2:9), apparently rearrested as part of Nero's persecution of Christians. Unlike Paul's confident hope of release during his first imprisonment (Phil. 1:19,25,26; 2:24; Philem. 22), this time he had no such hopes (4:6–8). In his first imprisonment in Rome (ca. A.D. 60–62), before Nero had begun the persecution of Christians (A.D. 64), he was only under house arrest and had opportunity for much interaction with people and ministry (Acts 28:16–31). At this time, five or six years later (ca. A.D. 66–67), however, he was in a cold cell (4:13), in chains (2:9), and with no hope of deliverance (4:6). Abandoned by virtually all of those close to him for fear of persecution (cf. 1:15; 4:9–12,16) and facing imminent execution, Paul wrote to Timothy, urging him to hasten to Rome for one last visit (4:9,21). Whether Timothy made it to Rome before Paul's execution is not known. According to tradition, Paul was not released from this second Roman imprisonment, but suffered the martyrdom he had foreseen (4:6).

In this letter, Paul, aware the end was near, passed the non-apostolic mantle of ministry to Timothy (cf. 2:2) and exhorted him to continue faithful in his duties (1:6), hold on to sound doctrine (1:13,14), avoid error (2:15–18), accept persecution for the gospel (2:3,4; 3:10–12), put his confidence in the Scripture, and preach it relentlessly (3:15–4:5).

KEY PEOPLE IN 2 TIMOTHY

Paul—wrote to encourage and instruct Timothy in his pastoral ministry at Ephesus (1:1–4:22)

Timothy—name means "one who honors God"; served as the pastor of the church at Ephesus (1:2–4:22)

Luke—Paul's traveling companion; only person to stay with Paul through his imprisonment (4:11)

Mark—traveled with Paul and Barnabas on their first missionary journey (4:11)

A Comparison of Paul's Two Roman Imprisonments

First Imprisonment	Second Imprisonment
Acts 28—Wrote the Prison Epistles	2 Timothy
Accused by Jews of heresy and sedition	Persecuted by Rome and arrested as a criminal against the Empire
Local sporadic persecutions (A.D. 60-63)	Nero's persecution (A.D. 64–68)
Decent living conditions in a rented house (Acts 28:30,31)	Poor conditions, in a cold, dark dungeon
Many friends visited him	Virtually alone (only Luke with him)
Many opportunities for Christian witness were available	Opportunities for witness were restricted
Was optimistic for release and freedom (Phil. 1:24-26)	Anticipated his execution (2 Tim. 4:6)

HISTORICAL AND THEOLOGICAL THEMES

It seems that Paul may have had reason to fear that Timothy was in danger of weakening spiritually. This would have been a grave concern for Paul since Timothy needed to carry on Paul's work (cf. 2:2). While there are no historical indications elsewhere in the NT as to why Paul was so concerned, there is evidence in the epistle itself from what he wrote. This concern is evident, for example, in Paul's encouragement to "stir up" his gift (1:6), to replace fear with power, love, and a sound mind (1:7), to not be ashamed of Paul and the Lord, but willingly suffer for the gospel (1:8), and to hold on to the truth (1:13,14). Summing up the potential problem of Timothy, who might be weakening under the pressure of the church and the persecution of the world, Paul calls him to (1) generally "be strong" (2:11), the key encouragement of the first part of the letter, and to (2) continue to "preach the word" (4:2), the main admonition of the last part. These final words to Timothy include few commendations but many admonitions, including about twenty-five commands.

CHRIST IN . . . 2 TIMOTHY

PAUL'S SECOND LETTER encourages Timothy to keep close to the "sound words which you have heard from me, in the faith and love which are in Christ Jesus" (1:13). Left to carry on Paul's ministry, Timothy was reminded of the person of Christ (2:8; 4:1,8), and his call to "preach the word" (4:2). Timothy was promised persecution by following Christ (3:12), yet he was urged to keep strong in the faith "which is in Christ Jesus" (3:15).

Since Timothy was well versed in Paul's theology, the apostle did not instruct him further doctrinally. He did, however, allude to several important doctrines, including salvation by God's sovereign grace (1:9,10; 2:10), the person of Christ (2:8; 4:1,8), and perseverance (2:11–13); plus Paul wrote the crucial text of the NT on the inspiration of Scripture (3:16,17).

Timothy's Ministry

Timothy must...	Because...
Share in suffering for the gospel (1:8; 2:3)	Through such sharing others will be saved (2:10)
Continue in sound doctrine (1:13; 2:15)	False doctrine spreads and leads to ungodliness (2:16,17)
Flee youthful lusts (2:22)	He must be cleansed and set apart for the Master's use (2:21)
Avoid contentiousness (2:23-25)	He must gently lead others to the truth (2:24–26)
Militantly preach the gospel (4:2)	Great apostasy is coming (4:3,4)

KEY DOCTRINES IN 2 TIMOTHY

Salvation by God's sovereign grace—comes through Jesus Christ alone (1:9,10; 2:10; Gen, 3:15; Pss. 3:8; 37:39; Is. 45:21,22; 49:6; 59:16; 63:9; Luke 1:69; John 1:1–18; 6:35,48; 8:12; 10:7,9; 10:11–14; 11:25; 14:6; 17:3; Acts 4:12; 16:31; Rom. 5:8; 10:9; Eph. 2:8; 5:23; 1 Tim. 1:14–16; 2:4–6; Heb. 2:10; 5:9; 1 Pet. 1:5; 1 John 1:1–4)

The person of Christ—both divine Judge over the world and the Messiah descending from the seed of David (2:8; 4:1,8; Is. 7:14; Matt. 4:11; John 1:14; Rom. 1:3,4; Acts 1:9; 1 Tim. 3:16; 6:15,16; 1 John 4:2,3; 5:6)

Perseverance—believers who persevere give evidence of the genuineness of their faith (2:11,13; Job 17:9; Ps. 37:24; Prov. 4:18; John 8:31; 1 Cor. 15:58; Gal. 6:9; Phil. 1:6; Col. 1:21–23; Heb. 3:6,14)

Inspiration of Scripture—God used the minds, vocabularies, and experiences of the biblical writers to produce His own infallible and inerrant Word (3:16,17; Acts 1:16; Rom. 3:2; 9:17; Gal. 3:8; Heb. 3:7; 1 Pet. 4:11; 2 Pet. 1:21)

GOD'S CHARACTER IN 2 TIMOTHY

God is powerful—1:8
God is a promise keeper—1:1
God is wise—2:19

INTERPRETIVE CHALLENGES

There are no major challenges in this letter involving theological issues. There is limited data regarding several individuals named in the epistle; e.g., Phygellus and Hermogenes (1:15), Onesiphorus (1:17; cf. 4:19), Hymenaeus and Philetus (2:17,18), Jannes and Jambres (3:8), and Alexander (4:14).

OUTLINE

    I. Greeting and Thanksgiving (1:1–5)

    II. The Perseverance of a Man of God (1:6–18)

        A. The Exhortation (1:6–11)

        B. The Examples (1:12–18)

            1. Paul (1:12–14)

            2. Onesiphorus (1:15–18)

    III. The Patterns of a Man of God (2:1–26)

        A. Paul (2:1,2)

        B. A Soldier (2:3,4)

        C. An Athlete (2:5)

        D. A Farmer (2:6,7)

        E. Jesus (2:8–13)

        F. A Worker (2:14–19)

        G. A Vessel (2:20–23)

        H. A Servant (2:24–26)

    IV. The Perils of a Man of God (3:1–17)

        A. Facing Apostasy (3:1–9)

        B. Defeating Apostasy (3:10–17)

    V. The Preaching of the Man of God (4:1–5)

        A. The Charge to Preach (4:1,2)

        B. The Need for Preaching (4:3–5)

    VI. Concluding Remarks (4:6–18)

        A. Paul's Triumph (4:6–8)

        B. Paul's Needs (4:9–18)

    VII. Paul's Farewells (4:19–22)

MEANWHILE, IN OTHER PARTS OF THE WORLD...

Events in Israel that will lead to the destruction of Jerusalem in A.D. 70 have begun.

ANSWERS TO TOUGH QUESTIONS

1. In 1:7, to what or whom does the term *spirit* refer?

This statement is contrasting two attitudes rather than describing the Holy Spirit, whose presence (1:14) produces the second "spirit" mentioned in 1:7. The spirit of fear, that could be translated "timidity," denotes a cowardly, shameful fear caused by a weak, selfish character. Since this is not a by-product of God's presence, it must be coming from somewhere else. The threat of Roman persecution, which was escalating under Nero, the hostility of those in the Ephesian church who resented Timothy's leadership, and the assaults of false teachers with their sophisticated systems of deception may have been overwhelming Timothy. But if he was fearful, his fear didn't come from God.

As an antidote to fear, Paul reminded Timothy of the resources God does supply. God has already given believers all the spiritual resources they need for every trial and threat (see Matt. 10:19,20). First, divine "power"—effective, productive spiritual energy—belongs to believers (see Zech. 4:6; Eph. 1:18–20; 3:20). Second, God provides "love." This love centers on pleasing God and seeking another's welfare before one's own (see Rom. 14:8; Gal. 5:22,25; Eph. 3:19; 1 Pet. 1:22; 1 John 4:18). Third, God promotes a "sound mind." This refers to a disciplined, self-controlled, and properly prioritized mind. This is the opposite of the fear and cowardice that causes disorder and confusion. Focusing on the sovereign nature and perfect purposes of our eternal God allows believers to control their lives with godly wisdom and confidence in every situation (see Rom. 12:3; 1 Tim. 3:2; Titus 1:8; 2:2).

2. How many generations of discipleship does 2:2 include?

As Paul directed Timothy in the process of transmitting the gospel message, he mentioned four generations of lives transformed by the grace of Christ. The first mentioned was Paul's own generation. He reminded Timothy that the source of his message for others was the countless hours of preaching and teaching he had heard the apostle deliver "among many witnesses." The next generation was Timothy's. What he had heard, he was charged to deliver to others. These others would be the next generation. They were not to be a random audience, but "faithful" believers with teaching abilities. These in

KEY WORDS IN

2 Timothy

Appearing: Greek *epiphaneia*—1:10; 4:1,8—literally means "a shining forth" and was used in Greek literature to denote a divine appearance. The English word *epiphany* is a close equivalent. The NT writers use the word to refer to Jesus' first coming, the time when He entered this world as a man (see 1:10). They also use the word to speak of Jesus' second coming, specifically to His appearance to all the world (see Matt. 24:27).

Books, Parchments: Greek *biblion*—4:13; Greek *membrana*—4:13, the word *biblion* is common in the NT but not the word *membrana*, which occurs only here. It is a word derived from Latin that means an animal skin used for writing. The two words in this passage have been interpreted in three different ways: (1) *the scrolls* were copies of OT books, and *the parchments* were copies of various NT books; (2) *the books* were copies of both OT and NT books, and *the parchments* were blank writing material or notebooks containing rough drafts; or (3) the two words signified the same thing: *the books—* that is, the *parchment notebooks.* If the third interpretation is correct, it suggests that Paul was anxious to recover some rough drafts he had left behind when he was arrested.

Inspiration of God: Greek *theopneustos*—3:16—means "God-breathed," from *theos* (God) and *pneō* (to breathe). Although it is difficult to fully recreate the thought of this Greek expression in English, we are sure that Paul meant to say that all Scripture was breathed out from God. This definition affirms the Bible's divine origin; thus God not only inspired the authors who wrote the words of the Bible but He also inspires those who read it with a heart of faith.

turn would teach the next generation about the "grace that is in Christ Jesus." The process of spiritual reproduction, which began in the early church, is to continue until the Lord returns.

3. What is a valedictory, and why did Paul include one in his second letter to Timothy? A valedictory is a speech or action done in parting. It is a farewell message. While hints of Paul's mood appear throughout the letter, 4:6–8 centers on Paul's self-evaluation. Nearing the end of his life, Paul was able to look back without regret or remorse. In these verses, he examined his life from three perspectives: (1) the present reality of the approaching end of his life, for which he was ready (verse 6); (2) the past, when he had been faithful (verse 7); (3) the future, as he anticipated his heavenly reward (verse 8).

FURTHER STUDY ON 2 TIMOTHY

1. What specific directions did Paul give Timothy about the attitude of a minister of the gospel?
2. What did Paul repeat in 2 Timothy that he emphasized in his first letter?
3. How does chapter 2 describe the process by which the gospel spreads?
4. How does Paul's statement in 2 Timothy 3:16 fit in with the rest of the letter?
5. What dangers did Paul point out to his young disciple about ministry in troubled times?
6. Who gives you the most encouragement in your Christian life, and what kind of response have you given them?

TITUS
Valued Messenger

TITLE
This epistle is named for its recipient, Titus, who is mentioned by name thirteen times in the NT (1:4; Gal. 2:1,3; 2 Tim 4:10; 2 Cor. 2:13; 7:6,13,14; 8:6,16,23; 12:18). The title in the Greek NT literally reads "To Titus." Along with 1 and 2 Timothy, these letters to Paul's sons in the faith are traditionally called "The Pastoral Epistles."

AUTHOR AND DATE
Authorship by the apostle Paul (1:1) is essentially uncontested (see 1 Timothy: Author and Date). Titus was written between A.D. 62–64, while Paul ministered to Macedonian churches between his first and second Roman imprisonments, from either Corinth or Nicopolis (cf. 3:12). Most likely, Titus served with Paul on both the second and third missionary journeys. Titus, like Timothy (2 Tim. 1:2), had become a beloved disciple (1:4) and fellow worker in the gospel (2 Cor. 8:23). Paul's last mention of Titus (2 Tim. 4:10) reports that he had gone for ministry in Dalmatia—modern Yugoslavia. The letter probably was delivered by Zenas and Apollos (3:13).

BACKGROUND AND SETTING
Although Luke did not mention Titus by name in the Book of Acts, it seems probable that Titus, a Gentile (Gal. 2:3), met and may have been led to faith in Christ by Paul (1:4) before or during the apostle's first missionary journey. Later, Titus ministered for a period of time with Paul on the Island of Crete and was left behind to continue and strengthen the work (1:5). After Artemas or Tychicus (3:12) arrived to direct the ministry there, Paul wanted Titus to join him in the city of Nicopolis, in the province of Achaia in Greece, and stay through the winter (3:12).

> ## CHRIST IN ... TITUS
> THE DEITY OF CHRIST is strongly maintained in the Book of Titus: "Looking for the blessed hope and glorious appearing of our great God and Savior Jesus Christ" (2:13). Paul refers to God and Christ as the Savior throughout the book, emphasizing both the person of Christ as God and the plan of salvation (1:3,4; 2:10,13; 3:4,6).

Because of his involvement with the church at Corinth during Paul's third missionary journey, Titus is mentioned nine times in 2 Corinthians (2:13; 7:6,13,14; 8:6,16,23; 12:18), where Paul refers to him as "my brother" (2:13) and "my partner and fellow worker" (8:23). The young elder was already familiar with Judaizers, false teachers in the church, who among other things insisted that all Christians, Gentile as well as Jew, were bound by the Mosaic law. Titus had accompanied Paul and Barnabas years earlier to the Council of Jerusalem where that heresy was the subject (Acts 15; Gal. 2:1–5).

Crete, one of the largest islands in the Mediterranean Sea, measuring 160 miles long by 35 miles at its widest, lying south of the Aegean Sea, had been briefly visited by Paul on his voyage to Rome (Acts 27:7–9,12,13,21). He returned there for ministry and later left Titus to continue the work, much as he left Timothy at Ephesus (1 Tim. 1:3), while he went on to Macedonia. He most likely wrote to Titus in response to a letter from Titus or a report from Crete.

KEY PEOPLE IN TITUS

Paul—wrote to give Titus encouragement and counsel regarding his leadership position in the church (1:1–3:15)

Titus—Greek believer sent by Paul to pastor the church on the island of Crete (1:4–3:15)

HISTORICAL AND THEOLOGICAL THEMES

Like Paul's two letters to Timothy, the apostle gives personal encouragement and counsel to a young pastor who, though well-trained and faithful, faced continuing opposition from ungodly men within the churches where he ministered. Titus was to pass on that encouragement and counsel to the leaders he was to appoint in the Cretan churches (1:5).

In contrast to several of Paul's other letters, such as those to the churches in Rome and Galatia, the Book of Titus does not focus on explaining or defending doctrine. Paul had full confidence in Titus's theological understanding and convictions, evidenced by the fact that he entrusted him with such a demanding ministry. Except for the warning about false teachers and Judaizers, the letter gives no theological correction, strongly suggesting that Paul also had confidence in the doctrinal grounding of most church members there, despite the fact that the majority of them were new believers. Doctrines that this epistle affirms include: (1) God's sovereign election of believers (1:1,2); (2) His saving grace (2:11; 3:5); (3) Christ's deity and second coming (2:13); (4) Christ's substitutionary atonement (dying in our place for our sin) (2:14); and (5) the regeneration and renewing of believers by the Holy Spirit (3:5).

KEY WORDS IN

Titus

God Our Savior: Greek *tou sōtēros hēmōn theou*—1:3; 2:10; 3:4—in the Pastoral Epistles, this expression or similar ones appear often. In each of these verses, the appellation describes God the Father. The OT writers speak of God as Savior (see Ps. 24:5; Is. 12:2; 45:15,21) and so do a few other NT writers (Luke 1:47; Jude 25). The Son is called Savior in the Pastoral Epistles (1:4; 2:13; 3:6; 2 Tim. 1:10), and in 2:13 the Son is called "our God and Savior," thus clearly identifying Jesus as God.

Washing of Regeneration: Greek *loutron palingenesias*—3:5—this word for "washing" can signify the receptacle of washing itself. In Ephesians 5:26, the only other NT occurrence of this word, the natural meaning is washing. Here the action of washing is also presented. Quite simply, the text says that regeneration is characterized by or accompanied by the action of washing. The regenerative activity of the Holy Spirit is characterized elsewhere in Scripture as cleansing and purifying (see Ezek. 36:25–27; John 3:5). The Greek term for *regeneration* literally means "being born again"—indicating the new birth put in effect by the Holy Spirit (see John 3:6; Rom. 8:16; Gal. 4:6). Thus God saved us through one process with two aspects: the washing of regeneration and the renewing of the Holy Spirit.

God and Christ are regularly referred to as *Savior* (1:3,4; 2:10,13; 3:4,6), and the saving plan is so emphasized in 2:11–14 that it indicates the major thrust of the epistle is that of equipping the churches of Crete for effective evangelism. This preparation required godly leaders who not only would shepherd believers under their care (1:5–9), but also would equip those Christians for evangelizing their pagan neighbors, who had been characterized by one of their own famous natives as "liars, evil beasts, and lazy gluttons" (1:12). In order to gain a hearing for the gospel among such people, the believers' primary preparation for evangelization was to live among themselves with the unarguable testimony of righteous, loving, selfless, and godly lives (2:2–14) in marked contrast to the debauched lives of the false teachers (1:10–16). How they behaved with reference to governmental authorities and unbelievers was also crucial to their testimony (3:1–8).

Several major themes repeat themselves throughout Titus. They include: work(s) (1:16; 2:7,14; 3:1,5,8,14); soundness in faith and doctrine (1:4,9,13; 2:1,2,7,8,10; 3:15); and salvation (1:3,4; 2:10,13; 3:4,6).

KEY DOCTRINES IN TITUS

God's sovereign election of believers—before time began, God intimately knew the life and future of His children (1:1–2; Deut. 7:6; Matt. 20:16; John 6:44; 13:18; 15:16; Acts 22:14; Eph. 1:4; 1 Thess. 1:4; 1 Tim. 6:12)

God's saving grace—God's gracious gift to fallen humanity is Jesus Christ (2:11; 3:5; Ps. 84:11; John 1:14; 3:16–18; Rom. 5:15,17; Eph. 1:6; 1 Tim. 2:5,6; 4:10; Heb. 4:16; James 1:17; 1 Pet. 5:10; 1 John 2:2)

Christ's deity and second coming—the second coming of Jesus Christ will reveal His full glory as God (2:13; Rom. 8:22,23; 1 Cor. 15:51–58; Phil. 3:20,21; 1 Thess. 4:13–18; 2 Pet. 1:1; 1 John 3:2,3)

Christ's substitutionary atonement—Christ gave Himself as a sacrifice so that believers in Him might be pardoned from sin (2:14; Is. 53:4–12; John 15:13; Acts 4:12; Rom. 5:8–11; 8:32; 2 Cor. 5:18,19; Gal. 1:4; Heb. 10:14; 1 Pet. 3:18; 1 John 2:2; 4:10)

The Holy Spirit's regeneration and renewing of believers—salvation brings the gift of a new, Spirit-generated, Spirit-empowered, Spirit-protected life as God's own children and heirs (3:5; Ezek. 36:25–29; Joel 2:28; John 3:3–6; Rom. 5:5; 8:2; Eph. 5:26; James 1:18; 1 Pet. 1:23; 1 John 2:29; 3:9; 4:7; 5:1)

GOD'S CHARACTER IN TITUS

God is kind—3:4–6
God is loving—3:4–7
God is merciful—1:18; 3:5
God is a promise keeper—1:2
God is true—1:2

INTERPRETIVE CHALLENGES

The letter to Titus presents itself in a straightforward manner that should be taken at face value. The few interpretive challenges include: (1) Are the children of 1:6 merely "faithful" or are they "believing"? The term "faithful" is always used in the NT of believers and never for unbelievers, so this refers to children who have saving faith in Christ and reflect it in ther conduct. (2) What is the "blessed hope" of 2:13? This is a general reference to the second coming of Jesus Christ, including the resurrection and the reign of the saints with Christ in glory (2 Tim. 2:10).

OUTLINE
  I. Salutation (1:1–4)
  II. Essentials for Effective Evangelism (1:5–3:11)
      A. Among Leaders (1:5–16)
          1. Recognition of elders (1:5–9)
          2. Rebuke of false teachers (1:10–16)
      B. In the Church (2:1–15)
          1. Holy living (2:1–10)
          2. Sound doctrine (2:11–15)
      C. In the World (3:1–11)
          1. Holy living (3:1–4)
          2. Sound doctrine (3:5–11)
  III. Conclusion (3:12–14)
  IV. Benediction (3:15)

MEANWHILE, IN OTHER PARTS OF THE WORLD...
Queen Boudicca of Britain leads a revolt against the Roman emperor Nero after his legions plundered and brutally annexed some of her lands. The proud British fight with such ferocity that the Romans had to send for additional troops. Rome is victorious, but at great cost.

ANSWERS TO TOUGH QUESTIONS
1. In what ways does Paul's letter to his disciple Titus indicate that the message was intended for more than just Titus and the Christians on Crete?

Titus 2:11–13 presents the heart of Paul's letter to Titus. The apostle had already emphasized God's sovereign purpose in calling out elders as leaders (1:5) and in commanding His people to live righteously (2:1–10). That purpose is to provide the witness that brings God's plan and purpose of salvation to fulfillment. As always, the apostle had a larger audience in mind. The gospel has a universal scope. Here Paul condensed God's saving plan into three realities: (1) salvation from the penalty of sin (verse 11); (2) salvation from the power of sin (verse 12); and (3) salvation from the presence of sin (verse 13).

As he described the "grace of God that brings salvation" (verse 11), Paul was not simply referring to the divine attribute of grace but to Jesus Christ Himself, grace incarnate, God's supremely gracious gift to fallen humankind (see John 1:14). The term "all men" (verse 11), in spite of efforts to make it a proof text for Universalism, does not provide support for that error. "Mankind" is translated as "man" in 3:4, to refer to humanity in general, as a category, not to every individual. Jesus Christ made a sufficient offering to cover the sins of everyone who believes (see John 3:16–18; 1 Tim. 2:5,6; 4:10; 1 John 2:2). The opening words of this letter to Titus make it clear that salvation becomes effective only through "the faith of God's elect" (1:1). Paul was well aware that the gospel had universal implications. Out of all humanity, only those who believe will be saved (see John 1:12; 3:16; 5:24,38,40; 6:40; 10:9; Rom. 10:9–17).

2. How does 3:1–11 make a case for the value of evangelism?

Throughout this letter, Paul made it clear that Titus had a larger role than simply to maintain the existing church in Crete. Paul's purpose was evangelistic. He wanted Titus's work to bring more people to faith in Christ. In order for this to occur, Paul's directions focused on equipping the churches of Crete for effective evangelism. Even Paul's standards for leadership required godly leaders who would not only shepherd believers under their care (1:5–9) but also equip those Christians for evangelizing their pagan neighbors. Paul's consistent pattern is best described in 2 Timothy 2:2.

Paul's closing remarks admonish Titus to remind believers under his care of (1) the importance of having a good attitude toward the unsaved rulers (3:1) and people in general (3:2); (2) their previous state as unbelievers lost in sin (3:3); (3) of their gracious salvation through Jesus Christ (3:4–7); (4) of their righteous testimony to the unsaved world (3:8); and (5) their responsibility to oppose false teachers and factious members within the church (3:9–11). All these matters prove essential to effective evangelism. A humble and compassionate witness by a well-ordered body of believers offers the most compelling message of the gospel.

FURTHER STUDY ON TITUS

1. As you study Titus, review the location of the island of Crete.
2. Compare Titus with 1 Timothy. What points of similarity do you note between the two letters?
3. How did Paul summarize the gospel for Titus?
4. What are the key church leadership roles according to Paul's guidelines for Titus?
5. To what degree did the character of church leaders matter to Paul?
6. What group of Christians do you represent, and how seriously do you take that responsibility?

PHILEMON
Spiritual Equality and
True Forgiveness

TITLE
Philemon, the recipient of this letter, was a prominent member of the church at Colosse (vv. 1,2; cf. Col. 4:9), which met in his house (v. 2). The letter was for him, his family, and the church.

AUTHOR AND DATE
The book claims that the apostle Paul was its writer (vv. 1,9,19), a claim that few in the history of the church have disputed, especially since there is nothing in Philemon that a forger would have been motivated to write. It is one of the Prison Epistles, along with Ephesians, Philippians, and Colossians. Its close connection with Colossians, which Paul wrote at the same time (ca. A.D. 60–62; cf. vv. 1,16), brought early and unquestioned vindication of Paul's authorship by the early church fathers (e.g., Jerome, Chrysostom, and Theodore of Mopsuestia). The earliest of NT canons, the Muratorian (ca. A.D. 170), includes Philemon. For biographical information on Paul, see Romans: Author and Date. For the date and place of Philemon's writing, see Ephesians and Philippians: Author and Date.

BACKGROUND AND SETTING
Philemon had been saved under Paul's ministry, probably at Ephesus (v. 19), several years earlier. Wealthy enough to have a large house (cf. v. 2), Philemon also owned at least one slave, a man named Onesimus (lit."useful"; a common name for slaves). Onesimus was not a believer at the time he stole some money (v. 18) from Philemon and ran away. Like countless thousands of other runaway slaves, Onesimus fled to Rome, seeking to lose himself in the Imperial capital's teeming and nondescript slave population. Through circumstances not recorded in Scripture, Onesimus met Paul in Rome and became a Christian.

The apostle quickly grew to love the runaway slave (vv. 12,16) and longed to keep Onesimus in Rome (v. 13), where he was providing valuable service to Paul in his imprisonment (v. 11). But by stealing and running away from Philemon, Onesimus had both broken Roman law and defrauded his master. Paul knew those issues had to be dealt with, and decided to send Onesimus back to Colosse. It was too hazardous for him to make the trip alone

CHRIST IN . . . PHILEMON
THE RELATIONSHIP between Paul, Onesimus, and Philemon presents a beautiful illustration of Christ's mediation between the Father and humanity. Paul freely accepted Onesimus's penalty in order to renew the relationship between Onesimus and Philemon, his former master. Paul's work of forgiveness also portrays the strength given to Christians by God to show compassion and mercy.

(because of the danger of slave-catchers), so Paul sent him back with Tychicus, who was returning to Colosse with the epistle to the Colossians (Col. 4:7–9). Along with Onesimus, Paul sent Philemon this beautiful personal letter, urging him to forgive Onesimus and welcome him back to service as a brother in Christ (vv. 15–17).

How Love Works in Philemon

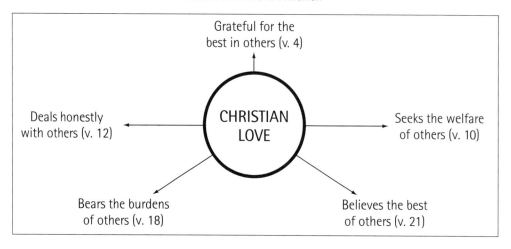

KEY PEOPLE IN PHILEMON

Paul—wrote to urge Philemon to forgive and accept Onesimus as his brother (verses 1–25)

Philemon—prominent member of the church at Colosse; former master of Onesimus (verses 1–25)

Onesimus—runaway slave of Philemon; became a Christian after meeting Paul in Rome (verses 10–22)

HISTORICAL AND THEOLOGICAL THEMES

Philemon provides valuable historical insights into the early church's relationship to the institution of slavery. Slavery was widespread in the Roman Empire (according to some estimates, slaves constituted one third, perhaps more, of the population) and an accepted part of life. In Paul's day, slavery had virtually eclipsed free labor. Slaves could be doctors, musicians, teachers, artists, librarians, or accountants; in short, almost all jobs could be and were filled by slaves.

Slaves were not legally considered persons, but were the tools of their masters. As such, they could be bought, sold, inherited, exchanged, or seized to pay their master's debt. Their masters had virtually unlimited power to punish them, and sometimes did so severely for the slightest infractions. By the time of the NT, however, slavery was beginning to change. Realizing that contented slaves were more productive, masters tended to treat them more leniently. It was not uncommon for a master to teach a slave his own trade, and some masters and slaves became close friends. While still not recognizing them as persons under the law, the Roman Senate in A.D. 20 granted slaves accused of crimes the right to a trial. It also became more common for slaves to be granted (or to purchase) their freedom. Some slaves enjoyed very favorable and profitable service under their masters and were better off than many freemen because they were assured of care and provision. Many freemen struggled in poverty.

The NT nowhere directly attacks slavery; had it done so, the resulting slave insurrections would have been brutally suppressed and the message of the gospel hopelessly confused with that of social reform. Instead, Christianity undermined the evils of slavery by changing the hearts of slaves and masters. By stressing the spiritual equality of master and slave (v. 16; Gal. 3:28; Eph. 6:9; Col. 4:1; 1 Tim. 6:1,2), the Bible did away with slavery's abuses. The rich theological theme that alone dominates the letter is forgiveness, a featured theme throughout NT Scripture (cf. Matt. 6:12–15; 18:21–35; Eph. 4:32; Col. 3:13). Paul's instruction here provides the biblical definition of forgiveness, without ever using the word.

KEY DOCTRINES IN PHILEMON
Forgiveness—Christ offers the perfect example of forgiveness (vv. 16,17; Matt. 6:12–15; 18:21–35; Eph. 4:32; Col. 3:13)

Equality—Christianity undermined the evils of slavery by changing the hearts of slaves and masters and stressing the spiritual equality of master and slave (verse 16; Matt. 20:1–16; Mark 10:31; Gal. 3:28; Eph. 6:9; Col. 4:1; 1 Tim. 6:1,2)

GOD'S CHARACTER IN PHILEMON
God is forgiving—verses 16,17

God is impartial—verse 16

INTERPRETIVE CHALLENGES
There are no significant interpretive challenges in this personal letter from Paul to his friend Philemon.

OUTLINE
    I. Greeting (1–3)
    II. The Character of One Who Forgives (4–7)
    III. The Actions of One Who Forgives (8–18)
    IV. The Motives of One Who Forgives (19–25)

MEANWHILE, IN OTHER PARTS OF THE WORLD...
The Romans begin to manufacture brass and develop a system to extract gold from its ores.

ANSWERS TO TOUGH QUESTIONS

1. Who was Onesimus, and why did Paul write a letter to Philemon about him?

Onesimus was a slave owned by Philemon, a prominent member of the church at Colosse. Through happy and divine coincidence, Onesimus met Paul after he ran away from Philemon. At the time, Onesimus was a double lawbreaker, on the run as a thief and an escaped slave. Shortly after meeting Paul, Onesimus became a Christian.

Although Onesimus was providing useful service to Paul, the apostle decided to send him back to Philemon. With him, he sent both Tychicus as an escort and a personal cover letter as an explanation to Philemon. The wealthy Colossian owed Paul much, for Paul was the messenger who had brought him the gospel. Paul didn't hesitate to mention that debt to awaken Philemon's awareness of the importance of welcoming and forgiving his vagabond slave.

Paul's letter to Philemon provides an insightful glimpse into the NT's handling of slavery. Rather than a direct attack on this terrible practice, Christianity disarmed the institution from within by radically changing the relationship between slaves and masters. See the introduction to this letter for more on this subject.

2. How did Paul intervene with Philemon on Onesimus's behalf?

Paul reintroduced the slave Onesimus to the master Philemon as his own son in the faith (verse 10). Paul had led the slave to Christ while in prison at Rome. Since *Onesimus* was a common slave name that meant "useful," Paul offered a play on words as a tribute to Onesimus's new life in Christ. Paul's description (verse 11) basically means, "Useful—formerly was useless, but now really is useful." Onesimus had been radically transformed by God's grace.

Although Paul did not challenge Onesimus's existing legal standing with Philemon as a slave (verse 16), he did challenge Philemon to a new relationship with Onesimus. Paul did not call for the slave's freedom (1 Cor. 7:20–22) but called for the master to receive his slave as a fellow-believer in Christ (see Eph. 6:9; Col. 4:1; 1 Tim. 6:2). Paul was not trying to abolish slavery but rather to make the relationship within this institution just and kind. The master and the slave were to enjoy spiritual oneness and fellowship as they worshiped and ministered together.

Paul also recognized that Philemon's forgiveness would involve a cost. The original theft as well as the loss due to Onesimus's absence were justifiable concerns that Paul was willing to address. If Philemon felt the need for restitution, Paul declared that he would pay Onesimus's debt. He also gently hinted, however, that Philemon might consider what he owed Paul as he was reckoning his losses.

FURTHER STUDY ON PHILEMON

1. How did Paul handle the issue of slavery in writing to Philemon?
2. On what principles did Paul base his encouragement to Philemon to forgive Onesimus?
3. What is the tone of Paul's letter?
4. How would you resolve the tension between Onesimus, Philemon, and Paul in such a way that each one would be satisfied?

HEBREWS
Christ Is Our High Priest

TITLE

When the various NT books were formally brought together into one collection shortly after A.D. 100, the titles were added for convenience. This epistle's title bears the traditional Greek title, "To the Hebrews," which was attested by at least the second century A.D. Within the epistle itself, however, there is no identification of the recipients as either Hebrews (Jews) or Gentiles. Since the epistle is filled with references to Hebrew history and religion and does not address any particular Gentile or pagan practice, the traditional title has been maintained.

AUTHOR AND DATE

The author of Hebrews is unknown. Paul, Barnabas, Silas, Apollos, Luke, Philip, Priscilla, Aquila, and Clement of Rome have been suggested by different scholars, but the epistle's vocabulary, style, and various literary characteristics do not clearly support any particular claim. It is significant that the writer includes himself among those people who had received confirmation of Christ's message from others (2:3). That would seem to rule out someone like Paul who claimed that he had received such confirmation directly from God and not from men (Gal. 1:12). Whoever the author was, he preferred citing OT references from the Greek OT (LXX) rather than from the Hebrew text. Even the early church expressed various opinions on authorship, and current scholarship admits the puzzle still has no solution. Therefore, it seems best to accept the epistle's author as being anonymous. Ultimately, of course, the author was the Holy Spirit (2 Pet. 1:21).

The use of the present tense in 5:1–4; 7:21,23,27,28; 8:3–5,13; 9:6–9,13,25; 10:1,3,4,8,11; and 13:10,11 would suggest that the Levitical priesthood and sacrificial system were still in operation when the epistle was composed. Since the temple was destroyed by General (later Emperor) Titus Vespasian in A.D. 70, the epistle must have been written prior to that date. In addition, it may be noted that Timothy had just been released from prison (13:23) and that persecution was becoming severe (10:32–39; 12:4; 13:3). These details suggest a date for the epistle around A.D. 67–69.

BACKGROUND AND SETTING

Emphases on the priesthood in the tradition of the Levites and on sacrifices, as well as the absence of any reference to the Gentiles, support the conclusion that a community of Hebrews was the recipient of the epistle. Although these Hebrews were primarily converts to Christ, there were probably a number of unbelievers in their midst, who were attracted by the message of salvation, but who had not yet made a full commitment of faith in Christ (see Interpretive Challenges). One thing is clear from the contents of the epistle: the community of Hebrews was facing the possibility of intensified persecution (10:32–39; 12:4). As they confronted this possibility, the Hebrews were tempted to cast aside any identification with Christ. They may have considered demoting Christ from God's Son to a mere angel. Such a precedent had already been set in the Qumran community of messianic Jews living near the Dead Sea. They had dropped out of society, established a religious commune, and included the worship of angels in their brand of reformed Judaism. The Qumran community had even gone so far as to claim that the angel Michael was higher in status than the coming Messiah. These kinds of doctrinal aberrations could explain the emphasis in Hebrews chapter one on the superiority of Christ over the angels.

Possible locations for the recipients of the epistle include Palestine, Egypt, Italy, Asia Minor, and Greece. The community that was the primary recipient may have circulated the epistle among those of Hebrew background in neighboring areas and churches. Those believers probably had not seen Christ personally. Apparently, they had been evangelized by "those who heard" Christ and whose ministries had been authenticated "with signs and wonders, with various miracles" (2:3,4). Thus the recipients could have been in a church outside Judea and Galilee or in a church in those areas, but established among people in the gen-

CHRIST IN . . . HEBREWS

DIRECTED TOWARDS JEWISH READERS, this is a work of contrasts. The Jewish believers were in danger of falling back into the rituals of the law. Yet Hebrews exhorts its readers to remember God's provision for a perfect priest and sacrifice in Christ to free those under the law. Hebrews presents Christ as the perfect sacrifice over the inadequate sacrifices of the Jews (9:9,12–15). Christ is also superior as the High Priest, Prophet, and King to all those who came before Him (4:14–16; 12:1,2).

eration following those who had been eyewitnesses of Christ. The congregation was not new or untaught ("by this time you ought to be teachers") yet some of them still needed "milk and not solid food" (5:12).

"Those from Italy" (13:24) is an ambiguous reference since it could mean either those who had left Italy and were living elsewhere, or those who were still in Italy and being singled out as native residents of that country. Greece or Asia Minor must also be considered because of the apparently early establishment of the church there, and because of the consistent use of the LXX.

The generation of Hebrews receiving this epistle had practiced the Jewish system of sacrifices at the temple in Jerusalem. Jews living in exile had substituted the synagogue for the temple but still felt a deep attraction to the temple worship. Some had the means to make regular pilgrimages to the temple in Jerusalem. The writer of this epistle emphasized the superiority of Christianity over Judaism and the superiority of Christ's once-for-all sacrifice over the repeated and imperfect Levitical sacrifices observed in the temple.

KEY PEOPLE IN HEBREWS

Abel—son of Adam and Eve; offered a more acceptable sacrifice to God than his brother did (11:4; 12:24)

Enoch—lived in close fellowship with God; taken up to heaven without dying (11:5)

Noah—obeyed God and built the ark (11:7)

Abraham—followed God to become the father of the Jewish nation (2:16; 6:13–11:19)

Sarah—trusted God to give her a child in her old age (11:11)

Isaac—son of Abraham and Sarah; blessed his sons, Jacob and Esau, according to the will of God (11:9–20)

Jacob—son of Isaac; blessed and adopted Joseph's sons before his death (11:9,20–21)

Joseph— believed God would deliver the nation of Israel out from Egypt (11:22)

Moses—courageously served God and led Israel out of Egypt (3:2–16; 7:14–12:25)

Rahab—obeyed God by sheltering Israelite spies in her home (11:31)

Old Testament people of faith—accomplished great deeds for God and also suffered great persecution (11:32–40)

HISTORICAL AND THEOLOGICAL THEMES

Since the Book of Hebrews is grounded in the work of the Levitical priesthood, an understanding of the Book of Leviticus is essential for properly interpreting Hebrews. During the OT times, Israel's sin had continually interrupted God's fellowship with His chosen and covenant people, Israel. Therefore, He graciously established a system of sacrifices that symbolized the inner repentance of sinners and His divine forgiveness. However, the need for sacrifices never ended because the people and priests continued to sin. The need of all mankind was for a perfect priest and a perfect sacrifice that would once and for all actually remove sin. God's provision for that perfect priest and sacrifice in Christ is the central message of Hebrews.

The epistle to the Hebrews is a study in contrast, between the imperfect and incomplete provisions of the Old Covenant, given under Moses, and the infinitely better provisions of the New Covenant offered by the perfect High Priest, God's only Son and the Messiah, Jesus Christ. Included in the "better" provisions are: a better hope, testament, promise, sacrifice, substance, country, and resurrection. Those who belong to the New Covenant dwell in a completely new and heavenly atmosphere, they worship a heavenly Savior, have a heavenly calling, receive a heavenly gift, are citizens of a heavenly country, look forward to a heavenly Jerusalem, and have their very names written in heaven.

One of the key theological themes in Hebrews is that all believers now have direct access to God under the New Covenant and, therefore, may approach the throne of God

KEY WORDS IN
Hebrews

Covenant: Greek *diathēkē*—8:6,8–10; 9:4; 10:16,29; 12:24—literally, "agreement," "will," or "testament." In 9:15–20, the author of Hebrews explains why the New Covenant (8:7) has completed the first covenant made at Mount Sinai. The author uses the word *diathēkē* throughout the section as an analogy to a "will." Just as the contents of a will go into effect when a person dies, so Christ's death initiated the New Covenant that frees us from bondage to the first covenant.

Mediator: Greek *mesitēs*—8:6; 9:15; 12:24—literally, "a go-between" or "intermediary." Paul characterizes Moses as a mediator of the covenant at Mount Sinai. Moses acted as a communication link between God and the Israelites. He informed the Israelites of their covenant obligations and also appealed to God on Israel's behalf (see Gal. 3:19,20). Acting in the same position, Jesus is the Mediator of the New Covenant. He activated this covenant through His own sacrifice on the cross. He now sits at the right hand of the Father interceding for us (7:25).

Redemption: Greek *apolutrōsis*—9:15—literally, "redemption." When used by the NT writers, this word, and its related term, *lutrōsis*, signify redemption. *Redemption* reflects the act of freeing, releasing, or buying back by paying a ransom price. The ransom price for humanity's sin is death. Yet, Christ paid this ransom price through His own sacrifice (1 Pet. 1:18,19) and thus freed us from the bondage of sin, to be brought back into the family of God (Gal. 3:13; 4:5).

boldly (4:16; 10:22). One's hope is in the very presence of God, into which he follows the Savior (6:19,20; 10:19,20). The primary teaching symbolized by the tabernacle service was that believers under the covenant of law did not have direct access to the presence of God (9:8), but were shut out of the Holy of Holies. The Book of Hebrews may briefly be summarized in this way: Believers in Jesus Christ, as God's perfect sacrifice for sin, have the perfect High-Priest through whose ministry everything is new and better than under the covenant of law.

Christ's Superiority

Jesus Is Greater Than the Prophets, 1:1-3	Jesus Is Greater Than the Angels, 1:4–14
Seven character affirmations:	Seven Scripture quotations:
Heir of all things (v. 2)	Psalm 2:7 (v. 5)
Creator (v. 2)	2 Samuel 7:14 (v. 3)
Manifested of God's Being (v. 3)	Deuteronomy 32:43 or Psalm 97:7 (v. 6)
Perfect representation of God (v. 3)	Psalm 104:4 (v. 7)
Sustainer of all things (v. 3)	Psalm 45:6, 7 (vv. 8,9)
Savior (v. 3)	Psalm 102:25-27 (vv. 10–12)
Exalted Lord (v. 3)	Psalm 110:1 (v. 13)

This epistle is more than a doctrinal statement, however. It is intensely practical in its application to everyday living (see chap. 13). The writer himself even refers to his letter as a "word of exhortation" (13:22; cf. Acts 13:15). Exhortations of warning and advice designed to stir the readers into action are found throughout the text. These encouragements are given in the form of six warnings:

- Warning against drifting from "the things we have heard" (2:1–4)
- Warning against disbelieving the "voice" of God (3:7–14)
- Warning against degenerating from "the elementary principles of Christ" (5:11–6:20)
- Warning against despising "the knowledge of the truth" (10:26–39)
- Warning against devaluing "the grace of God" (12:15–17)
- Warning against departing from Him "who speaks" (12:25–29)

Another significant aspect of this epistle is its clear explanatory teaching of selected OT passages. The writer was clearly a skilled expositor of the Word of God. His example is instructive for preachers and teachers:

- 1:1–2:4   Exposition of verses from Pss.; 2 Sam. 7; Deut. 32
- 2:5–18   Exposition of Ps. 8:4–6
- 3:1–4:13   Exposition of Ps. 95:7–11
- 4:14–7:28   Exposition of Ps. 110:4
- 8:1–10:18   Exposition of Jer. 31:31–34
- 10:32–12:3   Exposition of Hab. 2:3,4

- 12:4–13   Exposition of Prov. 3:11,12
- 12:18–29   Exposition of Ex. 19,20

KEY DOCTRINES IN HEBREWS

The New Covenant—all believers now have direct access to God and may approach God's throne without fear (4:16; 6:19,20; 9:8; 10:19–22; Deut. 4:7; Ps. 65:4; John 10:7,9; 14:6; Rom. 5:2; Eph. 2:18; 3:12; Col. 1:21,22; 1 Pet. 3:18)

Christ as High Priest—(3:1,2; 4:14; 5:5–11; 6:20; 7:15–17,26; 9:11; Zech. 6:13; Ps. 110:4)

GOD'S CHARACTER IN HEBREWS

God is accessible—4:16; 7:25; 9:6–15; 10:19–22; 11:16

God is a consuming fire—12:29

God is glorious—1:3

God is loving—12:6

God is a promise keeper—4:1; 6:12,15,17; 8:6,10,12; 10:23,36; 11:9,11,33

God is wrathful—3:17–19; 10:26.27

INTERPRETIVE CHALLENGES

A proper interpretation of this epistle requires the recognition that it addresses three distinct groups of Jews: (1) believers; (2) unbelievers who were intellectually convinced of the gospel; and (3) unbelievers who were attracted by the gospel and the person of Christ but who had reached no final conviction about Him. Failure to acknowledge these groups leads to interpretations inconsistent with the rest of Scripture.

The primary group addressed were Hebrew Christians who suffered rejection and persecution by fellow Jews (10:32–34), although none as yet had been martyred (12:4). The letter was written to give them encouragement and confidence in Christ, their Messiah and High-Priest. They were an immature group of believers who were tempted to hold on to the symbolic and spiritually powerless rituals and traditions of Judaism. The second group addressed were Jewish unbelievers who were convinced of the basic truths of the gospel but who had not placed their faith in Jesus Christ as their own Savior and Lord. These unbelievers are addressed in such passages as 2:1–3; 6:4–6; 10:26–29; and 12:15–17. The third group addressed were Jewish unbelievers who were not convinced of the gospel's truth but had had some exposure to it. Chapter 9 is largely devoted to them (see especially vv. 11,14,15,27,28).

By far, the most serious interpretive challenge is found in 6:4–6. The phrase "once enlightened" is often taken to refer to Christians, and the accompanying warning taken to indicate the danger of losing their salvation if "they fall away" and "crucify again for themselves the Son of God." But there is no mention of their being saved and they are not described with any terms that apply only to believers (such as holy, born again, righteous, or saints). This problem arises from inaccurately identifying the spiritual condition of the ones being addressed. In this case, they were unbelievers who had been exposed to God's redemptive truth, and perhaps made a profession of faith, but had not exercised genuine saving faith. In 10:26, the reference once again is to apostate Christians, not to genuine believers who are often incorrectly thought to lose their salvation because of their sins.

OUTLINE

I. The Superiority of Jesus Christ's Position (1:1–4:13)
A. A Better Name (1:1–3)
B. Better Than the Angels (1:4–2:18)
   1. A greater messenger (1:4–14)
   2. A greater message (2:1–18)
      a. A greater salvation (2:1–4)
      b. A greater savior (2:5–18)
C. Better Than Moses (3:1–19)
D. A Better Rest (4:1–13)

II. The Superiority of Jesus Christ's Priesthood (4:14–7:28)
A. Christ as High-Priest (4:14–5:10)
B. Exhortation to Full Commitment to Christ (5:11–6:20)
C. Christ's Priesthood like Melchizedek's (7:1–28)

III. The Superiority of Jesus Christ's Priestly Ministry (8:1–10:18)
A. Through a Better Covenant (8:1–13)
B. In a Better Sanctuary (9:1–12)
C. By a Better Sacrifice (9:13–10:18)

IV. The Superiority of the Believer's Privileges (10:19–12:29)
A. Saving Faith (10:19–25)
B. False Faith (10:26–39)
C. Genuine Faith (11:1–3)
D. Heroes of the Faith (11:4–40)
E. Persevering Faith (12:1–29)

V. The Superiority of Christian Behavior (13:1–21)
A. In Relation to Others (13:1–3)
B. In Relation to Ourselves (13:4–9)
C. In Relation to God (13:10–21)

Postscript (13:22–25)

MEANWHILE, IN OTHER PARTS OF THE WORLD...
In east Africa, the art of pottery developed in Tanzania and Kenya migrates to Mozambique.

ANSWERS TO TOUGH QUESTIONS

1. To which Hebrews was this book written?
Although the author and the original recipients of this letter are unknown, the title, dating as early as the second century A.D., has been "To the Hebrews." The title certainly fits the content. The epistle exudes a Jewish mindset. References to Hebrew his-

tory and religion abound. And since no particular Gentile or pagan practice gains any attention in the book, the church has kept the traditional title.

A proper interpretation of Hebrews, however, requires the recognition that it addresses three distinct groups of Jews:

- Hebrew Christians formed the primary addressees. These had already suffered rejection and persecution by fellow Jews (10:23–34), although none had yet been martyred (12:4). They were an immature group of believers who were tempted to hold on to the symbolic and spiritually powerless rituals and traditions of Judaism. This letter was written to give them encouragement and confidence in Christ, their Messiah and High Priest.
- Jewish unbelievers convinced of the truth but still uncommitted. This group had given mental assent to the truth of the gospel but had not placed their faith in Jesus Christ as their Savior and Lord. They were intellectually persuaded but spiritually uncommitted. These unbelievers are addressed in such passages as 2:1–3; 6:4–6; 10:26–29; 12:15–17.
- Jewish unbelievers who were attracted by the gospel and the person of Christ but who had reached no final conviction about Him. Chapter 9 of Hebrews speaks specifically to this group (particularly verses 11,14–15, 27–28).

2. What does 4:14–16 teach about prayer?

This passage offers two very personal benefits that come to those who have trusted in Jesus the Son of God as the great High Priest. First, we have Someone who can "sympathize with our weaknesses" because He "was in all points tempted as we are, yet without sin" (verse 15). Second, we can be confident of access to the "throne of grace" (verse 16) because Someone knows our need. Christian prayer accepts God's invitation to enjoy the access provided through Christ.

The Christian's unique access to God was a radical idea in the ancient world. Most ancient rulers were unapproachable by anyone but their highest advisers. In contrast, the Holy Spirit calls for all to come confidently before God's throne to receive mercy and grace through Jesus Christ (see 7:25; 10:22; Matt. 27:51). It was at the throne of God that Christ made atonement for sins, and it is there that grace is dispensed to believers for all the issues of life (see 2 Cor. 4:15; 9:8; 12:9; Eph. 1:7; 2:7).

3. To whom is 6:4–6, and particularly the phrase "once enlightened" directed?

The phrase "once enlightened" is often taken to refer to Christians. The accompanying warning, then, is taken to indicate the danger of losing their salvation if they "fall away" and "crucify again for themselves the Son of God." But the immediate context has no mention of their being saved. They are not described with any terms that apply only to believers (such as holy, born again, righteous, or saints).

The interpretive problem arises from inaccurately identifying the spiritual condition of the ones being addressed. In this case, they were unbelievers who had been exposed to God's redemptive truth and, perhaps, had made a profession of faith but had not exercised genuine saving faith. Another passage (10:26) addresses the same issue. The subject here is people who came in contact with the gospel but were spiritually unchanged by it. These apostates were Christians in name only and were never genuine believers, who are often incorrectly thought to lose their salvation because of their sins.

There is no possibility of these verses referring to someone losing salvation. Many Scripture passages make unmistakably clear that salvation is eternal (see, for example, John 10:27–29; Rom. 8:35,38,39; Phil. 1:6; 1 Pet. 1:4,5). Those who want to make this passage mean that believers can lose salvation will have to admit that it would then also make the point that one could never get it back again.

4. Who was Melchizedek and why was he so important?

Melchizedek shows up abruptly and briefly in the OT, but his special role in Abraham's life makes him a significant figure. He is mentioned again in Psalm 110:4, the passage under consideration in 4:14–7:28. As the king of Salem and priest of the Most High God in the time of Abraham, Melchizedek offered a historical precedent for the role of king-priest (Gen. 14:18–20) that was later filled perfectly by Jesus Christ.

By using the two OT references to Melchizedek, the writer (7:1–28) explains the superiority of Christ's priesthood by reviewing Melchizedek's unique role as a type of Christ and his superiority to the Levitical high priesthood. The Levitical priesthood was hereditary, but Melchizedek's was not. Through Abraham's honor, Melchizedek's rightful role was established. The major ways in which the Melchizedekan priesthood was superior to the Levitical priesthood are these:

- The receiving of tithes (7:2–10), as when Abraham the ancestor of the Levites gave Melchizedek a tithe of the spoils
- The giving of the blessing (7:1,6,7), as when Abraham accepted Melchizedek's blessing
- The continual replacement of the Levitical priesthood (7:11–19), which passed down from father to son the perpetuity of the Melchizedekan priesthood (7:3,8,16,17,20–28), since the record about his priesthood does not record his death

5. What significance can be found in the statement, "And as it is appointed for men to die once, but after this the judgment" (9:27)?

First, this passage offers a direct answer to those tempted to flirt with any form of reincarnation. Second, it states the general rule for all humankind, with very rare and only partial exceptions. Lazarus and the multitudes who were raised from the dead at Christ's resurrection had to die again (see Matt. 27:51–53; John 14:43,44). Those, like Lazarus, who were raised from the dead by a miraculous act of our Lord were not resurrected to a glorified body and unending life. They only experienced resuscitation. Another exception will be those who don't die even once, but who will be "caught up . . . to meet the Lord in the air" (1 Thess. 4:17). Enoch (Gen. 5:24) and Elijah (2 Kin. 2:11) are also part of this last group.

The general rule for all human beings includes another shared event—judgment. The judgment noted here refers to the judgment of all people, believers (2 Cor. 5:10) and unbelievers (Rev. 20:11–15).

6. Why are so many Old Testament people listed in chapter 11?

The eleventh chapter of Hebrews offers a moving account of faithful OT saints who remain models of faith. The chapter has received such titles as "The Saint's Hall of Fame," "The Honor Roll of OT Saints," and "Heroes of the Faith." Their lives attest to the value of living by faith. They compose the "cloud of witnesses" (12:1), who give powerful testimony to the Hebrews that they should come to faith in Christ.

This passage begins with an emphatic statement about the nature of faith. Faith involves the most solid possible conviction—the God-given guarantee of a future reality. True faith is not based on scientific evidence but on divine assurance, and it is a gift of God (Eph. 2:8).

The names, accomplishments and sufferings described in this chapter illustrate the range of faithfulness in the lives of saints. Some experienced great success in this world; whereas others suffered great affliction. The point is that they all courageously and uncompromisingly followed God, regardless of the earthly outcome. They placed their trust in Him and in His promises (see 6:12; 2 Tim. 3:12).

7. Does the Book of Hebrews contain any practical teaching?

The doctrine of salvation is the ultimate practical teaching. The significance of every other application flows from the reality of a right relationship with God through Christ. Once that is established, many other responses follow. Chapter 13 focuses on some of the essential practical ethics of Christian living. These ethics help portray the true gospel to the world, encourage others to believe in Christ, and bring glory to God. Marriage and general relationships among Christians also receive special attention. Verses 7–17 highlight the role of leaders and the submission required from believers. The chapter then concludes with a request for prayer, a benediction, and final greetings. In short, a careful reading of Hebrews, particularly the last chapter, will yield a wealth of godly direction for living.

8. Did the writer of Hebrews actually think Christians might entertain angels (13:2)?

This verse primarily highlights the importance of extending love to strangers (Rom. 13:3; 1 Tim. 3:2). Hospitality in the ancient world would often include putting up a guest overnight or longer. The possibility of an angelic visit was mentioned not as the ultimate motivation for hospitality but to demonstrate that one never knows how far-reaching an act of kindness might be (Matt. 25:40,45). The writer was appealing to historical precedents that his Jewish readers would have known well. Angels certainly had visited and had been entertained by Abraham and Sarah (Gen. 18:1–3), Lot (Gen. 19:1,2), Gideon (Judg. 6:11–24), and Manoah (Judg. 13:6–20).

FURTHER STUDY ON HEBREWS

1. In explaining Christ's uniqueness and excellence, what did the writer of Hebrews use for comparison?
2. What specific examples of practical teaching can you find in Hebrews?
3. What was the role of the Old Testament saints, particularly in chapter 11?
4. How does Hebrews explain Christ's dual role of priest and sacrifice?
5. What insights from Hebrews have you gained about your own prayer life?

JAMES
Faith in Action

TITLE
James, like all of the general epistles except Hebrews, is named after its author (v. 1).

AUTHOR AND DATE
Of the four men named James in the NT, only two are candidates for authorship of this epistle. No one has seriously considered James the Less, the son of Alphaeus (Matt. 10:3; Acts 1:13), or James the father of Judas, not Iscariot (Luke 6:16; Acts 1:13). Some have suggested James the son of Zebedee and brother of John (Matt. 4:21), but he was martyred too early to have written it (Acts 12:2). That leaves only James, the oldest half-brother of Christ (Mark 6:3) and brother of Jude (Matt. 13:55), who also wrote the epistle that bears his name (Jude). James had at first rejected Jesus as Messiah (John 7:5), but later believed (1 Cor. 15:7). He became the key leader in the Jerusalem church (cf. Acts 12:17; 15:13; 21:18; Gal. 2:12), being called one of the "pillars" of that church, along with Peter and John (Gal. 2:9). Also known as James the Just because of his devotion to righteousness, he was martyred ca. A.D. 62, according to the first-century Jewish historian Josephus. Comparing James's vocabulary in the letter he wrote, which is recorded in Acts 15, with that in the epistle of James further corroborates his authorship.

James		Acts 15
1:1	"greetings"	15:23
1:16,19; 2:5	"beloved"	15:25
1:21; 5:20	"your souls"	15:24,26
1:27	"visit"	15:14
2:10	"keep"	15:24
5:19,20	"turn"	15:19

James wrote with the authority of one who had personally seen the resurrected Christ (1 Cor. 15:7), who was recognized as an associate of the apostles (Gal. 1:19), and who was the leader of the Jerusalem church.

James most likely wrote this epistle to believers scattered (1:1) as a result of the unrest recorded in Acts 12 (ca. A.D. 44). There is no mention of the Council of Jerusalem described in Acts 15 (ca. A.D. 49), which would be expected if that Council had already taken place. Therefore, James can be reliably dated ca. A.D. 44–49, making it the earliest written book of the NT canon.

BACKGROUND AND SETTING
The recipients of this book were Jewish believers who had been dispersed (1:1), possibly as a result of Stephen's martyrdom (Acts 7, A.D. 31–34), but more likely due to the persecution under Herod Agrippa I (Acts 12, ca. A.D. 44). The author refers to his audience as "brethren" fifteen times (1:2,16,19; 2:1,5,14; 3:1,10,12; 4:11; 5:7,9,10,12,19), which was a common epithet among the first century Jews. Not surprisingly, then, James is Jewish in

its content. For example, the Greek word translated "assembly" (2:2) is the word for "synagogue." Further, James contains more than forty allusions to the OT (and more than twenty to the Sermon on the Mount, Matt. 5–7).

James and the Sermon on the Mount

James	Sermon on the Mount	Subject
1:2	Matt. 5:10-12 (Luke 6:22, 23)	Joy in the midst of trials
1:4	Matt. 5:48	God's desire and work in us: perfection
1:5	Matt. 7:7	Asking God for good gifts
1:17	Matt. 7:11	God is the giver of good gifts
1:19,20	Matt. 5:22	Command against anger
1:22,23	Matt. 7:24-27	Contrast between hearers and doers (illustrated)
1:26,27	Matt. 7:21-23	Religious person whose religion is worthless
2:5	Matt. 5:3	The poor as heirs of the kingdom
2:10	Matt. 5:19	The whole moral law to be kept
2:11	Matt. 5:21,22	Command against murder
2:13	Matt. 5:7; 6:14,15	The merciful blessed; the unmerciful condemned
2:14-26	Matt. 7:21–23	Dead, worthless (and deceiving) faith
3:12	Matt. 7:16 (Luke 6:44,45)	Tree producing what is in keeping with its kind
3:18	Matt. 5:9	Blessing of those who make peace
4:2,3	Matt. 7:7,8	Importance of asking God
4:4	Matt. 6:24	Friendship with the world = hostility toward God
4:8	Matt. 5:8	Blessing on and call for the pure in heart
4:9	Matt. 5:4	Blessing and call for those who mourn
4:11,12	Matt. 7:1-5	Command against wrongly judging others
4:13,14	Matt. 6:34	Not focusing too much on tomorrow
5:1	(Luke 6:24,25)	Woe to rich
5:2	Matt. 6:19,20	Moth and rust spoiling earthly riches
5:6	(Luke 6:37)	Against condemning the righteous man
5:9	Matt. 5:22; 7:1	Not judging–the Judge standing at the door
5:10	Matt. 5:12	The prophets as examples of wrongful suffering
5:12	Matt. 5:33–37	Not making hasty and irreverent oaths

KEY PEOPLE IN JAMES
The believers—persecuted Jewish believers dispersed throughout the Roman Empire (1:1–5:20)

HISTORICAL AND THEOLOGICAL THEMES
James, with its devotion to strong, direct statements on wise living, is reminiscent of the book of Proverbs. It has a practical emphasis, stressing godly behavior rather than simply theoretical knowledge. James wrote with a passionate desire for his readers to be uncompromisingly obedient to the Word of God. He used at least thirty references to nature (e.g., "wave of the sea" [1:6]; "reptile" [3:7]; and "heaven gave rain" [5:18]), as befits one who spent a great deal of time outdoors. He complements Paul's emphasis on justification by faith with his own emphasis on spiritual fruitfulness demonstrating true faith.

KEY DOCTRINES IN JAMES

Works—salvation is determined by faith alone and is demonstrated by faithfulness to obey God's will (2:14–26; Matt. 7:16,17,21–23,26; 21:28–32; Rom. 3:28; 11:6; Gal. 5:6; Eph. 2:8–10; 2 Tim. 1:9; Titus 3:5; 2 Pet. 1:3–11)

Godly behavior—wise living through uncompromising obedience to the Word of God (1:22; 3:13,17; 4:7–11; 5:7–12; Job 9:4,28; Pss. 104:24; 111:10; Prov. 1:7; 2:1–7; 3:19,20; 9:10; Jer. 10:7,12; Dan. 1:17; 2:20–23; Matt. 7:21,26; Luke 6:46–49; Rom. 2:13)

GOD'S CHARACTER IN JAMES

God is accessible—4:8

God is immutable—1:17

God is Light—1:17

God is a promise keeper—1:12; 2:5

God is unified—2:19–20

INTERPRETIVE CHALLENGES

At least two significant texts challenge the interpreter: 1) In 2:14–26, what is the relationship between faith and works? Does James's emphasis on works contradict Paul's focus on faith? (See Answers to Tough Questions for discussion on this difficult issue.) 2) In 5:13–18, do the promises of healing refer to the spiritual or physical realm? It seems clear in context that James is calling for prayer to deliver the sick from their physical suffering because they have been weakened by their infirmity, not from their sin, which was confessed.

CHRIST IN . . . JAMES

JAMES OPENLY REFERS to Christ only twice (1:1; 2:1), yet his epistle abounds with references to Christ's teachings, particularly to the Sermon on the Mount (see chart, James and the Sermon on the Mount). James's application of truth to his reader's lives gives believers a clearer understanding of Christ's wisdom.

Faith Alive

James wants his readers to demonstrate in their lives the qualities of a living faith. Such a living faith is more than mere knowledge and assent—it includes heartfelt trust that endures and obeys God.

Described as:	Results in:
Tested (1:2,3)	Patience (1:3)
Without doubt (1:6-8)	Answered prayer (1:5)
Enduring temptation (1:12)	Eternal life (1:12)
More than belief (2:19,20)	Faith perfected by works (2:22)
Believing God (2:23-25)	Righteousness before God (2:23)

James contrasts living faith to dead, or empty, faith. Dead faith does not result in the transformed life that is characteristic of living faith.

OUTLINE

There are a number of ways to outline the book to grasp the arrangement of its content. One way is to arrange it around a series of tests by which the genuineness of a person's faith may be measured.

Introduction (1:1)

    I. The Test of Perseverance in Suffering (1:2–12)
    II. The Test of Blame in Temptation (1:13–18)
    III. The Test of Response to the Word (1:19–27)
    IV. The Test of Impartial Love (2:1–13)
    V. The Test of Righteous Works (2:14–26)
    VI. The Test of the Tongue (3:1–12)
    VII. The Test of Humble Wisdom (3:13–18)
    VIII. The Test of Worldly Indulgence (4:1–12)
    IX. The Test of Dependence (4:13–17)
    X. The Test of Patient Endurance (5:1–11)
    XI. The Test of Truthfulness (5:12)
    XII. The Test of Prayerfulness (5:13–18)
    XIII. The Test of True Faith (5:19,20)

MEANWHILE, IN OTHER PARTS OF THE WORLD...

The sea route used for trade between India and Egypt becomes increasingly more important than the main land routes through Persia.

ANSWERS TO TOUGH QUESTIONS

1. How can James expect Christians to somehow "count it all joy" when they face difficulties and trials (1:2)?

The Greek word for *count* may also be translated "consider" or "evaluate." The natural human response to hardships and difficulties is rarely rejoicing. Therefore, the believer must make a conscious commitment to face trials with joy. Trials, then, are reminders to rejoice (Phil. 3:1).

Trials comes from a Greek word that connotes trouble, or something that breaks the pattern of peace, comfort, joy, and happiness in someone's life. The verb form of this word means "to put someone or something to the test," with the purpose of discovering that person's nature or that thing's quality. God brings such tests to prove—and increase—the strength and quality of one's faith and to demonstrate its validity (verses 2–12). Every trial becomes a test of faith designed to strengthen: If the believer fails the test by responding wrongly, that test then becomes a temptation, or a solicitation to evil. The choice to rejoice avoids greater trouble later.

2. When James writes about the "perfect law of liberty," how does he use those terms—*law* and *liberty*—that appear to be contradictory (1:25)?

In both the OT and the NT, God's revealed, inerrant, sufficient, and comprehensive Word is called "law" (Ps. 19:7). The presence of God's grace does not mean the absence of a moral law or code of conduct for believers to obey. Believers are enabled by the Spirit to keep God's standards.

True liberty is not the license to do what we want but rather the assistance to do what we ought. The law of liberty frees us from sin (2:12,13). It liberates us when we have sinned by showing us a gracious God, and it directs us away from sin as we obey Him. As the Holy Spirit applies the principles of Scripture to believers' hearts, they are freed from sin's bondage and enabled to live in true freedom (John 8:34–36).

3. What is the "royal law" (2:8)?

The phrase *royal law* translates better as "sovereign law." The idea is that this law is supreme or binding. James quotes the second half of what Jesus taught was the whole of the sovereign law. "Love your neighbor as yourself," which James quotes from Leviticus 19:18 as well as from Mark 12:31, when combined with the command to love God (Deut. 6:4,5), summarizes all the Law and the Prophets (Matt. 22:36–40; Rom. 13:8–10).

> **KEY WORDS IN**
>
> # James
>
> **Anointing:** Greek *aleiphō*—5:14—literally, "to daub" or "to smear." Greek *chriō*—5:14—literally, "to anoint." The term *aleiphō* was commonly used to describe a medicinal anointing. A similar Greek word *chriō* was used to express a sacramental anointing. In biblical times, oil was commonly used as a medicine (Luke 10:30–37). Yet, oil also symbolized the Spirit of God (1 Sam. 16:1–13).
>
> **Good Gift; Perfect Gift:** Greek *dosis agathē*—1:17—literally, "the act of giving" and "good." Greek *dōrēma teleion*—1:17—literally, "actual gifts" and "perfect." The Greek text uses two separate words to describe gifts from God. The first expression, *good gift*, reveals the value of receiving something from God, while *perfect gift* represents the flawless quality of God's gifts. God's giving is continuously good, and His gifts are always perfectly suited for His children.

James has already alluded to the first part of the great commandment (2:5). Here he focuses on the theme of this section, which is human relationships. James is not advocating some kind of emotional affection for oneself—self-love is clearly a sin (2 Tim. 3:2). Rather, the command is to pursue meeting the physical and spiritual needs of one's neighbors with the same intensity and concern as one does naturally for one's self (Phil. 2:3,4), while never forgetting we are under royal law to do so.

4. What is the relationship between faith and works? If salvation is by faith in Christ, how can James write, "Faith without works is dead" (2:14–26)?

This passage comes within a longer section, in which James provides his readers with a series of tests they can use to evaluate whether their faith is living or dead. Here is the central test—the one that pulls the others together: the test of works or righteous behavior. James defines this behavior as actions that obey God's Word and manifest a godly nature (1:22–25).

James's point is not that a person is saved by works. He has already strongly and clearly asserted that salvation is a gracious gift from God (1:17,18). Rather, his concern is to show that there is a kind of apparent faith that is dead and does not save (2:14,17,20,24,26). His teaching parallels the rest of Scripture (Matt. 3:7,8; 5:16; 7:21; 13:18–23; John 8:30,31; 15:6). It is possible that James was writing to Jews who had turned away from the works righteousness of Judaism and had instead embraced the mistaken notion that since righteous works and obedience to God's will were not efficacious for salvation, they were not necessary at all. Thus, they reduced faith to a mere mental aknowledgement of the facts about Christ, to which James rightly declares that such faith is dead.

5. What do the ten commands in 4:7–10 have to do with grace?

These verses contain a series of commands that prepare a person to receive saving grace. These commands delineate a person's response to God's gracious offer of salvation and reveal what it means to be humble. Each command uses a Greek imperative to define the expected action:

- Submit to God (verse 7)—James used the phrase to describe a willing, conscious submission to God's authority as sovereign ruler of the universe (Matt. 10:38).
- Resist the devil (verse 7)—Those who consciously "take their stand against" Satan and transfer their allegiance to God will find that Satan "will flee from" them; he is a defeated foe (John 8:44; Eph. 2:2; 1 John 3:8; 5:19).
- Draw near to God (verse 8)—Pursue an intimate relationship with God (Phil. 3:10).
- Cleanse your hands (verse 8)—The added term "sinners" addresses the unbeliever's need to recognize and confess his or her sin (5:20).
- Purify your hearts (verse 8)—Cleansing the hands symbolizes external behavior; this phrase refers to the inner thoughts, motives, and desires of the heart (Ps. 24:3,4; Jer. 4:4; 1 Tim. 1:5; 2 Tim. 2:22; 1 Pet. 1:22).
- Lament (verse 9)—To be afflicted, wretched and miserable. This is the state of those truly broken over their sin (Matt. 5:3).
- Mourn (verse 9)—The internal experience of brokenness over sin (Ps. 51:17; Matt. 5:4).
- Weep (verse 9)—The outward manifestation of inner sorrow over sin (Mark 14:72).
- Laughter to mourning, joy to gloom (verse 9)—mourn over sin, rather than flippant laughter of those foolishly indulging in worldly pleasures without regard to God.
- Humble yourself (verse 10)—This final command sums up the preceding nine. The word *humble* means, "to make oneself low." Those conscious of being in the presence of the majestic, infinitely holy God are humbled (Is. 6:5).

6. What does James mean by the closing words of his letter, "he who turns a sinner from the error of his way will save a soul from death and cover a multitude of sins" (5:20)?

The language used by James makes it clear that the "sinner" he has in mind here is someone whose faith is dead (2:14–26), not a believer who sins. The term is used throughout Scripture to describe those who are outside of Christ and lifeless in regard to the faith (Prov. 11:31; 13:6,22; Matt. 9:13; Luke 7:37,39; 15:7,10; 18:13; Rom. 5:8; 1 Tim. 1:9,15; 1 Pet. 4:18).

A person who wanders from the truth and never allows it to transform him puts his soul in jeopardy. This "death" is not physical death, but eternal death—eternal separation from God and eternal punishment in hell (Is. 66:24; Dan. 12:2; Matt. 13:40, 42,50; 25:41,46; Mark 9:43–49; 2 Thess. 1:8,9; Rom. 6:23; Rev. 20:11–15; 21:8). Knowing how high the stakes are should motivate Christians to aggressively pursue such people.

Since even one sin is enough to condemn a person to hell, James's use of the word *multitude* emphasizes the hopeless condition of lost, unregenerate sinners. The good news of the gospel is that God's forgiving grace (which is greater than any sin, Rom. 5:20) is available to those who turn from their sins and exercise faith in the Lord Jesus Christ (Eph. 2:8,9).

FURTHER STUDY ON JAMES

1. Explain James's view of the benefits of difficulties and suffering.
2. How did James view harmful discrimination between Christians?
3. How did James discuss the tension between faith and works?
4. How do the ten commands that fill James 4:7–10 relate to grace?
5. What command in James do you find most challenging to carry out?

FIRST PETER
Persecution of the Church

TITLE

The letter has always been identified (as are most general epistles, like James, John, and Jude) with the name of the author, Peter, and with the notation that it was his first inspired letter.

AUTHOR AND DATE

The opening verse of the epistle claims the book was written by Peter, who was clearly the leader among Christ's apostles. The gospel writers emphasize this fact by placing his name at the head of each list of apostles (Matt. 10; Mark 3; Luke 6; Acts (1), and including more information about him in the four gospels than any person other than Christ. Originally known as Simon (Greek) or Simeon (Hebrew), (cf. Mark 1:16; John 1:40,41), Peter was the son of Jonas (Matt. 16:17) who was also known as John (John 1:42). He was a member of a family of fishermen who lived in Bethsaida and later in Capernaum. Andrew, Peter's brother, brought him to Christ (John 1:40–42). He was married, and his wife apparently accompanied him in his ministry (Mark 1:29–31; 1 Cor. 9:5).

Peter was called to follow Christ in His early ministry (Mark 1:16,17), and was later appointed to apostleship (Matt. 10:2; Mark 3:14–16). Christ renamed him *Peter* (Greek), or *Cephas* (Aramaic), both words meaning "stone" or "rock" (John 1:42). The Lord clearly singled out Peter for special lessons throughout the gospels (e.g., Matt. 10; 16:13–21; 17:1–9; 24:1–7; 26:31–33; John 6:6; 21:3–7,15–17). He was the spokesman for the Twelve, articulating their thoughts and questions as well as his own. His triumphs and weaknesses are chronicled in the gospels and Acts 1–12.

After the resurrection and ascension, Peter initiated the plan for choosing a replacement for Judas (Acts 1:15). After the coming of the Holy Spirit (Acts 2:1–4), he was empowered to become the leading gospel preacher from the Day of Pentecost on (Acts 2:12). He also performed notable miracles in the early days of the church (Acts 3–9), and opened the door of the gospel to the Samaritans (Acts 8) and to the Gentiles (Acts 10). According to tradition, Peter had to watch as his wife

CHRIST IN . . . 1 PETER

SINCE THE CHRISTIANS addressed in 1 Peter lived in the midst of great persecution, Peter directs them to identify with the sufferings of Christ (1:10–12; 2:24; 4:12,13). First Peter balances this message with reminders of the numerous blessings bestowed on Christians for their perseverance (1:13–16). Christ remains the believer's "living hope" in a hostile world (1:3,4).

was crucified, but encouraged her with the words, "Remember the Lord." When it came time for him to be crucified, he reportedly pled that he was not worthy to be crucified like his Lord, but rather should be crucified upside down (ca. A.D. 67–68), which tradition says he was.

Because of his unique prominence, there was no shortage in the early church of documents falsely claiming to be written by Peter. That the apostle Peter is the author of 1 Peter, however, is certain. The material in this letter bears definite resemblance to his messages in the Book of Acts. The letter teaches, for example, that Christ is the Stone rejected by the builder (2:7,8; Acts 4:10,11), and that Christ is no respecter of persons (1:17; Acts 10:34). Peter teaches his readers to "gird yourself with humility" (5:5), an echo of the Lord's girding Himself with a towel and washing the disciples' feet (John 13:3–5). There are other statements in the letter similar to Christ's sayings (4:14; 5:7,8). Moreover, the author claims to have been a witness of the sufferings of Christ (5:1; cf. 3:18; 4:1). In addition to these internal evidences, it is noteworthy that the early Christians universally recognized this letter as the work of Peter.

The only significant doubt to be raised about Peter's authorship arises from the rather classical style of Greek employed in the letter. Some have argued that Peter, being an "unlearned" fisherman (Acts 4:13), could not have written in sophisticated Greek, especially in light of the less classical style of Greek employed in the writing of 2 Peter. However, this argument is not without a good answer. In the first place, that Peter was "unlearned" does not mean that he was illiterate, but only that he was without formal, rabbinical training in the Scriptures. Moreover, though Aramaic may have been Peter's primary language, Greek would have been a widely spoken second language in Palestine. It is also apparent that at least some of the authors of the NT, though not highly educated, could read the Greek of the OT Septuagint (see James' use of the LXX in Acts 15:14–18).

Beyond these evidences of Peter's ability in Greek, Peter also explained (5:12) that he wrote this letter "by Silvanus," also known as Silas. Silvanus was likely the messenger designated to take this letter to its intended readers. But more is implied by this statement in that Peter is acknowledging that Silvanus served as his secretary, or amanuensis. Dictation was common in the ancient Roman world (cf. Paul and Tertius; Rom. 16:22), and secretaries often could aid with syntax and grammar. So, Peter, under the superintendence of the Spirit of God, dictated the letter to Silvanus, while Silvanus, who also was a prophet (Acts 15:32), may have aided in some of the composition of the more classical Greek.

First Peter was most likely written just before or shortly after July, A.D. 64, when the city of Rome burned, thus a writing date of ca. A.D. 64–65.

KEY WORDS IN

1 Peter

Word: Greek *logos*—1:23; 2:8; 3:1—literally, "word" or "idea," also Greek *rhēma*—1:25. "The word of God" (1:23) is the gospel message about the Lord Jesus Christ. The Spirit uses the Word to produce life. It is the truth of the gospel that saves and regenerates men and women. Peter used Isaiah 40:6–8, which says "the word of our God" in a NT context.

Example: Greek *hupogrammos*—2:21—literally, "tracing tablet." In biblical times, this term denoted tablets that contained the entire Greek alphabet. Students would practice tracing each letter of the alphabet on these tablets. When believers use the life of Jesus as their example, His life of suffering becomes their tracing tablet. Christians who trace the life of Jesus learn godliness and wisdom in the face of persecution.

Love: Greek *agapē*—4:8—literally, "love." Most of the ancient occurrences of this Greek word appear in the NT. *Agapē* describes the love of one who shows kindness to strangers, gives hospitality, and acts charitably. In the NT, the word *agapē* took on a special meaning: It denoted a love in action as opposed to the purely emotional kind. *Agapē* love is the self-sacrificial love naturally demonstrated by God.

BACKGROUND AND SETTING

When the city of Rome burned, the Romans believed that their emperor, Nero, had set the city on fire, probably because of his incredible lust to build. In order to build more, he had to destroy what already existed.

The Romans were totally devastated. Their culture, in a sense, went down with the city. All the religious elements of their life were destroyed—their great temples, shrines, and even their household idols were burned up. This tragedy had great religious implications because it made them believe that their deities had been unable to deal with this conflagration and were also victims of it. The people were homeless and hopeless. Many had been killed. Their bitter resentment was severe, so Nero realized that he had to redirect the hostility.

The emperor's chosen scapegoat was the Christians, who were already hated because they were associated with Jews, and because they were seen as being hostile to the Roman culture. Nero spread the word quickly that the Christians had set the fires. As a result, a vicious persecution against Christians began, and soon spread throughout the Roman Empire, touching places north of the Taurus mountains, like Pontus, Galatia, Cappadocia, Asia, and Bithynia (1:1), and impacting the Christians, whom Peter calls "pilgrims." These "pilgrims," who were probably Gentiles, for the most part (1:14,18; 2:9,10; 4:3), possibly led to Christ by Paul and his associates, and established on Paul's teachings. But they needed spiritual strengthening because of their sufferings. Thus the apostle Peter, under the inspiration of the Holy Spirit, wrote this epistle to strengthen them.

Peter wrote that he was in "Babylon" when he penned the letter (5:13). Three locations have been suggested for this "Babylon." First, a Roman outpost in northern Egypt was named Babylon; but that place was too obscure, and there are no reasons to think that Peter was ever there. Second, ancient Babylon in Mesopotamia is a possibility; but it would be quite unlikely that Peter, Mark, and Silvanus were all at this rather small, distant place at the same time. Third, "Babylon" is an alias for Rome; perhaps even a code word for Rome. In times of persecution, writers exercised unusual care not to endanger Christians by identifying them. Peter, according to some traditions, followed James and Paul and died as a martyr near Rome about two years after he wrote this letter, thus he had written this epistle near the end of his life, probably while staying in the imperial city. He did not want the letter to be found and the church to be persecuted, so he may have hidden its location under the code word, "Babylon," which aptly fit because of the city's idolatry (cf. Rev. 17,18).

KEY PEOPLE IN 1 PETER

Peter—one of Jesus' twelve disciples; wrote to encourage persecuted believers (1:1–5:14)
Silas—missionary who traveled with Paul; assisted Peter in writing his letters (5:12)
Mark—leader in the church; used Peter's testimony to write the gospel of Mark (5:13)

HISTORICAL AND THEOLOGICAL THEMES

Since the believers addressed were suffering increasing persecution (1:6; 2:12,19–21; 3:9,13–18; 4:1,12–16,19), the purpose of this letter was to teach them how to live victoriously in the midst of that hostility: (1) without losing hope; (2) without becoming bitter;

(3) while trusting in their Lord; and (4) while looking for His second coming. Peter wished to impress on his readers that by living an obedient, victorious life under duress, a Christian can actually evangelize his hostile world (cf. 1:14; 2:1,12,15; 3:1–6,13–17; 4:2; 5:8,9).

Believers are constantly exposed to a world system energized by Satan and his demons. Their effort is to discredit the church and to destroy its credulity and integrity. One way these spirits work is by finding Christians whose lives are not consistent with the Word of God, and then parading them before the unbelievers to show what a sham the church is. Christians, however, must stand against the enemy and silence the critics by the power of holy lives.

In this epistle, Peter is rather effusive in reciting two categories of truth. The first category is positive and includes a long list of blessings bestowed on Christians. As he speaks about the identity of Christians and what it means to know Christ, Peter mentions one privilege and blessing after another. Interwoven into this list of privileges is the catalog of suffering. Christians, though most greatly privileged, should also know that the world will treat them unjustly. Their citizenship is in heaven and they are strangers in a hostile, Satan-energized world. Thus the Christian life can be summed up as a call to victory and glory through the path of suffering. So, the basic question that Peter answers in this epistle is: How are Christians to deal with animosity? The answer features practical truths and focuses on Jesus Christ as the model of one who maintained a triumphant attitude in the midst of hostility.

Suffering in Divine Perspective

Human Suffering	Divine Perspective
Various trials (1:6).	Rejoice; they are temporary (1:6).
Unjust authority (2:18).	Silence evil men by doing good. Follow the example of Christ (2:21).
Suffering for doing what is right (3:14).	Be ready to give testimony of your faith (3:15).
Suffering because of a determination to resist carnal desires (4:1).	Give up carnal pursuits (4:2).
Religious persecution (4:12–14).	Be partakers in Christ's sufferings (4:13,14).
Suffering as part of God's refining fire for spiritual growth (4:19).	Commit your life to Him; He is faithful (4:19).
Suffering from the attack of Satan (5:8).	Resist Satan; be steadfast in faith (5:9).

The Book of 1 Peter also answers other important practical questions about Christian living such as: Do Christians need a priesthood to intercede with God for them (2:5–9)? What should be the Christian's attitude to secular government and civil disobedience (2:13–17)? What should a Christian employee's attitude be toward a hostile employer (2:18)? How should a Christian lady conduct herself (3:3,4)? How can a believing wife win her unsaved husband to Christ (3:1,2)?

Living Among Pagans

Christians are exhorted to be...	Because...
Good citizens (2:13,14)	Foolish men will be silenced (2:15)
Obedient servants (2:18)	Christ is our example (2:21)
Submissive wives (3:1)	Some unbelieving husbands will be won by their example (3:1,2)
Considerate husbands (3:7)	Their prayers will be heard (3:7)
Compassionate brothers and sisters (3:8)	They will inherit a blessing (3:9)

KEY DOCTRINES IN 1 PETER
Persecution—Christians are able to identify with Christ's sufferings when they are persecuted for their faith (1:6; 2:12,19–21; 3:9,13–18; 4:1, 12–16,19; Ps. 69:26; Is. 50:6; 53:7; Jer. 15:15; Dan. 3:28; Zech. 2:8; Mark 10:30; Luke 21:12; John 5:16; 15:20; Rom. 8:35; 2 Cor. 1:10; 4:9; 2 Tim. 3:12)

GOD'S CHARACTER IN 1 PETER
God is accessible—1:17; 3:18
God is faithful—4:19
God is holy—1:15,16
God is just—1:17
God is long-suffering—3:20
God is merciful—1:3
God is righteous—2:23

INTERPRETIVE CHALLENGES
First Peter 3:18–22 stands as one of the most difficult NT texts to translate and then interpret. For example, does "Spirit" in 3:18 refer to the Holy Spirit, or to Christ's Spirit? Did Christ preach through Noah before the Flood, or did He preach Himself after the crucifixion (3:19)? Was the audience to this preaching composed of the people in Noah's day, or demons in the abyss (3:19)? Does 3:20,21 teach baptismal regeneration (salvation), or salvation by faith alone in Christ? A discussion of some of these questions is in Answers to Tough Questions.

OUTLINE
Salutation (1:1,2)
    I. Remember Our Great Salvation (1:3–2:10)
        A. The Certainty of Our Future Inheritance (1:3–12)
            1. Preserved by the power of God (1:3–5)
            2. Proven by the trials of persecution (1:6–9)
            3. Predicted by the prophets of God (1:10–12)

B. The Consequences of Our Future Inheritance (1:13–2:10)
    1. Perseverance of hope (1:13–16)
    2. Persistence of wonder (1:17–21)
    3. Power of love (1:22–2:3)
    4. Praises of Christ (2:4–10)

II. Remember Our Example Before Men (2:11–4:6)
  A. Honorable Living Before Unbelievers (2:11–3:7)
    1. Submission to the government (2:11–17)
    2. Submission to masters (2:18–25)
    3. Submission in the family (3:1–7)
  B. Honorable Living Before Believers (3:8–12)
  C. Honorable Living in the Midst of Suffering (3:13–4:6)
    1. The principle of suffering for righteousness (3:13–17)
    2. The paragon of suffering for righteousness (3:18–22)
    3. The purpose of suffering for righteousness (4:1–6)

III. Remember Our Lord Will Return (4:7–5:11)
  A. The Responsibilities of Christian Living (4:7–11)
  B. The Rewards of Christian Suffering (4:12–19)
  C. The Requirements for Christian Leadership (5:1–4)
  D. The Realization of Christian Victory (5:5–11)

Conclusion (5:12–14)

MEANWHILE, IN OTHER PARTS OF THE WORLD...

Fire destroys much of the city of Rome. Nero blames Christians for setting the fire, which begins an empire-wide persecution of all believers.

ANSWERS TO TOUGH QUESTIONS

1. Why does Peter call his readers "elect" (1:2)?

Peter uses a term here that in Greek also connotes "called out ones." The word means "to pick out" or "to select." In the OT, the word was used of Israel (Deut. 7:6), indicating that God sovereignly chose Israel from among all the nations of the world to believe in and belong to Him (Deut. 14:12; Ps. 105:43; 135:4). In 1 Peter, the *elect* is used for Christians, those chosen by God for salvation (Rom. 8:33; Col. 3:12; 2 Tim. 2:10). The word is also used for those who receive Christ during the tribulation time (Matt. 24:22,24) and for holy, unfallen angels (1 Tim. 5:21). To be reminded that they were elected by God was a great comfort to those persecuted Christians.

By using this and other terms of ownership, Peter was establishing the basis from which he would encourage them not to see their suffering as evidence of a different standing with God. Their ultimate security, even in the face of persecution and suffering, was in God's hands.

2. What is the "pure milk of the word" (2:2)?

The Scriptures frequently use startling but clear figurative language to teach spiritual truth. Daily life often mirrors heavenly realities. God's Word offers pure spiritual nourishment. Spiritual growth is always marked by a craving for and delight in God's Word with the same intensity with which a baby craves milk (Job 23:12; Pss. 1:1,2; 19:7–11; 119:16,24,35,47,48,72,92,97,103,111,113,127,159,167,174; Jer. 15:16). That initial by-product of spiritual rebirth ought to be a consistent part of the Christian's life.

Christians develop and maintain a desire for the truth of God's Word by remembering their life's source (1:25; Is. 55:10,11; John 15:3; Heb. 4:12), eliminating sin from their lives (2:1), admitting their need for God's truth (2:2, "as newborn babes"; Matt. 4:4), pursuing spiritual growth (2:2, "that you may grow thereby"), and surveying their blessings (2:3, "the Lord is gracious").

3. Do Christians need a priesthood to intercede for them with God (2:9)?

Along with "royal priesthood" Peter uses several OT concepts to emphasize the privileges of NT Christians (Deut. 7:6–8). This phrase gave rise to the theological expression "the priesthood of believers." For believers, the need for a representative priest has been met by Jesus Christ, the ultimate royal priest (Heb. 4:14–9:15). The role of priest is not eliminated but altered. This verse indicates that a central role of the priesthood of all believers is to "proclaim the praises of Him who called you out of darkness into His marvelous light."

The concept of a kingly priesthood is drawn from Exodus 19:6. Israel had temporarily forfeited this privilege because of its apostasy and because its wicked leaders executed the Messiah. At the present time, the church is a royal priesthood united with the royal priest, Jesus Christ. A royal priesthood is not only a priesthood that belongs to and serves the king, but is also a priesthood that exercises rule. This will ultimately be fulfilled in Christ's future kingdom (1 Cor. 6:1–4; Rev. 5:10; 20:6).

4. How does Peter use familiar terms like *spirit, abyss, flood,* and *baptism* in 1 Peter 3:18–22?

This passage proves to be one of the most difficult texts in the NT to translate and interpret. The line between OT allusions and NT applications gets blurred. Peter's overall purpose in this passage, which was to encourage his readers in their suffering, must be kept in mind during interpretation. The apostle repeatedly reminds them and demonstrates that even Christ suffered unjustly because it was God's will (verse 11) and was accomplishing God's purposes.

Therefore, although Jesus experienced a violent physical execution that terminated His earthly life when He was "put to death in the flesh" (verse 18; Heb. 5:7), He was nevertheless "made alive by the Spirit" (verse 18). This is not a reference to the Holy Spirit but to Jesus' true inner life, His own spirit. Contrasted with His flesh (humanness), which was dead for three days, His spirit (deity) remained alive, literally, "in spirit" (Luke 23:46).

Part of God's purpose in Christ's death involved His activities between His death and resurrection. His living spirit went to the demon spirits bound in the abyss and proclaimed victory in spite of death. Peter further explains that the *abyss* is inhabited by bound demons that have been there since the time of Noah. They were sent there because they overstepped the limits of God's tolerance with their wickedness. Not even 120 years of Noah's example and preaching had stemmed the tide of wickedness in his time (Gen. 6:1–8). Thus God bound these demons permanently in the abyss until their final sentencing.

Peter's analogy spotlights the ministry of Jesus Christ in saving us as surely as the ark saved Noah's family. He is not referring to water baptism in 3:21, but to a figurative immersion in Christ that keeps us safe from the flood of God's sure judgment. The resurrection of Christ demonstrates God's acceptance of Christ's substitutionary death for the sins of those who believe (Acts 2:30–31; Rom. 1:4). God's judgment fell on Christ just as the judgment of the floodwaters fell on the ark. The believer who is in Christ is thus in the ark of safety that will sail over the waters of judgment into eternal glory (Rom. 6:1–4).

FURTHER STUDY ON 1 PETER

1. Peter clearly wants his readers to be secure in their relationship with Christ. What points did he make about salvation?
2. What special titles, names, and roles did Peter assign to Christ in this letter?
3. In 1 Peter 2:21-25, how does Jesus serve as a model for those facing suffering for their faith?
4. Compare 1 Peter 3:1-7 with Ephesians 5:21–33. How does the teaching of these two apostles regarding marriage overlap and where does it differ in emphasis?
5. What did Peter have to say about the conduct of relationships among Christians in general?
6. In 1 Peter 1:14-25, the apostle includes a major section emphasizing the important of holy living. To what extent does your life match the pattern given by Peter?

SECOND PETER
False Teachers among God's People

TITLE

The clear claim to authorship in 1:1 by the apostle Peter gives the epistle its title. To distinguish it from Peter's first epistle, it was given the Greek title "*Petrou B*," or 2 Peter.

AUTHOR AND DATE

The author of 2 Peter is the apostle Peter (see 1 Peter: Author and Date). In 1:1, he makes that claim; in 3:1, he refers to his first letter; in 1:14, he refers to the Lord's prediction of his death (John 21:18,19); and in 1:16–18, he claims to have been at the Transfiguration (Matt. 17:1–4). However, critics have generated more controversy over 2 Peter's authorship and rightful place in the canon of Scripture than over any other NT book. The church fathers were slow in giving it their acceptance. No church father refers to 2 Peter by name until Origen near the beginning of the third century. The ancient church historian, Eusebius, included 2 Peter only in his list of disputed books, along with James, Jude, 2 John, and 3 John. Even the leading Reformers only hesitatingly accepted it.

The question about differences in Greek style between the two letters has been satisfactorily answered. Peter wrote that he used an amanuensis, Silvanus, in 1 Peter (cf. 1 Pet. 5:12). In 2 Peter, Peter either used a different scribe or wrote the letter by himself. The differences in vocabulary between the two letters can be explained by the differences in themes. First Peter was written to help suffering Christians. Second Peter was written to expose false teachers. On the other hand, there are remarkable similarities in the vocabulary of the two books. The salutation, "grace to you and peace be multiplied," is essentially the same in each book. The author uses such words as "precious," "virtue," "putting off," and "eyewitness," to name just a few examples, in both letters. Certain rather unusual words found in 2 Peter are also found in Peter's speeches in the Acts of the

> ## CHRIST IN . . . 2 PETER
>
> IN HIS SECOND LETTER, Peter anticipates the second coming of the Lord Jesus Christ "as a thief in the night" (3:10). He also speaks repeatedly of the knowledge of Christ that produces peace, grace, and power for the believer (1:2–3,8; 3:18).

Apostles. These include "obtained" (1:2; Acts 1:17); "godliness" (1:3,6,7; 3:11; Acts 3:12); and "wages of iniquity" (2:13,15; Acts 1:18). Both letters also refer to the same OT event (2:5; 1 Pet. 3:18–20). Some scholars have pointed out that there are as many similarities in vocabulary between 1 and 2 Peter as there are between 1 Timothy and Titus, two letters almost universally believed to have been written by Paul.

The differences in themes also explains certain emphases, such as why one letter teaches that the Second Coming is near, and one deals with its delay. First Peter, ministering especially to suffering Christians, focuses on the imminency of Christ as a means of encouraging the Christians. Second Peter, dealing with scoffers, emphasizes the reasons why the imminent return of Christ has not yet occurred. Other proposed differences invented by the critics, such as the contradiction between including the Resurrection of Christ in one letter and the Transfiguration of Christ in the other, seem to be contrived.

The Life of Peter

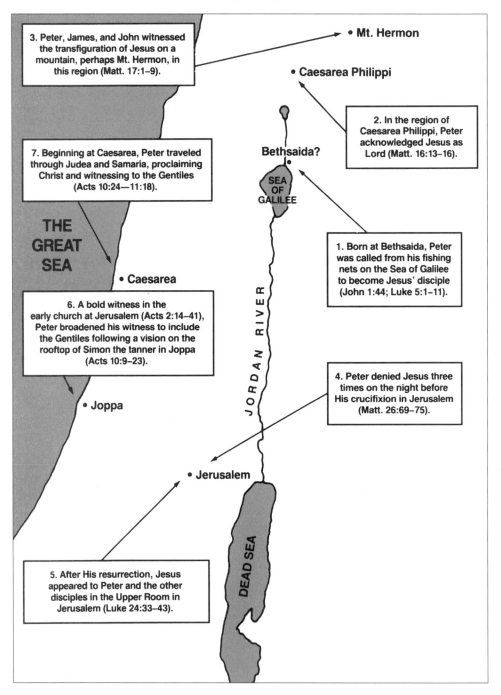

3. Peter, James, and John witnessed the transfiguration of Jesus on a mountain, perhaps Mt. Hermon, in this region (Matt. 17:1–9).

• Mt. Hermon

• Caesarea Philippi

2. In the region of Caesarea Philippi, Peter acknowledged Jesus as Lord (Matt. 16:13–16).

7. Beginning at Caesarea, Peter traveled through Judea and Samaria, proclaiming Christ and witnessing to the Gentiles (Acts 10:24—11:18).

Bethsaida?

SEA OF GALILEE

THE GREAT SEA

1. Born at Bethsaida, Peter was called from his fishing nets on the Sea of Galilee to become Jesus' disciple (John 1:44; Luke 5:1–11).

• Caesarea

6. A bold witness in the early church at Jerusalem (Acts 2:14–41), Peter broadened his witness to include the Gentiles following a vision on the rooftop of Simon the tanner in Joppa (Acts 10:9–23).

JORDAN RIVER

4. Peter denied Jesus three times on the night before His crucifixion in Jerusalem (Matt. 26:69–75).

• Joppa

• Jerusalem

5. After His resurrection, Jesus appeared to Peter and the other disciples in the Upper Room in Jerusalem (Luke 24:33–43).

DEAD SEA

Moreover, it is seemingly irrational that a false teacher would spuriously write a letter against false teachers. No unusual, new, or false doctrines appear in 2 Peter. So, if 2 Peter were a forgery, it would be a forgery written by a fool for no reason at all. This is too much to believe. The conclusion to the question of authorship is that, when the writer introduced the letter and referred to himself as Peter, he was writing the truth.

Nero died in A.D. 68, and tradition says Peter died in Nero's persecution. The epistle may have been written just before his death (1:14; ca. A.D. 67–68).

BACKGROUND AND SETTING

Since the time of the writing and sending his first letter, Peter had become increasingly concerned about false teachers who were infiltrating the churches in Asia Minor. Though these false teachers had already caused trouble, Peter expected that their heretical doctrines and immoral life-styles would result in more damage in the future. Thus Peter, in an almost last will and testament (1:13–15), wrote to warn the beloved believers in Christ about the doctrinal dangers they were facing.

Peter does not explicitly say where he was when he wrote this letter, as he does in 1 Peter (1 Pet. 5:13). But the consensus seems to be that Peter wrote this letter from prison in Rome, where he was facing imminent death. Shortly after this letter was written, Peter was martyred, according to reliable tradition, by being crucified upside down.

Peter says nothing in the salutation about the recipients of this letter. But according to 3:2, Peter was writing another epistle to the same people to whom he wrote 1 Peter. In his first letter, he spelled out that he was writing "to the pilgrims of the Dispersion in Pontus, Galatia, Cappadocia, Asia, and Bithynia" (1 Pet. 1:1). These provinces were located in an area of Asia Minor, which is modern Turkey. The Christians to whom Peter wrote were mostly Gentiles.

KEY PEOPLE IN 2 PETER

Peter—one of Jesus' twelve disciples; wrote his second letter to warn against false teachers in the church (1:1–3:18)

Paul—great missionary and apostle whose writings were twisted by false teachers in the church (3:15,16)

HISTORICAL AND THEOLOGICAL THEMES

Second Peter was written for the purpose of exposing, thwarting, and defeating the invasion of false teachers into the church. Peter intended to instruct Christians in how to defend themselves against these false teachers and their deceptive lies. This book is the most graphic and penetrating exposé of false teachers in Scripture, comparable only to Jude.

The description of the false teachers is somewhat generic. Peter does not identify some specific false religion, cult, or system of teaching. In a general characterization of false teachers, he informs that they teach destructive heresies. They deny Christ and twist the Scriptures. They bring true faith into disrepute. And they mock the second coming of Christ. But Peter was just as concerned to show the immoral character of these teachers as he was to expose their teaching. Thus, he describes them in more detail than he describes their doctrines. Wickedness is not the product of sound doctrine, but of "destructive heresies" (2:1).

Other themes for this letter can be discerned in the midst of Peter's polemic against the false teachers. He wanted to motivate his readers to continue to develop their Christian character (1:5–11). In so doing, he explains wonderfully how a believer can have assurance of his salvation. Peter also wanted to persuade his readers of the divine character of the apostolic writings (1:12–21). Near the end of the letter, he presents reasons for the delay in Christ's second coming (3:1–13).

Another recurring theme is the importance of knowledge. The word *knowledge* appears in some form sixteen times in these three short chapters. It is not too much to say that Peter's primary solution to false teaching is knowledge of true doctrine. Other distinctive features of 2 Peter include a precise statement on the divine origin of Scripture (1:20,21); the future destruction of the world by fire (3:8–13); and the recognition of Paul's letters as inspired Scripture (3:15,16).

KEY WORDS IN

2 Peter

Knowledge: Greek *gnōsis*—1:5–6; 3:18—literally, "knowledge." This Greek word expresses a knowledge that grows and progresses. As Christians, we need to grow in our personal knowledge of Jesus Christ. The greatest protection against false teachings comes from a solid foundation in the Word of God. Peter's epistle encourages believers to attain a fuller, more thorough knowledge of their Lord Jesus Christ (1:8; 2:20; 3:18).

Morning Star: Greek *phōsphoros*—1:19—literally, "light-bearer" or "light-bringer." In 2 Peter, Christ is called the "morning star." He is also called the "Bright and Morning Star" in Revelation 22:16, and the "Dayspring" in Luke 1:78. Christians today have the light of Christ within their hearts. When Jesus returns to earth, He will bring all believers into a perfect day. His outward coming will bring light to all people. On this day, the spirits of the godly will take on "an illuminating transformation" as the light of Christ fills them.

KEY DOCTRINES IN 2 PETER

False teachers—their teachings deny Christ and twist the Scriptures (chapt. 2; Deut. 13:1–18; 18:20; Jer. 23; Ezek. 13; Matt. 7:15; 23:1–36; 24:4,5; Rom. 16:17; 2 Cor. 11:13,14; Gal. 3:1,2; 2 Tim. 4:3,4)

Scripture—the Holy Spirit, as divine author and originator of all Scripture, worked through humans to convey the Word of God (1:20,21; Jer. 1:4; 3:2; John 10:34,35; 17:17; Rom. 3:2; 1 Cor. 2:10; 1 Thess. 2:13; 2 Tim. 3:16; Titus 1:2; 1 Pet. 1:10,11)

Christian character—God gives all believers the power to grow in faith, virtue, knowledge, self-control, perseverance, godliness, brotherly kindness, and love (1:5–11; Ps. 4:3; Prov. 28:1; 1 Cor. 9:27; Gal. 5:23; Col. 1:4; 1 Thess. 4:9; 1 Pet. 4:8; 1 John 4:20; Rev. 17:14)

Christ's second coming—God has continual patience to allow people to repent before Christ returns (3:1–13; Dan. 7:13; Matt. 24:30; 25:31; John 14:3; 1 Thess. 4:16; 2 Thess. 1:10; 1 Tim. 6:14; Heb. 9:28; Jude 14; Rev. 1:7)

GOD'S CHARACTER IN 2 PETER

God is long-suffering—3:9,15

God is a promise keeper—1:4; 3:3–4,13

INTERPRETIVE CHALLENGES

Perhaps the most important challenge in the epistle is to rightly interpret 1:19–21, because of its far-reaching implications with regard to the nature and authenticity of Scripture. That passage, along with 2 Timothy 3:15–17, is vital to a sound view of the Bible's inspiration. Peter's remark that the Lord "bought" false teachers (2:1) poses a challenge interpretively and theologically with regard to the nature of the atonement.

The identity of the angels who sinned (2:4) also challenges the interpreter. These angels, according to Jude 6, "did not keep their proper domain," i.e., they entered men who promiscuously cohabited with women. Apparently this is a reference to the fallen angels of Genesis 6 (sons of God): (1) before the flood (v. 5; Gen. 6:1–3), who left their normal state and lusted after women, and (2) before the destruction of Sodom and Gomorrah (v. 6; Gen. 19).

Many who believe that the saved can be lost again, use 2:18–22 for their argument. That passage, directed at false teachers, must be clarified so as not to contradict a similar statement to believers in 1:4. Further, whom does God not want to perish (3:9)? Fuller answers to these and other questions are located in Answers to Tough Questions.

OUTLINE

Salutation (1:1, 2)

    I. Know Your Salvation (1:3–11)
        A. Sustained by God's Power (1:3, 4)
        B. Confirmed by Christian Graces (1:5–7)
        C. Honored by Abundant Reward (1:8–11)

    II. Know Your Scriptures (1:12–21)
        A. Certified by Apostolic Witness (1:12–18)
        B. Inspired by the Holy Spirit (1:19–21)

    III. Know Your Adversaries (2:1–22)
        A. Deceptive in Their Infiltration (2:1–3)
        B. Doomed by Their Iniquity (2:4–10a)
        C. Disdainful in Their Impurity (2:10b-17)
        D. Devastating in Their Impact (2:18–22)

    IV. Know Your Prophecy (3:1–18)
        A. The Sureness of the Day of the Lord (3:1–10)
        B. The Sanctification of God's People (3:11–18)

MEANWHILE, IN OTHER PARTS OF THE WORLD...
Nero commits suicide in A.D. 68 and is succeeded by Galba.

ANSWERS TO TOUGH QUESTIONS

1. How can two letters (1 and 2 Peter) from the same author be so different in style?

The differences between 1 Peter and 2 Peter lie in three areas: style, vocabulary, and theme. These differences must be resolved in the context of the clear claim by the author of 2 Peter to be the author of 1 Peter (2 Peter 3:2). See Author and Date.

2. Who were the false teachers in the early church that Peter addressed in 2 Peter?

Second Peter offers the most graphic and penetrating exposé of false teachers in Scripture, comparable only to Jude. Peter does not identify a specific false religion, cult, or system of teaching. He is more concerned with general principles of recognizing and resisting false instruction in the church.

In his broadest characterization of false teachers, Peter points out that they teach destructive heresies. They deny Christ and twist the Scriptures. They bring true faith into disrepute. They mock the Second Coming of Christ. It is not too much to claim that Peter's primary response to false teaching is knowledge of true doctrine. Falsehood may come in a variety of shades, but they stand revealed as wrong when compared with the truth.

Peter was just as concerned to show the immoral character of false teachers as he was to expose their teaching. He describes them in more detail than he does their doctrine. He knows that the quality of fruit reveals the soundness of the tree. Wickedness is not the product of sound doctrine but of "destructive heresies" (2:1). Peter urges Christians to pursue a deliberate plan of spiritual growth (1:5–9), allowing a life of integrity to expose what is false.

3. What does Peter mean by the counsel to "make your call and election sure" (1:10)?

This phrase hits the theological bull's-eye Peter was aiming at in 1:5–9. Though God is "sure" who His elect are and has given them an eternally secure salvation (Rom. 8:31–39; 1 Pet. 1:1–5), the Christian might not always have inward assurance of salvation. Security is the fact revealed by the Holy Spirit that salvation is forever. Assurance is one's confidence that he or she possesses that eternal salvation. In other words, the believers who pursue the spiritual qualities mentioned in the context of this phrase will guarantee to themselves by spiritual fruit that they were called (Rom. 8:30; 1 Pet. 2:21) and chosen (1 Pet. 1:2) by God to salvation.

4. How does Peter explain the doctrine of the inspiration of Scripture (1:19–21)?

This particular section of 2 Peter provides crucial insights regarding the nature and authenticity of Scripture. Even the apostle expected his readers to provide a reasonable defense for their confidence in the Scriptures. He realized that false teachers would attempt to discredit his letter as well as his past ministry, so he countered their arguments. He knew they would accuse him of concocting fables and myths as a way to manipulate his audience. (This charge by the false teachers actually revealed their own approach and purpose.) So, Peter gave evidence in this passage to prove that he wrote the truth of God as a genuinely inspired writer.

Peter details the process of inspiration. Scripture, claims Peter, is not of human origin. Neither is Scripture the result of human will (1:21). The emphasis in this phrase is that no part of Scripture was produced solely because men wanted it so. The Bible is not the product of sheer human effort. The prophets, in fact, often wrote what they could not understand (1 Pet. 1:10–11), but they were nevertheless faithful to write what God revealed to them.

Instead of relying on their own purposes, men were "moved by the Holy Spirit" (1:21) to write. Grammatically, this means that they were continually carried or borne along by the Spirit of God (Luke 1:70; Acts 27:15,17). The Holy Spirit thus is the divine author and originator, the producer of the Scriptures. In the OT alone, the human writers refer to their writings as the words of God over 3,800 times (Jer. 1:4; 3:2; Rom.3:2). Though the human writers were active rather than passive in the process of writing Scripture, God the Holy Spirit superintended them so that, using their own individual personalities, thought processes, and vocabulary, they composed and recorded without error the exact words God wanted written. The original documents of Scripture are therefore inspired (God-breathed, 2 Tim. 3:16), and inerrant (without error, John 10:34,35; 17:17; Titus 1:2). Peter here has described the process of inspiration that created an inerrant original text (Prov. 30:5; 1 Cor. 14:36; 1 Thess. 2:13).

5. How does "with the Lord one day is as a thousand years, and a thousand years as one day" (3:8) affect our understanding of God's plan?

God understands time very differently from us. From a human point of view, Christ's coming seems like a long time away (Ps. 90:4). From God's viewpoint, it will not be long. Peter reminds his readers of this fact before pointing out that any delay in Christ's return from the human perspective should never be taken as an indication that God is loitering or late. The passage of time actually is a clearer signal of God's immense capacity for patience before He breaks forth in judgment (Joel 2:13; Luke 15:20; Rom. 9:22; 1 Pet. 3:15).

Beyond that general frame of reference, this text may be a specific indication of the fact that there are actually a thousand years between the first phase of the Day of the Lord at the end of the tribulation (Rev. 6:17) and the second phase at the end of the millennial kingdom when the Lord creates the new heaven and new earth.

6. If the Lord is "not willing that any should perish" (3:9), why does it appear that many will have that very end?

The "any" in this passage must refer to those whom the Lord has chosen and will call to complete the redeemed, the "us" mentioned earlier in the same verse. Since the whole passage is about God's destroying the wicked, His patience is not so He can save all of them, but so that He can receive all His own. He can't be waiting for everyone to be saved, since the emphasis is that He will destroy the world and the ungodly. Those who do perish and go to hell, go because they are depraved and worthy only of hell—they have rejected the only remedy, Jesus Christ—not because they were created for hell and predetermined to go there. The path to damnation is the path of an unrepentant heart; it is the path of one who rejects the person and provision of Jesus Christ and holds on to sin (Is. 55:1; Jer. 13:17; Ezek.l 18:32; Matt. 11:28; 13:37; Luke 13:3; John 3:16; 8:21,24; 1 Tim. 2:3,4; Rev. 22:17).

The word "all," which begins the next phrase "but that all should come to repentance," must refer to all who are God's people who will come to Christ to make up the full number of the people of God. The reason for the delay in Christ's coming and the attendant judgments is not because He is slow to keep His promise, or because He wants to judge more of the wicked, or because He is impotent in the face of wickedness. He delays His coming because He is patient and desires the time for His people to repent.

7. What do Peter's comments about Paul's writings mean (2 Pet. 3:15,16)?

In the final thoughts of his letter, Peter turns for biblical support to the writings of Paul. Since Paul had (by the time Peter wrote) written all his letters and died, the readers of 2 Peter would have already received letters about future events from Paul. Some of Paul's explanations were difficult (but not impossible) to interpret. Nevertheless, Peter does not hesitate to use Paul as a support for his own teaching.

Peter then goes on to add a word of caution in pointing out that there were those willing to "twist" (3:16) and pervert the apostle's teaching about the future. The fact that distorting Paul's writings can lead to eternal damnation proves that God inspired Paul's writings. Peter's further addition of the phrase, "the rest of the Scriptures" (3:16), offers one of the most clear-cut statements in the Bible to affirm that the writings of Paul are Scripture. Peter's testimony is that Paul wrote Scripture, but the false teachers distorted it. The NT apostles were aware that they spoke and wrote the Word of God (1 Thess. 2:13) as surely as did the OT prophets. Peter affirmed that the NT writers compiled the divine truth that completed the Bible (1 Pet. 1:10–12).

FURTHER STUDY ON 2 PETER

1. What indications can you discover in the letter that indicate it might have been Peter's last?
2. How did Peter explain the apparent delay in the return of Christ?
3. In what ways did Peter attack and undermine the false authority of the false teachers?
4. What practical steps for spiritual growth does Peter include in this letter?

FIRST JOHN
The Fundamentals of Faith

TITLE

The epistle's title has always been "1 John." It is the first and largest in a series of three epistles that bear the apostle John's name. Since the letter identifies no specific church, location, or individual to whom it was sent, its classification is as a "general epistle." Although 1 John does not exhibit some of the general characteristics of an epistle common to that time (e.g., no introduction, greeting, or concluding salutation), its intimate tone and content indicate that the term "epistle" still applies to it.

AUTHOR AND DATE

The epistle does not identify the author, but the strong, consistent and earliest testimony of the church ascribes it to John the disciple and apostle (cf. Luke 6:13,14). This anonymity strongly affirms the early church's identification of the epistle with John the apostle, for only someone so knowledgeable and well respected as John would be able to write with such unmistakable authority, expecting complete obedience from his readers, without clearly identifying himself (e.g., 4:6). He was well known to the readers so he didn't need to mention his name.

John and James, his older brother (Acts 12:2), were known as "the sons of Zebedee" (Matt. 10:2–4), whom Jesus gave the name "Sons of Thunder" (Mark 3:17). John was one of the three most intimate associates of Jesus (along with Peter and James—cf. Matt. 17:1; 26:37), being an eyewitness to and participant in Jesus' earthly ministry (1:1–4). In addition to the three epistles, John also authored the fourth gospel, in which he identified himself as the disciple "whom Jesus loved" and as the one who reclined on Jesus' breast at the Last Supper (John 13:23; 19:26; 20:2; 21:7,20). He also wrote the Book of Revelation (Rev. 1:1).

Precise dating is difficult because no clear historical indications of date exist in 1 John. Most likely John composed this work in the latter part of the first century. Church tradition consistently identifies John in his advanced age as living and actively writing during this time at Ephesus in Asia Minor. The tone of the epistle supports this evidence since the writer gives the strong impression that he is much older than his readers (e.g., "my little children"—2:1,18,28). The epistle and John's gospel reflect similar vocabulary and manner of expression (see Historical and Theological Themes). Such similarity causes many to date the writing of John's epistles as occurring soon after he composed his gospel. Since many date the gospel during the later part of the first century, they also prefer a similar date for the epistles. Furthermore, the heresy John combats most likely reflects the beginnings of Gnosticism (see Background and Setting), which was in its early stages during the latter third of the first century when John was actively writing. Since no mention is made of the persecution under Domitian, which began about A.D. 95, it may have been written before that began. In light of such factors, a reasonable date for 1 John is ca. A.D. 90–95. It was likely written from Ephesus to the churches of Asia Minor over which John exercised apostolic leadership.

The Life of John

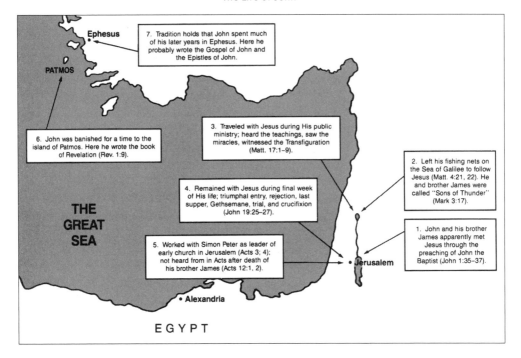

Ephesus

7. Tradition holds that John spent much of his later years in Ephesus. Here he probably wrote the Gospel of John and the Epistles of John.

PATMOS

6. John was banished for a time to the island of Patmos. Here he wrote the book of Revelation (Rev. 1:9).

3. Traveled with Jesus during His public ministry; heard the teachings, saw the miracles, witnessed the Transfiguration (Matt. 17:1–9).

2. Left his fishing nets on the Sea of Galilee to follow Jesus (Matt. 4:21, 22). He and brother James were called "Sons of Thunder" (Mark 3:17).

4. Remained with Jesus during final week of His life; triumphal entry, rejection, last supper, Gethsemane, trial, and crucifixion (John 19:25–27).

THE GREAT SEA

5. Worked with Simon Peter as leader of early church in Jerusalem (Acts 3; 4); not heard from in Acts after death of his brother James (Acts 12:1, 2).

1. John and his brother James apparently met Jesus through the preaching of John the Baptist (John 1:35–37).

Jerusalem

• **Alexandria**

E G Y P T

BACKGROUND AND SETTING

Although he was greatly advanced in age when he penned this epistle, John was still actively ministering to churches. He was the sole remaining apostolic survivor who had intimate, eyewitness association with Jesus throughout His earthly ministry, death, resurrection, and ascension. The church fathers (e.g., Justin Martyr, Irenaeus, Clement of Alexandria, Eusebius) indicate that after that time, John lived at Ephesus in Asia Minor, carrying out an extensive evangelistic program, overseeing many of the churches that had arisen, and conducting an extensive writing ministry (e.g., epistles, the gospel of John, and Revelation). One church father (Papias) who had direct contact with John described him as a "living and abiding voice." As the last remaining apostle, John's testimony was highly authoritative among the churches. Many eagerly sought to hear the one who had firsthand experience with the Lord Jesus.

Ephesus (cf. Acts 19:10) lay within the intellectual center of Asia Minor. As predicted years before by the apostle Paul (Acts 20:28–31), false teachers arising from within the church's own ranks, saturated with the prevailing climate of philosophical trends, began infecting the church with false doctrine, perverting the traditional teaching of the apostles. These false teachers advocated new ideas that eventually became known as "Gnosticism" (from the Greek word "knowledge"). After the Pauline battle for freedom from the law, Gnosticism was the most dangerous heresy that threatened the early church during the first three centuries. Most likely, John was combating the beginnings of this virulent heresy that threatened to destroy the fundamentals of the faith and the churches.

This heresy (false teaching) featured two basic forms. First, some asserted that Jesus' physical body was not real but only "seemed" to be physical (known as "Docetism" from a

Gr. word that means "to appear"). John forcefully affirmed the physical reality of Jesus by reminding his readers that he was an eyewitness to Him ("heard," "seen," " handled," "Jesus Christ has come in the flesh"—1:1–4; 4:2,3). According to early tradition (Irenaeus), there was another form of this heresy, which John may have attacked, that was led by a man named Cerinthus. Cerinthus contended that the Christ's "spirit" descended on the human Jesus at his baptism but left him just before his crucifixion. John wrote that the Jesus who was baptized at the beginning of His ministry was the same person who was crucified on the cross (5:6).

Such heretical views destroy not only the true humanity of Jesus, but also the atonement, for Jesus must not only have been truly God, but also the truly human (and physically real) man who actually suffered and died upon the cross in order to be the acceptable substitutionary sacrifice for sin (cf. Heb. 2:14–17). The biblical view of Jesus affirms His complete humanity as well as His full deity.

The Gnostic idea that matter was evil and only spirit was good led to the idea that either the body should be treated harshly, a form of asceticism (e.g., Col. 2:21–23), or sin committed in the body had no connection or effect on one's spirit. This led some, especially John's opponents, to conclude that sin committed in the physical body did not matter; absolute indulgence in immorality was permissible; one could deny sin even existed (1:8–10) and disregard God's law (3:4). John emphasized

CHRIST IN . . . 1 JOHN

IN THIS EPISTLE, John combats Gnostic doctrine that denied the humanity of Jesus Christ. John proclaims the identity of Jesus Christ as the incarnation of God the Son into human flesh: "This is He who came by water and blood" (5:6). This verse describes the genuine life and death of Christ as the Son of Man.

the need for obedience to God's laws, for he defined the true love of God as obedience to His commandments (5:3). (See Answers to Tough Questions for further discussion.)

A lack of love for fellow believers characterizes false teachers, especially as they react against anyone rejecting their new way of thinking (3:10–18). They separated their deceived followers from the fellowship of those who remained faithful to apostolic teaching, leading John to reply that such separation outwardly manifested that those who followed false teachers lacked genuine salvation (2:19). Their departure left the other believers, who remained faithful to apostolic doctrine, shaken. Responding to this crisis, the aged apostle wrote to reassure those remaining faithful and to combat this grave threat to the church. Since the heresy was so acutely dangerous and the time period was so critical for the church in danger of being overwhelmed by false teaching, John gently, lovingly, but with unquestionable apostolic authority, sent this letter to churches in his sphere of influence to stem this spreading plague of false doctrine.

KEY PEOPLE IN 1 JOHN

John—wrote to reassure believers about the fundamental truth of the Christian faith (1:1–5:21)

Jesus—Christ is the Word of Life who sacrificed Himself and rose from the grave to give eternal life to all who believe (1:1–5:20)

HISTORICAL AND THEOLOGICAL THEMES

In light of the circumstances of the epistle, the overall theme of 1 John is "a recall to the fundamentals of the faith" or "back to the basics of Christianity." The apostle deals with certainties, not opinions or conjecture. He expresses the absolute character of Christianity in very simple terms; terms that are clear and unmistakable, leaving no doubt as to the fundamental nature of those truths. A warm, conversational, and above all, loving tone occurs, like a father having a tender, intimate conversation with his children.

First John also is pastoral, written from the heart of a pastor who has concern for his people. As a shepherd, John communicated to his flock some very basic, but vitally essential, principles reassuring them regarding the basics of the faith. He desired them to have joy regarding the certainty of their faith rather than being upset by the false teaching and current defections of some (1:4).

The book's viewpoint, however, is not only pastoral but also polemical; not only positive but also negative. John refutes the defectors from sound doctrine, exhibiting no tolerance for those who pervert divine truth. He labels those departing from the truth as "false prophets" (4:1), "those who try to deceive" (2:26; 3:7), and "antichrists" (2:18). He pointedly identifies the ultimate source of all such defection from sound doctrine as demonic (4:1–7).

The constant repetition of three sub-themes reinforces the overall theme regarding faithfulness to the basics of Christianity: happiness (1:4), holiness (2:1), and security (5:13). By faithfulness to the basics, his readers will experience these three results continually in their lives. These three factors also reveal the key cycle of true spirituality in 1 John: a proper belief in Jesus produces obedience to His commands; obedience issues in love for God and fellow believers (e.g., 3:23,24). When these three (sound faith, obedience, love) operate in concert together, they result in happiness, holiness and assurance. They constitute the evidence, the litmus test, of a true Christian.

KEY DOCTRINES IN 1 JOHN

Fundamentals of the faith—sound faith, obedience, and love work together to produce happiness, holiness, and assurance in the lives of believers (1:4,9; 2:1,3,15; 4:4–6; 5:13; Ps. 32:3–5; Prov. 28:13; John 14:30; 16:11; Rom. 6:12–14; 8:12,13; 1 Cor. 15:34; Eph. 4:32; Col. 2:13)

Demonic teachings—false teachers denied the humanity of Jesus Christ (2:18,26; 3:7; 4:1–7; Is. 53:3,4; Matt. 1:18; Luke 1:31; 1 Cor. 15:21; Gal. 4:4; Heb. 2:14–17; 2 John 1:7)

GOD'S CHARACTER IN 1 JOHN

God is faithful—1:9
God is just—1:9
God is light—1:5
God is loving—2:5; 3:1; 4:8–10,12,16,19
God is a promise keeper—2:25
God is true—1:10; 5:10
God is unified—5:7

INTERPRETIVE CHALLENGES

Theologians debate the precise nature of the false teachers' beliefs in 1 John, because John does not directly specify their beliefs, but rather combats the heretics mainly through a positive restatement of the fundamentals of the faith. The main feature of the heresy, as noted above, seems to be a denial of the Incarnation, i.e., Christ had not come in the flesh. This was most likely an incipient or beginning form of Gnosticism, as was pointed out. (See Background and Setting).

The interpreter is also challenged by the rigidity of John's theology. John presents the basics or fundamentals of the Christian life in absolute, not relative, terms. Unlike Paul, who presented exceptions, and dealt so often with believers' failures to meet the divine standard, John does not deal with the "what if I fail" issues. Only in 2:1,2 does he give some relief from the absolutes. The rest of the book presents truths in black and white rather than shades of gray, often through a stark contrast, e.g., "light" vs. "darkness" (1:5,7; 2:8–11); truth vs. lies (2:21,22; 4:1); children of God vs. children of the devil (3:10). Those who claim to be Christians must absolutely display the characteristics of genuine

> ### KEY WORDS IN
> # 1 John
>
> **Sin:** Greek *hamartia*—1:7,8; 3:4,5,8,9; 5:16,17—literally, "to miss the mark." John speaks of a kind of sin one can recover from and another kind of sin from which one cannot recover. John's readers, unlike readers today, apparently understood the difference between these two kinds of sin. The overall teaching of this epistle suggests that those who denied the Christian community (2:18-19) to follow heretical, "antichrist" teachings were irrecoverable. Their rebellion and denial of Jesus' true identity (4:1-3) leads to unrepentant sin. In the end, their sin produces spiritual death.
>
> **Advocate:** Greek *paraklētos*—2:1—literally, "one who is called to our side." This Greek term refers to the position of a comforter, consoler, or defense attorney. In John 14:26 and 15:26, the Holy Spirit is called the Helper/Advocate for believers. The Holy Spirit works within us to comfort and help us and also pleads our case before the Father in heaven (Rom. 8:26,27,34).

Christians: sound doctrine, obedience, and love. Those who are truly born again have been given a new nature, which gives evidence of itself. Those who do not display characteristics of the new nature don't have it, so were never truly born again. The issues do not center (as much of Paul's writing does) in maintaining temporal or daily fellowship with God but in the application of basic tests in one's life to confirm that salvation has truly occurred. Such absolute distinctions were also characteristic of John's gospel.

In a unique fashion, John challenges the interpreter by his repetition of similar themes over and over to emphasize the basic truths about genuine Christianity. Some have likened John's repetition to a spiral that moves outward, becoming larger and larger, each time spreading the same truth over a wider area and encompassing more territory. Others have seen the spiral as moving inward, penetrating deeper and deeper into the same themes while expanding on his thoughts. (See Outline.) However one views the spiraling pattern, John uses repetition of basic truths as a means to accentuate their importance and to help his readers understand and remember them.

OUTLINE

I. The Fundamental Tests of Genuine Fellowship—SPIRAL I (1:1–2:17)

A. The Fundamental Tests of Doctrine (1:1–2:2)
  1. A biblical view of Christ (1:1–4)
  2. A biblical view of sin (1:5–2:2)

B. The Fundamental Tests of Morals (2:3–17)
  1. A biblical view of obedience (2:3–6)
  2. A biblical view of love (2:7–17)
    a. The love that God requires (2:7–11)
    b. The love that God hates (2:12–17)

II. The Fundamental Tests of Genuine Fellowship—SPIRAL II (2:18–3:24)

A. Part 2 of the Doctrinal Test (2:18–27)
  1. Antichrists depart from Christian fellowship (2:18–21)
  2. Antichrists deny the Christian faith (2:22–25)
  3. Antichrists deceive the Christian faithful (2:26,27)

B. Part 2 of the Moral Test (2:28–3:24)
  1. The purifying hope of the Lord's return (2:28–3:3)
  2. The Christian's incompatibility with sin (3:4–24)
    a. The requirement of righteousness (3:4–10)
    b. The requirement of love (3:11–24)

III. The Fundamental Tests of Genuine Fellowship—SPIRAL III (4:1–21)

A. Part 3 of the Doctrinal Test (4:1–6)
  1. The demonic source of false doctrine (4:1–3)
  2. The need for sound doctrine (4:4–6)

B. Part 3 of the Moral Test (4:7–21)
  1. God's character of love (4:7–10)
  2. God's requirement of love (4:11–21)

IV. The Fundamental Tests of Genuine Fellowship—SPIRAL IV (5:1–21)

A. The Victorious Life in Christ (5:1–5)

B. The Witness of God for Christ (5:6–12)

C. Christian Certainties Because of Christ (5:13–21)
  1. The certainty of eternal life (5:13)
  2. The certainty of answered prayer (5:14–17)
  3. The certainty of victory over sin and Satan (5:18–21)

MEANWHILE, IN OTHER PARTS OF THE WORLD...

The empires of Rome and China expand towards each other, separated only by the Armenian mountains and the Caspian Sea.

ANSWERS TO TOUGH QUESTIONS

1. How does 1 John help us understand some of the destructive teaching that attacked Christianity in the first century?

Paul, Peter, and John all faced early forms of a system of false teaching that later became known as Gnosticism. That term (derived from the Greek word for "knowledge") refers to the Gnostics' claim of an elevated knowledge, a higher truth known only to those in on the deep things. Those initiated into this mystical knowledge of truth had a higher internal authority than Scripture. This resulted in a chaotic situation in which instead of divine revelation standing as judge over man's ideas, man's ideas judged God's revelation (1 John 2:15–17).

Philosophically, the heresy relied on a distortion of Platonism. It advocated a dualism in which matter was inherently evil and spirit was good. One of the direct errors of this heresy involved attributing some form of deity to Christ but denying His true humanity, supposedly to preserve Him from evil (which they concluded He would be if He actually came in the flesh). Such a view destroys not only the true humanity of Jesus but also the atonement work of Christ in which his suffering and death paid for our sins. Jesus must not only have been truly God, but also the truly human (physically real) man who actually suffered and died upon the cross in order to be the acceptable substitutionary sacrifice for sin (Heb. 2:14–17). The biblical view of Jesus affirms His complete humanity as well as His full deity.

The Gnostic heresy, even in John's day, featured two basic forms: Docetism and the error of Cerinthus. Docetism (from a Greek word that means "to appear") asserted that Jesus' physical body was not real but only "seemed" to be physical. John forcefully and repeatedly affirmed the physical reality of Jesus. He reminded his readers that he was an eyewitness to Him ("heard," "seen," "handled," "Jesus Christ has come in the flesh"; 1 John 1:1–4; 4:2,3). The other form of early Gnosticism was traced back to Cerinthus by the early church apologist Irenaeus. Cerinthus taught that Christ's "spirit" descended on the human Jesus at His baptism but left Him shortly before His crucifixion. John asserted that the Jesus who was baptized at the beginning of His ministry was the same person who was crucified on the cross (1 John 5:6).

John does not directly specify the early Gnostic beliefs, but his arguments offer clear clues about his targets. Further, John's wisdom was to avoid direct attacks on rapidly shifting heresies, but to provide a timely and clear restatement of the basic truths about Christ that would provide a timeless foundation and answers for later generations of Christians.

2. What are the nonnegotiable basics of the faith that John spells out in 1 John?

John presents the basics or fundamentals of the Christian life in absolute terms. John recognizes the importance of forgiveness and Christ's role as Advocate when we fail (1:8,9; 2:1), but his stark contrasts allow little room for compromise: "light" versus "darkness" (1:5,7; 2:8–11); truth versus lies (2:21,22; 4:1); children of God versus children of the devil (3:10). Those who claim to be Christians must display the characteristics of genuine Christians: sound doctrine, obedience, and love. Such absolute distinctions were typical of John's gospel.

3. What does confession have to do with gaining forgiveness in 1 John 1:9?

The false teachers that John was resisting shared a characteristic with many modern people. They walked in spiritual darkness (sin) but went so far as to deny the existence of a sin nature in their lives. If someone never admits to being a sinner, salvation cannot result (see Matt. 19:16–22 for the account of the young man who refused to recognize his sin). Confession (admission of sin) is like opening a hand to release an object. Once the hand is open, it can receive forgiveness.

Continual confession of sin is an indication of genuine salvation. While the false teachers would not admit their sin, the genuine Christians admitted and forsook it (Ps. 32:3–5; Prov. 28:13). The term *confess* means to say the same thing about sin that God says, to acknowledge His perspective about sin. Confession of sin characterizes genuine Christians, and God continually cleanses those who are confessing. Rather than focusing on confession for every single sin as necessary, John has especially in mind here a settled recognition and acknowledgment that one is a sinner in need of cleansing and forgiveness (Eph. 4:32; Col. 2:13).

4. Why are we not to love the world (2:15)?

Although John often repeats the importance of love and that God is love (4:7–8), he also reveals that God hates a certain type of love: love of the world (John 15:18–20). An absence of love for the world must habitually characterize the love life of those to be considered born again. Conversely, Christians love God and their fellow Christians.

Love here signifies affection and devotion. God, not the world, must have the first place in the Christian's life (Matt. 10:37–39; Phil. 3:20). The term *world* is not a reference to the physical, material world but to the invisible spiritual system of evil, dominated by Satan, and all that it offers in opposition to God, His Word, and His people (5:19; John 12:31; 1 Cor. 1:21; 2 Cor. 4:4; James 4:4; 2 Pet. 1:4).

5. What four reasons does John give for why true Christians cannot habitually practice sin (1 John 3:4–10)?

This passage begins with the phrase "Whoever commits sin" (verse 4). "Commits" translates a Greek verb that conveys the idea of habitual practice. Although genuine Christians have a sin nature (1:8), and do behave sinfully, their confession of sin (1:9; 2:1) and acceptance of forgiveness prevent sin from becoming the unbroken pattern of their lives (John 8:31,34–36; Rom. 6:11; 2 John 9). God builds a certain growing awareness about sin that provides four effective reasons why true Christians cannot habitually practice sin: (1) Genuine Christians cannot practice sin because sin is incompatible with the law of God, which they love (3:4; Ps. 119:34,77,97; Rom. 7:12,22); whereas practicing habitual sin shows the ultimate sense of rebellion—living as if there were no law or ignoring what laws do exist (James 4:17). (2) Genuine Christians cannot practice sin because sin is incompatible with the work of Christ (3:5). Christ died to sanctify (make holy) the believer (2 Cor. 5:21; Eph. 5:25–27). Habitual sin contradicts Christ's work of breaking the dominion of sin in the believer's life (Rom. 6:1–15). (3) Genuine Christians cannot practice sin because Christ came to destroy the works of the arch-sinner, Satan (3:8). The devil is still operating, but he has been defeated, and in Christ we escape his tyranny. The day will come when all of Satan's activity will cease in the universe, and he will be sent to hell forever (Rev. 20:10). (4) Genuine Christians cannot practice sin because sin is incompatible with the ministry of the Holy Spirit, who has imparted a new nature to the believer (3:9; John 3:5–8). This new nature shuns sin and exhibits the habitual character of righteousness produced by the Holy Spirit (Gal. 5:22–24).

FURTHER STUDY ON 1 JOHN

1. What did John teach about confession and forgiveness in the first chapter?
2. John's letter includes five specific reasons why Christians love (4:7–21). What are they?
3. How did John use Cain as an example in his letter?
4. According to John, why is it impossible to love God and hate our neighbor?
5. How do you apply the statement "We love because He first loved us" in your life?

SECOND JOHN
A Lesson in Hospitality

TITLE
The epistle's title is "2 John." It is the second in a series of three epistles that bear the apostle John's name. Second and Third John present the closest approximation in the NT to the conventional letter form of the contemporary Greco-Roman world, since they were addressed from an individual to individuals. Second and Third John are the shortest epistles in the NT, each containing less than 300 Greek words. Each letter could fit on a single papyrus sheet (cf. 3 John 13).

AUTHOR AND DATE
The author is the apostle John. He describes himself in 2 John 1 as "The Elder" which conveys the advanced age of the apostle, his authority, and status during the foundational period of Christianity when he was involved with Jesus' ministry. The precise date of the epistle cannot be determined. Since the wording, subject matter, and circumstances of 2 John closely approximate 1 John (v. 5 [cf. 1 John 2:7; 3:11]; v. 6 [cf. 1 John 5:3]; v. 7 [cf. 1 John 2:18–26]; v. 9 [cf. 1 John 2:23]; v. 12; [cf. 1 John 1:4]), most likely John composed the letter at the same time or soon after 1 John, ca. A.D. 90–95, during his ministry at Ephesus in the latter part of his life.

BACKGROUND AND SETTING
Second John deals with the same problem as 1 John (see 1 John: Background and Setting). False teachers influenced by the beginnings of Gnostic thought were threatening the church (v. 7; cf. 1 John 2:18,19,22,23; 4:1–3). The strategic difference is that while 1 John has no specific individual or church specified to whom it was addressed, 2 John has a particular local group or house-church in mind (v. 1).

The focus of 2 John is that the false teachers were conducting an itinerant ministry among John's congregations, seeking to make converts, and taking advantage of Christian hospitality to advance their cause (vv. 10,11; cf. Rom. 12:13; Heb. 13:2; 1 Pet. 4:9). The individual addressed in the greeting (v. 1) inadvertently or unwisely may have shown hospitality to these false prophets, or John may have feared that the false teachers would attempt to take advantage of her kindness (vv. 10,11). The apostle seriously warns his readers against showing hospitality to such deceivers (vv. 10,11). Although his warning may appear on the surface to be harsh or unloving, the dangerous nature of their teaching justified such actions, especially since it threatened to destroy the very foundations of the faith (v. 9).

KEY PEOPLE IN 2 JOHN
John—apostle of Jesus writing to emphasize Christian fellowship and hospitality (vv. 1–13)
The elect lady—personal acquaintance of John and a believer (v. 1)
The lady's children—reference to the sons and daughters of the chosen lady (v. 1)

HISTORICAL AND THEOLOGICAL THEMES

The overall theme of 2 John closely parallels 1 John's theme of a "recall to the fundamentals of the faith" or "back to the basics of Christianity" (vv. 4–6). For John, the basics of Christianity are summarized by adherence to the truth (v. 4), love (v. 5), and obedience (v. 6).

The apostle, however, conveys an additional but related theme in 2 John: "the biblical guidelines for hospitality." Not only are Christians to adhere to the fundamentals of the faith, but the gracious hospitality that is commanded of them (Rom. 12:13) must be discriminating. The basis of hospitality must be common love of or interest in the truth, and Christians must share their love within the confines of that truth. They are not called to universal acceptance of anyone who claims to be a believer. Love must be discerning. Hospitality and kindness must be focused on those who are adhering to the fundamentals of the faith. Otherwise, Christians may actually aid those who are attempting to destroy those basic truths of the faith. Sound doctrine must serve as the test of fellowship and the basis of separation between those who profess to be Christians and those who actually are (vv. 10,11; cf. Rom. 16:17; Gal. 1:8,9; 2 Thess. 3:6,14; Titus 3:10).

CHRIST IN . . . 2 JOHN

SIMILAR TO JOHN'S FIRST LETTER, the apostle stresses the basic truth of Christ's identity (verses 7–11). To deny Christ's humanity is to deny the bodily suffering and sacrifice Christ endured to redeem the world of sin: "Many deceivers have gone out into the world who do not confess Jesus Christ as coming in the flesh. This is a deceiver and an antichrist" (vv. 7,8).

KEY DOCTRINES IN 2 JOHN

Christian fellowship—sound doctrine must serve as the test of fellowship and the basis of separation between those who profess to be Christians and those who actually are (vv 9–11; Rom. 16:17; Gal. 1:8,9; 2 Thess. 3:6,14; Titus 3:10).

Fundamentals of the faith—the basics of Christianity are summarized by adherence to the truth, love, and obedience (vv. 4–6; John 13:34,35; 14:15,21; 15:10,12,17; 1 Thess. 2:19,20; 1 John 2:7–11; 3:11; 4:7–12).

GOD'S CHARACTER IN 2 JOHN

God is loving—1:6
God is truth—1:1–2

INTERPRETIVE CHALLENGES

Second John stands in direct opposition to the frequent cry for unconditional acceptance and unity among believers. Love and truth are inseparable in Christianity. The main lesson of this book is that truth determines the bounds of love, and as a consequence, of unity. See Answers to Tough Questions for further discussion.

The reference to the "elect lady and her children" (v. 1) should be understood in a normal, plain sense referring to a particular woman and her children rather than interpreted in a non-literal sense as a church and its membership. Similarly, the reference to "the children of your elect sister" (v. 13) should be understood as a reference to the nieces and/or nephews of the individual addressed in verse 1, rather than metaphorically to a sister church and its membership. In these verses, John conveys greetings to personal acquaintances that he has come to know through his ministry.

OUTLINE
I. The Basis of Christian Hospitality (1–3)
II. The Behavior of Christian Hospitality (4–6)
III. The Bounds of Christian Hospitality (7–11)
IV. The Blessings of Christian Hospitality (12,13)

MEANWHILE, IN OTHER PARTS OF THE WORLD...
Most of northern Germany is still occupied by barbarians. However, Rome invades and conquers parts of the Black Forest, located between the Rhine and the Danube.

ANSWERS TO TOUGH QUESTIONS
1. Why was it so important to John to "confess Jesus Christ as coming in the flesh" (verse 7)?
John's purpose was to strengthen Christians to resist the tide of heresy that was rising against the church. Much of this false teaching was an early form of Gnosticism. (For more on the heresy itself, see 1 John: Answers to Tough Questions.)

The Gnostic idea that matter was evil and only spirit was good led to the idea that either the body should be treated harshly (Col. 2:21–23) or that sin committed in the body had no connection or effect on one's spirit. In other words, the false teaching sought to drive a wedge between body and soul. This is why Gnosticism often maintained that Jesus could not have been God and man at the same time.

The result of this error in teaching was compounded when some, including John's opponents, concluded that sins committed in the physical body did not matter. Absolute indulgence in immorality was permissible. One could deny sin even existed (1 John 1:8–10) and disregard God's law (1 John 3:4).

As a bulwark against this heresy, John lifted the confession that Jesus Christ came "in the flesh" (verse 7). What Christians do in their physical life is directly connected with what they do in their spiritual life. John emphasized the need for obedience to God's laws, for he defined the true love for God as obedience to His commandments (1 John 5:3). Jesus, in His human living, offered the perfect example of that kind of love.

2. How does John's teaching about truth and love affect discussions about Christian unity today (vv. 4–6)?

John's teaching stands in direct antithesis to the frequent cry for unconditional acceptance and unity among believers. Love and truth are inseparable in Christianity. Truth must always guide the exercise of love (Eph. 4:5). Love must stand the test of truth. The main lesson of John's second letter is that truth determines the bounds of love and, as a consequence, the bounds of unity. Therefore, truth must exist before love can unite, for truth generates love (1 Pet. 1:22). When someone compromises the truth, true Christian love and unity are destroyed. Only shallow sentimental feeling exists where truth is not the foundation of unity.

FURTHER STUDY ON 2 JOHN
1. How did John highlight his consistent theme of love in his short letter?
2. How did John emphasize the importance of truth?
3. What was the cause of John's warnings in this brief letter?
4. What positive counsel about Christian relationships did John offer?

THIRD JOHN

Serving the Servants of the Lord

TITLE

The epistle's title is "3 John." It is the third in a series of three epistles that bear the apostle John's name. Third John and 2 John present the closest approximation in the NT to the conventional letter form of the contemporary Greco-Roman world, since they were addressed from an individual to individuals. Both 2 and 3 John are the shortest epistles in the NT, each containing less than 300 Greek words, so as to fit on a single papyrus sheet (cf. v. 13).

AUTHOR AND DATE

The author is the apostle John. He describes himself in verse 1 as "The Elder," which conveys the advanced age of the apostle, his authority, and his eyewitness status, especially during the foundational period of Christianity when John was involved with Jesus' ministry (cf. 2 John 1). The precise date of the epistle cannot be determined. Since the structure, style, and vocabulary closely approximate 2 John (v. 1 [cf. 2 John 1]; v. 4 [cf. 2 John 4]; v. 13 [cf. 2 John 12]; v. 14 [cf. 2 John 12]), most likely John composed the letter at the same time or soon after 2 John, ca. A.D. 90–95. As with 1 and 2 John, the apostle probably composed the letter during his ministry at Ephesus in the latter part of his life.

BACKGROUND AND SETTING

Third John is perhaps the most personal of John's three epistles. While 1 John appears to be a general letter addressed to congregations scattered throughout Asia Minor, and 2 John was sent to a lady and her family (2 John 1), in 3 John the apostle clearly names the sole recipient as "the beloved Gaius" (v. 1). This makes the epistle one of a few letters in the NT addressed strictly to an individual (cf. Philemon). The name "Gaius" was very common in the first century (e.g., Acts 19:29; 20:4; Rom. 16:23; 1 Cor. 1:14), but nothing is known of this individual beyond John's salutation, from which it is inferred that he was a member of one of the churches under John's spiritual oversight.

CHRIST IN . . . 3 JOHN

UNLIKE 1 AND 2 JOHN, 3 John does not directly mention the name of Jesus Christ. However, in verse 7, John describes the missionaries as going "forth for His name's sake" (see Rom. 1:5). The truth of Christ's sacrifice on the cross remains the basis of spreading the Good News to all people.

As with 2 John, 3 John focuses on the basic issue of hospitality but from a different perspective. While 2 John warns against showing hospitality to false teachers (2 John 7–11), 3 John condemns the lack of hospitality shown to faithful ministers of the Word (vv. 9,10). Reports came back to the apostle that itinerant teachers known and approved by him (vv. 5–8) had traveled to a certain congregation and were refused hospitality (e.g., lodging and provision) by an individual named Diotrephes, who domineered the assembly (v. 10). Diotrephes went even further, for he also verbally slandered the apostle John with malicious accusations and excluded anyone from the assembly who dared challenge him (v. 10).

In contrast, Gaius, a beloved friend of the apostle and faithful adherent to the truth (vv. 1–4), extended the correct standard of Christian hospitality to traveling ministers. John wrote to commend the type of hospitality exhibited by Gaius to worthy representatives of the gospel (vv. 6–8) and to condemn the high-handed actions of Diotrephes (v. 10). The apostle promised to correct the situation personally and sent this letter through an individual named Demetrius, whom he commended for his good testimony among the brethren (vv. 10–12).

KEY PEOPLE IN 3 JOHN

John—wrote to commend Gaius for his generous hospitality (vv. 1–14)

Gaius—sole recipient of John's letter; member of one of the churches under John's spiritual oversight (v. 1)

Diotrephes—self-centered and domineering member of the church (vv. 9,10)

Demetrius—faithful servant and excellent role model in the church (v. 12)

> ### KEY WORDS IN
> # 3 John
>
> **Church:** Greek *ekklēsia*—verses 6,9–10—literally, "an assembly." In secular Greek literature, this term described any gathering of people to an important event or assembly. The writers of the NT used this term to mean a local assembly of believers, or the worldwide body of believers. John uses *ekklēsia* in two ways: "the church" in verse 6 refers to the general group of believers, whereas "the church" in verses 9 and 10 has to be a specific local church. In biblical times, Christians of each city were organized under one group of elders (see Acts 14:23; 15:2,4; 20:17–18; Titus 1:5). Several "assemblies" of believers, held in various homes, comprised the local church in each city.

HISTORICAL AND THEOLOGICAL THEMES

The theme of 3 John is the commendation of the proper standards of Christian hospitality and the condemnation for failure to follow those standards.

KEY DOCTRINE IN 3 JOHN

Hospitality—should be shown to faithful ministers of the Word (vv. 9,10; Gen. 14:18; 18:3–8; Ex. 2:20; 1 Sam. 9:22; 2 Kin. 6:22,23; Job 31:32; Is. 58:7; Luke 14:13,14; Rom. 12:13,20; 1 Tim. 3:2; 5:10; Titus 1:8; Heb. 13:2; 1 Pet. 4:9)

GOD'S CHARACTER IN 3 JOHN

God is good—verse 11

INTERPRETIVE CHALLENGES

Some think that Diotrephes may either have been a heretical teacher or at least favored the false teachers who were condemned by 2 John. However, the epistle gives no clear evidence to warrant such a conclusion, especially since one might expect that John would have mentioned Diotrephes' heretical views. The epistle indicates that his problems revolved around arrogance and disobedience, which is a problem for the orthodox as well as the heretic.

MEANWHILE, IN OTHER PARTS OF THE WORLD...
John's disciple Polycarp may already be ministering in Smyrna.

OUTLINE

I. The Commendation Regarding Christian Hospitality (1–8)
II. The Condemnation Regarding Violating Christian Hospitality (9–11)
III. The Conclusion Regarding Christian Hospitality (12–14)

ANSWERS TO TOUGH QUESTIONS

1. **What guidelines about Christian hospitality are found in 3 John?**

John offers both encouragement and counsel regarding hospitality. He certainly believed that Christians should practice the kind of hospitality that could be judged in a "manner worthy of God" (v. 6). First, Christians must show hospitality to those who have pure motives. He described these as itinerant missionaries who went out "for the sake of the name" (v. 7; Rom. 1:5). They must be doing ministry for God's glory, not their own. Second, Christians must show hospitality to those who are not in ministry for money. Since these missionaries were "taking nothing from the Gentiles" (v. 7), the church was their only means of support. Third, when Christians practice hospitality, they become participants in the ministry of those to whom they extend a welcome (v. 8).

2. **Why was John so upset about this person called Diotrephes in his third letter?**

John mentioned Diotrephes to Gaius as an example of the kind of negative effect caused by a leader who contradicts Jesus' teaching on servant-leadership in the church (Matt. 20:20–28; Phil. 2:5–11; 1 Tim. 3:3; 1 Pet. 5:3) and who violates the standards of hospitality required of Christians. John noted at least six errors in Diotrephes' behavior that form helpful warnings to others:

- He loved to have preeminence (the desire to be first, v. 9).
- He rejected John's authority and therefore the authority of God's Word by refusing to receive John's letter (v. 9).
- John charged Diotrephes with "prating against us" (a term that conveys the idea of someone talking nonsense, v. 10).
- Diotrephes acted "with malicious words" (his false accusations against John were also evil, v. 10).
- He "does not receive the brethren" (his hostility extended to other Christians, v. 10).
- He was even "putting them out of the church" (he was excommunicating those who resisted his authority, v. 10).

FURTHER STUDY ON 3 JOHN

1. What are the high points and low points of John's third letter?
2. In what ways is Christian hospitality important?
3. What character traits were creating problems in the church to whom John wrote?
4. For what actions and traits were Gaius and Demetrius complimented?
5. What has been your most memorable experience of giving or receiving Christian hospitality?

JUDE

TITLE
Jude, which is rendered "Judah" in Hebrew and "Judas" in Greek, was named after its author (v. 1), one of the four half-brothers of Christ (Matt. 13:55; Mark 6:3). As the fourth shortest NT book (Philem., 2 John, and 3 John are shorter), Jude is the last of eight general epistles. Jude does not quote the OT directly, but there are at least nine obvious allusions to it.

AUTHOR AND DATE
Although Jude (Judas) was a common name in Palestine (at least eight are named in the NT), the author of Jude generally has been accepted as Jude, the half-brother of Christ. He is to be differentiated from the apostle Judas, the son of James (Luke 6:16; Acts 1:13). Several lines of thought lead to this conclusion: (1) Jude's appeal to being the "brother of James," the leader of the Jerusalem Council (Acts 15) and another half-brother of Jesus (v. 1; cf. Gal. 1:19); (2) Jude's salutation being similar to James (cf. James 1:1); and (3) Jude's not identifying himself as an apostle (v. 1), but rather distinguishing between himself and the apostles (v. 17).

The doctrinal and moral dysfunction discussed by Jude (vv. 4–18) closely parallels that of 2 Peter (2:1–3:4), and it is believed that Peter's writing predated Jude for several reasons: (1) 2 Peter anticipates the coming of false teachers (2 Pet. 2:1,2; 3:3), while Jude deals with their arrival (vv. 4,11,12,17,18); and (2) Jude quotes directly from 2 Pet. 3:3 and acknowledges that it is from an apostle (vv. 17,18). Since no mention of Jerusalem's destruction in A.D. 70 was made by Jude, though Jude most likely came after 2 Peter (ca. A.D. 68–70), it was almost certainly written before the

> ## CHRIST IN . . . JUDE
> JUDE OPENS HIS ATTACK on apostasy by first addressing believers: "To those who are called, sanctified by God the Father, and preserved in Jesus Christ" (v. 1). Christ keeps believers secure for eternal life, which is not the fate of condemned apostates. Jude concludes his epistle by bolstering the courage of believers in Christ's power. Jude proclaims Jesus as "Him who is able to keep you from stumbling, and to present you faultless" (v. 24).

destruction of Jerusalem. Although Jude did travel on missionary trips with other brothers and their wives (1 Cor. 9:5), it is most likely that he wrote from Jerusalem. The exact audience of believers with whom Jude corresponded is unknown, but seems to be Jewish in light of Jude's illustrations. He undoubtedly wrote to a region recently plagued by false teachers.

Although Jude had earlier rejected Jesus as Messiah (John 7:1–9), he, along with other half-brothers of our Lord, was converted after Christ's resurrection (Acts 1:14). Because of his relation to Jesus, his eyewitness knowledge of the resurrected Christ, and the content of this epistle, it was acknowledged as inspired and was included in the Muratorian Canon (A.D. 170). The early questions about its canonicity also tend to support that it was written after 2 Peter. If Peter had quoted Jude, there would have been no question about canonicity, since Peter would thereby have given Jude apostolic affirmation. Clement of

Rome (ca. A.D. 96) plus Clement of Alexandria (ca. A.D. 200) also alluded to the authenticity of Jude. Its diminutive size and Jude's quotations from uninspired writings, account for any misplaced questions about its canonicity.

BACKGROUND AND SETTING

Jude lived at a time when Christianity was under severe political attack from Rome and aggressive spiritual infiltration from gnostic-like false teachers who sowed abundant seed for a gigantic harvest of doctrinal error. It could be that this was the forerunner to full-blown Gnosticism which the apostle John would confront over twenty-five years later in his epistles. Except for John, who lived at the close of the century, all of the other apostles had been martyred, and Christianity was thought to be extremely vulnerable. Thus, Jude called the church to fight, in the midst of intense spiritual warfare, for the truth.

KEY PEOPLE IN JUDE

Jude—Christ's half-brother who earlier rejected Jesus as Messiah and then converted after the Resurrection (1:1–25)

James—brother of Jude; well-known leader of the Jerusalem church and author of the Book of James (1:1)

HISTORICAL AND THEOLOGICAL THEMES

Jude is the only NT book devoted exclusively to confronting "apostasy," meaning abandonment of true, biblical faith (vv. 3,17). Apostates are described elsewhere in 2 Thessalonians 2:10, Hebrews 10:29, 2 Peter 2:1–22, and 1 John 2:18–23. He wrote to condemn the apostates and to urge believers to contend for the faith. He called for discernment on the part of the church and a rigorous defense of biblical truth. He followed the earlier examples of: (1) Christ (Matt. 7:15ff.; 16:6–12; 24:11ff; Rev. 2,3); (2) Paul (Acts 20:29,30; 1 Tim. 4:1; 2 Tim. 3:1–5; 4:3,4); (3) Peter (2 Pet. 2:1,2; 3:3,4); and (4) John (1 John 4:1–6; 2 John 6–11).

Jude is replete with historical illustrations from the OT which include: the Exodus (v. 5); Satan's rebellion (v. 6); Sodom and Gomorrah (v. 7); Moses' death (v. 9); Cain (v. 11); Balaam (v. 11); Korah (v. 11); Enoch (vv. 14,15); and Adam (v. 14).

Jude also vividly described the apostates in terms of their character and unthinkable activities (vv. 4,8,10,16,18,19). Additionally, he borrowed from nature to illustrate the futility of their teaching (vv. 12,13). While Jude never commented on the specific content of their false teaching, it was enough to demonstrate that their disfunctional personal lives and fruitless ministries betrayed their attempts to teach error as though it were truth. This emphasis on character repeats the constant theme regarding false teachers—their personal corruption. While their teaching is clever, subtle, deceptive, enticing, and delivered in myriads of forms, the common way to recognize them is to look behind their false spiritual fronts and see their wicked lives (2 Pet. 2:10,12,18,19).

KEY DOCTRINE IN JUDE

Apostasy—defection from the true, biblical faith (vv. 3,4,8,10,16–19; 2 Thess. 2:10; Heb. 10:29; 2 Pet. 2:1–22; 1 John 2:18–23)

GOD'S CHARACTER IN JUDE

God is glorious—verses 24,25
God is gracious—verse 4
God is judging—verses 5,6,14,15
God is Lord—verse 4
God is loving—verses 1–3,21
God is wise—verse 25

INTERPRETIVE CHALLENGES

Because there are no doctrinal issues discussed, the challenges of this letter have to do with interpretation in the normal process of discerning the meaning of the text. Jude does quote from sources that are not in the accepted canon, or body, of Scripture (i.e., the actual author was not the one named in its title), sources such as *1 Enoch* (v. 14) and the *Assumption of Moses* (v. 9), to support his points. Was this acceptable? Since Jude was writing under the inspiration of the Holy Spirit (2 Tim. 3:16; 2 Pet. 1:20,21) and included material that was accurate and true in its affirmations, he did no differently than Paul (cf. Acts 17:28; 1 Cor. 15:33; Titus 1:12).

Profile of an Apostate

1. Ungodly (v. 4)
2. Morally perverted (v. 4)
3. Deny Christ (v. 4)
4. Defile the flesh (v. 8)
5. Rebellious (v. 8)
6. Revile holy angels (v. 8)
7. Dreamers (v. 10)
8. Ignorant (v. 10)
9. Corrupted (v. 10)
10. Grumblers (v. 16)
11. Fault finders (v. 16)
12. Self seeking (v. 16)
13. Arrogant speakers (v. 16)
14. Flatterers (v. 16)
15. Mockers (v. 18)
16. Cause division (v. 19)
17. Worldly minded (v. 19)
18. Without the Spirit (v. 19)[1]

[1]John F. MacArthur, Jr., *The MacArthur Study Bible*, (Dallas: Word Publishing) 1997.

OUTLINE

    I. Desires of Jude (1,2)
    II. Declaration of War Against Apostates (3,4)
    III. Damnable Outcome of Apostates (5–7)
    IV. Denunciation of Apostates (8–16)
    V. Defenses Against Apostates (17–23)
    VI. Doxology of Jude (24,25)

MEANWHILE, IN OTHER PARTS OF THE WORLD...

Vespasian enters Rome triumphantly and is adopted as the new emperor by the senate.

ANSWERS TO TOUGH QUESTIONS

1. Since Jude quotes from books that are not in the Bible, does this give those other books a special value?

Jude quoted specifically from two extra-biblical books: *1 Enoch* (v. 14) and *Assumption of Moses* (v. 9). The authors of these books are unknown. Jude referred to them to support and illustrate his points.

Christians have held that Jude was writing under the inspiration of the Holy Spirit (2 Tim. 3:16; 2 Pet. 1:20,21) and included material that was accurate and true in its affirmations. His use of extra-biblical material was selective and not meant to extend any special authority to those texts. Paul followed the same pattern in quoting or referring to nonbiblical authors (Acts 17:28; 1 Cor. 15:33; Titus 1:12).

2. What does Jude mean by "the faith which was once delivered to the saints" (v. 3)?

Jude is referring to the whole body of revealed salvation truth contained in the Scriptures (Gal. 1:23; Eph. 4:5,13; Phil. 1:27; 1 Tim. 4:1). Here, and later in verse 20, Jude is describing a fixed body of spiritual revelation that can be known as sound doctrine (Eph. 4:14; Col. 3:16; 1 Pet. 2:2; 1 John 2:12–14), used in discerning and sorting out truth from error (1 Thess. 5:20–22), and effective in confronting and attacking error (2 Cor. 10:3–5; Phil. 1:17,27; 1 Tim. 1:18; 6:12; 2 Tim. 1:13; 4:7,8; Titus 1:13).

God's revelation was delivered once as a unit, at the completion of the Scripture, and is not to be edited by either deletion or addition (Deut. 4:2; 12:32; Prov. 30:6; Rev. 22:18,19). Scripture is complete, sufficient, and finished; therefore it is fixed for all time. Nothing is to be added to the body of the inspired Word (2 Tim. 3:16,17; 2 Pet. 1:19–21) because nothing else is needed.

3. Why are the last verses in Jude called a "doxology"?

The word itself is not found in the Bible but is an ancient term referring to special passages that express high praise to God. The first part of the word comes from the Greek word *doxa*, which means "glory." The second part of the word comes from the Greek word *logos*, which means "word." These words in Jude express in the most exalted terms the glory of God. They stand alongside other splendid examples in the NT (Rom. 11:33–36; 16:25–27; 2 Cor. 13:14; Heb. 13:20,21).

Jude's doxology includes Christians in a powerful way, highlighting what God can do for them that no one else can do. Jude reemphasized his theme of salvation and bolstered the courage of the believers to know that Christ would protect them from the present apostasy.

FURTHER STUDY ON JUDE

1. How did Jude describe himself in relation to his brother James and his half brother, Jesus? Why is that significant?
2. What figures and events from biblical history did Jude use to base his warnings?
3. In what way did he describe the false teachers?
4. What does the word *apostasy* mean, and how did Jude characterize an apostate?
5. What specific aspects of our relationship with God through Christ are lifted up in the doxology of verses 24–25?

REVELATION
The Final Judgment

TITLE
Unlike most books of the Bible, Revelation contains its own title: "The Revelation of Jesus Christ" (1:1). "Revelation" (Gr., *apokalupsis*) means "an uncovering," "an unveiling," or "a disclosure." In the NT, this word describes the unveiling of spiritual truth (Rom. 16:25; Gal. 1:12; Eph. 1:17; 3:3), the revealing of the sons of God (Rom. 8:19), Christ's incarnation (Luke 2:32), and His glorious appearing at His second coming (2 Thess. 1:7; 1 Pet. 1:7). In all its uses, "revelation" refers to something or someone, once hidden, becoming visible. What this book reveals or unveils is Jesus Christ in glory. Truths about Him and His final victory that the rest of Scripture merely allude to become clearly visible through revelation about Jesus Christ (see Historical and Theological Themes). This revelation was given to Him by God the Father, and it was communicated to the apostle John by an angel (1:1).

AUTHOR AND DATE
Four times the author identifies himself as John (1:1,4,9; 22:8). Early tradition unanimously identified him as John the apostle, author of the fourth gospel and three epistles. For example, important second-century witnesses to the apostle John's authorship include Justin Martyr, Irenaeus, Clement of Alexandria, and Tertullian. Many of the book's original readers were still alive during the lifetimes of Justin Martyr and Irenaeus—both of whom held to apostolic authorship.

There are differences in style between Revelation and John's other writings, but they are insignificant and do not preclude one man from writing both. In fact, there are some striking parallels between Revelation and John's other works. Only John's gospel and Revelation refer to Jesus Christ as the Word (19:13; John 1:1). Revelation (1:7) and John's gospel (19:37) translate Zech. 12:10 differently from the Septuagint, but in agreement with each other. Only Revelation and the gospel of John describe Jesus as the Lamb (5:6,8; John 1:29); both describe Jesus as a witness (cf. 1:5; John 5:31,32).

Revelation was written in the last decade of the first century (ca. A.D. 94–96), near the end of Emperor Domitian's reign (A.D. 81–96). Although some date it during Nero's reign (A.D. 54–68), their arguments are unconvincing and conflict with the view of the early church. Writing in the second century, Irenaeus declared that Revelation had been written toward the end of Domitian's reign. Later writers, such as Clement of Alexandria, Origen, Victorinus (who wrote one of the earliest commentaries on Revelation), Eusebius, and Jerome affirm the Domitian date.

The spiritual decline of the seven churches (chaps. 2,3) also argues for the later date. Those churches were strong and spiritually healthy in the mid-60s, when Paul last ministered in Asia Minor. The brief time between Paul's ministry there and the end of Nero's reign was too short for such a decline to have occurred. The longer time gap also explains the rise of the heretical sect known as the Nicolaitans (2:6,15), who are not mentioned in Paul's letters, not even to one or more of these same churches (Ephesians). Finally, dating Revelation during Nero's reign does not allow time for John's ministry in Asia Minor to reach the point at which the authorities would have felt the need to exile him.

BACKGROUND AND SETTING

Revelation begins with John, the last surviving apostle and an old man, in exile on the small, barren island of Patmos, located in the Aegean Sea southwest of Ephesus. The Roman authorities had banished him there because of his faithful preaching of the gospel (1:9). While on Patmos, John received a series of visions that laid out the future history of the world.

When he was arrested, John was in Ephesus, ministering to the church there and in the surrounding cities. Seeking to strengthen those congregations, he could no longer minister to them in person and, following the divine command (1:11), John addressed Revelation to them (1:4). The churches had begun to feel the effects of persecution; at least one man—probably a pastor—had already been martyred (2:13), and John himself had been exiled. But the storm of persecution was about to break in full fury upon the seven churches so dear to the apostle's heart (2:10). To those churches, Revelation provided a message of hope: God is in sovereign control of all the events of human history, and though evil often seems pervasive and wicked men all-powerful, their ultimate doom is certain. Christ will come in glory to judge and rule.

The Seven Churches

2. Message to Smyrna: "Be faithful until death, and I will give you the crown of life" (2:10).

3. Message to Pergamos: "I have a few things against you" (Rev. 2:14).

4. Message to Thyatira: "Hold fast what you have till I come" (2:25).

5. Message to Sardis: "You have a name that you are alive, but you are dead" (3:1).

6. Message to Philadelphia: "I have set before you an open door" (3:8).

7. Message to Laodicea: "You are neither cold nor hot" (3:15).

1. Message to Ephesus: "You have left your first love" (2:4).

John received his vision and wrote the Revelation while in exile on this island in the Aegean Sea (Rev. 1:1, 9).

ASIA

Pergamos
Thyatira
Sardis
Smyrna
Philadelphia
Ephesus
Laodicea

AEGEAN SEA

ISLE OF PATMOS

The Seven Churches of Revelation

COMMENDATION	CRITICISM	INSTRUCTION	PROMISE
Ephesus (2:1-7)			
Rejects evil, perseveres, has patience	Love for Christ no longer fervent	Do the works you did at first	The tree of life
Smyrna (2:8-11)			
Gracefully bears suffering	None	Be faithful until death	The crown of life
Pergamos (2:12-17)			
Keeps the faith of Christ	Tolerated immorality, idolatry, and heresies	Repent	Hidden manna and a stone with a new name
Thyatira (2:18-29)			
Love, service, faith, patience is greater than at first	Tolerates cult of idolatry and immorality	Judgment coming; keep the faith	Rule over nations and receive morning star
Sardis (3:1-6)			
Some have kept the faith	A dead church	Repent; strengthen what remains	Faithful honored and clothed in white
Philadelphia (3:7-13)			
Perseveres in the faith	None	Keep the faith	A place in God's presence, a new name, and the New Jerusalem
Laodicea (3:14-22)			
None	Indifferent	Be zealous and repent	Share Christ's throne

KEY PEOPLE IN REVELATION

John—apostle of Jesus Christ who received the revelation of Jesus Christ from an angel (1:1,4,9; 22:8)

Jesus—the revealed Son of God who will come again to claim His people (1:1–22:21)

HISTORICAL AND THEOLOGICAL THEMES

Since it is primarily prophetic, Revelation contains little historical material, other than that in chaps. 1–3. The seven churches to whom the letter was addressed were existing churches in Asia Minor (modern Turkey). Apparently, they were singled out because John had ministered in them.

Revelation is first and foremost a revelation about Jesus Christ (1:1). The book depicts Him as the risen, glorified Son of God ministering among the churches (1:10ff.), as "the faithful witness, the firstborn from the dead, and the ruler over the kings of the earth" (1:5), as "the Alpha and the Omega, the Beginning and the End" (1:8), as the one "who is and who was and who is to come, the Almighty" (1:8), as the "First and the Last" (1:11), as the "Son of Man" (1:13), as the one who was dead, but now is alive forevermore (1:18), as the "Son of God" (2:18), as the one who is holy and true (3:7), as "the Amen, the Faithful and True Witness, the Beginning of the creation of God" (3:14), as the "Lion of the tribe of Judah" (5:5), as the "Lamb" in heaven, with authority to open the title deed to the earth (6:1ff.), as the Lamb on the throne (7:17), as the Messiah who will reign forever (11:15), as the "Word of God" (19:13), as the majestic "King of kings and Lord of lords," returning in glorious splendor to conquer His foes (19:11ff.), and as "the Root and the Offspring of David, the Bright and Morning Star" (22:16).

CHRIST IN . . . REVELATION

IN THE LAST BOOK of the Bible, Jesus triumphantly reveals Himself as the Almighty One (1:8); the Alpha and Omega (1:8; 21:6); the Beginning and the End (1:8; 21:6). Other voices in the Book of Revelation proclaim Jesus Christ as the Lion of the tribe of Judah (5:5); Heir to David's throne (5:5); the Lamb of God (5:6–22:3); the Word of God (19:13); King of kings and Lord of lords (19:16).

Many other rich theological themes find expression in Revelation. The church is warned about sin and encouraged toward holiness. John's vivid pictures of worship in heaven both exhort and instruct believers. In few other books of the Bible is the ministry of angels so prominent. Revelation's primary theological contribution is to eschatology, i.e., the doctrine of end times. In it we learn about: the final political setup of the world; the last battle of human history; the career and ultimate defeat of Antichrist; Christ's 1,000-year earthly kingdom; the glories of heaven and the eternal state; and the final state of the wicked and the righteous. Finally, only Daniel rivals this book in declaring that God providentially rules over the kingdoms of men and will accomplish His sovereign purposes regardless of human or demonic opposition.

KEY DOCTRINES IN REVELATION

Revelation—Jesus Christ's true identity and saving work is unveiled (1:1–22:21; Is. 11:5; 53:1–11; Zech. 9:9; Luke 1:35; John 1:1–14; 7:18; Acts 4:27; 2 Cor. 8:9; Phil. 2:8; 1 Thess. 5:24; Heb. 1:9; 1 John 5:20)

Holiness—the church is warned about sin and exhorted to holiness (22:11; Lev. 11:45; 19:2; 20:7; Ps. 24:3,4; Rom. 8:29; 12:1; Eph. 5:1,8; Col. 3:12; Heb. 12:14; 1 Pet. 1:15,16; 1 John 2:6)

Worship—God is worthy of man's worship and praise (4:10,11; 5:12; 2 Sam. 22:44; Pss. 22:23; 50:23; 96:2; 145:3; Ezek. 3:12; Dan. 2:20; Matt. 2:1,2,11; 28:16,17; John 4:20–24; 9:30–38; Luke 1:68,69; Heb. 1:6; Jude 1:25)

Eschatology—the doctrine of the last things (4:1–22:21)

GOD'S CHARACTER IN REVELATION
God is eternal—4:8–10; 16:5
God is glorious—21:11,23
God is holy—4:8; 15:4; 21:27
God is just—19:2
God is powerful—4:11; 5:13; 11:17
God is righteous—16:5,7; 19:2
God is true—15:3; 16:7
God is wrathful—6:17; 11:18; 16:6.7; 19:15

INTERPRETIVE CHALLENGES
No other NT book poses more serious and difficult interpretive challenges than Revelation. The book's vivid imagery and striking symbolism have produced four main interpretive approaches:

The *preterist* approach interprets Revelation as a description of first-century events in the Roman Empire (see Author and Date). This view conflicts with the book's own often repeated claim to be prophecy (1:3; 22:7,10,18,19). It is impossible to see all the events in

KEY WORDS IN

Revelation

Hades: Greek *hadēs*—1:18; 6:8; 20:13,14—literally, "the place of the unseen." This Greek word, translated from the Hebrew word *sheol,* describes the invisible world of the dead. All people who die go to Hades in the sense that death leads from the visible world to the invisible. Therefore, death and Hades can be used interchangeably. Unfortunately, many people mistakenly associate Hades with hell, a place of eternal punishment. But the Greek word for hell is *gehenna* (see Mark 9:43–45). While we will all one day go to Hades, we can avoid hell by believing in Jesus Christ's work of salvation.

Almighty: Greek *pantokratōr*—1:8; 4:8; 11:17; 15:3; 16:7,14; 19:15; 21:22—literally, "one who has power over everything," in other words, the One in total control. God commands all the hosts of powers in heaven and earth, and He is able to overcome all His foes. The title *Almighty* occurs often in Revelation as this book unveils God's awesome control over the universe and throughout all history.

Devil; Satan: Greek *diabolos*—2:10; 12:9,12; 20:2,10—literally, "slanderer," and Greek *Satanas*—20:2,7—literally, "Adversary." The word *diabolos* signifies one who accuses another. Hence that other name given him: "the accuser of our brethren" (see 12:10). The name Satan signifies one who lies in wait for or sets himself in opposition to another. These and other names of the same fallen spirit point to different features of his evil character and deceitful operations.

New Jerusalem: Greek *Ierousalēm kainē*—3:12; 21:2,10. The New Jerusalem that comes out of heaven is plainly distinct from the earthly Jerusalem, the former capital of Israel. This is the city Abraham looked for, the city whose builder and maker is God (Heb. 11:10). This is the city that exists even now in heaven, for Paul calls it the Jerusalem that is above (Gal. 4:26).

The Alpha and the Omega: Greek *to Alpha kai to Ō*—1:8,11; 21:6; 22:13. Alpha and omega are the first and last letters of the Greek alphabet. This phrase is used of both God the Father and God the Son. God in Christ comprises everything, all that goes between the Alpha and the Omega, as well as being the First and the Last. This expresses God's fullness, comprehensiveness, and all-inclusiveness. He is the Source of all things and will bring all things to their appointed end.

Revelation as already fulfilled. The second coming of Christ, for example, obviously did not take place in the first century.

The *historicist* approach views Revelation as a panoramic view of church history from apostolic times to the present—seeing in the symbolism such events as the barbarian invasions of Rome, the rise of the Roman Catholic Church (as well as various individual popes), the emergence of Islam, and the French Revolution. This interpretive method robs Revelation of any meaning for those to whom it was written. It also ignores the time limitations the book itself places on the unfolding events (cf. 11:2; 12:6,14; 13:5). Historicism has produced many different—and often conflicting—interpretations of the actual historical events contained in Revelation.

The *idealist* approach interprets Revelation as a timeless depiction of the cosmic struggle between the forces of good and evil. In this view, the book contains neither historical allusions nor predictive prophecy. This view also ignores Revelation's prophetic character and, if carried to its logical conclusion, severs the book from any connection with actual historical events. Revelation then becomes merely a collection of stories designed to teach spiritual truth.

The *futurist* approach insists that the events of chaps. 6–22 are yet future, and that those chapters literally and symbolically depict actual people and events yet to appear on the world scene. It describes the events surrounding the second coming of Jesus Christ (chaps. 6–19), the Millennium and final judgment (chap. 20), and the eternal state (chaps. 21,22). Only this view does justice to Revelation's claim to be prophecy and interprets the book by the same grammatical-historical method as chaps. 1–3 and the rest of Scripture.

OUTLINE
    I. **The Things which You Have Seen (1:1–20)**
        A. The Prologue (1:1–8)
        B. The Vision of the Glorified Christ (1:9–18)
        C. The Apostle's Commission to Write (1:19,20)
    II. **The Things which Are (2:1–3:22)**
        A. The Letter to the Church at Ephesus (2:1–7)
        B. The Letter to the Church at Smyrna (2:8–11)
        C. The Letter to the Church at Pergamos (2:12–17)
        D. The Letter to the Church at Thyatira (2:18–29)
        E. The Letter to the Church at Sardis (3:1–6)
        F. The Letter to the Church at Philadelphia (3:7–13)
        G. The Letter to the Church at Laodicea (3:14–22)
    III. **The Things which Will Take Place after This (4:1–22:21)**
        A. Worship in Heaven (4:1–5:14)
        B. The Great Tribulation (6:1–18:24)
        C. The Return of the King (19:1–21)
        D. The Millennium (20:1–10)
        E. The Great White Throne Judgment (20:11–15)
        F. The Eternal State (21:1–22:21)

MEANWHILE, IN OTHER PARTS OF THE WORLD...
Clement I becomes bishop of Rome (A.D. 88–97). Emperor Trajan expands the Roman Empire to its largest state (A.D. 98–117).

ANSWERS TO TOUGH QUESTIONS

1. What do we know about these seven churches to which John wrote his letters?

Revelation 2:1–3:22 includes seven letters dictated to John by the Lord Jesus. Each of these churches displays a significant character trait about which the Lord was pleased or displeased. The churches were named for the cities in which they were located: Ephesus, Smyrna, Pergamos, Thyatira, Sardis, Philadelphia, Laodicea. Although these seven churches were actual, historical churches in Asia Minor, they also represent the types of churches that perennially exist throughout the church age. What Christ says to each of these churches is relevant in all times. (See Background and Setting for more about the seven churches.)

2. Does Revelation 3:20 mean that Christ is standing at each person's life, knocking to come in?

Rather than allowing for the common interpretation of Christ's knocking on a person's heart, the context demands that we say Christ was seeking to enter this church that bore His name, but which lacked a single true believer. The poignant letter to the church in Laodicea was Christ's "knocking." If one member would recognize his spiritual bankruptcy and respond in saving faith, Christ would enter the church.

3. What is the "tribulation" and where does it fit in the Book of Revelation?

The tribulation refers to that seven-year time period immediately following the removal of the church from the earth (John 14:1–3; 1 Thess. 4:13–18), when the righteous judgments of God will be poured out upon an unbelieving world (Jer. 30:7; Dan. 9:27; 12:1; 2 Thess. 2:7–12; Rev. 16). These judgments will be climaxed by the return of Christ in glory to the earth (Matt. 24:27–31; 25:31–46; 2 Thess. 2:7–12).

In the Book of Revelation, the lengthy section from 6:1 to 19:21 details the judgments and events of the time of tribulation from its beginning with the opening of the first seal through the seven seal, trumpet, and bowl judgments of God, to the return of Christ to destroy the ungodly (19:11–21). The passage of time during this period is tracked in Revelation (11:2,3; 12:6,14; 13:5). The second half of the seven-year period is specifically called in Revelation 7:14 "the great tribulation."

4. Why does the number 666 get so much attention?

Numbers are important in Scripture in two ways: (1) they speak to God's exactness; and (2) they represent certain recurring ideas. The number 666 is mentioned in

Revelation 13:18. The significance of the number itself is not emphasized, so speculation about the meaning must be cautious and limited.

The number represents the essential number of a man. The number 6 falls one short of God's perfect number, 7, and thus points to human imperfection. Antichrist, the most powerful human the world will ever know, will still be a man—a 6. The ultimate in human and demonic power is a 6, not perfect, as God is. The threefold repetition of the number is intended to emphasize man's identity. He is emphatically imperfect, not almost perfect. When Antichrist is finally revealed, there will be some way to identify him with this basic number, or his name may have the numerical equivalent of 666. In many languages, including Hebrew, Greek, and Latin, letters from the alphabet were used to represent numbers.

Beyond these basic observations, the text reveals very little about the meaning of 666. It is unwise, therefore, to speculate beyond what God's Word gives us.

5. Why does the great multitude in Revelation 19:1–6 keep saying "Alleluia"?
The term is a transliterated Hebrew that appears only four times in the NT, all in this chapter (vv. 1,3,4,6). This exclamation, meaning "Praise the Lord," occurs frequently in the OT (Pss. 104:35; 105:45; 106:1; 111:1; 112:1; 113:1; 117:1; 135:1; 146:1).

In the case of this great multitude gathered in heaven, they have five reasons for repeatedly shouting "Alleluia—Praise the Lord!"

- They praise God for delivering His people from their enemies (vv. 1,2).
- They praise God for meting out justice (v. 2).
- They praise God for permanently crushing man's rebellion (v. 3).
- They praise God for His sovereignty (v. 6).
- They praise God for communing (being) with His people (v. 7).

6. What is the Millennium and where does it fit in Revelation?
Revelation 20 includes six mentions of a kingdom that will last a thousand years (vv. 2–7). There are three main views regarding the nature and duration of this period:

Premillennialism sees this as a literal thousand-year period during which Jesus Christ, in fulfillment of numerous OT prophecies (2 Sam. 7:12–16; Ps. 2; Is. 11:6–12; 24:23; Hos. 3:4,5; Joel 3:9–21; Amos 9:8–15; Mic. 4:1–8; Zeph. 3:14–20; Zech. 14:1–11) and Jesus' own teaching (Matt. 24:29–31,36–44), will reign on the earth. Using the same general principles of interpretation for both prophetic and nonprophetic passages leads most naturally to premillennialism. This view is also strongly supported by the fact that so many biblical prophecies have already been literally fulfilled, and therefore it suggests that future prophecies will likewise be fulfilled literally.

Premillennial/posttribulational scholars assert that Christ will return at the end of a seven-year Great Tribulation to establish a millennial kingdom. This kingdom will end with a rebellion by the forces of evil and the final judgment. This view often interprets prophecy in a non-literal way and does not usually view Israel and the church as the objects of completely different divine historical plans. Rather, Israel and the church ultimately form one people of

God. Premillennialists of both types adopt the "Futurist" approach to the Book of Revelation.

Postmillennialism understands the reference to a thousand-year period as only symbolic of a golden age of righteousness and spiritual prosperity. It will be ushered in by the spread of the gospel during the present church age and brought to completion when Christ returns. According to this view, references to Christ's reign on earth primarily describe His spiritual reign in the hearts of believers in the church.

Amillennialism understands the thousand years to be merely symbolic of a long period of time. This view interprets OT prophecies of a Millennium as being fulfilled spiritually now in the church (either on earth or in heaven) or as references to the eternal state.

In summary, nothing in the text leads directly to the conclusion that "a thousand years" is symbolic. Never in Scripture when the term *year* is used with a number is its meaning not literal. The weight of biblical evidence points to the premillennialist position.

FURTHER STUDY ON REVELATION
1. What statements about its purpose does the Book of Revelation declare?
2. What are the seven churches to which John writes, and what comments does Jesus make about each one?
3. How does Revelation illustrate the sovereignty of God?
4. Throughout the Book of Revelation, what happens to people who continue to trust Christ?
5. What, according to chapter 20, will happen at the last judgment?
6. Whose names are recorded in the Book of Life, and why?

THEOLOGY

Overview of

THE HOLY SCRIPTURES

We teach that the Bible is God's written revelation to man, and thus the 66 books of the Bible given to us by the Holy Spirit constitute the plenary (inspired equally in all parts) Word of God (1 Cor. 2:7–14; 2 Pet. 1:20,21).

We teach that the Word of God is an objective, propositional revelation (1 Cor. 2:13; 1 Thess. 2:13), verbally inspired in every word (2 Tim. 3:16), absolutely inerrant in the original documents, infallible, and God-breathed. We teach the literal, grammatical-historical interpretation of Scripture, which affirms the belief that the opening chapters of Genesis present creation in six literal days (Gen. 1:31; Ex. 31:17).

We teach that the Bible constitutes the only infallible rule of faith and practice (Matt. 5:18; 24:35; John 10:35; 16:12,13; 17:17; 1 Cor. 2:13; 2 Tim. 3:15–17; Heb. 4:12; 2 Pet. 1:20,21).

We teach that God spoke in His written Word by a process of dual authorship. The Holy Spirit so superintended the human authors that, through their individual personalities and different styles of writing, they composed and recorded God's Word to man (2 Pet. 1:20,21) without error in the whole or in the part (Matt. 5:18; 2 Tim. 3:16).

We teach that, whereas there may be several applications of any given passage of Scripture, there is but one true interpretation. The meaning of Scripture is to be found as one diligently applies the literal, grammatical-historical method of interpretation under the enlightenment of the Holy Spirit (John 7:17; 16:12–15; 1 Cor. 2:7–15; 1 John 2:20). It is the responsibility of believers to ascertain carefully the true intent and meaning of Scripture, recognizing that proper application is binding on all generations. Yet the truth of Scripture stands in judgment of men; never do men stand in judgment of it.

GOD

We teach that there is but one living and true God (Deut. 6:4; Is. 45:5–7; 1 Cor. 8:4), an infinite, all-knowing Spirit (John 4:24), perfect in all His attributes, one in essence, eternally existing in three Persons—Father, Son, and Holy Spirit (Matt. 28:19; 2 Cor. 13:14)—each equally deserving worship and obedience.

GOD THE FATHER

We teach that God the Father, the first person of the Trinity, orders and disposes all things according to His own purpose and grace (Ps. 145:8,9; 1 Cor. 8:6). He is the Creator of all things (Gen. 1:1–31; Eph. 3:9). As the only absolute and omnipotent ruler in the universe, He is sovereign in creation, providence, and redemption (Ps. 103:19; Rom. 11:36). His fatherhood involves both His designation within the Trinity and His relationship with mankind. As Creator He is Father to all men (Eph. 4:6), but He is Spiritual Father only to believers (Rom. 8:14; 2 Cor. 6:18). He has decreed for His own glory all things that come to pass (Eph. 1:11). He continually upholds, directs, and governs all creatures and events (1 Chr. 29:11). In His sovereignty He is neither author nor approver of sin (Hab. 1:13), nor does He abridge the accountability of moral, intelligent creatures (1 Pet. 1:17). He has graciously chosen from eternity past those whom He would have as His own (Eph. 1:4–6); He saves from sin all those who come to Him; and He becomes, upon adoption, Father to His own (John 1:12; Rom. 8:15; Gal. 4:5; Heb. 12:5–9).

GOD THE SON
We teach that Jesus Christ, the second person of the Trinity, possesses all the divine excellencies, and in these He is coequal, consubstantial, and coeternal with the Father (John 10:30; 14:9).

We teach that God the Father created "the heavens and the earth and all that is in them" according to His own will, through His Son, Jesus Christ, by whom all things continue in existence and in operations (John 1:3; Col. 1:15–17; Heb. 1:2).

We teach that in the incarnation (God becoming man) Christ surrendered only the prerogatives of deity but nothing of the divine essence, either in degree or kind. In His incarnation, the eternally existing second person of the Trinity accepted all the essential characteristics of humanity and so became the God-man (Phil. 2:5–8; Col. 2:9).

We teach that Jesus Christ represents humanity and deity in indivisible oneness (Mic. 5:2; John 5:23; 14:9,10; Col. 2:9).

We teach that our Lord Jesus Christ was virgin born (Is. 7:14; Matt. 1:23,25; Luke 1:26–35); that He was God incarnate (John 1:1,14); and that the purpose of the incarnation was to reveal God, redeem men, and rule over God's kingdom (Ps. 2:7–9; Is. 9:6; John 1:29; Phil. 2:9–11; Heb. 7:25,26; 1 Pet. 1:18,19).

We teach that, in the incarnation, the second person of the Trinity laid aside His right to the full prerogatives of coexistence with God, assumed the place of a Son, and took on an existence appropriate to a servant while never divesting Himself of His divine attributes (Phil. 2:5–8).

We teach that our Lord Jesus Christ accomplished our redemption through the shedding of His blood and sacrificial death on the cross and that His death was voluntary, vicarious, substitutionary, propitiatory, and redemptive (John 10:15; Rom. 3:24,25; 5:8; 1 Pet. 2:24).

We teach that on the basis of the efficacy of the death of our Lord Jesus Christ, the believing sinner is freed from the punishment, the penalty, the power, and one day the very presence of sin; and that he is declared righteous, given eternal life, and adopted into the family of God (Rom. 3:25; 5:8,9; 2 Cor. 5:14,15; 1 Pet. 2:24; 3:18).

We teach that our justification is made sure by His literal, physical resurrection from the dead and that He is now ascended to the right hand of the Father, where He now mediates as our Advocate and High-Priest (Matt. 28:6; Luke 24:38,39; Acts 2:30,31; Rom. 4:25; 8:34; Heb. 7:25; 9:24; 1 John 2:1).

We teach that in the resurrection of Jesus Christ from the grave, God confirmed the deity of His Son and gave proof that God has accepted the atoning work of Christ on the cross. Jesus' bodily resurrection is also the guarantee of a future resurrection life for all believers (John 5:26–29; 14:19; Rom. 4:25; 6:5–10; 1 Cor. 15:20,23).

We teach that Jesus Christ will return to receive the church, which is His body, unto Himself at the Rapture and, returning with His church in glory, will establish His millennial kingdom on earth (Acts 1:9–11; 1 Thess. 4:13–18; Rev. 20).

We teach that the Lord Jesus Christ is the one through whom God will judge all mankind (John 5:22,23):
Believers (1 Cor. 3:10–15; 2 Cor. 5:10);
Living inhabitants of the earth at His glorious return (Matt. 25:31–46); and
Unbelieving dead at the Great White Throne (Rev. 20:11–15).

As the mediator between God and man (1 Tim. 2:5), the head of His body the church (Eph. 1:22; 5:23; Col. 1:18), and the coming universal King who will reign on the throne of David (Is. 9:6,7; Ezek. 37:24–28; Luke 1:31–33), He is the final judge of all who fail to place their trust in Him as Lord and Savior (Matt. 25:14–46; Acts 17:30,31).

GOD THE HOLY SPIRIT

We teach that the Holy Spirit is a divine person, eternal, underived, possessing all the attributes of personality and deity, including intellect (1 Cor. 2:10–13), emotions (Eph. 4:30), will (1 Cor. 12:11), eternality (Heb. 9:14), omnipresence (Ps. 139:7–10), omniscience (Is. 40:13,14), omnipotence (Rom. 15:13), and truthfulness (John 16:13). In all the divine attributes He is coequal and consubstantial with the Father and the Son (Matt. 28:19; Acts 5:3,4; 28:25,26; 1 Cor. 12:4–6; 2 Cor. 13:14; and Jer. 31:31–34 with Heb. 10:15–17).

We teach that it is the work of the Holy Spirit to execute the divine will with relation to all mankind. We recognize His sovereign activity in the creation (Gen. 1:2), the incarnation (Matt. 1:18), the written revelation (2 Pet. 1:20,21), and the work of salvation (John 3:5–7).

We teach that a unique work of the Holy Spirit in this age began at Pentecost when He came from the Father as promised by Christ (John 14:16,17; 15:26) to initiate and complete the building of the body of Christ. His activity includes convicting the world of sin, of righteousness, and of judgment; glorifying the Lord Jesus Christ and transforming believers into the image of Christ (John 16:7–9; Acts 1:5; 2:4; Rom. 8:29; 2 Cor. 3:18; Eph. 2:22).

We teach that the Holy Spirit is the supernatural and sovereign agent in regeneration, baptizing all believers into the body of Christ (1 Cor. 12:13). The Holy Spirit also indwells, sanctifies, instructs, empowers them for service, and seals them unto the day of redemption (Rom. 8:9–11; 2 Cor. 3:6; Eph. 1:13).

We teach that the Holy Spirit is the divine teacher who guided the apostles and prophets into all truth as they committed to writing God's revelation, the Bible (2 Pet. 1:19–21). Every believer possesses the indwelling presence of the Holy Spirit from the moment of salvation, and it is the duty of all those born of the Spirit to be filled with (controlled by) the Spirit (Rom. 8:9–11; Eph. 5:18; 1 John 2:20,27).

We teach that the Holy Spirit administers spiritual gifts to the church. The Holy Spirit glorifies neither Himself nor His gifts by ostentatious displays, but He does glorify Christ by implementing His work of redeeming the lost and building up believers in the most holy faith (John 16:13,14; Acts 1:8; 1 Cor. 12:4–11; 2 Cor. 3:18).

We teach, in this respect, that God the Holy Spirit is sovereign in the bestowing of all His gifts for the perfecting of the saints today and that speaking in tongues and the working of sign miracles in the beginning days of the church were for the purpose of pointing to and authenticating the apostles as revealers of divine truth, and were never intended to be characteristic of the lives of believers (1 Cor. 12:4–11; 13:8–10; 2 Cor. 12:12; Eph. 4:7–12; Heb. 2:1–4).

MAN

We teach that man was directly and immediately created by God in His image and likeness. Man was created free of sin with a rational nature, intelligence, volition, self-determination, and moral responsibility to God (Gen. 2:7,15–25; James 3:9).

We teach that God's intention in the creation of man was that man should glorify God, enjoy God's fellowship, live his life in the will of God, and by this accomplish God's purpose for man in the world (Is. 43:7; Col. 1:16; Rev. 4:11).

We teach that in Adam's sin of disobedience to the revealed will and Word of God, man lost his innocence; incurred the penalty of spiritual and physical death; became subject to the wrath of God; and became inherently corrupt and utterly incapable of choosing or doing that which is acceptable to God apart from divine grace. With no recuperative powers to enable him to recover himself, man is hopelessly lost. Man's salvation is thereby wholly of God's grace through the redemptive work of our Lord Jesus Christ (Gen. 2:16,17; 3:1–19; John 3:36; Rom. 3:23; 6:23; 1 Cor. 2:14; Eph. 2:1–3; 1 Tim. 2:13,14; 1 John 1:8).

We teach that because all men were in Adam, a nature corrupted by Adam's sin has been transmitted to all men of all ages, Jesus Christ being the only exception. All men are thus sinners by nature, by choice, and by divine declaration (Ps. 14:1–3; Jer. 17:9; Rom. 3:9–18,23; 5:10–12).

SALVATION
We teach that salvation is wholly of God by grace on the basis of the redemption of Jesus Christ, the merit of His shed blood, and not on the basis of human merit or works (John 1:12; Eph. 1:4–7; 2:8–10; 1 Pet. 1:18,19).

ELECTION
We teach that election is the act of God by which, before the foundation of the world, He chose in Christ those whom He graciously regenerates, saves, and sanctifies (Rom. 8:28–30; Eph. 1:4–11; 2 Thess. 2:13; 2 Tim. 2:10; 1 Pet. 1:1,2).

We teach that sovereign election does not contradict or negate the responsibility of man to repent and trust Christ as Savior and Lord (Ezek. 18:23,32; 33:11; John 3:18,19,36; 5:40; 2 Thess. 2:10–12; Rev. 22:17). Nevertheless, since sovereign grace includes the means of receiving the gift of salvation as well as the gift itself, sovereign election will result in what God determines. All whom the Father calls to Himself will come in faith and all who come in faith the Father will receive (John 6:37–40,44; Acts 13:48; James 4:8).

We teach that the unmerited favor that God grants to totally depraved sinners is not related to any initiative of their own part nor to God's anticipation of what they might do by their own will, but is solely of His sovereign grace and mercy (Eph. 1:4–7; Titus 3:4–7; 1 Pet. 1:2).

We teach that election should not be looked upon as based merely on abstract sovereignty. God is truly sovereign but He exercises this sovereignty in harmony with His other attributes, especially His omniscience, justice, holiness, wisdom, grace, and love (Rom. 9:11–16). This sovereignty will always exalt the will of God in a manner totally consistent with His character as revealed in the life of our Lord Jesus Christ (Matt. 11:25–28; 2 Tim. 1:9).

REGENERATION
We teach that regeneration is a supernatural work of the Holy Spirit by which the divine nature and divine life are given (John 3:3–8; Titus 3:5). It is instantaneous and is accomplished solely by the power of the Holy Spirit through the instrumentality of the Word of God (John 5:24), when the repentant sinner, as enabled by the Holy Spirit, responds in faith to the divine provision of salvation. Genuine regeneration is manifested by fruits worthy of repentance as demonstrated in righteous attitudes and conduct. Good works will be its proper evidence and fruit (1 Cor. 6:19,20; Eph. 5:17–21; Phil. 2:12b; Col. 3:12–17; 2 Pet. 1:4–11). This obedience causes the believer to be increasingly conformed to the image of our Lord Jesus Christ (2 Cor. 3:18). Such a conformity is climaxed in the believer's glorification at Christ's coming (Rom. 8:16,17; 2 Pet. 1:4; 1 John 3:2,3).

JUSTIFICATION
We teach that justification before God is an act of God (Rom. 8:30,33) by which He declares righteous those who, through faith in Christ, repent of their sins (Luke 13:3; Acts 2:38; 3:19; 11:18; Rom. 2:4; 2 Cor. 7:10; Is. 55:6,7) and confess Him as sovereign Lord

(Rom. 10:9,10; 1 Cor. 12:3; 2 Cor. 4:5; Phil. 2:11). This righteousness is apart from any virtue or work of man (Rom. 3:20; 4:6) and involves the placing of our sins on Christ (Col. 2:14; 1 Pet. 2:24) and the imputation of Christ's righteousness to us (1 Cor. 1:2,30; 6:11; 2 Cor. 5:21). By this means God is enabled to "be just, and the justifier of the one who has faith in Jesus" (Rom. 3:26).

SANCTIFICATION

We teach that every believer is sanctified (set apart) unto God by justification and is therefore declared to be holy and is therefore identified as a saint. This sanctification is positional and instantaneous and should not be confused with progressive sanctification. This sanctification has to do with the believer's standing, not his present walk or condition (Acts 20:32; 1 Cor. 1:2,30; 6:11; 2 Thess. 2:13; Heb. 2:11; 3:1; 10:10,14; 13:12; 1 Pet. 1:2).

We teach that there is also by the work of the Holy Spirit a progressive sanctification by which the state of the believer is brought closer to the likeness of Christ through obedience to the Word of God and the empowering of the Holy Spirit. The believer is able to live a life of increasing holiness in conformity to the will of God, becoming more and more like our Lord Jesus Christ (John 17:17,19; Rom. 6:1–22; 2 Cor. 3:18; 1 Thess. 4:3,4; 5:23).

In this respect, we teach that every saved person is involved in a daily conflict—the new creation in Christ doing battle against the flesh—but adequate provision is made for victory through the power of the indwelling Holy Spirit. The struggle nevertheless stays with the believer all through this earthly life and is never completely ended. All claims to the eradication of sin in this life are unscriptural. Eradication of sin is not possible, but the Holy Spirit does provide for victory over sin (Gal. 5:16–25; Eph. 4:22–24; Phil. 3:12; Col. 3:9,10; 1 Pet. 1:14–16; 1 John 3:5–9).

SECURITY

We teach that all the redeemed once saved are kept by God's power and are thus secure in Christ forever (John 5:24; 6:37–40; 10:27–30; Rom. 5:9,10; 8:1,31–39; 1 Cor. 1:4–9; Eph. 4:30; Heb. 7:25; 13:5; 1 Pet. 1:4,5; Jude 24).

We teach that it is the privilege of believers to rejoice in the assurance of their salvation through the testimony of God's Word, which however, clearly forbids the use of Christian liberty as an excuse for sinful living and carnality (Rom. 6:15–22; 13:13,14; Gal. 5:13,16,17,25,26; Titus 2:11–14).

SEPARATION

We teach that separation from sin is clearly called for throughout the Old and New Testaments, and that the Scriptures clearly indicate that in the last days apostasy and worldliness shall increase (2 Cor. 6:14–7:1; 2 Tim. 3:1–5).

We teach that out of deep gratitude for the undeserved grace of God granted to us and because our glorious God is so worthy of our total consecration, all the saved should live in such a manner as to demonstrate our adoring love to God and so as not to bring reproach upon our Lord and Savior. We also teach that separation from any association with religious apostasy, and worldly and sinful practices is commanded of us by God (Rom. 12:1,2; 1 Cor. 5:9–13; 2 Cor. 6:14–7:1; 1 John 2:15–17; 2 John 9–11).

We teach that believers should be separated unto our Lord Jesus Christ (2 Thess. 1:11,12; Heb. 12:1,2) and affirm that the Christian life is a life of obedient righteousness demonstrated by a beatitude attitude (Matt. 5:2–12) and a continual pursuit of holiness (Rom. 12:1,2; 2 Cor. 7:1; Heb. 12:14; Titus 2:11–14; 1 John 3:1–10).

THE CHURCH

We teach that all who place their faith in Jesus Christ are immediately placed by the Holy Spirit into one united spiritual body, the church (1 Cor. 12:12,13), the bride of Christ (2 Cor. 11:2; Eph. 5:23–32; Rev. 19:7,8), of which Christ is the head (Eph. 1:22; 4:15; Col. 1:18).

We teach that the formation of the church, the body of Christ, began on the day of Pentecost (Acts 2:1–21,38–47) and will be completed at the coming of Christ for His own at the Rapture (1 Cor. 15:51,52; 1 Thess. 4:13–18).

We teach that the church is thus a unique spiritual organism designed by Christ, made up of all born-again believers in this present age (Eph. 2:11–3:6). The church is distinct from Israel (1 Cor. 10:32), a mystery not revealed until this age (Eph. 3:1–6; 5:32).

We teach that the establishment and continuity of local churches is clearly taught and defined in the New Testament Scriptures (Acts 14:23,27; 20:17,28; Gal. 1:2; Phil. 1:1; 1 Thess. 1:1; 2 Thess. 1:1) and that the members of the one scriptural body are directed to associate themselves together in local assemblies (1 Cor. 11:18–20; Heb. 10:25).

We teach that the one supreme authority for the church is Christ (Eph. 1:22; Col. 1:18) and that church leadership, gifts, order, discipline, and worship are all appointed through His sovereignty as found in the Scriptures. The biblically designated officers serving under Christ and over the assembly are elders (males, who are also called bishops, pastors, and pastor-teachers; Acts 20:28; Eph. 4:11) and deacons, both of whom must meet biblical qualification (1 Tim. 3:1–13; Titus 1:5–9; 1 Pet. 5:1–5).

We teach that these leaders lead or rule as servants of Christ (1 Tim. 5:17–22) and have His authority in directing the church. The congregation is to submit to their leadership (Heb. 13:7,17).

We teach the importance of discipleship (Matt. 28:19,20; 2 Tim. 2:2), mutual accountability of all believers to each other (Matt. 18:15–17), as well as the need for discipline for sinning members of the congregation in accord with the standards of Scripture (Matt. 18:15–22; Acts 5:1–11; 1 Cor. 5:1–13; 2 Thess. 3:6–15; 1 Tim. 1:19,20; Titus 1:10–16).

We teach the autonomy of the local church, free from any external authority or control, with the right of self-government and freedom from the interference of any hierarchy of individuals or organizations (Titus 1:5). We teach that it is scriptural for true churches to cooperate with each other for the presentation and propagation of the faith. Local churches, however, through their pastors and their interpretation and application of Scripture, should be the sole judges of the measure and method of their cooperation (Acts 15:19–31; 20:28; 1 Cor. 5:4–7,13; 1 Pet. 5:1–4).

We teach that the purpose of the church is to glorify God (Eph. 3:21) by building itself up in the faith (Eph. 4:13–16), by instruction of the Word (2 Tim. 2:2,15; 3:16,17), by fellowship (Acts 2:47; 1 John 1:3), by keeping the ordinances (Luke 22:19; Acts 2:38–42) and by advancing and communicating the gospel to the entire world (Matt. 28:19; Acts 1:8).

We teach the calling of all saints to the work of service (1 Cor. 15:58; Eph. 4:12; Rev. 22:12).

We teach the need of the church to cooperate with God as He accomplishes His purpose in the world. To that end, He gives the church spiritual gifts. First, He gives men chosen for the purpose of equipping the saints for the work of the ministry (Eph. 4:7–12) and He also gives unique and special spiritual abilities to each member of the body of Christ (Rom. 12:5–8; 1 Cor. 12:4–31; 1 Pet. 4:10,11).

We teach that there were two kinds of gifts given the early church: miraculous gifts of divine revelation and healing, given temporarily in the apostolic era for the purpose of confirming the authenticity of the apostles' message (Heb. 2:3,4; 2 Cor. 12:12); and ministering gifts, given to equip believers for edifying one another. With the New Testament revelation now complete, Scripture becomes the sole test of the authenticity of a man's message, and confirming gifts of a miraculous nature are no longer necessary to validate a man or his message (1 Cor. 13:8–12). Miraculous gifts can even be counterfeited by Satan so as to deceive even believers (Matt. 24:24). The only gifts in operation today are those non-revelatory equipping gifts given for edification (Rom. 12:6–8).

We teach that no one possesses the gift of healing today but that God does hear and answer the prayer of faith and will answer in accordance with His own perfect will for the sick, suffering, and afflicted (Luke 18:1–8; John 5:7–9; 2 Cor. 12:6–10; James 5:13–16; 1 John 5:14,15).

We teach that two ordinances have been committed to the local church: baptism and the Lord's Supper (Acts 2:38–42). Christian baptism by immersion (Acts 8:36–39) is the solemn and beautiful testimony of a believer showing forth his faith in the crucified, buried, and risen Savior, and his union with Him in death to sin and resurrection to a new life (Rom. 6: 1–11). It is also a sign of fellowship and identification with the visible body of Christ (Acts 2:41,42).

We teach that the Lord's Supper is the commemoration and proclamation of His death until He comes, and should be always preceded by solemn self-examination (1 Cor. 11:23–32). We also teach that whereas the elements of communion are only representative of the flesh and blood of Christ, the Lord's Supper is nevertheless an actual

Communion with the risen Christ who is present in a unique way, fellowshiping with His people (1 Cor. 10:16).

ANGELS

Holy Angels

We teach that angels are created beings and are therefore not to be worshiped. Although they are a higher order of creation than man, they are created to serve God and to worship Him (Luke 2:9–14; Heb. 1:6,7,14; 2:6,7; Rev. 5:11–14).

Fallen Angels

We teach that Satan is a created angel and the author of sin. He incurred the judgment of God by rebelling against his Creator (Is. 14:12–17; Ezek. 28:11–19), by taking numerous angels with him in his fall (Matt. 25:41; Rev. 12:1–14), and by introducing sin into the human race by his temptation of Eve (Gen. 3:1–15).

We teach that Satan is the open and declared enemy of God and man (Is. 14:13,14; Matt. 4:1–11; Rev. 12:9,10), the prince of this world who has been defeated through the death and resurrection of Jesus Christ (Rom. 16:20) and that he shall be eternally punished in the lake of fire (Is. 14:12–17; Ezek. 28:11–19; Matt. 25:41; Rev. 20:10).

LAST THINGS (ESCHATOLOGY)

Death

We teach that physical death involves no loss of our immaterial consciousness (Rev. 6:9–11), that there is a separation of soul and body (James 2:26), that the soul of the redeemed passes immediately into the presence of Christ (Luke 23:43; 2 Cor. 5:8; Phil. 1:23), and that, for the redeemed, such separation will continue until the Rapture (1 Thess. 4:13–17) which initiates the first resurrection (Rev. 20:4–6), when our soul and body will be reunited to be glorified forever with our Lord (1 Cor. 15:35–44,50–54; Phil. 3:21). Until that time, the souls of the redeemed in Christ remain in joyful fellowship with our Lord Jesus Christ (2 Cor. 5:8).

We teach the bodily resurrection of all men, the saved to eternal life (John 6:39; Rom. 8:10,11,19–23; 2 Cor. 4:14), and the unsaved to judgment and everlasting punishment (Dan. 12:2; John 5:29; Rev. 20:13–15).

We teach that the souls of the unsaved at death are kept under punishment until the second resurrection (Luke 16:19–26; Rev. 20:13–15), when the soul and the resurrection body will be united (John 5:28, 29). They shall then appear at the Great White Throne judgment (Rev. 20:11–15) and shall be cast into hell, the lake of fire (Matt. 25:41–46), cut off from the life of God forever (Dan. 12:2; Matt. 25:41–46; 2 Thess. 1:7–9).

The Rapture of the Church

We teach the personal, bodily return of our Lord Jesus Christ before the seven-year tribulation (1 Thess. 4:16; Titus 2:13) to translate His church from this earth (John 14:1–3;

1 Cor. 15:51–53; 1 Thess. 4:15–5:11) and, between this event and His glorious return with His saints, to reward believers according to their works (1 Cor. 3:11–15; 2 Cor. 5:10).

The Tribulation Period

We teach that immediately following the removal of the church from the earth (John 14:1–3; 1 Thess. 4:13–18) the righteous judgments of God will be poured out upon an unbelieving world (Jer. 30:7; Dan. 9:27; 12:1; 2 Thess. 2:7–12; Rev. 16), and that these judgments will be climaxed by the return of Christ in glory to the earth (Matt. 24:27–31; 25:31–46; 2 Thess. 2:7–12). At that time the Old Testament and tribulation saints will be raised and the living will be judged (Dan. 12:2,3; Rev. 20:4–6). This period includes the seventieth week of Daniel's prophecy (Dan. 9:24–27; Matt. 24:15–31; 25:31–46).

The Second Coming and the Millennial Reign

We teach that after the tribulation period, Christ will come to earth to occupy the throne of David (Matt. 25:31; Luke 1:32,33; Acts 1:10,11; 2:29,30) and establish His messianic kingdom for a thousand years on the earth (Rev. 20:1–7). During this time the resurrected saints will reign with Him over Israel and all the nations of the earth (Ezek. 37:21–28; Dan. 7:17–22; Rev. 19:11–16). This reign will be preceded by the overthrow of the Antichrist and the False Prophet, and by the removal of Satan from the world (Dan. 7:17–27; Rev. 20:1–6).

We teach that the kingdom itself will be the fulfillment of God's promise to Israel (Is. 65:17–25; Ezek. 37:21–28; Zech. 8:1–17) to restore them to the land which they forfeited through their disobedience (Deut. 28:15–68). The result of their disobedience was that Israel was temporarily set aside (Matt. 21:43; Rom. 11: 1–26) but will again be awakened through repentance to enter into the land of blessing (Jer. 31:31–34; Ezek. 36:22–32; Rom. 11:25–29).

We teach that this time of our Lord's reign will be characterized by harmony, justice, peace, righteousness, and long life (Is. 11; 65:17–25; Ezek. 36:33–38), and will be brought to an end with the release of Satan (Rev. 20:7).

The Judgment of the Lost

We teach that following the release of Satan after the thousand year reign of Christ (Rev. 20:7), Satan will deceive the nations of the earth and gather them to battle against the saints and the beloved city, at which time Satan and his army will be devoured by fire from heaven (Rev. 20:9). Following this, Satan will be thrown into the lake of fire and brimstone (Matt. 25:41; Rev. 20:10) whereupon Christ, who is the judge of all men (John 5:22), will resurrect and judge the great and small at the Great White Throne judgment.

We teach that this resurrection of the unsaved dead to judgment will be a physical resurrection, whereupon receiving their judgment (John 5:28,29), they will be committed to an eternal conscious punishment in the lake of fire (Matt. 25:41; Rev. 20:11–15).

Eternity

We teach that after the closing of the Millennium, the temporary release of Satan, and the judgment of unbelievers (2 Thess. 1:9; Rev. 20:7–15), the saved will enter the eternal state of glory with God, after which the elements of this earth are to be dissolved (2 Pet. 3:10) and replaced with a new earth wherein only righteousness dwells (Eph. 5:5; Rev. 20:15,21,22). Following this, the heavenly city will come down out of heaven (Rev. 21:2) and will be the dwelling place of the saints, where they will enjoy forever fellowship with God and one another (John 17:3; Rev. 21,22). Our Lord Jesus Christ, having fulfilled His redemptive mission, will then deliver up the kingdom to God the Father (1 Cor. 15:23–28) that in all spheres the triune God may reign forever and ever (1 Cor. 15:28).

The Character of Genuine
SAVING FAITH
2 Corinthians 13:5

1: EVIDENCES THAT NEITHER PROVE NOR DISPROVE ONE'S FAITH

A. Visible Morality: . . . . Matt. 19:16–21; 23:27.

B. Intellectual Knowledge:. . . . . Rom. 1:21; 2:17ff.

C. Religious Involvement: . . . . Matt. 25:1–10

D. Active Ministry: . . . . Matt. 7:21–24

E. Conviction of Sin:. . . . . Acts 24:25

F. Assurance:. . . . . Matt. 23

G. Time of Decision: . . . . Luke 8:13, 14

2: THE FRUIT/PROOFS OF AUTHENTIC/TRUE CHRISTIANITY:

A. Love for God: . . . . Ps. 42:1ff; 73:25; Luke 10:27; Rom. 8:7

B. Repentance from Sin: . . . . Ps. 32:5; Prov. 28:13; Rom. 7:14ff;
2 Cor. 7:10; 1 John 1:8–10

C. Genuine Humility:. . . . . Ps. 51:17; Matt. 5:1–12; James 4:6, 9ff.

D. Devotion to God's Glory: . . . . Ps. 105:3; 115:1; Is. 43:7, 48:10ff.;
Jer. 9:23, 24; 1 Cor. 10:31.

E. Continual Prayer: . . . . Luke 18:1; Eph. 6:18ff.; Phil. 4:6ff.;
1 Tim. 2:1–4; James 5:16–18

F. Selfless Love:. . . . . 1 John 2:9ff, 3:14; 4:7ff.

G. Separation from the World:. . . . . 1 Cor. 2:12; James 4:4ff.; 1 John 2:15–17, 5:5

H. Spiritual Growth:. . . . . Luke 8:15; John 15:1–6; Eph. 4:12–16

I. Obedient Living:. . . . . Matt. 7:21; John 15:14ff.; Rom. 16:26;
1 Pet. 1:2, 22; 1 John 2:3–5

If List I is true of a person and List II is false, there is cause to question the validity of one's profession of faith. Yet if List II is true, then the top list will be also.

3: THE CONDUCT OF THE GOSPEL:

A. Proclaim it: . . . . Matt. 4:23

B. Defend it: . . . . Jude 3

C. Demonstrate it:. . . . . Phil. 1:27

D. Share it: . . . . Phil. 1:5

E. Suffer for it:. . . . . 2 Tim. 1:8

F. Don't hinder it: . . . . 1 Cor. 9:16

G. Be not ashamed: . . . . Rom. 1:16

H. Preach it:. . . . . 1 Cor. 9:16

I. Be empowered: . . . . 1 Thess. 1:5

J. Guard it: . . . . Gal. 1:6–8

THE BIBLE

Date	Morning	Evening	Date	Morning	Evening	Date	Morning	Evening
	JANUARY		11	26:1-25	11, 12	22	1:39-56	10, 11, 12
	Matt.	**Gen.**	12	26:26-50	13	23	1:57-80	13, 14, 15
1	1	1, 2, 3	13	26:51-75	14	24	2:1-24	16, 17, 18
2	2	4, 5, 6	14	27:1-26	15, 16	25	2:25-52	19, 20, 21
3	3	7, 8, 9	15	27:27-50	17, 18	26	3	22, 23, 24
4	4	10, 11, 12	16	27:51-66	19, 20			**Judg.**
5	5:1-26	13, 14, 15	17	28	21, 22	27	4:1-30	1, 2, 3
6	5:27-48	16, 17		**Mark**		28	4:31-44	4, 5, 6
7	6:1-18	18, 19	18	1:1-22	23, 24	29	5:1-16	7, 8
8	6:19-34	20, 21, 22	19	1:23-45	25	30	5:17-39	9, 10
9	7	23, 24	20	2	26, 27	31	6:1-26	11, 12
10	8:1-17	25, 26			**Num.**			
11	8:18-34	27, 28	21	3:1-19	1, 2			
12	9:1-17	29, 30	22	3:20-35	3, 4		*APRIL*	
13	9:18-38	31, 32	23	4:1-20	5, 6		**Luke**	**Judg.**
14	10:1-20	33, 34, 35	24	4:21-41	7, 8	1	6:27-49	13, 14, 16
15	10:21-42	36, 37, 38	25	5:1-20	9, 10, 11	2	7:1-30	16, 17, 18
16	11	39, 40	26	5:21-43	12, 13, 14	3	7:31-50	19, 20, 21
17	12:1-23	41, 42	27	6:1-29	15, 16			**Ruth**
18	12:24-50	43, 44, 45	28	6:30-56	17, 18, 19	4	8:1-25	1, 2, 3, 4
19	13:1-30	46, 47, 48	29	7:1-13	20, 21, 22			**1 Sam.**
20	13:31-58	49, 50				5	8:26-56	1, 2, 3
		Ex.				6	9:1-17	4, 5, 6
21	14:1-21	1, 2, 3		*MARCH*		7	9:18-36	7, 8, 9
22	14:22-36	4, 5, 6		**Mark**	**Num.**	8	9:37-62	10, 11, 12
23	15:1-20	7, 8	1	7:14-37	23, 24, 25	9	10:1-24	13, 14
24	15:21-39	9, 20, 11	2	8:1-21	26, 27	10	10:25-42	15, 16
25	16	12, 13	3	8:22-38	28, 29, 30	11	11:1-28	17, 18
26	17	14, 15	4	9:1-29	31, 32, 33	12	11:29-54	19, 20, 21
27	18:1-20	16, 17, 18	5	9:30-50	34, 35, 36	13	12:1-31	22, 23, 24
28	18:21-35	19, 20			**Deut.**	14	12:32-59	25, 26
29	19	21, 22	6	10:1-31	1, 2	15	13:1-22	27, 28, 29
30	20:1-16	23, 24	7	10:32-52	3, 4	16	13:23-35	30, 31
31	20:17-34	25, 26	8	11:1-18	5, 6, 7			**2 Sam.**
			9	11:19-33	8, 9, 10	17	14:1-24	1, 2
			10	12:1-27	11, 12, 13	18	14:25-35	3, 4, 5
	FEBRUARY		11	12:28-44	14, 15, 16	19	15:1-10	6, 7, 8
	Matt.	**Ex.**	12	13:1-20	17, 18, 19	20	15:11-32	9, 10, 11
1	21:1-22	27, 28	13	13:21-37	20, 21, 22	21	16	12, 13
2	21:23-46	29, 30	14	14:1-26	23, 24, 25	22	17:1-19	14, 15
3	22:1-22	31, 32, 33	15	14:27-53	26, 27	23	17:20-37	16, 17, 18
4	22:23-46	34, 35	16	14:54-72	28, 29	24	18:1-23	19, 20
5	23:1-22	36, 37, 38	17	15:1-25	30, 31	25	18:24-43	21, 22
6	23:23-29	39, 40	18	15:26-47	32, 33, 34	26	19:1-27	23, 24
		Lev.			**Josh.**			**1 Kin.**
7	24:1-28	1, 2, 3	19	16	1, 2, 3	27	19:28-48	1, 2
8	24:29-51	4, 5		**Luke**		28	20:1-26	3, 4, 5
9	25:1-30	6, 7	20	1:1-20	4, 5, 6	29	20:27-47	6, 7
10	25:31-46	8, 9, 10	21	1:21-38	7, 8, 9	30	21:1-19	8, 9

Date	Morning	Evening	Date	Morning	Evening	Date	Morning	Evening
	MAY			Acts	Ezra		Rom.	Pss.
	Luke	1 Kin.	14	1	9, 10	29	1	49, 50
1	21:20-38	10, 11			Neh.	30	2	51, 52, 53
2	22:1-20	12, 13	15	2:1-21	1, 2, 3	31	3	54, 55, 56
3	22:21-46	14, 15	16	2:22-47	4, 5, 6			
4	22:47-71	16, 17, 18	17	3	7, 8, 9			
5	23:1-25	19, 20	18	4:1-22	10, 11		*AUGUST*	
6	23:26-56	21, 22	19	4:23-37	12, 13		Rom.	Pss.
		2 Kin.			Esth.	1	4	57, 58, 59
7	24:1-35	1, 2, 3	20	5:1-21	1, 2	2	5	60, 61, 62
8	24:36-53	4, 5, 6	21	5:22-42	3, 4, 5	3	6	63, 64, 65
	John		22	6	6, 7, 8	4	7	66, 67
9	1:1-28	7, 8, 9	23	7:1-21	9, 10	5	8:1-21	68, 69
10	1:29-51	10, 11, 12			Job	6	8:22-39	70, 71
11	2	13, 14	24	7:22-43	1, 2	7	9:1-15	72, 73
12	3:1-18	15, 16	25	7:44-60	3, 4	8	9:16-33	74, 75, 76
13	3:19-38	17, 18	26	8:1-25	5, 6, 7	9	10	77, 78
14	4:1-30	19, 20, 21	27	8:26-40	8, 9, 10	10	11:1-18	79, 80
15	4:31-54	22, 23	28	9:1-21	11, 12, 13	11	11:19-36	81, 82, 83
16	5:1-24	24, 25	29	9:22-43	14, 15, 16	12	12	84, 85, 86
	1 Chr.		30	10:1-23	17, 18, 19	13	13	87, 88
17	5:25-47	1, 2, 3				14	14	89, 90
18	6:1-21	4, 5, 6				15	15:1-13	91, 92, 93
19	6:22-44	7, 8, 9		*JULY*		16	15:14-33	94, 95, 96
20	6:45-71	10, 11, 12		Acts	Job	17	16	97, 98, 99
21	7:1-27	13, 14, 15	1	10:24-28	20, 21		1 Cor.	
22	7:28-53	16, 17, 18	2	11	22, 23, 24	18	1	100, 101, 102
23	8:1-27	19, 20, 21	3	12	25, 26, 27	19	2	103, 104
24	8:28-59	22, 23, 24	4	13;1-25	28, 29	20	3	105, 106
25	9:1-23	25, 26, 27	5	13:26-52	30, 31	21	4	107, 108, 109
26	9:24-41	28, 29	6	14	32, 33	22	5	110, 111, 112
		2 Chr.	7	15:1-21	34, 35	23	6	113, 114, 115
27	10:1-23	1, 2, 3	8	15:22-41	36, 37	24	7:1-19	116, 117, 118
28	10:24-42	4, 5, 6	9	16:1-21	38, 39, 40	25	7:20-40	119:1-88
29	11:1-29	7, 8, 9	10	16:22-40	41, 42	26	8	119:89-176
30	11:30-57	10, 11, 12			Pss.	27	9	120, 121, 122
31	12:1-26	13, 14	11	17:1-15	1, 2, 3	28	10:1-18	123, 124, 125
			12	17:16-34	4, 5, 6	29	10:19-33	126, 127, 128
			13	18	7, 8, 9	30	11:1-16	129, 130, 131
	JUNE		14	19:1-20	10, 11, 12	31	11:17-34	132, 133, 134
	John	2 Chr.	15	19:21-41	13, 14, 15			
1	12:27-50	15, 16	16	20:1-16	16, 17			
2	13:1-20	17, 18	17	20:17-38	18, 19		*SEPTEMBER*	
3	13:21-38	19, 20	18	21:1-17	20, 21, 22		1 Cor.	Pss.
4	14	21, 22	19	21:18=40	23, 24, 25	1	12	135, 136
5	15	23, 24	20	22	26, 27, 28	2	13	137, 138, 139
6	16	25, 26, 27	21	23:1-15	29, 30	3	14:1-20	140, 141, 142
7	17	28, 29	22	23:16-35	31, 32	4	14:21-40	143, 144, 145
8	18:1-18	30, 31	23	24	33, 34	5	15:1-28	146, 147
9	18:19-40	32, 33	24	25	35, 36	6	15:29-58	148, 149, 150
10	19:1-22	34, 35, 36	25	26	37, 38, 39			Prov.
		Ezra	26	27;1-26	40, 41, 42	7	16	1, 2
11	19:23-42	1, 2	27	27:27-44	43, 44, 45		2 Cor.	
12	20	3, 4, 5	28	28	46, 47, 48	8	1	2, 3, 4
13	21	6, 7, 8				9	2	6, 7

Date	Morning	Evening	Date	Morning	Evening	Date	Morning	Evening
10	3	8, 9			2 Thess.			1 Pet.
11	4	10, 11, 12	18	1	53, 54, 55	24	1	22, 23
12	5	13, 14, 15	19	2	56, 57, 58	25	2	24, 25, 26
13	6	16, 17, 18	20	3	59, 60, 61	26	3	27, 28, 29
14	7	19, 20, 21			1Tim.	27	4	30, 31, 32
15	8	22, 23, 24	21	1	62, 63, 64	28	5	33, 34
16	9	25, 26	22	2	65, 66			2 Pet.
17	10	27, 28, 29			Jer.	29	1	35, 36
18	11:1-15	30, 31	23	3	1, 2	30	2	37, 38, 39
		Eccl.	24	4	3, 4, 5			
19	11:16-33	1, 2, 3	25	5	6, 7, 8			
20	12	4, 5, 6	26	6	9, 10, 11			DECEMBER
21	13	7, 8, 9			2 Tim.			2 Pet.	Ezek.
		Gal.	27	1	12, 13, 14	1	3	40, 41
22	1	10, 11, 12	28	2	15, 16, 17			1 John
		Song	29	3	18, 19	2	1	42, 43, 44
23	2	1, 2, 3	30	4	20, 21	3	2	45, 46
24	3	4, 5			Titus	4	3	47, 48
25	4	6, 7, 8	31	1	22, 23			Dan.
		Is.				5	4	1, 2
26	5	1, 2				6	5	3, 4
27	6	3, 4			NOVEMBER	7	2 John	5, 6, 7
		Eph.		Titus	Jer.	8	3 John	8, 9, 10
28	1	5, 6	1	2	24, 25, 26	9	Jude	11, 12
29	2	7, 8	2	3	27, 28, 29		Rev.	Hos.
30	3	9, 10	3	Philem.	30, 31	10	1	1, 2, 3, 4
				Heb.		11	2	5, 6, 7, 8
		OCTOBER	4	1	32, 33	12	3	9, 10, 11
	Eph.	Is.	5	2	34, 35, 36	13	4	12, 13, 14
1	4	11, 12, 13	6	3	37, 38, 39	14	5	Joel
2	5:1-16	14, 15, 16	7	4	40, 41, 42			Amos
3	5:17-33	17, 18, 19	8	5	43, 44, 45	15	6	1, 2, 3
4	6	20, 21, 22	9	6	46, 47	16	7	4, 5, 6
	Phil.		10	7	48, 49	17	8	7, 8, 9
5	1	23, 24, 25	11	8	50	18	8	Obad.
6	2	26, 27	12	9	51, 52	19	10	Jon.
7	3	28, 29			Lam.			Mic.
8	4	30, 31	13	10:1-18	1, 2	20	11	1, 2, 3
	Col.		14	10:20-40	3, 4, 5	21	12	4, 5
9	1	32, 33			Ezek.	22	13	6, 7
10	2	34, 35, 36	15	11:1-19	1, 2	23	14	Nah.
11	3	37, 38	16	11:20-40	3, 4	24	15	Hab.
12	4	39, 40	17	12	5, 6, 7	25	16	Zeph.
	1 Thess.		18	13	8, 9, 10	26	17	Hag.
13	1	41, 42		James				Zech.
14	2	43, 44	19	1	11, 12, 13	27	18	1, 2, 3, 4
15	3	45, 46	20	2	14, 15	28	19	5, 6, 7, 8
16	4	47, 48, 49	21	3	16, 17	29	20	9, 10, 11, 12
17	5	50, 51, 52	22	4	18, 19	30	21	13, 14
			23	5	20, 21	31	22	Mal.

MONIES,

Weights, and Measures

The Hebrews probably first used coins in the Persian period (500–350 B.C.). However, minting began around 700 B.C. in other nations. Prior to this, precious metals were weighed, not counted as money.

Some units appear as both measures of money and measures of weights. This comes from naming the coins after their weight. For example, the shekel was a weight long before it became the name of a coin.

It is helpful to relate biblical monies to current values. But we cannot make exact equivalents. The fluctuating value of money's purchasing power is difficult to determine in our own day. It is even harder to evaluate currencies used two- to three-thousand years ago.

Therefore, it is best to choose a value meaningful over time, such as a common laborer's daily wage. One day's wage corresponds to the ancient Jewish system (a silver shekel is four days' wages) as well as to the Greek and Roman systems (the drachma and the denarius were each coins representing a day's wage).

The monies chart below takes a current day's wage as thirty-two dollars. Though there are differences of economies and standards of living, this measure will help us apply meaningful value to the monetary units in the chart and in the biblical text.

John F. MacArthur, Jr., *The MacArthur Study Bible*, (Dallas: Word Publishing) 1997.

MONIES

UNIT	MONETARY VALUE	EQUIVALENTS	TRANSLATIONS
Jewish Weights			
Talent	gold—$5,760,000[1] silver—$384,000	3,000 shekels; 6,000 bekas	talent, one hundred pounds
Shekel	gold—$1,920 silver—$128	4 days' wages; 2 bekas: 20 gerahs	shekel
Beka	gold—$960 silver—$64	1/2 shekel; 10 gerahs	beka
Gerah	gold—$96 silver—$6.40	1/20 shekel	gerahs
Persian Coins			
Daric	gold—$1,280[2] silver—$64	2 days' wages; 1/2 Jewish silver shekel	daric, drachma
Greek Coins			
Tetradrachma	$128	4 drachmas	stater
Didrachma	$64	2 drachmas	two-drachma tax
Drachma	$32	1 day's wage	coin, silver coins
Lepton	$.25	1/2 of a Roman kodrantes	cents, small copper coin
Roman Coins			
Aureus	$800	25 denarii	gold
Denarius	$32	1 day's wage	denaril
Assarius	$2	1/16 of a denarius	cent
Kodrantes	$.50	1/4 of an assarius	cent

[1]Value of gold is fifteen times the value of silver
[2]Value of gold is twenty times the value of silver

LIQUID MEASURES

UNIT	MEASURES	EQUIVALENTS	TRANSLATIONS
Kor	60 gallons	10 baths	kor
Metretes	10.2 gallons		gallon
Bath	6 gallons	6 hins	measure, bath
Hin	1 gallon	2 kabs	hin
Kab	2 quarts	4 logs	kab
Log	1 pint	1/4 kab	log

DRY MEASURES

UNIT	MEASURES	EQUIVALENTS	TRANSLATIONS
Homer	6.52 bushels	10 ephahs	homer
Kor	6.52 bushels	1 homer; 10 ephahs	kor, measure
Lethech	3.26 bushels	1/2 kor	a homer and a half
Ephah	.65 bushel, 20.8 quarts	1/10 homer	ephah
Modius	7.68 quarts		peck-measure
Seah	7 quarts	1/3 ephah	measure, pecks
Omer	2.08 quarts	1/10 ephah; 1 4/5 kab	omer
Kab	1.16 quarts	4 logs	kab
Choenix	1 quart		quart
Xestes	1 1/16 pints		pitcher
Log	.58 pint	1/4 kab	log

MEASURES OF LENGTH

UNIT	LENGTH	EQUIVALENTS	TRANSLATIONS
Day's journey	ca. 20 miles		day's journey, day's walk
Roman mile	4,854 feet	8 stadia	mile
Sabbath day's journey	3, 637 feet	6 stadia	a Sabbath day's journey
Stadion	606 feet	1/8 Roman mile	mile, stadion
Rod	9 feet (10.5 feet in Ezekiel)	3 paces; 6 cubits	measuring rod
Fathom	6 feet	4 cubits	fathom
Pace	3 feet	1/3 rod; 2 cubits	pace
Cubit	18 inches	1/2 pace; 2 spans	cubit, yards
Span	9 inches	1/2 cubit; 3 handbreadths	span
Handbreadth	3 inches	1/3 span; 4 fingers	handbreadth
Finger	.75 inches	1/4 handbreadth	finger

WEIGHTS

UNIT	LENGTH	EQUIVALENTS	TRANSLATIONS
Jewish Weights			
Talent	ca. 75 pounds for common talent, ca. 150 pounds for royal talent	60 minas; 3000 shekels	talent, one hundred pounds
Mina	1.25 pounds	50 shekels	maneh, mina
Shekel	ca. .4 ounce (11.4 grams) for common shekel	2 bekas; 20 gerahs	shekel
	ca. .8 ounce for royal shekel		
Beka	ca. .2 ounce (5.7 grams)	1/2 shekel; 10 gerahs	half-shekel
Gerah	ca. .02 ounce (.57 grams)	1/20 shekel	gerah
Roman Weight			
Litra	12 ounces		pound, pint

TOPICAL INDEX

Aaron . . . 2, 5, 21, 30, 38, 43-44, 46, 56, 65, 91, 121, 124, 417
Abed-nego . . . 218, 221
Abijam . . . 80, 82, 103
Abimelech . . . 5, 65-68, 154
Abishag . . . 79, 175
Abner . . . 82, 95
Abraham . . . xi, 1, 3, 4, 5, 8-17, 21-22, 44, 50, 55, 57-58, 73, 90, 108, 113, 115, 124, 131, 137, 140, 143, 190, 200, 211, 274, 303, 312, 345, 365, 393, 395, 419, 462, 468-469, 521
Achaia . . . 353, 358-359, 365, 373, 423, 451
Adam . . . xiii, 8-10, 13, 15-17, 52, 113-114, 117, 143, 186, 209, 303, 312, 345, 365-366, 368-369, 377, 419, 462, 514, 530
Adonijah . . . 79
Adulterous . . . 79, 225
Adultery . . . 78, 90, 92, 95, 195, 226, 274, 379-380
Aesop . . . 213
Africa . . . 466
Agag . . . 139
agapē . . . 480
Agrippina . . . 378
Ahab . . . 80, 82, 100, 103, 104, 107
Ahasuerus . . . 124, 137, 138, 415
Ahaz . . . 81, 83, 103, 114, 118, 183-184, 195, 223, 238, 247
Ahaziah . . . 80, 82, 103, 108, 118
aleiphō . . . 475
Alexander the Great . . . 281, 284, 408
Alexandria . . . 162, 283, 285, 339, 348, 351, 353, 359, 399, 415, 424, 496, 514, 517
Alleluia . . . 524
Alpha and Omega . . . 345, 419, 520-521
ʾamal . . . 170
Amalekites . . . 57, 66, 94, 139
Amanuensis . . . 480, 487
Amenhotep . . . 5, 20, 59
Amillennialism . . . 525
Amittai . . . 241
Ammonites . . . 65, 66, 68, 91, 132

Amnon . . . 78, 95
Amon . . . 81, 83, 103, 109, 114, 119, 255, 259
Amos . . . 82, 223, 227, 233-236, 241, 247, 248, 256, 279
Amphipolis . . . 358, 423
anastasis . . . 375
Anata . . . 193
Anathoth . . . 193
ʿanav . . . 260
Andrew . . . 304, 316, 328, 343, 346, 479
Angels . . . xiii, 8, 11, 14, 91, 145, 147, 151, 211, 219, 222, 247, 268, 277, 305, 352, 385, 388, 416-417, 438, 461-462, 464, 466, 469, 484, 491, 515, 517, 519, 520, 535
antilutron . . . 440
Antioch . . . 162, 283, 298, 327, 336, 357-359, 360-361, 365, 391-392, 399, 424
Antiochus . . . 112, 220-221, 264, 281-282, 284-285, 415
ʿaph . . . 106
Apollonia . . . 358, 423-424
Apollos . . . 162, 353, 365, 374, 378, 423, 451, 461
apolutrōsis . . . 463
Apostasy . . . 65, 67, 99, 106, 108, 233, 433-434, 441, 447-448, 485, 513-516, 532-533
Apostate . . . 107, 465, 468, 513-516
Apostles . . . xi-xiv, xvii, xix, xxiii, 236, 298, 306, 324, 332, 351, 353, 361, 385, 403, 404, 479, 494, 496, 513-514, 530, 534
apostolos . . . 385
Aqueduct . . . 198
Arabia, Arabians . . . 7, 15, 100, 180, 191, 198, 237-238, 298, 361, 363, 393
Aram, Arameans . . . 14-15, 95, 102
Aramaic . . . xi, xxi, xxviii, 121, 217, 219, 220-221, 316, 479, 480
ʾarar . . . 52
Archippus . . . 415
aretē . . . 409
Aristarchus . . . 415-416, 424

Ark of the Covenant . . . 23, 27, 77, 78, 90-92, 94, 104, 118
Armenia, Armenian . . . 7, 285, 500
ʾaron . . . 91
Artaxerxes . . . 123-124, 129-130, 132, 135, 142, 284
Asa . . . 80, 82, 103, 107, 114, 118
Ascension . . . xi, xii, 298, 300-301, 336, 337, 339, 352, 377, 412, 479, 496
Asherah . . . 105
Asia Minor . . . 91, 284, 339, 340, 351, 357, 363, 373, 391, 399, 462, 489, 495-496, 509, 517, 519, 523
Assyria, Assyrians . . . 15, 82, 91, 95, 102, 105, 107, 109, 121, 123, 129, 184, 185, 190-191, 195, 208-209, 218, 223, 227, 233, 238, 241-242, 247-248, 251-253, 255, 259, 261, 274, 282
Athaliah . . . 80, 82, 103, 118
Athens . . . 119, 125, 330, 358-359, 373, 424, 437
Atone, Atonement . . . xv, 34-36, 39, 40, 43, 189, 310, 366, 384-385, 425, 438, 440, 443, 452-453, 467, 491, 497, 501
ʾazkarah . . . 36
baʿal . . . 105
Baal . . . 46, 104-105, 109, 114, 223, 247, 259, 281
Baasha . . . 80, 82, 103
Babel . . . 15-16, 143, 261
Babylon, Babylonians . . . xi, 7, 16, 31, 81, 83, 85, 90, 99-100, 102, 105-109, 112-115, 121-124, 129-130, 137, 153, 184-186, 190-191, 193-196, 198, 201-202, 205, 208-210, 214, 217-219, 227-228, 237-238, 248, 251-252, 255-256, 259-260, 263, 267-268, 273-274, 282-284, 481
bachan . . . 274
bakah . . . 204
Balaam . . . 44-47, 71, 514
bamah . . . 106
baptizō . . . 329

Barnabas . . . 162, 315, 353, 357, 365, 393, 404, 416, 445, 451, 461

Baruch . . . 193, 195, 201

Bathsheba . . . 73, 78, 90, 102, 154, 162

Battle of Actium . . . 336

Beijing . . . 166

Belshazzar . . . 83, 218, 220

ben . . . 115

ben ʾadam . . . 209

berakah . . . 190

Bethlehem . . . 66, 71-72, 75, 86, 140, 179, 248, 311, 340

Bethom . . . 227

Bethsaida . . . 301, 320, 322, 341, 479

biblion . . . 449

Bildad the Shuhite . . . 144, 148-149, 150

Bithynia . . . 284, 481, 489,

Black Forest . . . 507

Blessing . . . xii, xiv, xv, xxv, 3, 8, 10, 12, 14, 33, 36, 39, 46, 50, 52-54, 59, 100, 112, 115-116, 124, 145, 155, 163, 165, 167, 170, 172, 176, 186, 190, 210, 218-219, 228, 237, 238, 242, 248, 256, 261, 265, 268, 274, 275-276, 298, 305, 367, 395, 400- 401, 405, 440, 468, 472, 479, 482-483, 485, 507, 536

Boaz . . . 71-76, 179

Book of the Law . . . xxx, 29, 61, 114, 132, 193, 255, 259

boulē . . . 401

Bride . . . 147, 175, 177, 179, 180, 223, 400, 403, 533

Brutus . . . 408

Buddha, Buddhism . . . 266, 271, 369, 411

Caesar . . . 285, 328, 351, 363-364, 367, 407-408

Caiaphas . . . 290, 304, 311, 323

California . . . 95

Cambyses . . . 83, 267

Canaan, Canaanites . . . xi, 9, 11, 14-15, 19, 24, 26, 42-44, 49, 55-58, 63, 66-68, 97, 105, 237, 247

Canon . . . xix-xx, xxii-xxiii, 72, 85, 121, 131, 139, 159, 201, 227, 273, 281, 303, 351, 374, 423, 431, 457, 471, 487, 513-515

Capernaum . . . 251, 301, 321-322, 333, 340, 377, 424, 479

Cappadocia . . . 392, 424, 481, 489

Captivity . . . 31, 83, 85, 99-100, 108, 112-113, 115, 117, 121-124, 129, 137, 142, 184-186, 191, 195, 208, 210, 217-218, 241, 248, 256, 260, 274

Caractacus . . . 426

Carchemish . . . 102, 209, 255, 283

Cartimandua . . . 426

Caspian Sea . . . 7, 500

Cayster River . . . 399

Celtic . . . 250, 391

Cenchrea . . . 330, 363, 365, 389, 424

Cephas . . . 374, 378, 479

Cerinthus . . . 497, 501

chadash . . . 204

Chaldeans . . . 143, 208, 255-256

charam . . . 90

charis . . . 352

charisma . . . 375

chazon . . . 219

Chemosh . . . 71, 75

chidah . . . 65

China, Chinese . . . 46, 54, 68, 141, 159, 166, 173, 221, 235, 244, 271, 323, 348, 369, 411, 420, 500

Chloe . . . 330, 375

chokmah . . . 165

choq . . . 52

chotham . . . 265

Christ's Life and Ministry . . . 299-302, 307, 311, 316, 318, 320, 341, 343, 345, 377, 418-419, 464

Christos . . . 305

Chronicles . . . 111

Church . . . . xi-xii, xxiii, 38, 175, 179, 180-182, 188, 192, 197, 200, 212, 234-236, 351-357, 378-379, 385, 400-408, 418, 424-425, 427-452, 482, 485, 510, 514, 518-519, 529-530, 533-535

Cilicia . . . 357-358, 363, 391

Circus Maximus . . . 364

Claudius I . . . 290, 378, 433

Clement of Alexandria . . . 339, 348, 351, 415, 496, 514, 517

Clement of Rome . . . 373, 461, 513, 523

Cleopatra . . . 285, 336

Colosse . . . 415-416, 420, 424, 457, 458, 460

Confucius . . . 221, 271

Conquest . . . 56

Corinth . . . 298, 330, 358-359, 361, 363, 365, 373-374, 378-380, 383-386, 389, 393, 423-424, 431, 437, 451

Cornelius . . . 353, 368

Covenant . . . xii, xiv, 1, 3, 8, 10-14, 19, 21-22, 27, 30, 37-38, 40, 42, 45, 50, 52-55, 57, 65, 78-80, 91-93, 105-108, 114-118, 121-126, 129, 131-140, 143, 197, 198, 200, 211, 218, 224, 228, 233-234, 237, 239, 242, 248-249, 255-256, 268, 273-276, 335, 345, 353, 356, 385, 395, 419, 463-466

Coverdale, Myles . . . xxii

Creation . . . xi-xiii, xv, xix, xxiii, 1, 3, 8, 10-16, 146, 153, 170, 187, 211, 219, 228, 242, 345, 384, 387, 417-421, 520, 527, 529, 530, 532, 535

Cyrus . . . 81, 83, 109, 119, 122, 124-125, 130, 133, 135, 186, 263, 267

dabar . . . 199

Dalmatia . . . 451

dam . . . 36

Damascus . . . 82, 86, 100, 102, 178, 184-185, 198, 282-283, 298, 340, 357, 361, 363, 377, 385, 391, 424

Daniel . . . 59, 83, 129-130, 141-144, 194, 207, 209, 217-220, 255, 279, 281, 536

darash . . . 235

Darius . . . 83, 123, 138, 218, 263, 267, 281, 284

David . . . xi, 55-56, 58, 60, 63, 71-79, 85-98, 100-109, 111-118, 120, 123-126, 131-132, 140, 153-155, 158-159, 161-162, 169, 175, 179-180, 186, 189, 192, 195, 199-200, 208, 234-236, 238, 241, 247, 263, 264-265, 268, 274, 289, 303-304, 310, 365, 417, 447, 520, 529, 536

Day of Atonement . . . 37, 58, 138, 140

Day of the Lord . . . 58, 187, 227-230, 238, 260, 268, 274, 276-277, 425-426, 428-429, 432-434, 491, 493

Dead Sea . . . 71, 177, 227, 237-238, 358-359, 363, 392, 461

Dead Sea Scrolls . . . xxi, 192, 221

Deborah . . . 5, 64-68

Deity of Christ . . . xi, 11, 290, 342, 346, 411-412, 415-418, 420, 438, 451-453, 485, 497, 501, 528-529

Delilah . . . 65

Delphi . . . 276, 423

Demas . . . 415

Demetrius . . . 284-285, 384, 510

Demon . . . 93, 145, 147, 320-321, 330, 333, 352, 383, 388, 395, 408, 482-483, 486, 498, 500, 520, 524

diabolos . . . 521

Diaspora . . . 282, 283

diathēkē . . . 463

Diet of Worms . . . xxiii

dikaiōsis . . . 368

Diotrephes . . . 509-511

Docetism . . . 496-497, 501

Doctrine . . . xviii, xxi, xxiv, xxvii, 96, 117, 257, 305, 325, 332, 367-368, 375-376, 383, 392-394, 397, 411-412, 421, 441-447, 452-454, 469, 489-490, 492, 496-501, 506, 516, 520

dod . . . 180

Donkey . . . 47, 267

dosis agathē . . . 475

Dream . . . xix, 14, 79, 217, 219, 220, 228, 268, 312-313, 515

ʿebed . . . 190

Ebed-melech . . . 195

ʾeben . . . 58

Edom . . . 26, 86, 95, 154, 185, 191, 198, 204, 212, 236, 237-239

egō eimi . . . 342

Egypt . . . xi, 1, 3-5, 8, 13-15, 19-29, 42-45, 49, 54-55, 59, 75, 82, 90-91, 95, 99, 102, 117, 121, 123, 131, 135, 139, 150, 162, 184 186, 190 191, 194 195, 198, 200-201, 208-212, 218, 226, 237-238, 251, 255, 259, 267, 281, 283-285, 306, 312, 336, 399, 424, 462-463, 474, 481

Ehud . . . 5, 64-68

ekklēsia . . . 510

Elah . . . 80, 82, 103

Elam . . . 15, 198

Election . . . 200, 365, 367, 370, 416, 418, 438-439, 452-453, 492, 531

Elihu . . . 143, 144, 149-150

Elijah . . . 80, 82, 104, 109, 219, 228, 237, 241, 276-277, 322, 468

Eliphaz . . . 144, 148-150

Elisha . . . 82, 104, 109, 183, 219, 237

Elizabeth . . . 328-330

Elkosh, Elkoshite . . . 251, 253

ʾelohim . . . 11

elpis . . . 368

ʾemet . . . 158

Emperor Domitian . . . 290, 364, 495, 517

Emperor Trajan . . . 290, 399, 523

End times . . . 220, 228, 269, 317, 323-324, 385, 425, 432, 520

Enoch . . . 9, 462, 468, 514

Epaphras . . . 415-416

Epaphroditus . . . 409, 411

Ephesus . . . 162, 257, 283, 298, 330, 339, 340, 353, 358-359, 360-361, 365, 373-374, 383-384, 399-407, 415-416, 420, 422, 424, 431, 437-443, 445, 449, 451-452, 457, 486, 493, 495-496, 505, 509, 517-519, 522-523

Ephraim . . . 41, 66, 85, 223, 301, 340

epi to auto . . . 352

epichorēgia . . . 409

epiphaneia . . . 449

episkopos . . . 440

Erastus . . . 363

ʾerek ʾappayim . . . 242

ʾerets . . . 11

Esarhaddon . . . 83, 251

Eschatological Epistles . . . 425

Eschatology . . . xv, 228-230, 428, 432, 520, 535

Esther . . . 71, 83, 126, 130, 135, 137 142, 267

Ethiopia . . . 54, 190, 195, 261, 330

euangelion . . . 324

Eusebius . . . 303, 325, 327, 336, 339, 351, 415, 487, 496, 517

Eve . . . xiii, xvii, xx, 8, 10, 13, 15, 52, 143, 462, 535

ex nihilo . . . 12, 14

Exile . . . xi, 85, 99, 100, 106, 109, 112, 116, 122-126, 132, 191, 202, 209-210, 217-218, 243, 249, 251, 263, 267, 268, 282-283, 462, 518

Exodus . . . xi, 2, 5, 19-22, 24, 26-27, 29, 42-45, 49, 67, 121, 131, 143, 514

Ezekiel . . . 83, 108, 113, 194, 207-214, 217-218, 255, 264, 267

Faith (in James) . . . 473

Fall . . . xi, xii, 8, 10-16, 186, 439

Feasts . . . 29, 37, 122, 130, 138

Felix . . . 290, 330, 353, 363, 407, 422

Festus . . . 290, 353, 363, 407, 422

Foreknew . . . 370

Futurist . . . 306, 312, 522, 525

gaʾal . . . 75

Gad . . . 41, 85, 111, 227

Gaius . . . 363, 424, 509-511

Galatia . . . 391-392, 423, 437, 452, 481, 489

Galba . . . 491

Gamaliel . . . 162, 357, 363, 391

Gangites River . . . 408

Gath-hepher . . . 241

Gedaliah . . . 81

Genealogies . . . 13, 45, 71, 73, 77, 112-117, 123, 259, 289, 303-304, 312, 316, 399, 439

gennaō anōthen . . . 342

Gentiles . . . xiv, xv, xvii, 10, 73-74, 124-126, 186, 189, 192, 219, 220, 234-236, 316, 328, 329, 332, 353-354, 356, 357, 360, 367-368, 374, 392, 400, 403, 404, 415, 438, 461, 479, 481, 489, 511

Germany . . . 507

gibbor . . . 91

Gideon . . . 5, 64-68, 469

gillulim . . . 209

gnōsis . . . 490

Gnosticism . . . 416, 437-438, 495-496, 499, 501, 507, 514

Goliath . . . 161

Gomer . . . 179, 223-226

Goshen . . . 14, 24, 26

Gospel . . . xiv, 234, 289-290

Goths . . . 396

grammateus . . . 324

Great Britain . . . 250, 454

Guang Wudi . . . 420

Habakkuk . . . 83, 194, 217-218, 255-258
Hadassah . . . 137
hadēs . . . 521
Hades . . . 521
Haggai . . . 83, 112, 122-124, 126, 263-268, 273
hagiasmos . . . 427
hamartia . . . 499
Haran . . . 8, 255
Hasmonean . . . 282, 285
hē basileia tōn ouranōn . . . 305
hebel . . . 170
Hebrew . . . xi, xix-xxii, xxviii
Hellenism . . . 281, 283
Heresy . . . 392, 415-416, 420-421, 438, 446, 451, 495-497, 499, 501, 507
Hermogenes . . . 447
Herod Agrippa II . . . 290, 353
Herodian . . . 310
Heshbon . . . 19, 178
Hezekiah . . . 81, 83, 103-105, 109, 114, 118, 143, 161, 166, 163, 183-184, 186, 191, 195, 223-224, 247, 259
Hierapolis . . . 315
Hilkiah . . . 193, 259
High Priest . . . 21, 29-30, 34, 43-44, 55, 56, 64, 83, 86, 132, 259, 263, 265, 267-268, 270, 282-283, 285, 290, 304, 324, 345, 419, 421, 462-468, 529
Historicist . . . 522
ho anomos . . . 434
ho logos . . . 342
Holy . . . 22, 258, 375, 418, 427, 502
Holy Spirit . . . xii, xix, xxvii, 10, 11, 32, 57, 92, 93, 97, 111, 199, 229, 230, 341, 352, 355-356, 361, 363, 379, 385, 400, 493, 499
Homer . . . 239
Hosanna . . . 332
Hosea . . . 82-83, 179, 183, 223-226, 227, 233, 241, 247-248, 279
Hoshea . . . 81, 83, 103, 223
Humanity of Christ . . . 10, 32, 218, 290, 317, 345, 416, 419, 421, 497-498, 501, 506, 528
hupogrammos . . . 480
Hyksos . . . 4, 20
Hymenaeus . . . 399, 447
Iddo . . . 111, 267
Idealist . . . 522

Idols . . . 209, 329, 375, 481
Idolatry . . . 44, 63, 68, 90, 100, 102, 106, 109, 114, 116, 121, 123, 185, 194-195, 209-210, 223-224, 227, 234, 241, 247, 251-256, 259, 270, 275, 282, 519
Idumea, Idumeans . . . 237-238, 282, 290
Iēsous . . . 305
Iēsous Christos . . . 421
Ierousalēm kainē . . . 521
Iliad . . . 239
Immutable . . . xxiv, 156, 248, 473
Imprisonment . . . 193, 321, 327, 337, 351, 357, 361, 407-410, 422, 437-438, 445-446, 451, 457
India . . . 177, 230, 261, 411, 474
Inerrant . . . xviii, xxv, 111, 117, 119, 447, 475, 493, 527
Infallible . . . xviii, xxv, 447, 527
Inspiration . . . xix, xxii, 111, 319, 328, 341, 355, 438, 442, 446-447, 449, 481, 491, 492-493, 515-516
Intermarriage . . . 63, 124-126
Intertestamental Period . . . 281-285
Irenaeus . . . 315, 339, 351, 415, 496-497, 501, 517
Iron Age . . . 25
Isaac . . . xi, 4, 8-10, 13-14, 50, 179, 237, 462
Isaiah . . . xx, 75, 83, 105, 108, 111, 124, 140, 183-192, 195, 199, 204, 212, 218, 223, 233, 247, 279, 324
Ishbosheth . . . 82, 95
Italy . . . 192, 213, 315, 351, 373, 408, 424, 433, 462
ʾivvelet . . . 165
Jacob . . . xi, 1, 4, 8-10, 12-14, 19, 22, 50, 73, 124, 179, 237-238, 365, 462
James (brother of Jesus) . . . 147, 235, 287, 298, 471-477, 514
James (disciple) . . . 274, 287, 298, 304, 316, 327-328, 330, 339, 343, 352-353, 361, 394, 481, 495
Jannes and Jambres . . . 447
Japan . . . 253, 311, 420
Jehoahaz . . . 80-83, 103, 119, 194-195, 209, 217
Jehohanan . . . 131

Jehoiachin . . . 81, 100, 103, 119, 194-195, 198, 208-209, 217, 265
Jehoiakim . . . xx, 81, 83, 103, 105, 119, 193-195, 209, 217, 249, 255
Jehoram . . . 80, 82, 103, 114, 118, 237-238
Jehu . . . 80, 82, 103-104, 106-107, 111, 223
Jephthah . . . 5, 19, 64-68
Jeremiah . . . 52, 58, 83, 99, 124, 193-206, 207, 212, 217-218, 249, 255, 259, 265, 267, 279
Jeroboam . . . 80, 82, 101-103, 106, 109, 223, 233, 241, 247
Jerome . . . 111, 114, 183, 325, 327, 336, 351, 457, 517
Jerusalem . . . 122, 131, 198, 448
Jeshua . . . 265
Jethro . . . 21, 25
Jezebel . . . 104
Jezreel . . . 175, 224
Joab . . . 78, 90,
Joash . . . 66, 80, 82, 103-104, 118, 140, 227, 233
Job . . . 143-152, 163, 169, 171, 256, 388
Joel . . . 5, 82, 194, 227-231, 241, 279, 356
John (disciple) . . . xi, xix, xxiii, 10, 290, 298, 304, 316, 328, 339-349, 351, 353, 394, 400, 495-512, 514, 517-520
John the Baptist . . . xi, xiv, 290, 300, 301, 304, 308-309, 317, 321, 328-330, 333, 337, 356
Jonah . . . 82, 223, 233, 241-245, 251-252, 279
Jonathan . . . 77, 86, 94-95
Jordan River . . . 8, 42, 49, 55, 100, 329
Joseph (husband of Mary) . . . 200, 263, 304-305, 312
Joseph (of Arimathea) . . . 189, 323
Joseph (son of Jacob) . . . 1, 4, 8-10, 13-14, 19-20, 130, 462-463
Josephus . . . 346, 352, 402, 471
Joshua . . . 5, 9, 19, 21, 24, 43-44, 49, 50, 55-61, 63, 65, 201, 223, 263, 274, 279

Joshua (high priest) . . . 130, 263, 267-270
Josiah . . . 81, 83, 103, 105, 109, 114, 119, 194, 195, 201, 209, 217, 255, 259-260, 274
Jotham . . . 81-83, 103, 114, 118, 183-184, 223, 247
Judas Maccabeus . . . 282
Jude . . . xx, 287, 471, 513-516
Judges . . . 4-5, 63-69
Judgment of Nations . . . 185
Justin Martyr . . . 315, 496, 517
kabod . . . 209
Kadesh . . . 1, 26, 42, 46, 50, 86
kainos anthrōpos . . . 401
kashal . . . 224
katallagē . . . 368
Kedar and Hazor . . . 198
kenophōnia . . . 440
keseph . . . 106
Kings . . . 82-83, 103
Kinsman-Redeemer . . . 71, 73-76
Lake Fucino . . . 433
Laodicea . . . 365, 415, 420, 424, 519, 522, 523
laqat . . . 75
Latin Vulgate . . . 29, 41, 49, 85, 99, 111, 129, 175, 201, 227, 241
Law of Moses . . . xiii, 19, 27, 29, 38, 43, 49, 52, 75-76, 115, 117, 123, 132, 190, 274, 463
Law and Grace . . . 394
Lazarus . . . 301, 320, 330, 341-343, 347, 468
leitourgia . . . 385
Lemuel . . . 161-162, 166
Leprosy . . . 43, 104, 184, 223
Lo-Ammi . . . 224
Locust . . . 227-230, 235
logos . . . 480
Lord's Supper . . . 302, 311, 323, 335, 344, 349, 375-376, 378, 495, 534
Lo-Ruhamah . . . 224
loutron palingenesias . . . 452
Love (in Philemon) . . . 458
Luke . . . xi, xviii, 287, 289-290, 303, 312, 316-317, 319, 321, 327-337, 339, 341, 348-349, 351-353, 355, 407, 415, 445-446, 451, 462
Luther, Martin . . . xxiii
LXX . . . xx, xxi, 7, 29, 41, 49, 85, 93, 96, 99, 111, 129, 139, 153, 161, 169, 175, 201, 227, 241, 283, 332, 461, 462, 480

Lycus Valley . . . 415
Lydia (country) . . . 15, 102, 109
Lydia (person) . . . 330, 353, 408
Lystra . . . 358, 359, 391, 392, 424, 437
Maccabees . . . 282-283
Macedonian Vision . . . 327
Major Prophets . . . xi
makarios . . . 305
mal'ak . . . 268
Malachi . . . xix, xxiii, 83, 112, 124, 126, 130-131, 135, 273-277, 279
mamōnas . . . 329
Mamre . . . 14
manah . . . 242
Mahanaim . . . 14, 178
Manoah . . . 66
Marcion . . . 423
Mark . . . xi, 287, 289-290, 306, 312, 315-326, 332, 336-337, 341, 348, 349, 353, 357, 415-416, 445, 475, 481
Mark Antony . . . 285, 336
Mary . . . 189, 200, 263, 304, 328-330, 332, 343
Mary and Martha . . . 330, 334, 343
Mary Magdalene . . . 298, 304, 325, 329, 330, 343, 348, 377
Mashach . . . 43
Masoretic . . . xxi, , 93, 96, 175, 227, 241
Matthew . . . xi, 250, 287, 289, 303-313, 316-322, 332, 336, 341, 343, 348-349
Matthias . . . 404
Medes . . . 15, 109, 208
Megilloth . . . xx, 72, 139, 169, 179, 201
Melchizedek . . . 157, 417, 466, 468
melek . . . 90
membrana . . . 449
Menahem . . . 81-82, 103
Mentoring . . . 365
Mercy Seat . . . 39
Meshach . . . 218, 221
mesitēs . . . 463
Mesopotamia . . . 3, 5, 8, 65-66, 68, 90, 154, 282, 481
Messiah, Psalms of . . . 157
Mexico . . . 39
Micah . . . 83, 183, 194, 223, 241, 247-250, 256, 279
Midian . . . 8, 20, 21, 26, 65-68, 143

Millennium . . . xii, 113, 187, 200, 208, 214, 218, 228, 249, 264-266, 428-429, 493, 522, 524-525, 529, 536-537
Minor Prophets . . . xi, xx, 223, 233, 255, 259, 273
Miracles . . . 26-27, 59, 219, 221, 243-244, 308, 320, 337, 376, 379, 404, 479, 530
Miriam . . . 21, 43, 65
mizmor . . . 158
Moab, Moabites . . . 1, 8, 19, 22, 26, 42, 45-46, 49, 52, 55, 65-68, 71-75, 86, 95, 178, 179, 185, 190, 198, 212, 261
mor . . . 180
Mordecai . . . 137-142
Moresheth . . . 247
morphē theou . . . 409
Moses . . . xiii, xix, 1-2, 5, 7, 9, 19-21, 29-31, 42-47, 49-55, 57, 65, 68, 112, 143, 153, 159, 161, 197, 199, 219, 249, 264, 279, 305, 417, 463, 466, 514-516
Mt. Cadmus . . . 415
Mt. Nebo . . . 19, 20, 49
Muratorian Canon . . . 351, 457, 513
Naaman . . . 104
Nabatean Arabia . . . 238, 363, 393
nabi' . . . 199
Nabopolassar . . . 83, 195, 208, 251, 255
Naboth . . . 80
nachalah . . . 58
Nadab (king) . . . 80, 82, 103
Nadab and Abihu . . . 30, 38, 112, 264
Nahum . . . 83, 137, 242, 251-253, 279
Naomi . . . 72, 75, 76, 180
Nathan . . . 78, 85, 90, 92, 111, 114, 154, 200
Nathanael . . . 346
Nativity . . . 329, 332
natsal . . . 22
Nazareth . . . 241, 289, 301, 303, 309, 316, 332-333, 337, 340, 353, 423
Nebuchadnezzar . . . 83, 105, 112, 195, 201-202, 209-210, 218, 220, 237, 251, 255, 260, 264-265

Necho . . . 209, 255

neder . . . 43

Nehemiah . . . 83, 112, 121-126, 129-137, 141-142, 177, 251, 267, 273-274

Nero . . . 327, 352, 364, 373, 378, 387, 445-446, 449, 454, 481, 484, 489, 491, 517

Nevada . . . 95

New Covenant . . . 38, 40, 53, 115, 132, 197-198, 200, 335, 353, 463, 465

New Jerusalem . . . 91, 116, 220, 519, 521

Nicopolis . . . 424, 451

Nineveh . . . xiv, 102, 184, 195, 198, 208, 218, 233, 241-245, 251-253, 255, 259, 283

Noah . . . 8-9, 13, 15, 143-144, 158, 242, 310, 462, 483, 486

nomos . . . 368

Obadiah . . . 82, 179, 237-240, 279

Octavian . . . 285, 290, 336, 408

Odyssey . . . 239

Offerings . . . 31-35

Old Covenant . . . 37, 353, 356, 463

olethros . . . 434

Olivet Discourse . . . 302, 306, 310, 312, 324

Omnipotent . . . 12, 527, 529

Omnipresent . . . 156, 197, 529

Omniscient . . . 156, 164, 370, 529, 531

Omri . . . 80, 82, 103, 106-107, 109

Onesimus . . . 415-416, 457-458, 460

Onesiphorus . . . 447-448

ʿoni . . . 147

ʾor . . . 190

Origen . . . 303, 351, 415, 487, 517

Ostia . . . 364

Othniel . . . 5, 64-68

Palestine . . . 7, 25, 91, 102, 200, 209, 238, 251, 274, 281-284, 340, 346, 349, 351, 363, 383, 424, 462, 480, 513

pantokratōr . . . 521

Papias, bishop of Hieropolis . . . 315, 496

Parables . . . 165, 207, 289, 301, 304-310, 321, 332-333

paradeisos . . . 329

paraklētos . . . 499

Paran . . . 26, 42

parousia . . . 427

Passover . . . 2, 30, 37, 39, 117, 138, 142, 179, 299-300, 310, 335, 344, 346-347, 349

Pastoral Epistles . . . 437-438, 442, 445, 451-452

Patmos . . . 290, 340, 518

Patriarchs . . . xiii, xiv, 3-5, 9, 15, 29, 50, 77, 190, 219

Paul . . . xviii, 162, 287, 290, 298, 315, 321, 327, 330, 351-355, 357-361, 446

Pekah . . . 81-82, 103

Pekahiah . . . 81-82, 103

Peking . . . 166

Pelatiah . . . 210

Peloponnesus . . . 373

Penitential . . . 157, 160

Pentecost . . . 37, 38, 72, 93, 138, 169, 228, 230, 298, 352, 356, 360-362, 364, 373, 383, 479, 529, 533

Penuel . . . 14

Perga . . . 315, 358, 424

Pergamos . . . 283, 365, 424, 519, 522-523

Persecution . . . 143, 290, 327, 352, 354, 360, 411, 419, 431, 445-446, 461, 463, 465, 467, 471, 479-486, 489, 495, 518

Persia . . . 15, 83, 109, 112, 115, 119, 121-126, 129-135, 137-140, 186, 217-219, 227, 263, 267, 273-275, 281-284, 415, 474, 545

pesach . . . 117

pesel . . . 256

peshar . . . 219

Peter . . . 230, 287, 301, 304-305, 308, 311, 315-316, 320, 322, 324, 328, 330, 336, 339, 340, 343, 346, 348, 351, 353, 357, 360-361, 364, 377, 393, 394, 471, 479-494, 495, 501, 513-514

Pharaohs . . . 5, 20-25, 82, 175, 209, 365

Pharisee . . . 241-242, 283, 304, 316-317, 332, 346, 357, 360, 363, 391

Philadelphia . . . 282, 365, 424, 519, 522-523

Philemon . . . 373, 415-416, 457-460

Philetus . . . 447

Philip . . . 304, 316, 328, 343, 346, 351, 353, 461

Philistia, Philistines . . . 13, 65-68, 78, 89, 91, 94-95, 154, 185, 190, 198, 212, 227, 237, 238, 247, 261

Philippi . . . 301, 322, 330, 340, 358, 359, 384, 407-413, 423-424, 437

Phinehas . . . 55, 56, 115, 124, 132

phôsphoros . . . 490

Phoebe . . . 330, 363, 365

Phrygia . . . 213, 391, 415

Phygellus . . . 447

Pilate . . . xiii, 304, 311, 317, 323, 329, 336, 343

Pinto . . . 95

pisteuō . . . 342

pistis . . . 324

Plague . . . 23-26, 117, 227-230, 241

Plato, Platonism . . . 134, 501

pneuma . . . 352, 427

Poland . . . 396

Polycarp . . . 339, 373, 511

Postmillennialism . . . 525

Praetorium . . . 311, 323, 344

Predestination . . . xii, 370, 402

Premillennialism 220, 524-525

Preterist . . . 312, 521

Priscilla and Aquila . . . 162, 330, 353, 365, 374, 399, 461

prōtotokos . . . 421

Promised Land . . . 1-3, 8, 13, 21-22, 42-44, 50, 55-63, 68, 97, 112, 135

Prophets . . . 82-83

Prostitute . . . 56, 59, 105, 224-226, 374

prothesis . . . 401

Providence . . . xxii, 67, 73, 140-141, 149, 155, 171, 328, 364, 520, 527

Psalms, Types of . . . 155, 157

Ptolemy . . . 281, 283-285

pur . . . 140

Puteoli . . . 359, 364, 424

Pythagoras . . . 205

Q document . . . 319

qadash . . . 22

qannoʾ . . . 252

qorban . . . 36

Queen of Sheba . . . 65, 114

Qumran . . . 461-462

raʾah . . . 147

Rabbi . . . 72, 139, 153, 162, 169, 201, 282, 332, 363, 391

rachats . . . 22

Rahab . . . 55-56, 59, 60, 73, 126, 463

raham . . . 249

Ramses . . . 75

rapha' . . . 199

Rebekah . . . 8, 14, 179, 237, 365

Rechabites . . . 195

Redemption . . . xii, xiv, xv, 2, 8, 11-13, 20, 22, 74-75, 132, 144, 191, 204, 335, 387, 402, 416-417, 463, 527, 530-531

Regeneration . . . 22, 387, 394, 419, 452-453, 483, 530-531

Rehoboam . . . 80, 101-103, 109, 114, 118, 162, 163, 237

Restoration . . . 11, 91, 112, 115, 123, 129, 181, 185, 196, 198, 210-212, 221, 228-230, 233-235, 238-239, 261, 270, 367

rib . . . 249

ro'ah . . . 199

Road to Emmaus . . . 298, 311, 336, 377

Rock of Horeb . . . 39

Rome . . . 192, 219, 225, 281-282, 290, 298, 327, 330, 355, 359, 363-371, 424, 426, 454, 457, 459, 480-481, 484, 500, 507, 514-515, 523

ruach . . . 229

Ruth . . . 71-76, 126, 179

Sadducees . . . 283, 304-305, 316-317, 346

Salvation . . . xiv-xxvi, 57, 93, 96, 123, 162, 179, 183, 189-192, 199, 223, 255, 260, 267, 324, 328, 342-345, 352, 368, 385, 403-404, 421, 439, 442, 469, 475, 521

Samson . . . 5, 64-68

Samuel . . . 5, 63-64, 71, 77-97, 139, 161, 197, 199

Sanballat . . . 131-133, 135

Sarah . . . 8, 14, 365, 462, 469

Sardis . . . 102, 283, 365, 424, 519, 522, 523

Saronic Gulf . . . 373

sarx . . . 395

Satan . . . xiv, xvii, xx, xxvi, 11, 139-140, 144-151, 385-388, 400, 405-406, 408, 417, 434, 439-440, 476, 482, 500, 502-503, 514, 521, 534-537

Saul (king) . . . xi, 63, 71, 77-78, 82, 86, 90, 92-95, 103, 115, 118, 139, 154, 208, 238

Scribe . . . 121-123, 126, 129, 132, 162, 193, 195, 487

selah . . . 158

Seleucus . . . 281, 284-285

Semitic . . . 20, 159, 332

Sennacherib . . . 83, 105, 111, 183-184, 186, 191, 198, 247, 251

Septuagint (see LXX)

Serpent . . . 10-11, 39, 42, 47-48, 52, 196

Seventy-Year Captivity . . . 83, 112, 115, 117, 121-122, 129, 137, 217

sha'ar . . . 124

shaba' . . . 52

shachah . . . 52

Shadrach . . . 218, 221

Shallum . . . 81, 82, 103

shama' . . . 90

shamayim . . . 11

shaphat . . . 65

shaqat . . . 58

Shechem . . . 14, 56, 86, 178

Shem . . . 8, 9, 13, 15

shem . . . 105

Sheol . . . 329, 521

shophar . . . 58

Shulamite . . . 147, 175-176, 179, 182

Shunem . . . 104, 175

Shushan . . . 137

Sidon . . . 56, 102, 212, 227, 282-283, 301, 322, 340, 359, 424

Signs . . . xiii, 207, 269, 341-343, 354, 404

Silas (Silvanus) . . . 353, 374, 404, 408-409, 423-425, 431-432, 461, 480-481, 487

Sinai . . . 2, 20, 22, 25-26, 29, 30, 42, 45, 50, 53, 58, 248, 256, 463

Smyrna . . . 365, 424, 511, 519, 522-523

Solomon . . . xi, 19, 67, 79-80, 82, 99-109, 112-118, 143, 161-182, 208, 238, 241, 247

Son of God . . . 222, 290, 317, 342-343, 345-347, 419, 421, 519-520

Sons of Zebedee . . . 339, 495

Spain . . . 235

Sparta . . . 118-119

Stephen . . . 298, 353, 360-361, 471

stoicheia . . . 395

Substitutionary Atonement . . . 43, 385, 438, 452-453

Suffering . . . 144-152, 163, 183, 187, 191, 201, 260, 317, 387, 434, 447, 469, 474, 479, 480-487

Sweden . . . 396

Synoptic Problem . . . 289, 303, 312, 317, 321, 332, 336

Syria . . . 15, 25, 80, 102, 104, 154, 178, 184-185, 190, 241, 247, 251, 281, 282-285

Tabernacle . . . 1-2, 22-34, 38-39, 41, 43, 104, 112, 161, 264

Table of Nations . . . 15

Talmud . . . 143

tam . . . 147

Tamar . . . 73, 95

Tarsus . . . 102, 283, 298, 357-359, 361, 363, 367, 391-392, 424

Tax collector . . . 303, 305, 307-308, 328-329

techinnah . . . 105

teleios . . . 421

Temple . . . 104, 112-113, 184, 207, 263-264, 325

Tertullian . . . 351, 373, 415, 517

thelēma . . . 401

Theodore of Mopsuestia . . . 457

Theophilus . . . 327, 328, 351-352, 355

theopneustos . . . 449

Therma . . . 423

Thessalonica . . . 358-359, 423-435

Thyatira . . . 365, 424, 519, 522-523

Tiber River . . . 364

Timothy . . . 162, 315, 330, 353, 365, 374-375, 383-384, 399, 404, 409, 415-416, 423-425, 431-432, 437-452, 461

Tobiah . . . 132-133

torah . . . 2, 45, 158, 281-283

tou sōtēros hēmōn theou . . . 452

Transjordan . . . 91

Tribes of Israel . . . 7-8, 14, 41, 45, 55-56, 77, 83, 86, 117, 213

Tribulation . . . 113, 220, 264, 324, 428, 434, 484, 493, 522-525, 535-536
tsemach . . . 268
tsum . . . 140
Turkey . . . 363, 367, 391, 399, 415, 437, 489, 519
Tychicus . . . 399-400, 416, 420, 451, 457, 460
Tyndale, William . . . xxii
Type of Christ . . . 39, 42, 50, 71, 73, 154, 468
Tyre . . . 56, 86, 100, 102, 108, 185-186, 191, 210, 212, 227, 282-283, 301, 322, 340, 353, 359, 424
United States . . . 95, 442
Universalism . . . 376, 380, 454
Uz . . . 143
Uzziah . . . 80, 82-83, 103, 111, 114, 118, 183-184, 223, 233, 247
Valedictory . . . 450
Vanity . . . 170-173

Vashti . . . 138, 141
Vespasian . . . 290, 461, 515
Vistula River . . . 396
Women in NT . . . 330
Wycliffe, John . . . xxii
Xerxes . . . 83, 137, 138, 267, 415
yachal . . . 158
yadah . . . 132
yam . . . 274
yare' . . . 132
yashar . . . 117
yehudi . . . 124
yerushalaim . . . 91
yeshu'ah . . . 190
yobel . . . 36
yom . . . 274
Yom Kippur . . . 37, 138
Yorkshire Brigantes . . . 426
Yugoslavia . . . 451
Zacchaeus . . . 332, 337
Zadok . . . 124, 131, 214, 282-283
zadon . . . 238
zahab . . . 105

zanah . . . 224
zaqen . . . 43
Zarephath . . . 241
zebach . . . 43
Zechariah (father of John) . . . 328
Zechariah (king) . . . 81-82, 103, 223
Zechariah (prophet) . . . 83, 112, 122-126, 207, 241, 263, 267-271, 273, 275
Zedekiah . . . 81, 83, 99, 103, 105, 119, 194-195, 209, 217
Zephaniah . . . 83, 194, 217-218, 241, 255, 259-262
zera' . . . 11
Zerubbabel . . . 83, 112-113, 122-125, 130, 134-137, 214, 263-265, 267-268, 273, 283
Zimri . . . 80, 82, 103
Zion . . . 191, 196, 237
Ziphites . . . 77, 154
Zophar the Naamathite . . . 144, 149-150